Nissan Qashqai
Owners Workshop Manual

Peter T Gill

(5610 - 8AX2 - 416)

Models covered
Qashqai & Qashqai+2 with two- and four-wheel drive
Petrol: 1.6 litre (1598cc) & 2.0 litre (1997cc)
Turbo-diesel: 1.5 litre (1461cc) & 2.0 litre (1995cc)

Does NOT cover models with 1.6 litre diesel engine or CVT automatic transmission
Does NOT cover new Qashqai range introduced February 2014

© Haynes Publishing 2018

A book in the **Haynes Owners Workshop Manual Series**

ABCDE
FGHIJ
KLMNO
PQ

ISBN 978 1 78521 437 0

British Library Cataloguing in Publication Data
A catalogue record for this book is available from the British Library.

Printed in Malaysia

Haynes Publishing
Sparkford, Yeovil, Somerset BA22 7JJ, England

Haynes North America, Inc
859 Lawrence Drive, Newbury Park, California 91320, USA

Printed using NORBRITE BOOK 48.8gsm (CODE: 40N6533) from NORPAC; procurement system certified under Sustainable Forestry Initiative standard. Paper produced is certified to the SFI Certified Fiber Sourcing Standard (CERT - 0094271)

Contents

LIVING WITH YOUR NISSAN QASHQAI

Roadside Repairs

Weekly Checks

Lubricants, fluids and tyre pressures

MAINTENANCE

Contents

The Nissan Qashqai 5-door hatchback, known as a "Crossover" vehicle was introduced in the UK in February 2007. During the course of production, various trim levels where introduced and in August 2008 the +2 version (7-seater) was launched. In 2010 the Qashqai had a facelift, which involved some small changes to the external and internal appearance of the vehicle.

The Qashqai range is available with two sizes of petrol engines and three diesel engines. Covered in this manual are the 1.6 litre and 2.0 litre petrol engines, both being of double overhead camshaft (DOHC) 16-valve design. Both engines feature multi-point fuel injection and are equipped with an extensive range of emissions control systems. Also covered in this manual are the 1.5 litre and 2.0 litre diesel engines, both being of double overhead camshaft (DOHC) 16-valve design. These are Renault diesel engines, which are of a well-proven design and have been used previously in Renault vehicles.

Fully independent front and rear suspension units are fitted, with MacPherson strut type at the front and multi-link suspension used at the rear.

A five or six-speed manual transmission is fitted as standard across the range, with a six-speed automatic transmission optionally available on 2.0 litre models.

A wide range of standard and optional equipment is available within the Qashqai range including central locking, electric windows, an electric sunroof, an anti-lock braking system and supplementary restraint system.

For the home mechanic, the Qashqai is a straightforward vehicle to maintain, and most of the items requiring frequent attention are easily accessible.

Your Nissan Qashqai Manual

The aim of this manual is to help you get the best value from your vehicle. It can do so in several ways. It can help you decide what work must be done (even should you choose to get it done by a garage), provide information on routine maintenance and servicing, and give a logical course of action and diagnosis when random faults occur. However, it is hoped that you will use the manual by tackling the work yourself. On simpler jobs, it may even be quicker than booking the car into a garage and going there twice, to leave and collect it. Perhaps most important, a lot of money can be saved by avoiding the costs a garage must charge to cover its labour and overheads.

The manual has drawings and descriptions to show the function of the various components, so that their layout can be understood. Then the tasks are described and photographed in a clear step-by-step sequence.

References to the 'left' or 'right' are in the sense of a person in the driver's seat, facing forward.

Acknowledgements

Thanks are due to Draper Tools Limited, who provided some of the workshop tools, and to all those people at Sparkford who helped in the production of this Manual.

We take great pride in the accuracy of information given in this manual, but vehicle manufacturers make alterations and design changes during the production run of a particular vehicle of which they do not inform us. No liability can be accepted by the authors or publishers for loss, damage or injury caused by any errors in, or omissions from, the information given.

Working on your car can be dangerous. This page shows just some of the potential risks and hazards, with the aim of creating a safety-conscious attitude.

General hazards

Scalding

• Don't remove the radiator or expansion tank cap while the engine is hot.

• Engine oil, transmission fluid or power steering fluid may also be dangerously hot if the engine has recently been running.

Burning

• Beware of burns from the exhaust system and from any part of the engine. Brake discs and drums can also be extremely hot immediately after use.

Crushing

• When working under or near a raised vehicle, always supplement the jack with axle stands, or use drive-on ramps.

Never venture under a car which is only supported by a jack.

• Take care if loosening or tightening high-torque nuts when the vehicle is on stands. Initial loosening and final tightening should be done with the wheels on the ground.

Fire

• Fuel is highly flammable; fuel vapour is explosive.

• Don't let fuel spill onto a hot engine.

• Do not smoke or allow naked lights (including pilot lights) anywhere near a vehicle being worked on. Also beware of creating sparks (electrically or by use of tools).

• Fuel vapour is heavier than air, so don't work on the fuel system with the vehicle over an inspection pit.

• Another cause of fire is an electrical overload or short-circuit. Take care when repairing or modifying the vehicle wiring.

• Keep a fire extinguisher handy, of a type suitable for use on fuel and electrical fires.

Electric shock

• Ignition HT and Xenon headlight voltages can be dangerous, especially to people with heart problems or a pacemaker. Don't work on or near these systems with the engine running or the ignition switched on.

• Mains voltage is also dangerous. Make sure that any mains-operated equipment is correctly earthed. Mains power points should be protected by a residual current device (RCD) circuit breaker.

Fume or gas intoxication

• Exhaust fumes are poisonous; they can contain carbon monoxide, which is rapidly fatal if inhaled. Never run the engine in a confined space such as a garage with the doors shut.

• Fuel vapour is also poisonous, as are the vapours from some cleaning solvents and paint thinners.

Poisonous or irritant substances

• Avoid skin contact with battery acid and with any fuel, fluid or lubricant, especially antifreeze, brake hydraulic fluid and Diesel fuel. Don't syphon them by mouth. If such a substance is swallowed or gets into the eyes, seek medical advice.

• Prolonged contact with used engine oil can cause skin cancer. Wear gloves or use a barrier cream if necessary. Change out of oil-soaked clothes and do not keep oily rags in your pocket.

• Air conditioning refrigerant forms a poisonous gas if exposed to a naked flame (including a cigarette). It can also cause skin burns on contact.

Asbestos

• Asbestos dust can cause cancer if inhaled or swallowed. Asbestos may be found in gaskets and in brake and clutch linings. When dealing with such components it is safest to assume that they contain asbestos.

Special hazards

Hydrofluoric acid

• This extremely corrosive acid is formed when certain types of synthetic rubber, found in some O-rings, oil seals, fuel hoses etc, are exposed to temperatures above 4000C. The rubber changes into a charred or sticky substance containing the acid. *Once formed, the acid remains dangerous for years. If it gets onto the skin, it may be necessary to amputate the limb concerned.*

• When dealing with a vehicle which has suffered a fire, or with components salvaged from such a vehicle, wear protective gloves and discard them after use.

The battery

• Batteries contain sulphuric acid, which attacks clothing, eyes and skin. Take care when topping-up or carrying the battery.

• The hydrogen gas given off by the battery is highly explosive. Never cause a spark or allow a naked light nearby. Be careful when connecting and disconnecting battery chargers or jump leads.

Air bags

• Air bags can cause injury if they go off accidentally. Take care when removing the steering wheel and trim panels. Special storage instructions may apply.

Diesel injection equipment

• Diesel injection pumps supply fuel at very high pressure. Take care when working on the fuel injectors and fuel pipes.

⚠️ *Warning: Never expose the hands, face or any other part of the body to injector spray; the fuel can penetrate the skin with potentially fatal results.*

Remember...

DO

• Do use eye protection when using power tools, and when working under the vehicle.

• Do wear gloves or use barrier cream to protect your hands when necessary.

• Do get someone to check periodically that all is well when working alone on the vehicle.

• Do keep loose clothing and long hair well out of the way of moving mechanical parts.

• Do remove rings, wristwatch etc, before working on the vehicle – especially the electrical system.

• Do ensure that any lifting or jacking equipment has a safe working load rating adequate for the job.

DON'T

• Don't attempt to lift a heavy component which may be beyond your capability – get assistance.

• Don't rush to finish a job, or take unverified short cuts.

• Don't use ill-fitting tools which may slip and cause injury.

• Don't leave tools or parts lying around where someone can trip over them. Mop up oil and fuel spills at once.

• Don't allow children or pets to play in or near a vehicle being worked on.

The following pages are intended to help in dealing with common roadside emergencies and breakdowns. You will find more detailed fault finding information at the back of the manual, and repair information in the main chapters.

If your car won't start and the starter motor doesn't turn

- [ ] If it's a model with automatic transmission, make sure the selector is in the P or N position.
- [ ] Open the bonnet and make sure that the battery terminals are clean and tight.
- [ ] Switch on the headlights and try to start the engine. If the headlights go very dim when you're trying to start, the battery is probably flat. Try jump starting using another car.

If your car won't start even though the starter motor turns as normal

- [ ] Is there fuel in the tank?
- [ ] Is there moisture on electrical components under the bonnet? Switch off the ignition, and then wipe off any obvious dampness with a dry cloth. Spray a water-repellent aerosol product (WD-40 or equivalent) on ignition and fuel system electrical connectors like those shown in the photos. Pay special attention to the ignition coils wiring connector. (Note that diesel engines do not normally suffer from damp.)

A Remove the plastic cover and check the condition and security of the battery connections.

B On diesel engines, squeeze the priming bulb a few times to make sure the fuel is up to the engine.

Check that electrical connections are secure (with the ignition switched off) and spray them with a water dispersant spray like WD-40 if you suspect a problem due to damp.

C Check the camshaft sensor wiring connectors are securely connected (1.5 litre diesel model shown).

D With the ignition switched off, remove the cover and check that all fuses are still in good condition and none have blown.

Jump starting

When jump-starting a car using a booster battery, observe the following precautions:

✔ Before connecting the booster battery, make sure that the ignition is switched off.

Caution: Remove the key in case the central locking engages when the jump leads are connected

✔ Ensure that all electrical equipment (lights, heater, wipers, etc) is switched off.

✔ Take note of any special precautions printed on the battery case.

✔ Make sure that the booster battery is the same voltage as the discharged one in the vehicle.

✔ If the battery is being jump-started from the battery in another vehicle, the two vehicles MUST NOT TOUCH each other.

✔ Make sure that the transmission is in neutral (or PARK, in the case of automatic transmission).

 HAYNES HiNT *Jump starting will get you out of trouble, but you must correct whatever made the battery go flat in the first place. There are three possibilities:*

1 *The battery has been drained by repeated attempts to start, or by leaving the lights on.*

2 *The charging system is not working properly (alternator drivebelt slack or broken, alternator wiring fault or alternator itself faulty).*

3 *The battery itself is at fault (electrolyte low, or battery worn out).*

1 Connect one end of the red jump lead to the positive (+) terminal of the flat battery

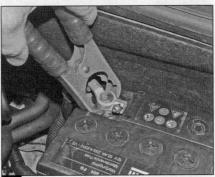

2 Connect the other end of the red lead to the positive (+) terminal of the booster battery.

3 Connect one end of the black jump lead to the negative (-) terminal of the booster battery

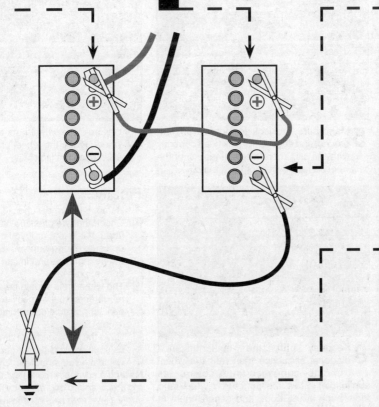

4 Connect the other end of the black jump lead to a bolt or bracket on the engine block, well away from the battery, on the vehicle to be started.

5 Make sure that the jump leads will not come into contact with the fan, drive-belts or other moving parts of the engine.

6 Start the engine using the booster battery and run it at idle speed. Switch on the lights, rear window demister and heater blower motor, then disconnect the jump leads in the reverse order of connection. Turn off the lights etc.

Wheel changing

 Warning: Do not change a wheel in a situation where you risk being hit by another vehicle. On busy roads, try to stop in a lay-by or a gateway. Be wary of passing traffic while changing the wheel – it is easy to become distracted by the job in hand.

Preparation

☐ When a puncture occurs, stop as soon as it is safe to do so.

☐ Park on firm level ground, if possible, and well out of the way of other traffic.

☐ Use hazard warning lights if necessary.

☐ If you have one, use a warning triangle to alert other drivers of your presence.

☐ Apply the handbrake and engage first or reverse gear (or Park on models with automatic transmission).

☐ If the ground is soft, use a flat piece of wood to spread the load under the foot of the jack.

☐ Place a chock against the wheel diagonally opposite the wheel to be removed, or use a large stone (or similar) to stop the car rolling.

Changing the wheel

1 The spare wheel and tools are stored in the luggage compartment, lift up the floor panel/carpet. The tool kit is located to the side of the spare wheel.

2 Unscrew the centre fastener and remove the spare wheel from the luggage compartment.

3 Where anti-theft wheel nuts are fitted, unscrew the anti-theft nut using the special tool provided – normally stored in the passenger glovebox or toolkit.

4 With the vehicle still on the ground, use the tool provided to slacken each wheel nut by half a turn.

5 Make sure the jack is located on firm ground, and engage the jack head correctly with the sill. Then raise the jack until the wheel is raised clear of the ground.

6 Unscrew the wheel nuts and remove the wheel. Place the wheel under the vehicle sill in case the jack fails.

7 Fit the spare wheel and screw in the bolts. Lightly tighten the nuts with the wheel brace then lower the car to the ground.

8 Securely tighten the wheel nuts in a diagonal sequence then refit the wheel trim/hub cap/wheel nut covers (as applicable). Stow the punctured wheel and tools back in the boot, and secure them in position.

Finally...

☐ Remove the wheel chock.

☐ Check the tyre pressure on the wheel just fitted. If it is low, or if you don't have a pressure gauge with you, drive slowly to the next garage and inflate the tyre to the correct pressure.

☐ The wheel nuts should be slackened and retightened to the specified torque at the earliest possible opportunity (see Chapter 1A or 1B).

☐ Have the damaged tyre or wheel repaired as soon as possible, or another puncture will leave you stranded.

Note: *If a compact spare wheel is fitted (as pictured), speed and distance restrictions apply. Drive with caution and refit the repaired tyre as soon as possible.*

Towing

When all else fails, you may find yourself having to get a tow home – or of course you may be helping somebody else. Long-distance recovery should only be done by a garage or breakdown service. For shorter distances, DIY towing using another car is easy enough, but observe the following points:

☐ Use a proper tow-rope – they are not expensive. The vehicle being towed must display an ON TOW sign in its rear window.

☐ Always turn the ignition key to the 'on' position when the vehicle is being towed, so that the steering lock is released, and that the direction indicator and brake lights work.

☐ The towing eye is kept with the spare wheel (see *Wheel changing*). To fit the eye, unclip the access cover from the relevant bumper and screw the eye firmly into position **(see illustrations)**.

☐ Before being towed, release the handbrake and select neutral on the transmission.
Caution: On models with automatic transmission, do not tow the car at speeds in excess of 30 mph or for a distance greater than 30 miles. If towing speeds/distances are to exceed these limits, then the car must be towed with its front wheels off the ground.

☐ Note that greater-than-usual pedal pressure will be required to operate the brakes, since the vacuum servo unit is only operational with the engine running.

☐ The driver of the car being towed must keep the tow-rope taut at all times to avoid snatching.

☐ Make sure that both drivers know the route before setting off.

☐ Only drive at moderate speeds and keep the distance towed to a minimum. Drive smoothly and allow plenty of time for slowing down at junctions.

The towing eye is located with the spare wheel

Unclip the access cover from the bumper ...

... and then screw the towing eye in securely ...

... using the wheel brace through eye to tighten

Access cover for the rear bumper

Identifying leaks

Puddles on the garage floor or drive, or obvious wetness under the bonnet or underneath the car, suggest a leak that needs investigating. It can sometimes be difficult to decide where the leak is coming from, especially if an engine undershield is fitted. Leaking oil or fluid can also be blown rearwards by the passage of air under the car, giving a false impression of where the problem lies.

 Warning: Most automotive oils and fluids are poisonous. Wash them off skin, and change out of contaminated clothing, without delay.

 The smell of a fluid leaking from the car may provide a clue to what's leaking. Some fluids are distinctively coloured. It may help to remove the engine undershield, clean the car carefully and to park it over some clean paper overnight as an aid to locating the source of the leak.
Remember that some leaks may only occur while the engine is running.

Sump oil

Engine oil may leak from the drain plug...

Oil from filter

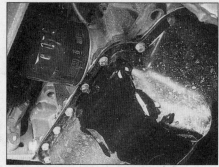

...or from the base of the oil filter.

Gearbox oil

Gearbox oil can leak from the seals at the inboard ends of the driveshafts.

Antifreeze

Leaking antifreeze often leaves a crystalline deposit like this.

Brake fluid

A leak occurring at a wheel is almost certainly brake fluid.

Power steering fluid

Power steering fluid may leak from the pipe connectors on the steering rack.

Introduction

There are some very simple checks which need only take a few minutes to carry out, but which could save you a lot of inconvenience and expense.

These checks require no great skill or special tools, and the small amount of time they take to perform could prove to be very well spent, for example;

☐ Keeping an eye on tyre condition and pressures, will not only help to stop them wearing out prematurely, but could also save your life.

☐ Many breakdowns are caused by electrical problems. Battery-related faults are particularly common, and a quick check on a regular basis will often prevent the majority of these.

☐ If your car develops a brake fluid leak, the first time you might know about it is when your brakes don't work properly. Checking the level regularly will give advance warning of this kind of problem.

☐ If the oil or coolant levels run low, the cost of repairing any engine damage will be far greater than fixing the leak, for example.

Underbonnet check points

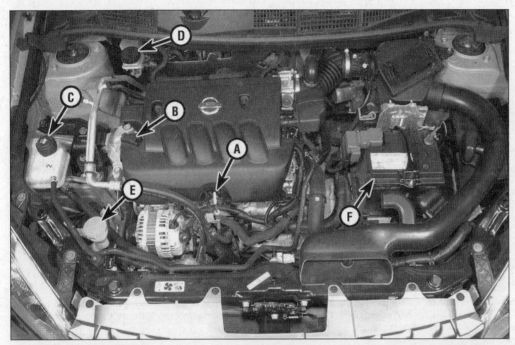

◀ 2.0 litre – petrol engine

A *Engine oil level dipstick*

B *Engine oil filler cap*

C *Coolant expansion tank*

D *Brake (and clutch) fluid reservoir*

E *Screen washer fluid reservoir*

F *Battery*

◀ 1.5 litre – diesel engine

A *Engine oil level dipstick*

B *Engine oil filler cap*

C *Coolant expansion tank*

D *Brake (and clutch) fluid reservoir*

E *Screen washer fluid reservoir*

F *Battery*

Engine oil level

Before you start
✔ Make sure that your car is on level ground.
✔ Check the oil level before the car is driven, or at least 5 minutes after the engine has been switched off.

The correct oil
Modern engines place great demands on their oil. It is very important that the correct oil for your car is used (see *Lubricants and fluids*).

Car care
● If you have to add oil frequently, you should check whether you have any oil leaks. Place some clean paper under the car overnight, and check for stains in the morning. If there are no leaks, the engine may be burning oil.
● Always maintain the level between the upper and lower dipstick marks (see photo 3). If the level is too low severe engine damage may occur. Oil seal failure may result if the engine is overfilled by adding too much oil.

 HAYNES HiNT *If the oil is checked immediately after driving the vehicle, some of the oil will remain in the upper engine components, resulting in an inaccurate reading on the dipstick.*

1 The dipstick is located at the front of the engine (see *Underbonnet check points*); the dipstick is brightly coloured (yellow or orange) or has a picture of an oil-can on the top for identification. Withdraw the dipstick (2.0 litre MR20DE engine shown). **Note:** *On 2.0 litre diesel models the dipstick is part of the oil filler cap.*

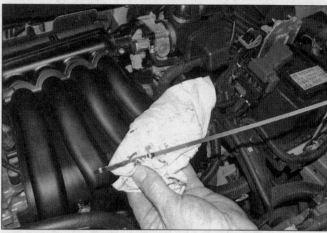

2 Using a clean rag or paper towel remove all oil from the dipstick. Insert the clean dipstick into the tube as far as it will go, then withdraw it again.

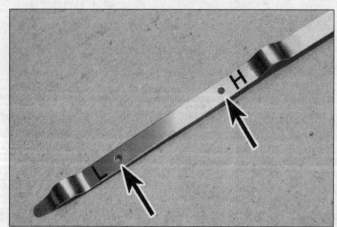

3 Note the oil level on the end of the dipstick, which should be between the upper (MAX) mark and lower (MIN) mark. Approximately 1.0 litre of oil will raise the level from the lower mark to the upper mark.

4 Oil is added through the filler cap. Unscrew the cap and top-up the level; a funnel may help to reduce spillage. Add the oil slowly, checking the level on the dipstick often. Don't overfill (see *Car care*).

Brake and clutch fluid level

Warning: Brake fluid can harm your eyes and damage painted surfaces, so use extreme caution when handling and pouring it.
Warning: Do not use fluid that has been standing open for some time, as it absorbs moisture from the air, which can cause a dangerous loss of braking effectiveness.

Before you start

✔ Make sure that your car is on level ground.

Safety first!

● If the reservoir requires repeated topping-up this is an indication of a fluid leak somewhere in the system, which should be investigated immediately.

● If a leak is suspected, the car should not be driven until the braking system has been checked. Never take any risks where brakes are concerned.

1 The upper (MAX) fluid level marking is on the side of the upper reservoir, which is located at the rear of the engine compartment.

2 If topping-up is necessary, first wipe clean the area around the filler cap with a clean cloth.

3 Unscrew the cap and remove it from the top of the reservoir, along with the rubber diaphragm.

4 Carefully add fluid, avoiding spilling it on the surrounding paintwork. Use only the specified hydraulic fluid. After filling to the correct level, refit the cap and diaphragm and tighten it securely. Wipe off any spilt fluid.

Coolant level

Warning: DO NOT attempt to remove the expansion tank pressure cap when the engine is hot, as there is a very great risk of scalding.
Warning: Do not leave open containers of coolant about, as it is poisonous.

Car care

● Adding coolant should not be necessary on a regular basis. If frequent topping-up is required, it is likely there is a leak. Check the radiator, all hoses and joint faces for signs of staining or wetness, and rectify as necessary.

● It is important that antifreeze is used in the cooling system all year round, not just during the winter months. Don't top-up with water alone, as the antifreeze will become too diluted.

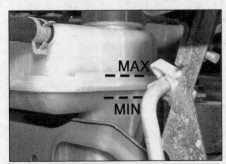

1 The coolant level must be checked with the engine cold; the coolant level should be between the MAX and MIN marks on the expansion tank.

2 If topping-up is necessary, remove the pressure cap (see *Warning*) from the expansion tank, which is located on the right-hand side of the engine compartment.

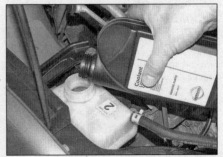

3 Add a mixture of water and antifreeze to the expansion tank until the coolant level is between the level marks. Once the level is correct, securely refit the cap.

Tyre condition and pressure

It is very important that tyres are in good condition, and at the correct pressure - having a tyre failure at any speed is highly dangerous. Tyre wear is influenced by driving style - harsh braking and acceleration, or fast cornering, will all produce more rapid tyre wear. As a general rule, the front tyres wear out faster than the rears. Interchanging the tyres from front to rear ("rotating" the tyres) may result in more even wear. However, if this is completely effective, you may have the expense of replacing all four tyres at once!

Remove any nails or stones embedded in the tread before they penetrate the tyre to cause deflation. If removal of a nail does reveal that the tyre has been punctured, refit the nail so that its point of penetration is marked. Then immediately change the wheel, and have the tyre repaired by a tyre dealer.

Regularly check the tyres for damage in the form of cuts or bulges, especially in the sidewalls. Periodically remove the wheels, and clean any dirt or mud from the inside and outside surfaces. Examine the wheel rims for signs of rusting, corrosion or other damage. Light alloy wheels are easily damaged by "kerbing" whilst parking; steel wheels may also become dented or buckled. A new wheel is very often the only way to overcome severe damage.

New tyres should be balanced when they are fitted, but it may become necessary to re-balance them as they wear, or if the balance weights fitted to the wheel rim should fall off. Unbalanced tyres will wear more quickly, as will the steering and suspension components. Wheel imbalance is normally signified by vibration, particularly at a certain speed (typically around 50 mph). If this vibration is felt only through the steering, then it is likely that just the front wheels need balancing. If, however, the vibration is felt through the whole car, the rear wheels could be out of balance. Wheel balancing should be carried out by a tyre dealer or garage.

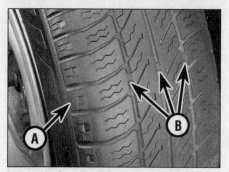

1 Tread Depth - visual check
The original tyres have tread wear safety bands (B), which will appear when the tread depth reaches approximately 1.6 mm. The band positions are indicated by a triangular mark on the tyre sidewall (A).

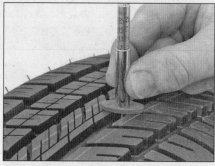

2 Tread Depth - manual check
Alternatively, tread wear can be monitored with a simple, inexpensive device known as a tread depth indicator gauge.

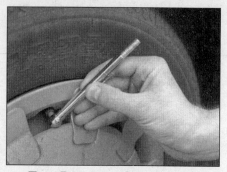

3 Tyre Pressure Check
Check the tyre pressures regularly with the tyres cold. Do not adjust the tyre pressures immediately after the vehicle has been used, or an inaccurate setting will result.

Tyre tread wear patterns

Shoulder Wear

Underinflation (wear on both sides)
Under-inflation will cause overheating of the tyre, because the tyre will flex too much, and the tread will not sit correctly on the road surface. This will cause a loss of grip and excessive wear, not to mention the danger of sudden tyre failure due to heat build-up.
Check and adjust pressures
Incorrect wheel camber (wear on one side)
Repair or renew suspension parts
Hard cornering
Reduce speed!

Centre Wear

Overinflation
Over-inflation will cause rapid wear of the centre part of the tyre tread, coupled with reduced grip, harsher ride, and the danger of shock damage occurring in the tyre casing.
Check and adjust pressures

If you sometimes have to inflate your car's tyres to the higher pressures specified for maximum load or sustained high speed, don't forget to reduce the pressures to normal afterwards.

Uneven Wear

Front tyres may wear unevenly as a result of wheel misalignment. Most tyre dealers and garages can check and adjust the wheel alignment (or "tracking") for a modest charge.
Incorrect camber or castor
Repair or renew suspension parts
Malfunctioning suspension
Repair or renew suspension parts
Unbalanced wheel
Balance tyres
Incorrect toe setting
Adjust front wheel alignment
Note: *The feathered edge of the tread which typifies toe wear is best checked by feel.*

Bulbs and fuses

✔ Check all external lights and the horn. Refer to Chapter 12, Section 2 for details if any of the circuits are found to be inoperative.

✔ Visually check all accessible wiring connectors, harnesses and retaining clips for security, and for signs of chafing or damage.

 HAYNES HiNT *If you need to check your brake lights and indicators unaided, back up to a wall or garage door and operate the lights. The reflected light should show if they are working properly.*

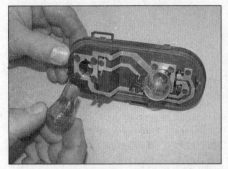

1 If a single indicator light, brake light, sidelight or headlight has failed, it is likely that a bulb has blown, and will need to be renewed. Refer to Chapter 12, Section 5 for details. If both brake lights have failed, it is possible that the switch has failed (see Chapter 9, Section 18).

2 If more than one indicator or tail light has failed, it is likely that either a fuse has blown or that there is a fault in the circuit. Fuses are located behind a cover on the drivers side lower facia panel.

3 Additional fuses are usually located in the fusebox. To renew a blown fuse, simply pull it out and fit a new fuse of the correct rating (see Wiring diagrams). If the fuse blows again, it is important that you find out why – a complete checking procedure is given in Chapter 12, Section 2.

Battery

Caution: Before carrying out any work on the vehicle battery, read the precautions given in 'Safety first!' at the start of this manual.

✔ Make sure that the battery tray is in good condition, and that the clamp is tight. Corrosion on the tray, retaining clamp and the battery itself can be removed with a solution of water and baking soda. Thoroughly rinse all cleaned areas with water. Any metal parts damaged by corrosion should be covered with a zinc-based primer, and then painted.

✔ Periodically (approximately every three months), check the charge condition of the battery, as described in Chapter 5A, Section 2.

✔ If the battery is flat, and you need to jump start your vehicle, see *Roadside repairs.*

1 Lift the plastic cover to gain access to the battery positive terminal, which is located on the left-hand side of the engine compartment. The exterior of the battery should be inspected periodically for damage such as a cracked case or cover.

2 Check the battery lead clamps for tightness to ensure good electrical connections, and check the leads for signs of damage.

HAYNES HiNT

Battery corrosion can be kept to a minimum by applying a layer of petroleum jelly to the clamps and terminals after they are reconnected.

3 If corrosion (white, fluffy deposits) is evident, remove the cables from the battery terminals, clean them with a small wire brush, then refit them. Automotive stores sell a tool for cleaning the battery post …

4 … as well as the battery cable clamps.

Wiper blades

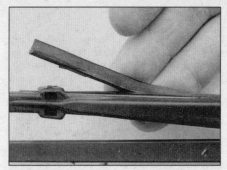

1 Check the condition of the wiper blades: if they are cracked or show signs of deterioration, or if the glass swept area is smeared, renew them. For maximum clarity of vision, wiper blades should be renewed annually.

2 To remove a windscreen wiper blade, turn the ignition on, then turn the ignition off, and press the wiper switch stalk down once. This places the arms in the 'service' position. Lift the wiper from the screen and squeeze the lower ends of the retaining clip together ...

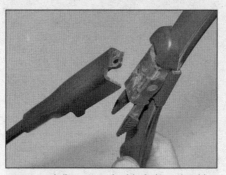

3 ... and disengage the blade by unhooking it from the end of the wiper arm, taking care not to allow the wiper arm to spring back and damage the windscreen. When completed, return the blades to the park position by pressing the wiper switch stalk again.

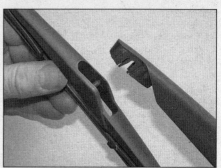

4 To remove the rear wiper blade, lift the wiper arm and then unclip it from the arm, taking care not to allow the arm to spring back and damage the rear screen.

Screen washer fluid level

● Screenwash additives not only keep the windscreen clean during foul weather, they also prevent the washer system freezing in cold weather – which is when you are likely to need it most. Don't top-up using plain water as the screenwash will become too diluted, and will freeze during cold weather.

 Warning: On no account use coolant antifreeze in the washer system, as this may damage the paintwork.

1 The washer fluid reservoir is located in the right-hand front corner of the engine compartment. To check the fluid level, open the cap and look down the filler neck.

2 If topping-up is necessary, add water and a screenwash additive in the quantities recommended on the bottle.

Lubricants and fluids

Engine

Petrol models:
HR16DE and MR20DE engines . . . . Engine oil – SAE 5W30, API SL/SM specification

Diesel models:
K9K engine:
Without particulate filter . . . . Engine oil – SAE 5W30 or SAE 5W30, low SAPS ACEA C4 specification
With particulate filter. . . . . Genuine Nissan engine oil - SAE 5W30 DPF or SAE 5W30, low SAPS ACEA C4 specification

M9R engine:
Without particulate filter . . . . Genuine Nissan engine oil – SAE 5W40 or 0W40, ACEA B4 specification
With particulate filter. . . . . Genuine Nissan engine oil - SAE 5W30 DPF or SAE 5W30, low SAPS ACEA C4 specification

Cooling system

All models. . . . . Genuine Nissan long life coolant or equivalant

Transmission

Manual
RS5F92R (5-speed) and RS6F94R (6-speed). . . . . Genuine Nissan MT-XZ gear oil TL/JR type or API GL-4, viscosity SAE 75W-80
RS6F52A (6-speed) . . . . Genuine Nissan MT-XZ gear oil sports & off-road vehicles or API GL-4, viscosity SAE 75W-85

Automatic:
Upto January 2009 . . . . Genuine Nissan Matic fluid J - ATF
From January 2009 . . . . Genuine Nissan Matic fluid J or S - ATF

Transfer gearbox & Final drive

All 4-wheel drive (4WD) models . . . . Genuine Nissan differential fluid or API GL-5, viscosity SAE 80W-90

Braking and clutch system

All models. . . . . Genuine Nissan brake fluid or equivalent hydraulic fluid to DOT 4

Tyre pressures

Note: *The make of tyres, the sizes and the pressures for each vehicle are given on a label attached to the driver's door A-pillar* **(see illustration)**. *On models with a space-saver spare wheel, a separate pressure is given for the spare tyre, and care must be taken not to misread the sticker; the space-saver wheel is inflated to a lot higher pressure than the standard tyres (typically 60 psi). On models with a space-saver spare wheel, note that the* spare is for temporary use only; whilst the spare is fitted, the vehicle should not be driven at speeds in excess of 50 mph.

Note: *Pressures on the label apply to original-equipment tyres listed, and may vary if any other makes or type of tyre is fitted; check with the tyre manufacturer or supplier for correct pressures if necessary.*

Note: *Tyre pressures must always be checked with the tyres cold to ensure accuracy.*

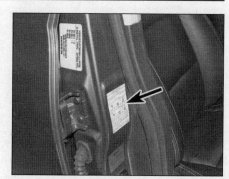

Driver's door A-pillar label

Chapter 1 Part A:
Routine maintenance and servicing – petrol models

Contents

Degrees of difficulty

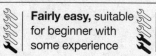

| **Easy,** suitable for novice with little experience | **Fairly easy,** suitable for beginner with some experience | **Fairly difficult,** suitable for competent DIY mechanic | **Difficult,** suitable for experienced DIY mechanic | **Very difficult,** suitable for expert DIY or professional |

Specifications

Lubricants and fluids
Refer to *Lubricants and fluids*

Capacities
Engine oil (with filter):
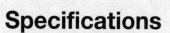

1.6 litre . . . . 4.3 litres
2.0 litre . . . . 4.4 litres
Difference between MAX and MIN dipstick marks . . . . Approx. 1.0 litre
Cooling system:
 1.6 litre . . . . 6.4 litres
 2.0 litre:
   Manual transmission . . . . 7.0 litres
   Automatic transmission . . . . 7.4 litres
Transmission:
 Manual transmission:
   5-speed models . . . . 2.3 litres
   6-speed models . . . . 2.0 litres
 Automatic transmission models . . . . 7.5 litres
 Transfer box – 4-WD models . . . . 0.4 litres
 Rear axle – 4-WD models . . . . 0.6 litres
Fuel tank . . . . 65.0 litres

Cooling system

	Antifreeze	Water
Antifreeze mixture (ethylene glycol antifreeze):		
Protection down to –15ºC	30%	70%
Protection down to –35ºC	50%	50%

Note: *Refer to antifreeze manufacturer for latest recommendations.*

Fuel system

Idle speed (not adjustable – controlled by ECU):
1.6 litre engine	650 ± 50 rpm
2.0 litre engine	700 ± 50 rpm
Idle mixture CO content	0.3 % Max. (Not adjustable – controlled by ECU)

Ignition system

Spark plug type (1.6 & 2.0 litre engines).........................	NGK PLZKAR6A or Bosch FR7ME
Electrode gap	1.1 mm
Ignition timing (not adjustable – controlled by ECU)	15º ± 5º BTDC @ 700rpm

Auxiliary drivebelts

Drivebelt deflection:

	Setting	Limit
1.6 litre engines (used belt):		
With air conditioning	4.8 to 5.3 mm	8.2 mm
Without air conditioning	4.3 to 4.7 mm	7.4 mm
1.6 litre engines (new belt):	Setting	
With air conditioning	4.1 to 4.4 mm	
Without air conditioning	3.7 to 3.9 mm	

Note: *In all cases, the drivebelt deflection is measured by applying a force of 98Nm (10 kg, 22 lb) as described in the text.*

Brakes

Minimum front brake pad friction material thickness...............	2.0 mm
Minimum rear brake pad friction material thickness	1.5 mm
Minimum handbrake shoe lining thickness	1.5 mm
Number of clicks required to fully apply handbrake...............	7 to 8 clicks
Number of clicks required operating handbrake 'on' warning light....	1 click
Disc runout limit (attached to vehicle)	0.035 mm

Suspension and steering

Front wheel toe setting..................................	2.0 mm ± 1.0 mm toe-in

Torque wrench settings

	Nm	lbf ft
Auxilliary drivebelt tensioning pulley nut (1.6 litre engines):		
Stage 1 (adjustment position)............................	5	4
Stage 2	35	26
Automatic transmission:		
Drain plug (hexagon outer plug)	8	7
Fluid level tube (inner plug/tube)	8	7
Cylinder block coolant drain plug..........................	10	8
Engine sump drain plug	34	25
Manual transmission:		
5-speed:		
Filler/level plug (plastic plug)	3	2
Drain plug...	25	18
6-speed:		
Filler/level plug (plastic plug)	3	2
Drain plug...	23	17
Rear axle (4WD):		
Filler/level plug	35	26
Drain plug..	35	26
Transfer box (4WD):		
Filler/level plug	35	26
Drain plug..	35	26
Turbine revolution sensor	6	5
Roadwheel nuts	113	83
Front seat belt mounting bolts:		
Upper pillar anchorage	25	18
Lower sill anchorage	49	36
Seat belt inertia reel bolt	40	30
Pre-tensioner-to-sill bolt	50	37
Rear seat belt mounting bolts (all bolts)...................	49	36
Spark plugs	20	15

The maintenance intervals in this manual are provided with the assumption that you, not the dealer, will be carrying out the work. These are the minimum maintenance intervals recommended by us for vehicles driven daily. If you wish to keep your vehicle in peak condition at all times, you may wish to perform some of these procedures more often. We encourage frequent maintenance because it enhances the efficiency, performance and resale value of your vehicle. If the vehicle is driven in dusty areas, used to tow a trailer, or driven frequently at slow speeds (idling in traffic) or on short journeys, more frequent maintenance intervals are recommended. Nissan recommend that many service intervals are halved for vehicles which are used under these conditions.

When the vehicle is new, it should be serviced by a dealer service department (or other workshop recognised by the vehicle manufacturer as providing the same standard of service) in order to preserve the warranty. The vehicle manufacturer may reject warranty claims if you are unable to prove that servicing has been carried out as and when specified, using only original equipment parts or parts certified to be of equivalent quality.

Every 250 miles or weekly
☐ Refer to Weekly checks

Every 12 500 miles or 12 months – whichever comes first
In addition to all the items listed above, carry out the following:

☐ Renew the engine oil and filter (Section 3)

* Note: *Frequent oil and filter changes are good for the engine and we recommend that the oil and filter be renewed at the interval specified here (or at least once every 12 months), especially if the vehicle is used on a lot of short journeys or covers a small annual mileage.*

☐ Check all underbonnet components and hoses for fluid leaks (Section 4)
☐ Check the brake pads and renew if necessary (Section 5)

Every 12 500 miles or 12 months – whichever comes first (continued)
☐ Check the operation of the handbrake (Section 6)
☐ Check the operation of the clutch (Section 7)
☐ Check the condition of the air conditioning system components (see Section 8)
☐ Check the condition of the emissions control system hoses and components (Section 9)
☐ Check the condition of the auxiliary drivebelts, and renew if necessary (Section 10)
☐ Check the steering and suspension components for condition and security (Section 11)
☐ Check the condition of the driveshaft rubber gaiters (Section 12)
☐ Check the wheel alignment (Section 13)
☐ Check the condition of the exhaust system and mountings (Section 14)
☐ Check the operation and security of all seat belts (Section 15)
☐ Check the operation of all electrical systems (Section 16)
☐ Lubricate all hinges and locks (Section 17)
☐ Renew the pollen filter (Section 18)
☐ Renew the air filter element (Section 19)
☐ Check the automatic transmission fluid level (Section 20)
☐ Check the manual transmission oil level (Section 21)
☐ Check the final drive oil level (Section 22)
☐ Check the transfer gearbox oil level (Section 23)
☐ Carry out a road test (Section 24)

Every 25 000 miles or 2 years – whichever comes first
In addition to all the items listed above, carry out the following:

☐ Renew the spark plugs (Section 25)
☐ Renew the brake fluid (Section 26)
☐ Renew the coolant (Section 27)

Front underbody view

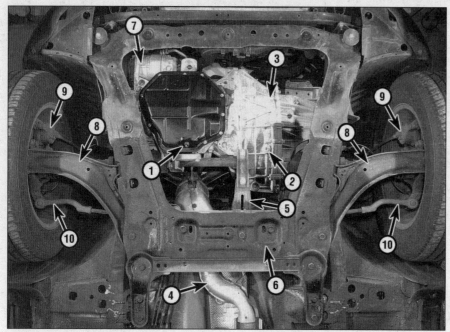

1 Engine oil drain plug
2 Transmission drain plug
3 Transmission
4 Exhaust front pipe
5 Rear engine steady bar
6 Subframe
7 AC compressor
8 Front suspension lower arm
9 Brake calipers
10 Steering track rod end

Rear underbody view

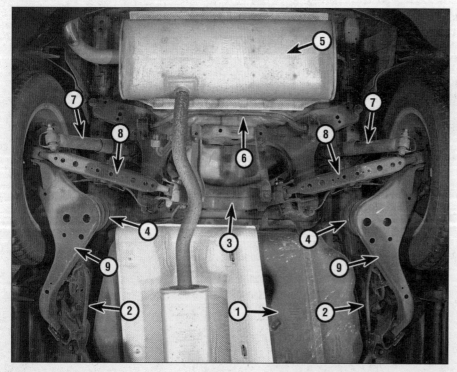

1 Fuel tank
2 Handbrake cables
3 Rear axle assembly
4 Coil springs
5 Exhaust rear silencer and tailpipe
6 Anti-roll bar
7 Shock absorbers (dampers)
8 Lower suspension arms
9 Rear trailing arms

Underbonnet view

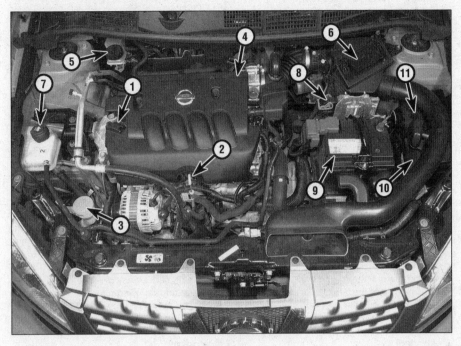

1 Engine oil filler cap
2 Engine oil level dipstick
3 Windscreen washer bottle
4 EGR valve
5 Brake fluid reservoir
6 Air cleaner element
7 Coolant expansion tank
8 Engine management control module (ECM)
9 Battery
10 Relay/fusebox
11 Intelligent Power Distribution Module (IPDM)

Maintenance procedures

1 General information

This Chapter is designed to help the home mechanic maintain his/her vehicle for safety, economy, long life and peak performance.

The Chapter contains a master maintenance schedule, followed by sections dealing specifically with each task on the schedule. Visual checks, adjustments, component renewal and other helpful items are included. Refer to the accompanying illustrations of the engine compartment and the underside of the vehicle for the locations of the various components.

Servicing of your vehicle in accordance with the mileage/time maintenance schedule and the following sections will provide a planned maintenance programme, which should result in a long and reliable service life. This is a comprehensive plan, so maintaining some items but not others at the specified service intervals, will not produce the same results.

As you service your vehicle, you will discover that many of the procedures can – and should – be grouped together, because of the particular procedure being performed, or because of the close proximity of two otherwise-unrelated components to one another. For example, if the vehicle is raised for any reason, the exhaust can be inspected at the same time as the suspension and steering components.

The first step in this maintenance programme is to prepare you before the actual work begins. Read through all the sections relevant to the work to be carried out, then make a list and gather all the parts and tools required. If a problem is encountered, seek advice from a parts specialist, or a dealer service department.

2 Regular maintenance

1 If, from the time the vehicle is new, the routine maintenance schedule is followed closely, and frequent checks are made of fluid levels and high-wear items, as suggested throughout this manual, the engine will be kept in relatively good running condition, and the need for additional work will be minimised.

2 It is possible that there will be times when the engine is running poorly, due to lack of regular maintenance. This is even more likely if a used vehicle, which has not received regular and frequent maintenance checks, is purchased. In such cases, additional work may need to be carried out, outside of the regular maintenance intervals.

3 If engine wear is suspected, a compression test (Chapter 2A, Section 2 or Chapter 2B, Section 2) will provide valuable information regarding the overall performance of the main internal components. Such a test can be used as a basis to decide on the extent of the work to be carried out. If for example a compression test indicates serious internal engine wear, conventional maintenance as described in this Chapter will not greatly improve the performance of the engine, and may prove a waste of time and money, unless extensive overhaul work (Chapter 2E) is carried out first.

4 The following series of operations are those most often required to improve the performance of a generally poor-running engine:

Primary operations

a) Check all the engine-related fluids (See 'Weekly checks').

b) Check the condition of all hoses, and check for fluid leaks (Section 4).

c) Clean, inspect and test the battery (See 'Weekly checks' and Chapter 5A, Section 2).

d) Renew the spark plugs (Section 25).

e) Check the condition and tension of the auxiliary drivebelts (Section 10).

f) Check the condition of the air filter, and renew if necessary (Section 19).

5 If the above operations do not prove fully effective, carry out the following secondary operations:

Secondary operations

All items listed under Primary operations, plus the following:

a) Check the charging system (Chapter 5A).

b) Check the ignition system (Chapter 5B).

c) Check the fuel, exhaust and emission control systems (Chapter 4A or Chapter 4C).

Every 12 500 miles or 12 months

3 Engine oil and filter renewal

1 Frequent oil and filter changes are the most important preventative maintenance procedures that can be undertaken by the DIY owner. As engine oil ages, it becomes diluted and contaminated, which leads to premature engine wear.

2 Before starting this procedure, gather together all the necessary tools and materials. Also make sure that you have plenty of clean rags and newspapers handy, to mop-up any spills. Ideally, the engine oil should be warm, as it will drain more easily, and more built-up sludge will be removed with it.

3 Take care not to touch the exhaust or any other hot parts of the engine when working under the vehicle. To avoid any possibility of scalding, and to protect yourself from possible

skin irritants and other harmful contaminants in used engine oils, it is advisable to wear gloves when carrying out this work.

4 Access to the underside of the vehicle will be greatly improved if it can be raised on a lift, driven onto ramps, or jacked up and supported on axle stands (see *Jacking and vehicle support*). Whichever method is chosen, make sure that the vehicle remains level, or if it is at an angle, that the drain plug is at the lowest point. The drain plug is located at the rear of the sump **(see illustration)**. Undo the retaining bolts and remove the engine undershield from under the front of the vehicle.

5 Remove the oil filler cap from the cylinder head camshaft cover at the timing chain end (twist it anti-clockwise and withdraw it) **(see illustration)**.

6 Using a spanner, or a suitable socket and bar, slacken the drain plug about half a turn. Position the draining container under the drain plug, and then remove the plug completely

(see illustrations). If possible, try to keep the plug pressed into the sump while unscrewing it by hand the last couple of turns.

7 Allow some time for the oil to drain, noting that it may be necessary to reposition the container as the oil flow slows to a trickle.

8 After all the oil has drained; wipe the drain plug with a clean rag. Remove the old sealing washer from the drain plug and fit a new one. Clean the area around the drain plug opening, and refit the plug complete with the new sealing washer **(see illustration)**. Tighten the drain plug securely – preferably to the specified torque, using a torque wrench.

9 The oil filter is located at the front of the cylinder block – access is most easily obtained from underneath the vehicle **(see illustration)**.

10 Move the container into position under the oil filter to catch the oil spillage.

11 Use an oil filter removal tool (if required) to slacken the filter initially, then unscrew it by

3.4 Engine oil drain plug (arrowed)

3.5 Remove oil filler cap

3.6a Use a spanner to slacken the drain plug ...

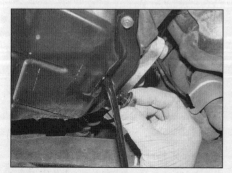

3.6b ... and then unscrew it from the sump

3.8 Fit a new sealing washer to the drain plug

3.9 Oil filter location on the front of the engine (arrowed)

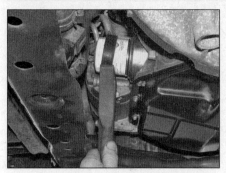

3.11 Slackening the oil filter with a removal tool

3.13a Apply clean oil to the seal ...

3.13b ... and then refit the oil filter

hand the rest of the way **(see illustration)**. Be prepared for some oil spillage as the filter is removed. Empty the oil from the old filter into the container, before disposal.

12 Use a clean rag to remove all oil, dirt and sludge from the filter sealing area on the engine cylinder block. Check the old filter to make sure that the rubber sealing ring has not stuck to the engine. If it has, carefully remove it.

13 Apply a light coating of clean engine oil to the sealing ring on the new filter, and then screw the filter into position on the engine **(see illustrations)**. Lightly tighten the filter until its sealing ring contacts the block, and then tighten it through a further two-thirds of a turn. Tighten the filter firmly by hand only – **do not** use any tools.

14 Remove the old oil and all tools from under the vehicle then, if applicable, refit the engine undershield and lower the vehicle to the ground.

15 Fill the engine through the oil filler hole in the cylinder head cover, using the correct grade and type of oil (see *Weekly checks*). Pour in half the specified quantity of oil first, and then wait a few minutes for the oil to drain into the sump. Continue to add oil, a small quantity at a time, until the level is up to the lower mark on the dipstick. Adding a further 1.0 litre will bring the level up to the upper mark on the dipstick. Refit the oil filler cap when correct level is achieved.

16 Start the engine and run it for a few minutes, while checking for leaks around the oil filter seal and the sump drain plug. Note that there may be a delay of a few seconds before the low oil pressure warning light goes out when the engine is first started, as the oil circulates through the new oil filter and the engine oil galleries before the pressure builds-up. Do not run the engine above idle speed while the warning light is on.

17 Stop the engine, and wait a few minutes for the oil to settle in the sump once more. With the new oil circulated and the filter now completely full, recheck the level on the dipstick, and add more oil as necessary.

18 Dispose of the used engine oil and filter safely, referring to *General repair procedures* in the Reference Chapter. Do not discard the old filter with domestic household waste. The facility for waste oil disposal provided by many local council refuse tips generally has a filter receptacle alongside.

4 Hose and fluid leak check

1 Visually inspect the engine joint faces, gaskets and seals for any signs of water or oil leaks. Pay particular attention to the areas around the cylinder head cover, cylinder head, oil filter and sump joint faces. Over a period of time, some very slight seepage from these areas is to be expected – what you are really looking for is any indication of a serious leak. Should a leak be found, renew the offending gasket or oil seal by referring to the appropriate Chapters in this manual.

2 Also check the security and condition of all the engine-related pipes and hoses. Ensure that all cable ties or securing clips are in place and in good condition. Clips, which are broken or missing, can lead to chafing of the hoses pipes or wiring which could cause more serious problems in the future.

3 Carefully check the radiator hoses and heater hoses along their entire length. Renew any hose, which is cracked, swollen or deteriorated. Cracks will show up better if the hose is squeezed. Pay close attention to the hose clips that secures the hoses to the cooling system components. Hose clips can pinch and puncture hoses, resulting in cooling system leaks. If the crimped-type hose clips are used, it may be a good idea to fit standard worm-drive clips.

4 Inspect all the cooling system components (hoses, joint faces, etc) for leaks. Where any problems of this nature are found on system components, renew the component or gasket with reference to Chapter 3 **(see Haynes Hint)**.

5 Where applicable, inspect the automatic transmission fluid cooler hoses for leaks or deterioration **(see illustration)**.

6 With the vehicle raised, inspect the petrol tank and filler neck for punctures, cracks and other damage. The connection between the filler neck and tank is especially critical. Sometimes a rubber filler neck or connecting hose will leak due to loose retaining clamps or deteriorated rubber.

7 Carefully check all rubber hoses and metal fuel lines leading away from the petrol tank. Check for loose connections, deteriorated hoses, crimped lines and other damage. Pay particular attention to the vent pipes and hoses, which often loop up around the filler neck and can become blocked or crimped. Follow the lines to the front of the vehicle,

A leak in the cooling system will usually show up as white - or antifreeze-coloured deposits on the area adjoining the leak

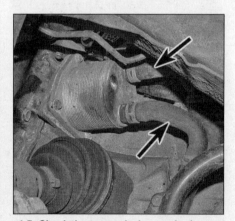

4.5 Check the transmission cooler hoses

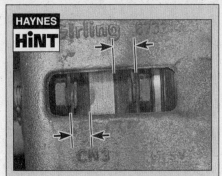

HAYNES HiNT

For a quick check, the thickness of friction material remaining on each brake pad can be measured through the aperture in the caliper body.

carefully inspecting them all the way. Renew damaged sections as necessary.
8 Check the condition of all brake fluid hoses.
9 From within the engine compartment, check the security of all fuel hose attachments and pipe unions, and inspect the fuel hoses and vacuum hoses for kinks, chafing and deterioration.

5 Brake pad condition check – front and rear

Front brake pads

1 Firmly apply the handbrake, and then jack up the front of the vehicle and support it securely on axle stands (see *Jacking and vehicle support*). Remove the front roadwheels.
2 If any pad's friction material is worn to the specified thickness or less; *all four pads must be renewed as a set* (**see Haynes Hint**). **Note:** *If any pad is approaching the minimum thickness, consider renewal as a precautionary measure in case the pads wear out before the next service.*
3 For a comprehensive check, the brake pads should be removed and cleaned. This will permit the operation of the caliper to be checked, and the condition of the brake disc itself to be fully examined on both sides. Refer to Chapter 9 for further information.

6.11a Remove the rubber grommet ...

6.8 Unclip the cup holder from the centre console

Rear brake pads

4 Chock the front wheels then jack up the rear of the vehicle and support it securely on axle stands (see *Jacking and vehicle support*). Remove the rear roadwheels.
5 Proceed as described for the front brake pads in paragraphs 2 and 3.

6 Handbrake check and adjustment

Check

1 The handbrake should be capable of holding the parked vehicle stationary, even on steep slopes, when applied with moderate force. The mechanism should be firm and positive in feel, with no trace of stiffness or sponginess from the cables, and the mechanism should release immediately the handbrake lever is released. If the mechanism does not operate satisfactorily, it should be checked immediately.
2 To check the operation of the handbrake, chock the front wheels then jack up the rear of the vehicle and support it securely on axle stands (see *Jacking and vehicle support*).
3 Fully release the handbrake, and check that the rear road wheels can be rotated by hand – slight dragging is acceptable, but it should be possible to turn each wheel easily without undue force.
4 Operate the handbrake lever up and down approx. 10 times, to establish the correct shoe-to-drum clearance.

6.11b ... and turn the adjuster ...

6.9 Measure the length of thread, before slackening the adjusting nut

5 With the handbrake lever released, again, check that the rear road wheels can still be rotated.
6 Apply normal moderate pressure to operate the handbrake lever, and count the number of clicks necessary to bring the lever to the fully applied position, (this should be approx. 7 to 8 clicks). Check that the road wheels are locked with the lever fully applied.

Adjustment

7 If the number of clicks required to fully apply the handbrake is not as specified, proceed as follows.
8 Working inside the vehicle, unclip the cup holder from the centre console (**see illustration**).
9 The handbrake adjuster nut is located under the cup holder on the threaded end of the front cable. Measure the length of thread, protruding through the nut, as a guide for refitting (**see illustration**). Slacken the adjuster nut until it is at the end of the threaded part of the cable.
10 If not already done, chock the front wheels then jack up the rear of the vehicle and support it securely on axle stands (see *Jacking and vehicle support*). Remove the rear road wheels.
11 Working on each side at a time, adjust the shoe positions as follows. Turn the rear disc until the access hole is positioned over the adjuster serrations. Using a screwdriver through the hole in the brake disc, tighten the adjuster until the brake disc cannot be rotated, then back the adjuster off, so that the brake disc is free to turn without any drag (**see illustrations**). Repeat the adjustment on

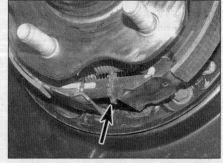

6.11c ... between the lower part of the brake shoes

6.13 Make sure the cables are still connected (arrowed)

10.2 Remove the inner wheel arch panel

10.3 Check for drivebelt wear

the other side of the vehicle, and then refit the plug to the access holes in the brake disc.

12 Working inside the vehicle, tighten the adjuster nut on the end of the front handbrake cable, until the handbrake operates correctly at approx. 7 to 8 clicks.

13 When tightening the adjuster nut on the end of the front cable, make sure the two rear cables are still located in the equalizer bar, under the rear end of the centre console **(see illustration)**.

14 Check that the handbrake 'on' warning light illuminates after the first click.

15 Refit the cup holder to the centre console and check the handbrake operation as described previously in this Section.

16 If this adjustment cannot be achieved, remove the handbrake shoes and cables as described in Chapter 9, and check their condition.

17 On completion, refit the road wheels, and then lower the vehicle to the ground.

7 Clutch operation check

Check that the clutch pedal moves smoothly and easily through its full travel. Check the hydraulic system for leaks; check also that the clutch itself functions correctly, with no trace of slip or drag. If excessive effort is required to operate the clutch, check the pedal assembly to ensure that its pivot is properly greased. Refer to Chapter 6 for further information.

8 Air conditioning system check

Note: *Before proceeding, refer to the precautions given in Chapter 3, Section 10, regarding work on the air conditioning system.*

1 Check the tension and condition of the auxiliary drivebelt, which drives the air conditioning compressor, as described in Section 10.

2 Check the condition of the condenser fins, and clean them out if necessary (remove the front bumper/grille panel for access). Clean any dirt and insects from the fins using compressed air, or a soft brush. Be careful not to damage the condenser.

3 Operate the air conditioning system for at least 10 minutes each month, even during cold weather, to keep the seals, etc, in good condition.

4 Regularly inspect the refrigerant pipes, hoses and unions for security and condition.

5 The most common cause of poor cooling is simply a low system refrigerant charge. If a noticeable drop in cool air output occurs, one of the following checks will help to determine if the refrigerant level is low.

6 Warm up the engine to normal operating temperature.

7 Move the temperature control knob to the coldest setting, and move the blower motor control knob to the highest setting. Open the doors (to ensure that the air conditioning system does not shut off as soon as it cools the passenger compartment).

8 With the compressor engaged – the compressor clutch will make an audible click, and the centre of the clutch will rotate – On some models, there is a sight glass in the top of the receiver/drier bottle, if air bubbles are present in the sight glass, or the refrigerant looks foamy, the charge is low.

9 If no sight glass is fitted, feel the inlet and outlet pipes at the compressor. One side should be cold, and the other hot. If there is no perceptible difference in temperature between the two pipes, this indicates a fault with the compressor, a low refrigerant charge, or some other system fault – consult a Nissan dealer or air conditioning specialist for advice.

10 The air conditioning system will lose a proportion of its charge through normal seepage – so it is as well to regard periodic recharging as a maintenance operation. Recharging must be done by a Nissan dealer or an air conditioning specialist.

11 **Do Not** under any circumstances attempt to open any of the refrigerant lines, or renew any of the components, until the system has been evacuated of its refrigerant, as it is potentially dangerous (see Chapter 3, Section 10).

9 Emissions control systems check

Details of the emissions control system components and testing are given in Chapter 4C, Section 2.

Checking consists simply of a visual check for obvious signs of damaged or leaking hoses and joints.

10 Auxiliary drivebelt checking and renewal

Checking drivebelt condition

1 Firmly apply the handbrake, and then jack up the front of the vehicle and support it securely on axle stands (see *Jacking and vehicle support*). Remove the right-hand front roadwheel.

2 Release the retaining clips and remove the inner panel from the front of the wheel arch liner, to gain access to the crankshaft pulley **(see illustration)**. If required, also undo the retaining bolts and remove the engine undershield to improve access.

3 Using a suitable socket and extension bar fitted to the crankshaft pulley bolt, rotate the crankshaft so that the entire length of the drivebelts can be examined. Examine the drivebelts for cracks, splitting, fraying or damage. Check also for signs of glazing (shiny patches) and for separation of the belt plies **(see illustration)**. Renew the belt if worn or damaged.

4 On 2.0 litre models, a spring-loaded tensioner is fitted to automatically maintain the correct tension on the belt. If the arrow on the tensioner body is outside the indicator

10.4 Tensioner indicator (arrowed) – 2.0 litre engines

10.7 Slacken the tensioner pulley securing nut

10.8a Slacken the tensioner pulley adjusting bolt (arrowed) ...

10.8b ... and remove the auxiliary belt

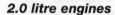

10.9 Make sure the belt is fitted correctly

range, then the belt will need to be renewed **(see illustration)**.

5 If the condition of the belt is satisfactory, check the drivebelt tension as described below under the relevant sub-heading.

1.6 litre engines

Removal

6 If not already done, proceed as described in paragraphs 1 and 2.

7 Working under the right-hand front wheel arch, slacken the nut securing the tensioner pulley to the mounting bracket, by a quarter of a turn **(see illustration)**. This nut does not require slackening too much, or it will cause the tensioner pulley to twist, and then it will prevent the belt from being adjusted correctly on refitting.

8 Rotate the adjuster bolt to slacken the tensioner pulley, until there is sufficient slack for the drivebelt to be removed from the

pulleys **(see illustrations)**. Note the routing of the belt as it is removed. If the belt is to be re-used mark the direction of rotation on the belt.

Refitting

9 Fit the belt around the pulleys, as noted on removal **(see illustration)**, and then take up the slack in the belt by tightening the adjuster bolt. If the belt is new, ensure that the belt is of the correct type and length.

10 Correct tensioning of the drivebelt will ensure that it has a long life. Beware, however, of over tightening, as this can cause wear in the bearings.

11 The belt tension is checked at the mid-point between the pulleys on the lower belt run. Referring to the Specifications given at the start of this Chapter, apply the specified force and check that the belt deflection is within the specified range.

12 To adjust the tension, rotate the adjuster bolt until the correct tension is achieved **(see illustration)**, see specifications at the beginning of this Chapter. Make sure the nut securing the tensioner pulley is tightened to the stage 1 (adjustment position), as described in the torque settings at the beginning of this Chapter. If this is not done, then the tensioner pulley could twist and prevent the belt from being adjusted correctly.

13 Once the belt is correctly tensioned, rotate the crankshaft a couple of times and recheck the tension.

14 When all is correct, tighten the tensioner pulley retaining nut to its stage 2, specified torque setting.

15 Refit the wheel arch liner and engine undershield, securely tightening their fasteners, then refit the roadwheel and lower the vehicle to the ground. Tighten the road wheels to the specified torque setting.

2.0 litre engines

Removal

16 If not already done, proceed as described in paragraphs 1 and 2.

17 Working under the right-hand front wheel arch, release the tension on the belt by using a spanner to move the tensioner clockwise (as viewed from the right-hand side of the car). If required, a 6 mm Allen key or drill bit can be inserted into a hole in the tensioner body to hold it in the released position **(see illustrations)**.

10.12 Check the deflection of the drive belt

10.17a Turning the spanner clockwise from under the vehicle ...

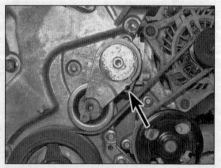

10.17b ... and lock the tensioner, when the holes are aligned (arrowed)

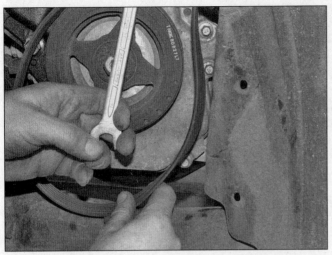

10.18 Remove the drive belt from around the pulleys

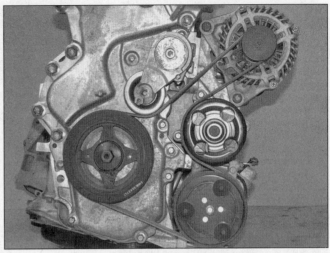

10.19 Auxilliary drivebelt configuration

18 Note the routing of the belt, then slip the belt off the pulleys **(see illustration)**. If the belt is to be re-used mark the direction of rotation on the belt.

Refitting

19 Fit the belt around the pulleys, as noted on removal **(see illustration)**. If the belt is new, ensure that the belt is of the correct type and length.

20 With the belt in position, use the spanner/socket to hold the tensioner in position while the 6 mm Allen key is removed, then carefully release the pressure and the spring loaded tensioner will move anti-clockwise so the belt will automatically become tensioned **(see illustration)**.

21 Once the belt is correctly fitted, rotate the crankshaft a couple of times and recheck the tension, as described in paragraph 4.

22 Refit the wheel arch liner and engine undershield, securely tightening their fasteners, then refit the roadwheel and lower the vehicle to the ground. Tighten the road wheels to the specified torque setting.

11 Steering and suspension check

Front suspension and steering

1 Firmly apply the handbrake, and then jack up the front of the vehicle and support it securely on axle stands (see *Jacking and vehicle support*).

2 Visually inspect the balljoint dust covers and the steering rack and pinion gaiters for splits, chafing or deterioration **(see illustrations)**. Any wear of these components will cause loss of lubricant, together with dirt and water entry, resulting in rapid deterioration of the balljoints or steering gear.

3 Grasp the roadwheel at the 12 o'clock

and 6 o'clock positions, and try to rock it **(see illustration)**. Very slight free play may be felt, but if the movement is appreciable, further investigation is necessary to determine the source. Continue rocking the wheel while an assistant depresses the footbrake. If the movement is now eliminated or significantly reduced, it is likely that the hub bearings are at fault. If the free play is still evident with the footbrake depressed, then there is wear in the suspension joints or mountings.

4 Now grasp the wheel at the 9 o'clock and 3 o'clock positions, and try to rock it as before

10.20 Hold the pressure on the tensioner whilst fitting the drive belt

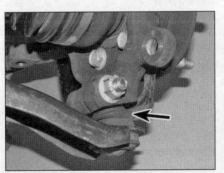

11.2a Check the ball joint dust covers (arrowed) ...

11.2b ... the steering rack gaiters (arrowed) ...

11.2c ... and the anti-roll bar drop link ball joint dust covers (arrowed)

11.3 Check for wear in the hub bearings by grasping the wheel and trying to rock it

(see illustration). Any movement felt now may again be caused by wear in the hub bearings or the steering track rod balljoints. If the inner or outer balljoint is worn, the visual movement will be obvious.

5 Using a large screwdriver or flat bar, check for wear in the suspension mounting bushes by levering between the relevant suspension component and its attachment point. Some movement is to be expected as the mountings are made of rubber, but excessive wear should be obvious. Also check the condition of any visible rubber bushes, looking for splits, cracks or contamination of the rubber.

6 With the car standing on its wheels, have an assistant turn the steering wheel back-and-forth about an eighth of a turn each way. There should be very little, if any, lost movement between the steering wheel and roadwheels. If this is not the case, closely observe the joints and mountings previously described, but in addition check the steering column universal joints for wear, and also check the rack-and-pinion steering gear itself.

Rear suspension

7 Chock the front wheels, then jack up the rear of the vehicle and support securely on axle stands (see *Jacking and vehicle support*).

8 Working as described previously for the front suspension, check the rear hub bearings, the suspension bushes and the shock absorber mountings for wear.

Strut/shock absorber check

9 Check for any signs of fluid leakage around the suspension strut/shock absorber body, or from the rubber gaiter around the piston rod. Should any fluid be noticed, the suspension strut/shock absorber is defective internally, and should be renewed. **Note:** *Suspension struts/shock absorbers should always be renewed in pairs on the same axle.*

10 The efficiency of the suspension strut/shock absorber may be checked by bouncing the vehicle at each corner. Generally speaking, the body will return to its normal position and stop after being depressed. If it rises and returns on a rebound, the suspension strut/shock absorber is probably suspect. Examine the suspension strut/shock absorber upper and lower mountings for any signs of wear.

12 Driveshaft gaiter check

With the vehicle raised and securely supported on stands (see *Jacking and vehicle support*), turn the steering onto full lock, then slowly rotate the roadwheel. Inspect the condition of the outer constant velocity (CV) joint rubber gaiters, squeezing the gaiters to open out the folds **(see illustration)**. Check for signs of cracking, splits or deterioration of the rubber, which may allow the grease to escape, and lead to water and grit entry into the joint.

11.4 Check for wear in the steering rack or ball joints by grasping the wheel and trying to rock it

Also check the security and condition of the retaining clips. Repeat these checks on the inner CV joints. If any damage or deterioration is found, the gaiters should be renewed as described in Chapter 8, Section 3.

At the same time, check the general condition of the CV joints themselves by first holding the driveshaft and attempting to rotate the wheel. Repeat this check by holding the inner joint and attempting to rotate the driveshaft. Any appreciable movement indicates wear in the joints, wear in the driveshaft splines, or a loose driveshaft retaining nut.

13 Wheel alignment check

Definitions

A vehicle's steering and suspension geometry is defined in four basic settings – all angles are expressed in degrees (toe settings are also expressed as a measurement); the relevant settings are camber, castor, steering axis inclination and toe setting. Some of these settings are adjustable, and in all cases special equipment is necessary to check them. Note that front wheel toe setting is often referred to as 'tracking' or 'front wheel alignment'.

Checking

Due to the special measuring equipment necessary to check the wheel alignment, and the skill required to use it properly, the

14.2 Check the exhaust system securing bolts

12.1 Check the driveshaft rubber gaiters (arrowed)

checking and adjustment of these settings is best left to a Nissan dealer or similar expert. Note that most tyre-fitting shops now possess sophisticated checking equipment.

14 Exhaust system check

1 With the engine cold (at least an hour after the vehicle has been driven), check the complete exhaust system from the engine to the end of the tailpipe. The exhaust system is most easily checked with the vehicle raised on a hoist, or suitably supported on axle stands, so that the exhaust components are readily visible and accessible.

2 Check the exhaust pipes and connections for evidence of leaks, severe corrosion and damage. Make sure that all brackets and mountings are in good condition, and that all relevant nuts and bolts are tight **(see illustration)**. Leakage at any of the joints or in other parts of the system will usually show up as a black sooty stain in the vicinity of the leak.

3 Rattles and other noises can often be traced to the exhaust system, especially the brackets and mountings **(see illustration)**. Try to move the pipes and silencers. If the components are able to come into contact with the body or suspension parts, secure the system with new mountings. Otherwise separate the joints (if possible) and twist the pipes as necessary to provide additional clearance.

14.3 Check the exhaust system rubber mountings

15 Seat belt check

1 All models are fitted with three-point diagonal inertia reel seat belts for all seats.
2 Inspect the belts for signs of fraying or other damage. Also check the operation of the buckles and retractor mechanisms, and ensure that all mounting bolts are securely tightened. Note that the bolts are shouldered so that the belt anchor points are free to rotate.
3 If there is any sign of damage, or any doubt about the condition of a belt, it must be renewed. If the vehicle has been involved in a collision, any belts in use at the time should be renewed as a matter of course, and all other belts should be checked carefully.
4 Use only warm water and non-detergent soap to clean the belts. Never use any chemical cleaners, strong detergents, dyes or bleaches. Keep the belts fully extended until they have dried naturally – do not apply heat to dry them.

16 Electrical systems check

1 Check the operation of all electrical equipment, i.e. lights, direction indicators, horn, etc. Refer to the appropriate Sections of Chapter 12 for details if any of the circuits are found to be inoperative.
2 Note that stop-light switch adjustment is described in Chapter 9, Section 18.
3 Visually check all accessible wiring connectors, harnesses and retaining clips for security, and for signs of chafing or damage. Rectify any faults found.

18.2 Disconnect the wiring connector

17 Hinge and lock lubrication

1 Work around the vehicle, and lubricate the hinges of the bonnet, doors and tailgate or boot lid with a light machine oil.
2 Lightly lubricate the bonnet release mechanism and the exposed sections of the inner cable with a smear of grease. Similarly, lubricate the tailgate/boot lid/fuel filler flap release mechanisms, where accessible.
3 Check carefully the security and operation of all hinges, latches and locks, adjusting them where required (see Chapter 11). Check the operation of the central locking system.
4 Check the condition and operation of the tailgate struts, renewing them if either is leaking or no longer able to support the tailgate securely when raised.

18 Pollen filter renewal

1 Remove the glovebox as described in Chapter 11, Section 26.
2 Disconnect the wiring connector from the control flap motor, on the left-hand rear of the heater housing unit (see illustration).

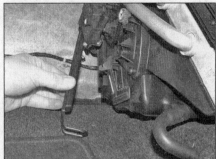

18.3 Unclip the filter cover

18.4 Withdraw the pollen filter from the housing

3 Release the lower part of the filter cover and unclip it from the rear of the heater housing unit (see illustration).
4 Collapse the pollen filter inside the housing and withdraw it, then wipe clean the area around the housing (see illustration).
5 Fit the new filter to the housing, in the same way as it was removed, making sure it is fitted in the correct position, with the arrows facing towards the inside of the vehicle (see illustration).
6 Refit the filter cover on the housing, making sure the lower part of the cover is clipped into position (see illustration).
7 Refit the wiring connector to the control flap motor, then refit the glovebox back into the facia panel.

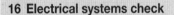

18.5 Note the markings on the filter for refitting

18.6 Make sure the lower part of the filter cover is secured

19.2a Release the two retaining clips …

19.2b … and withdraw the filter and plastic tray

19.3 Remove the filter element from the plastic tray

19.5 make sure the filter assembly is secured in the housing corectly

19 Air filter element renewal

1 The air filter is situated in the air filter housing at the left-hand rear of the engine compartment.

2 Open the bonnet, release the two retaining clips, and then withdraw the air filter element and plastic tray, out from the top of the air filter housing **(see illustrations)**.

3 Lift the old air filter element out of the plastic tray; noting which way round it is fitted and fit a new filter element to the tray **(see illustration)**.

4 Wipe the inside of the air filter housing and filter cover with a clean cloth to remove all traces of dirt and debris.

5 Install the new filter element and tray, ensuring that it is correctly seated in the housing and secure it in position with the two retaining clips **(see illustration)**.

20 Automatic transmission fluid level check

Note: *The fluid temperature must be at 40ºC, before the following procedure can be carried out. Nissan have special equipment for this procedure, so if in any doubt contact your local dealer.*

Note: *Some transmissions do not have a fluid drain/level check plug; on these transmissions*

it will be necessary to have the fluid level check carried out by a Nissan dealer or transmission specialist.

1 Park the vehicle on level ground and firmly apply the handbrake, remove the engine undershield and check around the transmission casing for and fluid leaks.

2 Start the engine and move the gear selector lever through each of the gear positions, then place the selector lever in the P position.

3 The transmission fluid needs to be at approximately 40ºC to be able to get the correct fluid level in the transmission. Nissan dealers have diagnostic equipment, which they can connect to the vehicle to give them the fluid temperature. **Note:** *The fluid in the transmission will reach approximately 40ºC, after ten minutes of the engine idling.*

4 Position a suitable container under the

20.5 Automatic transmission fluid level/ drain hole

A Drips of fluid, when level is correct

drain/level plug arrangement, situated on the base of the transmission. Unscrew the outer plug and recover the sealing washer, a new one will be required for refitting.

> ⚠ *Warning: If the fluid is hot, take precautions against scalding.*

5 If the transmission fluid overflows the level tube inside the drain hole and runs out into the container, the fluid level is correct **(see illustration)**.

6 If no transmission fluid flows out of the drain hole, then the transmission will need to be topped up as follows.

7 There is no filler plug on this transmission, so the sensor in the top of the transmission housing has to be removed and the fluid is poured in through the sensor mounting hole. Note that Nissan recommend the sensor, O-ring seal and bolt should be renewed, if they are removed. To improve access to the sensor, remove the battery as described in Chapter 5A, Section 3.

8 Locate the turbine revolution sensor on top of the transmission and wipe clean the area around the sensor **(see illustration)**. Disconnect the wiring connector, and then undo the retaining bolt and remove the sensor from the top of the transmission housing. Nissan recommend that the O-ring and retaining bolt be renewed when refitting.

9 Carefully add fluid to the top of the transmission, until there is a small flow of fluid coming out from the level tube inside the drain hole under the vehicle. (Refer to *Lubricants and fluids* for the specified type of transmission fluid used).

10 When there is a constant flow of fluid coming out from the level tube inside the drain hole, fit a new sealing washer to the outer plug and refit it to the underside of the transmission housing. Tighten to the specified torque setting.

11 Fit the new O-ring seal to the sensor, and then refit the sensor to the top of the transmission housing, tightening the new bolt to the specified torque.

12 Refit the battery and battery tray/box as described in Chapter 5A, Section 3.

13 After topping-up, take the vehicle on a short run to distribute the fresh fluid, and then recheck the level again, topping-up if necessary.

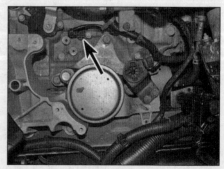

20.8 Remove the turbine revolution sensor (arrowed)

21 Manual transmission oil level check

1 Park the car on a level surface. The oil level must be checked before the car is driven, or at least 5 minutes after the engine has been switched off. If the oil is checked immediately after driving the car, some of the oil will remain distributed around the transmission components, resulting in an inaccurate level reading. To improve access, position the car over an inspection pit, or raise the car off the ground and position it on axle stands, (see *Jacking and vehicle support*) making sure the vehicle remains level to the ground.

2 Wipe clean the area around the filler/level plug, and unscrew it from the casing. On 5-speed transmissions the filler/level plug is situated on the front of the transmission and on 6-speed transmissions it is situated on the left-hand rear of the transmission unit, behind the driveshaft **(see illustrations)**.

3 The oil level should reach the lower edge of the filler/level hole. A certain amount of oil will have gathered behind the filler/level plug and will trickle out when it is removed; this does **not** necessarily indicate that the level is correct. To ensure that a true level is established, wait until the initial trickle has stopped, then add oil as necessary until a trickle of new oil can be seen emerging. The level will be correct when the flow ceases; use only good-quality oil of the specified type.

4 On 6-speed transmissions, remove the left-hand front road wheel for better access to the filler/level plug. Use a length of hose and a funnel to make topping up easier **(see illustrations)**.

5 Refilling the transmission is an extremely awkward operation; above all, allow plenty of time for the oil level to settle properly before checking it. If a large amount had to be added to the transmission and a large amount flows out on checking the level, refit the filler/level plug, and take the vehicle on a short journey. This will allow the new oil to be distributed fully around the transmission components. On

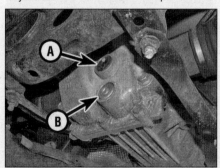

22.2 Final drive unit

A *Oil filler/level plug – upper*
B *Oil drain plug - lower*

21.2a Transmission oil filler/level plug (arrowed) – 5-speed transmissions

21.4a Using a funnel and hose …

21.2b Transmission oil filler/level plug (arrowed) – 6-speed transmissions

21.4b … to fill up the transmission

returning, recheck the level when the oil has settled again.

6 If the transmission has been overfilled so that oil flows out as soon as the filler/level plug is removed, check that the car is completely level (front-to-rear and side-to-side). If necessary, allow the surplus to drain off into a suitable container.

7 When the level is correct, refit the filler/level plug, tightening it to the specified torque wrench setting. Wash off any spilt oil.

22 Final drive oil level check – 4WD models

1 Park the car on a level surface. The oil level must be checked before the car is driven, or at least 5 minutes after the engine has been switched off. If the oil is checked immediately after driving the car, some of the oil will remain distributed around the axle components, resulting in an inaccurate level reading. To improve access, position the car over an inspection pit, or raise the car off the ground and position it on axle stands, (see *Jacking and vehicle support*) making sure the vehicle remains level to the ground.

2 Wipe clean the area around the filler/level plug, and unscrew it from the casing **(see illustration)**. The filler/level plug is situated on the rear of the final drive casing.

3 The oil level should reach the lower edge of the filler/level hole. A certain amount of

oil will have gathered behind the filler/level plug and will trickle out when it is removed; this does **not** necessarily indicate that the level is correct. To ensure that a true level is established, wait until the initial trickle has stopped, then add oil as necessary until a trickle of new oil can be seen emerging. The level will be correct when the flow ceases; use only good-quality oil of the specified type.

4 Allow plenty of time for the oil level to settle properly before checking it. If a large amount had to be added to the axle and a large amount flows out on checking the level, refit the filler/level plug, and take the vehicle on a short journey. This will allow the new oil to be distributed fully around the axle components. On returning, recheck the level when the oil has settled again.

5 If the final drive unit has been overfilled so that oil flows out as soon as the filler/level plug is removed, check that the car is completely level (front-to-rear and side-to-side). If necessary, allow the surplus to drain off into a suitable container.

6 When the level is correct, fit a new sealing washer and refit the filler/level plug, tightening it to the specified torque wrench setting. Wash off any spilt oil.

7 If the final drive needs to have the oil drained at any time, the plug at the lower part of the final drive casing is the drain plug, this also has a sealing washer that will need to be renewed if the plug is removed **(see illustration 22.2)**. Refer to Chapter 7C, Section 6, for draining and refilling.

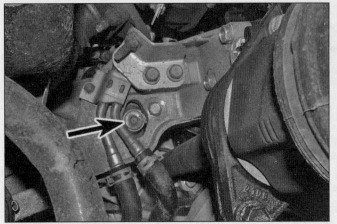
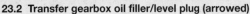

23.2 Transfer gearbox oil filler/level plug (arrowed)

23.7 Transfer gearbox oil drain plug (arrowed)

23 Transfer gearbox oil level check – 4WD models

1 Park the car on a level surface. The oil level must be checked before the car is driven, or at least 5 minutes after the engine has been switched off. If the oil is checked immediately after driving the car, some of the oil will remain distributed around the transfer box components, resulting in an inaccurate level reading. To improve access, position the car over an inspection pit, or raise the car off the ground and position it on axle stands, (see *Jacking and vehicle support*) making sure the vehicle remains level to the ground.

2 Wipe clean the area around the filler/level plug, and unscrew it from the casing **(see illustration)**. The filler/level plug is situated on the right-hand side of the transfer box, above the driveshaft.

3 The oil level should reach the lower edge of the filler/level hole. A certain amount of oil will have gathered behind the filler/level plug and will trickle out when it is removed; this does **not** necessarily indicate that the level is correct. To ensure that a true level is established, wait until the initial trickle has stopped, then add oil as necessary until a trickle of new oil can be seen emerging. The level will be correct when the flow ceases; use only good-quality oil of the specified type.

4 Allow plenty of time for the oil level to settle properly before checking it. If a large amount had to be added to the transfer box and a large amount flows out on checking the level, refit the filler/level plug, and take the vehicle on a short journey. This will allow the new oil to be distributed fully around the transfer box components. On returning, recheck the level when the oil has settled again.

5 If the transfer box has been overfilled so that oil flows out as soon as the filler/level plug is removed, check that the car is completely level (front-to-rear and side-to-side). If necessary, allow the surplus to drain off into a suitable container.

6 When the level is correct, fit a new sealing washer and refit the filler/level plug, tightening it to the specified torque wrench setting. Wash off any spilt oil.

7 If the transfer box needs to have the oil drained at any time, make sure the correct plug is removed from the lower part of the casing, as there are two plugs fitted. The plug nearest the right-hand side of the casing is the drain plug; this also has a sealing washer that will need to be renewed if the plug is removed **(see illustration)**. Refer to Chapter 7C, Section 2, for draining and refilling.

24 Road test

Instruments and electrical equipment

1 Check the operation of all instruments and electrical equipment.

2 Make sure that all instruments read correctly, and switch on all electrical equipment in turn to check that it functions properly.

Steering and suspension

3 Check for any abnormalities in the steering, suspension, handling or road feel.

4 Drive the vehicle, and check that there are no unusual vibrations or noises.

5 Check that the steering feels positive, with no excessive 'sloppiness', or roughness, and check for any suspension noises when cornering and driving over bumps.

Drivetrain

6 Check the performance of the engine, clutch (where applicable), transmission and driveshafts.

7 Listen for any unusual noises from the engine, clutch and transmission.

8 Make sure that the engine runs smoothly when idling, and that there is no hesitation when accelerating.

9 Check that, where applicable, the clutch action is smooth and progressive, that the drive is taken up smoothly, and that the pedal travel is not excessive. Also listen for any noises when the clutch pedal is depressed.

10 On manual transmission models, check that all gears can be engaged smoothly without noise, and that the gear lever action is smooth and not abnormally vague or 'notchy'.

11 On automatic transmission models, make sure that all the gearchanges occur smoothly, without snatching, and without an increase in engine speed between changes. Check that all the gear positions can be selected with the vehicle at rest. If any problems are found, they should be referred to a Nissan dealer.

12 Listen for a metallic clicking sound from the front of the vehicle as the vehicle is driven slowly in a circle with the steering on full lock. Carry out this check in both directions. If a clicking noise is heard, this indicates wear in a driveshaft joint; in which case, the complete driveshaft must be renewed (see Chapter 8, Section 2).

Braking system

13 Make sure that the vehicle does not pull to one side when braking, and that the wheels do not lock when braking hard.

14 Check that there is no vibration through the steering when braking.

15 Check that the handbrake operates correctly without excessive movement of the lever, and that it holds the vehicle stationary on a slope.

16 Test the operation of the brake servo unit as follows. Depress the footbrake four or five times to exhaust the vacuum, and then start the engine. As the engine starts, there should be a noticeable 'give' in the brake pedal as vacuum builds-up. Allow the engine to run for at least two minutes and then switch it off. If the brake pedal is depressed again, it should be possible to detect a hiss from the servo as the pedal is depressed. After about four or five applications, no further hissing should be heard, and the pedal should feel considerably harder.

Every 25 000 miles or 2 years

25 Spark plug renewal

1 The correct functioning of the spark plugs is vital for the correct running and efficiency of the engine. It is essential that the plugs fitted are appropriate for the engine (the suitable type is specified at the beginning of this Chapter). If this type is used and the engine is in good condition, the spark plugs should not need attention between scheduled renewal intervals. Spark plug cleaning is rarely necessary, and should not be attempted unless specialised equipment is available, as damage can easily be caused to the firing ends.

2 Open the bonnet and remove the inlet manifold as described in Chapter 4A, Section 11.

3 Disconnect the wiring connectors from the four ignition coils (see illustration).

4 Undo the retaining bolts and withdraw the ignition coils from the top of the spark plugs (see illustrations).

5 It is advisable to remove the dirt from the spark plug recesses using a clean brush, vacuum cleaner or compressed air before removing the plugs, to prevent dirt dropping into the cylinders (see illustration).

6 Unscrew the plugs using a spark plug spanner, suitable box spanner or a deep socket and extension bar. Keep the socket aligned with the spark plug; otherwise if it is forcibly

moved to one side, the ceramic insulator may be broken off. As each plug is removed (see illustration), examine it as follows.

7 Examination of the spark plugs will give a good indication of the condition of the engine. If the insulator nose of the spark plug is clean and white, with no deposits, this is indicative of too hot a plug (a hot plug transfers heat away from the electrode slowly, a cold plug transfers heat away quickly) or a possible engine management system fault.

8 If the tip and insulator nose are covered with hard black-looking deposits, then this is also indicative of a possible problem in the engine management system. Should the plug be black and oily, and then it is likely that the engine is fairly worn.

9 It is normal for the insulator nose to be covered with light tan to greyish-brown deposits, indicating that both the spark plug and the engine are in good condition.

10 The spark plug electrode gap is of considerable importance as, if it is too large or too small, the size of the spark and its efficiency will be seriously impaired. The gap should be set to the value given in the Specifications at the beginning of this Chapter.

11 To set it, measure the gap with a feeler blade and then bend open, or closed, the outer plug electrode until the correct gap is achieved (see illustration). The centre electrode should never be bent, as this may crack the insulator and cause plug failure, if nothing worse.

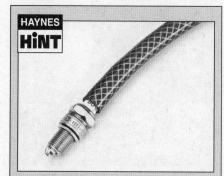

HAYNES HINT

It is very often difficult to insert spark plugs into their holes without cross-threading them. To avoid this possibility, fit a short length of 8 mm internal diameter rubber hose over the end of the spark plug. The flexible hose acts as a universal joint to help align the plug with the plug hole. Should the plug begin to cross-thread, the hose will slip on the spark plug, preventing thread damage to the cylinder head.

12 Special spark plug electrode gap adjusting tools are available from most motor accessory shops, or from some spark plug manufacturers.

13 Before fitting the spark plugs, check that the threaded connector sleeves (where fitted) are tight, and that the plug exterior surfaces and threads are clean. Insert each spark plug by hand, taking care to enter the plug threads correctly (see Haynes Hint).

25.3 Disconnect the coil wiring connectors

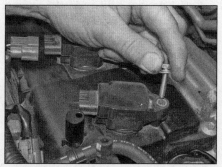

25.4a Remove the retaining bolts ...

25.4b ... and withdraw the ignition coils

25.5 Clean out the spark plug recesses in the top of the cover

25.6 Using a spark plug deep socket to remove the spark plugs

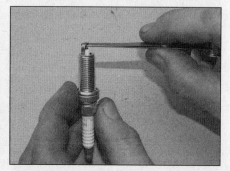

25.11 Measuring the spark plug gap with feeler blades

26.3 Topping-up the brake fluid

26.4 Using a brake bleeding bottle

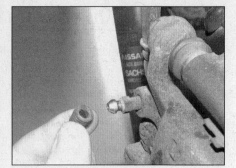

26.5 Make sure all bleed screws are fitted with dust caps

14 Tighten the plug to the specified torque using the spark plug socket and a torque wrench. Refit the remaining spark plugs in the same manner.

15 Refit the ignition coils to the top of the spark plugs and tighten the retaining bolts, ensuring the wiring connectors are fitted securely to the ignition coils.

16 Refit the inlet manifold, with reference to Chapter 4A, Section 11.

26 Brake fluid renewal

⚠ *Warning: Brake hydraulic fluid can harm your eyes and damage painted surfaces, so use extreme caution when handling and pouring it. Do not use fluid that has been standing open for some time, as it absorbs moisture from the air. Excess moisture content can cause a dangerous loss of braking effectiveness. Caution: On models equipped with ABS, disconnect the battery before carrying out this operation and do not reconnect the battery until after the operation is complete. Failure to do this could lead to air entering the hydraulic unit. If air enters the hydraulic unit pump, it will prove very difficult (in some cases impossible) to bleed the unit. Refer to 'Disconnecting the battery' in the Reference Section.*

1 The procedure is similar to that for the bleeding of the hydraulic system as described in Chapter 9, Section 2. The brake fluid reservoir should be emptied by syphoning, using a clean antifreeze tester or similar before starting, then refilled with fresh fluid. Allowance should be made for the old fluid to be expelled when bleeding a section of the circuit.

2 Working as described in Chapter 9, Section 2, open the first bleed screw in the sequence and pump the brake pedal gently until nearly all the fluid has been emptied from the master cylinder reservoir.

3 Top-up to the MAX level with more fresh fluid, and continue pumping until new fluid can be seen emerging from the bleed screw. Tighten the screw and top the reservoir level up to the MAX level line **(see illustration)**.

4 Work through all the remaining bleed screws in the sequence until new fluid can be seen at all of them **(see illustration)**. Be careful to keep the master cylinder reservoir topped-up to above the MIN level at all times, or air may enter the system and greatly increase the length of the task.

5 When the operation is complete, check that all bleed screws are securely tightened, and that their dust caps are refitted **(see illustration)**. Wash off all traces of spilt fluid, and recheck the master cylinder reservoir fluid level.

6 Check the operation of the brakes before taking the car on the road.

7 Dispose safely of the used brake fluid with reference to *General repair procedures*.

27 Coolant renewal

⚠ *Warning: Wait until the engine is cold before starting this procedure. Do not allow antifreeze to come in contact with your skin, or with the painted surfaces of the vehicle. Rinse off spills immediately with plenty of water. Never leave antifreeze lying around in an open container, or in a puddle in the driveway or garage floor. Children and pets are attracted by its sweet smell, but antifreeze can be fatal if ingested.*

Cooling system draining

1 To drain the cooling system, first cover the radiator pressure tank cap with a wad of

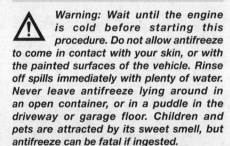

27.3 Remove the lower radiator hose to drain coolant

rag, and slowly turn the cap anti-clockwise to relieve the pressure in the cooling system (a hissing sound will normally be heard). Wait until any pressure remaining in the system is released, then continue to turn the cap until it can be removed.

2 Inside the car, move the heater temperature control lever fully to the HOT position.

3 Remove the engine undershield and position a suitable container beneath the radiator bottom hose. Slacken the retaining clip and withdraw the hose from the radiator, and allow the coolant to drain into the container **(see illustration)**.

4 If necessary, remove the coolant expansion tank, drain out the coolant, and then refit the tank, ensuring that the hoses are securely reconnected. Take care not to spill coolant on the surrounding components.

5 Reposition the container under the cylinder block drain plug (when fitted), which is usually located at the rear of the cylinder block, at the timing chain end **(see illustration)**.

6 Remove the cylinder block drain plug, and drain the coolant from the cylinder block.

7 If the coolant has been drained for a reason other than renewal, then provided it is clean and less than two years old, it can be re-used.

Cooling system flushing

8 If coolant renewal has been neglected, or if the antifreeze mixture has become diluted, then in time, the cooling system may gradually lose efficiency, as the coolant passages become restricted due to rust, scale deposits,

27.5 Cylinder block coolant drain plug (arrowed)

and other sediment. The cooling system efficiency can be restored by flushing the system clean.

9 The radiator should be flushed independently of the engine, to avoid unnecessary contamination.

10 To flush the radiator, fit and tighten the radiator pressure cap, and if the radiator is fitted to the vehicle, clamp the hose running from the top of the radiator to the coolant expansion tank.

11 Disconnect the top and bottom hoses at the radiator, and then insert a garden hose into the radiator top inlet. Direct a flow of clean water through the radiator, and continue flushing until clean water emerges from the radiator bottom outlet. If after a reasonable period the water still does not run clear, the radiator can be flushed with a good proprietary cleaning agent. It is important that the cleaning agent manufacturer's instructions are followed carefully. If the contamination is particularly bad, insert the hose in the radiator bottom outlet, and flush the radiator in reverse ('reverse-flushing').

12 Remove the thermostat as described in Chapter 3, Section 4, and then temporarily refit the thermostat cover.

13 With the radiator top and bottom hoses disconnected from the radiator, insert a hose into the radiator bottom hose. Direct a clean flow of water through the engine, and continue flushing until clean water emerges from the radiator top hose.

14 On completion of flushing, refit the thermostat with reference to Chapter 3, Section 4, and reconnect the hoses.

Cooling system filling

15 Before attempting to fill the cooling system, make sure that all hoses and clips are in good condition, and that the clips are tight. Note that an antifreeze mixture must be used all year round, to prevent corrosion of the alloy engine components.

16 If not already done, reconnect the radiator

27.16 Disconnect the heater upper hose

bottom hose, then disconnect the upper heater hose from the rear of the bulkhead **(see illustration)**, and raise it until it is above the 'MAX' line on the coolant reservoir.

17 Position the container under the cylinder block drain plug, then refill the cooling system through the reservoir tank, until coolant runs from the cylinder block drain plug aperture. Coat the threads of the drain plug with suitable sealant, then refit and tighten the plug to the specified torque.

18 Continue to fill the system through the reservoir until the coolant, free from air bubbles, emerges from the heater hose. Refit the heater hose back to the bulkhead heater connection, once the coolant escaping is free from air bubbles.

19 Continue to fill the reservoir tank until the coolant level reaches the MAX mark.

20 Start the engine, and increase the engine speed to approx 1500rpm for two to three minutes, keeping the coolant level at 'MAX', then refit the reservoir tank cap.

21 Run the engine for approximately 10 minutes at 2500 rpm (until the thermostat operates). Check the coolant temperature gauge for signs of overheating.

22 Stop the engine; allow it to cool completely, and then check for leaks, particularly around

27.23 Check the coolant is up to the 'MAX' level in the reservoir

the disturbed components. With the system cold (the system must be cold for an accurate coolant level indication), check the level in the reservoir.

23 If necessary, top-up the coolant level in the reservoir tank to the MAX level mark **(see illustration)**. On completion, refit the reservoir tank cap. Where applicable, refit the engine under shield.

Antifreeze mixture

24 Always use an ethylene glycol based antifreeze, which is suitable for use in mixed-metal cooling systems. The quantity of antifreeze and levels of protection are indicated in the Specifications.

25 Before adding antifreeze, the cooling system should be completely drained, preferably flushed, and all hoses and clips checked for condition and security.

26 After filling with antifreeze, a label should be attached to the radiator or expansion tank stating the type and concentration of antifreeze used, and the date installed. Any subsequent topping-up should be made with the same type and concentration of antifreeze.

Caution: Do not use engine antifreeze in the windscreen/tailgate/headlight washer system, as it will cause damage to the vehicle paintwork.

Chapter 1 Part B:
Routine maintenance and servicing – diesel models

Contents

Degrees of difficulty

Easy, suitable for novice with little experience 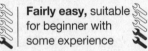	**Fairly easy,** suitable for beginner with some experience	**Fairly difficult,** suitable for competent DIY mechanic	**Difficult,** suitable for experienced DIY mechanic	**Very difficult,** suitable for expert DIY or professional

Specifications

Lubricants and fluids
Refer to *Lubricants and fluids*

Capacities

Engine oil (Including filter)

1.5 litre engines	4.5 litres
2.0 litre engines	7.4 litres
Difference between MAX and MIN dipstick marks	Approx. 1.0 litre

Cooling system

1.5 litre engines:	
Without DPF	7.9 litres
With DPF	9.1 litres
2.0 litre engines:	
Manual transmission	8.4 litres
Automatic transmission	8.8 litres

Transmission

Manual transmission:	
5-speed models	2.3 litres
6-speed models	2.0 litres
Automatic transmission models	7.5 litres
Transfer box – 4-WD models	0.4 litres
Rear axle – 4-WD models	0.6 litres
Fuel tank	65.0 litres

Cooling system

	Antifreeze	Water
Antifreeze mixture (ethylene glycol antifreeze):		
Protection down to –15°C	30%	70%
Protection down to –35°C	50%	50%

Note: *Refer to antifreeze manufacturer for latest recommendations.*

Fuel system

Idle speed (not adjustable – controlled by ECU):
1.5 litre engine	800 ± 50 rpm
2.0 litre engine	750 ± 50 rpm

Brakes

Minimum front brake pad friction material thickness.............	2.0 mm
Minimum rear brake pad friction material thickness	1.5 mm
Minimum handbrake shoe lining thickness	1.5 mm
Number of clicks required to fully apply handbrake...............	7 to 8 clicks
Number of clicks required operating handbrake 'on' warning light....	1 click
Disc runout limit (attached to vehicle)	0.035 mm

Suspension and steering

Front wheel toe setting......................................	2.0 mm ± 1.0 mm toe-in

Torque wrench settings

	Nm	lbf ft
Auxiliary belt tensioner mounting bolt (1.5 litre engine)	40	30
Roadwheel nuts	113	83
Front seat belt mounting bolts:		
Upper pillar anchorage	25	18
Lower sill anchorage	49	36
Seat belt inertia reel bolt	40	30
Pre-tensioner-to-sill bolt	50	37
Rear seat belt mounting bolts (all bolts)........................	49	36
Final drive (4WD):		
Filler/level plug	35	26
Drain plug	35	26
Automatic transmission:		
Drain plug (hexagon outer plug)	8	7
Fluid level tube (inner plug/tube)	8	7
Manual transmission:		
5-speed:		
Filler/level plug (plastic plug)	3	2
Drain plug	25	18
6-speed:		
Filler/level plug (plastic plug)	3	2
Drain plug	23	17
Sump oil drain plug		
1.5 litre engine	20	15
Turbine revolution sensor	6	5
Transfer box (4WD):		
Filler/level plug	35	26
Drain plug	35	26

The maintenance intervals in this manual are provided with the assumption that you, not the dealer, will be carrying out the work. These are the minimum maintenance intervals based on the schedule recommended by the manufacturer for vehicles driven daily. If you wish to keep your vehicle in peak condition at all times, you may wish to perform some of these procedures more often. We encourage frequent maintenance because it enhances the efficiency, performance and resale value of your vehicle. If the vehicle is driven in dusty areas, used to tow a trailer, or driven frequently at slow speeds (idling in traffic) or on short journeys, more frequent maintenance intervals are recommended. Nissan recommend that many service intervals are halved for vehicles which are used under these conditions.

When the vehicle is new, it should be serviced by a dealer service department (or other workshop recognised by the vehicle manufacturer as providing the same standard of service) in order to preserve the warranty. The vehicle manufacturer may reject warranty claims if you are unable to prove that servicing has been carried out as and when specified, using only original equipment parts or parts certified to be of equivalent quality.

Every 250 miles or weekly

☐ Refer to Weekly checks

Every 9000 miles or 12 months – whichever comes first

☐ Renew the engine oil and filter (Section 3)*
☐ Drain any water from the fuel filter (Section 4)
* Note: *Frequent oil and filter changes are good for the engine and we recommend that the oil and filter be renewed at the interval specified here (or at least once every 12 months), especially if the vehicle is used on a lot of short journeys or covers a small annual mileage.*

Every 18 000 miles or 2 years – whichever comes first

In addition to all the items listed previously, carry out the following:
☐ Check all underbonnet components and hoses for fluid leaks (Section 5)
☐ Check the brake pad thickness – front and rear (Section 6)
☐ Check the operation of the handbrake (Section 7)
☐ Check the operation of the clutch (Section 8)
☐ Check the operation of the air conditioning system (Section 9)

Every 18 000 miles or 2 years – whichever comes first (continued)

☐ Check the condition of the auxiliary drivebelts (Sections 10 and 11)
☐ Check the steering and suspension components for condition and security (Section 12)
☐ Check the condition of the driveshaft rubber gaiters (Section 13)
☐ Check the wheel alignment (Section 14)
☐ Check the condition of the exhaust system and mountings (Section 15)
☐ Check the condition of the seat belts (Section 16)
☐ Check the operation of all electrical systems (Section 17)
☐ Lubricate all hinges and locks (Section 18)
☐ Renew the pollen filter (Section 19)
☐ Renew the air filter element (Section 20)*
☐ Renew the fuel filter (Section 21)
☐ Check the automatic transmission fluid level (Section 22)
☐ Check the manual transmission oil level (Section 23)
☐ Check the final drive oil level (Section 24)
☐ Check the transfer box oil level (Section 25)
☐ Carry out a road test (Section 26)
* Note: *Although Nissan recommend this task to be carried out every 36 000 miles (60 000 km) we recommend that the filter be renewed more frequently, perhaps every 18 000 miles or every two years, especially if the vehicle is used in a dusty environment.*

Every 36 000 miles or 4 years – whichever comes first

In addition to all the items listed previously, carry out the following:
☐ Renew the timing belt – 1.5 diesel engines (Section 27)*
☐ Renew the brake fluid (Section 28)
☐ Renew the coolant (Section 29)

* Note: *Although the normal interval for timing belt renewal is 72 000 miles (120 000 km), it is strongly recommended that the interval is reduced to 36 000 miles (60 000 km) on vehicles which are subjected to intensive use, i.e. mainly short journeys or a lot of stop-start driving. The actual belt renewal interval is therefore very much up to the individual owner, but bear in mind that severe engine damage may result if the belt breaks.*

Front underbody view

1 Engine oil drain plug
2 Transmission drain plug
3 Transmission
4 Exhaust front pipe
5 Rear engine steady bar
6 Subframe
7 AC compressor
8 Front suspension lower arm
9 Brake calipers
10 Steering track rod end

Rear underbody view

1 Fuel tank
2 Handbrake cables
3 Rear axle assembly
4 Coil springs
5 Exhaust rear silencer and tailpipe
6 Anti-roll bar
7 Shock absorbers (dampers)
8 Lower suspension arms
9 Rear trailing arms

Underbonnet view

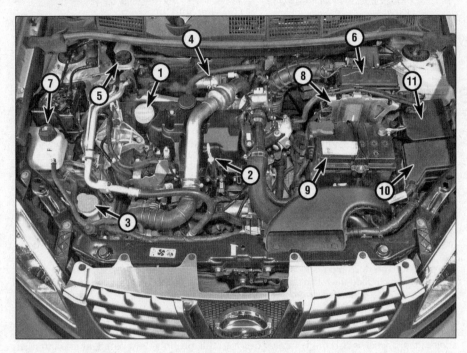

1 Engine oil filler cap
2 Engine oil level dipstick
3 Windscreen washer bottle
4 EGR valve
5 Brake fluid reservoir
6 Air cleaner element
7 Coolant expansion tank
8 Engine management control module (ECM)
9 Battery
10 Relay/fusebox
11 Intelligent Power Distribution Module (IPDM)

Maintenance procedures

1 General information

This Chapter is designed to help the home mechanic maintain his/her vehicle for safety, economy, long life and peak performance.

The Chapter contains a master maintenance schedule, followed by Sections dealing specifically with each task in the schedule. Visual checks, adjustments, component renewal and other helpful items are included. Refer to the accompanying illustrations of the engine compartment and the underside of the vehicle for the locations of the various components.

Servicing your vehicle in accordance with the mileage/time maintenance schedule and the following Sections will provide a planned maintenance programme, which should result in a long and reliable service life. This is a comprehensive plan, so maintaining some items but not others at the specified service intervals will not produce the same results.

As you service your vehicle, you will discover that many of the procedures can –

and should – be grouped together, because of the particular procedure being performed, or because of the close proximity of two otherwise-unrelated components to one another. For example, if the vehicle is raised for any reason, the exhaust can be inspected at the same time as the suspension and steering components.

The first step in this maintenance programme is to prepare yourself before the actual work begins. Read through all the Sections relevant to the work to be carried out, then make a list and gather together all the parts and tools required. If a problem is encountered, seek advice from a parts specialist, or a dealer service department.

2 Regular maintenance

1 If, from the time the vehicle is new, the routine maintenance schedule is followed closely, and frequent checks are made of fluid levels and high-wear items, as suggested throughout this manual, the engine will be kept

in relatively good running condition, and the need for additional work will be minimised.

2 It is possible that there will be times when the engine is running poorly due to the lack of regular maintenance. This is even more likely if a used vehicle, which has not received regular and frequent maintenance checks, is purchased. In such cases, additional work may need to be carried out, outside of the regular maintenance intervals.

3 If engine wear is suspected, a compression test or leakdown test (refer to Chapter 2C or Chapter 2D) will provide valuable information regarding the overall performance of the main internal components. Such a test can be used as a basis to decide on the extent of the work to be carried out. If, for example, a compression test indicates serious internal engine wear, conventional maintenance as described in this Chapter will not greatly improve the performance of the engine, and may prove a waste of time and money, unless extensive overhaul work is carried out first.

4 The following series of operations are those most often required to improve the performance of a generally poor-running engine:

Primary operations

a) Clean, inspect and test the battery (see 'Weekly checks').
b) Check all the engine-related fluids (see 'Weekly checks').
c) Check the condition and tension of the auxiliary drivebelt (Sections 10 and 11).
d) Check the condition of the air filter element, and renew if necessary (Section 20).
e) Check the fuel filter – drain off any water and renew filter if necessary (Section 21).
f) Check the condition of all hoses, and check for fluid leaks (Section 5).

5 If the above operations do not prove fully effective, carry out the following secondary operations:

Secondary operations

All items listed under *Primary operations*, plus the following:
a) Check the charging system (Chapter 5A).
b) Check the preheating system (Chapter 5C).
c) Check the fuel system (Chapter 4B).

Every 9000 miles (15 000 km) or 12 months

3 Engine oil and filter renewal

1 Frequent oil and filter changes are the most important preventative maintenance procedures that can be undertaken by the DIY owner. As engine oil ages, it becomes diluted and contaminated, which leads to premature engine wear.

2 Before starting this procedure, gather together all the necessary tools and materials. Also make sure that you have plenty of clean rags and newspapers handy, to mop-up any spills. Ideally, the engine oil should be warm, as it will drain more easily, and more built-up sludge will be removed with it.

3 Take care not to touch the exhaust or any other hot parts of the engine when working under the vehicle. To avoid any possibility of scalding, and to protect yourself from possible skin irritants and other harmful contaminants in used engine oils, it is advisable to wear gloves when carrying out this work.

4 Access to the underside of the vehicle will be greatly improved if it can be raised on a lift, driven onto ramps, or jacked up and supported on axle stands (see *Jacking and vehicle support*). Whichever method is chosen, make sure that the vehicle remains level, or if it is at an angle, that the drain plug is at the lowest point. The drain plug is located at the rear of the sump. Undo the retaining bolts and remove the engine undershield from under the front of the vehicle.

5 Remove the oil filler cap from the top of the engine camshaft cover. **Note:** *On 2.0 litre engines the dipstick is part of the oil filler cap* **(see illustration)**.

6 Slacken the drain plug about half a turn, position the draining container under the drain plug, and then remove the plug completely **(see illustrations)**. Note that on some engines an 8 mm square section drain plug key will be needed to unscrew the drain plug. If possible, try to keep the plug pressed into the sump while unscrewing it by hand the last couple of turns.

7 Allow some time for the oil to drain, noting that it may be necessary to reposition the container as the oil flow slows to a trickle.

8 After all the oil has drained; wipe the drain plug with a clean rag. Remove the old sealing washer from the drain plug and fit a new one. Clean the area around the drain plug opening, and refit the plug complete with the new sealing washer **(see illustration)**. Tighten the drain plug securely – preferably to the specified torque, using a torque wrench.

9 The oil filter is located at the front of the cylinder block – access is most easily obtained from underneath the vehicle on 2.0 litre engines, and from the top on 1.5 litre engines **(see illustrations)**.

3.5 Remove oil filler cap/dipstick – 2.0 litre engines

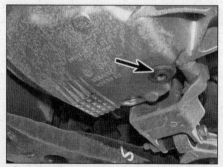

3.6a Engine oil drain plug – 1.5 litre engines

3.6b Engine oil drain plug – 2.0 litre engines

3.8 Fit a new sealing washer to the drain plug

3.9a Oil filter location on the front of the engine – 1.5 litre engines

3.9b Oil filter location on the front of the engine – 2.0 litre engines

3.11 Slacken the oil filter with a removal tool

3.13 Apply clean oil to the seal on the oil filter

3.14 Withdraw the filter from the cap

10 Move the container into position under the oil filter, to catch any oil spillage.

1.5 litre engines

11 Use an oil filter removal tool to slacken the filter initially, then unscrew it by hand the rest of the way **(see illustration)**. Position it with its open end uppermost to prevent further spillage of oil, then empty the oil from the old filter into the container.

12 Use a clean rag to remove any oil, dirt and sludge from the filter sealing area on the engine. Check the old filter to make sure that the rubber sealing ring has not stuck to the engine. If it has, carefully remove it.

13 Apply a light coating of clean engine oil to the sealing ring on the new filter **(see illustration)**, then screw the filter into position on the engine. Lightly tighten the filter until its sealing ring contacts the block, and then tighten it through a further two-thirds of a turn. Tighten the filter firmly by hand only – **do not** use any tools.

2.0 litre engines

14 The filter is a cartridge inside the oil filter housing. Using a bar and socket, unscrew the filter housing cap and withdraw the filter cartridge, draining the oil into the container **(see illustration)**.

15 Use a clean rag to remove any oil, dirt and sludge from inside the oil filter housing. Remove any old rubber seals from the oil filter housing and filter cap and fit the new seals, which should be supplied with the filter **(see illustration)**.

16 Apply a light coating of clean engine oil to the sealing rings **(see illustration)**, then insert the filter cartridge. Screw the filter cap into position on the engine. Tighten the filter cap firmly by hand at first, then use spanner to tighten securely

All models

17 Refit the undertray and securely tighten its retaining screws. Remove the old oil and all tools from under the vehicle then lower the vehicle to the ground.

18 Fill the engine through the filler hole in the cylinder head cover, using the correct grade and type of oil (refer to *Weekly checks* for details of topping-up). Pour in half the specified quantity of oil first, and then wait a few minutes for the oil to drain into the sump. Continue to add oil, a small quantity at a time, until the level is up to the lower mark on the dipstick. Adding approximately a further 1.0 litre will bring the level up to the upper mark on the dipstick. Refit the oil filler cap when correct level is achieved.

19 Start the engine and run it for a few minutes, while checking for leaks around the oil filter seal and the sump drain plug. Note that there may be a delay of a few seconds before the low oil pressure warning light goes out when the engine is first started, as the oil circulates through the new oil filter and the engine oil galleries before the pressure builds-up. Do not run the engine above idle speed while the warning light is on.

20 Stop the engine, and wait a few minutes for the oil to settle in the sump once more. With the new oil circulated and the filter now completely full, recheck the level on the dipstick, and add more oil as necessary.

21 Where applicable, refit the plastic engine cover(s).

22 Dispose of the used engine oil safely with reference to *General repair procedures* in the Reference Chapter. Do not discard the old filter with domestic household waste. The facility for waste oil disposal provided by many local council refuse tips generally has a filter receptacle alongside.

3.15 Fit new seal to the filter cap

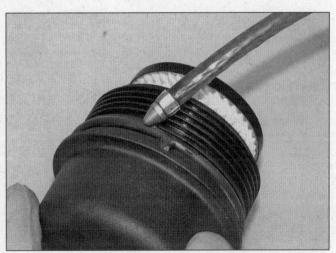

3.16 Lubricate the seal with clean engine oil

4 Fuel filter water draining

1 On most models a water drain screw is provided on the base of the fuel filter **(see illustration)**.

2 Place a suitable container beneath the drain screw. To make draining easier, a suitable length of tubing can be attached to the outlet pipe at the centre of the screw to direct the fuel flow – on some models a drain tube is provided as standard. **Note:** *If desired, access can be improved by unscrewing the nuts securing the filter head bracket to the body and by raising the complete filter assembly to a more convenient position – if this is done, take care not to strain the fuel hoses and electrical wiring.*

3 Open the drain screw by turning it anti-clockwise, operate the hand priming pump

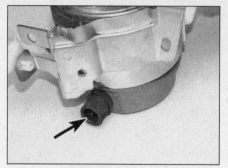

4.1 Water drain screw (arrowed) fitted to base of filter

a couple of times to allow the fuel to flow through the filter **(see illustration)**.

4 Allow the entire contents of the filter to drain into the container, and then securely tighten the drain screw.

5 Prime and bleed the fuel system as described in Chapter 4B, Section 5.

4.3 Hand priming pump location (arrowed)

6 Dispose of the used fuel safely with reference to *General repair procedures* in the Reference Chapter. Do not discard the fuel with domestic household waste. The facility for waste oil/fuel disposal provided by many local council refuse tips generally has a filter receptacle alongside.

Every 18 000 miles (30 000 km) or 2 years

5 Hose and fluid leak check

See Chapter 1A, Section 4.

6 Brake pad condition check – front and rear

See Chapter 1A, Section 5.

7 Handbrake check and adjustment

See Chapter 1A, Section 6.

8 Clutch operation check

See Chapter 1A, Section 7.

9 Air conditioning system check

See Chapter 1A, Section 8.

10 Auxiliary drivebelt check and renewal – 1.5 litre engine

Note: *Nissan recommend that the belt be always renewed if it is removed, along with the automatic tensioner. The belt and tensioner should be renewed every 72 000 miles or 5 years regardless of condition.*

Checking

1 The auxiliary drivebelt is located on the right-hand side of the engine.

2 Due to their function and material makeup, drivebelts are prone to failure after a period of time and should therefore be inspected, and if necessary adjusted periodically.

3 A basic check for obvious faults can be made from the engine compartment. However,

10.4 Remove the inner wheel arch panel

because the belt runs very close to the right hand inner wing a through inspection can only be made from below.

4 Jack up the front of the car, and support it on axle stands (see *Jacking and vehicle support*). Remove the right-hand wheel and the inner wing panel **(see illustration)**.

5 With the engine stopped, inspect the full length of the drivebelt for cracks and separation of the belt plies **(see illustration)**. It will be necessary to turn the engine (using a spanner or socket and bar on the crankshaft pulley bolt) in order to move the belt from the pulleys so that the belt can be inspected thoroughly. Twist the belt between the pulleys so that both sides can be viewed. Also, check for fraying and glazing which gives the belt a shiny appearance. Check the pulleys for nicks, cracks, distortion and corrosion.

10.5 Check for drivebelt wear

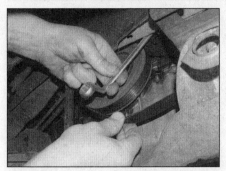

10.6a Turning the spanner clockwise from under the vehicle …

Renewal

Note: *Before removal of the belt, note the fitted position. On some models, the compressor pulley has six grooves and the belt has five. In this case the inner groove on the compressor pulley is left unused, so that the run of the belt is straight.*

6 Using a spanner on the outer nut on the tensioner, turn the tensioner clockwise to release the tension on the belt **(see illustrations)**, then lift the drivebelt from the pulleys, noting its fitted position on the pulleys.

7 If the belt is removed, it is recommended by Nissan that it must be renewed.

8 Unbolt the tensioner unit and fit a new one, tightening the retaining bolt to the specified torque.

9 Using the spanner on the outer nut on the tensioner, hold the tensioner clockwise, to allow the new belt to be fitted around the pulleys, making sure that it is correctly located in the grooves.

10 Fit a socket to the crankshaft pulley and rotate the engine several times to check the belt alignment.

11 Refit the wing liner and wheel, then lower the vehicle to the ground. Tighten the road wheels to the specified torque setting.

11 Auxiliary drivebelt check and renewal – 2.0 engine

Note: *Nissan recommend that the belt be always renewed if it is removed, along with the automatic tensioner and idler pulley. These should be renewed every 72 000 miles or 5 years regardless of condition.*

Checking

1 The auxiliary drivebelt is located at the right-hand side of the engine.

2 Due to their function and material makeup, drivebelts are prone to failure after a period of time and should therefore be inspected, and if necessary adjusted periodically.

3 Since the drivebelt is located very close to the right-hand side of the engine

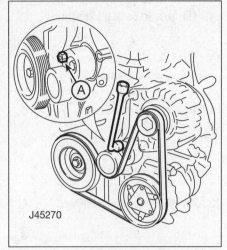

J45270

10.6b … or from above, using hexagon (A) on the tensioner pulley

compartment, it is possible to gain better access by raising the front of the vehicle and removing the right-hand wheel, then removing the inner panel **(see illustration 10.4)**, from inside the wheel arch, and if required the engine undertray.

4 With the engine stopped, inspect the full length of the drivebelt for cracks and separation of the belt plies **(see illustration 10.5)**. It will be necessary to turn the engine (using a spanner or socket and bar on the crankshaft pulley bolt) in order to move the belt from the pulleys so that the belt can be inspected thoroughly. Twist the belt between the pulleys so that both sides can be viewed. Also check for fraying, and glazing which gives

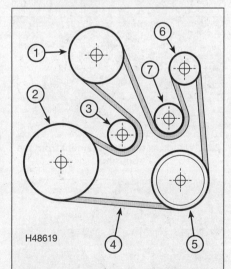

H48619

11.7 Auxilliary drivebelt configuration – 2.0 litre engines

1 Coolant pump
2 Crankshaft pulley
3 Drive belt tensioner
4 Drivebelt
5 Air-conditioning compressor
6 Alternator
7 Idler pulley

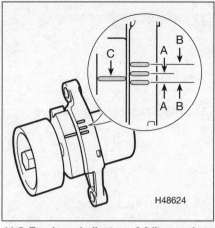

H48624

11.5 Tensioner indicator – 2.0 litre engines

A-A *New drive belt range*
B-B *Used drive belt range*
C   *Indicator marking on tensioner*

the belt a shiny appearance. Check the pulleys for nicks, cracks, distortion and corrosion.

5 A spring-loaded tensioner is fitted to automatically maintain the correct tension on the belt. If the line on the tensioner body is outside the indicator range, then the belt will need to be renewed **(see illustration)**. If problems with belt squeal or slip are encountered, the belt should be renewed. If the problem continues, it will be necessary to renew the tensioner assembly.

Renewal

6 To remove the belt, use a Torx key in the hole provided to turn the tensioner clockwise (as viewed from the right-hand side of the car). A 3.0mm Allen key or drill bit can be inserted into a hole in the tensioner body to hold it in the released position.

7 Note the routing of the belt, then slip the belt off the pulleys **(see illustration)**.

8 Fit the new belt ensuring that it is routed correctly.

9 With the belt in position, use the Torx key to hold the tensioner in position while the 3.0mm Allen key is removed, then carefully release the Torx key anti-clockwise so the belt will automatically become tensioned.

10 Fit a socket to the crankshaft pulley and rotate the engine several times to check the belt alignment. Check the position of the line on the tensioner body, to make sure it is between the two outer wear lines on the tensioner.

11 Refit the wing liner and wheel, then lower the vehicle to the ground. Tighten the road wheels to the specified torque setting.

12 Steering and suspension check

See Chapter 1A, Section 11.

13 Driveshaft gaiter check

See Chapter 1A, Section 12.

14 Wheel alignment check

See Chapter 1A, Section 13.

15 Exhaust system check

See Chapter 1A, Section 14.

16 Seat belt check

See Chapter 1A, Section 15.

17 Electrical systems check

See Chapter 1A, Section 16.

18 Hinge and lock lubrication

See Chapter 1A, Section 17.

19 Pollen filter renewal

See Chapter 1A, Section 18.

20 Air filter element renewal

1.5 litre engines

1 The air filter is situated in the air filter housing at the left-hand rear of the engine compartment.

2 Open the bonnet, release the two retaining clips (one at each end of the cover), and remove it from the air cleaner housing **(see illustration)**.

3 Withdraw the old air filter element out of the housing; noting which way round it is fitted **(see illustration)**.

4 Wipe the inside of the air filter housing and cover with a clean cloth to remove all traces of dirt and debris.

5 Install the new filter element, ensuring that it is correctly seated in the housing, and then secure the cover in position, making sure the securing clips are located correctly **(see illustration)**.

2.0 litre engines

6 The air filter is situated in the air filter housing at the left-hand rear of the engine compartment.

7 Open the bonnet, release the two retaining clips, and then withdraw the air filter element and plastic tray, out from the top of the air filter housing **(see illustrations)**.

8 Lift the old air filter element out of the plastic tray; noting which way round it is fitted and fit a new filter element to the tray **(see illustration)**.

9 Wipe the inside of the air filter housing and filter cover with a clean cloth to remove all traces of dirt and debris.

10 Install the new filter element and tray, ensuring that it is correctly seated in the housing and secure it in position with the two retaining clips.

21 Fuel filter renewal

Caution: Do not allow dirt to enter the fuel system during this procedure.

1 The contents of the fuel filter can be drained, as described in Section 4, of this Chapter. Place a piece of clean cloth around the fuel filter to soak up any spilt fuel, as the fuel lines are disconnected.

20.2 Unclip the cover from the filter housing

20.3 Withdraw the filter element from the housing

20.5 Make sure the filter cover is fitted the correctly on refitting

20.7a Release the two retaining clips ...

20.7b ... and withdraw the filter and plastic tray

20.8 Remove the filter element from the plastic tray

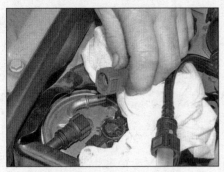

21.3a Disconnect the fuel lines …

21.3b … plug the ends of the lines …

21.3c … and remove the priming bulb with the fuel lines

2 Where applicable, disconnect the fuel heater wiring connector from the top of the filter housing.

3 Release the retaining clips and disconnect the fuel lines from the priming bulb to the fuel filter housing **(see illustrations)**. Unclip the priming bulb from the inner wing panel and move it to one side. Take care not to damage the fuel lines as they are removed; cover the ends of the fuel lines to prevent any dirt ingress.

4 Undo the two retaining nuts and remove the fuel filter housing bracket, from the inner wing panel **(see illustration)**.

5 Note the fitted position of the fuel lines on top of the fuel filter, and then disconnect them. Take care not to damage the fuel lines as they are removed; cover the ends of the fuel lines to prevent any dirt ingress **(see illustration)**.

6 Unclip the fuel line from the retaining clip on the fuel filter bracket and withdraw the fuel filter from the engine compartment **(see illustration)**.

7 With the fuel filter housing removed from the vehicle, slacken the mounting bracket securing bolt, and slide the fuel filter out from the bracket **(see illustration)**.

8 Release the retaining clip on the top of the fuel filter, and then withdraw the fuel connector. Check the seal on the fuel connector is not damaged and renew seal if required.

9 Fit the new fuel filter into the mounting bracket and tighten the securing bolt. Refit the fuel connector to the top of the fuel filter, and secure it in position with the retaining clip.

21.4 Remove the filter housing bracket

21.5 Note the fitted position of the fuel lines

21.6 Withdraw the fuel filter from the engine compartment

21.7 Filter mounting bracket securing bolt (arrowed)

10 Make sure the drain plug in the bottom of the fuel filter housing is tight.

11 Refit the filter and mounting bracket to the inner wing panel and reconnect the fuel lines to the top of the filter, taking care not to damage the pipes **(see illustration)**.

12 Clip the fuel line back into the retaining clip on the side of the fuel filter bracket **(see illustration)**.

13 Refit the fuel filter housing bracket to the inner wing panel and tighten the two retaining nuts **(see illustration)**.

21.11 Make sure the fuel line securing clips are not damaged

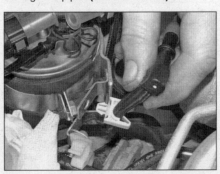

21.12 Refit the fuel lines into the securing clips

21.13 Tighten the bracket retaining nuts (arrowed)

14 Refit the priming bulb fuel lines to the fuel filter, and then clip the priming bulb back in position.

15 Where applicable, reconnect the fuel heater wiring connector to the top of the filter housing.

16 With all the fuel line connectors refitted, squeeze the priming bulb several times to pump the fuel back through the filter.

17 Turn the ignition key and crank the engine to start the engine. If required squeeze the priming bulb, to help the fuel flow through the system.

18 With engine running, check for leaks around the fuel filter and that the pipes are secure.

22 Automatic transmission fluid level check

See Chapter 1A, Section 20.

23 Manual transmission oil level check

See Chapter 1A, Section 21.

24 Final drive oil level check – 4WD models

See Chapter 1A, Section 22.

25 Transfer gearbox oil level check – 4WD models

See Chapter 1A, Section 23.

26 Road test

See Chapter 1A, Section 24.

Every 36 000 miles (60 000 km) or 4 years

27 Timing belt renewal – 1.5 litre models

Note: *This Section applies to 1.5 litre engines only.*

Refer to Chapter 2C, Section 6, for the removal and refitting procedure.

28 Brake fluid renewal

See Chapter 1A, Section 26.

29 Coolant renewal

See Chapter 1A, Section 27.

Chapter 2 Part A:
1.6 litre petrol engine in–car repair procedures

Contents

Degrees of difficulty

Easy, suitable for novice with little experience	**Fairly easy,** suitable for beginner with some experience	**Fairly difficult,** suitable for competent DIY mechanic	**Difficult,** suitable for experienced DIY mechanic	**Very difficult,** suitable for expert DIY or professional

Specifications

Engine (general)

Engine code	HR16DE
Capacity.	1598 cc
Bore	78.0 mm
Stroke	83.6 mm
Direction of crankshaft rotation	Clockwise (viewed from right-hand side of vehicle)
No. 1 cylinder location	At timing chain end of block
Firing order	1-3-4-2
Compression ratio	10.7: 1
Cylinder compression pressures:	
Standard.	15.0 bars
Minimum.	14.7 bars
Maximum difference between cylinders (all engines).	0.6 bar

Valve clearances

Cold engine:

Inlet	0.26 to 0.34 mm
Exhaust	0.29 to 0.37 mm

Camshaft and followers

Drive	Chain
Number of bearings	5
Endfloat	0.075 to 0.153 mm
Camshaft lobe height:	
Inlet	41.705 to 41.895 mm
Exhaust	40.175 to 40.365 mm
Camshaft bearing journal outer diameter:	
No 1 bearing	27.935 to 27.955 mm
Nos 2 to 5 bearings	24.950 to 24.970 mm
Camshaft cylinder head bearing journal internal diameter:	
No 1 bearing	28.000 to 28.021 mm
Nos 2 to 5 bearings	25.000 to 25.021 mm
Camshaft journal-to-bearing clearance:	
No 1 bearing	0.045 to 0.086 mm
Nos 2 to 5 bearings	0.030 to 0.071 mm
Camshaft run-out:	
Standard	0.075 to 0.153 mm
Limit	0.02 mm
Camshaft sprocket run-out	Less than 0.15 mm
Camshaft follower outer diameter	29.977 to 29.987 mm
Cylinder head hole diameter for follower	30.000 to 30.021 mm
Camshaft follower to cylinder head clearance	0.013 to 0.044 mm

Lubrication system

Oil pump type	Rotor-type, driven off crankshaft right-hand end
Minimum oil pressure at normal operating temperature (approx. 80°C):	
At Idle speed	0.60 bars (minimum)
At 2000 rpm	2.70 bars (minimum)

Torque wrench settings

	Nm	lbf ft
Big-end bearing cap nuts:		
Stage 1	27	20
Stage 2	Completely slacken	
Stage 3	20	14
Stage 4	Angle-tighten a further 60°	
Camshaft bearing cap bolts (see text):		
Stage 1 – bolts 9 to 11	2	1.5
Stage 2 – bolts 1 to 8	2	1.5
Stage 3 – bolts 1 to 11	6	4.5
Stage 4 – bolts 1 to 11	11	8
Camshaft sprocket retaining bolts (Variable valve timing):		
Inlet	79	58
Exhaust	79	58
Crankshaft pulley bolt:		
Stage 1	35	26
Stage 2	Angle-tighten 60°	
Cylinder head bolts:		
Stage 1	67	49
Stage 2	Fully slacken all the bolts	
Stage 3	40	30
Stage 4	Angle-tighten 75°	
Stage 5	Angle-tighten a further 75°	
Cylinder head cover bolts	10	8
Driveplate (automatic transmission)	98	72
Engine-to-transmission fixing bolts	48	35
Flywheel (manual transmission)	108	80
Left-hand transmission mounting:		
Through-bolt/stud nut	65	48
Through-bolt/stud-to-bracket	65	48
Mounting-to-bracket nuts	105	77
Mounting bracket-to-inner wing panel bolts	80	59
Mounting-to-transmission bolts	45	33

Torque wrench settings (continued)

	Nm	lbf ft
Main bearing cap bolts:		
Stage 1	33	24
Stage 2	Angle-tighten 60º	
Oil level sensor retaining bolt	8	6
Oil pump sprocket retaining nut.	25	18
Rear engine/transmission torque/link arm mounting:		
Mounting-to-front subframe bolt	110	81
Mounting bracket-to-transmission bolt	110	81
Right-hand engine mounting:		
Bracket bolts to engine	55	41
Mounting bolts to inner wing	55	41
Mounting bolt to engine bracket (horizontal).	125	92
Stay bracket to mounting bracket (small bolts – where fitted)	12	9
Sump oil drain plug	35	26
Lower sump oil pan bolts	10	8
Upper sump pan bolts to transmission	48	35
Upper sump casing bolts to cylinder block	25	18
Timing chain cover bolts (see text):		
Lower bolts x 9 (6mm)	25	18
Upper bolts x 5 (8mm)	55	41
Timing chain tensioner access plug in cover	20	14
Timing chain guide bolts	25	18
Timing chain tensioner bolts	10	8

1 General information

Using this Chapter

This part of Chapter 2 is devoted to in-car repair procedures for the 1.6 litre petrol engine. Similar information covering the other engine types can be found in Parts B, C and D. All procedures concerning engine removal and refitting, and engine block/cylinder head overhaul can be found in Part E of this Chapter.

Note that, while it may be possible physically to overhaul items such as the piston/connecting rod assemblies while the engine is in the car, such tasks are not normally carried out as separate operations. Usually, several additional procedures (not to mention the cleaning of components and of oilways) have to be carried out. For this reason, all such tasks are classed as major overhaul procedures, and are described in Part E of this Chapter.

In Parts A, B, C and D, the assumption is made that the engine is installed in the car, with all ancillaries connected. If the engine has been removed for overhaul, the preliminary dismantling information, which precedes each operation, may be ignored.

Engine description

The engine is of the sixteen-valve, in-line four-cylinder, double overhead camshaft (DOHC) type, mounted transversely at the front of the car with the transmission attached to the left-hand end.

The crankshaft runs in five main bearings. Thrustwashers are fitted to No 3 main bearing (upper half) to control crankshaft endfloat.

The connecting rods rotate on horizontally split bearing shells at their big ends. The pistons are attached to the connecting rods by gudgeon pins, which are a press fit in the small end of the connecting rod. The aluminium-alloy pistons are fitted with three piston rings – two compression rings and an oil control ring.

The cylinder block is made of aluminium alloy and the cylinder bores are an integral part of the block. On this type of engine the cylinder bores are sometimes referred to as having dry liners.

The inlet and exhaust valves are each closed by coil springs, and operate in guides pressed into the cylinder head; the valve seat inserts are also pressed into the cylinder head, and can be renewed separately if worn. The inlet camshaft has a variable valve sprocket to the end which is oil fed through a control solenoid valve.

The camshaft is driven by a timing chain, and operates the sixteen valves via bucket-type followers. The followers are situated directly below the camshafts. Valve clearances are adjusted by replacing the relevant follower with a different thickness. The camshafts rotate directly in the cylinder head.

Lubrication is by means of an oil pump, which is driven off the right-hand end of the crankshaft. It draws oil through a strainer located in the sump, and then forces it through an externally mounted filter into galleries in the cylinder block/crankcase. From there, the oil is distributed to the crankshaft (main bearings) and camshaft. The big-end bearings are supplied with oil via internal drillings in the crankshaft, while the camshaft bearings also receive a pressurised supply. The camshaft lobes and valves are lubricated by splash, as are all other engine components.

Repairs with engine in car

The following work can be carried out with the engine in the car:

a) Compression pressure – testing.
b) Cylinder head cover – removal and refitting.
c) Timing chain cover – removal and refitting.
d) Timing chain – removal, inspection and refitting.
e) Timing chain tensioner, guides and sprockets – removal, inspection and refitting.
f) Camshaft and followers – removal, inspection and refitting.
g) Valve clearances – adjustment.
h) Cylinder head – removal and refitting.
i) Cylinder head and pistons – decarbonising.
j) Sump oil pan – removal and refitting.
k) Oil pump – removal, inspection and refitting.
l) Crankshaft oil seals – renewal.
m) Engine/transmission mountings – inspection and renewal.
n) Flywheel/driveplate – removal, inspection and refitting.

2 Compression test – description and interpretation

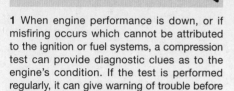

1 When engine performance is down, or if misfiring occurs which cannot be attributed to the ignition or fuel systems, a compression test can provide diagnostic clues as to the engine's condition. If the test is performed regularly, it can give warning of trouble before any other symptoms become apparent.

2 The engine must be fully warmed-up to normal operating temperature, the battery must be fully charged, and the aid of an assistant will also be required.

3 Depressurise the fuel system by removing the fuel pump fuse from the fusebox – the fuses can usually be identified from the label inside the fusebox cover, or from the wiring diagrams at the end of this manual (see Chapter 12). With the fuse removed, start the engine, and allow it to run until it stalls. Try to start the engine at least twice more, to ensure that all residual pressure has been relieved.

4 Remove the spark plugs as described in Chapter 1A, Section 25.

5 Fit a compression tester to the No 1 cylinder spark plug hole – the type of tester which screws into the plug thread is to be preferred.

6 Have the assistant hold the throttle wide open, and crank the engine on the starter motor; after two or three revolutions, the compression pressure should build-up to a maximum figure, and then stabilise. Record the highest reading obtained.

7 Repeat the test on the remaining cylinders, recording the pressure in each.

8 All cylinders should produce very similar pressures; any difference greater than that specified indicates the existence of a fault. Note that the compression should build-up quickly in a healthy engine; low compression on the first stroke, followed by gradually increasing pressure on successive strokes, indicates worn piston rings. A low compression reading on the first stroke, which does not build-up during successive strokes, indicates leaking valves or a blown head gasket (a cracked head could also be the cause). Deposits on the undersides of the valve heads can also cause low compression.

9 If the pressure in any cylinder is reduced to the specified minimum or less, carry out the following test to isolate the cause. Introduce a teaspoonful of clean oil into that cylinder through its spark plug hole and repeat the test.

10 If the addition of oil temporarily improves the compression pressure, this indicates that bore or piston wear is responsible for the pressure loss. No improvement suggests that leaking or burnt valves, or a blown head gasket, may be to blame.

11 A low reading from two adjacent cylinders is almost certainly due to the head gasket having blown between them; the presence of coolant in the engine oil will confirm this.

12 If one cylinder is about 20 percent lower than the others and the engine has a slightly rough idle; a worn camshaft lobe could be the cause.

13 If the compression reading is unusually high, the combustion chambers are probably coated with carbon deposits. If this is the case, the cylinder head should be removed and decarbonised.

14 On completion of the test, refit the spark plugs, inlet manifold and fuel pump fuse.

3 Top dead centre (TDC) – locating

1 Disconnect the battery negative terminal (refer to Disconnecting the battery in the Reference Chapter), then remove all the spark plugs as described in Chapter 1A, Section 25.

2 Apply the handbrake and ensure that the transmission is in neutral, then jack up the front of the car and support it on axle stands (see Jacking and vehicle support). Remove the right-hand roadwheel.

3 From underneath the front of the car, release the retaining clips and remove the wheel arch liner inner panel from underneath the wing to gain access to the crankshaft pulley (see illustrations). If necessary, also undo the retaining bolts and remove the engine undershield to improve access.

4 The timing marks are in the form of notches on the crankshaft pulley rim, which align with a pointer on the timing chain cover. The TDC mark is the notch on its own to the left of the two other notches in the pulley, as viewed from under the right-hand front wheel arch.

5 Using a spanner (or socket and extension bar) applied to the crankshaft pulley bolt, rotate the crankshaft clockwise until the TDC notch on the crankshaft pulley rim is aligned with the pointer on the timing chain cover (see illustration).

6 With the crankshaft in this position, Nos 1 and 4 cylinders are now at TDC, one of them on the compression stroke.

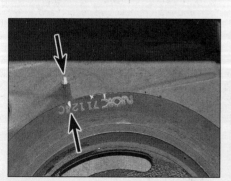

3.3a Release the retaining clips …

3.3b … and remove the inner wing panel

3.5 Align the TDC markings (arrowed)

4.3 Cover the inlet ports using duct tape

4 Cylinder head cover – removal and refitting

Removal

1 Disconnect the battery negative terminal (refer to Disconnecting the battery in the Reference Chapter).

2 Remove the inlet manifold as described in Chapter 4A, Section 11.

3 To prevent anything dropping down into the inlet ports in the cylinder head, use duct tape or similar to cover up the ports (see illustration).

4.4 Remove the ignition coils

4.5a Disconnect the wiring connector from the solenoid valve ...

4.5b ... and the fuel injectors

4 Disconnect the wiring connectors from the ignition coils, undo the retaining bolts and withdraw the ignition coils from the cylinder head cover (see illustration).

5 Release the securing clips and disconnect the wiring connectors from the intake valve timing control solenoid and the four fuel injectors (see illustrations).

6 Undo the two retaining bolts and remove the injector rail protector plate from the cylinder head cover and move it to one side. If required, release the retaining clips and disconnect the wiring loom from the protector plate (see illustrations).

7 Release the retaining clips and disconnect the breather hose from the transmission end of the cover (see illustration).

8 Using a jack support the engine (see

4.6a Undo the retaining bolts (arrowed) ...

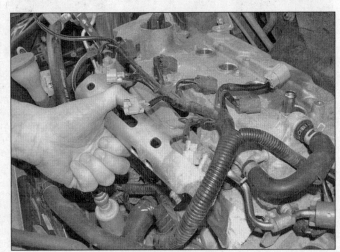

4.6b ... remove the protector plate ...

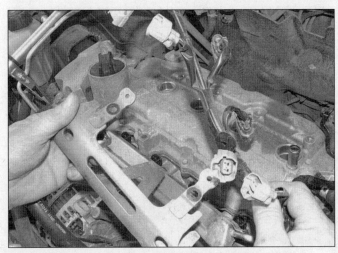

4.6c ... and unclip the wiring loom retaining clips

4.7 Disconnect the breather hose

4.8 Use a jack to support the engine

4.10a Remove the cylinder head cover …

4.10b … and recover the rubber seal

4.13a Apply sealant to the joint …

4.13b … at both sides of the camshaft sprockets

14 Fit the rubber seal to the cylinder head cover groove, ensuring that it is correctly located along its entire length, and around the four spark plug holes in the centre of the cover **(see illustration)**.

15 Carefully lower the cylinder head cover onto the cylinder head, taking great care not to displace any of the rubber seal.

16 Make sure the cover is correctly seated, and then install the retaining bolts. Working in sequence, tighten all the cover screws to the specified torque **(see illustration)**. Note bolts 13 and 14 also secure the fuel injector rail protector plate in place.

17 Refit the injector rail protector plate to the cylinder head cover and tighten the bolts as specified in paragraph 16. If removed, clip the wiring loom back into position on the protector plate

18 Reconnect the wiring connectors to the intake valve timing control solenoid and the four fuel injectors.

19 Refit the breather hose to the end of the cover and secure in position with the retaining clip.

20 Refit the ignition coils and reconnect their wiring connectors.

21 Refit the right-hand engine mounting as described in Section 15 of this Chapter. When

illustration), and then undo the retaining bolts and remove the right-hand engine mounting as described in Section 15 of this Chapter.

9 Working in the **reverse** of the tightening sequence **(see illustration 4.16)**, slacken and remove the cylinder head cover retaining bolts. Note bolts 13 and 14 have already been removed, as they also secure the fuel injector rail protector plate.

10 Lift off the cylinder head cover **(see illustrations)**, and recover the rubber seal, which goes around the outer edge of the cover, and also around each of the spark plug holes.

11 Inspect the cover seals for signs of damage and deterioration, and renew as necessary. Nissan recommends that the cylinder head cover seal should always be renewed, if the cover is removed.

Refitting

12 Carefully clean the cylinder head and cover mating surfaces, and remove all traces of oil.

13 Apply a small amount of sealant to where the timing chain upper cover joins the cylinder head **(see illustrations)**.

4.14 Fit the new rubber gasket to the cylinder head cover

4.16 Tighten the retaining bolts in the sequence shown

5.3 Using a homemade tool to hold the pulley

5.4 Remove the crankshaft pulley bolt

5.5a Remove the pulley using a puller ...

the engine mounting is in place, remove the jack from under the engine.

22 Remove the duct tape (where used) from the intake ports in the cylinder head, and clean the inlet manifold mating surface. Refit the inlet manifold as described in Chapter 4A, Section 11.

23 Reconnect the battery negative terminal. Run the engine and check for any oil leaks around the engine cylinder head cover.

5 Crankshaft pulley – removal and refitting

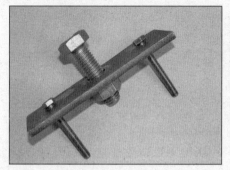

5.5b ... which can be made out of a piece of flat metal bar

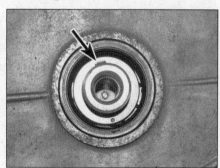

5.6 Make sure the woodruff key (arrowed) is located securely

Removal

1 Remove the auxiliary drivebelt as described in Chapter 1A, Section 10.

2 If necessary, position No 1 cylinder at TDC on its compression stroke as described in Section 3.

3 To prevent crankshaft rotation while the pulley bolt is unscrewed, the pulley should be held by a suitable tool which locates in the slots in the pulley to prevent it from turning **(see illustration)**. If this is not available, on manual transmission models, select top gear

and have an assistant apply the brakes firmly. On automatic transmission models lock the flywheel; the starter motor may need to be removed to do this.

4 Unscrew the pulley bolt, along with its washer (where applicable), and remove the pulley from the crankshaft **(see illustration)**.

5 If the pulley is a tight fit on the end of the crankshaft, use a puller to withdraw the pulley from the end of the shaft. Refit the pulley bolt and screw it back into the end of the crankshaft, leaving it approx. 5mm out from the pulley face. Fit the puller (this can be a homemade puller, using a piece of flat bar and three bols/nuts) to the pulley and tighten the

centre bolt to withdraw the pulley from the end of the crankshaft **(see illustrations)**.

6 If the pulley Woodruff key is a loose fit in the end of the crankshaft **(see illustration)**, remove it and store it with the pulley for safekeeping.

Refitting

7 Refit the Woodruff key (where removed).

8 Align the crankshaft pulley groove with the key **(see illustration)**, then slide the sprocket onto the crankshaft.

9 Lubricate under the head of the bolt, also the bolt threads with new engine oil **(see illustration)**, and then refit the retaining bolt/ washer.

5.8 Align the slot in the pulley centre hub with the woodruff key

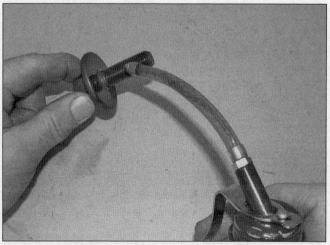

5.9 Apply a small amount of oil to the threads

5.10a Make alignments marks at 60° on the pulley and bolt …

5.10b … and turn the bolt until the marks are aligned

10 Lock the crankshaft by the method used on removal, and tighten the pulley retaining bolt to the specified torque settings. The head of the bolt/washer has markings around its edge, dividing it into 60° segments. To carry out the final stage of the tightening procedure (angle tighten 60°), paint one of the marks on the bolt head, and also paint a mark on the pulley alongside the following 60° mark to the right of the first mark. As the bolt is tightened, when the two paint marks are aligned, the bolt has then been tightened through 60° **(see illustrations).**

11 Refit the auxiliary drivebelt and adjust it as described in Chapter 1A, Section 10.

6 Timing chain cover – removal and refitting

Removal

1 Disconnect the battery negative terminal (refer to *Disconnecting the battery* in the Reference Chapter).

2 Firmly apply the handbrake, and then jack up the front of the vehicle and support it securely on axle stands (see *Jacking and vehicle support*). Remove right-hand front road wheel.

3 Undo the fasteners and remove the plastic inner wheel arch liner **(see illustration),** and undershields from beneath the right-hand front wing and the engine.

4 Drain the engine oil, then clean and refit the engine oil drain plug using a new sealing washer, tightening it to the specified torque. If the engine is nearing its service interval when the oil and filter are due for renewal, it is recommended that the filter is also removed, and a new one fitted. After reassembly, the engine can then be refilled with fresh oil. Refer to Chapter 1A, Section 3 for further information.

5 Remove the cylinder head cover as described in Section 4.

6 Remove the crankshaft pulley as described in Section 5.

7 Remove the alternator as described in Chapter 5A, Section 5.

8 Undo the three retaining bolts and remove the coolant pump pulley **(see illustration).**

9 Working in the **reverse** of the tightening sequence **(see illustration 6.17)**, slacken and remove the timing chain cover retaining bolts. Note the correct fitted location of each bolt, as some of the bolts are different lengths. Also the five upper bolts are a larger diameter than the nine lower bolts **(see illustration).**

10 Bolts 10 and 12 in the tightening sequence can be accessed easier from under the front wheel arch **(see illustration)**. Note it may be necessary to raise or lower the jack supporting the engine, to align the bolts with the access holes in the inner wing panel.

11 The timing chain cover has been fitted using a liquid gasket, and is bonded to the engine block/cylinder head. Taking care not to damage the timing chain cover work your way around the outside of the cover to release it from the engine. Nissan show the

6.3 Remove the inner wing liner

6.8 Remove the coolant pump pulley

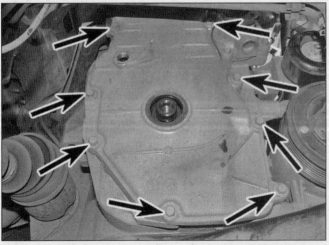

6.9 Timing chain cover lower retaining bolts

6.10 Two of the bolts (arrowed) can be accessed through the inner wing panel

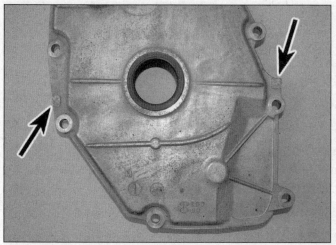

6.11a Nissan show the starting point (arrowed) to start prying the cover

6.11b Two steel dowels are located in holes at the top of the cover (arrowed)

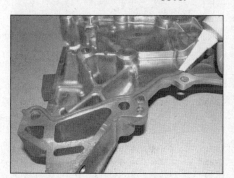

6.14a Apply a bead of sealant around the outside of the cover ...

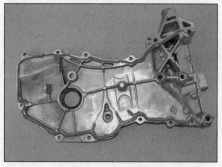

6.14b ... and around the centre mountings as shown

6.15 Apply sealant to the joints (arrowed) at both sides of the cylinder block

starting point at each side of the lower part of the casing, where there is an area to start prying. Also note that at the top of the timing chain cover there are two steel dowels, which can become very tight in the alloy cover **(see illustrations)**.

Refitting

12 Prior to refitting the cover, it is recommended that the crankshaft oil seal should be renewed. Note the seals fitted position and the carefully lever the old seal out of the cover using a large flat-bladed screwdriver. Fit the new seal to the cover, making sure its sealing lip is facing inwards. Drive the seal into position until it seats squarely in the position noted on removal, for further information see Section 13, of this Chapter.

13 Ensure that the timing chain cover and engine cylinder block/cylinder head mating surfaces are clean/dry and free from any silicone sealer. Clean the steel dowels on the cylinder block, and apply a small amount of oil to aid fitting.

14 Apply a thin bead of suitable sealant (3mm to 4mm diameter) to the timing chain cover surface, not forgetting to apply sealant to the area around the two engine mounting

bolt passages in the upper centre of the cover **(see illustrations)**.

15 Also apply a small amount of sealant to where the cylinder block joins the cylinder head, and where the cylinder block joins the upper sump housing **(see illustration)**.

16 For this procedure the help of an assistant would be advisable; lower the timing chain cover into position taking care not to wipe the sealer off the face of the cover. With the assistant under the right-hand front wheel arch manoeuvre the cover into position over the end of the crankshaft, taking great care not to damage the oil seal lip.

17 Make sure the cover is correctly seated, and then install the retaining bolts. Working in sequence, tighten all the cover screws to the specified torque **(see illustration)**. Note bolts 10 and 12 can be accessed easier from under the front wheel arch.

18 Refit the coolant pump pulley and tighten the three retaining bolts.

19 Refit the alternator with reference to Chapter 5A, Section 5.

20 Refit the crankshaft pulley as described in Section 5, of this Chapter.

21 Refit the cylinder head cover as described in Section 4, of this Chapter.

22 After reassembly, the engine can then

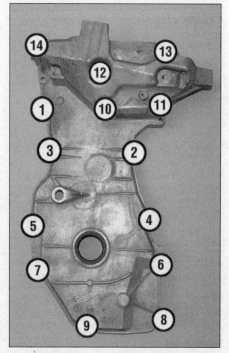

6.17 Tightening sequence for timing chain cover

7.4a Align the markings on the camshaft sprockets (arrowed) ...

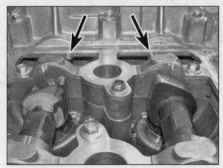

7.4b ... in this position the cam lobes should be pointing as shown

7.5a Push the tensioner lever down ...

7.5b ... and insert locking pin through tensioner

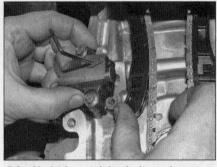

7.6a Undo the retaining bolts and remove the tensioner ...

7.6b ... keeping the locking pin in place

be refilled with fresh oil. Refer to Chapter 1A, Section 3 for further information.

23 Refit the plastic inner wheel arch liner and engine undershield.

24 Refit the front road wheel and lower the vehicle to the ground, then remove the jack from underneath the vehicle. Tighten the road wheel to the specified torque setting.

7 Timing chain, tensioner, guides and sprockets – removal, inspection and refitting

Removal

1 Position No 1 cylinder at TDC on its compression stroke, as described in Section 3.

2 Remove the cylinder head cover as described in Section 4.

3 Remove the timing chain cover as described in Section 6.

4 With No 1 cylinder set at TDC, the markings on the camshaft sprockets should be in line. Apply paint marks to the timing chain links which are in line with the markings on the sprockets (see illustrations). *If the markings on the camshaft are not aligned, it may be that it is set to be firing on No. 4 cylinder. Temporarily refit the crankshaft pulley bolt and turn the crankshaft one complete turn clockwise to get it firing on number 1 cylinder. Note the cam lobes on number 1 cylinder, should be pointing upwards and towards each other when firing on this cylinder.*

5 Whilst holding down the tensioner lever,

push the tensioner plunger back into its body. With the plunger retracted, align the hole in the lever with the hole in the tensioner body and hold it in position by inserting a small-diameter rod through the plate hole and into the body of the tensioner (see illustrations).

6 Undo the two retaining bolts, and remove the tensioner from the end of the cylinder block. Keep the rod inserted into the tensioner to prevent the plunger from springing out (see illustrations).

7 Release the upper pivot point of the chain tensioner guide, and remove it from the rear of the crankcase (see illustrations).

8 Unscrew the two mounting bolts, and remove the chain front guide from the crankcase (see illustration).

9 Disengage the timing chain from the

7.7a Release the upper pivot point (arrowed) ...

7.7b ... and withdraw the tensioner guide

7.8 Removing the fixed chain guide

7.9 Disengage the timing chain from the crankshaft sprocket

7.10a Using an open ended spanner to counter hold the camshaft …

7.10b … and remove the camshaft sprocket retaining bolt

crankshaft sprocket, and manoeuvre it out from the engine **(see illustration)**.

⚠️ *Warning: Do not turn the crankshaft or camshafts while the timing chain is removed, otherwise piston and valve contact may occur causing damage.*

10 Slacken the exhaust camshaft sprocket retaining bolt, whilst retaining the camshafts with a large open-ended spanner fitted to the hexagonal section of each shaft. Remove the bolt along with its washer (where applicable), disengage the sprocket from the end of its camshaft **(see illustrations)**.

11 To remove the variable valve inlet sprocket from the inlet camshaft, requires the inlet camshaft to be removed. See Section 9 for further information.

12 To remove the crankshaft sprocket from the end of the crankshaft, requires removing the oil pump chain and sprocket as a complete unit. See Section 12 for further information.

Inspection

13 Examine the teeth on the camshaft and crankshaft sprockets for any sign of wear or damage such as chipped, hooked or missing teeth. If there is any sign of wear or damage on either sprockets or timing chain then they should be renewed as a set.

14 Inspect the links of the timing chain for signs of wear or damage on the rollers. The extent of wear can be judged by checking the amount by which the chain can be bent sideways; a new chain will have very little sideways movement. If there is an excessive amount of side play in either timing chain, it must be renewed.

15 Note that it is a sensible precaution to renew the timing chain, regardless of apparent condition, if the engine has covered a high mileage, or if it has been noted that the chain has sounded noisy when the engine running. Although not strictly necessary, it is always worth renewing the chain and sprockets as a matched set, since it is false economy to run a new chain on worn sprockets and *vice versa*. If there is any doubt about the condition of the timing chain and sprockets, seek the advice of a Nissan dealer service department, who will be able to advise you as to the best course of action.

16 Examine the chain guides for signs of wear or damage to their chain contact faces, renewing any which are badly marked.

17 Check the chain tensioner for signs of wear, and check that the plunger is free to slide freely in the tensioner body. The condition of the tensioner spring can only be judged in comparison to a new component. Renew the

tensioner if it is worn or there is any doubt about the condition of its tensioning spring.

Refitting

18 Check the crankshaft is still positioned at TDC (the keyway will be in the 12 o'clock position, seen from the right-hand end of the engine).

19 Manoeuvre the exhaust camshaft sprocket into position, ensuring that the timing marks are facing the position noted on removal. Engage the sprocket with the chain and align the two dark blue chain links with the alignment marks on the camshaft sprockets **(see illustrations)**.

7.19a Align the slot in the rear of the sprocket …

7.19b … then align the dark coloured link with the sprocket alignment marks …

7.19c … and also on the inlet camshaft sprocket (arrowed)

7.21 Align the coloured link with the dot on the crankshaft sprocket

7.23 Locate the tensioner guide into place

20 Tighten the exhaust camshaft bolt to the specified torque setting, whilst retaining the camshafts with a large open-ended spanner fitted to the hexagonal section of each shaft **(see illustrations 7.10a)**.

21 Manoeuvre the chain into position, engaging it with the crankshaft sprocket so that its coloured link is aligned with the timing mark on the crankshaft sprocket **(see illustration)**. Check that all the timing marks are correctly aligned with the chain links.

22 Fit the chain front fixed guide to the cylinder block, and tighten its retaining bolts to the specified torque.

23 Fit the chain rear tensioner guide to the upper pivot point and locate it in position **(see illustration)**.

24 Fit the chain tensioner to the cylinder block, and tighten its retaining bolts to the specified torque. Whilst holding the guide against the tensioner plunger, withdraw the rod, and check that the tensioner plunger is forced out against the guide to take up the slack in the chain **(see illustration)**.

25 Check that all the timing marks are still correctly aligned with the chain links. If all timing marks are aligned, fit the crankshaft pulley and turn the engine two complete turns, and check the timing marks on the sprockets are all re-aligned. **Note:** *The coloured links on the chain will not be re-aligned with the marks on the sprockets. The coloured links are just for the initial set up, and will take many turns before they will line up again, with the marks on the sprockets.*

26 Remove the crankshaft pulley and refit the timing chain cover as described in Section 6.

27 Refit the crankshaft pulley as described in Section 5, of this Chapter.

28 Refit the cylinder head cover as described in Section 4.

8 Valve clearances – checking and adjustment

Note: *This is not a routine operation. It should only be necessary at high mileage,* *after overhaul, or when investigating noise or power loss which may be attributable to the valve gear. Adjustment involves removing the camshaft and changing the cam followers (valve lifters) that are available in 26 different thicknesses (ranging from 3.00mm to 3.50mm, in steps of 0.02mm).*

Checking

1 The importance of having the valve clearances correctly adjusted cannot be overstressed, as they vitally affect the performance of the engine. The clearances are checked as follows.

2 Draw the outline of the engine on a piece of paper, numbering the cylinders 1 to 4, with No 1 cylinder at the timing chain end of the engine. Show the position of each valve, together with the specified valve clearance. Above each valve, draw two lines for noting the actual clearance and the amount of adjustment required.

3 Remove the cylinder head cover as described in Section 4.

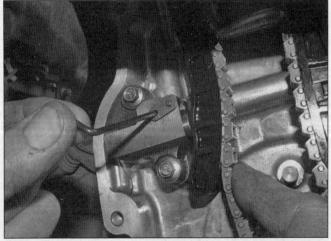

7.24 Hold pressure against the tensioner and remove the locking pin

8.5a Check the clearances between the camshafts and the followers (arrowed)

8.5b Check clearances as shown

Cylinder 1 –
    Inlet and Exhaust valves

Cylinder 2 – Inlet valves
Cylinder 3 – Exhaust valves

8.7 Check clearances as shown

Cylinder 2 – Exhaust valves
Cylinder 3 – Inlet valves

Cylinder 4 –
    Inlet and Exhaust valves

4 Position No 1 cylinder at TDC on its compression stroke, as described in Section 3.

5 Using feeler gauges, measure the clearance between the base of the cam and the follower of the following valves, recording each clearance on the paper **(see illustrations)**.

    No 1 cylinder inlet and exhaust valves
    No 2 cylinder inlet valves
    No 3 cylinder exhaust valves

6 Rotate the crankshaft through one complete turn (360°) clockwise until the TDC notch on the crankshaft pulley is realigned with the pointer. No 4 cylinder is now at TDC on its compression stroke.

7 Check the clearances of the following valves, and record them on the paper **(see illustration)**.

    No 2 cylinder exhaust valves
    No 3 cylinder inlet valves
    No 4 cylinder inlet and exhaust valves

8 Calculate the difference between each measured clearance and the desired value, and record it on the piece of paper.

Adjustment

Note: *A micrometer or dial gauge and probe will be required for this operation.*

9 Where a valve clearance differs from the specified value, then the cam follower (valve lifter) for that valve must be substituted with a thinner or thicker one accordingly. The cam followers have the thickness stamped on the bottom face of the follower; e.g. 324 indicates the follower is 3.24 mm thick at the top centre of the follower **(see illustration)**.

10 If required use a micrometer or dial gauge to measure the true thickness of any follower removed, as it may have been reduced by wear. **Note:** *Followers are available in thicknesses between 3.00 mm and 3.50 mm, in steps of 0.02 mm.*

11 To access the cam followers (valve lifters), first remove the camshafts as described in

Section 9. Remove and refit each follower separately, to avoid any confusion.

12 The size of follower required is calculated as follows. If the measured clearance is less than specified, subtract the measured clearance from the specified clearance, and deduct the result from the thickness of the existing follower. For example:

Sample calculation – clearance too small

    Clearance measured (A) = 0.16 mm
    Desired clearance (B) = 0.30 mm
    Difference (B – A) = 0.14 mm
    Cam follower thickness fitted = 3.50 mm
    Cam follower thickness required = 3.50 – 0.14 = 3.36 mm

13 If the measured clearance is greater than specified, subtract the specified clearance from the measured clearance, and add the result to the thickness of the existing follower. For example:

Sample calculation – clearance too big

    Clearance measured (A) = 0.40 mm
    Desired clearance (B) = 0.30 mm
    Difference (A – B) = 0.10 mm
    Cam follower thickness fitted = 3.26 mm
    Cam follower thickness required = 3.26 + 0.10 = 3.36 mm

8.9 Markings inside the follower for thickness

14 Working on each separately, lift out the follower to be renewed, then oil the new one and carefully locate it in the cylinder head, on top of the valve.

15 Refit the camshafts with reference to Section 9.

16 It will be helpful for future adjustment if a record is kept of the thickness of cam followers (valve lifters) fitted at each position. The cam followers required could be purchased in advance once the clearances and the existing follower thicknesses are known.

17 Once all valve clearances have been adjusted, rotate the crankshaft through at least four complete turns in the correct direction of rotation, to settle all disturbed followers, then recheck the clearances as described above.

18 With all valve clearances correctly adjusted, refit the cylinder head cover as described in Section 4, and refit all components removed to gain access to the crankshaft pulley.

9 Camshafts and followers – removal, inspection and refitting

Note: *Before the variable valve inlet sprocket can be removed from the camshaft, a minimum of 3.0 bars air pressure will need to be applied to the variable valve inlet sprocket, and a 3 mm locking pin to hold the sprocket in position.*

Removal

1 Position No 1 cylinder at TDC on its compression stroke, as described in Section 3.

2 Remove the cylinder head cover as described in Section 4.

9.3 Remove the camshaft position sensor

9.4 Check the alignment marks on the camshaft sprockets (arrowed)

3 Undo the retaining bolt and remove the camshaft position sensor from the end of the cylinder head **(see illustration)**.

4 With No 1 cylinder set at TDC, the markings on the camshaft sprockets should be in line. Apply paint marks to the timing chain link, which are in line with the markings on the sprockets **(see illustration)**. If the markings on the camshaft are not aligned, turn the crankshaft one turn clockwise to get it firing on number 1 cylinder. Note the cam lobes on number 1 cylinder, should be pointing upwards and towards each other when firing on this cylinder.

5 Working inside the right-hand front wheel arch, remove the blanking plug from the timing chain cover **(see illustration)**.

6 Use a thin screwdriver to hold the tensioner lever downwards, which will allow the tensioner plunger to be pushed back into its body **(see illustration)**.

7 With the aid of an assistant, turn the crankshaft sprocket anticlockwise slightly, whilst turning the exhaust camshaft sprocket clockwise slightly. This will pull the timing chain taut, causing the tensioner plunger to be pushed back. With the plunger retracted, align the hole in the lever with the hole in the tensioner body and hold it in position by inserting a small-diameter rod through the plate hole and into the body of the tensioner **(see illustration)**. **Note:** *For further information on the removal and refitting of the timing*

chain tensioner, with the cover removed, see Section 7 of this Chapter.

8 With the tensioner locked, turn the crankshaft sprocket clockwise slightly to let the chain become slack around the camshaft sprockets.

9 Slacken the exhaust camshaft sprocket retaining bolt, whilst retaining the camshaft with a large open-ended spanner fitted to the hexagonal section on the shaft **(see illustration)**.

10 Remove the bolt along with its washer (where applicable), disengage the sprocket from the end of its camshaft, and then release it from the timing chain **(see illustrations)**.

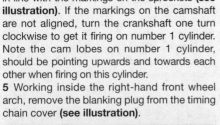

9.5 Remove the blanking plug

9.6 Push the tensioner lever down …

9.7 … and insert locking pin (allen key) through tensioner

9.9 Using an open ended spanner to counter hold the camshaft

9.10a Remove the camshaft sprocket retaining bolt …

9.10b … and remove the sprocket

9.11 Remove the bearing cap housing

9.12a Using an air gun to apply pressure …

9.12b … through the oil gallery hole (arrowed) in the camshaft

⚠ *Warning: Do not turn the crankshaft or camshafts while the timing chain is removed, otherwise piston and valve contact may occur causing damage.*

11 At the timing chain end of the camshafts the bearing cap housing covers both of the camshafts, undo the three retaining bolts and remove it from the cylinder head **(see illustration)**.

12 Using an air gun apply a minimum of 3 bars air pressure to the oil passage leading to the variable valve inlet sprocket **(see illustrations)**.

13 While keeping the air pressure applied, slowly turn the camshaft sprocket from anti-clockwise to clockwise. During this procedure a click (locking pin disengaging) is heard from the inlet sprocket. **Note:** *If a click has not been heard, then waggle the camshaft sprocket very slightly and gently tap the variable valve inlet sprocket with a plastic mallet* **(see illustration)**.

14 Still keeping the air pressure applied, after the click (locking pin disengaging) has been heard, slowly turn the inlet camshaft in the anti-clockwise direction (to the rear of the vehicle) setting it to the most advanced position. In this position the groove and the pinhole should be in line.

15 Insert a 2.5 mm Allen key into the hole in the inlet sprocket to hold it in position **(see illustrations)**. Use the short end of the Allen key to insert into the sprocket, as the inserted part should be approximately 15 mm; tape the Allen key into position. Air pressure can now be released.

⚠ *Warning: Do not remove the Allen key from the inlet sprocket until it has been refitted to the vehicle. If the Allen key is removed while the sprocket is off the engine, the locking pin inside the sprocket will be damaged by lateral load and could shear. If this happens a new sprocket will be required.*

16 All remaining camshaft bearing caps have identification markings stamped into their top surface; the exhaust camshaft caps being marked 2 to 5 and the inlet camshaft caps being marked A to D; the No 2 and A caps are fitted nearest the timing chain end of the engine **(see illustration)**. Note the markings on the caps for refitting. If the caps are not marked, suitable identification marks should be made prior to removal. Using white paint or suitable marker pen, mark each cap in some way to indicate its correct fitted orientation and position. This will avoid the possibility of installing the caps in the wrong positions and/or the wrong way around on refitting.

17 Working in the **reverse** of the tightening sequence **(see illustration 9.35)**, evenly and progressively slacken the sixteen remaining camshaft bearing cap retaining bolts by one turn at a time, to relieve the pressure of the valve springs on the bearing caps gradually and evenly. Once the valve spring pressure has been relieved, the bolts can be fully unscrewed and the caps removed **(see illustration)**.

18 With the bearing caps removed the exhaust camshaft can be simply lifted off the top of the cylinder head, noting its fitted position. Note the position of the dowel on the sprocket end of the camshaft, and the position of the cam lobes, so that it can be refitted in the correct position for TDC on no.1 cylinder.

19 To remove the inlet camshaft, the variable valve inlet sprocket will need to be removed from the end of the camshaft. To do this, the

9.13 Turn the camshaft sprocket while air pressure is applied

9.15a Insert a 2.5 mm pin to lock the sprocket …

9.15b … and secure it in place to prevent it falling out

9.16 Camshaft bearing cap markings

9.17 Remove the bearing caps

9.19 Using an open ended spanner to counter hold the camshaft

9.20a Remove the camshaft sprocket retaining bolt …

9.20b … remove the camshaft …

9.20c … and unhook the timing chain from the sprocket

9.21 Remove the cam followers

camshaft will require lifting slightly to access the retaining bolt. With the camshaft raised slightly and supported on a clean piece of cloth, slacken the camshaft sprocket securing bolt, whilst retaining the camshaft with a large open-ended spanner fitted to the hexagonal section on the shaft **(see illustration)**.

20 Remove the securing bolt, disengage the sprocket from the end of its camshaft, and then release it from the timing chain **(see illustrations)**. The timing chain cannot drop down into the timing chain cover, or drop off the bottom of the crankshaft sprocket, so it can be left in position ready for refitting.

21 Obtain sixteen small, clean plastic containers, and number them 1 to 16. Alternatively, divide a larger container into sixteen compartments. Using a rubber sucker, withdraw each follower (valve lifter) in

turn, and place it in its respective container **(see illustration)**. Do not interchange the cam followers, or the rate of wear will be increased.

22 If required, undo the retaining bolt and remove the inlet variable valve timing control solenoid from the front of the cylinder head **(see illustration)**.

Inspection

23 Remove the plug from below the timing control solenoid and clean-out or renew the oil filter for the variable valve system **(see illustration)**.

24 Inspect the cam bearing surfaces of the head and the bearing caps. Look for score marks and deep scratches. Check the camshaft lobes for heat discoloration (blue appearance), score marks, chipped areas or flat spots.

25 Camshaft run-out can be checked by supporting each end of the camshaft on V-blocks, and measuring any run-out at the centre of the shaft using a dial gauge. If the run-out exceeds the specified limit, a new camshaft will be required.

26 Measure the height of each lobe with a micrometer **(see illustration)**, and compare the results to the figures given in the Specifications. If damage is noted or wear is excessive, new camshaft(s) must be fitted.

27 The camshaft bearing oil clearance should now be checked.

28 Fit the bearing caps to the cylinder head, using the identification markings or the marks made on removal to ensure that they are correctly positioned. Tighten the retaining bolts to the specified torque in sequence **(see illustration 9.35)**. Measure the diameter of each bearing cap journal, and compare the measurements obtained with the results given in the Specifications at the start of this Chapter. If any journal is worn beyond the service limit, the cylinder head must be renewed. The camshaft bearing oil clearance can then calculated by subtracting the camshaft bearing journal diameter from the bearing cap journal diameter.

29 Check the cam follower and cylinder head bearing surfaces for signs of wear or damage.

Refitting

30 Liberally oil the cylinder head cam follower bores and the followers. Carefully refit the followers to the cylinder head; ensuring that each follower is refitted to its original

9.22 Inlet variable valve timing control solenoid valve

9.23 Remove plug (arrowed) to renew the solenoid valve filter

9.26 Checking the cam lobe height with a micrometer

9.30 Lubricate the camshaft bearing surfaces

bore. Some care will be required to enter the followers squarely into their bores. Liberally oil the camshaft bearing and lobe contact surfaces **(see illustration)**.

31 Refit the exhaust camshaft to its correct location in the cylinder head, in the position noted on removal.

32 Locate the variable valve inlet sprocket onto the inlet camshaft as the camshaft is being placed on the cylinder head **(see illustration)**. This will need to be tightened to the camshaft, before the camshaft is secured into place, so as to access the securing bolt. With the camshaft raised slightly and supported on a clean piece of cloth, tighten the camshaft sprocket securing bolt, whilst retaining the camshaft with a large open-ended spanner fitted to the hexagonal section on the shaft **(see illustration 9.19)**. Note: *Make sure the timing chain is located around the sprocket before the camshaft is secured into place.*

33 Ensure that the bearing cap and head mating surfaces are completely clean, unmarked and free from oil.

34 Refit the bearing caps, using the identification markings or the marks made on removal to ensure that each is installed the correct way round and in its original location.

35 Working in sequence, evenly and progressively tighten the camshaft bearing cap bolts by one turn at a time until the caps touch the cylinder head **(see illustration)**. Then go round again and tighten all the bolts to the specified torque setting (see Torque wrench settings for sequence). Work only as described, to impose the pressure of the valve springs gradually and evenly on the bearing caps.

36 Refit the exhaust camshaft sprocket, making sure it is located correctly on the dowel on the end of the camshaft **(see illustrations)**. Tighten the camshaft sprocket securing bolt, whilst retaining the camshaft with a large open-ended spanner fitted to the hexagonal section on the shaft, as done on removal. Make sure the chain is correctly located around the sprocket and the timing marks are aligned, as noted on removal.

37 With the crankshaft pulley and camshaft sprockets timing marks all aligned for TDC (see Section 7, for further information), remove

9.32 Align the locating peg on the end of the camshaft with the sprocket

9.35 Tighten the bearing caps in the sequence shown

9.36a Align the locating peg with the slot in the sprocket …

9.36b … then using an open ended spanner to counter hold the camshaft, tighten the sprocket bolt

9.37 Remove the locking pin

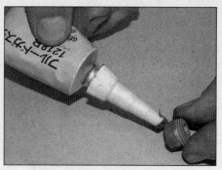

9.38a Apply some sealant to the threads …

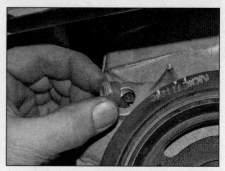

9.38b … and refit the blanking plug

the locking pin from the timing chain tensioner **(see illustration)**. With the pin removed turn the crankshaft clockwise slightly, so that the tension on the chain releases the tensioner to take up the slack in the chain.

38 Apply sealant to the blanking plug and refit it to the timing chain cover **(see illustrations)**.

39 Remove the tape and withdraw the locking pin from the variable valve inlet sprocket **(see illustration)**, slowly turn the crankshaft clockwise, to allow the sprocket to reach its most retarded position.

40 Check that the camshaft timing marks are still correctly aligned with the painted chain links and the crankshaft pulley is still set to TDC. If all timing marks are aligned, then turn the engine two complete turns, and check the timing marks on the sprockets are all re-aligned. **Note:** *The painted links on the chain will not be re-aligned with the marks on the sprockets. If required, see Section 7 for further information on setting the timing.*

41 If the cylinder head/camshafts have been overhauled, check and adjust the valve clearances as described in Section 8.

42 Refit the camshaft position sensor to the end of the cylinder head.

43 Refit the cylinder head cover as described in Section 4.

44 If the cylinder head/camshafts have been overhauled, check the valve clearances 'cold' prior to refitting the cylinder head cover (see Section 8).

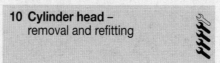

10 Cylinder head –
removal and refitting

Removal

1 Depressurise the fuel system as described in Chapter 4A, Section 6.

2 Disconnect the battery negative terminal (refer to *Disconnecting the battery* in the Reference Chapter).

3 Remove the timing chain as described in Section 7.

4 Remove the camshafts as described in Section 9.

5 Carry out the following operations as described in Chapter 4A.

a) *Disconnect the exhaust system front pipe from the manifold.*

b) *Disconnect the fuel feed and return hoses from the fuel rail (plug all openings, to prevent loss of fuel and entry of dirt into the fuel system).*

c) *Disconnect the vacuum servo unit hose, coolant hose(s) and all the other relevant/ breather hoses from the manifold and associated valves.*

6 Slacken the retaining clip(s) and disconnect the coolant hose(s) from the cylinder head.

7 Working in the **reverse** of the tightening sequence **(see illustration 10.21)**, progressively slacken the ten main cylinder head bolts by half a turn at a time, until all bolts can be unscrewed by hand.

8 Lift out the cylinder head bolts and recover the washers (where applicable), noting which way around they are fitted.

9 Lift the cylinder head away with the aid of an assistant, as it is a heavy assembly. Remove the gasket from the top of the block, noting the locating dowels fitted to the top of the cylinder block. If they are a loose fit in the block, remove the locating dowels, noting which way round they are fitted, and store them with the head for safekeeping.

10 If the cylinder head is to be dismantled for overhaul, then refer to Chapter 2E, Section 6.

Preparation for refitting

11 Check the condition of the cylinder head bolts, and particularly their threads, whenever they are removed. Wash the bolts and wipe dry, then check each for any sign of visible wear or damage, renewing any bolt if necessary.

Checking cylinder head bolt (see illustration): –

a) *Measure 10mm up from the threaded end of the bolt and note the reading = D1.*

b) *Measure 40mm up from the threaded end of the bolt and note the reading = D2*

c) *Take the second reading away from the first reading (D1 – D2), and it should be no more than 0.15mm.*

Although Nissan do not specify that the bolts must be renewed, it is strongly recommended, that the bolts should be renewed as a complete set whenever they are disturbed.

12 The mating faces of the cylinder head and cylinder block/crankcase must be perfectly clean before refitting the head. Use a hard plastic or wood scraper to remove all traces of gasket and carbon; also clean the piston crowns. Take particular care, as the surfaces are damaged easily. Also, make sure that the carbon is not allowed to enter the oil and water passages – this is particularly important for the lubrication system, as carbon could block the oil supply to any of the engine's components. Using adhesive tape and paper, seal the water, oil and bolt holes in the cylinder block/crankcase. To prevent carbon entering the gap between the pistons and bores, smear a little grease in the gap. After cleaning each piston, use a small brush to remove all traces of grease and carbon from the gap, and then wipe away the remainder with a clean rag. Clean all the pistons in the same way.

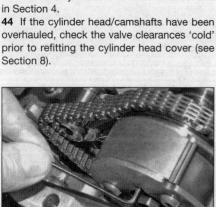

9.39 Remove the locking pin

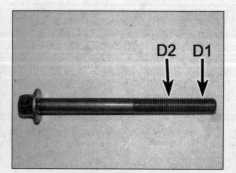

10.11 Check the cylinder head bolt for wear

13 Check the mating surfaces of the cylinder block/crankcase and the cylinder head for nicks, deep scratches and other damage. If slight, they may be removed carefully with a file, but if excessive, machining may be the only alternative to renewal.

14 If warpage of the cylinder head gasket surface is suspected, use a straight-edge to check it for distortion. If necessary, refer to Chapter 2E, Section 7.

Refitting

15 Wipe clean the mating surfaces of the cylinder head and cylinder block/crankcase. Check the locating dowels are in position at each end of the cylinder block/crankcase surface.

16 Fit a new gasket to the cylinder block/ crankcase surface, aligning it with the locating dowels.

17 With the aid of an assistant, carefully refit the cylinder head assembly to the block, aligning it with the locating dowels.

18 Apply a smear of clean oil to the threads, and to the underside of the heads, of the cylinder head bolts.

19 Fit the washer to each head bolt, making sure it is fitted with its tapered edge uppermost.

20 Carefully enter each bolt into its relevant hole (*do not drop them in*) and screw in, by hand only, until finger-tight.

21 Working progressively and in sequence, tighten the cylinder head bolts to their Stage 1 torque setting, using a torque wrench and suitable socket **(see illustration)**. See specifications at the beginning of this Chapter.

22 For stage 2, leave the bolts a minute then, working in the **reverse** of the specified sequence, progressively slacken the head bolts by half a turn at a time, until all bolts can be unscrewed by hand.

23 Tighten the head bolts again by hand, then go around again in the specified sequence and tighten these ten bolts to the specified Stage 3 torque setting.

24 Go around in the specified sequence and tighten the ten cylinder head bolts through the specified Stage 4 angle setting.

25 Finally, go around again in the specified sequence and tighten the ten cylinder head bolts through the specified Stage 5 angle setting.

26 Reconnect the coolant hoses to the cylinder head and securely tighten the retaining clips.

27 Working as described in Chapter 4A, carry out the following operations:

a) *Refit all disturbed wiring, hoses and control cable(s) to the inlet manifold and fuel system components.*

b) *Reconnect the exhaust system front pipe to the manifold, and reconnect the exhaust gas sensor wiring connector.*

c) *Refit the inlet manifold.*

28 Refit the camshafts to the cylinder head as described in Section 9.

29 Fit the timing chains and sprockets as described in Section 7. **Note:** *If the cylinder head has been overhauled, check the valve*

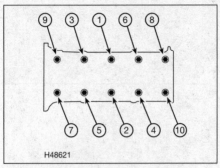

10.21 Cylinder head bolt tightening sequence

clearances 'cold' prior to refitting the cylinder head cover (see Section 8).

30 Start the engine and warm it up to normal operating temperature, check for any leaks from the engine, cooling circuit and fuel system.

11 Sump – removal and refitting

Note: *The oil sump is made up of two parts; it has an upper alloy part and a lower steel oil pan. The following procedure is for the lower oil pan part. To remove the upper alloy part, the engine will need to be removed and the upper alloy sump then split from the cylinder block.*

Removal

1 Firmly apply the handbrake, and then jack up the front of the vehicle and support it securely on axle stands (see *Jacking and vehicle support*).

2 Slacken and remove the retaining bolts and remove the plastic undershield from beneath the engine.

3 Drain the engine oil, then clean and refit the engine oil drain plug, fit a new sealing washer

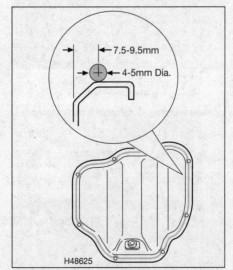

11.7 Apply a bead of sealant around the sump as shown

11.5 Using a flat ended scraper to prise the sump away

on refitting. And then tighten it to the specified torque. If the engine is nearing its service interval when the oil and filter are due for renewal, it is recommended that the filter is also removed, and a new one fitted. Refer to Chapter 1A, Section 3 for further information.

4 Progressively slacken and remove all of the steel oil pan retaining bolts.

5 The lower steel oil pan is sealed to the upper alloy sump casing with strong liquid gasket sealer, which is very difficult to remove, however methodical use of a spatula or thin knife will release the sump **(see illustration)**. Take care not to distort or damage the mating surfaces of the lower oil pan and upper alloy sump. Take adequate precautions to catch any oil remaining inside the sump housing, as the oil pan is removed.

Refitting

6 Clean all traces of sealant from the mating surfaces of the upper alloy part of the sump and steel oil pan, then use a clean rag to wipe out the oil pan and the sump interior.

7 Ensure that the lower oil pan and upper alloy casing mating surfaces are clean and dry. Apply a continuous bead of suitable sealant to the mating surface of the oil pan. Apply a 4mm to 5mm diameter bead of sealant to the oil pan, going around the inner edge of each bolt hole **(see illustration)**.

8 Offer up the sump, locating it in the correct position, and refit its retaining bolts. Tighten the bolts evenly and progressively to the specified torque and in the correct sequence **(see illustration)**.

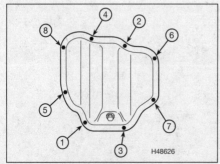

11.8 Tighten the bolts in the sequence shown

12.3 Remove the tensioner from the cylinder block

12.4 Remove the sprocket securing nut

12.5 Remove the drive chain complete with sprockets

9 Refit the engine undershield and securely tighten the retaining bolts.

10 After reassembly, the engine can then be refilled with fresh engine oil. Refer to Chapter 1A, Section 3, for further information.

11 Start the engine and warm it up to normal operating temperature, check for any leaks from the sump area.

12 Oil pump, drive chain and sprockets – removal, inspection and refitting

Removal

1 Remove the timing chain as described in Section 7.

2 Remove the sump oil pan as described in Section 11.

12.6 Oil pump retaining bolts

3 Release the spring from the hole in the cylinder block and withdraw the chain tensioner from the pivot on the cylinder block (see illustration).

4 Unscrew the oil pump drive sprocket retaining nut, use a socket on the end of the oil pump drive shaft to slacken the retaining nut (see illustration).

5 Remove the oil pump drive chain complete with sprockets from the oil pump drive shaft and crankshaft (see illustration).

6 Undo the retaining bolts and remove the oil pump from the upper sump housing (see illustration).

Inspection

7 Clean the components and carefully examine the chain, sprockets and pump for any signs of excessive wear. If evident, it is recommended that all the components are renewed as a set (see illustration).

12.7 Check the condition of all components

8 Before refitting the oil pump, prime it by filling with clean engine oil whilst rotating the pump clockwise.

Refitting

9 Fit the oil pump back in place in the sump upper housing and tighten the retaining bolts.

10 Make sure the chain is located around the two sprocket correctly, and then refit them as a complete assembly to the oil pump drive shaft and crankshaft (see illustration).

11 Refit the oil pump sprocket retaining nut and tighten to the specified torque setting.

12 Refit the chain tensioner to the pivot on the cylinder block, making sure the tensioner spring is located correctly in the cylinder block (see illustration).

13 Refit the sump oil pan as described in Section 11.

14 Refit the timing chain cover as described in Section 7.

13 Crankshaft oil seals – renewal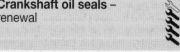

Timing chain cover oil seal

1 Remove the crankshaft pulley as described in Section 5.

2 Carefully lever the oil seal out of position, using a large flat-bladed screwdriver, taking care not to damage the end of the crankshaft or timing cover (see illustration).

12.10 Make sure the chain is located around the sprocket correctly

12.12 Make sure the tensioner spring (arrowed) is located correctly

13.2 Carefully prise out the oil seal

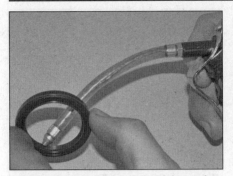

13.4a Lubricate the inner lip of the seal ...

13.4b ... press the seal into position ...

13.4c ... carefully fit the seal into the cover

3 Clean the seal housing, and polish off any burrs or raised edges, which may have caused the seal to fail in the first place.

4 Lubricate the lips of the new seal with a smear of clean oil and offer up the seal ensuring its sealing lip is facing inwards. Carefully ease the seal into position, taking care not to damage its sealing lip. Drive the seal into position until it seats flush with the face of the timing chain cover **(see illustrations)**. Take care not to damage the seal lips during fitting.

5 Wash off any traces of oil, then refit the crankshaft pulley as described in Section 5.

Flywheel oil seal

6 Remove the flywheel, as described in Section 14.

7 Note the fitted position of the old seal, then prise it out of the right-hand cover/housing using a screwdriver or suitable hooked instrument, taking care not to damage the surface of the crankshaft. Alternatively, the oil seal can be removed by drilling a hole in the seal, and then inserting a self-tapping screw. A pair of grips/pliers can then be used to pull out the oil seal **(see illustrations)**. Note: *Take care when drilling the hole, to not drill into anything other than the seal.*

8 Clean the seal housing, and polish off any burrs or raised edges, which may have caused the seal to fail in the first place **(see illustration)**.

9 Lubricate with clean oil the lips of the new seal and the crankshaft shoulder, then offer up the seal to the cylinder block/crankcase. Ease the sealing lip of the seal over the crankshaft shoulder by hand only, and press the seal evenly into its recess to make it square in the casing **(see illustrations)**.

10 With the seal still protruding out from the cylinder block, apply a coat of liquid gasket/sealant all the way around the outer edge of the seal. Carefully drive the seal into position until it seats flush with the face of the cylinder block, and then wipe off the excess liquid gasket/sealant from the casing

13.7a Carefully drill a hole in the seal ...

13.7b ... insert a self tapping screw ...

13.7c ... and lever the seal out from the casing

13.8 Clean around the seal fitting surface area

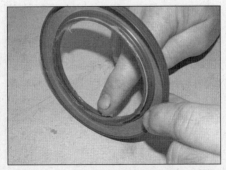

13.9a Using clean oil to lubricate the inner lip of the seal ...

13.9b ... press the seal into position ...

13.10a Apply some sealant around the outer edge of the seal ...

13.10b ... press the seal fully into position ...

13.10c ... then clean off the excess sealant from around the casing

(see illustrations). Make sure the outer edge of the seal is sitting flush with the cylinder block casing.

11 Wash off any traces of oil or sealant, then refit the flywheel as described in Section 14.

14 Flywheel – removal, inspection and refitting

Removal

1 Remove the manual transmission as described in Chapter 7A, Section 6.
2 Remove the clutch assembly as described in Chapter 6, Section 6.
3 Prevent the flywheel from turning by locking the ring gear teeth (see illustration). Alternatively, bolt a strap between the flywheel and the cylinder block.
4 Slacken and remove the retaining bolts (see illustration), then remove the flywheel from the end of the crankshaft. Do not drop it, as it is very heavy.

Inspection

5 If the flywheel's clutch mating surface is deeply scored, cracked or otherwise damaged, the flywheel must be renewed. Seek the advice of a Nissan dealer or engine reconditioning specialist.

6 If the ring gear is badly worn or has missing teeth, it must be renewed. Check with your Nissan dealer or engine reconditioning specialist, to see if the flywheel can be repaired.

Refitting

7 Install the locating dowels (where removed).
8 Clean the mating surfaces of the flywheel and crankshaft.
9 Offer up the flywheel, and refit the retaining bolts.
10 Lock the ring gear using the method employed on dismantling, and tighten the retaining bolts to the specified torque.
11 Refit the clutch as described in Chapter 6, Section 6.
12 Remove the locking tool, and refit the transmission as described in Chapter 7A, Section 6.

15 Engine/transmission mountings – inspection and renewal

Inspection

1 If improved access is required, firmly apply the handbrake, and then jack up the front of the vehicle and support it securely on axle stands (see *Jacking and vehicle support*).

2 Check the mounting rubber to see if it is cracked, hardened or separated from the metal at any point; renew the mounting if any such damage or deterioration is evident.
3 Check that all the mounting's fasteners are securely tightened; use a torque wrench to check if possible.
4 Using a large screwdriver or a crowbar, check for wear in the mounting by carefully levering against it to check for free play. Where this is not possible, enlist the aid of an assistant to move the engine/transmission back-and-forth, or from side-to-side, while you watch the mounting. While some free play is to be expected even from new components, excessive wear should be obvious. If excessive free play is found, check first that the fasteners are correctly secured, and then renew any worn components as described below.

Renewal

Right-hand mounting

5 Disconnect the battery negative terminal (refer to *Disconnecting the battery* in the Reference Chapter).
6 Place a jack beneath the engine, with a block of wood on the jack head. Raise the jack until it is supporting the weight of the engine (see illustration).
7 Slacken the securing bolt and disconnect

14.3 Using a tool to prevent the flywheel from turning ...

14.4 ... when slackening the flywheel bolts

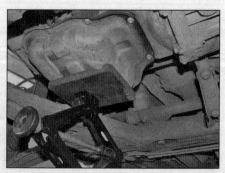

15.6 Supporting the engine on a jack

15.7 Undo the earth cable securing bolt (arrowed)

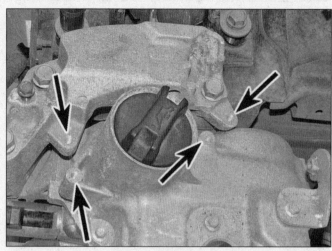

15.8 Some engines have support brackets in the position arrowed

15.9a Remove the mounting retaining bolts (arrowed) …

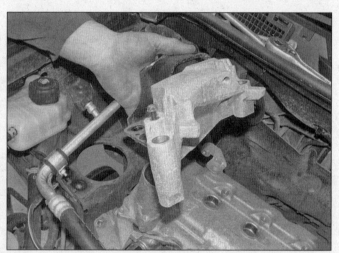

15.9b … and remove the mounting from the engine compartment

the earth wire from the top of the mounting bracket **(see illustration)**.

8 On some models, it may be necessary to undo the retaining bolts and remove the small stay brackets from the mounting bracket to the cylinder head cover **(see illustration)**.

9 Slacken and remove the three retaining bolts from the inner wing panel, remove the three retaining bolts from the engine mounting bracket, and then withdraw the complete mounting from the engine compartment **(see illustrations)**.

10 Check carefully for signs of wear or damage on all components, and renew them where necessary.

11 On refitting, fit the engine mounting and bracket to the inner wing panel and engine, and then securely tighten its retaining bolts to the specified torque setting.

12 Where applicable, refit the small stay brackets back to the cylinder head cover.

13 With the engine mounting back in position, lower the jack and remove it from underneath the engine.

14 Reconnect the earth cable to the top of the engine mounting and then reconnect the battery negative terminal.

Left-hand mounting

15 Remove the battery and tray, as described in Chapter 5A, Section 3.

16 Place a jack and block of wood beneath the transmission, and raise the jack to take the weight of the transmission.

17 Slacken and remove the through-bolt/stud retaining nut from the centre of the mounting **(see illustration)**.

18 Slacken and remove the two outer retaining nuts, and withdraw the mounting from the upper mounting bracket **(see illustration)**.

15.17 Undo the centre retaining nut (arrowed)

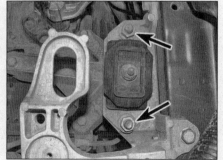

15.18 Undo the two outer securing nuts (arrowed)

15.20 Mounting bracket securing bolts (arrowed)

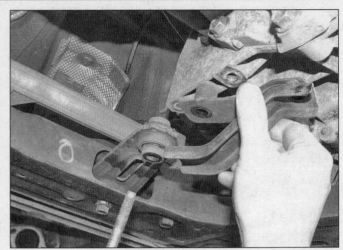

15.28 Remove the mounting bracket from the transmission

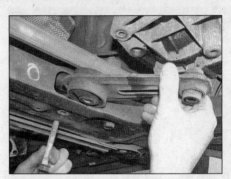

15.29 Remove the link arm from the subframe

19 If required, undo the retaining bolts from the inner wing panel to remove the upper mounting bracket.

20 Also, if required, undo the retaining bolts from the transmission to remove the lower mounting bracket (see illustration).

21 Check carefully for signs of wear or damage on all components, and renew them where necessary.

22 On refitting, fit the upper and lower mounting brackets (where removed) and securely tighten the retaining bolts.

23 Align the left-hand rubber mounting with the bolt/stud on the lower mounting bracket and tighten its nut to the specified torque setting.

24 Refit the two outer retaining nuts, and tighten to the specified torque setting.

25 With the transmission mounting back in position, lower the jack and remove it from underneath the transmission.

26 Refit the battery and battery tray, with reference to Chapter 5, Section 3.

Rear lower mounting

27 If not already done, firmly apply the handbrake, and then jack up the front of the vehicle and support it securely on axle stands (see *Jacking and vehicle support*).

28 Slacken and remove the bolts securing the rear mounting bracket to the transmission, and then withdraw the bracket from transmission (see illustration).

29 Slacken and remove the bolt securing the rear mounting link to the subframe, and then withdraw the mounting link from subframe (see illustration).

30 Check carefully for signs of wear or damage on all components, and renew them where necessary.

31 On reassembly, fit the rear mounting to the subframe, and tighten the retaining bolt to the specified torque.

32 Refit the mounting bracket to the lower part of the transmission and tighten its retaining bolts to the specified torque.

33 With the transmission rear mounting link arm back in position, lower the vehicle to the ground.

Chapter 2 Part B:
2.0 litre petrol engine in–car repair procedures

Contents

Degrees of difficulty

Easy, suitable for novice with little experience	**Fairly easy,** suitable for beginner with some experience	**Fairly difficult,** suitable for competent DIY mechanic	**Difficult,** suitable for experienced DIY mechanic	**Very difficult,** suitable for expert DIY or professional

Specifications

Engine (general)

Engine code	MR20DE
Capacity	1997 cc
Bore	84.0 mm
Stroke	90.1 mm
Direction of crankshaft rotation	Clockwise (viewed from right-hand side of vehicle)
No 1 cylinder location.	At timing chain end of block
Firing order	1-3-4-2
Compression ratio	10.2 : 1
Cylinder compression pressures:	
Standard.	13.9 bars
Minimum.	11.4 bars
Maximum difference between cylinders (all engines).	1.0 bar

Valve clearances

Cold engine:	
Inlet	0.26 to 0.34 mm
Exhaust.	0.29 to 0.37 mm

Camshaft and followers

Drive	Chain
Number of bearings	5
Endfloat	0.075 to 0.153 mm
Camshaft lobe height:	
Inlet	45.265 to 45.455 mm
Exhaust.	43.775 to 43.965 mm
Camshaft bearing journal outer diameter:	
No 1 bearing.	27.935 to 27.955 mm
Nos 2 to 5 bearings	24.950 to 24.970 mm
Camshaft cylinder head bearing journal internal diameter:	
No 1 bearing.	28.000 to 28.021 mm
Nos 2 to 5 bearings	25.000 to 25.021 mm
Camshaft journal-to-bearing clearance:	
No 1 bearing.	0.045 to 0.086 mm
Nos 2 to 5 bearings	0.030 to 0.071 mm
Camshaft run-out:	
Standard.	0.02 mm
Limit	0.05 mm
Camshaft sprocket run-out	Less than 0.15 mm
Camshaft follower outer diameter:	
Inlet	33.977 to 33.987 mm
Exhaust.	29.977 to 29.987 mm
Cylinder head hole diameter for follower:	
Inlet	34.000 to 34.021 mm
Exhaust.	30.000 to 30.021 mm
Camshaft follower to cylinder head clearance	0.013 to 0.044 mm

Lubrication system

Oil pump type.	Rotor-type, driven off crankshaft right-hand end
Minimum oil pressure at normal operating temperature (approx. 80ºC):	
At Idle speed	0.80 bars (minimum)
At 2000 rpm	4.50 bars (minimum)

Torque wrench settings

	Nm	lbf ft
Balance shaft sprocket retaining bolt.	55	41
Balance shaft chain tensioner bolts	10	8
Big-end bearing cap nuts:		
Stage 1	27	20
Stage 2	Fully slacken bolts	
Stage 3	20	14
Stage 4	Angle-tighten a further 60°	
Camshaft ladder bracket bolts (see text):		
Stage 1	2	1.5
Stage 2	6	4.5
Stage 3	10	8
Camshaft sensor retaining bolt	7	6
Camshaft signal plate retaining bolt (end of inlet camshaft)	55	41
Camshaft sprocket retaining bolts:		
Inlet:		
Stage 1	35	26
Stage 2	Angle-tighten a further 67°	
Exhaust.	88	65
Crankshaft pulley bolt:		
Stage 1	68	51
Stage 2	Fully slacken bolt	
Stage 3	30	22
Stage 4	Angle-tighten 60°	
Cylinder head bolts:		
Stage 1	40	30
Stage 2	Angle-tighten 100°	
Stage 3	Fully slacken all the bolts	
Stage 4	40	30
Stage 5	Angle-tighten 100°	
Stage 6	Angle-tighten a further 100°	
Cylinder head cover bolts:		
Stage 1	3	2
Stage 2	9	7

Torque wrench settings (continued)

	Nm	lbf ft
Driveplate (automatic transmission)	98	72
Engine-to-transmission fixing bolts:		
Manual transmission	62	46
Automatic transmission	48	35
Flywheel (manual transmission)	108	80
Left-hand transmission mounting:		
Through-bolt/stud nut	65	48
Through-bolt/stud-to-bracket	65	48
Mounting-to-bracket nuts	105	77
Mounting bracket-to-inner wing panel bolts	80	59
Mounting-to-transmission bolts	45	33
Main bearing cap bolts:		
Stage 1	34	25
Stage 2	Angle-tighten 60°	
Oil level sensor	25	18
Oil filter cooler centre bolt/stud	50	36
Rear engine/transmission torque/link arm mounting:		
Mounting-to-front subframe bolt	110	81
Mounting bracket-to-transmission bolt	110	81
Right-hand engine mounting:		
Bracket bolts to engine	55	41
Mounting bolts to inner wing	55	41
Dynamic damper (bobbin) nut	21	16
Stay bracket to mounting bracket and inner wing bolts	21	16
Sump oil drain plug	35	26
Lower sump oil pan bolts	10	8
Upper sump pan bolts to transmission	26	19
Upper sump casing bolts to cylinder block	25	18
Timing chain cover bolts:		
M6 bolts	10	8
M8 bolts	25	18
M10 bolts	55	41
M12 bolts	75	55
Timing chain guide bolts	25	18
Timing chain tensioner bolts	10	8

1 General information

Using this Chapter

This part of Chapter 2 is devoted to in-car repair procedures for the 2.0 litre petrol engine. Similar information covering the other engine types can be found in Parts A, C and D. All procedures concerning engine removal and refitting, and engine block/cylinder head overhaul can be found in Part E of this Chapter.

Note that, while it may be possible physically to overhaul items such as the piston/connecting rod assemblies while the engine is in the car, such tasks are not normally carried out as separate operations. Usually, several additional procedures (not to mention the cleaning of components and of oilways) have to be carried out. For this reason, all such tasks are classed as major overhaul procedures, and are described in Part E of this Chapter.

In Parts A, B, C and D, the assumption is made that the engine is installed in the car, with all ancillaries connected. If the engine has been removed for overhaul, the preliminary dismantling information, which precedes each operation, may be ignored.

Engine description

The engine is of the sixteen-valve, in-line four-cylinder, double overhead camshaft (DOHC) type, mounted transversely at the front of the car with the transmission attached to the left-hand end.

The crankshaft runs in five main bearings. Thrustwashers are fitted to No 3 main bearing (upper half) to control crankshaft endfloat.

The connecting rods rotate on horizontally split bearing shells at their big ends. The pistons are attached to the connecting rods by gudgeon pins, which are a sliding fit in the connecting rod small-end eyes and retained in the pistons by circlips. The aluminium-alloy pistons are fitted with three piston rings – two compression rings and an oil control ring.

The cylinder block is made of aluminium alloy and the cylinder bores are an integral part of the block. On this type of engine the cylinder bores are sometimes referred to as having dry liners.

The inlet and exhaust valves are each closed by coil springs, and operate in guides pressed into the cylinder head; the valve seat inserts are also pressed into the cylinder head, and can be renewed separately if worn. The inlet camshaft has a variable valve sprocket to the end which is oil fed through a control solenoid valve.

The camshaft is driven by a timing chain, and operates the sixteen valves via bucket-type followers. The followers are situated directly below the camshafts. Valve clearances are adjusted by replacing the relevant follower with a different thickness. The camshafts rotate directly in the cylinder head.

Lubrication is by means of an oil pump, which is driven off the end of a balance shaft, which is positioned below the crankshaft in the upper alloy sump housing. The balance shaft has a sprocket on the end, which is driven by a chain from the right-hand end of the crankshaft. The oil pump draws oil through a strainer located in the sump, and then forces it through an externally mounted filter into galleries in the cylinder block/crankcase. From there, the oil is distributed to the crankshaft (main bearings) and camshaft. The big-end bearings are supplied with oil via internal drillings in the crankshaft, while the camshaft bearings also receive a pressurised supply. The camshaft lobes and valves are lubricated by splash, as are all other engine components.

Repairs with engine in car

The following work can be carried out with the engine in the car:

a) *Compression pressure – testing.*
b) *Cylinder head cover – removal and refitting.*
c) *Timing chain cover – removal and refitting.*
d) *Timing chain – removal, inspection and refitting.*
e) *Timing chain tensioner, guides and sprockets – removal, inspection and refitting.*
f) *Camshaft and followers – removal, inspection and refitting.*
g) *Valve clearances – adjustment.*
h) *Cylinder head – removal and refitting.*
i) *Cylinder head and pistons – decarbonising.*
j) *Sump oil pan – removal and refitting.*
k) *Crankshaft oil seals – renewal.*
l) *Engine/transmission mountings – inspection and renewal.*
m) *Flywheel/driveplate – removal, inspection and refitting.*

2 Compression test – description and interpretation

1 When engine performance is down, or if misfiring occurs which cannot be attributed to the ignition or fuel systems, a compression test can provide diagnostic clues as to the engine's condition. If the test is performed regularly, it can give warning of trouble before any other symptoms become apparent.

2 The engine must be fully warmed-up to normal operating temperature, the battery must be fully charged, and the aid of an assistant will also be required.

3 Depressurise the fuel system by removing the fuel pump fuse from the fusebox – usually the fuses can be identified from the label inside the fusebox cover, or from the wiring diagrams at the end of this manual (see Chapter 12). With the fuse removed, start the engine, and allow it to run until it stalls. Try to start the engine at least twice more, to ensure that all residual pressure has been relieved.

4 Remove the spark plugs as described in Chapter 1A, Section 25.

5 Fit a compression tester to the No 1 cylinder spark plug hole – the type of tester which screws into the plug thread is to be preferred.

6 Have the assistant hold the throttle wide open, and crank the engine on the starter motor; after two or three revolutions, the compression pressure should build-up to a maximum figure, and then stabilise. Record the highest reading obtained.

7 Repeat the test on the remaining cylinders, recording the pressure in each.

8 All cylinders should produce very similar pressures; any difference greater than that specified indicates the existence of a fault. Note that the compression should build-up quickly in a healthy engine; low compression on the first stroke, followed by gradually increasing pressure on successive strokes, indicates worn piston rings. A low compression reading on the first stroke, which does not build-up during successive strokes, indicates leaking valves or a blown head gasket (a cracked head could also be the cause). Deposits on the undersides of the valve heads can also cause low compression.

9 If the pressure in any cylinder is reduced to the specified minimum or less, carry out the following test to isolate the cause. Introduce a teaspoonful of clean oil into that cylinder through its spark plug hole and repeat the test.

10 If the addition of oil temporarily improves the compression pressure, this indicates that bore or piston wear is responsible for the pressure loss. No improvement suggests that leaking or burnt valves, or a blown head gasket, may be to blame.

11 A low reading from two adjacent cylinders is almost certainly due to the head gasket having blown between them; the presence of coolant in the engine oil will confirm this.

12 If one cylinder is about 20 percent lower than the others and the engine has a slightly rough idle; a worn camshaft lobe could be the cause.

13 If the compression reading is unusually high, the combustion chambers are probably coated with carbon deposits. If this is the case, the cylinder head should be removed and decarbonised.

14 On completion of the test, refit the spark plugs, inlet manifold and fuel pump fuse.

3 Top dead centre (TDC) – locating

1 Disconnect the battery negative terminal (refer to *Disconnecting the battery* in the Reference Chapter), then remove all the spark plugs as described in Chapter 1A, Section 25.

2 Apply the handbrake and ensure that the transmission is in neutral, then jack up the front of the car and support it on axle stands (see *Jacking and vehicle support*). Remove the right-hand roadwheel.

3 From underneath the front of the car, release the retaining clips and remove the wheel arch liner inner panel from underneath the wing to gain access to the crankshaft pulley (see illustrations). If necessary, also undo the retaining bolts and remove the engine undershield to improve access.

4 The timing marks are in the form of notches on the crankshaft pulley rim, which align with a pointer on the timing chain cover. The TDC mark is the notch on its own to the left of the two other notches in the pulley, as viewed from under the right-hand front wheel arch.

5 Using a spanner (or socket and extension bar) applied to the crankshaft pulley bolt, rotate the crankshaft clockwise until the TDC notch on the crankshaft pulley rim is aligned with the pointer on the timing chain cover (see illustration).

6 With the crankshaft in this position, Nos 1 and 4 cylinders are now at TDC, one of them on the compression stroke.

4 Cylinder head cover – removal and refitting

Removal

1 Disconnect the battery negative terminal (refer to *Disconnecting the battery* in the Reference Chapter).

2 Remove the inlet manifold as described in Chapter 4A, Section 11.

3 To prevent anything dropping down into the intake ports in the cylinder head, use duct

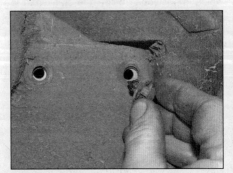

3.3a Release the retaining clips ...

3.3b ... and remove the inner wing panel

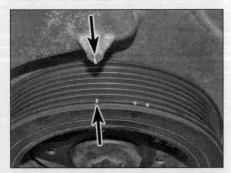

3.5 Align the TDC markings (arrowed)

4.3 Cover the inlet ports using duct tape

4.4 Remove the ignition coils

4.5 Unclip the wiring loom from the cylinder head cover

4.8a Unclip the wiring loom connector ...

4.8b ... and remove the cylinder head cover

4.11 Fit the new rubber gasket to the cylinder head cover

tape or similar to cover up the ports **(see illustration)**.

4 Disconnect the wiring connectors from the ignition coils, undo the retaining bolts and withdraw the ignition coils from the cylinder head cover **(see illustration)**.

5 Release the retaining clips and disconnect the wiring loom from the front and the transmission end of the cylinder head cover **(see illustration)**.

6 If not already disconnected, release the retaining clip and disconnect the PCV hose from the timing chain end of the cylinder head cover.

7 Working in the **reverse** of the tightening sequence **(see illustration 4.13)**, slacken and remove the cylinder head cover retaining bolts.

8 Lift off the cylinder head cover, and disconnect the wiring loom securing clip from the timing chain end of the cover **(see**

illustrations). Recover the rubber seal, which goes around the outer edge of the cover, and also around each of the spark plug holes.

9 Inspect the cover seals for signs of damage and deterioration, and renew as necessary. Nissan recommends that the cylinder head cover seal should always be renewed, if the cover is removed.

Refitting

10 Carefully clean the cylinder head and cover mating surfaces, and remove all traces of oil.

11 Fit the rubber seal to the cylinder head cover groove, ensuring that it is correctly located along its entire length, and around the four spark plug holes in the centre of the cover **(see illustration)**.

12 Carefully lower the cylinder head cover onto the cylinder head, taking great care not to

displace any of the rubber seal **(see illustration)**.

13 Make sure the cover is correctly seated, and then install the retaining bolts. Working in sequence, tighten all the cover screws to the specified torque **(see illustration)**.

14 Refit the wiring loom securing clips to the locating holes in the outer edge of the cylinder head cover.

15 Refit the ignition coils and reconnect their wiring connectors.

16 Refit the PCV hose and secure in position with the retaining clip.

17 Remove the duct tape (where used) from the intake ports in the cylinder head, and clean the inlet manifold mating surface. Refit the inlet manifold as described in Chapter 4A, Section 11.

18 Reconnect the battery negative terminal. Run the engine and check for any oil leaks around the engine cylinder head cover.

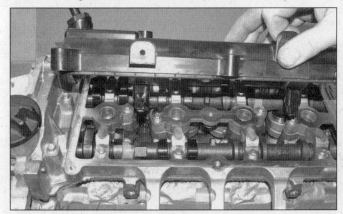

4.12 Refit the cylinder head cover

4.13 Tighten the retaining bolts in the sequence shown

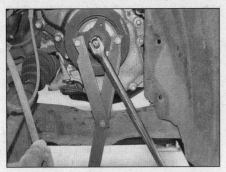

5.3 Using a homemade tool to hold the pulley

5.4 Remove the crankshaft pulley bolt

5.5a Remove the pulley using a puller

5 Crankshaft pulley – removal and refitting

Removal

1 Remove the auxiliary drivebelt as described in Chapter 1A, Section 10.

2 If necessary, position No 1 cylinder at TDC on its compression stroke as described in Section 3.

3 To prevent crankshaft rotation while the pulley bolt is unscrewed, the pulley should be held by a suitable tool which locates in the slots in the pulley to prevent it from turning **(see illustration)**. If this is not available, on manual transmission models, select top gear and have an assistant apply the brakes firmly. On automatic transmission models lock the

flywheel; the starter motor may need to be removed to do this.

4 Unscrew the pulley bolt, along with its washer (where applicable), and remove the pulley from the crankshaft **(see illustration)**.

5 If the pulley is a tight fit on the end of the crankshaft, use a puller to withdraw the pulley from the end of the shaft. Refit the pulley bolt and screw it back into the end of the crankshaft, leaving it approx. 5mm out from the pulley face. Fit the puller (this can be a homemade puller, using a piece of flat bar and three bols/nuts) to the pulley and tighten the centre bolt to withdraw the pulley from the end of the crankshaft **(see illustration)**.

6 If the pulley Woodruff key is a loose fit in the end of the crankshaft **(see illustration)**, remove it and store it with the pulley for safekeeping.

Refitting

7 Refit the Woodruff key (where removed).

8 Align the crankshaft pulley groove with the key **(see illustration)**, then slide the sprocket onto the crankshaft.

9 Lubricate under the head of the bolt, also the bolt threads with new engine oil **(see illustration)**, and then refit the retaining bolt/washer.

10 Lock the crankshaft by the method used on removal, and tighten the pulley retaining bolt to the specified torque settings. The head of the bolt/washer has markings around its edge, dividing it into 60° segments. To carry out the final stage of the tightening procedure (angle tighten 60°), paint one of the marks on the bolt head, and also paint a mark on the pulley alongside the following 60° mark to the right of the first mark. As the bolt is tightened, when the two paint marks are aligned, the bolt has then been tightened through 60° **(see illustrations)**.

11 Refit the auxiliary drivebelt and adjust it as described in Chapter 1A, Section 10.

5.5b A puller made out of a piece of flat metal bar and bolts

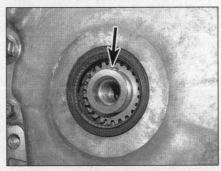

5.6 Make sure the woodruff key (arrowed) is located securely

5.8 Align the slot in the pulley centre hub with the Woodruff key

5.9 Apply a small amount of oil to the bolt

5.10a Make alignments marks at 60° on the pulley and bolt ...

5.10b ... and turn the bolt until the marks are aligned

6.3 Remove the inner wing liner

6.7 Using a trolley jack to support the engine

6 Timing chain cover – removal and refitting

Removal

1 Disconnect the battery negative terminal (refer to *Disconnecting the battery* in the Reference Chapter).

2 Firmly apply the handbrake, and then jack up the front of the vehicle and support it securely on axle stands (see *Jacking and vehicle support*). Remove right-hand front road wheel.

3 Undo the retaining bolts and remove the plastic inner wheel arch liner **(see illustration)**, and undershields from beneath the right-hand front wing and the engine.

4 Drain the engine oil, then clean and refit the engine oil drain plug using a new sealing washer, tightening it to the specified torque. If the engine is nearing its service interval when the oil and filter are due for renewal, it is recommended that the filter is also removed, and a new one fitted. After reassembly, the engine can then be refilled with fresh oil. Refer to Chapter 1A, Section 3 for further information.

5 Remove the cylinder head cover as described in Section 4.

6 Remove the crankshaft pulley as described in Section 5.

7 Using a jack support the engine **(see illustration)**, and then undo the retaining bolts and remove the right-hand engine mounting as described in Section 16 of this Chapter.

8 Disconnect the wiring connector from the intake valve timing control solenoid, and release the wiring loom securing clips from the timing chain cover **(see illustration)**.

9 Undo the retaining bolt and withdraw the intake valve timing control solenoid from the timing chain cover **(see illustrations)**. To make access easier, the engine can be lifted slightly using the jack supporting the engine. **Note:** *As the control solenoid is withdrawn, there will be oil spillage. Renew the control solenoid on refitting.*

10 Undo the retaining bolt and withdraw the auxiliary belt automatic tensioner the timing chain cover **(see illustration)**.

11 Working in the **reverse** of the tightening sequence **(see illustration 6.20)**, slacken and remove the timing chain cover retaining bolts. Note the correct fitted location of each bolt, as some of the bolts are different lengths. Also there are three sizes (diameter) of bolts.

12 The timing chain cover has been fitted using a liquid gasket, and is bonded to the engine block/cylinder head. Taking care not to damage the timing chain cover work your way around the outside of the cover to release it from the engine. Nissan show the starting point at each side of the lower part of the casing, where there is an area to start prying. Also note at the lower end of the cover there are two steel dowels, which

6.8 Release the wiring loom clip from the cover

6.9a Undo the retaining bolt ...

6.9b ... and remove the intake valve timing control solenoid

6.10 Remove the auxiliary belt tensioner

6.12a Two steel dowels are located in holes at each side of the cover (arrowed)

6.12b Carefully work your way around the cover …

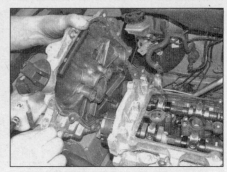

6.12c … to remove it from the engine

can become very tight in the alloy cover **(see illustrations)**.

13 There is an O-ring oil seal fitted to the cylinder block, to the front of the fixed timing chain guide **(see illustration)**. Discard the O-ring oil seal, as a new one will be required on refitting.

Refitting

14 Prior to refitting the cover, it is recommended that the crankshaft oil seal should be renewed. Note the seals fitted position and the carefully lever the old seal out of the cover using a large flat-bladed screwdriver. Fit the new seal to

the cover, making sure its sealing lip is facing inwards. Drive the seal into position until it seats squarely in the position noted on removal, for further information see Section 13, of this Chapter.

15 Ensure that the timing chain cover and engine cylinder block/cylinder head mating surfaces are clean/dry and free from any silicone sealer.

16 Fit a new O-ring oil seal to the cylinder block, use a small amount of grease to hold it in position **(see illustration)**.

17 Apply a thin bead of suitable sealant (3mm to 4mm diameter) to the timing chain

cover surface, not forgetting to apply sealant to the area around the three engine mounting bolt passages in the upper centre of the cover **(see illustrations)**.

18 Also apply a small amount of sealant to where the cylinder block joins the cylinder head, and where the cylinder block joins the upper sump housing **(see illustration)**.

19 For this procedure the help of an assistant would be advisable; lower the timing chain cover into position taking care not to wipe the sealer of the face off the cover or dislodge the O-ring seal on the cylinder block. With the assistant under the right-hand front wheel

6.13 Retrieve the O-ring seal from the cylinder block

16.16 Fit a new O-ring seal to the cylinder block

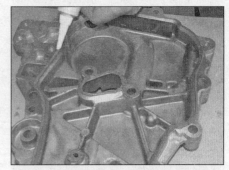

6.17a Apply a bead of sealant around the outside of the cover …

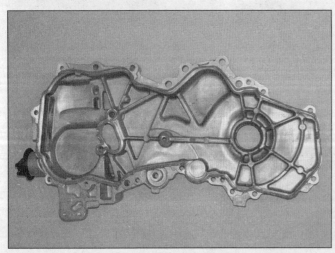

6.17b … and around the centre mountings as shown

6.18 Apply sealant to the joints (arrowed) at both sides of the cylinder block

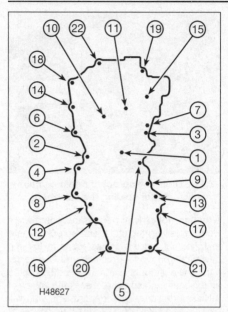

6.20 Tightening sequence for timing chain cover

arch manoeuvre the cover into position over the end of the crankshaft, taking great care not to damage the oil seal lip.

20 Make sure the cover is correctly seated, and then install the retaining bolts. Working in sequence, tighten all the cover screws to the specified torque **(see illustration)**. Note the different sizes of bolts used, as noted on removal.

21 Refit the auxiliary belt automatic tensioner to the timing chain cover and tighten the retaining bolt.

22 Refit the intake valve timing control solenoid to the timing chain cover and tighten the retaining bolt. Reconnect the wiring connector and clip the loom securing clips into the cover.

23 Refit the right-hand engine mounting as described in Section 16 of this Chapter. When the engine mounting is in place, remove the jack from under the engine.

24 Refit the crankshaft pulley as described in Section 5, of this Chapter.

25 Refit the cylinder head cover as described in Section 4, of this Chapter.

26 After reassembly, the engine can then be refilled with fresh oil. Refer to Chapter 1A, Section 3 for further information.

27 Refit the plastic inner wheel arch liner and engine undershield.

28 Refit the front road wheel and lower the vehicle to the ground, then remove the jack from underneath the vehicle. Tighten the road wheel to the specified torque setting.

7 Timing chain, tensioner, guides and sprockets – removal, inspection and refitting

Removal

1 Position No 1 cylinder at TDC on its compression stroke, as described in Section 3.

2 Remove the cylinder head cover as described in Section 4.

3 Remove the timing chain cover as described in Section 6.

4 With No 1 cylinder set at TDC, the markings on the camshaft sprockets should be in line. Apply paint marks to the timing chain links which are in line with the markings on the sprockets **(see illustrations)**. **Note:** *If the markings on the camshaft are not aligned, it may be that it is set to be firing on No. 4 cylinder. Turn the crankshaft one complete turn clockwise to get it firing on number 1 cylinder. Note the cam lobes on number 1 cylinder, should be pointing upwards and towards each other when firing on this cylinder.*

5 Check the crankshaft sprocket is positioned at TDC **(see illustration)**. **Note:** *The keyway will also be in the 12 o'clock position, as seen from the right-hand end of the engine.*

6 Whilst holding the plunger back into the body of the tensioner, insert a small-diameter rod through the hole in the body to lock the plunger **(see illustration)**.

7 Undo the two retaining bolts, and remove the tensioner from the end of the cylinder block. Keep the rod inserted into the tensioner to prevent the plunger from springing out **(see illustration)**.

8 Undo the chain tensioner guide upper pivot bolt, and remove it from the rear of the crankcase **(see illustration)**.

9 Unscrew the two mounting bolts, and

7.4a Align the markings on the camshaft sprockets (arrowed) ...

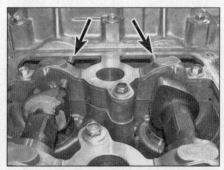
7.4b ... in this position the cam lobes should be pointing as shown

7.5 Crankshaft alignment marks

7.6 Insert locking pin through tensioner body

7.7 Undo the retaining bolts and remove the tensioner

7.8 Remove upper pivot bolt and withdraw the tensioner guide

7.9 Removing the fixed chain guide

7.10 Disengage the timing chain from the crankshaft sprocket

7.11a Undo the sprocket retaining bolts, while counter holding the camshaft ...

7.11b ... with an open-ended spanner on the hexagonal on the camshaft ...

7.11c ... then remove the camshaft sprockets

remove the chain front guide from the crankcase (see illustration).

10 Disengage the timing chain from the crankshaft sprocket, and manoeuvre it out from the engine (see illustration).

⚠ **Warning: Do not turn the crankshaft or camshafts while the timing chain is removed, otherwise piston and valve contact may occur causing damage.**

11 Slacken the camshaft sprocket retaining bolts, whilst retaining the camshafts with a large open-ended spanner fitted to the hexagonal section of each shaft. Remove the bolts along with its washers (where applicable), disengage the sprockets from the end of the camshafts (see illustrations).

12 To remove the crankshaft sprocket from the end of the crankshaft requires removing the balancer shaft drive chain. See Section 15 for further information.

Inspection

13 Examine the teeth on the camshaft and crankshaft sprockets for any sign of wear or damage such as chipped, hooked or missing teeth. If there is any sign of wear or damage on either sprockets or timing chain then they should be renewed as a set.

14 Inspect the links of the timing chain for signs of wear or damage on the rollers. The extent of wear can be judged by checking the amount by which the chain can be bent sideways; a new chain will have very little sideways movement. If there is an excessive amount of side play in either timing chain, it must be renewed.

15 Note that it is a sensible precaution to renew the timing chain, regardless of apparent condition, if the engine has covered a high mileage, or if it has been noted that the chain has sounded noisy when the engine running.

Although not strictly necessary, it is always worth renewing the chain and sprockets as a matched set, since it is false economy to run a new chain on worn sprockets and *vice versa*. If there is any doubt about the condition of the timing chain and sprockets, seek the advice of a Nissan dealer service department, who will be able to advise you as to the best course of action.

16 Examine the chain guides for signs of wear or damage to their chain contact faces, renewing any which are badly marked.

17 Check the chain tensioner for signs of wear, and check that the plunger is free to slide freely in the tensioner body. The condition of the tensioner spring can only be judged in comparison to a new component. Renew the tensioner if it is worn or there is any doubt about the condition of its tensioning spring.

Refitting

18 Check the crankshaft is still positioned at TDC (see illustration), and that the timing marks on the balance shaft drive chain and sprockets have not been disturbed. See Section 15 for further information.

19 Refit the inlet camshaft sprocket into position, ensuring that the locating peg is aligned (see illustrations). Tighten the camshaft bolt to the specified torque setting, whilst retaining the camshaft with a large open-ended spanner as used on removal.

20 Refit the exhaust camshaft sprocket into position, ensuring that the timing marks are facing the position noted on removal (see

7.18 Check the crankshaft is still at TDC

7.19a Align the locating peg on the end of the camshaft with the sprocket

7.19b Tighten the sprocket retaining bolt, while counter holding the camshaft

7.20a Align the slot in the sprocket with the locating peg in the camshaft

7.20b Tighten the sprocket retaining bolt, while counter holding the camshaft

7.21a Align the coloured links with the camshaft sprockets (arrowed) …

7.21b … and the crankshaft markings (arrowed)

illustrations). Tighten the camshaft bolt to the specified torque setting, whilst retaining the camshaft with a large open-ended spanner as used on removal.

21 Manoeuvre the chain around the sprockets, making sure the coloured links on the chain align with the camshaft and crankshaft timing marks. The orange link

aligns with the crankshaft sprocket timing mark and the two dark blue links align with the camshaft sprockets alignment marks **(see illustrations).**

22 Fit the timing chain front and rear guides to the cylinder block, and tighten the retaining bolts to the specified torque **(see illustration).**

23 Fit the chain tensioner to the cylinder block,

and tighten its retaining bolts to the specified torque. Whilst holding the guide against the tensioner plunger, withdraw the rod, and check that the tensioner plunger is forced out against the guide to take up the slack in the chain **(see illustrations).**

24 Check that all the timing marks are still correctly aligned with the chain links. If all

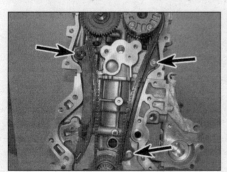

7.22 Fit the timing chain guides to the cylinder block

7.23a Refit the tensioner

7.23b Hold pressure against the tensioner and remove the locking pin

timing marks are aligned, fit the crankshaft pulley and turn the engine two complete turns, and check the timing marks on the sprockets are all re-aligned. **Note:** *The coloured links on the chain will not be re-aligned with the marks on the sprockets. The coloured links are just for the initial set up, and will take many turns before they will line up again, with the marks on the sprockets.*

25 Remove the crankshaft pulley and refit the timing chain cover as described in Section 6.

26 Refit the crankshaft pulley as described in Section 5, of this Chapter.

27 Refit the cylinder head cover as described in Section 4.

8 Valve clearances – checking and adjustment

Note: *This is not a routine operation. It should only be necessary at high mileage, after overhaul, or when investigating noise or power loss which may be attributable to the valve gear. Adjustment involves removing the camshaft and changing the cam followers (valve lifters) that are available in 26 different*

8.5a Check the clearances between the camshafts and the followers (arrowed)

thicknesses (ranging from 3.00mm to 3.50mm, in steps of 0.02mm).

Checking

1 The importance of having the valve clearances correctly adjusted cannot be overstressed, as they vitally affect the performance of the engine. The clearances are checked as follows.

2 Draw the outline of the engine on a piece of paper, numbering the cylinders 1 to 4, with No 1 cylinder at the timing chain end of the engine. Show the position of each valve, together with the specified valve clearance. Above each valve, draw two lines for noting the actual clearance and the amount of adjustment required.

3 Warm the engine up to normal operating temperature, then switch off. Remove the cylinder head cover as described in Section 4.

4 Position No 1 cylinder at TDC on its compression stroke, as described in Section 3.

5 Using feeler gauges, measure the clearance between the base of the cam and the follower of the following valves, recording each clearance on the paper **(see illustrations)**.

    No 1 cylinder inlet and exhaust valves
    No 2 cylinder inlet valves
    No 3 cylinder exhaust valves

6 Rotate the crankshaft through one complete turn (360°) clockwise until the TDC notch on the crankshaft pulley is realigned with the pointer. No 4 cylinder is now at TDC on its compression stroke.

7 Check the clearances of the following valves, and record them on the paper **(see illustration)**.

    No 2 cylinder exhaust valves
    No 3 cylinder inlet valves
    No 4 cylinder inlet and exhaust valves

8 Calculate the difference between each measured clearance and the desired value, and record it on the piece of paper.

Adjustment

Note: *A micrometer or dial gauge and probe will be required for this operation.*

9 Where a valve clearance differs from the specified value, then the cam follower (valve lifter) for that valve must be substituted with a thinner or thicker one accordingly. The cam followers have the thickness stamped on the bottom face of the follower; e.g. 324 indicates the follower is 3.24 mm thick at the top centre of the follower **(see illustration)**.

10 If required use a micrometer or dial gauge to measure the true thickness of any follower removed, as it may have been reduced by wear. **Note:** *Followers are available in thicknesses between 3.00 mm and 3.50 mm, in steps of 0.02 mm.*

11 To access the cam followers (valve lifters), first remove the camshafts as described in Section 9. Remove and refit each follower separately, to avoid any confusion.

12 The size of follower required is calculated as follows. If the measured clearance is less than specified, subtract the measured clearance from the specified clearance, and deduct the result from the thickness of the existing follower. For example:

Sample calculation – clearance too small

    Clearance measured (A) = 0.16 mm
    Desired clearance (B) = 0.30 mm
    Difference (B – A) = 0.14 mm
    Cam follower thickness fitted = 3.50 mm
    Cam follower thickness required = 3.50 –
      0.14 = 3.36 mm

13 If the measured clearance is greater than specified, subtract the specified clearance from the measured clearance, and add the result to the thickness of the existing follower. For example:

Sample calculation – clearance too big

    Clearance measured (A) = 0.40 mm
    Desired clearance (B) = 0.30 mm
    Difference (A – B) = 0.10 mm
    Cam follower thickness fitted = 3.26 mm
    Cam follower thickness required = 3.26 +
      0.10 = 3.36 mm

8.5b Check clearances as shown

Cylinder 1 – Inlet and Exhaust valves
Cylinder 2 – Inlet valves
Cylinder 3 – Exhaust valves

8.7 Check clearances as shown

Cylinder 2 – Exhaust valves
Cylinder 3 – Inlet valves
Cylinder 4 – Inlet and Exhaust valves

8.9 Markings inside the follower for thickness

14 Working on each separately, lift out the follower to be renewed, then oil the new one and carefully locate it in the cylinder head, on top of the valve.

15 Refit the camshafts with reference to Section 9.

16 It will be helpful for future adjustment if a record is kept of the thickness of cam followers (valve lifters) fitted at each position. The cam followers required could be purchased in advance once the clearances and the existing follower thicknesses are known.

17 Once all valves clearances have been adjusted, rotate the crankshaft through at least four complete turns in the correct direction of rotation, to settle all disturbed followers, then recheck the clearances as described above.

18 With all valve clearances correctly adjusted, refit the cylinder head cover as described in Section 4, and refit all components removed to gain access to the crankshaft pulley.

9 Camshafts and followers – removal, inspection and refitting

Removal

1 Remove the timing chain cover, as described in Section 6.

2 Remove the camshaft sprockets, as described in Section 7.

3 Remove the fuel rail from across the front of the cylinder head, as described in Chapter 4A, Section 10. Plug all openings, to prevent loss of fuel and entry of dirt into the fuel system.

4 To prevent anything dropping down into the intake ports or injector holes in the cylinder head, use duct tape or similar to cover up the ports **(see illustration)**.

5 Release the wiring loom and hoses from the mounting brackets on the transmission end of the cylinder head, then undo the retaining bolts and remove the brackets **(see illustrations)**.

6 Undo the retaining bolt and remove the camshaft position sensor from the top of the camshaft ladder bracket **(see illustration)**.

7 Working in the **reverse** of the tightening sequence **(see illustration 9.23)**, evenly and progressively slacken the seventeen camshaft bearing ladder bracket retaining bolts by one turn at a time, to relieve the pressure of the valve springs on the bearing ladder gradually and evenly. Once the valve spring pressure

9.4 Covering up the injector holes using duct tape

9.5a Remove the bracket from the front left-hand corner of the cylinder head

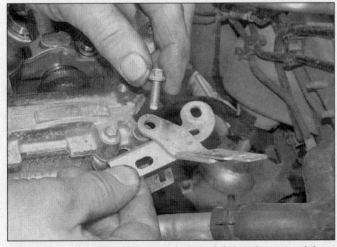

9.5b Remove the bracket from the rear left-hand corner of the cylinder head

9.6 Remove the camshaft position sensor

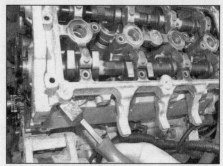

9.8a Carefully prise the camshaft ladder …

9.8b … noting the steel dowels at the rear …

9.8c … and front of the camshaft ladder

9.8d Remove the camshaft ladder from the top of the cylinder head

9.9a Lift the camshafts from the cylinder head …

9.9b … noting the inlet camshaft has the target ring for the position sensor

has been relieved, the bolts can be fully unscrewed and removed. **Note:** *Bolts 13, 14 and 15 are longer than the other bolts.*

8 The camshaft ladder bracket has been fitted using a liquid gasket, and is bonded to the cylinder head. Taking care not to damage the ladder bracket or cylinder head work your way around the outside of the housing to release it from the cylinder head. Nissan show the starting point at the front left-hand corner, and the rear right-hand corner of the ladder bracket (as viewed from the front of the vehicle), where there is an area to start prying. Also note that at the rear left-hand corner, and front right-hand corner of the ladder bracket (as viewed from the front of the vehicle), there are two steel dowels, which can become very tight in the alloy ladder bracket **(see illustrations)**.

9 With the camshaft bearing ladder bracket removed the camshafts can now be simply

lifted off the top of the cylinder head, noting their fitted position. Note the position of the dowel on the sprocket end of the camshafts, and the position of the cam lobes, so that they can be refitted in the correct position for TDC on no.1 cylinder **(see illustrations)**. **Note:** *Take care not to damage the signal plate for the camshaft position sensor on the end of the inlet camshaft.*

10 Obtain sixteen small, clean plastic containers, and number them 1 to 16. Alternatively, divide a larger container into sixteen compartments. Using a rubber sucker, withdraw each follower (valve lifter) in turn, and place it in its respective container **(see illustration)**. Do not interchange the cam followers in the cylinder head, or the rate of wear will be increased. **Note:** *The diameter of the inlet cam followers is larger than the exhaust cam followers.*

Inspection

11 Inspect the cam bearing surfaces of the head and the bearing ladder bracket. Look for score marks and deep scratches. Check the camshaft lobes for heat discoloration (blue appearance), score marks, chipped areas or flat spots.

12 Camshaft run-out can be checked by supporting each end of the camshaft on V-blocks, and measuring any run-out at the centre of the shaft using a dial gauge. If the run-out exceeds the specified limit, a new camshaft will be required.

13 Measure the height of each lobe with a micrometer **(see illustration)**, and compare the results to the figures given in the Specifications. If damage is noted or wear is excessive, new camshaft(s) must be fitted.

14 The camshaft bearing oil clearance should now be checked.

15 Fit the bearing ladder bracket to the cylinder head, and tighten the retaining bolts to the specified torque in sequence **(see illustration 9.23)**. Measure the diameter of each bearing cap journal, and compare the measurements obtained with the results given in the Specifications at the start of this Chapter. If any journal is worn beyond the service limit, the cylinder head must be renewed. The camshaft bearing oil clearance can then calculated by subtracting the camshaft bearing journal diameter from the bearing cap journal diameter.

16 Check the cam follower and cylinder head bearing surfaces for signs of wear or damage. Clean the steel dowels on the cylinder head, and apply a small amount of oil to aid fitting.

9.10 Remove the cam followers

9.13 Checking the cam lobe height with a micrometer

9.17a Lubricate the cam followers outer surface ...

9.17b ... and slide them back into place

9.17c Lubricate the camshaft bearing lower surfaces

Refitting

17 Liberally oil the cylinder head cam follower bores and the followers. Carefully refit the followers to the cylinder head; ensuring that each follower is refitted to its original bore **(see illustrations)**. Some care will be required to enter the followers squarely into their bores. Liberally oil the camshaft bearing and lobe contact surfaces.

18 Refit the camshafts to their correct locations in the cylinder head, as noted on removal **(see illustration)**.

19 Check that the crankshaft is still in the TDC position, as positioned on removal **(see illustration)**.

20 Liberally oil the camshaft bearing surfaces in the ladder bracket **(see illustration)**.

21 Ensure that the ladder bracket and head mating surfaces are completely clean, unmarked and free from oil. Apply a thin bead of suitable sealant (3.4mm to 4.4mm diameter) to the under side of the bearing ladder bracket surface, not forgetting to apply sealant to the area around the spark plug hole recesses in the centre of the ladder bracket **(see illustrations)**.

22 Lower the bearing ladder bracket into position, taking care not to wipe the sealer of the face of the ladder bracket. Make sure

9.18 Align the locating pegs on the end of the camshaft

9.19 Check the crankshaft is still aligned

9.20 Lubricate the camshaft bearing upper surfaces

9.21a Apply a bead of sealant around the outside of the ladder ...

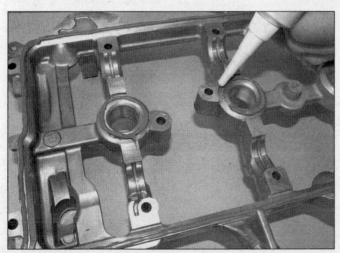

9.21b ... and around the centre mountings ...

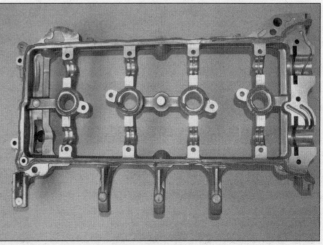

9.21c ... as shown

9.22 Align the dowels when fitting the ladder

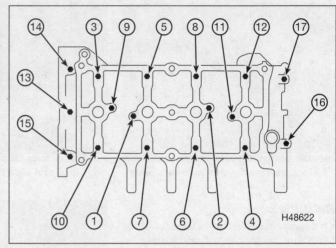

9.23 Tightening sequence for the camshaft ladder

the two locating dowels are aligned **(see illustration)**, before tightening the bolts fully.

23 Working in sequence, evenly and progressively tighten the camshaft bearing ladder bracket bolts by one turn at a time until the ladder touches the cylinder head **(see illustration)**. Then go round again and tighten all the bolts to the specified torque setting (see Torque wrench settings for sequence). Work only as described, to impose the pressure of the valve springs gradually and evenly on the bearing ladder bracket.

24 Refit the camshaft position sensor to the top of the camshaft ladder bracket and tighten the retaining bolt.

25 Refit the mounting brackets to the transmission end of the cylinder head, and tighten the retaining bolts, clip the wiring loom and hoses back into the brackets.

26 Remove the duct tape (where used) from the intake ports in the cylinder head, and clean the inlet manifold mating surface. Refit the fuel rail as described in Chapter 4A, Section 10.

27 Refit the camshaft sprockets and timing chain, as described in Section 7.

28 Refit the timing chain cover, as described in Section 6.

29 If the cylinder head/camshafts have been overhauled, check the valve clearances 'cold' prior to refitting the cylinder head cover (see Section 8).

10 Cylinder head –
  removal and refitting

Removal

1 Depressurise the fuel system as described in Chapter 4A, Section 6.

2 Disconnect the battery negative terminal (refer to *Disconnecting the battery* in the Reference Chapter).

3 Remove the timing chain as described in Section 7.

4 Remove the camshafts as described in Section 9.

5 Remove the exhaust manifold as described in Chapter 4A, Section 12.

6 Disconnect the wiring connector from the temperature sensor **(see illustration)**.

7 Noting their fitted position, slacken the retaining clips and disconnect the coolant hoses from the coolant housing on the transmission end of the cylinder head **(see illustrations)**.

10.6 Disconnect the temperature sensor wiring connector

10.7a Note the fitted position of the hoses ...

10.7b ... and disconnect them from the coolant housing

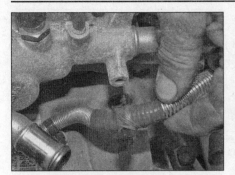

10.8 Unclip the wiring loom from the coolant housing

10.9a Undo the two retaining bolts …

10.9b … and remove the earth wires from the front of the cylinder head

8 Unclip the wiring loom securing clip from the coolant housing **(see illustration)**.

9 Undo the retaining bolts and disconnect the two earth cables from the front of the cylinder head **(see illustrations)**.

10 Working in the **reverse** of the tightening sequence, progressively slacken the ten cylinder head bolts by half a turn at a time, until all bolts can be unscrewed by hand **(see illustration 10.24)**.

11 Withdraw the cylinder head bolts and then lift the cylinder head away from the dowels on the cylinder block. If required, have an assistant to help removal, as it is a heavy assembly **(see illustrations)**.

12 Remove the gasket from the top of the block, noting the two locating dowels fitted to the top of the cylinder block **(see illustration)**. If they are a loose fit in the block, remove the locating dowels, noting which way round they are fitted, and store them with the head for safekeeping.

13 If the cylinder head is to be dismantled for overhaul, then refer to Chapter 2E, Section 6.

Preparation for refitting

14 Check the condition of the cylinder head bolts, and particularly their threads, whenever they are removed. Wash the bolts and wipe dry, then check each for any sign of visible wear or damage, renewing any bolt if necessary.
Checking cylinder head bolt (see illustration): –
a) Measure 11mm up from the threaded end of the bolt and note the reading = D1.

b) Measure 45mm up from the threaded end of the bolt and note the reading = D2.
c) Take the second reading away from the first reading (D1 – D2), and it should be no more than 0.15mm.

Although Nissan do not specify that the bolts must be renewed, it is strongly recommended, that the bolts should be renewed as a complete set whenever they are disturbed.

15 The mating faces of the cylinder head and cylinder block/crankcase must be perfectly clean before refitting the head. Use a hard plastic or wood scraper to remove all traces of gasket and carbon; also clean the piston crowns. Take particular care, as the surfaces are damaged easily. Also, make sure that the carbon is not allowed to enter the oil and water passages – this is particularly important for the lubrication system, as carbon could block the oil supply to any of the engine's components. Using adhesive tape and paper, seal the water, oil and bolt holes

in the cylinder block/crankcase. To prevent carbon entering the gap between the pistons and bores, smear a little grease in the gap. After cleaning each piston, use a small brush to remove all traces of grease and carbon from the gap, and then wipe away the remainder with a clean rag. Clean all the pistons in the same way.

16 Check the mating surfaces of the cylinder block/crankcase and the cylinder head for nicks, deep scratches and other damage. If slight, they may be removed carefully with a file, but if excessive, machining may be the only alternative to renewal.

17 Remove the oil filter for the intake valve timing control, which is situated in the front right-hand corner of the cylinder block. Clean the oil filter and refit it to the cylinder block making sure it does not protrude above the surface of the cylinder block. If filter is damaged or blocked, a new one will be required **(see illustration)**.

10.11a Remove the cylinder head bolts …

10.11b … and remove the cylinder head

10.12 Remove the cylinder head gasket

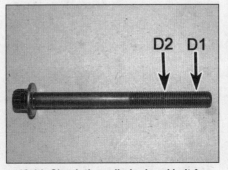

10.14 Check the cylinder head bolt for wear

10.17 Check the oil filter in the cylinder block

10.20 Align the new gasket with the locating dowels in the cylinder block

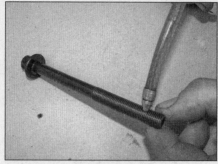

10.22 Lubricate the threads and underside of the head

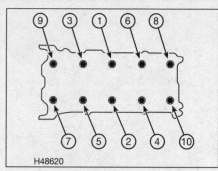

10.24 Tightening sequence for the cylinder head

18 If warpage of the cylinder head gasket surface is suspected, use a straight-edge to check it for distortion. If necessary, refer to Chapter 2E, Section 7.

Refitting

19 Wipe clean the mating surfaces of the cylinder head and cylinder block/crankcase. Check the locating dowels are in position at each end of the cylinder block/crankcase surface.

20 Fit a new gasket to the cylinder block/crankcase surface, aligning it with the locating dowels **(see illustration)**.

21 With the aid of an assistant, carefully refit the cylinder head assembly to the block, aligning it with the locating dowels.

22 Apply a smear of clean oil to the threads, and to the underside of the heads, of the ten cylinder head bolts **(see illustration)**.

23 Carefully enter each bolt into its relevant hole (do not drop them in) and screw in, by hand only, until finger-tight.

24 Working progressively and in sequence, tighten the cylinder head bolts to their Stage 1 torque setting, using a torque wrench and suitable socket **(see illustration)**. See specifications at the beginning of this Chapter.

25 Go around again in the specified sequence and tighten the head bolts through the specified Stage 2 angle setting **(see illustration)**.

26 For stage 3, leave the bolts a minute then, working in the **reverse** of the specified sequence **(see illustration 10.24)**,

progressively slacken the head bolts by half a turn at a time, until all bolts can be unscrewed by hand.

27 Tighten the head bolts again by hand, then go around again in the specified sequence and tighten these ten bolts to the specified Stage 4 torque setting.

28 Go around again in the specified sequence and tighten the head bolts to the specified Stage 5 angle setting.

29 Finally, go around again in the specified sequence and tighten the head bolts through the specified Stage 6 angle setting.

30 Reconnect the coolant hoses to the coolant housing, on the transmission end of the cylinder head, and then securely tightening the retaining clips.

31 Reconnect the wiring connector to the temperature sensor and clip the wiring loom securing clip back into the coolant housing.

32 Refit the two earth cables to the front of the cylinder head and tighten retaining bolts

33 Refit the exhaust manifold, as described in Chapter 4A, Section 12.

34 Refit the camshafts as described in Section 9.

35 Refit the timing chain as described in Section 7. **Note:** If the cylinder head has been overhauled, check the valve clearances 'cold' prior to refitting the cylinder head cover (see Section 8).

36 Start the engine and warm it up to normal operating temperature, check for any leaks from the engine, cooling circuit and fuel system.

11 Sump – removal and refitting

Note: The oil sump is made up of two parts; it has an upper alloy part and a lower steel oil pan. The following procedure is for the lower oil pan part. To remove the upper alloy part, the engine will need to be removed and the upper alloy sump then split from the cylinder block.

Removal

1 Firmly apply the handbrake, and then jack up the front of the vehicle and support it securely on axle stands (see Jacking and vehicle support).

2 Slacken and remove the retaining bolts and remove the plastic undershield from beneath the engine.

3 Drain the engine oil, then clean and refit the engine oil drain plug, fit a new sealing washer on refitting. And then tighten it to the specified torque. If the engine is nearing its service interval when the oil and filter are due for renewal, it is recommended that the filter is also removed, and a new one fitted. Refer to Chapter 1A, Section 3 for further information.

4 Progressively slacken and remove all of the steel oil pan retaining bolts.

5 The lower steel oil pan is sealed to the upper alloy sump casing with strong liquid gasket sealer, which is very difficult to remove, however methodical use of a spatula or thin knife will release the sump **(see illustration)**. Take care not to distort or damage the mating surfaces of the lower oil pan and upper alloy sump. Take adequate precautions to catch any oil remaining inside the sump housing, as the oil pan is removed.

Refitting

6 Clean all traces of sealant from the mating surfaces of the upper alloy part of the sump and steel oil pan, then use a clean rag to wipe out the oil pan and the sump interior.

7 Ensure that the lower oil pan and upper alloy casing mating surfaces are clean and dry. Apply a continuous bead of suitable sealant

10.25 Using an angle gauge to tighten bolts

11.5 Using a flat ended scraper to prise the sump away

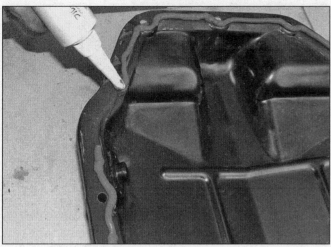

11.7a Apply a bead of sealant …

11.7b … around the outside of the sump pan, as shown

to the mating surface of the oil pan. Apply a 4mm to 5mm diameter bead of sealant to the oil pan, going around the inner edge of each bolt hole **(see illustrations)**.

8 Offer up the sump, locating it in the correct position, and refit its retaining bolts. Tighten the bolts evenly and progressively to the specified torque.

9 Refit the engine undershield and securely tighten the retaining bolts.

10 After reassembly, the engine can then be refilled with fresh engine oil. Refer to Chapter 1A, Section 3, for further information.

ensuring its sealing lip is facing inwards. Carefully ease the seal into position, taking care not to damage its sealing lip. Drive the seal into position until it seats flush with the face of the timing chain cover **(see illustrations)**. Take care not to damage the seal lips during fitting.

5 Wash off any traces of oil, then refit the crankshaft pulley as described in Section 5.

Flywheel/driveplate oil seal

6 Remove the flywheel or driveplate, as applicable, as described in Section 14.

11.8 Align the bolts and refit the sump pan

---

12 Oil pump – removal and refitting

The oil pump is driven from the balancer shaft assembly, which is located in the upper sump alloy housing. At the time of writing there was no procedure for the removal and refitting of the oil pump. Refer to your local dealer for further information.

13 Crankshaft oil seals – renewal

Timing chain cover oil seal

1 Remove the crankshaft pulley as described in Section 5.

2 Carefully lever the oil seal out of position, using a large flat-bladed screwdriver, taking care not to damage the end of the crankshaft or timing cover **(see illustration)**.

3 Clean the seal housing, and polish off any burrs or raised edges, which may have caused the seal to fail in the first place.

4 Lubricate the lips of the new seal with a smear of clean oil and offer up the seal;

13.2 Carefully prise out the oil seal

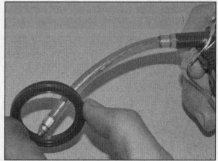

13.4a Lubricate the inner lip of the seal …

13.4b … press the seal into position …

13.4c … carefully fit the seal into the cover

13.7a Carefully drill a hole in the seal …

13.7b … insert a self tapping screw …

13.7c … and lever the seal out from the casing

7 Note the fitted position of the old seal, then prise it out of the right-hand cover/housing using a screwdriver or suitable hooked instrument, taking care not to damage the surface of the crankshaft. Alternatively, the oil seal can be removed by drilling a hole in the seal, and then inserting a self-tapping screw. A pair of grips/pliers can then be used to pull out the oil seal **(see illustrations)**. **Note:** *Take care when drilling the hole to not drill into anything other than the seal.*

8 Clean the seal housing, and polish off any burrs or raised edges, which may have caused the seal to fail in the first place **(see illustration)**.

9 Lubricate with clean oil the lips of the new seal and the crankshaft shoulder, then offer up the seal to the cylinder block/crankcase. Ease the sealing lip of the seal over the crankshaft shoulder by hand only, and press the seal evenly into its recess to make it square in the casing **(see illustrations)**.

10 With the seal still protruding out from the cylinder block, apply a coat of liquid gasket/sealant all the way around the outer edge of the seal. Carefully drive the seal into position until it seats flush with the face of the cylinder block, and then wipe off the excess liquid gasket/sealant from the casing **(see illustrations)**. Make sure the outer edge of the seal is sitting flush with the cylinder block casing.

11 Wash off any traces of oil or sealant, then refit the flywheel/driveplate as described in Section 14.

14 Flywheel/driveplate –
removal, inspection and refitting

Removal

1 Remove the transmission as described in Chapter 7A, Section 6 for manual transmissions or Chapter 7B, Section 11 for automatic transmissions. Ensure the engine is well supported during this and subsequent procedures in this Section.

2 On manual transmission, remove the clutch assembly as described in Chapter 6, Section 6.

3 Prevent the flywheel/driveplate from turning by locking the ring gear teeth (see

13.8 Clean around the seal fitting surface area

13.9a Using clean oil to lubricate the inner lip of the seal …

13.9b … press the seal into position …

13.10a Apply some sealant around the outer edge of the seal …

13.10b … press the seal fully into position …

13.10c … then clean off the excess sealant from around the casing

14.3 Using a tool to prevent the flywheel from turning ...

14.4 ... when slackening the flywheel bolts

14.10 Checking the end thrust of the flywheel

illustration). Alternatively, bolt a strap between the flywheel/driveplate and the cylinder block.
4 Slacken and remove the retaining bolts **(see illustration)**, then remove the flywheel/driveplate from the end of the crankshaft. Do not drop it, as it is very heavy.

Inspection

5 On manual transmission models, if the flywheel's clutch mating surface is deeply scored, cracked or otherwise damaged, the flywheel must be renewed. Seek the advice of a Nissan dealer or engine reconditioning specialist.
6 If the ring gear is badly worn or has missing teeth, it must be renewed. This job is best left to a Nissan dealer or engine reconditioning specialist. The temperature to which the new ring gear must be heated for installation is critical and, if not done accurately, the hardness of the teeth will be destroyed.

Checking – Dual Mass

7 If not already done refit the flywheel back to the end of the crankshaft.
8 To inspect the dual mass flywheel a dial test indicator (DTI) gauge will be required, along with a spring balance to apply force on the flywheel.
9 The run-out (deflection) of the flywheel can be checked, by setting the dial gauge at 105mm from the centre onto the flywheel surface. Rotate the crankshaft one complete turn and check the deflection reading on the gauge. This should be no more than 0.45mm, if the measured value is more than 0.45mm the flywheel will need to be renewed.

10 To measure the fore and aft (thrust) direction of the flywheel, set the dial gauge at 125mm from the centre onto the flywheel surface. Then apply 10.2 Kg (100N) of force to the flywheel at 125mm from the centre of the flywheel and take a reading of the distance traveled **(see illustration)**. This should be no more than 1.8mm, if the measured value is more than 1.8mm the flywheel will need to be renewed.
11 To check the radial direction of the flywheel, insert one of the clutch cover bolts to the flywheel and tighten.
a) *Put a force of 1.0 Kgm (9.8 Nm) to the bolt in a clockwise direction and mark one of the flywheel teeth and the dual mass surface plate with a paint mark (see illustration).*
b) *Again putting a force of 1.0 Kgm (9.8 Nm) to the bolt, but this time in an anti-*

14.11a Putting pressure clockwise make a mark on the flywheel ...

clockwise direction, make a paint mark on the flywheel tooth that is now inline with the mark you made originally on the dual mass surface plate (see illustration).
c) *Measure the distance between the two paint marks on the teeth of the flywheel and it should be no more than 33.2mm (see illustration). If the measured value is more than 33.2mm the flywheel will need to be renewed.*

Refitting

12 Clean the mating surfaces of the flywheel/driveplate and crankshaft.
13 Apply a smear of clean oil to the threads, and to the underside of the heads, of the flywheel bolts **(see illustration)**.
14 Offer up the flywheel/driveplate, and refit the retaining bolts **(see illustration)**.
15 Lock the ring gear using the method

14.11b ... then put pressure on in anti-clockwise direction and make another mark ...

14.11c ... then measure the distance between the marks

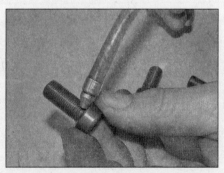

14.13 Lubricate the threads on the bolt

14.14 Fit the flywheel retaining bolts

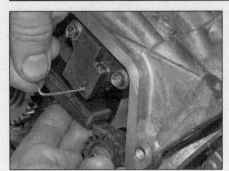

15.3 Hold pressure against the tensioner and fit locking pin

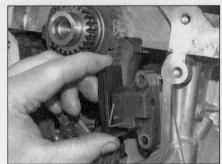

15.4 Remove the tensioner from the cylinder block

15.5a Slacken the sprocket retaining bolt ...

employed on dismantling, and tighten the retaining bolts to the specified torque.

16 On manual transmission models, refit the clutch as described in Chapter 6, Section 6.

17 Remove the locking tool, and refit the transmission as described in Chapter 7A, Section 6 or Chapter 7B, Section 11.

15 Balancer shaft, drive chain and sprockets – removal, inspection and refitting

Removal

1 Remove the timing chain as described in Section 7.

2 Remove the sump oil pan as described in Section 11.

3 Whilst holding the plunger back into the body of the tensioner, insert a small-diameter

rod through the hole in the body to lock the plunger **(see illustration)**.

4 Undo the two retaining bolts, and remove the tensioner from the end of the upper sump housing. Keep the rod inserted into the tensioner to prevent the plunger from springing out **(see illustration)**.

⚠️ **Warning: Do not turn the crankshaft or camshafts while the timing chain is removed, otherwise piston and valve contact may occur causing damage.**

5 Slacken the balancer shaft sprocket retaining bolt. Use a large open-ended spanner fitted to the flat section on the shaft (accessed through the sump aperture), to retain the balance shaft whilst slackening the bolt **(see illustrations)**.

6 Remove the bolt, then disengage the balancer shaft sprocket and drive chain from the crankshaft sprocket **(see illustrations)**.

7 If required, slide the crankshaft sprocket of the end of the crankshaft, noting its fitted position **(see illustration)**.

Inspection

8 The balance shaft unit is bolted to the underside of the upper sump housing **(see illustration)**. The oil pump is also driven from the balancer shaft assembly. At the time of writing there was no procedure for the removal and refitting of the balancer shaft unit. Refer to your local dealer for further information.

9 Clean the components and carefully examine the chain, sprockets and tensioner for any signs of excessive wear. If evident, it is recommended that all the components be renewed as a set.

10 Before refitting the balancer shaft drive chain and sprocket, refit the crankshaft sprocket and check it is positioned at TDC **(see illustration)**. **Note:** *The keyway will also*

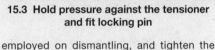

15.5b ... whilst counter holding the shaft (arrowed) with an open-ended spanner

15.6a Remove the sprocket bolt ...

15.6b ... then remove the sprocket and chain from the balance shaft

15.7 Removing the crankshaft sprocket

15.8 Balance shaft unit retaining bolts

15.10 Crankshaft alignment marks (arrowed)

15.11 Align the coloured link with the mark on the crankshaft sprocket

15.12 Align the coloured link with the mark on the balance shaft sprocket

be in the 12 o'clock position, as seen from the right-hand end of the engine.

Refitting

11 Fit the drive chain around the crankshaft sprocket, aligning the orange link on the chain with the balancer shaft timing mark on the crankshaft sprocket **(see illustration)**.

12 Fit the balancer shaft sprocket into the drive chain, aligning the dark blue link on the chain with the timing mark on the balancer shaft sprocket **(see illustration)**.

13 Apply a smear of clean oil to the threads, and to the underside of the head of the retaining bolt, and then run it by hand into the balancer shaft.

14 With the timing marks in position **(see illustration)**, tighten the balancer shaft sprocket retaining bolt to the specified torque setting, whilst retaining the shaft with a large open-ended spanner as used on removal.

15 Fit the chain tensioner to the upper sump housing, and tighten its retaining bolts to the specified torque. Whilst holding some pressure against the tensioner plunger, withdraw the rod, and check that the tensioner plunger is forced out to take up the slack in the chain **(see illustration)**.

16 Refit the sump oil pan as described in Section 11.

17 Refit the timing chain as described in Section 7.

16 Engine/transmission mountings – inspection and renewal

Inspection

1 If improved access is required, firmly apply the handbrake, and then jack up the front of the vehicle and support it securely on axle stands (see *Jacking and vehicle support*).

2 Check the mounting rubber to see if it is cracked, hardened or separated from the metal at any point; renew the mounting if any such damage or deterioration is evident.

3 Check that all the mounting's fasteners are securely tightened; use a torque wrench to check if possible.

4 Using a large screwdriver or a crowbar, check for wear in the mounting by carefully levering against it to check for free play. Where this is not possible, enlist the aid of an assistant to move the engine/transmission back-and-forth, or from side-to-side, while you watch the mounting. While some free play is to be expected even from new components, excessive wear should be obvious. If excessive free play is found, check first that the fasteners are correctly secured, and then renew any worn components as described below.

Renewal
Right-hand mounting

5 Disconnect the battery negative terminal (refer to *Disconnecting the battery* in the Reference Chapter).

15.14 Check the timing marks (arrowed)

15.15 Refit the tensioner and remove the pin

16.6 Supporting the engine on a jack

16.7 Undo the earth cable securing bolt

16.8a Undo the retaining bolts ...

6 Place a jack beneath the engine, with a block of wood on the jack head. Raise the jack until it is supporting the weight of the engine **(see illustration)**.

7 Slacken the securing bolt and disconnect the earth wire from the top of the mounting bracket **(see illustration)**.

8 Undo the retaining bolts and remove the stay bracket from the mounting bracket to the inner wing panel **(see illustrations)**.

9 Undo the retaining nut and remove the dynamic damper bobbin from the front of the mounting bracket **(see illustrations)**.

10 Slacken and remove the three retaining bolts

from the inner wing panel, remove the three retaining bolts from the engine mounting bracket, and then withdraw the complete mounting from the engine compartment **(see illustration)**.

11 Check carefully for signs of wear or damage on all components, and renew them where necessary.

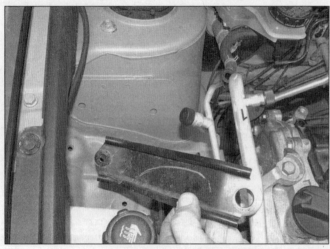

16.8b ... and remove the support bracket

16.9a Undo the retaining nut ...

16.9b ... and remove the dynamic damper

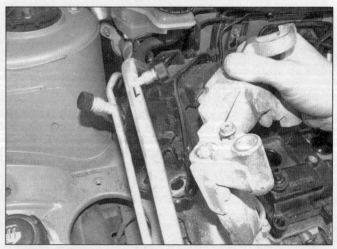

16.10 Undo the bolts and remove the mounting from the engine compartment

16.17 Supporting the transmission on a trolley jack

16.18 Undo the centre retaining nut and remove vibration damper

16.19 Undo the two outer securing nuts and remove the mounting

12 On refitting, fit the engine mounting and bracket to the inner wing panel and engine, and then securely tighten its retaining bolts to the specified torque setting.

13 Refit the stay bracket and dynamic damper bobbin, back to the engine mounting bracket.

14 With the engine mounting back in position, lower the jack and remove it from underneath the engine.

15 Reconnect the earth cable to the top of the engine mounting and then reconnect the battery negative terminal.

Left-hand mounting

16 Remove the battery and tray, as described in Chapter 5A, Section 3.

17 Place a jack and block of wood beneath the transmission, and raise the jack to take the weight of the transmission **(see illustration)**.

18 Slacken and remove the through-bolt/stud retaining nut from the centre of the mounting, and (where fitted) the vibration damper **(see illustration)**.

19 Slacken and remove the two outer retaining nuts, and withdraw the mounting from the upper mounting bracket **(see illustration)**.

20 If required, undo the retaining bolts from the inner wing panel to remove the upper mounting bracket.

21 Also, if required, undo the retaining bolts from the transmission to remove the lower mounting bracket **(see illustration)**.

22 Check carefully for signs of wear or damage on all components, and renew them where necessary.

23 On refitting, fit the upper and lower mounting brackets (where removed) and securely tighten the retaining bolts.

24 Align the left-hand rubber mounting with the bolt/stud on the lower mounting bracket and tighten its nut to the specified torque setting.

25 Refit the two outer retaining nuts, and tighten to the specified torque setting.

26 With the transmission mounting back in position, lower the jack and remove it from underneath the transmission.

27 Refit the battery and battery tray, with reference to Chapter 5, Section 3.

Rear lower mounting

28 If not already done, firmly apply the handbrake, and then jack up the front of the vehicle and support it securely on axle stands (see *Jacking and vehicle support*).

29 Slacken and remove the bolts securing the rear mounting bracket to the transmission, and then withdraw the bracket from transmission **(see illustration)**.

30 Slacken and remove the bolt securing the rear mounting link to the subframe, and then withdraw the mounting link from subframe **(see illustration)**.

31 Check carefully for signs of wear or damage on all components, and renew them where necessary.

32 On reassembly, fit the rear mounting to the subframe, and tighten the retaining bolt to the specified torque.

33 Refit the mounting bracket to the lower part of the transmission and tighten its retaining bolts to the specified torque.

34 With the transmission rear mounting link arm back in position, lower the vehicle to the ground.

16.21 Remove the mounting bracket from the transmission

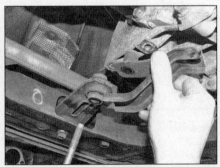

16.29 Remove the mounting bracket from the transmission

16.30 Remove the link arm from the subframe

Chapter 2 Part C:
1.5 litre diesel engine in-car repair procedures

Contents

Degrees of difficulty

Easy, suitable for novice with little experience	**Fairly easy,** suitable for beginner with some experience	**Fairly difficult,** suitable for competent DIY mechanic	**Difficult,** suitable for experienced DIY mechanic	**Very difficult,** suitable for expert DIY or professional

Specifications

General

Type	Four cylinder, in-line, single overhead camshaft
Designation	K9K
Capacity	1461 cc
Bore 76.0 mm	
Stroke	80.5 mm
Firing order	1-3-4-2 (No 1 cylinder at flywheel end)
Direction of crankshaft rotation	Clockwise viewed from timing belt end
Compression ratio	15.3 : 1

Compression pressures

Engine warm – approximately 80°C:

Minimum pressure	18 bars
Maximum difference between cylinders	4 bars

Camshaft

Drive	Toothed belt
Number of bearings	6
Camshaft endfloat	0.080 o 0.178 mm

Valve clearances

Inlet	0.125 to 0.250 mm
Exhaust	0.325 to 0.450 mm

Lubrication system

System pressure (at 80°C):

At idle	1.2 bars minimum
At 3000 rpm	3.5 bars minimum
Oil pump type	Gear-type, chain-driven off the crankshaft right-hand end
Oil level sensor resistance	6.0 to 20 ohms

Torque wrench settings

	Nm	lbf ft
Alternator	21	15
Big-end bearing caps:		
Stage 1	20	15
Stage 2	Angle-tighten a further 45° ± 6°	
Brake vacuum pump	21	15
Camshaft bearing caps	11	8
Camshaft sprocket:		
Stage 1	30	22
Stage 2	Angle-tighten a further 86°	
Clutch pressure plate	12	9
Crankshaft main bearing caps:		
Stage 1	25	18
Stage 2	Angle-tighten a further 47°	
Crankshaft pulley bolt:		
Stage 1	120	89
Stage 2	Angle-tighten a further 95°	
Crankshaft seal end cover	11	8
Cylinder block TDC blanking plug	20	15
Cylinder head bolts:*		
Stage 1	25	18
Stage 2	Angle-tighten a further 255°	
Cylinder head coolant outlet	10	7
Cylinder head cover bolts	12	9
Exhaust gas recirculation valve	21	15
Exhaust manifold	26	19
Flywheel*		
Stage 1	20	15
Stage 2	Angle-tighten a further 36°	
Glow plugs	15	11
High-pressure fuel pump bolts	21	15
High-pressure fuel pump sprocket	70	52
High-pressure pipe nuts	24	18
High-pressure rail nuts	28	21
Injector flange mounting bolts	30	22
Knock sensor	20	15
Left-hand transmission mounting:		
Through-bolt/stud nut	65	48
Through-bolt/stud-to-bracket	65	48
Mounting-to-bracket nuts	105	77
Mounting bracket-to-inner wing panel bolts	70	52
Mounting bracket-to-transmission bolts	45	33
Oil cooler – through bolt	45	33
Oil filter body – through bolt	45	33
Oil level sensor	22	16
Oil pressure sensor	35	26
Oil pump	25	18
Rear lower engine torque/link arm mounting:		
Torque link arm to front subframe bolt	110	81
Torque link arm to mounting bracket bolt	155	114
Mounting bracket-to-sump bolts	80	59
Right-hand engine mounting:		
Mounting bracket to cylinder head	25	18
Alloy mounting bracket to cylinder head mounting bracket	55	41
Mounting bracket bolts to inner wing	55	41
Mounting bolt to engine bracket (horizontal)	75	55
Torque arm mounting bolts	140	103
Sump (refer to sequence in text)	14	10
Timing belt tensioner	27	20
Turbocharger oil delivery pipe	23	17
Turbocharger oil return pipe	12	9
Turbocharger to exhaust manifold	26	19
Water pump	11	8
Water pump inlet pipe	20	15

* **Note:** *Use new bolts.*

1 General information

How to use this Chapter

1 This Part of Chapter 2 is devoted to in-car repair procedures for the 1.5 litre diesel engine. Similar information covering the other engine types can be found in Parts A, B and D. All procedures concerning engine removal and refitting, and engine block/cylinder head overhaul can be found in Part E of this Chapter.
2 Refer to *Vehicle identification numbers* in the Reference Section at the end of this manual for details of engine code locations.
3 Most of the operations included in this Part are based on the assumption that the engine is still installed in the car. Therefore, if this information is being used during a complete engine overhaul, with the engine already removed, many of the steps included here will not apply.

Engine description

4 The engine is of four cylinder, in-line, single overhead camshaft type, mounted transversely at the front of the vehicle.
5 The cylinder block is of cast iron with conventional dry liners bored directly into the cylinder block. The crankshaft is supported in five shell-type main bearings. Thrustwashers are fitted to No 3 main bearing to control crankshaft endfloat.
6 The connecting rods are attached to the crankshaft by 'cracked' horizontally split shell-type big-end bearings and to the pistons by gudgeon pins. The gudgeon pins are fully-floating and are retained by circlips. The aluminium alloy pistons are fitted with three piston rings, comprising two compression rings and a scraper-type oil control ring.
7 The single overhead camshaft is mounted directly in the cylinder head, and is driven by the crankshaft via a toothed timing belt.
8 The camshaft operates the valves via inverted bucket type tappets (cam followers), which operate in bores machined directly in the cylinder head. The valve clearances are adjusted by changing the cam followers, which are available in 25 different thicknesses. The inlet and exhaust valves are mounted vertically in the cylinder head and are each closed by a single valve spring.
9 The high-pressure fuel injection pump is driven by the timing belt and is described in further detail in Chapter 4B, Section 9.
10 A semi-closed crankcase ventilation system is employed, and crankcase fumes are drawn from the cylinder block and passed via a hose to the inlet tract (see Chapter 4C, Section 3 for further details).
11 Engine lubrication is by pressure feed from a gear type oil pump located beneath the crankshaft. Engine oil is fed through an externally mounted oil filter to the main oil gallery feeding the crankshaft and camshaft. Oil spray jets are fitted to the cylinder block to supply oil to the underside of the pistons. An oil cooler is mounted between the oil filter and the cylinder block.

Operations with engine in place

12 The following operations can be carried out without having to remove the engine from the vehicle:
 a) *Removal and refitting of the cylinder head.*
 b) *Removal and refitting of the timing belt and sprockets.*
 c) *Renewal of the camshaft oil seals.*
 d) *Removal and refitting of the camshaft.*
 e) *Removal and refitting of the sump.*
 f) *Removal and refitting of the connecting rods and pistons. ***
 g) *Removal and refitting of the oil pump.*
 h) *Renewal of the crankshaft oil seals.*
 i) *Renewal of the engine mountings.*
 j) *Removal and refitting of the flywheel.*
* *Although the operation marked with an asterisk can be carried out with the engine in the car after removal of the sump, it is better for the engine to be removed in the interests of cleanliness and improved access. For this reason, the procedure is described in Chapter 2E.*

2 Compression and leakdown tests – description and interpretation

Compression test

Note: *A compression tester specifically designed for diesel engines must be used for this test.*

1 When engine performance is down, or if misfiring occurs which cannot be attributed to a fault in the fuel system, a compression test can provide diagnostic clues as to the engine's condition. If the test is performed regularly it can give warning of trouble before any other symptoms become apparent.
2 A compression tester is connected to an adaptor that screws into the glow plug hole. It is unlikely to be worthwhile buying such a tester for occasional use, but it may be possible to borrow or hire one – if not, have the test performed by a garage.
3 Unless specific instructions to the contrary are supplied with the tester, observe the following points:
 a) *The battery must be in a good state of charge, the air filter must be clean and the engine should be at normal operating temperature.*
 b) *All the glow plugs must be removed before starting the test and the wiring disconnected from the injectors.*
4 There is no need to hold the accelerator pedal down during the test because the diesel engine air inlet is not throttled.
5 The actual compression pressures measured are not so important as the balance between cylinders. Values are given in the Specifications.
6 The cause of poor compression is less easy to establish on a diesel engine than on a petrol one. The effect of introducing oil into the cylinders ('wet' testing) is not conclusive, because there is a risk that the oil will sit in the swirl chamber or in the recess on the piston crown instead of passing to the rings. However, the following can be used as a rough guide to diagnosis.
7 All cylinders should produce very similar pressures; any difference greater than that specified indicates the existence of a fault. Note that the compression should build-up quickly in a healthy engine; low compression on the first stroke, followed by gradually increasing pressure on successive strokes, indicates worn piston rings. A low compression reading on the first stroke, which does not build-up during successive strokes, indicates leaking valves or a blown head gasket (a cracked head could also be the cause).
8 A low reading from two adjacent cylinders is almost certainly due to the head gasket having blown between them.

Leakdown test

9 A leakdown test measures the rate at which compressed air fed into the cylinder is lost. It is an alternative to a compression test and in many ways it is better, since the escaping air provides easy identification of where pressure loss is occurring (piston rings, valves or head gasket).
10 The equipment needed for leakdown testing is unlikely to be available to the home mechanic. If poor compression is suspected, have the test performed by a suitably equipped garage.

3 Top Dead Centre (TDC) for No 1 piston – locating

Note: *Special Nissan/Renault timing tools are required for this work, or tools obtained from an automotive accessory shop.*

1 Top Dead Centre (TDC) is the highest point in the cylinder that each piston reaches as the crankshaft turns. Each piston reaches TDC at the end of the compression stroke and again at the end of the exhaust stroke; however, for the purpose of timing the engine, TDC refers to the position of No 1 piston at the end of its compression stroke. No 1 piston is at the flywheel end of the engine.
2 When No 1 piston is at TDC, the timing hole in the camshaft sprocket will be aligned with the hole in the cylinder head so that the timing pin can be inserted. Additionally, if the crankshaft timing pin is fully screwed into the cylinder block, it will just contact the timing flat on the crankshaft web.
3 Setting the TDC timing is necessary to ensure that the valve timing is maintained

during operations that require removal and refitting of the timing belt. Note that the engine does not have a conventional diesel injection pump, however it is still necessary to align a mark on the pump sprocket with a bolt head on the cylinder head.

4 To set the engine at TDC, the right-hand engine mounting support and upper timing belt cover must be removed for access to the camshaft sprocket. First jack up the right-hand front of the car and support on axle stands. Remove the front right wheel, engine undertray and wheel arch liner.

5 Remove the auxiliary drivebelt with reference to Chapter 1B, Section 10.

6 Support the right-hand end of the engine with a support bar across the engine compartment, with a hoist, or alternatively with a jack and block of wood beneath the sump. Unbolt the right-hand engine mounting from the engine and body.

7 Undo the retaining bolts and remove the engine mounting support bracket from the end of the cylinder head as described in Section 15. Then release the retaining clips and remove the upper timing belt cover.

8 Release the fasteners and remove the lower timing belt cover.

9 Unscrew and remove the plug from the TDC hole on the front (transmission end) of the cylinder block. If required, remove the starter motor as described in Chapter 5A, Section 8, to make access to the TDC plug easier.

10 The crankshaft must now be turned using a spanner on the crankshaft pulley bolt. To enable the engine to be turned more easily, remove the glow plugs (Chapter 5C, Section 3) or the fuel injectors (Chapter 4B, Section 10). Before removing the injectors, consider that Nissan stipulate the high-pressure fuel lines must be renewed after removing them. New high-pressure fuel lines are expensive.

11 Turn the crankshaft clockwise until the timing hole in the camshaft sprocket is approaching the hole in the cylinder head.

12 Insert and tighten the special TDC pin into the cylinder block timing hole **(see illustration)**.

Note: *If the pin is not available, an alternative method of determining the TDC position is to use a dial gauge on the top of piston No 1 after removing the fuel injector or glow plug.*

13 Slowly turn the crankshaft clockwise until

3.12 Fitting the crankshaft TDC pin

3.13b ... or using a bolt to align the camsahft

its web contacts the timing pin. Now insert the remaining timing pin through the hole in the camshaft sprocket and into the cylinder head **(see illustrations)**. The engine is now positioned with No 1 piston at TDC on its compression stroke.

Caution: Do not attempt to rotate the engine whilst the crankshaft and camshaft timing pins are in position. If the engine is to be left in this state for a long period of time, it is a good idea to place suitable warning notices inside the vehicle, and in the engine compartment. This will reduce the possibility of the engine being accidentally cranked on the starter motor, which would cause considerable damage.

14 Check that the mark on the high-pressure injection pump sprocket is aligned with the bolt head on the cylinder head **(see illustration)**.

15 On completion, remove the timing pins and refit all removed components.

3.13a Fitting the camshaft TDC pin ...

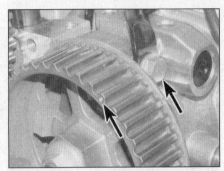
3.14 The mark on the high-pressure pump sprocket must be aligned with the bolt head on the cylinder head

4 Cylinder head cover – removal and refitting

Removal

1 Disconnect the battery negative terminal (refer to *Disconnecting the battery* in the Reference Chapter),

2 Unclip the engine plastic cover from the top of the engine **(see illustration)**.

3 Slacken the retaining clip and disconnect the intercooler pipe rubber hose **(see illustration)**.

4 Undo the retaining bolt, then release the securing clip at the turbo end of the pipe and pull the pipe upwards to remove it from across the top of the engine **(see illustrations)**.

5 Loosen the securing clip, and disconnect

4.2 Unclip the upper trim cover

4.3 Disconnecting the intercooler rubber hose

4.4a Undo the retaining bolt (arrowed) ...

4.4b ... and remove the air intake pipe

4.5 Disconnecting the intercooler rubber hose

4.6 Disconnect the wiring connector

4.7a Undo the retaining nut and securing clip (arrowed) ...

4.7b ... and remove the intake tube

4.8 Unclip the wiring loom from the cover

4.9a Undo the retaining bolt/nut ...

4.9b ... release the securing clips ...

the air intake hose from the plastic air intake tube (see illustration).

6 Disconnect the wiring connector from the turbocharger boost sensor (see illustration).

7 Slacken the securing clip, undo the retaining nut and then remove the plastic air intake tube (see illustrations).

8 Unclip the wiring loom retaining clip from the plastic shield/cover (see illustration).

9 Undo the retaining bolt and nut, release the two securing clips and lift off the plastic shield/cover (see illustrations).

10 Disconnect the wiring connector from the camshaft position sensor, undo the retaining bolt and remove it from the cylinder head cover (see illustrations). Note: *Twist the*

4.9c ... and remove the plastic cover

4.10a Disconnect the wiring connector ...

4.10b ... and remove the camshaft sensor

4.11 Remove the mounting bracket (arrowed)

4.12 Disconnect the breather hose (arrowed)

4.14a Release the clips . . .

sensor slightly to remove it completely from the cover, as it will catch on the lug on the alloy air intake housing.

11 Undo the retaining bolts and remove the EGR control valve mounting bracket from the rear of the cylinder head cover **(see illustration)**.

12 Slacken the retaining clip and disconnect the breather hose from the rear of the cylinder head cover **(see illustration)**.

13 Using a jack support the engine, and then undo the retaining bolts and remove the right-hand engine mounting as described in Section 15 of this Chapter.

14 Release the retaining clip, and then remove the plastic upper timing belt cover **(see illustrations)**.

15 Disconnect the wiring connectors from the fuel injectors, then unclip the wiring and the fuel return lines from across the front of the cylinder head cover and move them to one side **(see illustration)**.

16 Working from the outer ends of the cover, spiraling inwards to the centre, slacken and remove the cylinder head cover retaining bolts.

17 Lift off the cylinder head cover, and

4.14b . . . and remove the plastic upper timing cover

recover the rubber seal, which goes around the outer edge of the cover.

18 Inspect the cover seal for signs of damage and deterioration, and renew as necessary. Nissan recommends that the cylinder head cover seal should always be renewed, if the cover is removed.

Refitting

19 Carefully clean the cylinder head and cover mating surfaces, and remove all traces

4.15 Disconnect the wiring connectors

of oil. Then apply four beads of sealant, 2.0 mm wide, to the camshaft end bearing caps (No's 1 and 6) **(see illustration)**.

20 Fit the rubber seal to the cylinder head cover groove, ensuring that it is correctly located along its entire length. Carefully lower the cylinder head cover onto the cylinder head, taking great care not to displace any of the rubber seal

21 Make sure the cover is correctly seated, and then install the retaining bolts. Working from the centre of the cover and spiraling outwards, tighten all the cover bolts to the specified torque.

22 The remainder of the refitting procedure is the reversal of removal, bearing in mind the following points.

 a) *Make sure the two securing clips on the front of the plastic shield/cover are secure* **(see illustration)**.

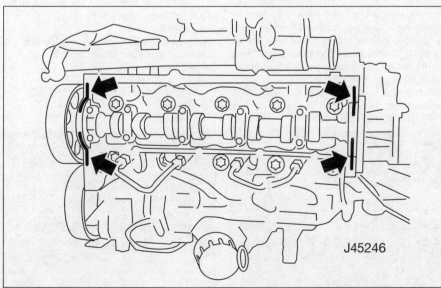

4.19 Apply 2.0 mm wide beads of sealant to the camshaft end bearing caps as shown

J45246

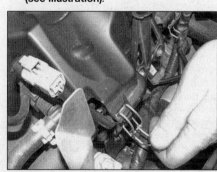

4.22a Check the retaining clips are secure

4.22b Check the retaining clip is located securely in the intake pipe

b) *Make sure the securing clip in the intercooler metal pipe is fitted correctly* **(see illustration)**.

c) *Ensure that the engine mounting is fitted securely (see Section 15), before removing the jack from under the engine.*

d) *Check all wiring connectors and retaining clips are correctly fitted and routed, as noted on removal.*

e) *Tighten all the hose clips securely*

23 Reconnect the battery negative terminal. Run the engine and check for any oil leaks around the engine cylinder head cover.

5 Valve clearances – checking and adjustment

Note: *This operation is not part of the maintenance schedule. It should be undertaken if noise from the valve gear becomes evident, or if loss of performance gives cause to suspect that the clearances may be incorrect. Adjustment involves removing the camshaft and changing the cam followers (valve lifters) that are available in 25 different thicknesses.*

Checking

1 Remove the cylinder head cover as described in Section 4.

2 During the following procedure, the crankshaft must be turned using a spanner on the crankshaft pulley bolt. Improved access to the pulley bolt can be obtained by jacking up the front right-hand corner of the vehicle and removing the roadwheel and placing the vehicle on an axle stand. Remove the fasteners and withdraw the plastic inner wheel arch panel.

3 If desired, to enable the crankshaft to be turned more easily, remove the glow plugs (Chapter 5C, Section 3) or the fuel injectors (Chapter 4B, Section 10). Before removing the injectors, consider that Nissan stipulate the high-pressure fuel lines must be renewed after removing them. New high-pressure fuel lines are expensive.

4 Draw the valve positions on a piece of paper, numbering them 1 to 8 from the flywheel end of the engine. Identify them as inlet or exhaust (i.e. 1E, 2I, 3E, 4I, 5E, 6I, 7E, 8I).

5 Turn the crankshaft until the valves of No 1

5.6 Using a feeler blade to check the valve clearances

cylinder (flywheel end) are 'rocking'. The exhaust valve will be closing and the inlet valve will be opening. The piston of No 4 cylinder will be at the top of its compression stroke, with both valves fully closed. The clearances for both valves of No 4 cylinder may be checked at the same time.

6 Insert a feeler blade of the correct thickness (see Specifications) between the cam lobe and the top of the cam follower (valve lifter), and check that it is a firm sliding fit **(see illustration)**. If it is not, use the feeler blades to ascertain the exact clearance, and record this for use when calculating the thickness of the new cam follower required. Note that the inlet and exhaust valve clearances are different (see Specifications).

7 With No 4 cylinder valve clearances checked, turn the engine through half a turn so that No 3 valves are 'rocking', then check the valve clearances of No 2 cylinder in the same way. Similarly check the remaining valve clearances in the sequence shown **(see illustration)**.

Adjustment

Note: *A micrometer or dial gauge and probe will be required for this operation.*

8 Where a valve clearance differs from the specified value, the cam follower for that valve must be changed with a thinner or thicker one accordingly. On new follower, the thickness is stamped on the bottom face of the tappet; however, the original followers may not have any thickness stamped on them. It is therefore prudent to use a micrometer or dial gauge to measure the true thickness of any follower removed, as it may have been reduced by wear **(see illustration)**.

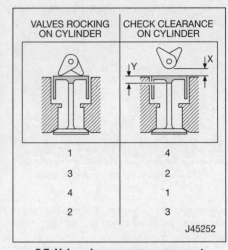

5.7 Valve clearance measurement

X Clearance   Y Cam follower thickness

9 To access the cam followers, first remove the camshaft as described in Section 9. Remove and refit each follower separately, to avoid confusion **(see illustration)**.

10 The size of follower required is calculated as follows. If the measured clearance is less than specified, subtract the measured clearance from the specified clearance, and deduct the result from the thickness of the existing follower. For example:

Sample calculation – clearance too small

Clearance measured (A) = 0.15 mm
Desired clearance (B) = 0.20 mm
Difference (B – A) = 0.05 mm
Cam follower thickness fitted = 7.70 mm
Cam follower thickness required = 7.70 – 0.05
* = 7.65 mm*

11 If the measured clearance is greater than specified, subtract the specified clearance from the measured clearance, and add the result to the thickness of the existing follower. For example:

Sample calculation – clearance too big

Clearance measured (A) = 0.50 mm
Desired clearance (B) = 0.40 mm
Difference (A – B) = 0.10 mm
Cam follower thickness fitted = 7.55 mm
Cam follower thickness required =
* 7.55 + 0.10 = 7.65 mm*

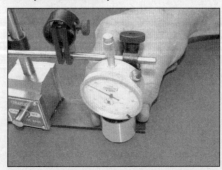

5.8 Using a dial gauge to measure the thickness of the removed cam follower

5.9 Removing a cam follower

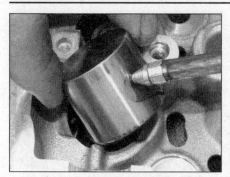

5.12 Lubricate the cam follower before refitting it

6.2 Remove the engine trim cover

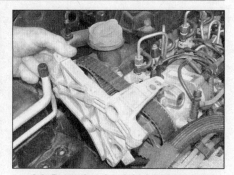

6.6 Removing the right-hand engine mounting support bracket (note the bracket extension is fitted beneath the timing belt)

12 Working on each separately, lift out the follower to be renewed, then oil the new one and carefully locate it in the cylinder head **(see illustration)**.
13 Refit the camshaft with reference to Section 9.
14 Where removed, refit the glow plugs (Chapter 5C, Section 3) or the fuel injectors (Chapter 4B, Section 10).
15 Remove the spanner from the crankshaft pulley bolt and refit the plastic inner wheel arch panel.
16 Refit the cylinder head cover as described in Section 4.

6 Timing belt – removal, inspection and refitting

Caution: If the timing belt breaks in service,

6.9a Unscrew and remove the crankshaft pulley bolt . . .

extensive engine damage will result. Renew the belt at the intervals specified in Chapter 1B, or earlier if its condition is at all doubtful.

Removal

1 Disconnect the battery negative lead (refer to *Disconnecting the battery* in Reference).
2 Jack up the right-hand front of the car and support on axle stands. Remove the front right wheel, engine/radiator undertray and wheel arch liner. Also remove the engine top cover **(see illustration)**.
3 Remove the auxiliary drivebelt with reference to Chapter 1B, Section 10, and then unbolt and remove the drivebelt tensioner.
4 Remove the right-hand engine mounting, as described in Section 15.
5 Release the retaining clips and remove the upper timing belt cover from around the engine mounting support bracket.
6 Unbolt and remove the engine mounting support bracket **(see illustration)**.
7 The crankshaft must now be turned to the TDC position using a spanner on the crankshaft pulley bolt. Set the engine to Top Dead Centre (TDC), as described in Section 3.
8 Temporarily remove the timing pins while the crankshaft pulley bolt is being loosened.
Caution: Do not use the timing pins to lock the engine when removing the crankshaft pulley bolt, as the timing pins may break and cause damage to the engine.
9 Before loosening the crankshaft pulley bolt, note that the crankshaft sprocket is not keyed to the crankshaft as is the normal arrangement, therefore if the crankshaft pulley is removed it is important to have an accurate

method of determining the TDC position of No 1 piston. Although the sprocket is not keyed to the crankshaft, there is still a groove in the crankshaft nose, which is at the 12 o'clock position when piston No 1 is at TDC. Unscrew the crankshaft pulley bolt while holding the crankshaft stationary. Have an assistant engage 4th gear and firmly depress the brake pedal. Alternatively, remove the starter motor or where applicable remove the cover plate from the transmission bellhousing, and have an assistant insert a screwdriver or similar tool in the starter ring gear teeth. With the bolt removed, ease the pulley from the crankshaft **(see illustrations)**.
10 Reposition the crankshaft at TDC and insert both timing pins again, as described in Section 3.
11 Loosen the tensioner locknut, then turn the tensioner clockwise to release the tension. If necessary, use a 6.0 mm Allen key in the eccentric hub plate to move the tensioner **(see illustration)**.
12 If the original belt is to be re-used (contrary to Nissan's recommendation), check if the belt is marked with arrows to indicate its running direction, and if necessary mark it. Similarly, make accurate alignment marks on the belt, corresponding to the timing marks on the camshaft, high-pressure fuel injection pump and crankshaft sprockets. Check that there are 18 inclusive teeth between the timing marks on the camshaft and injection pump sprockets, then release the timing belt from the camshaft sprocket, high-pressure injection pump, water pump pulley, crankshaft sprocket and tensioner **(see illustration)**.

6.9b . . . and remove the pulley

6.11 Loosen the tensioner locknut . . .

6.12 . . . then release the timing belt

6.20 Align the timing marks on the belt with those on the camshaft and fuel injection pump sprockets

13 Do not turn the camshaft or the crankshaft whilst the timing belt is removed, as there is a risk of piston-to-valve contact. If it is necessary to turn the camshaft for any reason, before doing so, turn the crankshaft anti-clockwise (viewed from the timing belt end of the engine) by a quarter turn to position all four pistons half-way down their bores. Leave the TDC pin tightened into the cylinder block.

14 Clean the sprockets, water pump pulley and tensioner and wipe them dry, although do not apply excessive amounts of solvent to the water pump and tensioner pulleys otherwise the bearing lubricant may be contaminated. Also clean the rear timing belt cover, and the cylinder head and block.

Inspection

15 Examine the timing belt carefully for any signs of cracking, fraying or general wear, particularly at the roots of the teeth. Renew the belt if there is any sign of deterioration of this nature, or if there is any oil or grease contamination. The belt must, of course, be renewed if it has completed the maximum mileage given in Chapter 1B.

16 It is recommended, that the timing belt should be renewed whenever it is disturbed. Due to the extent of damage that can be caused to the engine by belt failure, it is always best to renew the belt if it has been removed.

17 Thoroughly clean the nose of the crankshaft and the bore of the crankshaft sprocket, and also the contact surfaces of the sprocket and pulley. This is necessary to prevent the possibility of the sprocket slipping in use.

Refitting

18 Check that the crankshaft, camshaft and high-pressure fuel injection pump sprockets are still positioned at TDC, and that the groove in the crankshaft nose is pointing upwards. If the pistons have been positioned halfway down their bores, turn the crankshaft clockwise until the web contacts the TDC tool.

19 Check that the tensioner peg is correctly located in the groove in the cylinder head.

20 Align the timing marks on the belt with

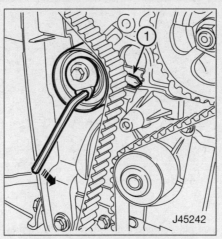

6.21a Pretension the timing belt by positioning the tensioner pointer (1) as shown

those on the camshaft and fuel injection pump sprockets **(see illustration)**, ensuring that the running direction arrows on the belt are pointing clockwise (viewed from the timing belt end of the engine). Note that the belt should be marked with lines across its width to act as timing marks. Fit the timing belt over the crankshaft sprocket first, followed by the water pump pulley, fuel injection pump sprocket, camshaft sprocket, and tensioner. There are 18 inclusive teeth between the timing marks on the camshaft and injection pump sprockets.

21 With the timing marks still aligned, use the 6.0 mm Allen key to pretension the belt by turning the tensioner anti-clockwise until the index pointer is positioned below the timing window **(see illustrations)**. Hold the tensioner stationary and tighten the locknut to the specified torque. This torque is critical, since if the nut were to come loose, considerable engine damage would result.

22 Remove the timing pins from the cylinder block and camshaft sprocket.

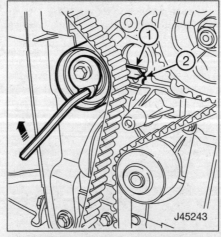

6.25 Position the pointer (1) to its final setting in the middle of the timing window (2)

6.21b Pretensioning the timing belt

23 Refit the crankshaft pulley, then insert the bolt and tighten to the specified torque and angle.

24 Turn the crankshaft two complete turns in the normal direction of rotation, but just before the camshaft sprockets are aligned, refit and tighten the crankshaft timing pin. Slowly turn the crankshaft clockwise until its web is contacting the timing pin, and then check that it is possible to insert the remaining timing pin through the hole in the camshaft sprocket and into the cylinder head. If all is aligned, then the timing pins can be removed again.

25 Hold the tensioner with the Allen key, then loosen the locknut a maximum of one turn, and turn the tensioner clockwise until the index pointer is positioned in the middle of the timing window **(see illustration)**. Tighten the locknut to the specified torque.

26 Apply sealant to the threads, then refit the blanking plug to the cylinder block and tighten it to the specified torque.

27 Refit the engine mounting support bracket and tighten the bolts to the specified torque.

28 Refit the lower timing cover and locate the fuel pipes in their clips (where applicable).

29 Clip the upper timing cover onto the lower cover, then refit the right-hand engine mounting to the engine and body and tighten the bolts to the specified torque (see Section 15).

30 Refit the auxiliary drivebelt with reference to Chapter 1B, Section 10.

31 Refit the engine undertray and wheel arch liner.

32 Refit the front right wheel and lower the car to the ground. Tighten the wheel bolts to the specified torque.

33 Reconnect the battery negative lead (refer to *Disconnecting the battery* in the Reference Section).

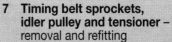

7 Timing belt sprockets, idler pulley and tensioner – removal and refitting

Crankshaft sprocket

Removal

1 Remove the timing belt as described in Section 6.

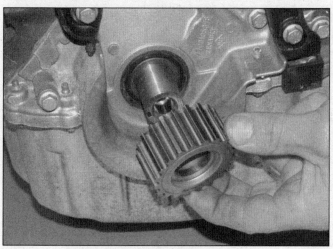

7.2 Removing the crankshaft sprocket

7.13 Removing the sprocket from the end of the camshaft – note the integral spline

2 Slide the sprocket from the crankshaft; noting which way around it is fitted **(see illustration)**.

Refitting

3 Thoroughly clean the nose of the crankshaft and the bore of the crankshaft sprocket, and also the contact surfaces of the sprocket and pulley. This is necessary to prevent the possibility of the sprocket slipping in use.
4 Slide the sprocket onto the crankshaft the correct way around.
5 Refit the timing belt as described in Section 6.

High-pressure pump sprocket

Note: *A suitable puller will be required for this operation.*

Removal

6 Sprocket may be removed as follows, however, note that if it is being removed for pump renewal, a special Nissan tool is available to enable the pump to be removed without removing the timing belt. Check with your Nissan dealer for the availability of a sprocket support tool.
7 Remove the timing belt as described in Section 6.
8 Hold the sprocket stationary using a suitable

gear holding tool. Alternatively, an old timing belt can be wrapped around the sprocket and held firmly with a pair of grips. Unscrew and remove the central securing nut.
9 Use a puller to release the sprocket from the taper on the pump shaft. Recover the Woodruff key from the groove in the pump shaft.

Refitting

10 Refitting is a reversal of removal, bearing in mind the following points.
a) Ensure that the Woodruff key is correctly engaged with the pump shaft and sprocket.
b) Tighten the sprocket securing nut to the specified torque.
c) Refit and tension the timing belt as described in Section 6. Make sure that the mark on the sprocket is aligned with the bolt on the cylinder head.

Camshaft sprocket

Removal

11 Remove the timing belt as described in Section 6.
12 Hold the sprocket stationary using a suitable gear holding tool. Alternatively, an old timing belt can be wrapped around the

sprocket and held firmly with a pair of grips. Unscrew and remove the central securing nut.
13 Release the sprocket from the camshaft, noting the integral spline on the sprocket and the corresponding cut-out in the end of the camshaft **(see illustration)**.

Refitting

14 Refit the camshaft sprocket.
15 Insert the bolt and tighten it to the specified torque and angle, holding the sprocket stationary as during removal **(see illustration)**.
16 Refit and tension the timing belt as described in Section 6.

Tensioner

Removal

17 Remove the timing belt as described in Section 6.
18 Unscrew the securing nut and remove the washer and pivot bolt, then withdraw the tensioner assembly from the engine **(see illustration)**.

Refitting

19 Refitting is a reversal of removal. Refit and tension the timing belt as described in Section 6.

7.15 Angle-tightening the camshaft sprocket retaining bolt

7.18 Removing the timing belt tensioner

8 Camshaft oil seals – renewal

Timing belt end oil seal

1 Remove the camshaft sprocket as described in Section 7.
2 Note the fitted depth of the old oil seal. Using a small screwdriver, prise out the oil seal from the cylinder head taking care not to damage the sealing surface on the camshaft. Alternatively, the oil seal can be removed by

8.4a Screw the rod into the end of the camshaft . . .

8.4b . . . locate the new oil seal and protector onto the camshaft . . .

8.4c . . . then tighten the tool to press the seal into position

drilling two small holes diagonally opposite each other and inserting self tapping screws in them. A pair of grips can then be used to pull out the oil seals, by pulling on each side in turn.

3 Inspect the seal rubbing surface on the camshaft. If it is grooved or rough in the area where the old seal was fitted, the new seal should be fitted slightly less deeply, so that it rubs on an unworn part of the surface.

4 Nissan technicians use a tool (Mot. 1632) to fit the oil seal. The tool consists of a threaded rod, metal tube and nut, and a machined shoulder to locate the protector/guide on. The rod is screwed into the end of the camshaft, and the protector/guide located on the shoulder. The metal tube is then fitted against the oil seal and the nut tightened to press the seal into the cylinder head/bearing cap **(see illustrations)**. If the Nissan tool cannot be obtained, a similar tool can be made out of a threaded rod, metal tube, washer and nut.

5 Wipe clean the oil seal seating, then press the oil seal squarely into position. Note that the Nissan tool is designed to locate the seal at the original depth, however, if the camshaft sealing surface is excessively worn, position it less deeply so that it locates on the unworn surface.

6 After fitting the oil seal, remove the protector/guide and tool.

7 Wipe away any excess oil, then refit the camshaft sprocket as described in Section 7.

Flywheel end sealing

8 No oil seal is fitted to the flywheel end of the camshaft. The sealing is provided by a gasket between the cylinder head and the brake vacuum pump housing, and on certain models by an O-ring fitted between the vacuum pump and the housing. The gasket and the O-ring, where applicable, can be renewed after unbolting the vacuum pump from the cylinder head (see Chapter 9, Section 13).

---

9 Camshaft and followers
– removal, inspection and refitting

Note: A new camshaft oil seal will be required, and suitable sealant will be required for the camshaft bearing caps and valve cover.

Removal

1 Removal of the camshaft will normally only be required for access to the cam followers (e.g. for valve clearance adjustment) or during cylinder head overhaul. For cylinder head overhaul, remove the head as described in Section 10.

2 Remove the cylinder head cover as described in Section 4.

3 Remove the camshaft sprocket as described in Section 7.

4 Disconnect the wiring connector, then remove the mounting bracket bolts, and actuator retaining nuts then remove the throttle control actuator from the intake manifold as described in Chapter 4B, Section 8.

5 Remove the brake vacuum pump with reference to Chapter 9, Section 13. Note the position of the offset drive inside the pump, which engages the slot in the end of the camshaft **(see illustrations)**.

6 Using a dial gauge, measure the camshaft endfloat, and compare with the value given in the Specifications. This will give an indication of the amount of wear present on the thrust surfaces.

7 If the original camshaft is to be refitted, it is advisable to measure the valve clearances at this stage as described in Section 5, so that any different thickness followers required can be obtained before the camshaft is refitted.

8 Check the camshaft bearing caps for identification marks, and if none are present, make identifying marks so that they can be refitted in their original positions and the same way round. Number the caps from the flywheel end of the engine **(see illustration)**.

9 Progressively slacken the bearing cap bolts until the valve spring pressure is relieved. Remove the bolts and the bearing caps themselves.

10 Lift out the camshaft out from the top of the cylinder head, together with the oil seal.

11 Remove the cam followers, keeping each

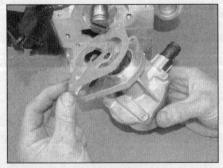

9.5a Removing the brake vacuum pump and gasket

9.5b Offset drive in the pump which engages the slot in the end of the camshaft

9.8 The camshaft bearing caps are numbered from the flywheel end of the engine

9.11 Removing the cam followers

9.17 Removing the camshaft from the cylinder head

10 Cylinder head – removal, inspection and refitting

Note: *A new cylinder head gasket must be fitted and all cylinder head bolts must be renewed. Sealant for the valve cover will also be required.*

Note: *Before removing any of the high-pressure fuel pipes, consider that Nissan stipulate they must be renewed after removing them.*

Removal

1 Before starting work, allow the engine to cool for as long as possible, to ensure the fuel pressure in the high-pressure lines, and the fuel temperature, are at a minimum.
2 Disconnect the battery negative lead (see *Disconnecting the battery* in Reference).
3 Drain the cooling system with reference to Chapter 1B, Section 29. Refit and tighten the plug after draining.
4 Remove the cylinder head cover as described in Section 4.
5 Slacken the retaining clips and remove the

identified for position **(see illustration)**. Place them in a compartment box, or on a sheet of card marked into eight sections, so that they may be refitted to their original locations. If any of the valve clearances measured in paragraph 7 is incorrect, use a micrometer to measure the thickness of the old follower from its upper surface to the inner surface, at the centre, which contacts the valve stem. Refer to Section 5 and obtain new followers of the correct thickness.

Inspection

12 Examine the camshaft bearing surfaces and cam lobes for wear ridges, pitting or scoring. Renew the camshaft if evident.
13 Renew the oil seal at the end of the camshaft as a matter of course. Lubricate the lips of the new seal before fitting, and store the camshaft so that its weight is not resting on the seal. Alternatively, the seal may be fitted after refitting the camshaft.
14 Examine the camshaft bearing surfaces in the cylinder head and bearing caps. Deep scoring or other damage means that the cylinder head must be renewed.
15 Inspect the cam followers for scoring, pitting and wear ridges. Renew as necessary.

Refitting

16 Oil the cam followers (inside and out) and fit them to the bores from which they were removed; where applicable, fit the new followers to their correct bores.
17 Oil the camshaft bearings. Place the camshaft without the oil seal onto the cylinder head **(see illustration)**.
18 Wipe clean the upper sealing edge of the cylinder head, then apply four beads of sealant, 1.0 mm wide, to the camshaft end bearing cap (Nos 1 and 6) contact areas as shown **(see illustrations)**.
19 Refit the camshaft bearing caps to their original locations, then insert the bearing cap bolts and progressively tighten them to the specified torque **(see illustration)**.
20 If a new camshaft has been fitted, measure the endfloat using a dial gauge, and check that it is within the specified limits.

21 Fit the new camshaft oil seal with reference to Section 8.
22 Refit the brake vacuum pump with reference to Chapter 9, Section 13.
23 Refit the throttle control actuator to the intake manifold, tighten the retaining bolts/nuts and reconnect the wiring connector.
24 Refit the camshaft sprocket as described in Section 7.
25 Refit the cylinder head cover as described in Section 4.

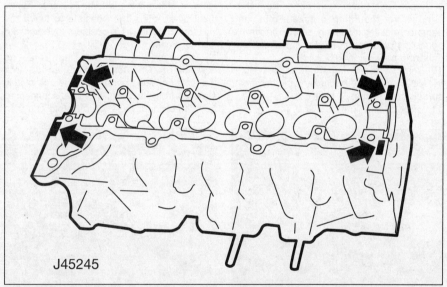

J45245

9.18a Apply 1.0 mm wide beads of sealant to the camshaft end bearing cap-to-cylinder head contact areas as shown

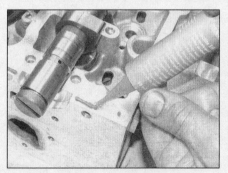

9.18b Apply the beads of sealant ...

9.19 ... then refit the camshaft bearing caps

10.5a Release the breather hose …

10.5b … and remove the air intake hose

10.6 Remove the bracket from the end of the cylinder head

air intake hose from the air flow meter to the turbocharger **(see illustrations)**.

6 Undo the retaining bolts and remove the bracket from the left-hand end of the cylinder head **(see illustration)**.

7 Disconnect the quick-release vacuum pipe from the brake vacuum pump on the left-hand end of the cylinder head **(see illustration)**.

8 Remove the hoses and coolant temperature sensor wiring connector, from the left-hand end of the cylinder head **(see illustrations)**.

9 Disconnect the wiring connector, then remove the mounting bracket bolts, and actuator retaining nuts then remove the throttle control actuator from the intake manifold **(see illustrations 9.4a, 9.4b & 9.4c)**

10 Remove the timing belt, as described in Section 6, and if necessary, the camshaft sprocket (in Section 7).

11 Unbolt and remove the timing belt tensioner roller from the cylinder head **(see illustration)**.

12 If required, unbolt and remove the auxiliary drivebelt tensioner from the cylinder block.

13 Unbolt and remove the inner timing cover from the cylinder block and head **(see illustration)**.

14 Remove the high-pressure fuel pump, as described in Chapter 4B, Section 9.

15 If required, remove the fuel rail as described in Chapter 4B, Section 11. If the removal of the cylinder head is just to renew the gasket, then it is possible to leave the injectors and fuel rail in position, together with the fuel pipes.

16 Remove the exhaust manifold, as described in Chapter 4B, Section 13. Note the manifold does not have to be completely removed from the vehicle, once disconnected from the cylinder head the manifold can then

be positioned to one side to allow the cylinder head to be removed.

17 The cylinder head assembly complete with ancillaries is very heavy. If required, seek the aid of an assistant to help lift the cylinder head from the vehicle.

18 Before removing the cylinder head, turn the crankshaft anti-clockwise (viewed from the timing belt end of the engine) by a quarter turn to position all four pistons halfway down their bores. The TDC pin can remain in the cylinder block if necessary, however, remember that it is in position and do not turn the crankshaft further anti-clockwise.

19 Progressively slacken the cylinder head bolts in the **reverse** sequence to that shown **(see illustration 9.29)**. With all the bolts loose, remove them **(see illustration)**.

20 Lift the cylinder head upwards off the cylinder block. If it is stuck, tap it with a

10.7 Disconnect the vacuum hose (arrowed)

10.8a Note the position of the coolant hoses on the left-hand end of the cylinder head

10.8b Disconnecting the wiring from the coolant temperature sensor

10.11 Removing the timing belt tensioner roller

10.13 Removing the inner timing cover

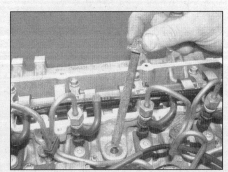

10.19 Removing the cylinder head bolts

10.27 Locate the new gasket on the cylinder block

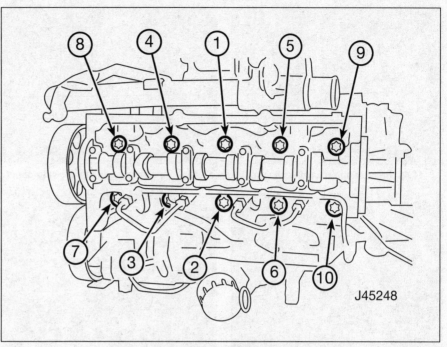

10.29 Cylinder head bolt tightening sequence

hammer and block of wood to release it. **Do not** try to turn the cylinder head (it is located by two dowels), nor attempt to prise it free using a screwdriver inserted between the block and head faces.

21 If necessary, remove the camshaft and followers, as described in Section 9.

Inspection

22 The mating faces of the cylinder head and block must be perfectly clean before refitting the head. Use a scraper to remove all traces of gasket and carbon, and also clean the tops of the pistons. Take particular care with the aluminium cylinder head, as the soft metal is damaged easily. Also, make sure that debris is not allowed to enter the oil and water channels – this is particularly important for the oil circuit, as carbon could block the oil supply to the camshaft or crankshaft bearings. Using adhesive tape and paper, seal the water, oil and bolt holes in the cylinder block. Clean the piston crowns in the same way.

23 Check the block and head for nicks, deep scratches and other damage. If slight, they may be removed carefully with a file. Machining of the cylinder head or cylinder block is not recommended by the manufacturers.

24 If warpage of the cylinder head is suspected, use a straight-edge to check it for distortion. Refer to Chapter 2E if necessary; if the warpage is more than the maximum, the cylinder head must be renewed, as regrinding is not allowed.

25 Clean out the cylinder head bolt holes in the block using a pipe cleaner, or a rag and screwdriver. Make sure that all oil is removed, otherwise there is a possibility of the block being cracked by hydraulic pressure when the bolts are tightened. Examine the bolt threads in the cylinder block for damage, and if necessary, use the correct size tap to chase out the threads. The cylinder head bolts must be renewed each time they are removed, and must not be oiled before being fitted.

Refitting

26 Where removed, refit the cam followers, camshaft and camshaft sprocket with

reference to Section 9 and Section 7. Turn the camshaft so that the sprocket is at its TDC position.

27 Ensure that the cylinder head locating dowels are fitted to the cylinder block, then fit the new gasket the right way round on the cylinder block **(see illustration)**.

28 Carefully lower the cylinder head onto the dowels and gasket, then insert the new bolts and hand-tighten. **Do not** oil the threads or heads of the new bolts.

29 Tighten the bolts in sequence, and in the stages given in the Specifications **(see illustration)**.

30 Turn the crankshaft clockwise by a quarter turn until the internal web contacts the TDC timing pin.

31 Refit the inner timing cover back to the cylinder block and head.

32 If removed, refit the auxiliary drivebelt tensioner to the cylinder block.

33 Refit the timing belt tensioner roller to the cylinder head.

34 Refit the timing belt, as described in Section 6.

35 Refit the exhaust manifold, as described in Chapter 4B, Section 13.

36 If removed, refit the fuel rail as described in Chapter 4B, Section 11.

37 Refit the high-pressure fuel pump, as described in Chapter 4B, Section 9.

38 Refit the hoses and coolant temperature sensor wiring connector, to the housing on the left-hand end of the cylinder head.

39 Reconnect the quick-release vacuum pipe to the brake vacuum pump on the left-hand end of the cylinder head.

40 Refit the throttle control actuator to the intake manifold, tighten the retaining bolts/nuts and reconnect the wiring connector.

41 Refit the bracket to the left-hand end of the cylinder head.

42 Refit the air intake hose between the air flow meter and turbocharger, also connecting the breather pipe.

43 Refit the cylinder head cover as described in Section 4.

44 Reconnect the battery negative lead (refer to *Disconnecting the battery* in the Reference Section).

45 Prime and bleed the fuel system as described in Chapter 4B, Section 5.

46 Refill and bleed the cooling system as described in Chapter 1B, Section 29.

11 Sump – removal and refitting

Removal

1 Disconnect the battery negative lead (refer to *Disconnecting the battery* in the Reference Section).

2 Jack up the front of the vehicle and support on axle stands. Remove the engine compartment undertray and right-hand front road wheel.

3 Drain the engine oil referring to Chapter 1B, Section 3, and then refit and tighten the drain plug, using a new washer.

4 Release the fasteners and remove the

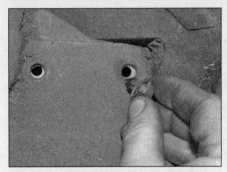

11.4a Release the retaining clips ...

11.4b ... and remove the inner wing panel

11.6 Oil level sensor (arrowed)

11.7 Unclip the fuel overflow pipe from below the sump

11.8 Remove the bolts (arrowed) through the transmission bell housing

11.12 Apply sealant where the right-hand cover meets the cylinder block ...

right-hand front wheel arch inner trim panel **(see illustrations)**.

5 Remove the rear lower engine mounting (torque link), and mounting bracket from the rear of the sump, as described in Section 15.

6 Disconnect the wiring connector and unscrew the oil level sensor from the front of the alloy sump housing **(see illustration)**. Also, if not already done, withdraw the oil level dipstick.

7 Unclip the fuel rail drain/overflow tube from the side and the lower part of the sump and move it to one side **(see illustration)**.

8 Slacken and remove the four bolts securing the sump to the lower part of the transmission housing **(see illustration)**.

9 Progressively slacken the bolts working in the **reverse** of the tightening sequence **(see illustration 11.14)** remove all the sump retaining bolts.

10 Tap the sump with a hide or plastic mallet to break the joint, and then remove the sump.

11.13 ... then locate a new gasket on the sump

Recover the gasket and discard it, as a new one must be used on refitting. There may be sealant at each end of the sump, use a spatula or thin knife to release the ends of the sump. Take care not to distort or damage the mating surfaces of the alloy sump or cylinder block. Take adequate precautions to catch any oil remaining inside the sump housing, as it is removed.

Refitting

11 Thoroughly clean the mating surfaces of the sump and cylinder block.

12 With the cylinder block lower surface clean and no traces of oil, apply four beads

of sealant, 5.0 mm wide, to the crankshaft end bearing caps (No's 1 and 5), where they meet the cylinder block. Also apply a bead of sealant at the right-hand end of the cylinder block where the crankshaft oil seal housing is bolted **(see illustration)**.

13 Locate a new gasket on the sump, and then lift the sump into position on the cylinder block and use a straight-edge to align the flywheel end of the sump with the corresponding end face of the cylinder block **(see illustration)**.

14 Insert the bolts and working in the sequence shown **(see illustration)**, tighten

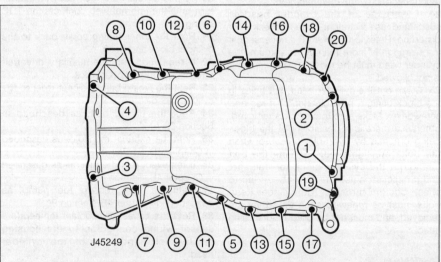

11.14 Sump bolt tightening sequence

sump retaining bolts, to the torque setting given in the Specifications.

15 Refit the four remaining bolts from the sump to the lower part of the transmission and tighten them to the specified torque setting.

16 Refit the oil level sensor and clip the fuel drain/overflow pipe back in position under the sump.

17 Refit the engine rear lower mounting (torque link) and tighten the bolts to the specified torque.

18 Refit the right-hand front wheel arch liner panel.

19 Refit the engine compartment undertray and right-hand front road wheel, and then lower the car to the ground. Tighten the wheel bolts to the specified torque setting.

20 Reconnect the battery negative lead (refer to *Disconnecting the battery* in the Reference Section).

21 Fill the engine with fresh engine oil, with reference to Chapter 1B, Section 3. Note: Wait at least 30mins after the sump has been fitted, before refilling with engine oil.

22 Start the engine and warm it up to normal operating temperature, check for any leaks from the sump area.

12 Oil pump and sprockets
– removal, inspection and refitting
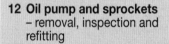

Removal

1 Remove the sump as described in Section 11.

2 Unscrew the two mounting bolts and withdraw the oil pump, tilting it to disengage its sprocket from the drive chain **(see illustrations)**. If the two locating dowels are displaced, refit them in their locations.

3 To remove the drive chain, first remove the crankshaft sprocket as described in Section 7, then unbolt the crankshaft seal end cover from the cylinder block. Where applicable, recover the gasket and discard, as a new one will be required on refitting.

4 Prise out the oil seal with a screwdriver, and discard it as a new one must be fitted on reassembly. If necessary, the new oil seal may be fitted with the right-hand cover on the bench **(see illustration)**.

5 Slide the oil pump drive sprocket and drive chain from the nose of the crankshaft. Note that the drive sprocket is not keyed to the crankshaft, but relies on the pulley bolt being tightened correctly to clamp the sprocket. It is most important that the pulley bolt is correctly tightened otherwise there is the possibility of the oil pump not functioning properly.

6 Unhook the drive chain from the drive sprocket.

Inspection

7 Clean the components and carefully examine the chain, sprockets and pump for any signs of excessive wear. If evident, it is

12.2a Oil pump and mounting bolts

12.4 Fitting a new oil seal to the right-hand cover

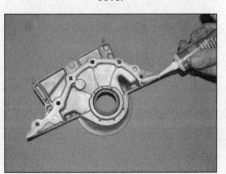

12.11b ... apply sealant to the mating faces ...

recommended that all the components be renewed as a set.

8 Before refitting the oil pump, prime it by filling with clean engine oil whilst rotating the pump clockwise.

Refitting

9 Wipe clean the oil pump and cylinder block mating surfaces and check that the two locating dowels are fitted in the cylinder block.

10 Engage the drive chain with the drive sprocket, then slide the sprocket onto the nose of the crankshaft.

11 Fit new gasket to the end of the cylinder block and refit the crankshaft seal end cover, insert the bolts and tighten them to the specified torque setting. If a new oil seal has already been fitted to the cover, wrap tape around the nose of the crankshaft to protect the oil seal, and then remove it on completion.

12.2b Removing the oil pump and drive chain

12.11a Wrap some tape around the nose of the crankshaft ...

12.11c ... and fit the right-hand cover

If there was no gasket fitted to the cover, apply a 2.0 mm wide bead of silicone sealant to the cover sealing face, making sure that the bead runs below the bolt holes **(see illustrations)**

12 Tilt the oil pump and engage the sprocket with the drive chain, then position it on the dowels and insert the two mounting bolts. Tighten the bolts to the specified torque.

13 Refit the sump with reference to Section 11.

13 Crankshaft oil seals –
renewal

Timing end cover oil seal

Note: *The new oil seal is extremely fragile and must only be handled by the protector.* **Do not** *touch the surface of the oil seal.*

Oil seals can be removed by drilling a small hole and inserting a self-tapping screw. A pair of grips can then be used to pull out the oil seal by pulling on the screw. If difficulty is experienced, insert two screws diagonally opposite each other.

1 Remove the crankshaft sprocket, as described in Section 7.

2 Note the fitted position of the old seal, then prise it out of the right-hand cover/housing using a screwdriver or suitable hooked instrument, taking care not to damage the surface of the crankshaft. Alternatively, the oil seal can be removed by drilling two small holes diagonally opposite each other and inserting self tapping screws in them. A pair of grips can then be used to pull out the oil seal, by pulling on each side in turn **(see Haynes Hint)**.

3 Inspect the seal rubbing surface on the crankshaft. If it is grooved or rough in the area where the old seal was fitted, the new seal should be fitted slightly less deeply, so that it rubs on an unworn part of the crankshaft surface.

4 Nissan technicians use a tool (drift set SST:KV113B0220 – Mot. 1586) to fit this oil seal. The tool consists of a threaded rod, metal tube and nut, and a machined shoulder to locate the protector/guide on. The rod is screwed into the end of the crankshaft, and the protector/guide located on the shoulder. The metal tube is then fitted against the oil seal and the nut tightened to press the seal into the right-hand cover. If the Nissan tool cannot be

13.9 Fitting a new oil seal to the flywheel end of the crankshaft

obtained, a similar tool can be made out of a threaded rod, metal tube, washer and nut.

5 Wipe clean the oil seal seating, then press the oil seal squarely into position. Note that the Nissan tool is designed to locate the seal at the original depth, however, if the crankshaft sealing surface is excessively worn, position it less deeply so that it locates on the unworn surface.

6 After fitting the oil seal, remove the protector/guide and tool.

7 Refit the crankshaft sprocket as described in Section 7.

Flywheel end oil seal

8 Remove the flywheel as described in Section 14.

9 Renew the oil seal as described in paragraphs 2 to 6 inclusive **(see illustration)**. Nissan technicians use a tool (drift set SST:KV113B0210 – Mot. 1585) to fit the flywheel end oil seal.

10 Refit the flywheel with reference to Section 14.

14 Flywheel – removal, inspection and refitting

Note: *New flywheel bolts must be used on refitting.*

Removal

1 Remove the manual transmission as described in Chapter 7A, Section 6.

2 Remove the clutch assembly as described in Chapter 6, Section 6.

3 Prevent the flywheel from turning by locking the ring gear teeth with a special tool. Alternatively, locate a long bolt in one of the engine-to-gearbox mounting bolt holes and insert a wide-bladed screwdriver or similar into the starter ring gear **(see illustrations)**.

4 Unscrew the securing bolts and withdraw the flywheel from the crankshaft. Note that the flywheel bolt holes are offset so that the flywheel can only be fitted in one position. Discard the old bolts as new ones must be used on refitting.

Inspection

5 On manual transmission models, if the flywheel's clutch mating surface is deeply scored, cracked or otherwise damaged, the flywheel must be renewed. Seek the advice of a Nissan dealer or engine reconditioning specialist.

6 If the ring gear is badly worn or has missing teeth, it must be renewed. Check with your Nissan dealer or engine reconditioning specialist, to see if the flywheel can be repaired.

Refitting

7 Clean the flywheel and crankshaft faces, and then coat the locating face on the crankshaft with Loctite Autoform, or an equivalent compound.

8 Locate the flywheel on the crankshaft and insert the new securing bolts, then tighten them in a diagonal sequence to the specified torque. Hold the flywheel stationary as during removal **(see illustration)**. **Do not** oil the new bolt threads as they are supplied with locking compound.

9 Refit the clutch as described in Chapter 6, Section 6.

10 Remove the locking tool (where used), and refit the transmission as described in Chapter 7A, Section 6.

15 Engine/transmission mountings – inspection and renewal

Inspection

1 If improved access is required, firmly apply the handbrake, and then jack up the

14.3a Using a home made tool to prevent the flywheel from turning ...

14.3b ... or hold the flywheel stationary using a screwdriver in the starter ring gear

14.8 Fit new flywheel bolts

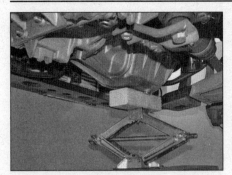

15.6 Support the engine with a suitable jack

15.7 Remove the filter support bracket

15.8a Unclip the fuel lines ...

front of the vehicle and support it securely on axle stands (see *Jacking and vehicle support*).

2 Check the mounting rubber to see if it is cracked, hardened or separated from the metal at any point; renew the mounting if any such damage or deterioration is evident.

3 Check that all the mounting's fasteners are securely tightened; use a torque wrench to check if possible.

4 Using a large screwdriver or a crowbar, check for wear in the mounting by carefully levering against it to check for free play. Where this is not possible, enlist the aid of an assistant to move the engine/transmission back-and-forth, or from side-to-side, while you watch the mounting. While some free play is to be expected even from new components, excessive wear should be obvious. If excessive free play is found, check first that the fasteners are correctly secured, and then

renew any worn components as described below.

Renewal

Right-hand mounting

5 Disconnect the battery negative terminal (refer to *Disconnecting the battery* in the Reference Chapter).

6 Place a jack beneath the engine, with a block of wood on the jack head. Raise the jack until it is supporting the weight of the engine **(see illustration)**.

7 To make access easier, remove the fuel filter and support bracket **(see illustration)**, as described in Chapter 1B, Section 21.

8 Unclip the fuel lines then slacken the securing bolt and disconnect the earth wire and bracket from the top of the engine mounting bracket **(see illustrations)**.

9 Slacken the retaining bolts and remove

the torque link from the rear of the engine mounting **(see illustration)**.

10 Slacken and remove the three retaining bolts from the inner wing panel, remove the three retaining bolts from the engine mounting bracket, and then withdraw the complete mounting from the engine compartment **(see illustrations)**.

11 Check carefully for signs of wear or damage on all components, and renew them where necessary.

12 On refitting, fit the engine mounting and bracket to the inner wing panel and engine, and then securely tighten its retaining bolts to the specified torque setting.

13 Refit the torque link to the rear of the engine mounting and tighten the retaining bolts to the specified torque setting.

14 With the engine mounting back in position, refit the fuel filter and mounting bracket as described in Chapter 1B, Section 21

15 Lower the jack and remove it from underneath the engine.

16 Reconnect the earth cable and bracket to the top of the engine mounting and secure the fuel lines back in the clips, and then reconnect the battery negative terminal.

Left-hand mounting

17 Remove the battery and tray, as described in Chapter 5A, Section 3.

18 Place a jack and block of wood beneath the transmission, and raise the jack to take the weight of the transmission **(see illustration)**.

19 Slacken and remove the through-bolt/stud retaining nut from the centre of the mounting,

15.8b ... and unbolt the bracket from the mounting

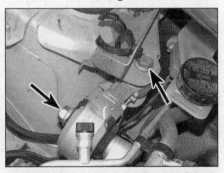

15.9 Unbolt the torque link (arrowed) from the rear of the bulkhead

15.10a Unbolt the inner wing panel bolts ...

15.10b ... and the engine mounting bolts

15.18 Support the transmission with a trolley jack

15.19 Undo the centre retaining nut and remove vibration damper

15.20 Undo the two outer securing nuts and remove the mounting

15.22 Remove the mounting bracket from the transmission

and (where fitted) the vibration damper **(see illustration)**.

20 Slacken and remove the two outer retaining nuts, and withdraw the mounting from the upper mounting bracket **(see illustration)**.

21 If required, undo the retaining bolts from the inner wing panel to remove the upper mounting bracket.

15.30 Remove the torque link arm bolts

22 Also, if required, undo the retaining bolts from the transmission to remove the lower mounting bracket **(see illustration)**.

23 Check carefully for signs of wear or damage on all components, and renew them where necessary.

24 On refitting, fit the upper and lower mounting brackets (where removed) and securely tighten the retaining bolts.

25 Align the left-hand rubber mounting with the bolt/stud on the lower mounting bracket and tighten its nut to the specified torque setting.

26 Refit the two outer retaining nuts, and tighten to the specified torque setting.

27 With the transmission mounting back in position, lower the jack and remove it from underneath the transmission.

28 Refit the battery and battery tray, with reference to Chapter 5, Section 3.

Rear lower mounting

29 If not already done, firmly apply the handbrake, and then jack up the front of the

vehicle and support it securely on axle stands (see *Jacking and vehicle support*). Remove engine undertray.

30 Slacken and remove the bolts securing the rear mounting link to the subframe and the mounting bracket, and then withdraw the mounting link from under the vehicle **(see illustration)**.

31 If required, slacken and remove the three bolts securing the rear mounting bracket to the sump, and then withdraw the bracket from under the vehicle.

32 Check carefully for signs of wear or damage on all components, and renew them where necessary.

33 Refit the mounting bracket to the rear of the sump housing and tighten its retaining bolts to the specified torque.

34 Fit the rear mounting link to the mounting bracket and subframe, and then tighten the retaining bolts to the specified torque.

35 With the transmission rear mounting link arm back in position, lower the vehicle to the ground.

Chapter 2 Part D:
2.0 litre diesel engine in-car repair procedures

Contents

Degrees of difficulty

Easy, suitable for novice with little experience	Fairly easy, suitable for beginner with some experience	Fairly difficult, suitable for competent DIY mechanic	Difficult, suitable for experienced DIY mechanic	Very difficult, suitable for expert DIY or professional

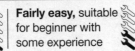

Specifications

General

Type	Four-cylinder, in-line, double overhead camshaft, 16-valve
Designation	M9R
Output:	
Euro 4	146bhp
Euro 5 'Pure Drive' version.	148bhp
Bore	84.0 mm
Stroke	90.0 mm
Capacity.	1995 cc
Compression ratio	15.6:1
Firing order.	1-3-4-2 (No 1 cylinder at flywheel end of engine)
Direction of crankshaft rotation	Clockwise, viewed from timing chain end

Compression pressures

Engine warm – approximately 80°C:

Standard pressure	26 bars
Minimum pressure	21 bars
Maximum difference between cylinders.	5 bars

Camshafts

Drive.	Timing chain to exhaust camshaft sprocket
Number of bearings on each	6
Camshaft endfloat	0.05 to 0.13 mm

Lubrication system

Minimum oil pressure at 80°C:

At 800 rpm	0.9 bars (13.3 psi)
At 3000 rpm	4.0 bars (58.0 psi)

Torque wrench settings

	Nm	lbf ft
Balancer shaft unit:		
Stage 1	15	11
Stage 2	Angle-tighten through 85° ± 5°	
Camshaft bearing caps	10	7
Camshaft housing	12	9
Connecting rod (big-end) cap bolts:		
Stage 1	25	18
Stage 2	Angle-tighten through 55° ± 6°	
Crankshaft main bearing cap bolts:		
Stage 1	20	15
Stage 2	Angle-tighten through 70° ± 6°	
Crankshaft oil seal:		
Timing end	47	35
Transmission end:		
Stage 1	5	4
Stage 2	10	7
Crankshaft position ring to crankshaft:		
Stage 1	3	2
Stage 2	20	15
Crankshaft pulley bolt:		
Stage 1	50	37
Stage 2	Angle-tighten through 85° ± 6°	
Cylinder block baseplate	25	18
Cylinder head bolts*:		
Stage 1	5	4
Stage 2	30	22
Stage 3	Angle-tighten through 300° ± 6°	
Exhaust camshaft sprocket to timing gear:		
Stage 1	10	7
Stage 2	Angle-tighten through 40° ± 6°	
Flywheel (dual mass) bolts*:		
Stage 1	25	18
Stage 2	Angle-tighten through 45° ± 6°	
High-pressure pump drivegear to exhaust camshaft:		
Stage 1	40	30
Stage 2	Angle-tighten through 34° ± 6°	
High-pressure pump sprocket	90	66
Inlet manifold	25	18
Inlet timing gear:		
Stage 1	20	15
Stage 2	Angle-tighten through 35° ± 6°	
Left-hand transmission mounting:		
Mounting-to-bracket bolts	110	81
Mounting bracket-to-inner wing panel bolts	80	59
Mounting bracket-to-transmission bolts	45	33
Main timing chain tensioner guide	25	18
Oil cooler/filter housing to block:		
Stage 1	5	4
Stage 2	25	18
Oil level dipstick guide tube	10	7
Oil level sensor	25	18
Oil pressure sensor	30	22
Oil pump strainer	10	7
Oil pump to cylinder block:		
Stage 1	5	4
Stage 2	25	18
Oil separator	12	9
Oil splash plate to oil pump	10	7
Rear lower engine torque/link arm mounting:		
Torque link arm to front subframe bolt	110	81
Torque link arm to mounting bracket bolt	155	114
Mounting bracket-to-sump bolts	80	59
Right-hand engine mounting:		
Alloy mounting bracket to cylinder head mounting bracket	55	41
Mounting bracket bolts to inner wing	55	41
Reinforcement bracket	45	33
Torque arm mounting bolts	130	96

Torque wrench settings (continued)	Nm	lbf ft
Static timing chain guide:		
Stage 1	5	4
Stage 2	25	18
Sump:		
Stage 1	5	4
Stage 2	16	12
TDC setting pin hole plug	25	18
Timing chain hydraulic tensioner	10	7
Timing cover bolts:		
Stage 1	5	4
Stage 2:		
M8 bolt	18	13
M6 bolt	16	12
Turbocharger outlet air duct bolt on the inlet manifold	8	6
Turbocharger pressure sensor nut on damper valve	8	6

* New bolts must be used.

1 General information

How to use this Chapter

1 This Part of Chapter 2 is devoted to in-car repair procedures for the 2.0 litre diesel engine. Similar information covering the other engine types can be found in Parts A, B and C. All procedures concerning engine removal and refitting, and engine block/cylinder head overhaul can be found in Part E of this Chapter.

2 Refer to *Vehicle identification numbers* in the Reference Section at the end of this manual for details of engine code locations.

3 Most of the operations included in this Part are based on the assumption that the engine is still installed in the car. Therefore, if this information is being used during a complete engine overhaul, with the engine already removed, many of the steps included here will not apply.

Engine description

4 The engine is a four-cylinder overhead camshaft 16-valve design, mounted transversely at the front of the vehicle with the transmission bolted to the left-hand side. The power steering pump, coolant pump, alternator and air conditioning compressor are driven by the auxiliary drivebelt. The brake servo vacuum pump is driven directly by the exhaust camshaft at the flywheel end.

5 The crankshaft is supported in five shell-type main bearings. Thrustwashers are fitted to No 2 main bearing to control crankshaft endfloat. The connecting rods are attached to the crankshaft by horizontally split shell-type big-end bearings, and to the pistons by gudgeon pins. The gudgeon pins are a sliding fit in the connecting rods and are retained by circlips. The aluminium alloy pistons are of the slipper type, and are fitted with three piston rings – two compression rings and a scraper-type oil control ring.

6 The double overhead camshafts are mounted in the cylinder head, and are driven by a timing chain direct from the crankshaft to the exhaust camshaft sprocket. The inlet camshaft is driven by gear direct from the exhaust camshaft at the timing end. The high-pressure fuel pump is gear-driven from the flywheel-end of the inlet camshaft.

7 The camshaft operates the 16 valves, which are mounted in the cylinder head, through rocker arms situated directly above the camshaft. Automatic adjustment of the valve-to-rocker arm clearance is provided by hydraulic lifters located in the cylinder head.

8 A balancer shaft unit is bolted to the crankcase and driven by gear direct from the crankshaft. The unit incorporates two shafts with counter-weights that rotate in opposite directions in order to minimise vertical oscillation of the engine caused by the pistons and connecting rods.

9 A dual-mass flywheel acts as an acoustic filter to reduce boom at low engine speeds.

10 Engine lubrication is by pressure feed from a gear-type oil pump, chain-driven off the timing end of the crankshaft. Engine oil is fed through an externally mounted oil filter and oil cooler to the main oil gallery feeding the crankshaft and camshaft. The oil cooler helps keep the oil temperature constant under arduous operating conditions.

Operations with engine in car

11 The following operations can be carried out without having to remove the engine from the vehicle:

a) *Removal and refitting of the crankshaft pulley.*

b) *Removal and refitting of the sump.*

c) *Removal and refitting of the oil pump.*

d) *Removal and refitting of the cylinder block baseplate.*

e) *Removal and refitting of the big-end bearings, connecting rods, and pistons.* *

f) *Removal and refitting of the balancer shaft unit.*

g) *Renewal of the crankshaft oil seals.*

h) *Removal and refitting of the flywheel.*

i) *Renewal of the engine/transmission mountings.*

* Although the operation marked with an asterisk can be carried out with the engine in the car after removal of the sump and baseplate, it is better for the engine to be removed, in the interests of cleanliness and improved access. For this reason, the procedure is described in Chapter 2E.

2 Compression test – description and interpretation

Refer to Chapter 2C, Section 2.

3 Top Dead Centre (TDC) for No 1 piston – locating

1 Top dead centre (TDC) is the highest point in the cylinder that each piston reaches as the crankshaft turns. Each piston reaches TDC at the end of the compression stroke and again at the end of the exhaust stroke. However, for the purpose of timing the engine, TDC refers to the position of No 1 piston at the end of its compression stroke. No 1 piston is at the flywheel end of the engine.

2 Disconnect the battery negative terminal (refer to *Disconnecting the battery* in the Reference Section of this manual).

3 Apply the handbrake, and then jack up the front of the car and support it on axle stands (see *Jacking and vehicle support*). Remove the right-hand roadwheel.

4 Remove the engine undertray and the right-hand wheel arch liner in order to gain access to the crankshaft pulley bolt.

5 To facilitate turning the engine easily, remove the glow plugs as described in Chapter 5C, Section 3.

6 With the help of an assistant and using a socket on the crankshaft pulley bolt, turn the engine clockwise until pressure can be felt in the No 1 glow plug hole, indicating that the No 1 piston is rising on its compression stroke.

7 Continue to turn the crankshaft clockwise until the pressure in No 1 cylinder ceases,

3.8a Unscrew the TDC plug . . .

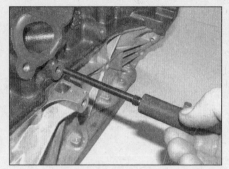

3.8b . . . then insert the crankshaft TDC
setting tool . . .

3.8c . . . and tighten securely

then turn the crankshaft an additional quarter turn so the piston is approximately midway down its bore.

8 Unscrew the TDC plug from the front of the cylinder block and insert Nissan TDC tool Mot 1766, tightening it securely **(see illustrations)**.

9 Turn the crankshaft anti-clockwise until it just contacts the TDC tool.

10 The engine is now positioned with No 1 piston at TDC on its compression stroke. For further information on setting the timing up see timing chain removal and refitting in Section 5.

Caution: Do not attempt to rotate the engine whilst the crankshaft and camshaft timing pins are in position. If the engine is to be left in this state for a long period of time, it is a good idea to place suitable warning notices inside the vehicle, and in the engine compartment. This will reduce the possibility of the engine being accidentally cranked on the starter motor, which would cause considerable damage.

4 Crankshaft pulley –
removal and refitting

Removal

1 Disconnect the battery negative terminal (refer to *Disconnecting the battery* in the Reference Section of this manual). Apply the handbrake, and then jack up the front of the car and support it on axle stands (see *Jacking*

and vehicle support). Remove the right-hand roadwheel.

2 Unbolt and remove the plastic undertray from the beneath the engine/transmission and the wheel arch liner from within the right-hand wheel arch.

3 Unbolt and remove the tie-bar fitted between the underbody and front subframe.

4 Remove the auxiliary drivebelt as described in Chapter 1B, Section 11.

5 Slacken the crankshaft pulley retaining bolt. To prevent crankshaft rotation whilst the retaining bolt is slackened, select 4th gear and have an assistant apply the brakes firmly. If this fails to prevent rotation, lock the flywheel ring gear; the starter motor may need to be removed to access the flywheel ring gear. *Do not* be tempted to use the crankshaft timing pin to prevent the crankshaft from rotating (see Section 3).

6 Remove the retaining bolt, spacer and pulley from the end of the crankshaft **(see illustrations)**.

Refitting

7 Remove all traces of locking compound from the crankshaft threads.

8 Clean the threads of the crankshaft pulley retaining bolt and apply a few drops of thread locking compound.

9 Refit the pulley to the crankshaft followed by the spacer, then screw in the retaining bolt. Tighten the bolt first to the specified Stage 1 torque and then through the specified Stage 2 angle, using the method employed on removal to prevent rotation **(see illustration)**.

10 Refit the auxiliary drivebelt as described in Chapter 1B, Section 11.

11 Refit the subframe-to-underbody tie-bar and tighten the bolts.

12 Refit the wheel arch liner and roadwheel, and lower the car to the ground.

5 Timing chain, sprockets and
guides – removal, inspection
and refitting

Note: *Removal of the engine from the car is necessary in order to carry out the procedure in this Section. Also, special Nissan tool Mot. 1766 is required to set the engine to TDC, and tool Mot. 1769 to tighten the exhaust camshaft sprocket bolts. When renewing the timing chain, Nissan recommend renewal of the sprockets, guides and the hydraulic tensioner at the same time.*

Removal

1 Remove the engine and gearbox assembly as described in Chapter 2E and place on a workbench. If not already done, drain the engine oil.

2 Remove the auxiliary drivebelt as described in Chapter 1B, Section 11.

3 Remove the coolant pump as described in Chapter 3, Section 7.

4 Remove the crankshaft pulley as described in Section 4.

5 A new crankshaft oil seal will be required for refitting, so it is recommended that the old one is removed from the timing cover now as described in Section 14.

4.6a Unscrew and remove the crankshaft
pulley bolt and spacer . . .

4.6b . . . then remove the pulley

4.9 Angle-tightening the crankshaft pulley
bolt

5.7 Right-hand engine mounting bracket

5.9 Removing the timing cover

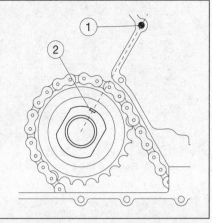

5.11 Align the groove (2) in the crankshaft nose with the bolt hole (1) on the cylinder block to position the pistons half way up the cylinder bores

6 From the right-hand top of the cylinder head, unbolt the engine mounting reinforcement bracket.

7 Unbolt the right-hand engine mounting bracket from the engine **(see illustration)**.

8 Progressively unscrew the bolts securing the timing cover to the engine, including the bolt concealed in the hole where the engine mounting bracket was fitted. Note the location of the M8 bolt at the bottom of the engine.

9 Ease the timing cover away while cutting the silicone sealant/adhesive to release it **(see illustration)**. This is a very difficult and time consuming job, however methodical use of a suitable spatula or thin knife will eventually release the cover.

10 If fitted, remove the crankshaft/flywheel locking device used in the crankshaft pulley removal procedure.

11 Using a spanner on the crankshaft nose flats, turn the crankshaft **clockwise** until the crankshaft groove is aligned with the bolt hole on the cylinder block **(see illustration)**. This will position the pistons half way up the cylinder bores.

12 Unscrew the TDC plug/bolt from the front of the cylinder block and insert Nissan TDC tool Mot. 1766, tightening it securely.

13 Turn the crankshaft **anti-clockwise** until it

just contacts the TDC tool. The engine is now set with No 1 piston at TDC on its compression stroke

14 If the timing chain is to be re-used, mark it with a dab of paint to ensure it is refitted the same way round. Loosen only the three exhaust camshaft sprocket retaining bolts.

15 Compress the timing chain hydraulic tensioner piston by pressing the guide, then lock it by inserting a 3.0 mm diameter Allen key or pin in the hole provided **(see illustration)**.

16 Unscrew the bolts and remove the tensioner **(see illustration)**.

17 Unscrew the single bolt and remove the dynamic tensioner guide **(see illustrations)**.

18 Completely remove the three exhaust camshaft sprocket bolts, remove the special washer and withdraw the sprocket and chain from the camshaft. If available, use the Nissan

5.15 Locking the hydraulic tensioner piston in its retracted position with a 3.0 mm rod

5.16 Removing the hydraulic tensioner

5.17a Unscrew the bolt . . .

5.17b . . . and remove the dynamic tensioner guide

5.18a Remove the bolts . . .

5.18b . . . and special washer . . .

5.18c . . . and withdraw the sprocket and chain from the exhaust camshaft

5.19 Removing the timing chain sprocket from the nose of the crankshaft

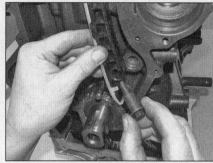

5.20 Removing the static timing chain guide

tool Mot. 1769 to hold the sprocket stationary. Release the timing chain from the camshaft and crankshaft sprockets **(see illustrations)**.
19 Withdraw the sprocket from the nose of the crankshaft **(see illustration)**.
20 Unbolt and remove the static timing chain guide **(see illustration)**.
21 Unscrew and remove the TDC tool from the front of the cylinder block.

Inspection

22 Thoroughly clean then visually inspect all parts for wear and damage. Check the timing chain for loose pins, cracks, worn rollers and side plates. Check the sprockets for hook-shaped, chipped and broken teeth. Also check the timing chain for wear by extending it horizontally, holding each end and attempting to flex the chain. Renew the timing chain and sprockets as a set if the engine has high mileage or fails inspection. Check the chain guides for excessive wear and scoring and renew them if necessary. Note that some scoring is normal but if they are deeply grooved they must be renewed.

Refitting

23 Carefully clean the surfaces of the timing cover, cylinder block and cylinder head, taking care not to damage the surfaces.
24 Check that the engine is still set to its TDC position as described in Section 3 using the TDC setting tool Mot 1766.
25 Position the timing mark on the inlet camshaft timing gear at 12 o'clock and align it with the boss on the camshaft housing. Make sure that the groove on the exhaust camshaft is horizontal with the larger offset uppermost **(see illustration)**.
26 Refit the static timing chain guide and tighten the bolts to the specified torque.
27 Locate the timing chain on the crankshaft sprocket so that the copper link is aligned with the timing mark, and then locate the sprocket on the nose of the crankshaft. Raise the chain to keep it engaged with the crankshaft sprocket while locating it onto the rigid tensioner guide, and then locate the exhaust camshaft sprocket in the upper loop so that the copper link aligns with the TDC hole in the sprocket **(see illustrations)**. **Note:** *A new timing chain may be fitted either way round,*

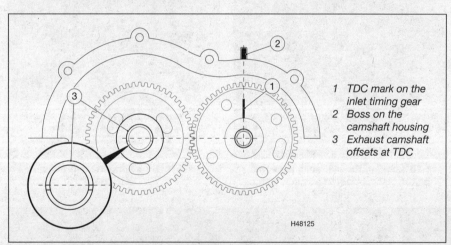

1 TDC mark on the inlet timing gear
2 Boss on the camshaft housing
3 Exhaust camshaft offsets at TDC

H48125

5.25 Setting the camshafts to TDC

5.27a Align the copper link with the TDC mark on the crankshaft sprocket . . .

5.27b . . . then fit the exhaust camshaft sprocket with the copper link aligned with the TDC hole

5.34 Angle-tightening the exhaust camshaft sprocket bolts

5.35 Refitting the TDC hole plug

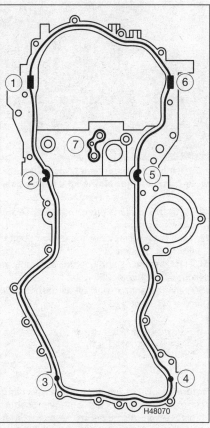

5.36a Sealant application for the timing cover

however a re-used chain should be fitted in its original position as noted during removal.

28 Fit the exhaust camshaft sprocket onto its timing gear.

29 Locate the new special washer and bolts on the exhaust camshaft timing gear and finger-tighten the bolts at this stage. The sprocket must be free to rotate within the elongated holes

30 Locate the dynamic tensioner guide in position and tighten the single bolt.

31 Refit the hydraulic tensioner together with locking Allen key, insert the bolts and tighten to the specified torque. Make sure the tensioner is in contact with the cylinder block before tightening the bolts.

32 Remove the locking Allen key or pin to allow the tensioner piston to tension the timing chain.

33 At this stage Nissan tool Mot. 1769 is required to hold the gears and sprocket in position while the exhaust sprocket bolts are tightened. Engage the tool with the slot on the end of the exhaust camshaft then turn the tool until it is possible to locate the dowels in the inlet camshaft timing gear. Insert the bolt through the top of the tool and tighten into the hole in the camshaft housing.

34 Tighten the exhaust camshaft sprocket bolts in the two stages given in Specifications.

The special tool has a hole for access to one of the bolts **(see illustration)**.

35 Remove tool Mot. 1769 and the TDC tool. Apply locking fluid to the threads of the TDC hole plug, then insert and tighten it to the specified torque **(see illustration)**.

36 Apply a bead of silicone adhesive/sealant to the timing cover contact face on the engine of the dimensions shown **(see illustrations)**.

37 Refit the timing cover and finger-tighten the bolts, then tighten them in the two stages given in Specifications starting at the bottom right M8 bolt and working in an anti-clockwise direction so that the final bolt to tighten is the M6 bolt.

38 Refit the right-hand engine mounting bracket and finger-tighten the bolts. Tighten the lower 5 bolts to the torque given in Specifications starting at the upper front bolt and working in a clockwise direction. Finally, tighten the upper rear bolt to the torque given in Specifications.

39 Refit the engine mounting reinforcement bracket and finger-tighten the bolts, then tighten them to the specified torque.

40 Fit a new crankshaft oil seal as described in Section 14.

41 Refit the crankshaft pulley as described in Section 4.

Bead diameter 5 ± 2 mm from points 1 to 6 passing around the lower part of the engine

Bead diameter 11 ± 2 mm for a length of 10 to 15 mm on points 1, 2, 3, 4, 5, 6

Bead diameter 3.5 ± 1 mm from points 6 to 1 passing around the upper part of the cylinder head

Bead diameter 3.5 ± 1 mm around the inner edge 7

5.36b Apply a bead of silicone adhesive/sealant to the timing cover contact face . . .

5.36c . . . including the central 'island'

6.7 Using the Nissan bench tool to set the wear compensator on the inlet timing gear

6.8 Locate the inlet timing gear on the inlet camshaft . . .

6.9 . . . and fit the spacer and bolt

42 Refit the coolant pump as described in Chapter 3, Section 7.
43 Refit the auxiliary drivebelt as described in Chapter 1B, Section 11.
44 Refit the engine and gearbox assembly as described in Chapter 2E.
45 Refill the engine with oil as described in Chapter 1B, Section 3.

6 Timing gears – removal, inspection and refitting

Note: *Removal of the engine from the car is necessary in order to carry out the procedure in this Section. Also, special Nissan tool Mot. 1769 is required to lock the camshaft gears, and tool Mot. 1773 to set the inlet camshaft timing gear automatic play compensator. The gear is in two parts, which are spring-loaded to keep the gear teeth accurately engaged.*

Removal

1 Remove the timing chain, sprockets and guides as described in Section 5.
2 Fit tool Mot. 1769 to hold the inlet timing gear stationary, then loosen the bolt securing the timing gear to the inlet camshaft.

3 Remove the tool, then insert a screwdriver in the inlet timing gear special hole, and compress the wear compensation spring by lifting the screwdriver in order to release it from the exhaust timing gear.
4 Slide the exhaust timing gear from the exhaust camshaft extension and release the screwdriver from the inlet timing gear.
5 Completely unscrew the inlet timing gear bolt and remove the spacer followed by the timing gear.

Inspection

6 Thoroughly clean then visually inspect the timing gears for wear and damage. Check for chipped and broken gear teeth and renew the gears if necessary.

Refitting

7 Before the inlet timing gear can be refitted, the wear compensation spring must be compressed and a 4.0 mm diameter pin inserted in the special hole to lock it. Moderate force is necessary to compress the spring and it is recommended that Nissan bench tool Mot. 1773 be used to carry out the work safely, however a similar home-made tool may be used. Clamp the baseplate of the tool in a vice and locate the inlet timing gear on it

making sure that the key is engaged to lock it. Now locate the tool lever on its pivot and tighten the wing nut. Engage the lever teeth with the lower wear compensation teeth and turn the lever anti-clockwise until the wear compensation teeth are aligned with the gear teeth. Lock the two gear sections in this position using a 4.0 mm diameter pin inserted in the special hole **(see illustration)**. **Note:** *New inlet timing gears are supplied with a plastic locking pin already fitted.*
8 Remove the inlet timing gear from the tool and locate it on the inlet camshaft **(see illustration)**.
9 Refit the spacer and finger-tighten the bolt **(see illustration)**.
10 Position the timing mark on the inlet camshaft timing gear at 12 o'clock and align it with the boss on the camshaft housing. Make sure that the groove on the exhaust camshaft is horizontal with the larger offset uppermost.
11 Offer the exhaust camshaft timing gear onto the camshaft so that the mounting holes are central within the gear elongated slots, then engage the gear teeth with the inlet timing gear and press it fully into position **(see illustrations)**.
12 Check the alignment of the inlet timing gear with the boss, and the exhaust timing

6.11a Locate the exhaust timing gear on the exhaust camshaft . . .

6.11b . . . so that the mounting holes are central within the gear elongated slots

6.12 Removing the locking pin from the inlet timing gear

6.13a Hold the gear with the special Nissan tool, then tighten the bolt to the specified torque . . .

gear with the camshaft slots, then remove the locking pin from the inlet timing gear **(see illustration)**.

13 The inlet timing gear bolt must now be tightened. Fit Nissan tool Mot. 1769 to hold the gear then tighten the bolt in the two stages given in Specifications. Remove the tool **(see illustrations)**.

14 Refit the timing chain, sprockets and guides as described in Section 5.

7 Camshafts – removal, inspection and refitting

Note: *Removal of the engine from the car is necessary in order to carry out the procedure in this Section.*

Removal

1 Remove the timing chain, sprockets and gears as described in Section 5 and Section 6. This involves removal of the engine from the car.

2 Remove the intercooler air inlet pipe by disconnecting the end fittings and unscrewing the mounting bolts, then remove the protector seat **(see illustrations)**.

3 Remove the brake vacuum pump as described in Chapter 9, Section 13.

4 Remove the high-pressure pipe between the pump and fuel rail, and the exhaust gas pressure sensor as described in Chapter 4B, Section 10.

5 Unbolt and remove the injector cover then the oil separator from the top of the engine **(see illustrations)**.

6 Remove the injector fuel return rail, the high-pressure pipes between the rail and injectors, then the injectors as described in Chapter 4B, Section 11.

7 Unscrew the bolts and remove the fuel

6.13b . . . and angle

7.2a Disconnect the intercooler air inlet pipe end fittings . . .

7.2b . . . note the O-ring seals inside the pipe end fittings

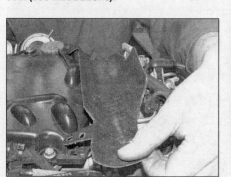

7.2c Removing the intercooler air inlet pipe protector seat

7.5a Removing the injector cover . . .

7.5b . . . and the oil separator from the top of the engine

7.9a Inlet camshaft bearing cap marking

7.9b Exhaust camshaft bearing cap marking

collector outlet pipe from the rear of the cylinder head.

8 Progressively unscrew the camshaft housing retaining bolts then carefully remove the housing complete with camshafts from the top of the cylinder head. If necessary, use a screwdriver and block of wood to lever the housing but take care not to damage the joint faces of the housing and cylinder head. There is no need to remove the camshaft followers and hydraulic tappets from the cylinder head.

9 With the housing upside down on the workbench, note the location of the inlet and exhaust camshafts, and the marks on the bearing caps to identify their position. The caps are marked ADM1 and ADM2 for the inlet camshaft, and ECH1 and ECH2 for the exhaust camshaft **(see illustrations)**.

10 Progressively unscrew the bolts, remove the bearing caps and lift the camshafts from the housing **(see illustrations)**.

11 If the exhaust camshaft is to be renewed, remove the high-pressure pump drivegear from it as follows **(see illustration)**. Grip the gear in a vice equipped with soft metal plates to protect the gear, then loosen the bolt, support the camshaft and fully unscrew the bolt.

Inspection

12 Thoroughly clean all components taking care to remove all traces of sealant from the joint faces.

13 Examine the camshaft bearing surfaces and cam lobes for signs of wear ridges and scoring. Renew the camshaft if any of these conditions are apparent. Examine the condition of the bearing surfaces, both on the camshaft journals and in the cylinder head/bearing caps/housing. If the bearing surfaces are worn excessively, the cylinder head, camshafts and housing will need to be renewed. Check the teeth of the high-pressure pump drivegear for wear and chipping, and if necessary renew the gear.

Refitting

14 If removed, refit the high-pressure pump drivegear by gripping it in the soft metal jawed vice, locating the camshaft from beneath, then screwing on the bolt. Tighten the bolt in the stages given in Specifications.

15 Lubricate the bearing surfaces with clean engine oil then locate the camshafts in the housing in their previously-noted positions **(see illustration)**.

16 Refit the bearing caps, making sure they make contact with the housing before inserting the bolts finger-tight. Finally, tighten the bolts to their specified torque.

17 The camshafts must now be set to their TDC positions. Temporarily place the housing on the bench in its normal position with the camshafts facing downward. Turn the exhaust camshaft as necessary so that the timing end grooves are horizontal with the larger offset uppermost. Turn the inlet camshaft as necessary so that the timing mark is at 12 o'clock and aligned with the boss on the camshaft housing **(see illustration)**.

18 Ensure the contact faces are clean, then apply a bead of silicone 1.5 ± 1.0 mm in diameter around the edges and central 'islands' of the cylinder head upper face.

7.10a Removing the camshaft bearing caps

7.10b Removing the inlet camshaft . . .

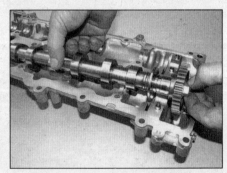

7.10c . . . and exhaust camshaft

7.11 High-pressure pump drivegear on the exhaust camshaft

7.15 Oil the bearing surfaces before fitting the camshafts

7.17 Camshafts set to their TDC positions

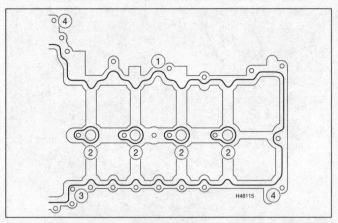

7.18a Silicone adhesive/sealant application to the cylinder head

1 *Exhaust side bead*
2 *Central 'islands'*
3 *Inlet side bead*
4 *Locations for guide studs*

7.18b Apply sealant to the edges . . .

7.18c . . . and central 'islands' of the cylinder head upper face

7.19 Use two M6 studs as guides when refitting the camshaft housing

7.21 Locating the camshaft housing on the cylinder head

Make sure the bead runs on the inner side of the outer bolt holes **(see illustrations)**.

19 To assist in locating the camshaft housing correctly on the cylinder head, temporarily screw two M6 studs, 60 mm long in the diagonally opposite holes **(see illustration)**.

20 Set the crankshaft in its TDC position with pistons 1 and 4 at the top of their cylinders.

21 Carefully locate the camshaft housing complete with camshafts onto the top of the cylinder head, making sure that the guide studs enter the correct holes before lowering it into position **(see illustration)**.

22 Referring to the diagram **(see illustration)** first insert then progressively tighten bolts 12, 15, 18 and 21 to the specified torque. Remove the two guide studs.

23 Insert the remaining retaining bolts and finger-tighten them at this stage.

24 Completely loosen bolts 12, 15, 18 and 21, then finger-tighten them.

25 Tighten the camshaft housing bolts to the specified torque in the sequence shown **(see illustration 7.22)**. Wipe away excess sealant from the outer joint face.

26 Refit the fuel collector outlet pipe and tighten the bolts.

27 Refit the injectors, high-pressure pipes and fuel return rail as described in Chapter 4B, Section 11, and then refit the injector cover to

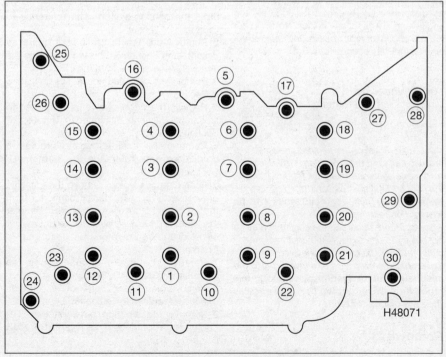

7.22 Camshaft housing bolt tightening sequence

7.27 Make sure the leak-off pipes are located correctly when refitting the injector cover

7.28a Fitting a new gasket . . .

the top of the cylinder head, making sure that the leak-off pipes are correctly located **(see illustration)**.

28 Refit the oil separator together with a new gasket and new sealing rings **(see illustrations)**.

29 Refit the high-pressure pipe between the pump and common rail, and also the exhaust gas pressure sensor, as described in Chapter 4B, Section 10.

30 Refit the brake vacuum pump as described in Chapter 9, Section 13.

31 Refit the camshaft gears, timing chain and sprockets as described in Section 6 and Section 5.

32 On completion check the engine oil level as described in *Weekly checks*. Start the engine and check for any noises. **Note:** *Do not run the engine at high speeds until the correct oil pressure has been reached.*

7.28b . . . entry sealing ring . . .

7.28c . . . and return sealing rings

8 Cylinder head – removal and refitting

Note 1: *Removal of the engine is necessary in order to carry out the procedure in this Section. Also, special Nissan tools are required to lock the inlet and exhaust camshafts.*

Note 2: *New cylinder head bolts will be required on refitting.*

Note 3: *Before restarting the engine, it may be necessary to use a diagnostic tool to clear any faults that may be stored in the injection ECU.*

Caution: Be careful not to allow dirt into the injection pump or injector pipes during this procedure. Cover or plug the open ends as they are disconnected.

Removal

1 Disconnect the battery negative terminal (refer to *Disconnecting the battery* in the Reference Section of this manual), then

drain the cooling system with reference to Chapter 1B, Section 29.

2 Remove the timing chain and gears as described in Section 5. This work involves the removal of the engine from the car.

3 Remove the camshaft housing as described in Section 7.

4 Remove the throttle valve (also referred to as damper valve) as described in Chapter 4B, Section 8.

5 Remove the exhaust gas recirculation rigid pipes with reference to Chapter 4C, Section 3.

6 According to version, remove the catalytic pre-converter or the catalytic converter from the turbocharger outlet as described in Chapter 4B, Section 17. Remove the turbocharger oil feed and return pipes as described in Chapter 4B.

7 Remove the brake vacuum pump as described in Chapter 9, Section 13.

8 Remove the oil level dipstick/filler cap then unbolt and remove the guide tube.

9 Remove the air pipe between the EGR cooler control solenoid valve and the EGR cooler.

10 Progressively slacken the cylinder head bolts by half a turn at a time until all bolts can be unscrewed by hand and removed.

11 Lift the cylinder head upwards and off the cylinder block. If it is stuck, tap it upwards using a hammer and block of wood. *Do not try to rotate it (it is located by two dowels), nor attempt to prise it free using a screwdriver inserted between the block and head faces.* If the locating dowels are a loose fit, remove them and store them with the head for safe-keeping. As the head is removed, check around the cylinder head to make sure everything has been disconnected.

12 Remove the cylinder head gasket. Note that new gaskets are supplied in two thicknesses according to engine code – the thickness is not measurable as it is defined as the 'crushed' thickness. Make sure the correct one is obtained for refitting.

13 Before removing the hydraulic tappets and rockers, have ready a container with 16 compartments and fill the container with engine oil to the depth of the tappets. **Note:** *The tappets must remain immersed in oil during the period they are removed from the cylinder head to prevent air entering them.*

14 Remove each hydraulic tappet and follower assembly and place in the container so that they can each be identified for location in the cylinder head. It is important

8.14a Hydraulic tappet and follower assembly in position

8.14b Removing the hydraulic tappet and follower assemblies

8.14c Keep the inlet and exhaust camshaft hydraulic tappet and follower assemblies identified for location and immersed in oil while removed from the cylinder head

they are each refitted to their correct bore on reassembly **(see illustrations)**.

Inspection

15 The mating faces of the cylinder head and block must be perfectly clean before refitting the head. Use a scraper (taking care not to damage the surface of the head) to remove all traces of gasket and carbon, and also clean the tops of the pistons. Take particular care with the aluminium cylinder head, as the soft metal is damaged easily. Also, make sure that debris is not allowed to enter the oil and water channels – this is particularly important for the oil circuit, as carbon could block the oil supply to the camshaft or crankshaft bearings. Using adhesive tape and paper, seal the water, oil and bolt holes in the cylinder block. To prevent carbon entering the gap between the pistons and bores, smear a little grease in the gap. After cleaning the piston, rotate the crankshaft so that the piston moves down the bore, and then wipe out the grease and carbon with a cloth rag. Clean the piston crowns in the same way.

16 Check the block and head for nicks, deep scratches and other damage. If slight, they may be removed carefully with a file. More serious damage may be repaired by machining, but this is a specialist job.

17 If warpage of the cylinder head is suspected, use a straight-edge to check it for distortion. Refer to Chapter 2E if necessary.

18 Ensure that the cylinder head bolt holes in the block are clean and free of oil. Syringe or soak up any oil left in the bolt holes. This is most important in order that the correct bolt tightening torque can be applied and to prevent the possibility of the block being cracked by hydraulic pressure when the bolts are tightened.

19 Examine the cylinder head bolt threads in the cylinder block for damage. If necessary, use the correct-size tap to chase out the threads in the block, and use a die to clean the threads on the bolts. The cylinder head bolts must be discarded and renewed, regardless of their apparent condition. Also, check that the locating dowels are in good condition and correctly located in the cylinder block **(see illustration)**.

Refitting

20 Ensure that the mating faces of the cylinder block and head are spotlessly clean,

that the retaining bolt threads are also clean and dry, and that they screw easily in and out of their locations.

21 Ensure that the locating dowels are correctly fitted to the block, and then apply 2 drops of silicone adhesive/sealant (5 to 7 mm diameter) to the surface of the two extremities at the timing end of the block **(see illustration)**.

22 Locate the new cylinder head gasket on the block; then again apply 2 drops of silicone adhesive/sealant (5 to 7 mm diameter) to the timing end extremities of the gasket **(see illustrations)**.

23 Using a spanner on the crankshaft nose flats; turn the crankshaft clockwise until the groove is aligned with the bolt hole on the cylinder block **(see illustration 5.11)**. This will

8.19 Head locating dowel in the cylinder block

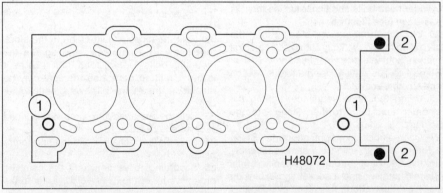

8.21 Make sure the locating dowels (1) are correctly in place, then apply sealant to the areas (2) shown

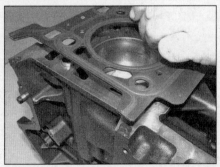

8.22a Locate the cylinder head gasket on the block . . .

8.22b . . . and apply silicone adhesive sealant to the timing end extremities

8.24a Lower the cylinder head onto the block . . .

8.27 Angle-tightening the cylinder head bolts

position the pistons half way up the cylinder bores.

24 Carefully lower the cylinder head onto the block, engaging it over the dowels. Insert the cylinder head bolts and finger-tighten them at this stage (see illustrations).

25 Working progressively, starting from the centre bolts and working outwards in a spiral motion, tighten the cylinder head bolts to their Stage 1 torque setting, using a torque wrench and suitable socket.

26 Using the same sequence, tighten the cylinder head bolts to their Stage 2 torque setting.

27 Once all bolts are tightened to the Stage 2 torque setting, using the same sequence, tighten each bolt through its specified final Stage 3 angle, using a socket and extension bar (see illustration). It is recommended that

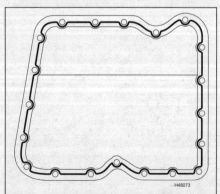

9.8a Apply silicone adhesive/sealant to the sump perimeter as shown

8.24b . . . and insert the retaining bolts

an angle-measuring gauge be used during this stage of the tightening, to ensure accuracy.

28 Clean away any excess sealant from the timing end of the head gasket.

29 If the hydraulic tappets and rockers have remained immersed in oil, no air will have entered them, however if there is any doubt, compress the piston head of the tappet and check that it does not move. If it does, the tappet may be reprimed by immersing it in clean diesel fuel. Also, check that the rocker-to-tappet clips are correctly in place.

30 Lubricate the tappet bores in the cylinder head with engine oil, then refit each hydraulic tappet and rocker assembly to its previously-noted location making sure that the rockers are correctly positioned on the valves.

31 Refit the air pipe between the EGR cooler control solenoid valve and the EGR cooler, tightening the upper-outer mounting bolt first, the upper-inner bolt next, and the lower bolt last.

32 Refit the dipstick guide tube to the block together with a new seal, and tighten the mounting bolts. Do not rotate the tube as it is being refitted otherwise the seal may be displaced. Insert the oil level dipstick/filler cap.

33 Refit the brake vacuum pump as described in Chapter 9, Section 13.

34 Refit the turbocharger oil feed and return pipes.

35 According to version, refit the catalytic pre-converter or the catalytic converter to the turbocharger outlet.

36 Refit the exhaust gas recirculation rigid pipes.

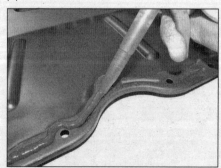

9.8b Applying silicone adhesive/sealant to the sump

37 Refit the throttle valve (also referred to as damper valve) as described in Chapter 4B, Section 8.

38 Refit the camshaft housing as described in Section 7.

39 Refit the timing chain and gears as described in Section 5.

40 Reconnect the battery negative terminal, and then refill the cooling system with reference to Chapter 1B, Section 29.

---

9 Sump – removal and refitting

Removal

1 Apply the handbrake, then jack up the front of the car and support it on axle stands (see Jacking and vehicle support). Undo the retaining screws and remove the plastic undertray from beneath the engine/transmission.

2 Drain the engine oil as described in Chapter 1B, Section 3, and then refit and tighten the drain plug, using a new sealing washer. Ensure all the oil is completely drained.

3 Remove the engine oil level dipstick.

4 Unscrew and remove the bolts securing the sump to the cylinder block baseplate.

5 The sump is sealed to the cylinder block baseplate with strong silicone adhesive/sealant that is very difficult to cut, however methodical use of a suitable spatula or thin knife will release the sump.

6 Take care not to distort or damage the mating surfaces of the sump and baseplate, and take adequate precautions to catch any oil remaining in the sump.

Refitting

7 Thoroughly clean the mating surfaces of the sump and cylinder block baseplate, taking care not to damage their surfaces.

8 Apply a 5 ± 2 mm diameter bead of silicone adhesive/sealant to the sump as shown (see illustrations).

9 Lift the sump into position making sure it is correctly aligned with the holes in the baseplate, then insert the bolts and finger-tighten them (see illustration).

10 Tighten the sump bolts to the Stage 1

9.9 Lift the sump into position on the crankcase

torque given in Specifications using the sequence shown **(see illustration)**.
11 Tighten the sump bolts to the Stage 2 torque using the same sequence.
12 Refit the undertray and lower the vehicle to the ground.
13 Fill the engine with fresh oil with reference to Chapter 1B, Section 3.

10 Oil pump, drive chain and sprocket – removal, inspection and refitting

Note: *Drive chain removal is only possible after removal of the engine.*

Removal

Oil pump

1 Remove the sump as described in Section 9.
2 Unscrew the two bolts and remove the oil pump strainer from the baseplate **(see illustration)**.
3 Unscrew the bolt securing the splash plate to the oil pump. The bolt goes through the oil pump housing to the splash plate located on the crankshaft side of the oil pump.
4 Unscrew the mounting bolts then release the drive sprocket from the drive chain and withdraw the oil pump **(see illustrations)**. If necessary, a length of bent wire may help to unhook the chain from the sprocket.
5 If necessary, remove the splash plate through the access aperture – this is quite difficult as there is limited room **(see illustration)**.

Drive chain and sprocket

6 Remove the engine and transmission from the car as described in Chapter 2E.
7 To remove the drive chain and sprocket first remove the oil pump as described in paragraphs 1 to 4.
8 Remove the timing chain and crankshaft sprocket as described in Section 5.
9 Unhook the drive chain from the drive sprocket on the crankshaft and remove the chain **(see illustration)**.
10 Slide the drive sprocket from the nose of

the crankshaft, while noting its fitted position **(see illustration)**.

Inspection

11 Clean the components and carefully examine the chain, sprockets and pump for any signs of excessive wear. If evident, it is recommended that all the components be renewed as a set.
12 Before refitting the oil pump, prime it by filling with clean engine oil whilst rotating the sprocket clockwise.

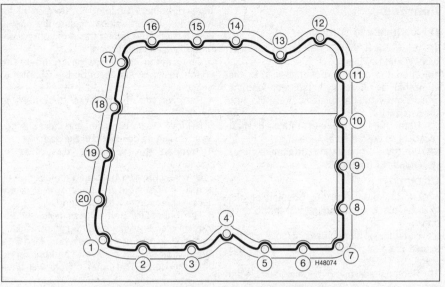

9.10 Tightening sequence for the sump bolts

10.2 Removing the oil pump strainer

10.4a Unscrew the mounting bolts . . .

10.4b . . . then unhook the drive chain and remove the oil pump

10.5 Oil pump splash plate

10.9 Unhook the chain from the drive sprocket . . .

10.10 . . . then slide the drive sprocket from the nose of the crankshaft

Refitting

Drive chain and sprocket

13 Wipe clean the oil pump and cylinder block mating surfaces.

14 Slide the drive sprocket fully onto the crankshaft as previously noted, then feed the chain through the baseplate aperture and onto the sprocket.

15 Refit the timing chain and crankshaft sprocket as described in Section 5.

16 Refit the engine and transmission as described in Chapter 2E.

Oil pump

17 Lift the oil pump into position on the cylinder block, then engage it with the drive chain.

18 Insert the oil pump mounting bolts and the splash plate-to-pump bolt finger-tight at this stage.

19 Tighten the oil pump mounting bolts in the two stages given in the Specifications.

20 Tighten the splash plate to pump bolt to the specified torque.

21 Refit the oil pump strainer together with a new seal and finger-tighten the bolts, then fully tighten the bolts to the specified torque.

22 Refit the sump as described in Section 9.

11 Cylinder block baseplate – removal and refitting

Note: *Removal of the engine is not essential to carry out this procedure; however, removal of the timing cover with the engine in position is extremely difficult.*

Removal

1 Remove the timing cover with reference to Section 5, paragraphs 1 to 10.

2 Remove the transmission as described in Chapter 7A, Section 6 for manual transmissions or Chapter 7B, Section 11 for automatic transmissions. Ensure the engine is well supported during this and subsequent procedures in this Section.

3 On manual transmission, remove the clutch assembly as described in Chapter 6, Section 6.

4 Remove the flywheel as described in Section 13.

5 Remove the transmission end crankshaft oil seal housing as described in Section 14.

6 Remove the sump as described in Section 9.

7 Unscrew the two bolts and remove the oil pump strainer from the baseplate. It is not necessary to remove the oil pump.

8 The baseplate bolt access holes at the transmission end may be fitted with blanking covers. If so, drill and cut them out using a 13 mm drill bit so that a socket can be inserted onto the bolts. The outer covers will have to be cut with a chisel, and the inner covers driven out using a suitable tube or drift **(see illustrations)**. Obtain new covers for refitting. Where blanking covers are not fitted, extra long bolts are used instead.

9 Progressively unscrew and remove the 16 baseplate bolts.

10 The baseplate is sealed to the crankcase with silicone adhesive/sealant and is likely to be difficult to remove. To help break the seal, insert two long studs into the outer bolt holes at the transmission end, and fit a nut and washer to each stud as shown. Progressively tighten the nuts to force the baseplate off of the crankcase **(see illustrations)**. On completion, remove the studs.

Refitting

11 Thoroughly clean the mating surfaces of the baseplate, crankcase and timing cover, taking care not to damage their surfaces.

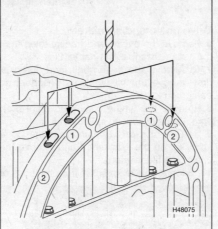

11.8a Drill out the blanking covers using a 13 mm drill bit . . .

1 Inner cover locations
2 Outer cover locations

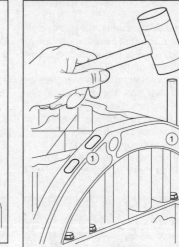

11.8b . . . then drive out the inner covers using a suitable tube or drift

1 Method of removing inner covers

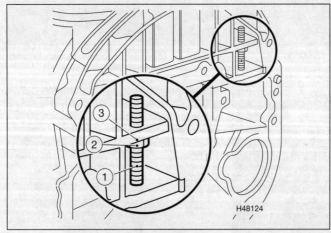

11.10a Use two studs to release the base plate from the crankcase

1 Stud   2 Nut   3 Washer

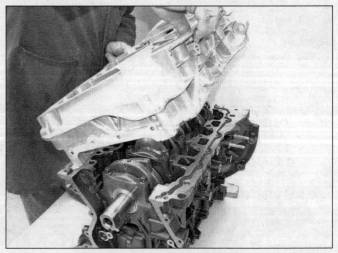

11.10b Removing the baseplate

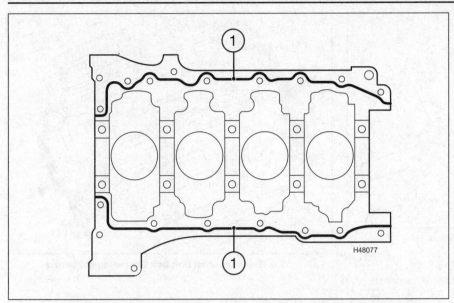

11.12a Apply silicone adhesive/sealant to the cylinder block as shown (1)

11.12b Apply sealant to the cylinder block

11.13 Insert the baseplate retaining bolts

12 Apply a 5 ± 2 mm diameter bead of silicone adhesive/sealant to the cylinder block as shown **(see illustrations)**.
13 If necessary, the studs used to separate the baseplate from the crankcase may be used without their nuts and washers as guides during refitting. Locate the baseplate on the crankcase making sure the bolt holes are correctly aligned, then insert the bolts and finger-tighten them **(see illustration)**.
14 Tighten the baseplate bolts to the specified torque, working in sequence from the timing end near the oil pump, then around the

transmission end and returning to the timing end on the opposite side **(see illustration)**. Wipe away any excess sealant.
15 Remove the guide studs.
16 Where blanking covers are fitted, apply a 5 ± 2 mm diameter bead of silicone adhesive/sealant to the new covers before pressing them into position by hand initially. Finally, use a suitable tube or drift to drive in new blanking covers to a depth of 3.0 mm from the lower edge of the holes **(see illustration)**.
17 Refit the oil pump strainer together with a new seal and finger-tighten the bolts,

then fully-tighten the bolts to the specified torque.
18 Refit the sump as described in Section 9.
19 Fit a new transmission end crankshaft oil seal housing as described in Section 14.
20 Refit the flywheel as described in Section 13.
21 On manual transmission models, refit the clutch as described in Chapter 6, Section 6.
22 Refit the transmission as described in Chapter 7A, Section 6 or Chapter 7B, Section 11.
23 Refit the timing cover with reference to Section 5, paragraphs 36 to 45.

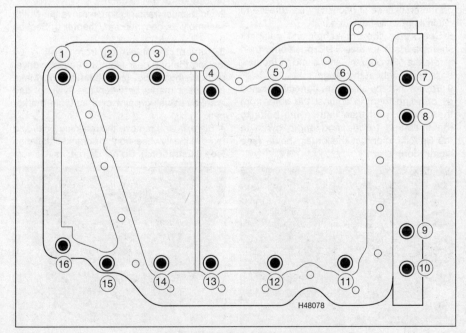

11.14 Baseplate bolt tightening sequence

11.16 Apply adhesive/sealant to the new covers (1) before driving them into the holes (2)

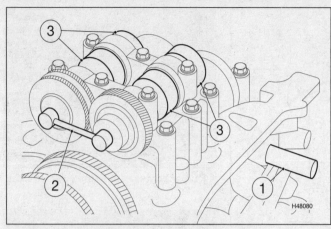

12.4 Balancer shaft unit removal

1 *TDC setting tool for crankshaft*
2 *TDC setting tool for balancer shafts*
3 *The balance shaft weights must face away from the crankshaft*

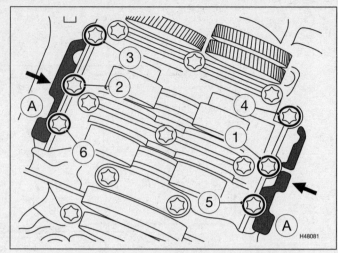

12.9 Balancer shaft unit bolt tightening sequence

A Shims

12 Balancer shaft unit – removal and refitting

Note 1: *Removal of the engine is not essential to carry out this procedure, however refer to the note at the beginning of Section 11.*
Note 2: *Nissan tool Mot. 1802 or an alternative pin will be required to set the balancer shaft.*

Removal

1 The M9R engine is equipped with a balancer shaft unit fitted between the cylinder block and the baseplate. The unit consists of two counter-rotating balance shafts driven by the crankshaft.
2 Remove the cylinder block baseplate as described in Section 11.
3 Before removing the balancer shaft unit, first set the engine to its TDC position with reference to Section 3.
4 Insert a suitable close-fitting pin through the balance shaft extensions to lock them in their TDC position (Nissan technicians use tool Mot. 1802). The weights on both shafts must be facing away from the crankshaft **(see illustration)**.
5 Progressively unscrew the mounting bolts

and lift the balancer shaft unit from the crankcase. Note the location of the adjustment shims then remove them. Discard the bolts and new ones must be used during refitting.
Caution: The shims are very sharp, and protective gloves should be worn when handling them.
6 Clean the balancer shaft unit, the shims and the drive ring on the crankshaft.

Refitting

7 To ensure the correct clearance between the balance shaft and crankshaft gears, the correct thickness shims must always be fitted. The thickness is indicated on the shims; therefore if new shims are fitted they must be of identical thickness to those removed. Locate the shims on the crankcase (if necessary use grease to retain them while fitting the unit).
8 Check that the crankshaft and balancer shafts are set to their TDC positions, then locate the unit onto the shims and fit the new bolts finger-tight at this stage.
9 Ensure that the shims are correctly located by pressing them in against the bolts from the outside, and then tighten the bolts to the specified torque and angle given in the Specifications in the order shown **(see illustration)**.

10 Remove the TDC pin from the balance shaft extensions.
11 Refit the cylinder block baseplate as described in Section 11.

13 Flywheel – removal, inspection and refitting

Removal

1 Remove the transmission as described in Chapter 7A, Section 6 for manual transmissions or Chapter 7B, Section 11 for automatic transmissions. Ensure the engine is well supported during this and subsequent procedures in this Section.
2 On manual transmission, remove the clutch assembly as described in Chapter 6, Section 6.
3 Prevent the flywheel from turning by locking the ring gear teeth with a screwdriver or homemade tool **(see illustration)**. Make alignment marks between the flywheel and crankshaft using paint or a suitable marker pen.
4 Slacken and remove the retaining bolts and remove the flywheel from the crankshaft flange **(see illustrations)**. Do not drop it, as it is very

13.3 Home-made tool for locking the flywheel

13.4a Unscrew and remove the bolts . . .

13.4b . . . and withdraw the flywheel from the crankshaft flange

13.5 Old flywheel bolt with three hacksaw cuts on the threads is ideal to clean the threads in the crankshaft

13.8 Mark the bolts and holes to ensure correct angle-tightening of the flywheel bolts

14.4 Locate the new oil seal on the timing cover with the raised segments aligned with the cut-outs

heavy. If the locating dowel (where fitted) is a loose fit in the crankshaft end, remove and store it with the flywheel for safekeeping. Discard the bolts, as they should be renewed whenever they are disturbed.

Inspection

5 Examine the flywheel for scoring of the clutch face, and for wear or chipping of the ring gear teeth. If the clutch face is scored, the flywheel may be surface-ground, but renewal is preferable. Seek the advice of a Nissan dealer or engine-reconditioning specialist to see if machining is possible. If the ring gear is worn or damaged, the flywheel must be renewed, as it is not possible to renew the ring gear separately. Clean the bolt hole threads in the crankshaft – an old retaining bolt with three cuts on the threads is ideal for doing this **(see illustration)**.

Refitting

6 Clean the mating surfaces of the flywheel and crankshaft.
7 Ensure that the locating dowel is in position (where fitted) and offer up the flywheel, locating it on the dowel, and fit the new retaining bolts. If the original is being refitted, align the marks made prior to removal.
8 Lock the flywheel using the method employed on dismantling, and tighten the retaining bolts to the specified torque and angle. To ensure all the bolts are tightened to the correct angle, make marks on the bolts and flywheel bolt holes **(see illustration)**.
9 On manual transmission models, refit the clutch as described in Chapter 6, Section 6.
10 Refit the transmission as described in Chapter 7A, Section 6 or Chapter 7B, Section 11.

14 Crankshaft oil seals – renewal

Timing end oil seal

Note: *Unlike conventional oil seals, the timing end oil seal is screwed into the timing cover.*
1 Remove the crankshaft pulley as described in Section 4.

2 A socket adapter is provided with the new crankshaft oil seal. Using the adapter, unscrew the old oil seal from the timing cover.
3 Clean the crankshaft and timing cover.
4 The new oil seal must not be lubricated during fitting. First, position the seal with its three raised segments aligned with the cut-outs in the timing cover and push the seal into the cover using hand pressure only. This will force the plastic protector from the centre of the oil seal **(see illustration)**.
5 Using the adapter, tighten the oil seal to the specified torque given in the Specifications **(see illustrations)**.
6 Refit the crankshaft pulley as described in Section 4.

Transmission end oil seal

Note: *The transmission end oil seal is supplied*

together with the oil seal housing and cannot be renewed separately.
7 Remove the flywheel as described in Section 13.
8 Unscrew the bolts and remove the oil seal housing from the cylinder block/baseplate **(see illustration)**.
9 Clean the contact faces of the cylinder block and baseplate. Do not remove the protector or touch the lip of the new oil seal during fitting as this will result in oil leakage.
10 Carefully locate the oil seal and housing onto the crankshaft and insert three 90 mm long M6 bolts loosely to act as guides **(see illustration)**. Do not press the housing into position at this stage.
11 Apply even pressure to the housing and press it into position until it contacts the

14.5a Fit the adapter . . .

14.5b . . . and tighten to the specified torque

14.8 Removing the transmission end oil seal housing

14.10 Use 3 bolts to act as guides when fitting the new oil seal housing

cylinder block. Now remove the protector and the three guide bolts (see illustration).

12 Insert the retaining bolts and finger-tighten, and then tighten them to the initial torque given in the Specifications in the sequence shown (see illustration).

13 Tighten the bolts to their final torque using the same sequence.

14 Refit the flywheel as described in Section 13.

15 Engine/transmission mountings – inspection and renewal

Inspection

1 If improved access is required, apply the handbrake, then jack up the front of the car and support it on axle stands (see *Jacking and vehicle support*).

2 Check the mounting rubber to see if it is cracked, hardened or separated from the metal at any point; renew the mounting if any such damage or deterioration is evident.

3 Check that all the mounting's fasteners are securely tightened; use a torque wrench to check if possible.

4 Using a large screwdriver or a crowbar, check for wear in the mounting by carefully levering against it to check for free play. Where this is not possible, enlist the aid of an assistant to move the engine/transmission back-and-forth, or from side-to-side, while you watch the mounting. While some free play is

14.11 Press the housing into position and remove the protector

to be expected, even from new components, excessive wear should be obvious. If excessive free play is found, check first that the fasteners are correctly secured, and then renew any worn components as described below.

Renewal

Right-hand mounting

5 Disconnect the battery negative terminal (refer to *Disconnecting the battery* in the Reference Chapter).

6 Place a jack beneath the engine, with a block of wood on the jack head. Raise the jack until it is supporting the weight of the engine.

7 To make access easier, remove the fuel filter and support bracket (see illustration), as described in Chapter 1B, Section 21.

8 Unclip the fuel lines then slacken the

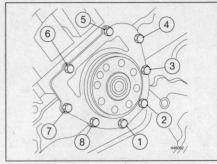

14.12 Tightening sequence for the transmission end crankshaft oil seal

securing bolt and disconnect the earth wire and bracket from the top of the engine mounting bracket (see illustrations).

9 Slacken the retaining bolts and remove the torque link from the rear of the engine mounting (see illustration).

10 Slacken and remove the three retaining bolts from the inner wing panel, remove the three retaining bolts from the engine mounting bracket, and then withdraw the complete mounting from the engine compartment (see illustrations).

11 Check carefully for signs of wear or damage on all components, and renew them where necessary.

12 On refitting, fit the engine mounting and bracket to the inner wing panel and engine, and then securely tighten its retaining bolts to the specified torque setting.

15.7 Remove the filter support bracket

15.8a Unclip the fuel lines ...

15.8b ... and unbolt the bracket from the mounting

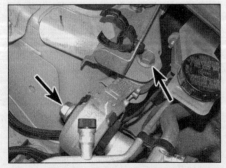

15.9 Unbolt the torque link (arrowed) from the rear of the bulkhead

15.10a Unbolt the inner wing panel bolts ...

15.10b ... and the engine mounting bolts

15.18 Support the transmission with a trolley jack

15.19 Unbolt the air filter housing lower mounting bracket (arrowed)

15.20 Undo the two outer securing bolts and remove the mounting

13 Refit the torque link to the rear of the engine mounting and tighten the retaining bolts to the specified torque setting.

14 With the engine mounting back in position, refit the fuel filter and mounting bracket as described in Chapter 1B, Section 21

15 Lower the jack and remove it from underneath the engine.

16 Reconnect the earth cable and bracket to the top of the engine mounting and secure the fuel lines back in the clips, and then reconnect the battery negative terminal.

Left-hand mounting

17 Remove the battery and tray, as described in Chapter 5A, Section 3.

18 Place a jack and block of wood beneath the transmission, and raise the jack to take the weight of the transmission **(see illustration)**.

19 Undo the retaining bolts and remove the air filter housing lower locating bracket from the top of the transmission mounting **(see illustration)**.

20 Slacken and remove the two outer retaining bolts, and withdraw the mounting from the upper mounting bracket **(see illustration)**.

21 If required, undo the retaining bolts from the inner wing panel to remove the upper mounting bracket.

22 Also, if required, undo the retaining bolts

from the transmission to remove the lower mounting bracket **(see illustration)**.

23 Check carefully for signs of wear or damage on all components, and renew them where necessary.

24 On refitting, fit the upper and lower mounting brackets (where removed) and securely tighten the retaining bolts.

25 Align the left-hand rubber mounting with the bolt/stud on the lower mounting bracket and tighten its nut to the specified torque setting.

26 Refit the two outer retaining nuts, and tighten to the specified torque setting.

27 With the transmission mounting back in position, lower the jack and remove it from underneath the transmission.

28 Refit the battery and battery tray, with reference to Chapter 5, Section 3.

Rear lower mounting

29 If not already done, firmly apply the handbrake, and then jack up the front of the vehicle and support it securely on axle stands (see *Jacking and vehicle support*). Remove engine undertray.

30 Slacken and remove the bolts securing the rear mounting link to the subframe and the mounting bracket, and then withdraw the mounting link from under the vehicle **(see illustration)**.

31 If required, slacken and remove the three bolts securing the rear mounting bracket to the lower cylinder block base plate, and then withdraw the bracket from under the vehicle.

32 Check carefully for signs of wear or damage on all components, and renew them where necessary.

33 Refit the mounting bracket to the rear of the sump housing and tighten its retaining bolts to the specified torque.

34 Fit the rear mounting link to the mounting bracket and subframe, and then tighten the retaining bolts to the specified torque.

35 With the transmission rear mounting link arm back in position, lower the vehicle to the ground.

16 Oil cooler – removal and refitting

Note: *The oil cooler is part of the oil filter housing; it would be good practice to renew the oil and oil filter whenever the oil cooler is removed.*

Removal

1 Disconnect the battery negative terminal (refer to *Disconnecting the battery* in the Reference Section of this manual).

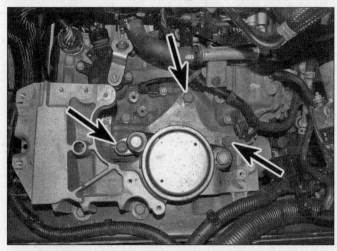

15.22 Mounting bracket-to-transmission retaining bolts (arrowed)

15.30 Remove the torque link arm bolts

16.5a Remove the oil level dipstick/filler cap . . .

16.5b . . . unscrew the mounting bolt . . .

16.5c . . . withdraw the guide tube from the cylinder block . . .

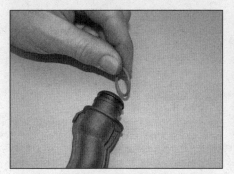

16.5d . . . and recover the O-ring seal

16.10a Remove the oil cooler/filter housing . . .

16.10b . . . and recover the gasket

2 Apply the handbrake, then jack up the front of the car and support it on axle stands (see *Jacking and vehicle support*). Undo the retaining screws and remove the engine undertray to gain access to the oil cooler, which is part of the oil filter housing and is mounted on the front of the cylinder block. Also remove the engine upper covers for access to the top of the engine.
3 Drain the engine oil and remove the oil filter as described in Chapter 1B, Section 3, and then refit and tighten the drain plug.
4 Drain the cooling system as described in Chapter 1B, Section 29. Alternatively, clamp the oil cooler coolant hoses as close to the cooler as possible, and be prepared for some coolant loss as the hoses are disconnected.
5 Withdraw the oil level dipstick/filler cap from the guide tube, then unscrew the upper mounting bolt and remove the guide tube from the engine. Discard the guide tube seal, as a new one must be used on refitting **(see illustrations)**.
6 Disconnect the wiring from the alternator and oil pressure sensor, and position to one side.
7 Where a coolant heating element unit is fitted to the bottom of the radiator, unscrew the mounting bolts from the bracket and position the unit to one side.
8 Unscrew the bolt securing the power steering high-pressure pipe to the engine and position the pipe to one side.
9 Release the clips and disconnect the coolant inlet (bottom) and outlet (top) hoses from the oil cooler/filter housing.

10 Unscrew the four mounting bolts and remove the oil cooler/filter housing from the front of the cylinder block. Discard the gasket, as a new one must be used on refitting **(see illustrations)**.

Refitting

11 Fit a new gasket to the oil cooler/filter housing, then offer the housing to the cylinder block. Ensure that the housing is correctly positioned then refit the mounting bolts and finger-tighten initially.
12 Tighten the bolts in diagonal sequence to the Stage 1 torque, and then tighten them to the Stage 2 torque using the same sequence.
13 Reconnect the inlet and outlet hoses and secure with the clips.
14 Where applicable, refit the coolant heating element to its mounting bracket and tighten the bolts securely.
15 Reconnect the wiring to the alternator and oil pressure sensor.
16 Fit a new seal to the dipstick guide tube and lubricate with engine oil, then refit the guide tube and tighten the mounting bolt to the specified torque. Check that the seal remains in position during fitting.
17 Insert the oil level dipstick/filler cap in the guide tube.
18 Reconnect the battery negative terminal (refer to *Disconnecting the battery* in the Reference Section of this manual).
19 Fit a new oil filter and refill the engine with oil as described in Chapter 1B, Section 3.
20 Refill or top-up the cooling system as

described in Chapter 1B, Section 29 or *Weekly checks* (as applicable). Start the engine, and check the oil cooler/filter housing for signs of leakage.
21 Refit the engine undertray and upper covers and lower the car to the ground.

17 Oil pressure sensor – removal and refitting

1 The oil pressure sensor gives a vital early warning of low oil pressure. The sensor operates the oil warning light on the instrument panel – the light should come on with the ignition, and go out almost immediately when the engine starts.
2 If the light does not come on, there could be a fault on the instrument panel, the switch wiring, or the switch itself. If the light does not go out, low oil level, worn oil pump (or sump pick-up blocked), blocked oil filter, or worn main bearings could be to blame – or again, the switch may be faulty.
3 If the light comes on while driving, the best advice is to turn the engine off immediately, and not to drive the car until the problem has been investigated – ignoring the light could mean expensive engine damage.

Removal

4 The oil pressure sensor is located on the front of the engine, in the top of the oil filter housing.
5 It may be easier to access the sensor from

18.6 Heat-resisting insulation fitted to the oil level sensor

18.7a Disconnect the wiring . . .

18.7b . . . then unscrew and remove the oil level sensor from the cylinder block

underneath the vehicle, jack up the front of the car, and support it on axle stands (see *Jacking and vehicle support*). Undo the retaining bolts and remove the engine undertray.

6 Disconnect the wiring plug from the sensor.

7 Unscrew the sensor from the housing, and remove it together with its sealing washer. There should only be a very slight loss of oil when this is done.

Inspection

8 Examine the sensor for signs of cracking or splits. If the top part of the sensor is loose, this is an early indication of impending failure.

9 Check that the wiring connector terminals are good, then trace the wire from the switch connector until it enters the main loom – any wiring defects will give rise to apparent oil pressure problems.

Refitting

10 Refitting is the reverse of the removal procedure, noting the following points:

a) *Clean the sensor threads before fitting. Tighten the switch to the specified torque.*

b) *Reconnect the sensor wiring, making sure it is routed away from any hot or moving parts.*

c) *Lower the car to the ground, then check the engine oil level and top-up if necessary (see 'Weekly checks').*

d) *Check for signs of oil leaks once the engine has been restarted and warmed-up to normal operating temperature.*

18 Oil level sensor – removal and refitting

Removal

1 The oil level sensor is located at the rear, right-hand side of the engine, above the right-hand driveshaft intermediate bearing.

2 Access to the sensor may be easiest from under the right-hand front wheel arch. First, jack up the front of the car, and support it on axle stands (see *Jacking and vehicle support*). Remove the front right-hand roadwheel.

3 Undo the fasteners and remove the wheel arch liner.

4 Refer to Chapter 10 and remove the anti-roll bar-to-strut link arm.

5 Unbolt and remove the short tie-bar between the front suspension subframe and underbody in order to gain access to the sensor.

6 The oil level sensor and wiring are fitted with heat-resisting insulating material **(see illustration)**. Cut the clip and move the material to one side.

7 Disconnect the wiring plug, and then unscrew the oil level sensor from the cylinder block **(see illustrations)**.

Refitting

8 Refitting is a reversal of removal. Tighten the sensor, tie-rod and link arm to their specified torques.

Chapter 2 Part E:
General engine removal and overhaul procedures

Contents

Degrees of difficulty

Easy, suitable for novice with little experience 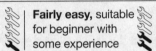	**Fairly easy,** suitable for beginner with some experience	**Fairly difficult,** suitable for competent DIY mechanic	**Difficult,** suitable for experienced DIY mechanic	**Very difficult,** suitable for expert DIY or professional

Specifications

General

Engine codes:

1.6 petrol engine	HR16DE
2.0 petrol engine	MR20DE
1.5 diesel engine	K9K
2.0 diesel engine	M9R

Cylinder head

Maximum gasket face distortion:

Petrol engines (HR16DE & MR20DE)	0.10 mm
Diesel engines (K9K & M9R)	0.05 mm

Cylinder head height:

HR16DE	125.0 mm
MR20DE	130.9 mm
K9K	127.0 mm
M9R	133.6 mm

Cylinder block

Maximum gasket face distortion:

Petrol engines (HR16DE & MR20DE)	0.10 mm
Diesel engines (K9K & M9R)	0.05 mm

Valve springs

Spring free height:

HR16DE	42.26 mm
MR20DE:	
Inlet	45.59 to 46.96 mm
Exhaust	45.13 to 46.40 mm
K9K	43.31 mm
M9R	46.90 mm

Spring squareness:

HR16DE	less than 1.8 mm
MR20DE	less than 1.9 mm
K9K	less than 1.2 mm
M9R	less than 1.2 mm

Valves

	Inlet	Exhaust
Valve head diameter:		
HR16DE	31.0 to 31.3 mm	25.3 to 25.6 mm
MR20DE	33.8 to 34.1 mm	27.6 to 27.9 mm
K9K	33.38 to 33.62 mm	28.88 to 29.12 mm
M9R	27.58 to 27.82 mm	25.88 to 26.12 mm
Valve stem diameter:		
HR16DE	4.965 to 4.980 mm	4.955 to 4.970 mm
MR20DE	5.465 to 5.480 mm	5.455 to 5.470 mm
K9K	5.969 to 5.985 mm	5.955 to 5.971 mm
M9R	5.970 to 5.990 mm	5.960 to 5.970 mm
Overall length:		
HR16DE	101.65 mm	102.46 mm
MR20DE	106.27 mm	105.26 mm
K9K	100.74 to 101.16 mm	100.54 to 100.96 mm
M9R	103.89 mm	103.78 mm

Pistons

Piston skirt diameter:	
HR16DE – (measured 37.1 mm from the top of the piston)	77.965 to 77.980 mm
MR20DE – (measured 39.9 mm from the top of the piston):	
Grade 1	83.970 to 83.980 mm
Grade 2	83.980 to 83.990 mm
K9K – (measured 56 mm from the top of the piston)	75.938 to 75.952 mm
M9R – (measured 56 mm from the top of the piston)	83.79 to 83.80 mm
Piston-to-bore clearance (petrol engines):	
HR16DE	0.020 to 0.050 mm
MR20DE	0.020 to 0.040 mm
Piston protrusion (diesel engines):	
K9K	0.030 to 0.288 mm
M9R:	
With 1.17 mm head gasket (crushed)	0.33 to 0.49 mm
With 1.20 mm head gasket (crushed)	0.36 to 0.52 mm

Piston rings

Ring-to-groove clearance:	
HR16DE:	
Top compression ring	0.04 to 0.08 mm – (limit 0.11 mm)
Second compression ring	0.03 to 0.07 mm – (limit 0.10 mm)
Oil control ring	0.045 to 0.125 mm
MR20DE:	
Top compression ring	0.04 to 0.08 mm – (limit 0.11 mm)
Second compression ring	0.03 to 0.07 mm – (limit 0.10 mm)
Oil control ring	0.015 to 0.185 mm
K9K:	
Top compression ring	0.10 to 0.12 mm
Second compression ring	0.08 to 0.10 mm
Oil control ring	0.03 to 0.05 mm
M9R:	
Top compression ring	0.10 to 0.12 mm
Second compression ring	0.08 to 0.10 mm
Oil control ring	0.03 to 0.05 mm
Ring end gaps (measured in cylinder):	
HR16DE:	
Top compression ring	0.20 to 0.30 mm – (limit 0.50 mm)
Second compression ring	0.35 to 0.50 mm – (limit 0.66 mm)
Oil control ring	0.20 to 0.60 mm – (limit 0.92 mm)
MR20DE:	
Top compression ring	0.20 to 0.30 mm – (limit 0.51 mm)
Second compression ring	0.50 to 0.65 mm – (limit 0.83 mm)
Oil control ring	0.15 to 0.45 mm – (limit 0.78 mm)
K9K:	
Top compression ring	0.20 to 0.35 mm
Second compression ring	0.70 to 0.90 mm
Oil control ring	0.25 to 0.50 mm
M9R:	
Top compression ring	0.23 to 0.38 mm
Second compression ring	0.60 to 0.80 mm
Oil control ring	0.25 to 0.50 mm

Crankshaft

Endfloat:
- HR16DE . . . . 0.098 to 0.260 mm – (limit 0.35 mm)
- MR20DE . . . . 0.10 to 0.26 mm – (limit 0.30 mm)
- K9K . . . . 0.045 to 0.252 mm – (limit 0.852 mm)
- M9R . . . . 0.05 to 0.70 mm

Main bearing running clearance:
- HR16DE . . . . 0.024 to 0.034 mm
- MR20DE:
  - Bearing caps 1, 4 & 5 . . . . 0.024 to 0.034 mm – (limit 0.065 mm)
  - Bearing caps 2 & 3 . . . . 0.012 to 0.022 mm – (limit 0.065 mm)
- K9K . . . . 0.010 to 0.054 mm
- M9R . . . . 0.030 to 0.070 mm

Big-end bearing running clearance:
- HR16DE . . . . 0.029 to 0.039 mm – (limit 0.10 mm)
- MR20DE . . . . 0.037 to 0.047 mm – (limit 0.07 mm)
- K9K . . . . 0.010 to 0.064 mm
- M9R . . . . 0.05 to 0.10 mm

Torque wrench settings

Refer to Chapter 2A, 2B, 2C and 2D Specifications, for relevant engine.

1 General information

Included in this Part of Chapter 2 are details of removing the engine/transmission from the vehicle, and general overhaul procedures for the cylinder head, cylinder block/crankcase and all other engine internal components.

The information given ranges from advice concerning preparation for an overhaul and the purchase of new parts, to detailed step-by-step procedures covering removal, inspection, renovation and refitting of engine internal components.

After Section 5, all instructions are based on the assumption that the engine has been removed from the vehicle. For information concerning in-car engine repair, as well as the removal and refitting of those external components necessary for full overhaul, refer to Part A, B, C or D of this Chapter and to Section 5. Ignore any preliminary dismantling operations described in Part A, B, C or D, that are no longer relevant once the engine has been removed.

Apart from torque wrench settings, which are given at the beginning of Part A, B, C or D, all specifications relating to engine overhaul are at the beginning of this Part of Chapter 2.

Engine overhaul

It is not always easy to determine when, or if, an engine should be completely overhauled, as a number of factors must be considered.

High mileage is not necessarily an indication that an overhaul is needed, while low mileage does not preclude the need for an overhaul. Frequency of servicing is probably the most important consideration. An engine, which has had regular and frequent oil and filter changes, as well as other required maintenance, should give many thousands of miles of reliable service. Conversely, a neglected engine may require an overhaul very early in its life.

Excessive oil consumption is an indication that piston rings, valve seals and/or valve guides are in need of attention. Make sure that oil leaks are not responsible before deciding that the rings and/or guides are worn. Perform a compression test, as described in Part A, B, C or D, of this Chapter, to determine the likely cause of the problem.

Check the oil pressure with a gauge fitted in place of the oil pressure switch, and compare it with that specified in Part A, B, C or D of this Chapter. If it is extremely low, the main and big-end bearings, and/or the oil pump, are probably worn out.

Loss of power, rough running, knocking or metallic engine noises, excessive valve gear noise, and high fuel consumption may also point to the need for an overhaul, especially if they are all present at the same time. If a complete service does not remedy the situation, major mechanical work is the only solution.

An engine overhaul involves restoring all internal parts to the specification of a new engine. During an overhaul, the cylinder bores are rebored (where necessary) and the pistons and piston rings are renewed. New main and big-end bearings are generally fitted; if necessary, the crankshaft may be reground, to restore the journals. The valves are also serviced as well, since they are usually in less-than-perfect condition at this point. The end result should be an as-new engine that will give many trouble-free miles.

Note: *Critical cooling system components such as the hoses, thermostat and coolant pump should be renewed when an engine is overhauled. The radiator should be checked carefully, to ensure that it is not clogged or leaking. Also, it is a good idea to renew the oil pump whenever the engine is overhauled.*

Before beginning the engine overhaul, read through the entire procedure, to familiarise yourself with the scope and requirements of the job. Check on the availability of parts, and make sure that any necessary special tools and equipment are obtained in advance. Most work can be done with typical hand tools, although a number of precision measuring tools are required for inspecting parts to determine if they must be renewed.

The services provided by an engineering machine shop or engine reconditioning specialist will almost certainly be required, particularly if major repairs such as crankshaft regrinding or cylinder reboring are necessary. Apart from carrying out machining operations, these establishments will normally handle the inspection of parts; offer advice concerning reconditioning or renewal and supply new components such as pistons, piston rings and bearing shells. It is recommended that the establishment used is a member of the Federation of Engine Re-Manufacturers, or a similar society.

Always wait until the engine has been completely dismantled, and until all components (especially the cylinder block and the crankshaft) have been inspected, before deciding what service and repair operations must be performed by an automotive engineering works. The condition of these components will be the major factor to consider when determining whether to overhaul the original engine, or to buy a reconditioned unit. Do not, therefore, purchase parts or have overhaul work done on other components until they have been thoroughly inspected.

As a final note, to ensure maximum life and minimum trouble from a reconditioned engine, everything must be assembled with care, in a spotlessly-clean environment.

2 Engine removal – methods and precautions

If you have decided that the engine must be removed for overhaul or major repair work, several preliminary steps should be taken.

Locating a suitable place to work is extremely important. Adequate workspace, along with storage space for the vehicle, will be needed. If a workshop or garage is not available, at the very least, a flat, level, clean work surface is required.

Cleaning the engine compartment and engine/transmission before beginning the removal procedure will help keep tools clean and organised.

An engine hoist will also be necessary. Make sure the equipment is rated in excess of the combined weight of the engine and transmission. Safety is of primary importance, considering the potential hazards involved in removing the engine/transmission from the vehicle.

The help of an assistant is essential. Apart from the safety aspects involved, there are many instances when one person cannot simultaneously perform all of the operations required during engine/transmission removal.

Plan the operation ahead of time. Before starting work, arrange for the hire of, or obtain, all of the tools and equipment you will need. Some of the equipment necessary to perform engine/transmission removal and installation safely (in addition to an engine hoist) is as follows: a heavy-duty trolley jack, complete sets of spanners and sockets as described at the rear of this manual, wooden blocks, and plenty of rags and cleaning solvent for mopping-up spilled oil, coolant and fuel. If the hoist must be hired, make sure that you arrange for it in advance, and perform all of the operations possible without it beforehand. This will save you money and time.

Plan for the vehicle to be out of use for quite a while. An engineering machine shop or engine reconditioning specialist will be required to perform some of the work, which cannot be accomplished without special equipment. These places often have a busy schedule, so it would be a good idea to consult them before removing the engine, in order to accurately estimate the amount of time required to rebuild or repair components that may need work.

During the engine/transmission removal procedure, it is advisable to make notes of the locations of all brackets, cable ties, earthing points, etc, as well as how the wiring harnesses, hoses and electrical connections are attached and routed around the engine and engine compartment. An effective way of doing this is to take a series of photographs of the various components before they are disconnected or removed. A simple inexpensive disposable or digital camera is ideal for this and the resulting photographs will prove invaluable when the engine is refitted.

Always be extremely careful when removing and refitting the engine/transmission. Serious injury can result from careless actions. Plan ahead and take your time, and a job of this nature, although major, can be accomplished successfully.

3 Engine and manual transmission – removal, separation, reconnection and refitting

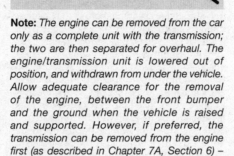

Note: *The engine can be removed from the car only as a complete unit with the transmission; the two are then separated for overhaul. The engine/transmission unit is lowered out of position, and withdrawn from under the vehicle. Allow adequate clearance for the removal of the engine, between the front bumper and the ground when the vehicle is raised and supported. However, if preferred, the transmission can be removed from the engine first (as described in Chapter 7A, Section 6) – this leaves the engine free to be either lifted out from above or lowered to the ground.*

Removal

1 Release the pressure in the fuel system as described in Chapter 4A, Section 6, for petrol engines, and Chapter 4B, Section 5, for diesel engines.

2 Disconnect the battery negative terminal (refer to *Disconnecting the battery* in the Reference Chapter). Remove the battery and tray from the vehicle with reference to Chapter 5A, Section 3.

3 Firmly apply the handbrake, then jack up the front of the vehicle and support it securely on axle stands (see *Jacking and vehicle support*), bearing in mind the note at the start of this Section, about the height required. Remove both front roadwheels.

4 Undo all the retaining screws, and remove the undershields from underneath and around the engine.

5 Drain the cooling system as described in Chapter 1A, Section 27 for petrol engine, or Chapter 1B, Section 29, for diesel engines. Save the coolant in a clean container, if it is fit for re-use.

6 Drain the transmission oil as described in Chapter 7A, Section 2. Refit the drain and filler plugs, and tighten them to their specified torque settings, fit new sealing washers where required.

7 If the engine is to be dismantled, working as described in Chapter 1A, Section 3 for petrol engines, or Chapter 1B, Section 3, for diesel engines. Drain the oil and if required remove the oil filter. Clean and refit the drain plug, tightening it to the specified torque, fit new sealing washers where required.

8 Working as described in Chapter 8, Section 2, remove both front driveshafts.

9 Working around the engine, disconnect the wiring connectors from the alternator, starter motor, oil pressure switch, oil level switch, knock sensor, crankshaft sensor etc…

depending on model. If necessary label the connectors as they are unplugged.

10 Carry out the following operations as described in the relevant parts of Chapter 4A.

a) *Remove the air cleaner assembly.*

b) *Disconnect the fuel feed and return hoses from the fuel rail (plug all openings, to prevent loss of fuel and entry of dirt into the fuel system).*

c) *Disconnect the relevant electrical connectors from the throttle housing, inlet manifold and associated components. Free the wiring from the manifold, and position it clear of the cylinder head so that it does not hinder removal.*

d) *Disconnect the vacuum servo unit hose, coolant hose(s), and all the other relevant/ breather hoses from the manifold and associated valves.*

e) *Remove the inlet manifold.*

f) *Disconnect the exhaust front pipe.*

11 Slacken the retaining clips, and disconnect the heater hoses and all other relevant cooling system hoses from the engine, noting each hose's correct fitted location.

12 On models with air conditioning, unbolt the compressor and position it clear of the engine. Support the weight of the compressor by tying it to the vehicle body, to prevent any excess strain being placed on the compressor lines whilst the engine is removed. **Do not** disconnect the refrigerant lines from the compressor (see the warnings given in Chapter 3, Section 10).

13 Disconnect the clutch fluid pipe with reference to Chapter 6, Section 7.

14 Working as described in Chapter 7A, Section 3, disconnect the gear linkage cables from the operating levers on the transmission.

15 Note their fitted positions and harness routing, then disconnect all wiring plugs from the transmission. If necessary label the connectors as they are unplugged.

16 Secure the radiator to the upper crossmember, making sure that the cooling fins do not get damaged.

17 Remove the front engine subframe from under the front of the vehicle **(see illustration)**, as described in Chapter 10, Section 12.

18 Manoeuvre the engine hoist into position, and attach it to the engine/transmission using suitable lifting brackets. Raise the hoist until

3.17 Removing the subframe

it is supporting the weight of the engine/transmission.

19 Mark the outline of the front engine/transmission mounting bracket bolts to use as a guide on refitting. Slacken and remove the bolts/nut and remove both right and left-hand side mountings from the inner wing panels, as described in the relevant part of Chapter 2A, B, C or D.

20 Make a final check that any components, which would prevent the removal of the engine/transmission from the car, have been removed or disconnected. Ensure that components such as the gearchange cables are secured so that they cannot be damaged on removal.

21 If available, a low trolley should be placed under the engine/transmission assembly, to facilitate its easy removal from under the vehicle. Lower the engine/transmission assembly, making sure that nothing is trapped or damaged. Note that it may be necessary to tilt the assembly slightly to clear the body panels. Great care must be taken to ensure that no components are trapped and damaged during the removal procedure.

22 Withdraw the assembly from under the vehicle.

Separation

23 Unscrew the retaining bolts, and remove the starter motor from the transmission.

24 Ensure that both engine and transmission are adequately supported, then slacken and remove the bolts securing the transmission housing to the engine. Note the correct fitted positions of each bolt (and, where fitted, the relevant brackets) as they are removed, to use as a reference on refitting.

25 Carefully withdraw the transmission from the engine, ensuring that the weight of the transmission is not allowed to hang on the input shaft while it is engaged with the clutch friction disc.

26 If they are loose, remove the locating dowels from the engine or transmission, and keep them in a safe place.

Reconnection

27 Apply a smear of high melting-point grease to the splines of the transmission input shaft. Do not apply too much; otherwise there is a possibility of the grease contaminating the clutch friction disc.

28 Ensure that the locating dowels are correctly positioned in the engine or transmission, and that the release bearing is correctly engaged with the fork.

29 Carefully offer the transmission to the engine, until the locating dowels are engaged. Ensure that the weight of the transmission is not allowed to hang on the input shaft as it is engaged with the clutch friction disc.

30 Refit the transmission housing-to-engine bolts, ensuring that all the necessary brackets are correctly positioned, and tighten them to the specified torque setting.

31 Refit the starter motor and tighten the retaining bolts.

Refitting

32 Position the engine/transmission assembly under the vehicle, then reconnect the hoist and lifting tackle to the engine lifting brackets.

33 Lift the assembly up into the engine compartment; making sure that it clears the surrounding components.

34 Refit the left-hand engine/transmission mounting bracket, ensuring that it is correctly seated in position. Manoeuvre the mounting into position, then fit the bolts securing it to the transmission and tighten them to the specified torque setting. Insert the through-bolt and nut, tightening it by hand only at this stage.

35 Fit the right-hand body mounting bracket, ensuring that it is correctly seated in position. Refit the mounting to the top of its bracket, and tighten its retaining bolts to the specified torque setting. Insert the through-bolt and nut, tightening it by hand only at this stage.

36 Refit the front engine subframe to the underside of the vehicle, as described in Chapter 10, Section 12.

37 Rock the engine/transmission to settle it in position, and then tighten all the engine/transmission mounting through-bolts to their specified torque settings.

38 The remainder of the refitting procedure is a direct reversal of the removal sequence, noting the following points:

a) Ensuring that the wiring harness is correctly routed and retained by all the relevant retaining clips, and all connectors are correctly and securely reconnected.

b) Prior to refitting the driveshafts to the transmission, renew the driveshaft oil seals as described in Chapter 7A.

c) Ensure that all coolant hoses are correctly reconnected and securely retained by their retaining clips.

d) Adjust the accelerator cable as described in Chapter 4A.

e) Connect and adjust the clutch cable as described in Chapter 6.

f) Refill the engine and transmission unit with correct quantity and type of lubricant, as described in the relevant Sections of Chapter 1.

g) Refill the cooling system as described in Chapter 1A or Chapter 1B.

h) On completion, start the engine and check for leaks.

4 Engine and automatic transmission – removal, separation, reconnection and refitting

Note: *The engine can be removed from the car only as a complete unit with the transmission; the two are then separated for overhaul. The engine/transmission unit is lowered out of position, and withdrawn from under the vehicle. Allow adequate clearance for the removal of the engine, between the front bumper and the ground when the vehicle is raised and supported. However, if preferred, the transmission can be removed from the engine first (as described in Chapter 7B, Section 11) – this leaves the engine free to be either lifted out from above or lowered to the ground.*

Removal

1 Release the pressure in the fuel system as described in Chapter 4A, Section 6, for petrol engines, and Chapter 4B, Section 5, for diesel engines.

2 Disconnect the battery negative terminal (refer to *Disconnecting the battery* in the Reference Chapter). Remove the battery and tray from the vehicle with reference to Chapter 5A, Section 3.

3 Firmly apply the handbrake, then jack up the front of the vehicle and support it securely on axle stands (see *Jacking and vehicle support*), bearing in mind the note at the start of this Section, about the height required. Remove both front roadwheels.

4 Undo all the retaining screws, and remove the undershields from underneath and around the engine.

5 Drain the cooling system as described in Chapter 1A, Section 27 for petrol engine, or Chapter 1B, Section 29, for diesel engines. Save the coolant in a clean container, if it is fit for re-use.

6 Drain the transmission oil as described in Chapter 7B, Section 2. Refit the drain and filler plugs, and tighten them to their specified torque settings, fit new sealing washers where required.

7 If the engine is to be dismantled, working as described in Chapter 1A, Section 3 for petrol engines, or Chapter 1B, Section 3, for diesel engines. Drain the oil and if required remove the oil filter. Clean and refit the drain plug, tightening it to the specified torque, fit new sealing washers where required.

8 Working as described in Chapter 8, Section 2, remove both front driveshafts.

9 Working around the engine, disconnect the wiring connectors from the alternator, starter motor, oil pressure switch, oil level switch, knock sensor, crankshaft sensor etc... depending on model. If necessary label the connectors as they are unplugged.

10 Carry out the following operations as described in the relevant parts of Chapter 4A.

a) Remove the air cleaner assembly.

b) Disconnect the fuel feed and return hoses from the fuel rail (plug all openings, to prevent loss of fuel and entry of dirt into the fuel system).

c) Disconnect the relevant electrical connectors from the throttle housing, inlet manifold and associated components. Free the wiring from the manifold, and position it clear of the cylinder head so that it does not hinder removal.

d) Disconnect the vacuum servo unit hose, coolant hose(s), and all the other relevant/breather hoses from the manifold and associated valves.

e) Remove the inlet manifold.

f) Disconnect the exhaust front pipe.

11 Slacken the retaining clips, and disconnect the heater hoses and all other relevant cooling system hoses from the engine, noting each hose's correct fitted location.

12 On models with air conditioning, unbolt the compressor and position it clear of the engine. Support the weight of the compressor by tying it to the vehicle body, to prevent any excess strain being placed on the compressor lines whilst the engine is removed. **Do not** disconnect the refrigerant lines from the compressor (see the warnings given in Chapter 3, Section 10).

13 Disconnect the fluid cooler hoses from the rear of the transmission.

14 Working as described in Chapter 7A, Section 3, disconnect the gear linkage cables from the operating levers on the transmission.

15 Note their fitted positions and harness routing, then disconnect all wiring plugs from the transmission. If necessary label the connectors as they are unplugged.

16 Secure the radiator to the upper crossmember, making sure that the cooling fins do not get damaged.

17 Remove the front engine subframe from under the front of the vehicle as described in Chapter 10, Section 12.

18 Manoeuvre the engine hoist into position, and attach it to the engine/transmission using suitable lifting brackets. Raise the hoist until it is supporting the weight of the engine/transmission.

19 Mark the outline of the front engine/transmission mounting bracket bolts to use as a guide on refitting. Slacken and remove the bolts/nut and remove both right and left-hand side mountings from the inner wing panels, as described in the relevant part of Chapter 2A, B, C or D.

20 Make a final check that any components, which would prevent the removal of the engine/transmission from the car, have been removed or disconnected. Ensure that components such as the gearchange cables are secured so that they cannot be damaged on removal.

21 If available, a low trolley should be placed under the engine/transmission assembly, to facilitate its easy removal from under the vehicle. Lower the engine/transmission assembly, making sure that nothing is trapped or damaged. Note that it may be necessary to tilt the assembly slightly to clear the body panels. Great care must be taken to ensure that no components are trapped and damaged during the removal procedure.

22 Withdraw the assembly from under the vehicle.

Separation

23 Unscrew the retaining bolts, and remove the starter motor from the transmission.

24 Undo the retaining bolts, and remove the cover plate from the sump flange to gain access to the torque converter retaining bolts. Slacken and remove the visible bolt then, using a socket and extension bar to rotate the crankshaft pulley, undo the remaining bolts securing the torque converter to the driveplate as they become accessible. There are four bolts in total.

25 To ensure that the torque converter does not fall out as the transmission is removed, secure it in position using a length of metal strip bolted to one of the starter motor bolt holes.

26 Ensure that both engine and transmission are adequately supported, then slacken and remove the bolts securing the transmission housing to the engine. Note the correct fitted positions of each bolt (and, where fitted, the relevant brackets) as they are removed, to use as a reference on refitting.

27 Carefully withdraw the transmission from the engine. If they are loose, remove the locating dowels from the engine or transmission, and keep them in a safe place.

Reconnection

28 Prior to joining the engine and transmission units, ensure that the torque converter is correctly engaged with the transmission. This can be checked by measuring the distance from the converter mounting bolt holes to the transmission mating surface; if the converter is correctly seated, this distance will be at least 20.4 mm.

29 Ensure that the locating dowels are correctly positioned in the engine or transmission. Carefully offer the transmission to the engine, and engage it on the locating dowels. Refit the transmission housing-to-engine bolts, ensuring that all the necessary brackets are correctly positioned, and tighten them to the specified torque settings.

30 Remove the torque converter retaining strap (where fitted) installed prior to removal. Align the torque converter holes with those in the driveplate, and install the retaining bolts.

31 Tighten the torque converter retaining bolts to the specified torque setting, then refit the cover plate to the sump and securely tighten its retaining bolts.

32 Refit the starter motor and tighten the retaining bolts.

Refitting

33 Position the engine/transmission assembly under the vehicle, then reconnect the hoist and lifting tackle to the engine lifting brackets.

34 Lift the assembly up into the engine compartment; making sure that it clears the surrounding components.

35 Refit the left-hand engine/transmission mounting bracket, ensuring that it is correctly seated in position. Manoeuvre the mounting into position, then fit the bolts securing it to the transmission and tighten them to the specified torque setting. Insert the through-bolt and nut, tightening it by hand only at this stage.

36 Fit the right-hand body mounting bracket, ensuring that it is correctly seated in position. Refit the mounting to the top of its bracket, and tighten its retaining bolts to the specified torque setting. Insert the through-bolt and nut, tightening it by hand only at this stage.

37 Refit the front engine subframe to the underside of the vehicle, as described in Chapter 10, Section 12.

38 Rock the engine/transmission to settle it in position, and then tighten all the engine/transmission mounting through-bolts to their specified torque settings.

39 The remainder of the refitting procedure is a direct reversal of the removal sequence, noting the following points:

a) *Ensuring that the wiring harness is correctly routed and retained by all the relevant retaining clips, and all connectors are correctly and securely reconnected.*

b) *Prior to refitting the driveshafts to the transmission, renew the driveshaft oil seals as described in Chapter 7B.*

c) *Ensure that all coolant hoses are correctly reconnected and securely retained by their retaining clips.*

d) *Refill the engine and transmission unit with correct quantity and type of lubricant, as described in the relevant Sections of Chapter 1.*

e) *Refill the cooling system as described in Chapter 1A or Chapter 1B.*

f) *On completion, start the engine and check for leaks*

5 Engine overhaul – dismantling sequence

1 It is preferable to dismantle and work on the engine with it mounted on a portable engine stand. These stands can often be hired from a tool hire shop. Before the engine is mounted on a stand, the flywheel/driveplate should be removed, so that the stand bolts can be tightened into the end of the cylinder block/crankcase.

2 If a stand is not available, it is possible to dismantle the engine with it blocked up on a sturdy workbench, or on the floor. Be extra careful not to tip or drop the engine when working without a stand.

3 If a reconditioned engine is to be obtained, or if the original engine is to be overhauled, the external components in the following list must be removed first. These components can then be transferred to the reconditioned engine, or refitted to the existing engine after overhaul.

a) *Alternator and air conditioning compressor mounting brackets (as applicable).*

b) *Coolant pump and thermostat/coolant outlet housing(s) (Chapter 3).*

c) *Fuel system components (Chapter 4A).*

d) *All electrical switches and sensors, and the engine wiring harness.*

e) *Inlet and exhaust manifolds (Chapter 4A).*

f) *Engine mountings (Part A, B, C or D, of this Chapter).*

g) *Flywheel/driveplate (Part A, B, C or D, of this Chapter).*

Note: *When removing the external components from the engine, pay close attention to details that may be helpful or important during refitting. Note the fitted position of gaskets, seals, spacers, pins, washers, bolts, and other small items.*

6.7a Remove the spring collets . . .

6.7b . . . then lift off the cap . . .

6.7c . . . valve spring . . .

4 If a 'short' engine is to be obtained (cylinder block, crankshaft, pistons and connecting rods all assembled), then the cylinder head, sump, oil pump, and timing chain will have to be removed also.

5 If a complete overhaul of the existing engine is being undertaken, the engine can be dismantled, in the order given below, referring to Part A, B, C or D, of this Chapter unless otherwise stated.

a) Inlet and exhaust manifolds (Chapter 4A).
b) Timing chain/belt and sprockets.
c) Cylinder head.
d) Sump.
e) Flywheel/driveplate.
f) Piston/connecting rod assemblies (Section 9 of this Chapter).
g) Crankshaft (Section 10 of this Chapter).

6 Before beginning the dismantling and overhaul procedures, make sure that you have all of the correct tools necessary. Refer to *Tools and working facilities* for further information.

6 Cylinder head – dismantling

Note: *New and reconditioned cylinder heads are available from the manufacturer, and from engine reconditioning specialists. Some specialist tools are required for dismantling and inspection, and new components may not be readily available. It may therefore be more practical and economical for the home mechanic to purchase a reconditioned head,*

6.7d . . . and the spring seat (where fitted)

rather than dismantle, inspect and recondition the original head.

1 Remove the cylinder head as described in Part A, B, C or D, of this Chapter.

2 Remove the inlet manifold with reference to Chapter 4A, Section 11 on petrol engines or Chapter 4B Section 12, diesel engines

3 Remove the exhaust manifold with reference to Chapter 4A, Section 12 on petrol engines or Chapter 4B Section 13, diesel engines

4 If not already done, remove the camshaft followers and shims as described in Part A, B, C or D, of this Chapter.

5 On petrol models, remove the spark plugs as described in Chapter 1A, Section 25.

6 On diesel models, remove the glow plugs as described in Chapter 5C, Section 3.

7 Using a valve spring compressor, compress each valve spring in turn until the split collets can be removed. Release the compressor, and lift off the spring retainer, spring and spring

6.7e Removing the oil seal from the top of the valve guide

seat. Using a pair of pliers, carefully extract the valve stem seal from the top of the guide **(see illustrations)**.

8 If, when the valve spring compressor is screwed down, the spring retainer refuses to free and expose the split collets, gently tap the top of the tool, directly over the retainer, with a light hammer. This will free the retainer.

9 Withdraw the valve through the combustion chamber **(see illustration)**.

10 It is essential that each valve is stored together with its collets, retainer, spring, and spring seat. The valves should also be kept in their correct sequence, unless they are so badly worn that they are to be renewed. If they are going to be kept and used again, place each valve assembly in a labelled polythene bag or similar small container **(see illustrations)**. Note that No 1 valve is nearest to the timing chain end of the engine.

6.9 Withdrawing a valve from the cylinder head

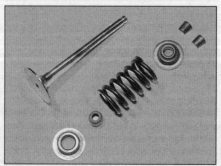

6.10a The valve components

6.10b Store the components in a labelled plastic bag

7.5 Check the cylinder head for distortion with feeler blades

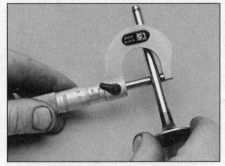

7.10 Measuring a valve stem using a micrometer

7.13 Grinding in a valve – lift the valve to distribute the paste evenly

7 Cylinder head and valves – cleaning and inspection

Cleaning

1 Scrape away all traces of old gasket material from the cylinder head.

2 Scrape away the carbon from the combustion chambers and ports, then wash the cylinder head thoroughly with paraffin or a suitable solvent.

3 Scrape off any heavy carbon deposits that may have formed on the valves, then use a power-operated wire brush to remove deposits from the valve heads and stems.

Inspection

Cylinder head

4 Inspect the head very carefully for cracks, evidence of coolant leakage, and other damage. If significant defects are found, a new cylinder head should be obtained.

5 Use a straight-edge and feeler blade to check for distortion of the cylinder head gasket surface **(see illustration)**. If the head is distorted beyond the limit given in the Specifications, seek the advice of an engine reconditioning specialist as to whether machining is possible.

6 Examine the valve seats in each of the combustion chambers. If they are severely pitted, cracked, or burned, they will need to be renewed or recut by an engine reconditioning specialist. If they are only slightly pitted, this can be removed by grinding-in the valve heads and seats with fine valve-grinding compound, as described below.

7 Check the valve guides for wear by inserting the relevant valve, and checking for side-to-side motion of the valve. A very small amount of movement is acceptable. If the movement seems excessive, remove the valve. Measure the valve stem diameter (see below), and renew the valve if it is worn. If the valve stem is not worn, the wear must be in the valve guide, and the guide must be renewed. The renewal of valve guides should be carried out by an engine reconditioning

specialist, who will have the necessary tools available.

8 If renewing the valve guides, the valve seats are to be recut or reground only *after* the guides have been fitted.

Valves

9 Examine the head of each valve for pitting, burning, cracks, and general wear. Check the valve stem for scoring and wear ridges. Rotate the valve, and check for any obvious indication that it is bent. Look for pits and excessive wear on the tip of each valve stem. Renew any valve that shows any such signs of wear or damage.

10 If the valve appears satisfactory at this stage, measure the valve stem diameter at several points using a micrometer **(see illustration)**. Any significant difference in the readings obtained indicates wear of the valve stem. Should any of these conditions be apparent, the valve(s) must be renewed.

11 If the valves are in satisfactory condition, they should be ground (lapped) into their respective seats, to ensure a smooth, gas-tight seal. If the seat is only lightly pitted, or if it has been recut, fine grinding compound *only* should be used to produce the required finish. Coarse valve-grinding compound should *not* be used, unless a seat is badly burned or deeply pitted. If this is the case, the cylinder head and valves should be inspected by a specialist, to decide whether seat recutting, or even the renewal of the valve or seat insert (where possible) is required.

12 Valve grinding is carried out as follows, with the head supported upside-down on blocks.

13 Smear a trace of (the appropriate grade of) valve-grinding compound on the seat face, and press a suction grinding tool onto the valve head. With a semi-rotary action, grind the valve head to its seat, lifting the valve occasionally to redistribute the grinding compound **(see illustration)**. A light spring placed under the valve head will greatly ease this operation.

14 If coarse grinding compound is being used, work only until a dull, matt even surface is produced on both the valve seat and the valve, then wipe off the used compound, and repeat the process with fine compound. When

a smooth unbroken ring of light grey matt finish is produced on both the valve and seat, the grinding operation is complete. *Do not* grind-in the valves any further than absolutely necessary, or the seat will be prematurely sunk into the cylinder head.

15 When all the valves have been ground-in, carefully wash off *all* traces of grinding compound using paraffin or a suitable solvent, before reassembling the cylinder head.

Valve components

16 Examine the valve springs for signs of damage and discoloration. The specified Nissan procedure for checking the condition of valve springs involves measuring the force necessary to compress each spring to a specified height. This is not possible without the use of the Nissan special test equipment, and therefore spring checking must be entrusted to a Nissan dealer. A rough idea of the condition of the spring can be gained by measuring the spring free length, and comparing it with a new one **(see illustration)**.

17 Stand each spring on a flat surface, and position a square alongside the edge of the spring.

18 If any of the springs are damaged, distorted or have lost their tension, obtain a complete new set of springs. It is normal to renew the valve springs as a matter of course if a major overhaul is being carried out.

19 Renew the valve stem oil seals regardless of their apparent condition.

7.16 Checking the height of a valve spring

8 Cylinder head – reassembly

1 Refit the spring seat then, working on the first valve, dip the new valve stem seal in fresh engine oil. Place it on the valve guide and use a suitable socket or metal tube to press the seal firmly onto the guide **(see illustrations)**.

2 Lubricate the stems of the valves, and insert the valves into their original locations **(see illustration)**. If new valves are being fitted, insert them into the locations to which they have been ground.

3 Locate the valve spring on top of its seat; ensuring that the spring is fitted with its closer-pitched coils at the bottom, and then refit the spring retainer.

4 Compress the valve spring, and locate the split collets in the recess in the valve stem **(see illustration)**. Release the compressor, then repeat the procedure on the remaining valves.

5 With all the valves installed, place the cylinder head on blocks on the bench and, using a hammer and interposed block of wood, tap the end of each valve stem to settle the components.

6 The cylinder head and associated components may now be refitted as described in Part A, B, C or D of this Chapter, and in Chapter 4A.

9 Piston/connecting rod assembly – removal

1 Remove the sump, cylinder block base plate (2.0 litre engines), timing chain/belt and cylinder head as described in Part A, B, C or D, of this Chapter.

2 If there is a pronounced wear ridge at the top of any bore, it may be necessary to remove it with a scraper or ridge reamer, to avoid piston damage during removal. Such a ridge indicates excessive wear of the cylinder bore.

3 Each connecting rod and bearing cap should be stamped with its respective cylinder number, No 1 cylinder being at the timing chain end of the engine **(see illustration)**. If

8.1a Fit the valve stem oil seal ...

8.1b ... and press it into the previously-noted position on the guide

8.2 Lubricate the valve stems before fitting the valves

8.4 Use a little grease to hold the collets in place

no markings are visible, using quick-drying paint or similar, mark each connecting rod and big-end bearing cap with its respective cylinder number on the flat machined surface provided.

4 Turn the crankshaft to bring pistons 1 and 4 to BDC (bottom dead centre).

5 On petrol engines, slacken the retaining bolts and remove the upper alloy part of the sump from the bottom of the cylinder block.

6 Unscrew the nuts from No 1 piston big-end bearing cap. Take off the cap **(see illustration)**, and recover the bottom half bearing shell. If the bearing shells are to be re-used, tape the cap and the shell together.

7 Using a hammer handle, push the piston up through the bore, and remove it from the top of the cylinder block. Recover the bearing shell **(see illustration)**, and tape it to the connecting rod for safekeeping.

8 Loosely refit the big-end cap to the connecting rod, and secure with the nuts – this will help to keep the components in their correct order.

9 Remove No 4 piston assembly in the same way.

10 Turn the crankshaft through 180° to bring pistons 2 and 3 to BDC (bottom dead centre), and remove them in the same way.

10 Crankshaft – removal

1 Remove the sump, cylinder block base plate (2.0 litre diesel engines), timing chain/belt and cylinder head as described in Part A, B, C or D, of this Chapter.

9.3 Big-end caps marked with a centre punch

9.6 Removing a big-end bearing cap

9.7 Removing a big-end bearing upper shell

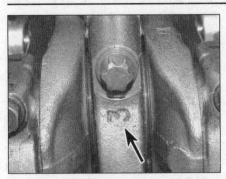

10.5 The main bearing caps are numbered for position

10.6 Removing a main bearing cap bolt

10.8 Lifting the crankshaft from the crankcase

2 Remove the pistons and connecting rods, as described in Section 9. If no work is to be done on the pistons and connecting rods, there is no need to remove the cylinder head, or to push the pistons out of the cylinder bores. The pistons should just be pushed far enough up the bores that they are positioned clear of the crankshaft journals.

3 Check the crankshaft endfloat as described in Section 13, then proceed as follows.

4 On diesel engines, undo the retaining bolts, and remove the oil seal housing from the left-hand (flywheel) end of the cylinder block. If the locating dowels are a loose fit, remove them and store them with the housing for safekeeping.

5 The main bearing caps should be numbered 1 to 5 from the timing chain end of the engine **(see illustration)**. If not, using quick-drying paint or similar, mark each cap so as to indicate its correct fitted orientation and position.

6 Working from the outer ends to the centre; progressively slacken the main bearing cap retaining bolts by a turn at a time. Once all bolts are loose, unscrew and remove them from the cylinder block **(see illustration)**.

7 Withdraw the bearing caps, and recover the lower main bearing shells. Tape each shell to its respective cap for safekeeping.

8 Carefully lift out the crankshaft, taking care not to displace the upper main bearing shells **(see illustration)**.

9 Recover the upper bearing shells from the cylinder block, and tape them to their respective caps for safekeeping.

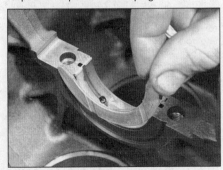

10.10 Removing the crankshaft thrustwashers – diesel engine

10 Remove the thrustwasher halves from the side of No 3 main bearing **(see illustration)**, and store them with the bearing cap.

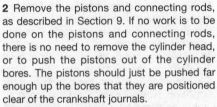

11 Cylinder block/crankcase – cleaning and inspection

Cleaning

1 Remove all external components and electrical switches/sensors from the block.

2 Scrape all traces of sealant from the cylinder block/crankcase, taking care not to damage the gasket sealing surfaces.

3 Where piston oil jet spray tubes are fitted, to the lower part of the cylinder, these should only be removed by a specialist, as damage may occur on removal.

4 Remove all oil gallery plugs (where fitted). The plugs are usually very tight – they may have to be drilled out, and the holes retapped. Use new plugs when the engine is reassembled.

5 If any of the castings are extremely dirty, all should be steam-cleaned, or cleaned with a suitable degreasing agent.

6 After cleaning, clean all oil holes and oil galleries one more time. Flush all internal passages with warm water until the water runs clear. Dry thoroughly, and apply a light film of oil to the cylinder bores to prevent rusting. If possible, use compressed air to speed up the drying process, and to blow out all the oil holes and galleries.

Warning: Wear eye protection when using compressed air.

7 If the castings are not very dirty, you can do an adequate cleaning job with very hot, soapy water and a stiff brush. Take plenty of time, and do a thorough job. Regardless of the cleaning method used, be sure to clean all oil holes and galleries very thoroughly, and to dry all components well. Protect the cylinder bores as described above, to prevent rusting.

8 All threaded holes must be clean, to ensure accurate torque readings during reassembly. To clean the threads, run the correct-size tap into each of the holes to remove rust, corrosion, thread sealant or sludge, and to

restore damaged threads. If possible, use compressed air to clear the holes of debris produced by this operation.

9 Apply suitable sealant to the new oil gallery plugs, and insert them into the holes in the block. Tighten them securely.

10 If the engine is not going to be reassembled right away, cover it with a large plastic bag to keep it clean; protect all mating surfaces and the cylinder bores as described above, to prevent rusting.

Inspection

11 Visually check the casting for cracks and corrosion. Look for stripped threads in the threaded holes. If there has been any history of internal water leakage, it may be worthwhile having an engine reconditioning specialist check the cylinder block/crankcase with special equipment. If defects are found, have them repaired if possible, or obtain a new block.

12 Check each cylinder bore for scuffing and scoring. Check for signs of a wear ridge at the top of the cylinder, indicating that the bore is excessively worn.

13 Accurate measuring of the cylinder bores requires specialised equipment and experience. We recommend having the bores measured by an automotive engineering workshop, which will also be able to supply appropriate pistons should a rebore be necessary.

14 If the cylinder bores and pistons are in reasonably good condition, and not worn to the specified limits, and if the piston-to-bore clearances can be maintained properly, then it will only be necessary to renew the piston rings. If this is the case, the bores should be honed, to allow the new rings to bed in correctly and provide the best possible seal. An engine reconditioning specialist will carry out this work at moderate cost.

12 Piston/connecting rod assembly – inspection

1 Before the inspection process can begin, the piston/connecting rod assemblies must be cleaned, and the original piston rings removed from the pistons. **Note:** *Always use new piston rings when the engine is reassembled.*

2 Carefully expand the old rings over the top of the pistons. The use of two or three old feeler blades will be helpful in preventing the rings dropping into empty grooves **(see illustration)**. Be careful not to scratch the piston with the ends of the ring. The rings are brittle, and will snap if they are spread too far. They're also very sharp – protect your hands and fingers.

3 Scrape away all traces of carbon from the top of the piston. A hand-held wire brush (or a piece of fine emery cloth) can be used, once the majority of the deposits have been scraped away.

4 Remove the carbon from the ring grooves in the piston, using an old ring. Break the ring in half to do this. Be careful to remove only the carbon deposits – do not remove any metal, and do not nick or scratch the sides of the ring grooves.

5 Once the deposits have been removed, clean the piston/connecting rod assembly with paraffin or a suitable solvent, and dry thoroughly. Make sure that the oil return holes in the ring grooves are clear.

6 If the pistons and cylinder bores are not damaged or worn excessively, and if the cylinder block does not need to be rebored, the original pistons can be refitted. Normal piston wear shows up as even vertical wear on the piston thrust surfaces, and slight looseness of the top ring in its groove. New piston rings, however, should always be used when the engine is reassembled.

7 Carefully inspect each piston for cracks around the skirt, around the gudgeon pin holes, and at the piston ring 'lands' (between the ring grooves).

8 Look for scoring and scuffing on the piston skirt, holes in the piston crown, and burned areas at the edge of the crown. If the skirt is scored or scuffed, the engine may have been suffering from overheating, and/or abnormal combustion, which caused excessively high operating temperatures. The cooling and lubrication systems should be checked thoroughly. Scorch marks on the sides of the pistons show that blow-by has occurred. A hole in the piston crown, or burned areas at the edge of the piston crown, indicates that abnormal combustion (pre-ignition, knocking, or detonation) has been occurring. If any of the above problems exist, the causes must be investigated and corrected, or the damage will occur again.

9 Corrosion of the piston, in the form of pitting, indicates that coolant has been leaking into the combustion chamber and/or the crankcase. Again, the cause must be corrected, or the problem may persist in the rebuilt engine.

10 Measure the piston ring-to-groove clearance by placing a new piston ring in each ring groove and measuring the clearance with a feeler blade. Check the clearance at three or four places around each groove. If the

12.2 Removing a piston ring with the aid of a feeler gauge

measured clearance is greater than specified, new pistons will be required.

11 Accurate measurement of the pistons requires specialised equipment and experience. We recommend having the piston measured by an automotive engineering workshop, which will also be able to supply appropriate pistons should a rebore be necessary.

12 Check the fit of the gudgeon pin by twisting the piston and connecting rod in opposite directions. Any noticeable play indicates excessive wear of the gudgeon pin, piston, or connecting rod small-end bearing.

13 If necessary, on models with circlips securing the gudgeon pin in place, the pistons and connecting rods can be separated and reassembled as follows. Before removing the piston from the connecting rod, mark both components to make sure they are fitted in the same position on reassembly. **Note:** *On models with no circlips fitted, the gudgeon pin is a press fit in the top of the connecting rod. On these types, we recommend having the pistons removed by an automotive engineering workshop.*

14 Using a small screwdriver, prise out the circlips, and push out the gudgeon pin. If necessary, support the piston, and tap the pin out using a suitable hammer and punch, taking great care not to mark the piston/connecting rod bores. Identify the piston, gudgeon pin and rod to ensure correct reassembly. Discard the circlips – new ones *must* be used on refitting.

15 On models where the gudgeon pins are an interference fit in the connecting rod small-end bearing (no circlips). The piston and/or connecting rod renewal should be entrusted to a Peugeot dealer or engine repair specialist, who will have the necessary tooling to remove and install the gudgeon pins.

16 Examine each connecting rod carefully for signs of damage, such as cracks around the big-end and small-end bearings. Check that the rod is not bent or distorted. Damage is highly unlikely, unless the engine has been seized or badly overheated. Detailed checking of the connecting rod assembly and any remedial action necessary can only be carried out by an engine reconditioning specialist with the necessary equipment.

13.2 Checking the crankshaft endfloat with a dial gauge

17 To refit the pistons, position the piston on the connecting rod so that the markings noted on removal are positioned correctly in relation to both components.

18 Where applicable, apply a smear of clean engine oil to the gudgeon pin. Slide it into the piston and through the connecting rod small-end. **Note:** *Gudgeon pin installation will be greatly eased if the piston is first warmed.* If necessary, tap the pin into position using a hammer and suitable punch, whilst ensuring that the piston is securely supported. Check that the piston pivots freely on the rod, then secure the gudgeon pin in position with two new circlips (where applicable). Ensure that each circlip is correctly located in its groove in the piston.

13 Crankshaft – inspection

Checking endfloat

1 If the crankshaft endfloat is to be checked, this must be done when the crankshaft is still installed in the cylinder block/crankcase, but is free to move (see Section 10).

2 Check the endfloat using a dial gauge in contact with the end of the crankshaft. Push the crankshaft fully one way, and then zero the gauge. Push the crankshaft fully the other way, and check the endfloat **(see illustration)**. The result can be compared with the specified amount, and will give an indication as to whether new thrustwashers are required.

3 If a dial gauge is not available, feeler blades can be used. First push the crankshaft fully towards the flywheel/driveplate end of the engine, then use feeler blades to measure the gap between the No 4 crankpin web and No 3 main bearing thrustwasher.

Inspection

4 Clean the crankshaft using paraffin or a suitable solvent, and dry it, preferably with compressed air if available. Be sure to clean the oil holes with a pipe cleaner or similar probe, to ensure that they are not obstructed.

 Warning: Wear eye protection when using compressed air.

5 Check the main and big-end bearing journals for uneven wear, scoring, pitting and cracking.

6 Big-end bearing wear is accompanied by distinct metallic knocking when the engine is running (particularly noticeable when the engine is pulling from low speed) and some loss of oil pressure.

7 Main bearing wear is accompanied by severe engine vibration and rumble – getting progressively worse as engine speed increases – and again by loss of oil pressure.

8 Check the bearing journal for roughness by running a finger lightly over the bearing surface. Any roughness (which will be accompanied by obvious bearing wear) indicates that the crankshaft requires regrinding (where possible) or renewal.

9 Check the oil seal contact surfaces at each end of the crankshaft for wear and damage. If the seal has worn a deep groove in the surface of the crankshaft, consult an engine overhaul specialist; repair may be possible, but otherwise a new crankshaft will be required.

10 Accurate measurement of the crankshaft requires specialised equipment and experience. We recommend having the crankshaft measured by an automotive engineering workshop, which will also be able to supply appropriate journal bearings should a regrind be necessary.

11 If the crankshaft has been reground, check for burrs around the crankshaft oil holes (the holes are usually chamfered, so burrs should not be a problem unless regrinding has been carried out carelessly). Remove any burrs with a fine file or scraper, and thoroughly clean the oil holes as described previously.

12 At the time of writing, it was not clear whether Nissan produce undersize bearing shells for all of these engines. On some engines, if the crankshaft journals have not already been reground, it may be possible to have the crankshaft reconditioned, and to fit undersize shells. If no undersize shells are available and the crankshaft has worn beyond the specified limits, it will have to be renewed. Consult your Nissan dealer or engine specialist for further information on parts availability.

14 Main and big-end bearings – inspection

1 Even though the main and big-end bearings should be renewed during the engine overhaul, the old bearings should be retained for close examination, as they may reveal valuable information about the condition of the engine. The bearing shells are graded by thickness, the grade of each shell being indicated by the colour code marked on it.

2 Bearing failure can occur due to lack of lubrication, the presence of dirt or other foreign particles, overloading the engine, or corrosion. Regardless of the cause of bearing failure, the cause must be corrected (where applicable)

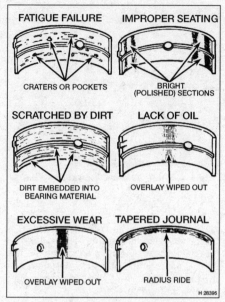

14.2 Typical bearing shell failures

before the engine is reassembled, to prevent it from happening again **(see illustration)**.

3 When examining the bearing shells, remove them from the cylinder block/crankcase, the main bearing caps, the connecting rods and the connecting rod big-end bearing caps. Lay them out on a clean surface in the same general position as their location in the engine. This will enable you to match any bearing problems with the corresponding crankshaft journal. *Do not* touch any shell's bearing surface with your fingers while checking it, or the delicate surface may be scratched.

4 Dirt and other foreign matter get into the engine in a variety of ways. It may be left in the engine during assembly, or it may pass through filters or the crankcase ventilation system. It may get into the oil, and from there into the bearings. Metal chips from machining operations and normal engine wear are often present. Abrasives are sometimes left in engine components after reconditioning, especially when parts are not thoroughly cleaned using the proper cleaning methods. Whatever the source, these foreign objects often end up embedded in the soft bearing material, and are easily recognised. Large particles will not embed in the bearing, and will score or gouge the bearing and journal. The best prevention for this cause of bearing failure is to clean all parts thoroughly, and keep everything spotlessly clean during engine assembly. Frequent and regular engine oil and filter changes are also recommended.

5 Lack of lubrication (or lubrication breakdown) has a number of interrelated causes. Excessive heat (which thins the oil), overloading (which squeezes the oil from the bearing face) and oil leakage (from excessive bearing clearances, worn oil pump or high engine speeds) all contribute to lubrication breakdown. Blocked oil passages, which

usually are the result of misaligned oil holes in a bearing shell, will also oil-starve a bearing, and destroy it. When lack of lubrication is the cause of bearing failure, the bearing material is wiped or extruded from the steel backing of the bearing. Temperatures may increase to the point where the steel backing turns blue from overheating.

6 Driving habits can have a definite effect on bearing life. Full-throttle, low-speed operation (labouring the engine) puts very high loads on bearings, tending to squeeze out the oil film. These loads cause the bearings to flex, which produces fine cracks in the bearing face (fatigue failure). Eventually, the bearing material will loosen in pieces, and tear away from the steel backing.

7 Short-distance driving leads to corrosion of bearings, because insufficient engine heat is produced to drive off the condensed water and corrosive gases. These products collect in the engine oil, forming acid and sludge. As the oil is carried to the engine bearings, the acid attacks and corrodes the bearing material.

8 Incorrect bearing installation during engine assembly will lead to bearing failure as well. Tight-fitting bearings leave insufficient bearing running clearance, and will result in oil starvation. Dirt or foreign particles trapped behind a bearing shell result in high spots on the bearing, which lead to failure.

9 *Do not* touch any shell's bearing surface with your fingers during reassembly; there is a risk of scratching the delicate surface, or of depositing particles of dirt on it.

10 As mentioned at the beginning of this Section, the bearing shells should be renewed as a matter of course during engine overhaul; to do otherwise is false economy. Refer to Sections 17 and 18 for details of bearing shell selection.

15 Engine overhaul – reassembly sequence

1 Before reassembly begins, ensure that all new parts have been obtained, and that all necessary tools are available. Read through the entire procedure, to familiarise yourself with the work involved, and to ensure that all items necessary for reassembly of the engine are at hand. In addition to all normal tools and materials, thread–locking compound will be needed. A suitable tube of liquid sealant will also be required for the joint faces that are fitted without gaskets; it is recommended that Nissan's Genuine Liquid Gasket (available from your Nissan dealer) is used.

2 In order to save time and avoid problems, engine reassembly can be carried out in the following order:

a) *Crankshaft (Section 17).*
b) *Piston/connecting rod assemblies (Section 18).*
c) *Cylinder head (See Part A, B, C or D, of this Chapter).*

16.3 Use the piston to push the rings into the cylinder bores ...

16.4 ... then measure the ring end gaps

16.9 Fit the oil control ring expander

d) *Timing chain and cover (See Part A, B, C or D, of this Chapter).*
e) *Sump (See Part A, B, C or D, of this Chapter).*
f) *Flywheel/driveplate (See Part A, B, C or D, of this Chapter).*
g) *Engine external components.*

3 At this stage, all engine components should be absolutely clean and dry, with all faults repaired. The components should be laid out (or in individual containers) on a completely clean work surface.

16 Piston rings – refitting

1 Before fitting new piston rings, the ring end gaps must be checked as follows.
2 Lay out the piston/connecting rod assemblies and the new piston ring sets, so that the ring sets will be matched with the same piston and cylinder during the end gap measurement and subsequent engine reassembly.
3 Insert the top ring into the first cylinder,

and push it down the bore using the top of the piston **(see illustration)**. This will ensure that the ring remains square with the cylinder walls. Push the ring down into the bore until the piston skirt is level with the block mating surface, then withdraw the piston.
4 Measure the end gap using feeler gauges, and compare the measurements with the figures given in the Specifications **(see illustration)**.
5 If the gap is too small (unlikely if reputable parts are used), it must be enlarged, or the ring ends may contact each other during engine operation, causing serious damage. Ideally, new piston rings providing the correct end gap should be fitted. As a last resort, the end gap can be increased by carefully filing the ring ends with a fine file. Mount the file in a vice with soft jaws, slip the ring over the file with the ends contacting the file face, and slowly move the ring to remove material from the ends. Take care, as piston rings are sharp, and are easily broken.
6 With new piston rings, it is unlikely that the end gap will be too large. If the gaps are too large, check that you have the correct rings for the engine and for the particular cylinder bore size.
7 Repeat the checking procedure for each ring in the first cylinder, and then for the rings in the remaining cylinders. Remember to keep rings, pistons and cylinders matched up.
8 Once the ring end gaps have been checked and if necessary corrected, the rings can be fitted to the pistons. **Note:** *Always follow any instructions supplied with the new piston ring sets – different manufacturers may specify different procedures. Do not mix up the top and second compression rings, as they have different cross-sections.*
9 The oil control ring (lowest on the piston) is installed first. It is composed of three separate components. Slip the expander into the groove, then install the upper side rail into the groove between the expander and the ring land, and then install the lower side rail in the same manner **(see illustration)**.
10 Install the second ring next. **Note:** *The second ring and top ring are different, and can be identified by their cross-sections.* Making sure the ring is the correct way up, fit the ring

into the middle groove on the piston, taking care not to expand the ring any more than is necessary **(see illustration)**.
11 Install the top ring in the same way; making sure the ring is the correct way up. Where the ring is symmetrical, fit it with its identification marking facing upwards.
12 With all the rings in position on the piston, space the ring end gaps correctly **(see illustration)**.
13 Repeat the above procedure for the remaining pistons and rings.

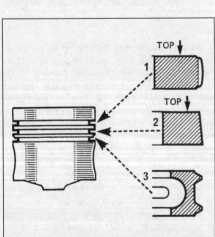

16.10 Piston ring profiles

1 Top compression ring
2 Lower compression ring
3 Oil control ring
Position the TOP markings as shown

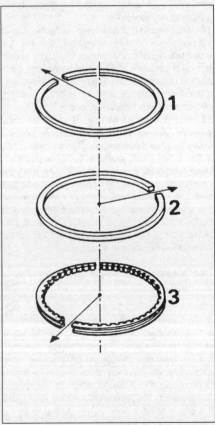

16.12 Position the piston ring end gaps 120° apart

1 Top compression ring
2 Lower compression ring
3 Oil control ring

17.4 Lubricate the main bearing shells before fitting the crankshaft

17.5a Smear a little grease on the crankshaft thrustwashers . . .

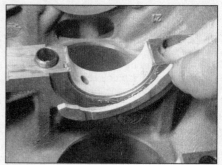

17.5b . . . and stick them to the centre main bearing

17 Crankshaft – bearing selection and refitting

Bearing selection

1 Main bearings for the engines described in this Chapter are available in standard sizes and a range of undersizes to suit reground crankshafts. Refer to your Nissan dealer or automotive engineering workshop for details.

Refitting

2 Clean the backs of the bearing shells, and the bearing locations in both the cylinder block and the main bearing caps.
3 Press the bearing shells into their locations, ensuring that the tab on each shell engages in the notch in the cylinder block/crankcase. Take care not to touch any shell's bearing surface with your fingers. Note that all the upper bearing shells have oil holes in them; and are sometimes grooved, the lower shells are plain.
4 Wipe dry the shells with a lint-free cloth. Liberally lubricate each bearing shell in the cylinder block/crankcase with clean engine oil **(see illustration)**.
5 Using a little grease, stick the upper thrustwashers to each side of the No 3 main bearing upper location; ensure that the oilway grooves on each thrustwasher face outwards (away from the cylinder block) **(see illustrations)**.
6 Lower the crankshaft into position **(see illustration)**, and check the crankshaft endfloat as described in Section 13.
7 Thoroughly degrease the mating surfaces of the cylinder block and the main bearing caps.
8 Lubricate the lower bearing shells in the main bearing caps with clean engine oil. Make sure that the locating lugs on the shells engage with the corresponding recesses in the caps.
9 Fit the main bearing caps **(see illustration)**, using the identification marks to ensure that they are installed in the correct locations and are fitted the correct way round. Insert the retaining bolts, tightening them by hand only.
10 Working in sequence, starting from the centre and working outwards, tighten the

bearing cap retaining bolts to approximately half the specified torque setting **(see illustrations)**. Then go around in the same sequence and tighten the bolts to the full specified torque setting. Check that the crankshaft rotates freely before proceeding any further.
11 Fit the piston/connecting rod assemblies as described in Section 18.
12 Ensure that the mating surfaces of the oil seal housing and cylinder block are clean and dry. Note the correct fitted depth of the oil seal then, using a large flat-bladed screwdriver, lever the seal out of the housing.
13 Fit the new crankshaft seal to the housing, making sure that its sealing lip is facing inwards. Tap the seal squarely into the housing until it is positioned at the same depth as the original was noted prior to removal.
14 Apply a bead of suitable sealant to the oil seal housing mating surface, and make sure

17.6 Lay the crankshaft in position in the crankcase

17.10a Tighten the main bearing cap bolts to the specified torque . . .

that the locating dowels are in position. Slide the housing over the end of the crankshaft, and into position on the cylinder block. Tighten the housing retaining bolts to the specified torque setting.
15 Refit the flywheel, timing chain and sump as described in Part A, B, C or D, of this Chapter.

18 Piston/connecting rod assembly – bearing selection and refitting

Bearing selection

1 Big-end bearings for the engines described in this Chapter are available in standard sizes and a range of undersizes to suit reground crankshafts. Refer to your Nissan dealer or automotive engineering workshop for details.

17.9 Fitting No 5 main bearing cap – petrol engine

17.10b . . . and angle

Refitting

2 Clean the backs of the bearing shells, and the bearing locations in both the connecting rod and bearing cap.

3 Press the bearing shells into their locations, ensuring that the tab on each shell engages in the recess in the connecting rod and cap. Take care not to touch any shell's bearing surface with your fingers, and ensure that the shells are correctly installed so that the upper shell oil hole is correctly aligned with connecting rod oil hole.

4 Note that the following procedure assumes that the crankshaft and main bearing caps are in place (see Section 17).

5 Wipe dry the shells and connecting rods with a lint-free cloth.

6 Lubricate the cylinder bores, the pistons, and piston rings **(see illustration)**, then lay out each piston/connecting rod assembly in its respective position.

7 Start with assembly No 1. Make sure that the piston rings are still spaced as described in Section 16, and then clamp them in position with a piston ring compressor.

8 Insert the piston/connecting rod assembly into the top of cylinder No 1. Ensure that the piston marking (in the form of either an arrow, letter or a dot) on the piston crown is on the correct side of the bore, as noted on removal. Using a block of wood or hammer handle against the piston crown, tap the assembly into the cylinder until the piston crown is flush with the top of the cylinder **(see illustration)**.

9 Ensure that the bearing shell is still correctly installed. Liberally lubricate the crankpin and both bearing shells. Taking care not to mark the cylinder bores, tap the piston/connecting rod assembly down the bore and onto the crankpin. Refit the big-end bearing cap **(see illustrations)**, tightening its retaining nuts finger-tight at first. Note that the faces with the identification marks must match (which means that the bearing shell locating tabs abut each other).

10 Tighten the bearing cap retaining nuts to their Stage 1 torque setting, using a torque wrench and suitable socket. Then tighten them either through the specified Stage 2 angle setting

11 Rotate the crankshaft. Check that it turns freely; some stiffness is to be expected if new components have been fitted, but there should be no signs of binding or tight spots.

12 Refit the three remaining piston/connecting rod assemblies in the same way.

13 Refit the cylinder head, timing chain and sump as described in Part A, B, C or D of this Chapter.

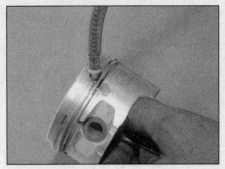

18.6 Lubricating the piston rings

18.9a Lubricate the big-end cap bearing shell …

19 Engine – initial start-up after overhaul

1 With the engine refitted in the vehicle, double-check the engine oil and coolant levels. Make a final check that everything has been reconnected, and that there are no tools or rags left in the engine compartment.

Petrol engine models

2 Remove the spark plugs and disable the fuel system by disconnecting the wiring connectors from the fuel injectors, referring to Chapter 4A, Section 5, for further information.

3 Turn the engine on the starter until the oil pressure warning light goes out. Refit the spark plugs, and reconnect the wiring.

Diesel engine models

4 On the models covered in this Manual, the oil pressure warning light is linked to the STOP warning light, and is not illuminated when the ignition is initially switched on. Therefore it is not possible to check the oil pressure warning light when turning the engine on the starter motor.

5 Prime the fuel system (refer to Chapter 4B, Section 5).

18.8 Using the wooden handle of a hammer to drive the piston into the bore

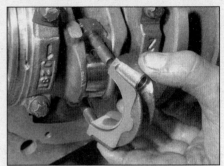

18.9b … then refit the cap

6 Fully depress the accelerator pedal, turn the ignition key to position M, and wait for the preheating warning light to go out.

All models

7 Start the engine, noting that this may take a little longer than usual, due to the fuel system components having been disturbed.

8 While the engine is idling, check for fuel, water and oil leaks. Don't be alarmed if there are some odd smells and smoke from parts getting hot and burning off oil deposits.

9 Assuming all is well; keep the engine idling until hot water is felt circulating through the top hose, then switch off the engine.

10 After a few minutes recheck the oil and coolant levels as described in *Weekly checks*, and top-up as necessary.

11 Note that there is no need to retighten the cylinder head bolts once the engine has first run after reassembly.

12 If new pistons, rings or crankshaft bearings have been fitted, the engine must be treated as new, and run-in for the first 500 miles. Do not operate the engine at full-throttle, or allow it to labour at low engine speeds in any gear. It is recommended that the oil and filter be changed at the end of this period.

Chapter 3
Cooling, heating and ventilation systems

Contents

Degrees of difficulty

Easy, suitable for novice with little experience 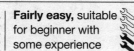	**Fairly easy,** suitable for beginner with some experience 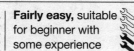	**Fairly difficult,** suitable for competent DIY mechanic 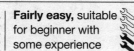	**Difficult,** suitable for experienced DIY mechanic 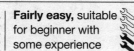	**Very difficult,** suitable for expert DIY or professional

Specifications

General

Cooling system type .... Pressurised sealed system, with front mounted radiator and electric cooling fan(s)

Cooling system pressure:
  Brown cap .... 1.2 bar
  Black cap with yellow hand mark .... 1.4 bar
Reservoir capacity .... 0.8 litres

Thermostat

Petrol engines:
  Opening temperature .... 80.5 to 83.5°C
  Closing temperature .... 77°C
  Maximum valve lift .... 8.0 mm
Water control thermostat (2.0 litre petrol engine):
  Opening temperature .... 93.5 to 96.5°C
  Closing temperature .... 90°C
  Maximum valve lift .... 8.0 mm
Diesel engines:
  1.5 litre (K9K) engine:
    Start of opening .... 89°C
    End of opening .... 97 to 101°C
  2.0 litre (M9R) engine:
    Opening temperature .... 86 to 89°C
    Maximum valve lift .... 8.5 mm

Engine coolant temperature sensor

Resistance at approx:

At 20°C	2.1 to 2.9 kilohms
At 90°C	0.24 to 0.26 kilohms
At 110°C	0.14 to 0.15 kilohms

Air conditioning

Compressor model:

1.6 litre petrol engine	Calsonic Kansei
2.0 litre petrol engine:	
Upto August 2008	Calsonic Kansei
From August 2008	Calsonic Kansei FVC17
1.5 litre diesel engine	Delphi 5 CVC
2.0 litre diesel engine:	
Upto August 2008	Delphi 5 CVC
From August 2008	Calsonic Kansei FVC17
Compressor type	Variable displacement swash plate
Compressor oil:	
Quantity	150 ml
Type	S (DH–PS)
Refrigerant	
Quantity	500 ± 25 g
Type	R134a

Torque wrench settings

	Nm	lbf ft
Petrol engines:		
Coolant pump pulley securing bolts (1.6 litre engine)	7	5
Coolant pump securing bolts	25	18
Cylinder block drain plug	10	8
Thermostat cover securing bolts	17	12
Coolant housing (end of cylinder head) bolts	25	18
Coolant temperature switch	25	18
Air-conditioning compressor mounting bolts	25	18
Air-conditioning compressor clutch disc plate bolt::		
1.6 litre engine	13	10
2.0 litre engine	25	18
Diesel engines:		
Coolant pump pulley securing bolts (2.0 litre engine)	21	15
Coolant pump securing bolts:		
1.5 litre engine	11	8
2.0 litre engine	25	18
Thermostat housing assembly (end of cylinder head) bolts	17	12
Air-conditioning compressor mounting bolts		
1.5 litre engine	21	15
2.0 litre engine	25	18
Air-conditioning compressor clutch disc plate bolt (2.0 litre engine)	25	18

1 General information and precautions

General information

The cooling system is of pressurised type, comprising a coolant pump driven by the auxiliary drivebelt from the crankshaft pulley, crossflow radiator, coolant expansion tank, electric cooling fan(s), thermostat, heater matrix, and all associated hoses and switches.

The system functions as follows. The coolant pump pumps cold coolant around the cylinder block and head passages, and through the inlet manifold, heater and throttle housing to the thermostat housing.

When the engine is cold, the coolant is returned from the thermostat housing to the coolant pump. When the coolant reaches a predetermined temperature, the thermostat opens, and the coolant passes through the top hose to the radiator. As the coolant circulates through the radiator, it is cooled by the inrush of air when the car is in forward motion. The airflow is supplemented by the action of the electric cooling fan(s) when necessary. Upon reaching the bottom of the radiator, the coolant has now cooled, and the cycle is repeated.

When the engine is at normal operating temperature, the coolant expands, and some of it is released through the valve in the radiator pressure cap into the expansion tank. Coolant collects in the tank, and is returned to the radiator when the system cools.

A single or twin electric cooling fan arrangement is used according to model and equipment fitted. The fan assembly is mounted behind the radiator and controlled by the engine management electronic control unit in conjunction with the engine coolant temperature sensor.

Precautions

⚠ *Warning: Do not attempt to remove the radiator pressure cap, or to disturb any part of the cooling system, while the engine is hot, as there is a high risk of scalding. If the radiator pressure cap must be removed before the engine and radiator have fully cooled (even though this is not recommended), the pressure in the cooling system must first be relieved. Cover the cap with a thick layer of cloth, to avoid scalding, and slowly unscrew the pressure cap until a hissing sound is heard. When the hissing has stopped, indicating that*

3.2a Remove the upper intercooler hose

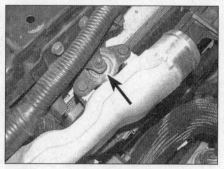

3.2b Undo the mounting bracket and remove the intake pipe

3.3 Disconnect the hoses from the radiator

the pressure has reduced, slowly unscrew the pressure cap until it can be removed; if more hissing sounds are heard, wait until they have stopped before unscrewing the cap completely. At all times, keep your face well away from the pressure cap opening, and protect your hands.

• *Do not allow antifreeze to come into contact with your skin, or with the painted surfaces of the vehicle. Rinse off spills immediately, with plenty of water. Never leave antifreeze lying around in an open container, or in a puddle in the driveway or on the garage floor. Children and pets are attracted by its sweet smell, but antifreeze can be fatal if ingested.*

• *If the engine is hot, the electric cooling fan may start rotating even if the engine is not running. Be careful to keep your hands, hair, and any loose clothing well clear when working in the engine compartment.*

• *Refer to Section 10 for precautions to be observed when working on models equipped with air conditioning.*

2 Cooling system hoses – disconnection and renewal

1 The number, routing and pattern of hoses will vary according to model, but the same basic procedure applies. Before commencing work, make sure that the new hoses are to hand, along with new hose clips if needed. It is good practice to renew the hose clips at the same time as the hoses.

2 Drain the cooling system, as described in Chapter 1A, Section 27 or Chapter 1B, Section 29, saving the coolant if it is fit for re-use. Squirt a little penetrating oil onto the hose clips if they are corroded.

3 Release the hose clips from the hose concerned. Three types of clip are used; worm-drive, spring and 'sardine-can'. The worm-drive clip is released by turning its screw anti-clockwise. The spring clip is released by squeezing its tangs together with pliers, at the same time working the clip away from the hose stub. The 'sardine-can' clip is not re-usable, and is best cut off with snips or side-cutters.

4 Unclip any wires, cables or other hoses, which may be attached to the hose being removed. Make notes for reference when reassembling if necessary.

5 Release the hose from its stubs with a twisting motion. Be careful not to damage the stubs on delicate components such as the radiator. If the hose is stuck fast, the best course is often to cut it off using a sharp knife, but again be careful not to damage the stubs.

6 Before fitting the new hose, smear the stubs with washing-up liquid or a suitable rubber lubricant to aid fitting. Do not use oil or grease, which may attack the rubber.

7 Fit the hose clips over the ends of the hose, and then fit the hose over its stubs. Work the hose into position. When satisfied, locate and tighten the hose clips.

8 Refill the cooling system as described in Chapter 1A, Section 27 or Chapter 1B, Section 29. Run the engine, and check that there are no leaks.

9 Recheck the tightness of the hose clips on any new hoses after a few hundred miles.
10 Top-up the coolant level if necessary.

3 Radiator – removal, inspection and refitting

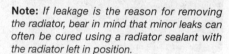

Note: *If leakage is the reason for removing the radiator, bear in mind that minor leaks can often be cured using a radiator sealant with the radiator left in position.*

Removal

1 Drain the cooling system as described in Chapter 1A, Section 27 or Chapter 1B, Section 29.

2 On diesel engines, slacken the retaining clips and remove the intercooler air intake hose from above the radiator, then undo the mounting bracket and move the air intake to one side **(see illustrations)**.

3 Disconnect the remaining coolant hose(s) from the radiator **(see illustration)**.

4 Remove the cooling fan and cowling as described in Section 5

5 On some models it will be necessary to undo the retaining bolts and disconnect the air-conditioning receiver/dryer from the side of the radiator **(see illustration)**.

6 Working at the top of the radiator, unscrew the bolts securing the radiator mounting brackets to the upper body panel, on both sides **(see illustrations)**.

7 Carefully tilt the radiator back towards the engine, and then lift the condenser to

3.5 Disconnect the receiver/dryer from the side of the radiator

3.6a Undo the retaining bolt (arrowed)

3.6b ... and remove the upper mounting bracket

3.7 Condenser lower securing clip (arrowed)

3.8a Lift the radiator …

3.8b … releasing it from the rubber mountings

3.12 Check the rubber mountings

release it from the retaining clips on the front of the radiator **(see illustration)**. Secure the condenser in position to prevent any strain on the air conditioning pipes.

8 Lift the radiator out from the engine compartment; recover the lower mounting rubbers as the radiator is withdrawn **(see illustrations)**.

Inspection

9 If the radiator has been removed due to suspected blockage, reverse-flush it as described in Chapter 1A, Section 27, or Chapter 1B, Section 29. Clean dirt and debris from the radiator fins, using an airline (in which case, wear eye protection) or a soft brush. Be careful, as the fins are sharp, and easily damaged.

10 If necessary, a radiator specialist can perform a 'flow test' on the radiator, to establish whether an internal blockage exists.

11 A leaking radiator must be referred to a specialist for permanent repair. Do not attempt to weld or solder a leaking radiator, as damage to the plastic components may result.

12 Inspect the condition of the radiator mounting rubbers **(see illustration)**, and renew them if necessary.

Refitting

13 Refitting is a reversal of removal, bearing in mind the following points:
  a) *Ensure that the radiator lower lugs engage correctly with the lower mounting rubbers.*
  b) *On completion, refill the cooling system as described in Chapter 1A, Section 27, or Chapter 1B, Section 29.*

4   Thermostat – removal, testing and refitting

Note: *A new seal will be required when refitting the thermostat housing.*

Removal

1 The thermostat is located in a housing bolted to the left-hand side of the cylinder head, at the transmission end of the engine.

2 Depending on model, it may be necessary to remove the air intake ducting to make access easier.

3 Drain the cooling system as described in Chapter 1A, Section 27 or Chapter 1B, Section 29.

4 Disconnect the wiring connector from the temperature sensor in the coolant housing **(see illustration)**.

5 Noting their fitted position slacken the retaining clips and disconnect the cooling system hoses from the housing bolted to the left-hand end of the cylinder head **(see illustration)**.

6 Unscrew the securing bolts **(see illus-**

4.4 Disconnect the wiring connector from the temperature sensor

4.5 Disconnect the coolant hoses

4.6a Undo the coolant housing bolts (arrowed) …

4.6b … and withdraw it from the end of the cylinder head

trations), and remove the thermostat cover and gasket (where applicable), from the housing.

7 Lift the thermostat and seal from the housing, noting the fitted position of the thermostat **(see illustration)**. The small air bleed valve in the thermostat should be in the upper most position.

MR20DE engines only

8 The 2.0 litre (MR20DE) petrol engine has two thermostats fitted, one as above (para-

graphs 1 to 6), and also another one fitted to the housing at the front right-hand end of the engine to the rear of the coolant pump **(see illustration)**.

9 If not already done, drain the cooling system as described in Chapter 1A, Section 27 or Chapter 1B, Section 29.

10 Slacken the retaining clip and disconnect the coolant hose from the thermostat housing **(see illustration)**.

11 Undo the two securing bolts, and remove

the thermostat cover from the housing **(see illustration)**.

12 Lift the thermostat and seal from the housing, noting the fitted position of the thermostat **(see illustrations)**. The small air bleed valve in the thermostat should be in the upper most position.

Testing

Note: *If there is any question about the operation of the thermostat, it's best to renew*

4.7 Note the fitted position of the thermostat

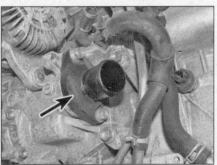

4.8 Coolant thermostat cover (arrowed)

4.10 Disconnect the coolant hose

4.11 Remove cover from housing

4.12a Withdraw the thermostat …

4.12b … noting its fitted position

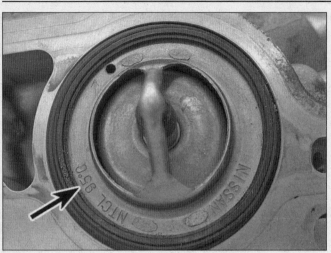

4.14 The temperature opening figure is stamped on the thermostat

4.18 Fit a new gasket to the housing

it – they are not usually expensive items. Testing involves heating in, or over, an open pan of boiling water, which carries with it the risk of scalding. A thermostat that has seen more than five years' service may well be past its best already.

13 A rough test of the thermostat may be made by suspending it with a piece of string in a container full of water. Heat the water to bring it to the boil – the thermostat must open by the time the water boils. If not, renew it.

14 If a thermometer is available, the precise opening temperature of the thermostat may be determined; compare with the figures given in the Specifications. The opening temperature is also marked on the thermostat **(see illustration)**.

15 A thermostat, which fails to close as the water cools down, must also be renewed.

Refitting

16 Commence refitting by thoroughly cleaning the mating faces of the cover and the housing.

17 Refit the thermostat and new seal to the housing, making sure it is fitted in the position noted on removal.

18 Fit the thermostat housing and gasket **(see illustration)**, refit the securing bolts and tighten to the specified torque.

19 Refit the coolant hoses to the housing in the positions noted on removal.

20 Reconnect the wiring plug to the temperature sensor on the coolant housing.

21 On completion, refill the cooling system as described in Chapter 1A, Section 27, or Chapter 1B, Section 29.

---

5 Electric cooling fan and resistor – removal and refitting

1 Disconnect the battery negative terminal (refer to *Disconnecting the battery* in the Reference Chapter).

2 Release the two retaining clips and remove the air intake ducting from the top of the front crossmember **(see illustrations)**.

Cooling fan

3 Release the securing clips, and then disconnect the wiring plug connectors from the fan resistor and the cooling fan motor **(see illustrations)**. Release the wiring loom retaining clips from the fan cowling.

5.2a Release the two retaining clips …

5.2b … and remove the air intake ducting

5.3a Disconnect the wiring connector from the resistor …

5.3b … the cooling fan …

5.3c … then unclip the wiring loom retaining clip

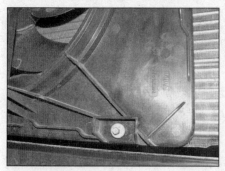

5.4 Undo the fan cowling lower securing bolt

5.5a Release the securing clips from the upper left …

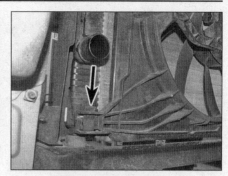

5.5b … the lower left …

4 Slacken and remove the retaining bolt from the right-hand side lower part of the fan cowling **(see illustration)**.

5 Release the two retaining clips from the left-hand side of the fan cowling and the one from the upper right-hand side of the fan cowling **(see illustrations)**.

6 With the retaining clips released, carefully withdraw the cooling fan and cowling upward out from the engine compartment **(see illustration)**. Take care not to damage the radiator fins as the fan cowling is withdrawn.

7 Refitting is a reversal of removal.

Cooling fan resistor

8 The cooling fan resistor is fitted to the top left-hand side of the fan cowling.

9 Release the securing clip, and disconnect the wiring plug connector from the fan resistor **(see illustration 5.3a)**.

10 Undo the retaining bolt, release the locating clips and then slide the resistor out from the fan cowling **(see illustrations)**.

11 Refitting is a reversal of removal.

5.5c … and the upper right of the cowling

5.6 Withdraw the fan cowling

temperature gauge and the cooling fan are all operated by the engine management ECM using the signal supplied by this sensor.

2 The unit contains a thermistor – an electronic component whose electrical resistance decreases at a predetermined rate as its temperature rises.

3 The engine management ECM supplies the sensor with a set voltage and then, by measuring the current flowing in the sensor circuit, it determines the engine temperature. This information is then used, in conjunction with other inputs, to control the engine management system and associated components.

4 If the sensor circuit should fail to provide plausible information, the ECM back-up facility will override the sensor signal. In this event, the ECM assumes a predetermined setting which will allow the engine management system to operate, albeit at

reduced efficiency. When this occurs, the engine warning light on the instrument panel will come on, and the advice of a Nissan dealer should be sought. The sensor itself can be tested by removing it, and checking the resistances at various temperatures using an ohmmeter (heat the sensor in a container of water, and monitor the temperature with a thermometer. The resistance values are given in the Specifications. *Do not* attempt to test the circuit with the sensor fitted to the engine, and the wiring connector fitted, as there is a high risk of damaging the ECM.

Removal

5 Disconnect the battery negative terminal (refer to *Disconnecting the battery* in the Reference Chapter).

6 Partially drain the cooling system to just below the level of the sensor (see Chapter 1A, Section 27 or Chapter 1B, Section 29). Alternatively, have ready a suitable bung to

<table>
<tr><td>

6 Cooling system electrical sensors – testing, removal and refitting

</td></tr>
</table>

Coolant temperature sensor

Testing

1 The coolant temperature sensor is fitted to the coolant/thermostat housing on the left-hand end of the cylinder head. The coolant

5.10a Undo the retaining bolt (arrowed) …

5.10b … slide the resistor (arrowed) …

5.10c … and withdraw the resistor

6.7a Disconnect the wiring connector – petrol model

6.7b Disconnect the wiring connector – diesel model

6.9a Withdraw the retaining clip ...

6.9b ... and remove the sensor and seal

6.13 Wiring connector to evaporator sensor (arrowed)

6.14 Temperature probe is clipped to the evaporator

plug the aperture in the housing when the sensor is removed.

7 Disconnect the wiring connector from the sensor (see illustrations).

8 On petrol engines, carefully unscrew the sensor and recover the sealing ring. If the system has not been drained, plug the sensor aperture to prevent further coolant loss.

9 On diesel engines, the sensor is clipped in place; prise out the sensor retaining circlip then remove the sensor and sealing ring from the housing (see illustrations). If the system has not been drained, plug the sensor aperture to prevent further coolant loss.

Refitting

10 Check the condition of the sealing ring and renew it if necessary.

11 Refitting is a reversal of removal, but refill (or top-up) the cooling system as described in Chapter 1A, Section 27 or Chapter 1B, Section 29, and Weekly checks.

12 On completion, start the engine and run it until it reaches normal operating temperature. Continue to run the engine until the cooling fan cuts in and out correctly.

Air conditioning temperature sensor

13 The sensor is clipped into the fins on the evaporator, located inside the heater/air conditioning unit behind the facia. To access the temperature sensor wiring connector, remove the centre console right-hand front trim panel (see illustration).

14 Remove the air-conditioning evaporator, as

described in Section 11, then the temperature sensor can be unclipped from the fins in the evaporator (see illustration).

7	Coolant pump – removal, inspection and refitting

Note: *A new gasket will be required when refitting the coolant pump.*

Removal

1 Disconnect the battery negative terminal (refer to *Disconnecting the battery* in the Reference Chapter).

2 Drain the cooling system as described in Chapter 1A, Section 27 or Chapter 1B, Section 29.

3 Remove the auxiliary drivebelts as described

7.5 Remove the coolant pump pulley

in Chapter 1A, Section 10 or Chapter 1B, Section 10.

1.6 litre petrol engine

4 To make access easier remove the alternator as described in Chapter 5A, Section 5.

5 Unscrew the three retaining bolts, and remove the pulley from the coolant pump (see illustration). If required, counterhold the pulley in order to unscrew the bolts. This is most easily achieved by wrapping an old drivebelt tightly around the pulley to act in a similar manner to a strap wrench.

6 Unscrew the retaining bolts, and withdraw the coolant pump from the cylinder block (see illustration). Remove the gasket and discard, as a new one will be required for refitting.

2.0 litre petrol engine

7 To make access easier remove the alternator as described in Chapter 5A, Section 5.

7.6 Undo the coolant pump bolts – 1.6 litre petrol

7.8a Undo the two coolant pump bolts (arrowed) …

7.8b … and the two bolts at the rear …

7.8c … then remove the pump and gasket – 2.0 litre petrol

7.10 Unscrew the securing bolts (arrowed)

7.11a Undo the pump retaining bolts (arrowed)

7.11b Fitting a new gasket to the coolant pump

8 Unscrew the four retaining bolts, and remove the coolant pump from the housing. Note two of the bolts are accessed from the front of the pump and two from the rear **(see illustrations)**. Remove the gasket and discard, as a new one will be required for refitting.

1.5 litre diesel engine

9 Remove the timing belt as described in Chapter 2C, Section 6.
10 Undo the retaining bolts and remove the rear timing belt cover from the cylinder block **(see illustration)**.
11 Unscrew the retaining bolts, and remove the coolant pump from the cylinder block **(see illustrations)**. Remove the gasket and discard, as a new one will be required for refitting.

2.0 litre diesel engine

12 To make access easier remove the alternator as described in Chapter 5A, Section 5.
13 Unscrew the three retaining bolts, and remove the pulley from the coolant pump **(see illustrations)**. If required, counterhold the pulley in order to unscrew the bolts. This is most easily achieved by wrapping an old drivebelt tightly around the pulley to act in a similar manner to a strap wrench.
14 Unscrew the retaining bolts, and withdraw the coolant pump from the cylinder block **(see illustrations)**. Prise out the O-ring seal from the groove in the pump body, discard, as a new one will be required for refitting.

7.13a Hold the pulley stationary using an oil filter removal strap, and undo the bolts

7.13b Removing the pulley

7.14a Unbolt and remove the coolant pump …

7.14b … then remove the O-ring seal

7.18 Fit new gasket to the coolant pump

8.9 Vehicle diagnostic plug location (arrowed)

Inspection

15 Check the pump body and impeller for signs of excessive corrosion. Turn the impeller, and check for stiffness due to corrosion, or roughness due to excessive endplay.

16 No spare parts are available for the pump, and if faulty, worn or corroded, a new pump should be fitted.

Refitting

17 Commence refitting by thoroughly cleaning all traces of gasket/sealant from the mating faces of the pump and cylinder block.

18 Where applicable, fit new gasket/seal to the coolant pump **(see illustration)**.

19 Place the pump in position in the cylinder block, refit the bolts to their correct locations and tighten to the specified torque.

20 On 1.6 litre petrol engines and 2.0 litre diesel engines, refit the pump pulley and tighten to the specified torque. Counterhold the pulley using an old drivebelt as during removal.

21 On 1.5 litre diesel engines refit the timing belt as described in Chapter 2C, Section 6.

22 Refit and tension the auxiliary drivebelts as described in Chapter 1A, Section 10 or Chapter 1B, Section 10.

23 Refill the cooling system as described in Chapter 1A, Section 27 or Chapter 1B, Section 29.

24 Reconnect the battery negative terminal (refer to *Disconnecting the battery* in the Reference Chapter).

8 Heater/ventilation system – general information

Note: *Refer to Section 10 for information on the air conditioning side of the system.*

Manually-controlled system

1 The heating/ventilation system consists of a four-speed blower motor (housed behind the facia), face level vents in the centre and at each end of the facia, and air ducts to the front footwells.

2 The control unit is located in the facia, and the controls operate flap valves to deflect and mix the air flowing through the various parts of the heating/ventilation system. The flap valves

are contained in the air distribution housing, which acts as a central distribution unit, passing air to the various ducts and vents.

3 Cold air enters the system through the grille in the scuttle. If required, the airflow is boosted by the blower, and then flows through the various ducts, according to the settings of the controls. Stale air is expelled through ducts at the rear of the vehicle. If warm air is required, the cold air is passed over the heater matrix, which is heated by the engine coolant.

4 A recirculation button enables the outside air supply to be closed off, while the air inside the vehicle is recirculated. This can be useful to prevent unpleasant odours entering from outside the vehicle, but should only be used briefly, as the recirculated air inside the vehicle will soon become stale.

5 On some diesel engine models an electric heater is fitted into the heater housing. When the coolant temperature is cold, the heater warms the air before it enters the heater matrix. This quickly increases the temperature of the heater matrix on cold starts, resulting in warm air being available to heat the vehicle interior soon after start-up.

Automatic climate control

6 A fully automatic electronic climate control system is fitted to some models. The main components of the system are exactly the same as those described for the manual system, the only major difference being that the temperature and distribution flaps in the heating/ventilation housing are operated by electric motors rather than cables.

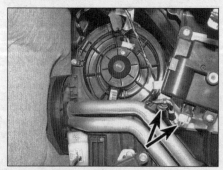

9.3 Disconnect the wiring connector and securing clip (arrowed)

7 The operation of the system is controlled by the electronic control module (which is incorporated in the blower motor assembly) along with the following sensors.

a) *The passenger compartment sensor – informs the control module of the temperature of the air inside the passenger compartment.*

b) *Evaporator temperature sensor – informs the control module of the evaporator temperature.*

c) *Heater matrix temperature sensor – informs the control module of the heater matrix temperature.*

8 Using the information from the above sensors, the control module determines the appropriate settings for the heating/ventilation system housing flaps to maintain the passenger compartment at the desired setting on the control panel.

9 If the system develops a fault, the vehicle should be taken to a Nissan dealer. A complete test of the system can then be carried out, using a special electronic diagnostic test unit, which is simply plugged into the system's diagnostic connector. This is located inside the passenger compartment, below the fuse box on the drivers side of the facia panel **(see illustration)**.

9 Heater/ventilation components – removal and refitting

Heater blower motor

1 Disconnect the battery negative terminal (refer to *Disconnecting the battery* in the Reference Chapter).

2 Remove the glovebox as described in Chapter 11, Section 26.

3 To make removal of the motor easier, disconnect the wiring connector from the heater flap control motor and release the wiring loom securing clips and move it to one side **(see illustration)**.

4 Reaching up around the rear of the heater housing, disconnect the wiring connector from the top of the blower motor **(see illustration)**.

9.4 Disconnect the wiring connector

9.5a Remove the retaining screw (arrowed) – where fitted

9.5b Rotate the motor anti-clockwise ...

9.5c ... and remove it from the heater housing

5 Undo the retaining screw, then turn the blower motor anti-clockwise to withdraw it from the rear of the heater housing **(see illustrations)**.

6 Refitting is a reversal of removal.

Heater blower motor resistor

7 Disconnect the battery negative terminal (refer to *Disconnecting the battery* in the Reference Chapter).

8 Remove the glovebox as described in Chapter 11, Section 26.

9 The resistor is located below the blower motor, in the left-hand side of the heater housing **(see illustration)**.

10 Disconnect the wiring connector from the blower motor resistor **(see illustration)**.

11 Undo the retaining screws and withdraw the resistor from the rear of the heater housing **(see illustrations)**.

12 Refitting is a reversal of removal.

Heater control panel

13 Unclip the lower trim panel from around the heater control panel. Release the trim panel by carefully levering at each side of the trim, to release the securing clips **(see illustrations)**.

14 As the lower trim panel is withdrawn

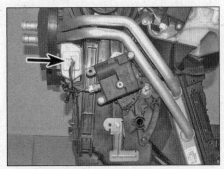

9.9 Location of heater blower resistor (arrowed)

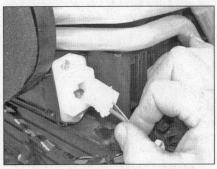

9.10 Disconnect the wiring connector

9.11a Remove the two retaining screws ...

9.11b ... and withdraw it from the heater housing

9.13a Unclip the trim panel ...

9.13b ... releasing the side securing clips ...

9.13c ... and the upper securing clips

9.14 Disconnect the wiring connectors as it is removed

9.15 Unclip the upper trim panel, releasing the side securing clips

9.16 Disconnect the wiring connectors as it is removed

disconnect the wiring connectors from the rear of the panel **(see illustration)**.

15 Unclip the upper vent trim panel from the centre of the facia. Release the trim panel by carefully levering at each side of the trim, to release the securing clips **(see illustration)**.

16 As the trim panel is withdrawn disconnect the wiring connectors from the rear of the panel **(see illustration)**.

Manually operated system

17 Remove the glovebox assembly, as described in Chapter 11, Section 26.

18 Release the retaining clips and remove the trim panel from the lower part of the steering column and the front of the centre console.

19 Disconnect the heater control cables from the right and left-hand side of the heater housing, noting their fitted positions.

20 Undo the three retaining screws, and slightly withdraw the heater control panel

from the facia. Tilt the control panel and disconnect the wiring connector from the rear of the control panel, then withdraw the heater control panel, complete with cables from the facia. Note the routing of the cables, as they are withdrawn through the facia.

21 Refitting is the reverse of removal. Ensure the control cables are correctly reconnected and securely held by the retaining clips; check the operation of the control knobs before refitting the trim panels and glovebox assembly.

Automatic climate system

22 Undo the three retaining screws, and withdraw the control panel from the facia **(see illustration)**.

23 Disconnect the wiring connectors from the rear of the control panel **(see illustration)**, and then withdraw the heater control panel from the facia.

24 Refitting is the reverse of removal. Check the operation of the controls before refitting the trim panels.

Control cables

25 Remove the manually operated system control panel as described previously in this Section.

26 Before disconnecting the cables from the rear of the control panel note their fitted position.

27 Release the retaining clip and then detach the relevant cable from the lever on the rear of the control panel.

28 Refitting is the reverse of removal, ensuring the cable is secured in place by its retaining clips. Check the operation of the control panel and cables.

Heater air flap motors

29 Depending on model, there is a number of air flap motors located on each side of the heater/blower motor housing **(see illustration)**.

30 To access the air intake door motor, the facia will need to be removed, as it is located in the top of the heater housing air duct **(see illustration)**.

31 To access the motors on the left-hand side of the heater housing, remove the glovebox assembly, as described in Chapter 11, Section 26.

32 To access the air mix door motor on the right-hand side of the heater housing, release the retaining clips and remove the trim panel from the front of the centre console **(see illustration)**.

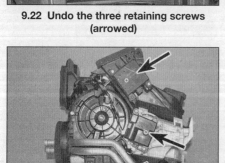

9.22 Undo the three retaining screws (arrowed)

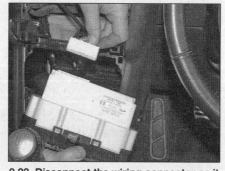

9.23 Disconnect the wiring connector as it is removed

9.29 Heater air control flap motors (arrowed) – left-hand side shown

9.30 Intake door control motor (arrowed)

9.32 Unclip the lower trim panel

33 Disconnect the motor wiring connector, then unscrew the retaining bolts and withdraw the motor **(see illustrations)**. Note, as the motor is withdrawn from the flap spindle, depending on the position of the flap, it may rotate in the heater housing.

34 Refitting is a reversal of removal, making sure the motors are located correctly on the housing. Before refitting the trim panels, check the operation of the motors, as they may need to be turned on the spindles to operate correctly.

Pollen filter

35 Remove and refit the pollen filter, as described in Chapter 1A, section 18, or Chapter 1B, Section 19.

Heater matrix

Note: *Depending on model, it may be possible to remove and refit the heater matrix without removing the facia and heater housing assembly. Remove the glovebox and lower trim panels from the left-hand side of the facia, to check the heater matrix pipe connections. Also check with your local Nissan dealer to see if the new heater matrix comes complete with coolant pipes for your model.*

Without facia removal

Note: *Check for the availability of parts with your local Nissan dealer, before commencing any work.*

36 Drain the cooling system as described in Chapter 1A, Section 27 or Chapter 1B, Section 29. Alternatively, clamp the heater matrix coolant hoses to minimise coolant loss.

37 Release the retaining clips and disconnect the coolant hoses from the heater matrix pipe unions on the engine compartment bulkhead **(see illustrations)**.

38 To access the heater matrix on the left-hand side of the heater housing, remove the glovebox assembly, as described in Chapter 11, Section 26. Check the coolant pipe connections on the heater matrix. If the pipes have retaining clips securing them to the heater matrix, carry out the following procedure.

39 On diesel models with additional heater, undo the retaining screw and move the wiring connector mounting bracket to one side (see paragraphs 51 to 56).

40 On models with manual heater control

9.33a Disconnect the wiring connector, undo the retaining screws …

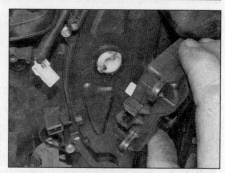
9.33b … and remove the motor from the housing

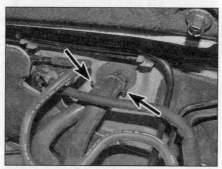
9.37a Release the retaining clips (arrowed) …

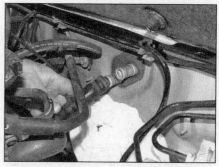
9.37b … and remove the heater hoses

panel, unclip the operating cable from the flap on the side of the heater housing and move it to one side, noting its fitted position.

41 Position a container beneath the heater matrix pipe unions on the left-hand side of the heating/ventilation housing to catch any spilt coolant.

42 Use a flat ended screwdriver to release the coolant pipe securing clips from the matrix, catching any spilt coolant in the container. Free the coolant pipes from the matrix and move them to one side, taking care not to damage them. Recover the sealing rings fitted to the pipe unions and discard them; new ones should be used on refitting.

43 Slide the matrix out from the housing and keep the matrix unions uppermost as the matrix is removed to prevent more coolant spillage.

With facia removal

Note: *Check for the availability of parts with*

your local Nissan dealer, before commencing any work.

44 To access the heater matrix on the left-hand side of the heater housing, remove the glovebox assembly, as described in Chapter 11, Section 26.

45 Check the coolant pipe connections on the heater matrix. If the pipes are fixed to the heater matrix, carry out the following procedure. As the coolant pipes go up through the bulkhead, if the pipes are part of the heater matrix assembly **(see illustration)**.

46 This work entails removal of the centre console, complete facia assembly, wiring loom, facia support braces and metal crossmember **(see illustration)**, as described in Chapter 11, Section 26.

47 With the heater assembly removed from the vehicle, remove the sealing foam from around the coolant pipes **(see illustration)**.

48 Undo the retaining screw and unclip the

9.45 Check the heater matrix pipes on the left-hand side of the heater housing

9.46 Removing the support brace from over the heater housing

9.47 Remove the sealing foam from around the heater matrix pipes

9.48a Undo the retaining screw (arrowed) ...

9.48b ... and unclip the plastic bracket

9.49 Slide the heater matrix out from the side of the housing

9.51 Location of the additional heater (arrowed)

9.55 Undo the retaining screws and remove the heater

9.57 Location of the ambient temperature sensor (arrowed)

plastic mounting bracket from around the coolant pipes **(see illustrations)**.

49 Slide the matrix out from the heater housing, keeping the coolant pipes uppermost to prevent any coolant spillage **(see illustration)**.

50 Refitting is a reversal of removal, making sure the foam seal around the heater matrix is located correctly, before sliding it back into the housing.

Additional heater (diesel models)

51 Depending on model, there may be an additional heater fitted, to the rear left-hand side of the heater housing **(see illustration)**.

52 On right-hand drive models, remove the glovebox and passenger's side central kick panel as described in Chapter 11, Section 26.

53 On left-hand drive models, remove the trim panel above the pedals, undo the two fasteners and remove the trim panel at the front of the centre console, adjacent to the pedals.

54 Release the wiring securing clip and disconnect the wiring plug connectors for the heater element.

55 Undo the two retaining screws, and slide the heater element out from the housing. **(see illustration)**.

56 Refitting is the reverse of removal.

Ambient temperature sensor

57 The ambient temperature sensor is located, at the front of the vehicle, behind the front bumper just below the bonnet catch **(see illustration)**.

58 To remove the sensor, remove the front bumper as described in Chapter 11, Section 6.

59 Disconnect the wiring connector from the sensor, and then unclip the sensor from the front support brace **(see illustrations)**.

60 Refitting is the reverse of removal.

9.59a Disconnect the wiring connector ...

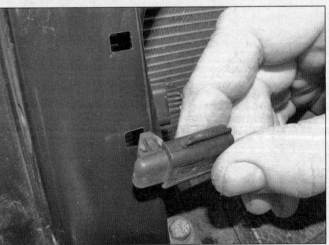

9.59b ... and unclip it from the front panel

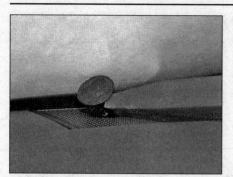

9.62a Unclip the sunlight sensor ...

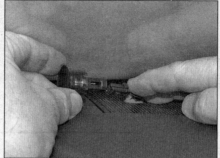

9.62b ... and disconnect the wiring connector

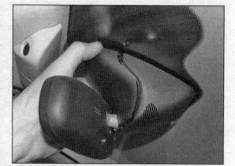

9.65a Unclip the mirror upper plastic cover ...

9.65b ... and the lower plastic cover ...

9.66 ... to access the rain sensor

Sunlight sensor

61 The sunlight sensor is fitted to the small speaker grill at the right-hand side, on the top of the facia, nearest to the windscreen.

62 Carefully unclip the sensor from the grill panel, and then disconnect the wiring connector **(see illustrations)**.

63 If the wiring is not very long, as it may be clipped to the underside of the facia, it may not be easy to remove the sensor. If required, unclip the speaker grill panel to make removal easier.

64 Refitting is the reverse of removal.

Rain sensor

65 Unclip the plastic trim from around the mirror base **(see illustrations)**.

66 Disconnect the wiring plug connector and then release the securing clips one at each side of the sensor to remove it from the mounting base on the windscreen **(see illustration)**.

67 Refitting is a reversal of removal.

10 Air conditioning system – general information and precautions

General information

1 An air conditioning system is available on all models. It enables the temperature of incoming air to be lowered, and also dehumidifies the air, which makes for rapid demisting and increased comfort.

2 The cooling side of the system works in the same way as a domestic refrigerator. Refrigerant gas is drawn into a belt-driven compressor, and passes into a condenser mounted on the front of the radiator, where it loses heat and becomes liquid. The liquid passes through an expansion valve to an evaporator, where it changes from liquid under high pressure to gas under low pressure. This change is accompanied by a drop in temperature, which cools the evaporator. The refrigerant returns to the compressor, and the cycle begins again.

3 Air blown through the evaporator passes to the heating/ventilation housing, where it is mixed with hot air blown through the heater matrix to achieve the desired temperature in the passenger compartment.

4 The heating side of the system works in the same way as on models without air conditioning (see Section 9).

5 The operation of the system is controlled electronically by the ECM integral with the control panel. Any problems with the system should be referred to a Nissan dealer, or suitably-equipped specialist.

Precautions

6 When an air conditioning system is fitted, it is necessary to observe special precautions whenever dealing with any part of the system, or its associated components. The refrigerant is potentially dangerous, and should only be handled by qualified persons. Uncontrolled discharging of the refrigerant is dangerous and damaging to the environment for the following reasons.

a) *If it is splashed onto the skin, it can cause frostbite.*

b) *The refrigerant is heavier then air and so displaces oxygen. In a confined space, which is not adequately ventilated, this could lead to a risk of suffocation. The gas is odourless and colourless so there is no warning of its presence in the atmosphere.*

c) *Although not poisonous, in the presence of a naked flame (including a cigarette) it forms a noxious gas that causes headaches, nausea, etc.*

⚠ *Warning: Never attempt to open any air conditioning system refrigerant pipe/hose union without first having the system fully discharged by an air conditioning*

specialist. On completion of work, have the system recharged with the correct type and amount of fresh refrigerant.

⚠ *Warning: Always seal disconnected refrigerant pipe/ hose unions as soon as they are disconnected. Failure to form an airtight seal on any union will result in the dehydrator reservoir become saturated, necessitating its renewal. Also renew all sealing rings disturbed.*

Caution: Do not operate the air conditioning system if it is known to be short of refrigerant as this could damage the compressor.

11 Air conditioning system components – removal and refitting

⚠ *Warning: Refer to the precautions given in Section 10 and have the system discharged by an air conditioning specialist before carrying out any work on the air conditioning system.*

Note: *If necessary for access to other components, the compressor can be unbolted and moved aside, without disconnecting its flexible hoses, after removing the auxiliary drivebelt.*

Compressor

1 Have the air conditioning system fully discharged and evacuated by an air conditioning specialist.

11.3a Undo the nut/bolt (arrowed) securing the refrigerant pipes to the compressor

11.3b Plug the compressor and pipes to prevent contamination

2 Remove the auxiliary drivebelt as described in Chapter 1A, Section 10 or Chapter 1B, Section 10 (as applicable).

3 Unscrew the nut and bolt securing the refrigerant pipe retaining plates to the compressor **(see illustrations)**. Separate the pipes from the compressor and quickly seal the pipe and compressor unions to prevent the entry of moisture into the refrigerant circuit. Discard the sealing rings, new ones must be used on refitting.

⚠️ **Warning: Failure to seal the refrigerant pipe unions will result in the dehydrator reservoir become saturated, necessitating its renewal.**

4 Disconnect the compressor wiring connector(s), and unclip the wiring harness from the retaining clips **(see illustration)**.

5 Unscrew the compressor mounting bolts, then free the compressor from its mounting bracket and remove it from the engine **(see illustrations)**. Where applicable, take care not to lose any spacers from the compressor mountings.

6 If the compressor is to be renewed, drain the refrigerant oil from the old compressor. The specialist who recharges the refrigerant system will need to add this amount of oil to the system.

7 Where fitted, ensure any spacers are correctly

fitted to the mounting bolts, then manoeuvre the compressor into position and fit the bolts.

8 Tighten the compressor front (drivebelt pulley end) mounting bolts to the specified torque first then tighten the rear bolts.

9 Lubricate the new refrigerant pipe sealing rings with compressor oil. Remove the plugs and install the sealing rings then quickly fit the refrigerant pipes to the compressor. Ensure the refrigerant pipes are correctly joined then refit the retaining bolt, tighten it securely.

10 Reconnect the wiring connector then refit the auxiliary drivebelt (see Chapter 1A, Section 10 or Chapter 1B, Section 10).

11 Have the air conditioning system recharged with the correct type and amount of refrigerant by a specialist before using the system. Remember to inform the specialist which components have been renewed, so they can add the correct amount of oil.

Condenser

12 Have the air conditioning system fully discharged by an air conditioning specialist.

13 Remove the radiator as described in Section 3.

14 Undo the retaining bolts and disconnect the refrigerant pipes from the right-hand side of the condenser. Recover the O-ring seals **(see illustrations)**. Separate the pipes from

11.4 Disconnect the compressor wiring connector

11.5a Remove the compressor mounting bolts (arrowed) ...

11.5b ... and remove the compressor

11.14a Undo the upper bolt ...

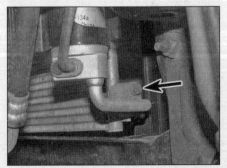

11.14b ... and lower bolt securing the refrigerant pipes to the condenser

11.16 Make sure the condenser retaining clips are secure

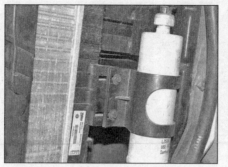

11.17a Undo the receiver/dryer securing bolts – petrol models

11.17b Undo the receiver/dryer securing bolts – diesel models

the condenser and quickly seal the pipe and condenser unions to prevent the entry of moisture into the refrigerant circuit. Discard the sealing rings, new ones must be used on refitting.

 Warning: Failure to seal the refrigerant pipe unions will result in the dehydrator reservoir become saturated, necessitating its renewal.

15 Move the top of the condenser to the rear and withdraw it out from the engine compartment.

16 Refitting is a reversal of removal. Noting the following points:

a) Ensure the condenser is seated in the locating clips on the radiator securely **(see illustration).**

b) Lubricate the sealing rings with compressor oil. Remove the plugs and install the sealing rings then quickly fit

the refrigerant pipes to the condenser. Securely tighten the dehydrator pipe union bolt/nut and ensure the compressor pipe is correctly joined.

c) Refit the radiator with reference to Section 3.

d) Have the air conditioning system recharged with the correct type and amount of refrigerant by a specialist before using the system.

Receiver/dryer

17 The receiver/dryer is located on the right-hand side of the condenser (as viewed from the drivers seat). It is bolted to the rear of the radiator on petrol models, and it is bolted to the front of the condenser on diesel engines **(see illustrations).**

18 On diesel models, remove the front bumper as described in Chapter 11, Sec-

tion 6. Then release the securing clips and remove the plastic shield/cover from the front of the receiver/dryer **(see illustrations).**

19 Have the air conditioning system fully discharged by an air conditioning specialist.

20 Disconnect the wiring connector from the top of the receiver/dryer **(see illustrations).**

21 Undo the retaining bolt and disconnect the refrigerant pipe from the bottom of the receiver/dryer **(see illustrations).** Separate the pipe from the condenser and quickly seal the pipe and condenser union to prevent the entry of moisture into the refrigerant circuit. Discard the sealing rings, new ones must be used on refitting.

 Warning: Failure to seal the refrigerant pipe unions will result in the dehydrator reservoir become saturated, necessitating its renewal.

11.18a Release the retaining clips ...

11.18b ... and remove the trim panel from the front of the radiator

11.20a Disconnect the wiring connector – petrol models

11.20b Disconnect the wiring connector – diesel models

11.21a Undo the bolt securing the refrigerant pipes to the receiver/dryer – petrol models

11.21b Undo the bolts securing the refrigerant pipes to the receiver/dryer – diesel models

11.22a Unbolt the mounting bracket – petrol models

11.22b Unbolt the mounting bracket – diesel models

11.30 Remove the sealing foam from the expansion valve

22 Unscrew the mounting bracket bolts/screws, then free the receiver/dryer from its mounting bracket and remove it from the engine compartment **(see illustrations)**.

23 Refitting is a reversal of removal. Noting the following points:

a) *Ensure the receiver/dryer is correctly fitted in position and the wiring connector is secure.*

b) *Lubricate the sealing rings with compressor oil. Remove the plugs and install the sealing rings then quickly fit the refrigerant pipes to the condenser and tighten them securely.*

c) *On diesel models, refit the plastic shield/cover, and then refit the front bumper as described in Chapter 11, Section 6.*

d) *Have the air conditioning system recharged with the correct type and amount of refrigerant by a specialist before using the system.*

Pressure switch

24 The switch is located in the top of the receiver/dryer **(see illustrations 11.17a & 11.17b)**.

25 Have the air conditioning system fully discharged by an air conditioning specialist.

26 Disconnect the wiring connector **(see illustrations 11.20a & 11.20b)**, and then unscrew the switch from the receiver/dryer. Quickly seal the union to prevent the entry of moisture into the refrigerant circuit.

Warning: Failure to seal the refrigerant pipe unions will result in the dehydrator reservoir become saturated, necessitating its renewal.

27 Refitting is a reversal of removal noting the following points:

a) *Lubricate the switch seal with compressor oil.*

b) *Have the air conditioning system recharged with the correct type and*

amount of refrigerant by a specialist prior to using the system.

Evaporator

28 Have the air conditioning system fully discharged and evacuated by an air conditioning specialist.

29 Remove the heating/ventilation housing as described in Section 9, for the removal of the heater matrix.

30 With the heater assembly removed from the vehicle, remove the sealing foam from around the refrigerant expansion valve connection **(see illustration)**.

31 Remove the air mix door motor on the right-hand side of the heater housing, as described in Section 9. Note, as the motor is withdrawn from the flap spindle, depending on the position of the flap, it may rotate in the heater housing.

32 Undo the retaining screws and remove the plastic evaporator cover from the right-hand side of the heater housing **(see illustration)**.

33 Release the temperature sensor wiring from the slot in the heater housing **(see illustration)**.

34 Slide the evaporator from the housing, withdrawing the temperature sensor with it, if required unclip the sensor from the evaporator **(see illustrations)**.

35 If required undo the retaining screws and remove the refrigerant pipes and expansion valve from the evaporator **(see illustration)**.

36 Refitting is a reversal of removal but have the air conditioning system recharged with the correct type and amount of refrigerant by a specialist prior to using the system.

11.32 Remove the cover from the evaporator

11.33 Unclip the wiring from the housing

11.34a Slide the evaporator out from the heater housing

11.34b Temperature sensor clipped to the evaporator

11.35 Undo the retaining screws to remove the pipes and expansion valve

11.38 Pull back the sound proofing ...

11.39a ... to access the refrigerant pipe retaining bolt ...

11.39b ... undo bolt and disconnect the refrigerant pipes

11.40a Plug the openings in the expansion valve ...

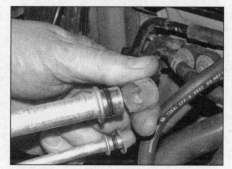

11.40b ... and the refrigerant pipes

11.42 Fit new O-ring seals on re-assembly

Expansion valve

37 Have the air conditioning system fully discharged and evacuated by an air conditioning specialist.

38 Release the fasteners and remove the sound insulation material from the engine compartment bulkhead **(see illustration)**.

39 Undo the retaining bolt and withdraw the refrigerant pipes from the connection at the engine compartment bulkhead **(see illustrations)**.

40 Plug/cover the openings in the refrigerant pipes and the expansion valve to prevent contamination/saturation **(see illustrations)**.

⚠ **Warning: Failure to seal the refrigerant pipe unions will result in the receiver/dryer becoming saturated, necessitating its renewal**

41 Pull the rubber seal from around the pipes connection at the bulkhead, and then undo the two bolts from the centre of the expansion valve, and remove it from the bulkhead.

42 Recover and discard the O-ring seals from the refrigerant pipes and expansion valve – new ones must be fitted **(see illustration)**.

43 Refitting is a reversal of removal but have the air conditioning system recharged with the correct type and amount of refrigerant by a specialist prior to using the system.

Chapter 4 Part A:
Petrol engine fuel and exhaust systems

Contents

Degrees of difficulty

Easy, suitable for novice with little experience	**Fairly easy,** suitable for beginner with some experience	**Fairly difficult,** suitable for competent DIY mechanic	**Difficult,** suitable for experienced DIY mechanic	**Very difficult,** suitable for expert DIY or professional

Specifications

General

System type . . . .   Nissan Electronic Concentrated Control System (ECCS) multi-point injection

Fuel system data

Idle speed (not adjustable – controlled by ECU):
   1.6 litre . . . .   650 ± 50 rpm
   2.0 litre . . . .   700 ± 50 rpm
Idle mixture CO content . . . .   Less than 1.0 % (not adjustable – controlled by ECU)
Fuel pump type . . . .   Electric, immersed in tank

Fuel system component test data

Fuel pump resistance at 25°C:

  Terminals 1 and 3 .... 0.2 to 5.0 ohms

Throttle housing position sensor voltages:

  Meter connected between terminal 33 and earth:

    Pedal fully released .... More than 0.36 volts

    Pedal fully depressed .... Less than 4.75 volts

  Meter connected between terminal 34 and earth:

    Pedal fully released .... Less than 4.75 volts

    Pedal fully depressed .... More than 0.36 volts

Throttle pedal position sensor voltages:

  Meter connected between terminal 110 and earth:

    Pedal fully released .... 0.6 to 0.9 volts

    Pedal fully depressed .... 3.9 to 4.7 volts

  Meter connected between terminal 103 and earth:

    Pedal fully released .... 0.3 to 0.6 volts

    Pedal fully depressed .... 1.9 to 2.4 volts

Fuel injector resistance (between 10 to 60°C) .... 11.1 to 14.5 ohms

Throttle control motor resistance at 25°C

  Terminals 5 and 6 .... Approximately 1.0 to 15.0 ohms

Heated oxygen sensor – resistance at 25°C

  Terminals 2 and 3 .... 3.3 to 4.4 ohms

  Terminals 1 and 2, 3, 4 .... Infinity (continuity should not exist)

  Terminals 4 and 1, 2, 3 .... Infinity (continuity should not exist)

Inlet air temperature sensor resistances (terminals 1 and 2):

  At 25°C (voltage 3.3 volts) .... 1.800 to 2.200 ohms

  At 80°C (voltage 1.2 volts) .... 0.283 to 0.359 ohms

Inlet valve timing control solenoid valve:

  Terminals 1 and 2 .... 6.7 to 7.7 ohms at 20°C

  Terminals 1 or 2 and earth .... Infinity (continuity should not exist)

Knock sensor:

  Between terminals 1 and 2 .... 5.3 to 5.9 ohms at 20°C

Mass airflow sensor:

  Supply voltage .... 11 to 14 volts (battery voltage)

  Ignition switched ON (engine stopped) .... 0.4 volts

  Output voltage at idle (at normal operating temperature) .... 0.8 to 1.1 volts

  Engine speed at approx. 4000rpm .... 1.1 to 2.4 volts

Coolant temperature sensor resistances (terminals 1 and 2):

  At -10°C (voltage 4.4 volts) .... 7.0 to 11.4 kilohms

  At 20°C (voltage 3.5 volts) .... 2.1 to 2.9 kilohms

  At 50°C (voltage 2.2 volts) .... 0.68 to 1.00 kilohms

  At 90°C (voltage 0.9 volts) .... 0.236 to 0.260 kilohms

Recommended fuel

Minimum octane rating .... 95 RON unleaded

Fuel tank capacity .... 65 litres

Torque wrench settings

	Nm	lbf ft
Camshaft position sensor	7	6
Crankshaft position sensor	7	6
Exhaust manifold nuts*	34	25
Exhaust flange nuts/springs	49	36
Fuel sender/pump unit securing ring	70	52
Fuel rail protector shield bolts (1.6 litre engines):		
Upper bolts	25	18
Lower bolts	10	8
Fuel rail retaining bolts:		
1.6 litre engine (HR16DE)	10	8
2.0 litre engine (MR20DE)	25	19
Fuel tank mounting bolts	43	32
Inlet manifold bolts	27	20
Inlet manifold mounting bracket bolts:		
1.6 litre engine (HR16DE)	11	9
2.0 litre engine (MR20DE)	20	14
Inlet valve timing solenoid valve	10	8
Knock sensor	23	17
Throttle housing retaining bolts	10	8
Oxygen sensor	50	37

* New nuts must be used

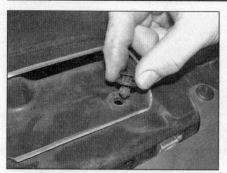

2.3a Release the retaining clips ...

2.3b ... and remove the air intake ducting

2.4 Slacken the air intake hose securing clip (arrowed)

1 General information and precautions

The fuel system consists of a fuel tank mounted under the car with an electric fuel pump immersed in it, a fuel filter, fuel feed and return lines. The fuel pump supplies fuel to the fuel rail which acts as a reservoir for the four fuel injectors which inject fuel into the inlet tracts. A fuel filter is incorporated in the fuel pump to ensure that the fuel supplied to the injectors is clean.

Refer to Section 5 for further information on the operation of the fuel injection system, and Section 13 for information on the exhaust system.

⚠ *Warning: Many of the procedures in this Chapter require the removal of fuel lines and connections, which may result in some fuel spillage. Before carrying out any operation on the fuel system refer to the precautions given in 'Safety first!' at the beginning of this Manual and follow them implicitly. Petrol is a highly dangerous and volatile liquid and the precautions necessary when handling it cannot be overstressed. Residual pressure will remain in the fuel lines long after the vehicle was last used, when disconnecting any fuel line, depressurise the fuel system as described in Section 6.*

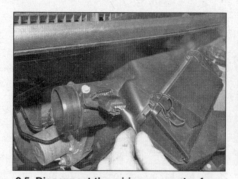

2.5 Disconnect the wiring connector from the airflow sensor

2 Air cleaner assembly – removal and refitting

Removal

1 To make removal of the air cleaner assembly easier, remove the battery, as described in Chapter 5A, Section 3.

2 Then remove the Electronic Control Module (ECM), from the battery tray mounting bracket as described in Section 10, of this Chapter.

3 Remove the two retaining clips and release the air intake ducting from the front crossmember, and then withdraw it from the air cleaner housing **(see illustrations)**. Where

2.6 Undo the air intake housing retaining nut (arrowed)

applicable, unclip the ducting from the lower resonator box.

4 Slacken the retaining clip and disconnect the air intake hose from the air cleaner assembly **(see illustration)**.

5 Disconnect the wiring connector from the mass airflow sensor **(see illustration)**; unclip the wiring from any retaining clips on the housing.

6 Undo the retaining nut that secures the air cleaner housing to the inner wing panel **(see illustration)**.

7 Pull the air cleaner upwards, disengaging the locating peg on the bottom of the air cleaner assembly, from the rubber mounting, and then remove it from the engine compartment **(see illustrations)**.

2.7a Remove the air cleaner housing ...

2.7b ... disengaging it from the lower mounting (arrowed)

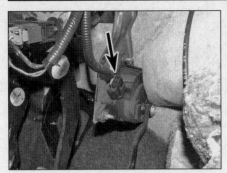

3.1 Disconnect the wiring connector

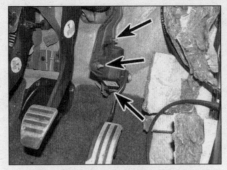

3.2 Undo the pedal retaining nuts (arrowed)

5.6 Diagnostic plug connector (arrowed)

8 If required remove the air filter element as described in Chapter 1A, Section 19.

Refitting

9 Refitting is a reversal of the removal procedure, ensuring that all hoses are properly reconnected, and that all ducts are correctly seated and securely held by their retaining clips.

3 Accelerator pedal – removal and refitting

Removal

1 Reach up behind the facia, and detach the wiring connector from the top of the accelerator pedal (see illustration).
2 Undo the three mounting nuts securing the pedal assembly to the bracket on the bulkhead, and remove it from underneath the facia (see illustration).
3 Examine the mounting bracket and pedal pivot points for signs of wear, and renew as necessary.

Refitting

4 Refitting is a reversal of the removal procedure, applying a little multipurpose grease to the pedal pivot shaft.

4 Unleaded petrol – general information and usage

Note: *The information given in this Chapter is correct at the time of writing. If updated information is thought to be required, check with a Nissan dealer. If travelling abroad, consult one of the motoring organisations (or a similar authority) for advice on the petrol's available, and their suitability for your vehicle.*

All Nissan petrol engine models are designed to run on fuel with a minimum octane rating of 95 (RON). All models have a catalytic converter must be run on unleaded fuel only. Under no circumstances should leaded fuel or lead replacement petrol be used, as this may damage the catalyst.

5 Fuel injection system – general information

1 All models are fitted with a combined fuel injection/ignition (engine management) system, controlled by the Engine Control Module (ECM), otherwise known as the Electronic Concentrated Control System (ECCS).
2 The fuel pump, immersed in the fuel tank, supplies fuel from the fuel tank to the fuel rail, via a filter that is built in to the fuel pump. Fuel supply pressure is controlled by a pressure regulator, which is located on the end of the fuel rail. This opens to allow excess fuel to return to the tank when the optimum operating pressure of the fuel system is exceeded.
3 The electrical control system consists of the Engine Control Module (ECM), along with the following sensors:
  a) *Throttle potentiometer – informs the ECM of the throttle valve position, and the rate of throttle opening/closing.*
  b) *Coolant temperature sensor – informs the ECM of engine temperature.*
  c) *Airflow meter – informs the ECM of the mass and temperature of the air passing through the inlet duct.*
  d) *Camshaft position sensor – housed in the transmission end of the cylinder head, the sensor informs the ECM of the engine speed and crankshaft position.*
  e) *Crankshaft position sensor – housed in the transmission end of the cylinder block at the rear of the engine, the sensor informs the ECM of the engine speed.*
  f) *Power steering and air conditioning system switches (where fitted) – informs the ECM if the system(s) are in operation, to allow it to adjust the idle speed to compensate for the extra load on the engine.*
  g) *Exhaust gas sensor – informs the ECM of the oxygen content of the exhaust gases (see Chapter 4C for further information).*
4 All the above signals are analysed by the Engine Control Module (ECM). Based on this information, the ECM selects the response appropriate to those values, and controls the fuel injectors (varying their pulse width – the length of time each injector is held open – to provide a richer or weaker mixture, as appropriate). The mixture and idle speed are constantly varied by the ECM to provide the best settings for cranking, starting (with either a hot or cold engine) and engine warm-up, idle, cruising, and acceleration.
5 If there is an abnormality in any of the readings obtained from the sensors, the ECM switches to its back-up mode. If this happens, it ignores the abnormal sensor signal, and assumes a preprogrammed value, which will allow the engine to continue running, albeit at reduced efficiency. If the ECM enters its back-up mode, the warning light on the instrument panel will come on, and the relevant fault code will be stored in the ECM memory.
6 If the warning light comes on, the vehicle should be taken to a Nissan dealer at the earliest opportunity. Once there, a complete test of the engine management system can be carried out, using a special electronic diagnostic test unit, which is simply plugged into the system's diagnostic connector (see illustration).

6 Fuel system – depressurisation

Note: *Refer to the warning note in Section 1 before proceeding.*

⚠ **Warning: The following procedure will merely relieve the pressure in the fuel system – remember that fuel will still be present in the system components, and take precautions accordingly before disconnecting any of them. Use clean rags wrapped around the connections to catch escaping fuel, and dispose of any fuel-soaked rags with care. Plug or tape over any open fuel lines, to prevent further loss of fuel or ingress of dirt.**

1 The fuel system referred to in this Section is defined as the tank-mounted fuel pump/fuel filter, the fuel rail and injectors, the pressure regulator, and the metal pipes and

flexible hoses of the fuel lines between these components. All these contain fuel, which will be under pressure while the engine is running and/or while the ignition is switched on. The pressure will remain for some time after the ignition has been switched off, and must be relieved before any of these components are disturbed for servicing work.

2 Identify and remove the fuel pump fuse (see wiring diagram in Chapter 12) from the fusebox – the fuses can also be identified from the label inside the fusebox cover.

3 Start the engine, and allow it to run until it stalls.

4 Try to start the engine at least twice more, to ensure that all residual pressure has been relieved.

5 Disconnect the battery negative terminal (refer to *Disconnecting the battery* in the Reference Chapter).

6 For safety, the fuel pump fuse should not be refitted until all work on the fuel system has been completed. If you refit the fuse now, **do not** switch on the ignition until completion of work.

7.4a Turn the four retaining clips ...

7.4b ... and remove the access cover

---

7 Fuel pump and fuel gauge sender unit – removal and refitting

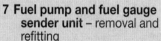

> ⚠ **Warning: Refer to the warning note in Section 1 before proceeding.**

Removal

1 Depressurise the fuel system as described in Section 6.

2 Disconnect the battery negative terminal (refer to *Disconnecting the battery* in the Reference Chapter).

3 To gain access to the sender unit, lift out the rear seat cushion, as described in Chapter 11, Section 22.

4 Turn the retaining clips through 90°, and lift up the access cover to expose the sender unit **(see illustrations)**.

5 Brush away any accumulated dust or dirt around the top of the sender unit so it does not drop into the fuel tank when the unit is removed.

2WD models

6 Disconnect the wiring connector from the top of the sender unit **(see illustration)**.

7 Release the retaining clip and disconnect the fuel hose from the top of the unit **(see illustration)**. Plug the hose end to prevent dirt ingress.

8 Note the fitted position of the sender unit and if necessary make an alignment mark on the sender unit and fuel tank to ensure correct refitting **(see illustration)**.

9 Twist the locking ring from the top of the fuel tank and carefully lift the sender unit out, taking care not to damage the sender unit or spill fuel onto the interior of the vehicle **(see illustrations)**.

7.6 Disconnect the pump wiring plug

7.7 Depress the release button and disconnect the fuel pipe(s)

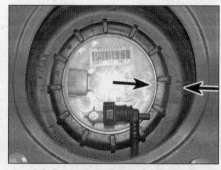
7.8 Fuel sender alignment marks (arrowed)

7.9a Using a home-made tool to slacken the locking ring ...

7.9b ... and remove it from the fuel pump ...

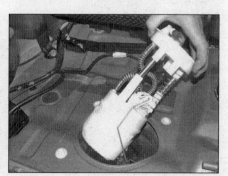
7.9c ... then withdraw the fuel pump, taking care not to damage the float arm

7.10 Fit a new sealing ring to the top of the tank

7.11 Two fuel level sensors are fitted to 4WD models

10 Remove the sealing ring from the top of the fuel tank and discard; as a new one will be required for refitting **(see illustration)**.

4WD models

11 There are two fuel level sensors; the one fitted to the left-hand side of the vehicle is called a sub fuel level sender unit. This is fitted due to the fuel tank having a tunnel moulded down the centre, which allows room for the prop-shaft to the rear axle **(see illustration)**.

12 Note the fitted position of the sender unit

and if necessary make an alignment mark on the sender unit and fuel tank to ensure correct refitting **(see illustration)**.

13 Twist the locking ring from the top of the fuel tank and carefully lift the sub fuel level sender unit out, taking care not to damage the sender unit or spill fuel onto the interior of the vehicle **(see illustrations)**. Disconnect the in-tank wiring as the unit is removed.

14 Remove the sealing ring from the top of the fuel tank and discard, as a new one will be required for refitting **(see illustration 7.10)**.

Refitting

15 Refitting is a reversal of the removal procedure, noting the following points:

a) Fit a new sealing ring to the top of the fuel tank.

b) Align the marks made on the sender unit and fuel tank during removal.

c) Where applicable, secure the unit with the locking ring, aligning the arrow on the locking ring between the MAX and MIN markings on the fuel tank **(see illustration)**.

d) Ensure that the fuel hose and the wiring connector are securely reconnected to the sender unit.

e) Prior to refitting the access cover, reconnect the battery, then start the engine and check the fuel hose(s) for signs of leaks.

8 Fuel tank – removal and refitting

Warning: Refer to the warning note in Section 1 before proceeding.

Removal

1 Before removing the fuel tank, all fuel must be drained from the tank. Since a fuel tank drain plug is not provided, it is therefore preferable to carry out the removal operation when the tank is nearly empty.

2 Depressurise the fuel system as described in Section 6.

3 Disconnect the battery negative terminal (refer to *Disconnecting the battery* in the Reference Chapter), then syphon or hand-pump the remaining fuel from the tank.

4 On 4WD vehicles, undo the retaining bolts and remove the rear section of the propeller shaft, as described in Chapter 8, Section 5.

5 Remove the relevant sections of the exhaust system from below the fuel tank

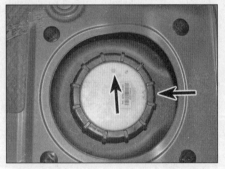

7.12 Note position of alignment marks (arrowed)

7.13a Using a special tool to slacken the locking ring …

7.13b … then remove the sender unit, taking care not to damage the float arm

7.15 Align the locking ring between the MIN and MAX markings

8.5 Remove the section of exhaust from below the fuel tank

8.7 Undo the fuel filler neck retaining clip (arrowed) …

8.8 Undo the fuel tank vent hose retaining clip (arrowed) …

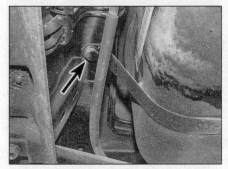

8.10a Undo the fuel tank retaining strap front bolts (arrowed) …

8.10b … and retaining strap rear bolts (arrowed)

and take great care to ensure that none of the hoses become trapped between the tank and vehicle body. Tighten the fuel tank mounting bolts to the specified torque setting.
b) Ensure that all pipes and hoses are correctly routed, and securely held in position with their retaining clips.
c) On completion, refill the tank with fuel, and check for signs of leakage prior to taking the vehicle on the road.

9 Throttle housing – removal and refitting

(see illustration), as described in Section 13. If required, release the fasteners and remove the heatshield from below the fuel tank.
6 Disconnect the wiring connector(s) and fuel hose(s) from the fuel pump/gauge sender unit, as described in Section 7.
7 Working at the right-hand side rear of the fuel tank, release the retaining clip and disconnect the filler neck hose from the fuel tank (see illustration).
8 Working at the rear of the fuel tank, release the retaining clip and disconnect the fuel vent pipe hose from the fuel tank (see illustration).
9 Place a trolley jack with an interposed block of wood beneath the tank, then raise the jack until it is supporting the weight of the tank.
10 Slacken and remove the bolts securing

the two fuel tank retaining straps to the vehicle body (see illustrations).
11 Slowly lower the fuel tank out of position and remove the tank from underneath the vehicle. Note, depending on model, it may be necessary to disconnect any other relevant vent/EVAP pipes as they become accessible.
12 If the tank is contaminated with sediment or water, remove the sender unit/fuel pump (Section 7) and swill the tank out with clean fuel. If any damage is evident, the tank should be renewed.

Refitting

13 Refitting is the reverse of the removal procedure, noting the following points:
a) When lifting the tank back into position, reconnect all the relevant breather hoses,

1 Disconnect the battery negative terminal (refer to Disconnecting the battery in the Reference Chapter).
2 Slacken the breather pipe retaining clip and disconnect it from the cylinder head cover (see illustration).
3 Slacken the retaining clips for the air intake hose between the throttle housing and the air cleaner assembly and remove it to one side (see illustrations).
4 On some models the throttle housing is water cooled, if required, partially drain the cooling system to below the level of the throttle housing (see Chapter 1A, Section 27 or Chapter 1B, Section 29). Alternatively, clamp the throttle housing coolant hoses to minimise coolant loss. Slacken the retaining

9.2 Disconnect the breather hose (arrowed)

9.3a Slacken the securing clips (arrowed) …

9.3b … and remove the air intake hose

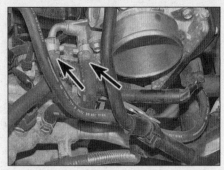

9.4 Disconnect the coolant hoses (arrowed)

9.5 Disconnect the wiring connector from the throttle housing

9.6 Remove the bracket

9.7a Undo the four retaining bolts …

9.7b … and remove the throttle housing

9.8 Fit a new seal to the inlet manifold

clips and disconnect the coolant hoses from the throttle housing body **(see illustration)**.

5 Disconnect the wiring connector from the throttle potentiometer **(see illustration)**.

6 On 1.6 litre models, slacken the retaining bolt and remove the bracket from below the throttle housing **(see illustration)**.

7 Slacken and remove the bolts securing the throttle housing assembly to the inlet manifold (working diagonally), and remove it from the engine compartment **(see illustrations)**. Remove the O-ring seal/gasket and discard it; a new one must be used on refitting. Plug the inlet manifold port with a wad of clean cloth, to prevent the possible entry of foreign matter.

Refitting

8 Refitting is a reverse of the removal procedure, bearing in mind the following points:

a) Ensure that the mating surfaces of the manifold and throttle housing are clean and dry, and fit a new O-ring seal/gasket to the manifold **(see illustration)**. Fit the throttle housing then, working in a diagonal sequence, tighten the retaining bolts to the specified torque setting.

b) Ensure that all hoses and wiring connectors are correctly reconnected and, where necessary, that there retaining clips are securely tightened.

---

10 Fuel injection system components – removal and refitting

Fuel rail and injectors

Note: Refer to the warning note in Section 1 before proceeding.

Note: If a faulty injector is suspected, before condemning the injector it is worth trying the effect of one of the proprietary injector-cleaning treatments.

1 Depressurise the fuel system as described in Section 6.

2 Disconnect the battery negative terminal (refer to Disconnecting the battery in the Reference Chapter).

3 Remove the inlet manifold as described in Section 11. Using duct tape (or similar), cover the intake ducts in the cylinder head to prevent anything being dropped down into the cylinders **(see illustration)**.

4 Disconnect the wiring harness from across the top of the cylinder head cover. Disconnect it from the coils, injectors and inlet valve timing solenoid valve, and then move it to one side **(see illustrations)**.

5 On 1.6 litre engines, undo the four retaining

10.3 Cover the intake ports with duct tape

10.4a Disconnect the fuel injector – 1.6 litre engine

10.4b Disconnect the fuel injector – 2.0 litre engine

10.5a Undo the upper mounting bolts …

10.5b … the lower mounting bolts …

10.5c … and remove the rail protector

10.6a Unclip the plastic cover from the connector – 1.6 litre engine

10.6b Unclip the plastic cover from the connector – 2.0 litre engine

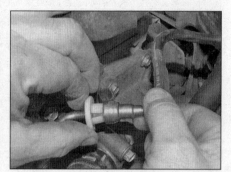

10.7a Using a plastic special tool to release fuel pipe

bolts and remove the fuel rail protector shield from the cylinder head **(see illustrations)**.

6 Unclip the plastic cover from the fuel rail connector at the left-hand side of the cylinder head **(see illustrations)**. Note its fitted position and the direction of the arrow on the side of the cover.

7 Using a special tool, release the securing clips and disconnect the fuel pipe from the end of the fuel rail **(see illustrations)**. Plug the fuel pipe and fuel rail end to prevent dirt ingress.

8 On 1.6 litre engines, undo the retaining bolt

10.7b Using a metal special tool to release fuel pipe

10.7c The four securing tangs need to be released …

10.7d … to disconnect the fuel pipe – 1.6 litre engine

10.7e Disconnecting the fuel pipe – 2.0 litre engine

10.7f Put caps over the ends of the fuel pipe

10.8 Undo the pipe bracket retaining bolt (arrowed) – 1.6 litre engine

10.9a Undo the mounting bolts (arrowed) …

10.9b … and remove the fuel rail – 1.6 litre engine

from the fuel pipe bracket on the front of the cylinder head (see illustration).

9 Slacken and remove the fuel rail retaining bolts (see illustrations), and then carefully ease the fuel rail and injectors out from the cylinder head, and remove it from the vehicle.

10 Using duct tape (or similar), cover the injector recesses in the cylinder head to prevent anything being dropped down inside them (see illustration).

11 Release the retaining clip from the relevant injector and remove the injector out of position, and recover the sealing rings

(see illustrations). Repeat the procedure as required to remove any other injectors.

12 Discard the seals and sealing rings; new ones must be used on refitting (see illustration).

13 Refitting is a reversal of the removal procedure, noting the following points:

a) Fit new O-rings to all disturbed injectors - Green O-ring seals cylinder head end of the injector and Black O-ring seals fuel rail side of the injector (see illustration).

b) Apply a smear of engine oil to the O-rings to aid installation (see illustration), and then ease the injectors into the fuel rail.

c) Make sure the injector retaining clips

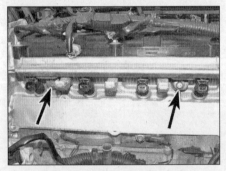

10.9c Undo the mounting bolts (arrowed) …

10.9d … and remove the fuel rail – 2.0 litre engine

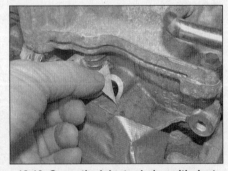

10.10 Cover the injector holes with duct tape

10.11a Remove the securing clip …

10.11b … and withdraw the fuel injector

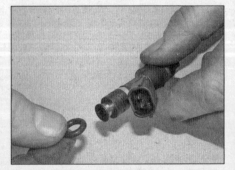

10.12 Remove the seal from the top of each injector

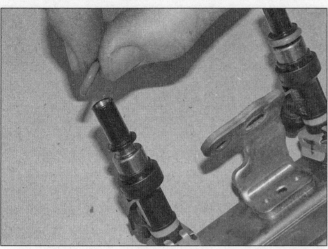

10.13a Renew all injector seals

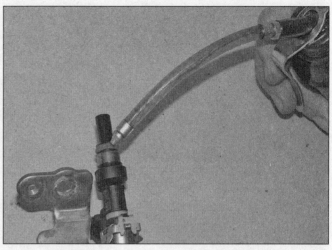

10.13b Apply a small amount of oil to the seals

on the fuel rail are fitted correctly **(see illustration)**.

d) *When fitting the plastic cover to the fuel pipe connection, make sure it is fitted securely* **(see illustration)**.

e) *On completion, start the engine and check for fuel leaks.*

Throttle potentiometer

14 The throttle potentiometer is mounted on the rear of the throttle housing and can only be renewed as a complete unit. See Section 9, for the removal and refitting procedure. Check with your local Nissan dealer for the availability of parts.

Mass airflow (MAF) sensor

15 The airflow sensor is mounted in the air cleaner housing, at the outlet end of the intake hose to the throttle housing. Prior to removal, disconnect the battery negative terminal (refer to *Disconnecting the battery* in the Reference Chapter).

16 Disconnect the wiring connector from the airflow sensor **(see illustration)**.

17 Undo the retaining bolts, and then remove the sensor from the air cleaner housing **(see illustration)**. Recover its sealing ring and renew.

18 Refitting is the reverse of removal, using

a new sealing ring (where applicable) and tightening its retaining screws securely.

Inlet valve timing solenoid valve

19 The inlet valve timing solenoid valve is fitted to the right-hand front of the cylinder head on 1.6 litre engines, and on the right-hand end of the engine in the centre of the timing chain cover, on 2.0 litre engines.

20 On 2.0 litre engines, support the engine and remove the right-hand engine mounting as described in Chapter 2B, Section 16.

21 Disconnect the wiring connector from the inlet solenoid valve **(see illustrations)**.

22 Undo the retaining bolt and withdraw the

10.13c Make sure the securing clip is fitted correctly

10.13d Note the direction arrows when refitting

10.16 Disconnect the wiring connector from the sensor

10.17 Undo the airflow sensor retaining bolts

10.21a Disconnect the wiring connector from the solenoid valve – 1.6 litre engine

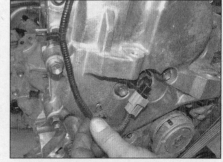

10.21b Disconnect the wiring connector from the solenoid valve – 2.0 litre engine

10.22a Undo the retaining bolt ...

10.22b ... then withdraw the solenoid valve

10.26a Disconnect the sensor wiring connector – 1.6 litre engine

10.26b Disconnect the sensor wiring connector – 2.0 litre engine

10.27 Remove the bracket from the cylinder head – 2.0 litre engine

29 Discard the O-ring seal; a new one must be used on refitting.
30 Refitting is a reversal of the removal procedure, noting the following points:
  a) *Fit a new O-ring seal to the sensor.*
  b) *Apply a smear of engine oil to the O-ring to aid installation, and then ease the sensor into position.*

Crankshaft position sensor

31 The crankshaft position sensor is fitted to the rear of the cylinder block at the transmission end.
32 Undo the retaining bolts and remove the heatshield from around the sensor **(see illustrations)**.
33 Disconnect the wiring connector from the position sensor **(see illustration)**.
34 Undo the retaining bolt and withdraw

solenoid valve from the cover **(see illustrations)**. Be prepared for some oil spillage, and have some cloth ready to catch it.
23 Refitting is the reverse of removal.

Inlet air temperature (IAT) sensor

24 The inlet air temperature sensor is built into the mass airflow sensor. See paragraphs 15 to 18 for the removal and refitting procedure.

Camshaft position sensor

25 The camshaft position sensor is fitted to the transmission end of the cylinder head cover.
26 Disconnect the wiring connector from the camshaft position sensor **(see illustrations)**.
27 On 2.0 litre engines, undo the retaining bolt and remove the bracket from the front

left-hand end of the cylinder head **(see illustration)**.
28 Undo the retaining bolt and withdraw the sensor from the cover **(see illustrations)**.

10.28a Undo the bolt and withdraw the sensor – 1.6 litre engine

10.28b Undo the bolt and withdraw the sensor – 2.0 litre engine

10.32a Undo the retaining bolts (arrowed) ...

10.32b ... and remove the sensor heatshield

10.33 Disconnect the sensor wiring connector

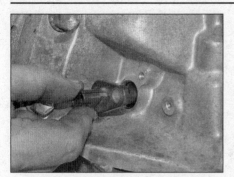

10.34 Undo the bolt and withdraw the sensor

10.35a Renew the O-ring seal ...

10.35b ... and lubricate with a smear of oil

the sensor from the cylinder block **(see illustration)**.

35 Refitting is a reversal of the removal procedure, noting the following points:

a) Fit a new O-ring seal to the sensor **(see illustration)**.

b) Apply a smear of engine oil to the O-ring to aid installation **(see illustration)**, and then ease the sensor into position.

Coolant temperature sensor

36 Refer to Chapter 3, Section 6.

Engine Control Module (ECM)

Note: *The engine management control module is electronically coded for the vehicle to which it is fitted; therefore new units are supplied without a code. If the ECM is being removed to enable a new unit to be fitted, a* Nissan dealer must program the new unit with the information from the old ECM.

37 The ECM is located in the left-hand side of the engine compartment, between the battery and the air cleaner housing **(see illustration)**.

38 First disconnect the battery negative lead (refer to *Disconnecting the battery* in the Reference Section).

39 Remove the battery, as described in Chapter 5A, Section 3.

40 Release the locking levers, and then withdraw the three electrical connectors from the side of the ECM **(see illustration)**.

41 Undo the retaining bolts and remove the mounting bracket, complete with control unit from the engine compartment **(see illustrations)**.

42 If required, undo the retaining nuts and remove the ECM from the mounting bracket.

43 Refitting is a reverse of the removal procedure ensuring that the wiring is securely reconnected.

Knock sensor

44 The knock sensor is fitted to the front of the cylinder block.

45 Disconnect the wiring connector from the sensor **(see illustration)**.

46 Undo the retaining bolt and withdraw the sensor from the cylinder block **(see illustration)**.

47 Refitting is a reversal of the removal procedure, making sure the mating face of the sensor and cylinder block are clean. Also make sure that the electrical connection on the sensor is facing towards the transmission when refitted.

Air conditioning pressure sensor

48 The air conditioning pressure sensor is screwed into the top of the receiver drier in the

10.37 Location of Engine Control Module (ECM)

10.40 Disconnect the wiring connectors

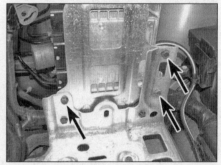

10.41a Undo the retaining bolts ...

10.41b ... and remove the ECM with mounting plate

10.45 Disconnect the sensor wiring connector

10.46 Undo the sensor retaining bolt

11.1 Remove the engine trim cover

11.3 Remove the breather hose –
2.0 litre engine

11.4a Undo the manifold left-hand rear
securing bolt – 1.6 litre engine

air conditioning circuit. Removal and refitting of the switch requires the air conditioning system to be discharged and recharged, and the home mechanic should not attempt this, (see Chapter 3, Section 11).

11 Inlet manifold – removal and refitting

Removal

1 Where fitted, undo the retaining bolts and remove the plastic trim cover from the top of the engine **(see illustration)**.

2 Remove the throttle housing as described in Section 9.

3 On 2.0 litre engines, disconnect the breather (PCV) hose from the rear of the manifold and move it to one side **(see illustration)**.

4 Slacken and remove the left-hand rear mounting bracket bolt from the manifold **(see illustrations)**.

5 Slacken and remove the right-hand rear mounting bracket bolt from the manifold **(see illustration)**.

6 Disconnect the brake vacuum hose from the right-hand rear of the manifold **(see illustration)**.

7 Disconnect the vacuum hose and wiring connector from the EVAP canister

purge solenoid valve, which is located on the left-hand side of the manifold **(see illustration)**.

8 On 2.0 litre engines, unclip the wiring loom retaining clip from the transmission end of the manifold **(see illustration)**.

9 On 2.0 litre engines, withdraw the oil level dipstick to make access to the manifold centre bolt easier.

10 Make a final check that all the necessary vacuum/breather hoses have been disconnected from the manifold then, working from the outside to the centre, slacken and remove the manifold retaining bolts **(see illustration)**.

11 Manoeuvre the manifold away from the

11.4b Undo the manifold left-hand rear
securing bolt (arrowed) – 2.0 litre engine

11.5 Undo the manifold right-hand rear
securing bolt

11.6 Disconnect the vacuum pipe from the
rear of the manifold

11.7 EVAP canister purge solenoid valve

11.8 Unclip the wiring loom bracket –
2.0 litre engine

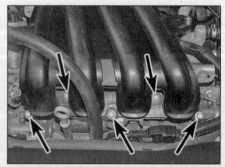

11.10 Undo the manifold securing bolts
(arrowed)

11.11a Remove the inlet manifold – 1.6 litre engine

11.11b Remove the inlet manifold – 2.0 litre engine

head (see illustrations), and out of the engine compartment. Remove the manifold rubber gasket and discard it, a new one will be required for refitting.

Refitting

12 Refitting is the reverse of the removal procedure, noting the following points:

a) Ensure that the manifold and cylinder head mating surfaces are clean and dry, and fit the new rubber gasket to the manifold (see illustration).

b) Refit the throttle housing as described in Section 9, using a new O-ring seal/gasket (see illustration).

c) Install the manifold, and tighten its retaining bolts to the specified torque, starting at the centre and working outwards.

d) Ensure that all relevant hoses are reconnected to their original positions, and are securely held (where necessary) by their retaining clips.

12 Exhaust manifold – removal and refitting

Note: On 2.0 litre models the exhaust manifold

and catalytic converter are a complete assembly, and cannot be renewed separately.

Removal

1 Firmly apply the handbrake, and then jack up the front of the vehicle and support it securely on axle stands (see Jacking and vehicle support).

2 Trace the wiring back from the two oxygen sensors, to there wiring connectors, and disconnect them from the main wiring harness. The upper oxygen sensor connection is on the top left-hand side of the exhaust manifold and the lower oxygen sensor connection is under the vehicle on the rear of the front subframe (see illustrations).

3 On 1.6 litre engines, undo the retaining nuts and bolts and remove the exhaust front pipe/catalytic converter, as described in Section 13.

4 On 2.0 litre engines, undo the retaining nuts and bolts and remove the exhaust front pipe/silencer, as described in Section 13.

5 Undo the retaining bolts and remove the mounting stay bracket from under the exhaust manifold (see illustration).

6 Working from the top in the engine compartment, undo the retaining bolts, and

11.12a Ensure new manifold seals are fitted …

11.12b … also to the throttle housing end

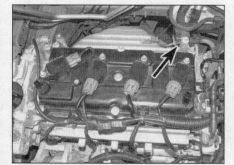

12.2a Disconnect oxygen sensor upper (arrowed) …

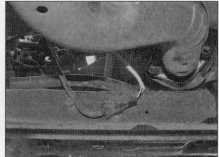

12.2b … and lower wiring connectors

12.5 Undo the lower support bracket bolt (arrowed)

12.6 Remove the upper heatshield

12.7 Undo the manifold securing nuts

12.9 Fit new manifold gasket

remove the heat shield from above the exhaust manifold **(see illustration)**.

7 Make sure there is nothing still attached to the manifold, and then working from the outside to the centre, slacken and remove the manifold retaining nuts **(see illustration)**.

8 Manoeuvre the manifold out of the engine compartment, and discard the manifold gasket.

Refitting

9 Refitting is the reverse of the removal procedure, noting the following points:

a) Examine all the exhaust manifold studs and nuts for signs of damage and corrosion; remove all traces of corrosion, and repair or renew any damaged studs. **Note:** Nissan recommends that the nuts and studs should always be renewed if removed.

b) Ensure that the manifold and cylinder

head sealing faces are clean and flat, and fit the new manifold gasket **(see illustration)**.

c) Install the manifold, and tighten its retaining bolts to the specified torque, starting at the centre and working outwards.

d) Refit the front pipe/catalytic converter to the manifold, with reference to Section 13.

13 Exhaust system – general information, component removal and refitting

Note: On 2.0 litre models the exhaust manifold and catalytic converter are a complete assembly, and cannot be renewed separately.

General information

1 The exhaust system consists of three sections: -

1.6 litre engines – a) Exhaust manifold - see Section 13. b) Front pipe/catalytic converter. c) Intermediate pipe/silencer/tailpipe.

2.0 litre engines – a) Exhaust manifold/catalytic converter - see Section 13. b) Front pipe/silencer. c) Intermediate pipe/silencer/tailpipe.

2 The system is suspended throughout its entire length by rubber mountings **(see illustration)**, and all exhaust sections are joined by flanged joints, which are then secured together by springs, nuts and/or bolts.

3 To remove the system or part of the system, firmly apply the handbrake, and then jack up the vehicle and support it securely on axle stands (see Jacking and vehicle support). Alternatively, position the car over an inspection pit, or on car ramps. Where fitted, remove the engine compartment undertray.

Front pipe/silencer (2.0 litre engines)

4 Undo the nuts securing the front pipe to the catalytic converter/manifold **(see illustration)**. With the nuts removed retrieve the washers and springs, and then separate the front pipe from the catalytic converter/manifold.

5 Trace the wiring back from the oxygen sensor to its wiring connector, which is located on the rear of the front subframe, and then disconnect it from the main wiring harness **(see illustration)**.

6 Slacken and remove the two bolts securing the front pipe/silencer flange joint to the intermediate pipe. Withdraw the front pipe from underneath the vehicle, and recover the gasket from the joint **(see illustrations)**.

13.2 Exhaust rubber mountings

13.4 Undo the front pipe-to-catalytic converter bolts/nuts

13.5 Disconnect the oxygen sensor wiring connector

13.6a Undo the retaining bolts …

13.6b … and remove the exhaust front pipe/silencer

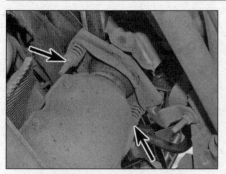

13.7 Undo the front pipe/catalytic converter to manifold bolts/nuts

13.8 Disconnect the oxygen sensor wiring connector

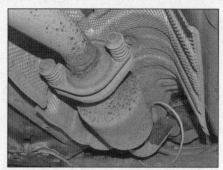

13.9 Undo the front pipe/catalytic converter to intermediate pipe bolts

Front pipe/Catalytic converter (1.6 litre engines)

7 Undo the nuts securing the front pipe/ catalytic converter to the exhaust manifold **(see illustration)**. With the nuts removed retrieve the washers and springs, and then separate the front pipe/catalytic converter from the exhaust manifold.

8 Trace the wiring back from the oxygen sensor to its wiring connector, which is located on the rear of the front subframe, and then disconnect it from the main wiring harness **(see illustration)**.

9 Slacken and remove the two bolts securing the front pipe/catalytic converter flange joint to the intermediate pipe. Withdraw the front pipe/catalytic converter from underneath the vehicle, and recover the gasket from the joint **(see illustration)**.

Intermediate pipe/silencer/tailpipe

10 Slacken and remove the two bolts securing the front pipe flange joint to the intermediate pipe **(see illustration)**, and then separate exhaust. Support the disconnected front pipe so as not to place undue strain on the front part of the exhaust system.

11 With the aid of an assistant, working along the underside of the vehicle, unhook the intermediate pipe/silencer/tailpipe from its mounting rubbers, and then manoeuvre the pipe out from underneath the vehicle.

Heat shield(s)

12 The heat shields are secured in position by a mixture of fasteners. Some heatshields are fitted to the underside of the vehicle. And also some are fitted to parts of the exhaust system. When an exhaust section is renewed, transfer any relevant heat shields from the

original over to the new section before installing the exhaust section on the vehicle **(see illustrations)**.

Refitting

13 Each section is refitted by a reverse of the removal sequence, noting the following points:

a) *Ensure that all traces of corrosion have been removed from the flanges, and renew all necessary gaskets* **(see illustrations)**.

b) *Inspect the rubber mountings for signs of damage or deterioration, and renew as necessary.*

c) *Prior to tightening the exhaust system fasteners, ensure that all rubber mountings are correctly located, and that there is adequate clearance between the exhaust system and vehicle underbody/ suspension components, etc.*

13.10 Undo the front pipe/silencer to intermediate pipe bolts

13.12a Heatshield to protect fuel tank

13.12b Heatshield around silencer/ catalytic converter …

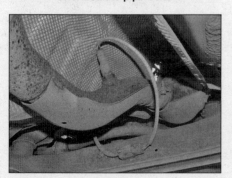

13.12c … and along the underside of the exhaust

13.13a Fit new sealing rings to the silencer …

13.13b … and the exhaust front pipe

Chapter 4 Part B:
Diesel engine fuel and exhaust systems

Contents

Degrees of difficulty

| Easy, suitable for novice with little experience 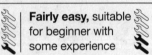 | Fairly easy, suitable for beginner with some experience | Fairly difficult, suitable for competent DIY mechanic | Difficult, suitable for experienced DIY mechanic | Very difficult, suitable for expert DIY or professional |

Specifications

General

System type . . . . Rear-mounted fuel tank, high-pressure pump with common-rail, direct injection, turbocharger

Type:
1.5 litre engine (K9K) . . . . Siemens
2.0 litre engine (M9R) . . . . Bosch EDC16

Fuel system data

1.5 litre engines

Firing order. . . . . 1-3-4-2 (number 1 at flywheel end)
Idle speed. . . . . 800 ± 50 rpm
Maximum no-load speed . . . . 4500 ± 150 rpm
Maximum under-load speed . . . . 5000 ± 150 rpm
High-pressure fuel pump:
    Type . . . . Delphi
    Direction of rotation . . . . Clockwise viewed from sprocket end
Injectors:
    Type . . . . Delphi solenoid injector
    Maximum pressure . . . . 1400 bars
    Resistance . . . . Not-measurable
Turbocharger:
    Type . . . . Garrett
    Boost pressure . . . . 1300 ± 2 mbars

Fuel system data (continued)

2.0 litre engines

Firing order . . . . 1-3-4-2 (number 1 at flywheel end)
Idle speed . . . . 750 ± 50 rpm
High-pressure fuel pump:
   Type . . . . Bosch
   Operating pressure . . . . 300 to 1350 bar
   Direction of rotation . . . . Clockwise viewed from sprocket end
Injectors:
   Type . . . . Bosch solenoid injector
   Solenoid resistance . . . . < 0.2 ohms
   Operating pressure . . . . 1350 bar
   Maximum pressure . . . . 1525 bar
Turbocharger:
   Operating vacuum . . . . 0.5 bar
   Valve rod movement 1.7mm
Glow plug:
   Resistance at 20° C – (connector removed) . . . . less than 2.0 ohms

Sensor resistances

Coolant temperature sensor resistances (terminals 1 and 2):
   At 25°C . . . . 2.252 ± 112 ohms
   At 50°C . . . . 810 ± 39 ohms
   At 80°C . . . . 283 ± 8 ohms
Crankshaft position sensor resistance:
   Terminals 1 and 2 . . . . 612 to 748 ohms
EGR volume control valve motor resistance:
   Terminals 2 and 6 . . . . 2.3 ohms
Fuel pump temperature sensor resistances (terminals 1 and 2):
   At 25°C . . . . 2.051 ± 123 ohms
   At 50°C . . . . 811 ± 47 ohms
   At 80°C . . . . 309 ± 17 ohms
Fuel injector resistance at 20°C:
   Terminals 1 and 2 . . . . 15.0 to 25.0 ohms
Fuel pump resistance at 25°C:
   Terminals 1 and 3 . . . . 0.2 to 5.0 ohms
Fuel volumetric control valve (on pump):
   Terminals 1 and 2 . . . . 1.5 to 15.0 ohms
High pressure fuel pump pressure control valve:
   Terminals 3 and 5 . . . . 1.5 to 15 ohms
Intake air temperature sensor (terminals 1 and 2):
   At 10° C . . . . 3.714 ± 161 ohms
   At 20° C . . . . 2.448 ± 95 ohms
   At 30° C . . . . 1.671 ± 58 ohms
Throttle pedal position sensor resistances:
   Terminals 2 and 4 . . . . 1.70 ohms
   Terminals 1 and 5 . . . . 2.85 ohms
Turbocharger boost control valve (at 23°C):
   Terminals 1 and 2 . . . . 19.9 to 23.1 ohms

Fuel tank

Capacity . . . . 65 litres

Torque wrench settings

	Nm	lbf ft
1.5 litre engines		
Catalytic converter:		
Rear mounting	21	15
To side mounting strut	25	18
To turbocharger	26	19
Strut to engine	44	32
EGR valve	21	15
EGR valve heat shield	12	9
Engine lifting eye	21	15
Exhaust manifold	26	19
Exhaust pipe clamp	21	15
Flow actuator	6	4
Fuel gauge sender unit	65	48

Torque wrench settings (continued)

	Nm	lbf ft
1.5 litre engines (continued)		
Fuel injectors to cylinder head	28	21
Fuel tank	21	15
Fuel temperature sensor (on high-pressure pump)	15	11
High-pressure fuel rail	28	21
High-pressure pipe union nuts	24	18
High-pressure pump	21	15
High-pressure pump sprocket nut	55	41
High-pressure pump venturi	6	4
Throttle valve housing	12	9
Turbocharger oil supply pipe:		
On cylinder head	23	17
On turbocharger	12	9
Turbocharger to exhaust manifold	26	19
2.0 litre engines		
Catalytic converter-to-turbocharger nuts	21	15
Throttle/damper unit:		
Mounting bracket to unit	12	9
Mounting bracket to inlet manifold	12	9
Turbocharger pressure sensor mounting nut	8	6
Turbocharger oil pipe bolts on turbocharger	10	7
Turbocharger oil pipe union bolt on the cylinder block	16	12
Turbocharger oil pipe support bolt	25	18
Turbocharger air outlet pipe	8	6
Turbocharger to exhaust manifold nuts	26	19
Fuel rail mounting bolts	25	18
Fuel pipe mounting on valve cover	10	7
High-pressure pipe union nuts	32	24
High-pressure pump pinion	90	66
High-pressure pump mounting	25	18
Injector clamp bolt	35	26
Inlet manifold	25	18
Exhaust manifold:		
Studs	9	7
Mounting nuts:		
Stage 1	18	13
Stage 2	30	22
EGR rigid pipe:		
To cooler	35	26
To exhaust manifold	35	26
EGR rigid pipe on cylinder head	10	7
EGR rigid pipe heatshield	10	7

1 General information and precautions

General information

1 The fuel system consists of a fuel tank, a fuel filter, a high-pressure pump with common rail injection system, electronic injectors and associated components.

2 The main components of the system are as follows:

a) Priming bulb on the low-pressure circuit.
b) Fuel filter.
c) High-pressure fuel pump.
d) Injector rail.
e) Pressure sensor located on the injector rail.
f) Four electronic solenoid injectors.
g) Fuel temperature sensor.
h) Coolant temperature sensor.
i) Air temperature sensor.
l) Cylinder reference sensor.
k) Engine speed sensor.
l) Turbocharging pressure sensor.
m) EGR solenoid valve.
n) Accelerator pedal potentiometer.
o) Atmospheric pressure sensor.
p) Engine Control Module (ECM).

3 The common rail injection system operates as follows. Fuel is drawn from the fuel tank to the high-pressure pump by a low-pressure transfer pump integrated in the high-pressure pump. Some versions have an electric pump mounted in the fuel tank. Before reaching the high-pressure pump, the fuel passes through a fuel filter, where foreign matter and water are removed. As the fuel passes through the filter, it is heated by an electric heater. On reaching the high-pressure pump, the fuel is pressurised according to demand, and accumulates in the injection common-rail. The pressure in the rail is accurately maintained using a pressure sensor in the rail and a pressure regulator under the control of the engine management ECM. This arrangement keeps heat generation to a minimum, and improves engine output. The rail pressure is also maintained by the injectors themselves; short electrical pulses which are not long enough to open the injector allow fuel into the return (leak-off) circuit, and also the normal pulses which open the injectors cause a reduction in pressure. The ECM determines the exact timing and duration of the injection period according to engine operating conditions.

4 The four fuel injectors inject a homogeneous spray of fuel into the combustion chambers located in the cylinder head. The injectors operate sequentially according to the firing order of the cylinders, and each injector needle is lubricated by fuel, which accumulates in the spring chamber. Each injector has its own unique flow characteristics, which are used by the system ECM to calculate the exact quantity of fuel to inject.

5 In terms of the sensors used by the ECM to control a modern common-rail diesel system, these engines are very similar to

1.8 Vehicle diagnostic connector (arrowed)

2.3a Release the retaining clips ...

2.3b ... and remove the air intake ducting – 2.0 litre engine

their petrol equivalents. The ECM determines engine speed and position from a TDC sensor fitted to the transmission bellhousing, which detects a reference tooth on the flywheel ring gear, and signals the ECM. A similar sensor is fitted to monitor the camshaft, to give a reference for No 1 cylinder. Further sensors are used to monitor airflow into the engine, air temperature, and turbocharging pressure. On the fuel side, fuel pressure, temperature and flow rate are all monitored, according to model, via sensors on the high-pressure pump and/or the fuel rail. As with the petrol-engine models, an 'electronic' throttle is fitted, with an accelerator position sensor instead of the mechanical cable previously used.

6 Provided that the specified maintenance is carried out, the fuel injection equipment will give long and trouble-free service. The main potential cause of damage to the high-pressure pump and injectors is dirt or water in the fuel. It is highly recommended that a set of fuel line plugs is obtained – these are available from motor accessory shops and better motor factors.

7 Servicing of the high-pressure pump, injectors, and electronic equipment and sensors is very limited for the home mechanic, and any dismantling or adjustment other than that described in this Chapter must be entrusted to a Nissan dealer or a diesel fuel injection specialist.

8 If a fault appears in the injection system, first ensure that all the system wiring connectors are securely connected and free of corrosion. Should the fault persist, the vehicle should be taken to a Nissan dealer or specialist who can test the system on a diagnostic tester **(see illustration)**. The tester will locate the fault quickly and simply, alleviating the need to test all the system components individually, which is a time-consuming operation that carries a risk of damaging the ECM. It is advisable to have any faulty components renewed by the dealer as in many instances the tester is required to reprogramme the ECM in the event of component or sensor renewal.

Precautions

⚠️ *Warning: It is necessary to take certain precautions when working on the fuel system components, particularly the fuel injectors and high-pressure pump. Before carrying out any operations on the fuel system, refer to the precautions given in 'Safety first!' at the beginning of this manual, and to any additional warning notes at the start of the relevant Sections. Allow the engine to cool for 5 to 10 minutes to ensure the fuel pressure and temperatures are at a minimum.*

⚠️ *Warning: Exercise extreme caution when working on the high-pressure fuel system. Do*

not attempt to test the fuel injectors or disconnect the high-pressure lines with the engine running. Never expose the hands or any part of the body to injector spray, as the high working pressure can cause the fuel to penetrate the skin, with possibly fatal results. You are strongly advised to have any work that involves testing the injectors under pressure carried out by a dealer or fuel injection specialist.

2 Air cleaner assembly – removal and refitting

Removal

1 To make removal of the air cleaner assembly easier, remove the battery, as described in Chapter 5A, Section 3.

2 Remove the Engine Control Module (ECM), from the battery tray mounting bracket as described in Section 8, of this Chapter.

3 On 2.0 litre engines, remove the two retaining clips and release the air intake ducting from the front crossmember, and then withdraw it from the air cleaner housing **(see illustrations)**.

4 Unclip the turbocharger boost control solenoid valve from the air filter mounting bracket, and move it to one side **(see illustrations)**.

2.4a Unclip the turbo boost valve – 1.5 litre engine

2.4b Unclip the turbo boost valve – 2.0 litre engine

2.5a Disconnect the wiring connector (arrowed) ...

2.5b ... and unclip the wiring loom – 1.5 litre engine

2.5c Disconnect the wiring connector ...

2.5d ... and unclip the breather hose securing clip – 2.0 litre engine

2.6 Slacken the hose retaining clip (arrowed)

2.7 Undo the air filter housing securing nut (arrowed)

2.8a Remove the air cleaner housing – 1.5 litre engine

5 Disconnect the wiring connector from the mass airflow sensor **(see illustrations)**; unclip the wiring from any retaining clips on the housing.
6 Slacken the retaining clip and disconnect the air intake hose from the air cleaner assembly **(see illustration)**.
7 Undo the retaining nut that secures the air cleaner housing to the inner wing panel **(see illustration)**.
8 Pull the air cleaner upwards, disengaging the locating pegs on the bottom of the air cleaner assembly, from the rubber mountings, and then remove it from the engine compartment **(see illustrations)**.
9 On 1.5 litre engines, release the air intake ducting from bottom of the air cleaner housing, as it is being withdrawn **(see illustration)**.

10 If required remove the air filter element, as described in Chapter 1B, Section 20.

Refitting

11 Refitting is a reversal of the relevant removal procedure, ensuring that all hoses are properly reconnected, and that all ducts are correctly seated and securely held by their retaining clips.

3 Fuel pump and fuel gauge sender unit – removal and refitting

The diesel engine fuel pump/gauge sender unit has the same removal procedure as the petrol engines. Remove the fuel pump/gauge sender unit, as described in Chapter 4A, Section 7.

2.8b Remove the air cleaner housing – 2.0 litre engine

2.8c Withdrawing it from the lower mountings (arrowed)

2.9 Release the air intake ducting (arrowed)

4 Fuel tank –
removal and refitting

The diesel engine fuel tank has the same removal procedure as the petrol engines. Remove the fuel tank, as described in Chapter 4A, Section 8.

5 Fuel system –
priming and bleeding

Warning: Refer to the precautions in Section 1 before proceeding. Do not attempt to bleed the system by loosening any of the unions on the high-pressure circuit.
Note: *Priming of the fuel system after filter renewal will be improved if the filter is filled with clean diesel fuel before securing it to the filter head. To avoid spillages of fuel, keep the filter upright during refitting.*

1 After disconnecting part of the fuel supply system or running out of fuel, it is necessary to prime the system and bleed off any air that may have entered the system components.
2 There is a priming pump to enable the system to be bled; this consists of a hand-operated priming bulb located next to the filter assembly on the right-hand side rear of the inner wing panel **(see illustration)**.
3 Squeeze the priming bulb several times to purge the low-pressure circuit of air **(see illustration)**.
4 Attempt to start the engine normally, however, do not operate the starter motor for more than 5 seconds at a time. If necessary, operate the starter motor in 4 to 5 second bursts followed by pauses of 8 to 10 seconds. As soon as the engine starts, let it run at fast idle speed until a regular idle speed is reached.
5 If difficulty in purging the air from the system is experienced (engine may hunt), it is possible to bleed the system through the return pipe **(see illustrations)**.
6 Place some clean rags around the fuel pipe, and then using a flat bladed screwdriver, lift the cap on the fuel return pipe connection

5.2 Diesel hand priming pump location

(see illustration), and crank the engine until the air is removed. When complete push the cap down to seal the return pipe and check for any leaks.
7 Start the engine, let it run at fast idle speed until a regular idle speed is reached, and then check for any fuel leaks.

6 Idle speed – general

1 The engine management ECM uses the following inputs to calculate the recommended idle speed according to the varying load on the engine by peripheral electrical or mechanical components.
 a) Engine coolant temperature.
 b) Battery voltage.
 c) The gear selected.
 d) Electrical consumers (heater fan, climate control system, etc).
2 At normal engine temperature with no electrical consumers switched on and neutral selected, the engine idle speed will be 700 to 800 rpm, depending on engine type.
3 If the accelerator pedal potentiometer internal tracks are faulty, the ECM will override the idle speed to approx. 1200 rpm, and the injection warning light will be illuminated on the instrument panel. If the brake pedal is depressed, the idle speed will revert to its normal level.

5.3 Squeeze the priming pump to purge the circuit

4 If there is an injector fault, the idle speed will be set to 1200 rpm and the warning light will be illuminated.
5 Should the idle speed be repeatedly incorrect, the car should be taken to a Nissan dealer who will have the necessary diagnostic equipment to pinpoint the faulty component responsible.

7 Accelerator pedal –
removal and refitting

The diesel accelerator pedal has the same removal procedure as the petrol engines. Remove the accelerator pedal, as described in Chapter 4A, Section 3.

8 Fuel system components –
removal and refitting

Engine Control Module (ECM)

Note: *The engine management control module is electronically coded for the vehicle to which it is fitted; therefore new units are supplied without a code. If the ECM is being removed to enable a new unit to be fitted, a Nissan dealer must program the new unit with the information from the old ECM.*
1 On all engines the ECM is located in the

5.5a Fuel bleed point – 1.5 litre engine

5.5b Fuel bleed point – 2.0 litre engine

5.6 Lift the cap (arrowed) to get rid of the air

8.1 Location of Engine Control Module (ECM)

8.4 Unclip the vacuum pipes from the mounting bracket

8.5 Disconnect the wiring connectors

8.6 Release the wiring loom retaining clips (arrowed)

8.7a Undo the retaining bolts ...

4 Uncip the vacuum pipes from across the top of the mounting bracket **(see illustration)**.

5 Release the locking levers, and then withdraw the three electrical connectors from the side of the ECM **(see illustration)**.

6 Release the wiring loom retaining clips from the bottom of the mounting bracket **(see illustration)**.

7 Undo the retaining bolts and remove the mounting bracket, complete with control unit from the engine compartment **(see illustrations)**.

8 If required, undo the four retaining nuts and remove the ECM from the mounting bracket **(see illustration)**.

9 Refitting is a reverse of the removal procedure ensuring that the wiring is securely reconnected.

Crankshaft position sensor

10 On 2.0 litre engines the crankshaft position sensor is fitted to the rear of the cylinder block at the transmission end. On 1.5 litre engines, it is fitted at the rear of the transmission bell-housing **(see illustration)**.

11 Disconnect the wiring connector from the position sensor.

12 Undo the retaining bolt and withdraw the sensor from the cylinder block/bellhousing **(see illustration)**.

13 Refitting is a reversal of the removal procedure, noting the following points:
a) Fit a new O-ring seal to the sensor.
b) Apply a smear of engine oil to the O-ring to aid installation **(see illustration)**, and then ease the sensor into position.

8.7b ... and remove the ECM with mounting plate

8.8 Undo the four retaining nuts to remove the ECM

left-hand side of the engine compartment, between the battery and the air cleaner housing **(see illustration)**.
2 First disconnect the battery negative lead

(refer to *Disconnecting the battery* in the Reference Section).
3 Remove the battery, as described in Chapter 5A, Section 3.

8.10 Location of crankshaft position sensor – 1.5 litre engine

8.12 Removing the crankshaft position sensor – 2.0 litre engine

8.13 Lubricate seal with a smear of oil

Camshaft position sensor

14 The camshaft position sensor is fitted to the transmission end of the cylinder head cover **(see illustrations)**.

15 On 2.0 litre engines, undo the retaining bolts and remove the air intake pipe from across the top of the cylinder head, then unclip the heat protector shield from the cylinder head cover **(see illustrations)**.

16 Disconnect the wiring connector from the camshaft position sensor **(see illustrations)**.

17 Undo the retaining bolt and withdraw the sensor from the cover **(see illustration)**.

18 Discard the O-ring seal; a new one must be used on refitting.

19 Refitting is a reversal of the removal procedure, noting the following points:

a) *Fit a new O-ring seal to the sensor.*

b) *Apply a smear of engine oil to the O-ring to aid installation, and then ease the sensor into position.*

Coolant temperature sensor

20 Refer to Chapter 3, Section 6.

Mass airflow (MAF) sensor

21 The airflow sensor is mounted in the air cleaner housing, at the outlet end of the intake hose to the throttle housing. Prior to removal, disconnect the battery negative terminal (refer to *Disconnecting the battery* in the Reference Chapter).

1.5 litre engines

22 Slacken the retaining clip and disconnect the air intake hose from the mass airflow sensor **(see illustration)**.

23 Disconnect the wiring connector from the airflow sensor **(see illustration)**.

24 Undo the retaining screws, and then remove the airflow sensor from the air cleaner housing **(see illustration)**. Recover its sealing ring and renew.

25 Refitting is the reverse of removal, using

8.14a Location of camshaft sensor – 1.5 litre engine

8.14b Location of camshaft sensor – 2.0 litre engine

8.15a Remove the air intake pipe …

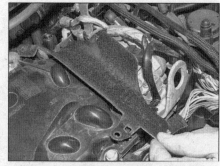

8.15b … and heat protection shield – 2.0 litre engine

8.16a Disconnect the wiring connector – 1.5 litre engine

8.16b Disconnect the wiring connector – 2.0 litre engine

8.17 Undo the bolt and remove the sensor

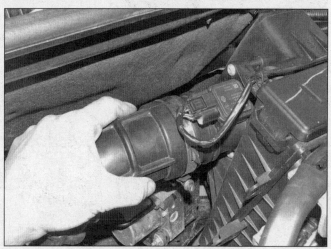

8.22 Disconnect the air intake hose

8.23 Disconnect the wiring connector

8.24 Undo the air flow sensor retaining screws (arrowed)

8.26 Disconnect the wiring connector

8.27 Undo the sensor retaining screws

8.30a Slacken the retaining clip ...

8.30b ... and remove the air intake pipe

a new sealing ring (where applicable) and tightening its retaining screws securely.

2.0 litre engines

26 Disconnect the wiring connector from the airflow sensor (see illustration).

8.31 Disconnect the wiring connector

27 Undo the retaining bolts, and then remove the sensor from the air cleaner housing (see illustration). Recover its sealing ring and renew.

28 Refitting is the reverse of removal, using a new sealing ring (where applicable) and tightening its retaining screws securely.

Inlet air temperature (IAT) sensor

29 The inlet air temperature sensor is combined with the mass airflow sensor. Remove the mass airflow sensor as described in paragraphs 21 to 28.

Throttle valve housing

1.5 litre engines

30 Slacken the retaining clip and disconnect

the air intake pipe from the throttle/damper unit (see illustrations). Move the hose to one side.

31 Disconnect the wiring from the throttle/damper unit (see illustration).

32 Unscrew the bolt from the mounting bracket and also the nuts from the intake manifold, and remove the unit from the engine. Remove and discard the gasket/seal (see illustrations).

33 Refitting is a reversal of removal, using a new gasket/seal and tightening to the specified torque.

2.0 litre engines

34 Disconnect the wiring connector from the turbocharger pressure sensor and the EGR solenoid valve.

35 Slacken the retaining clip and disconnect the air intake hose from the throttle/damper unit (see illustration), then move the hose to one side.

8.32a Undo the retaining bolt (arrowed) ...

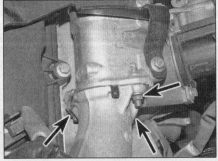

8.32b ... and the securing nuts to the manifold

8.35 Disconnect the air inlet hose from the throttle valve housing

8.36 Disconnect the wiring connector

8.37a Unbolt the throttle valve housing ...

8.37b ... and recover the gasket

36 Disconnect the wiring from the throttle/ damper unit **(see illustration)**.

37 Unscrew the bolts from the mounting bracket and also the bolts from the intake manifold, and remove the unit from the engine. Remove and discard the gasket/seal **(see illustrations)**.

38 Refitting is a reversal of removal, using a new gasket/seal and tightening to the specified torque.

---

9 High-pressure pump – removal and refitting

> ⚠️ **Warning: Refer to the warning note in Section 1 before proceeding.**

Caution: Before starting work, allow the engine to cool for 5 to 10 minutes, to ensure the fuel pressure and temperature are at a minimum.

Note: *The high-pressure pump is removed after first removing the timing belt as described in Chapter 2C. All high-pressure pipes removed must be renewed as a matter of course.*

Note: *Cleanliness is of critical importance*
when working on the fuel system of any modern diesel engine. The smallest speck of grit or dirt can cause extensive damage to the pump and injectors. Always clean thoroughly the pump and injector unions before dismantling. Immediately plug and seal all pipes and components. Components that are removed from the engine should immediately be placed in clean plastic bags.

Removal

1.5 litre engine

1 Disconnect the battery negative lead (refer
to *Disconnecting the battery* in the Reference Chapter).

2 Remove the plastic trim cover from the top of the engine **(see illustration)**.

3 Slacken the retaining clip and disconnect the intercooler pipe rubber hose **(see illustration)**.

4 Undo the retaining bolt, then release the securing clip at the turbo end of the pipe and pull the pipe upwards to remove it from across the top of the engine **(see illustrations)**.

5 Undo the upper bolt and retaining nut, release the two lower securing clips and

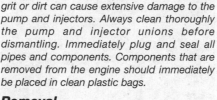

9.2 Remove the upper trim panel

9.3 Disconnect the intake hose

9.4a Undo the retaining bolt ...

9.4b ... and remove the air intake pipe

9.5a undo the nut and bolt …

9.5b …release the securing clips …

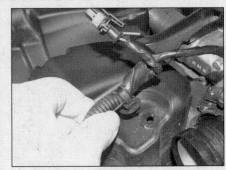

9.5c … unclip the wiring clip …

9.5d … and remove the upper plastic cover

9.6a Undo the bolt and nut …

9.6b … and remove the bracket from the fuel pump

9.7a Undo the two bolts …

9.7b … and pull back the dipstick bracket

remove the upper protective cover (see illustrations).

6 Undo the bolt and retaining nut and remove the bracket from the front of the fuel pump (see illustrations).

7 Undo the two retaining bolts and pull back the dipstick bracket from the front of the cylinder head (see illustrations).

8 Disconnect the wiring connector from the pressure switch on the bottom of the fuel rail (see illustration).

9 Release the securing clip and remove the wiring loom from the top of the lower cover (see illustration).

9.8 Disconnect the pressure sensor wiring connector

9.9 Unclip the wiring loom from the plastic cover

9.10a Unclip the drain tube …

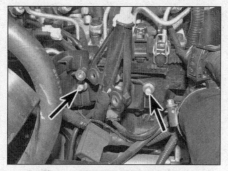

9.10b … undo the retaining nuts …

9.10c … and remove the lower plastic cover

10 Release the drain tube from the bottom of the cover, undo the two retaining nuts and remove the lower protective cover **(see illustrations)**.
11 Jack up the right-hand front of the car and support on axle stands. Remove the front right wheel, engine undertray and wheel arch liner.
12 Remove the auxiliary drivebelt with reference to Chapter 1B, Section 10.
13 Loosen the alternator lower bolt and remove the top bolt. Tip the alternator away from the engine.
14 Disconnect the three wiring connectors from the fuel pump **(see illustrations)**.
15 Place a clean rag over the alternator and then remove the fuel pipe/hoses from the pump **(see illustrations)**. As a precaution against

remaining pressure in the pipes, first wrap them loosely in cloth/rag. The high-pressure pipe will need to be renewed. Seal the pump and pipe/hoses immediately. Do not allow fuel to contaminate the alternator.
16 Remove the timing belt as described in Chapter 2C, Section 6. Note it would be a sensible precaution to renew the timing belt anyway.
17 Unbolt and remove the fuel pump, and then place the pump in a vice to remove the sprocket. Use a strap wrench and a ring spanner to do this. A puller will then be required to remove the sprocket from the pump.

2.0 litre engines

18 Remove the cylinder head cover, then

unscrew the union nut and disconnect the high-pressure pipe from the fuel rail **(see illustration)**, refer to Section 11, to gain access to the fuel rail. As a precaution against remaining pressure in the pipes, first wrap them loosely in cloth/rag. Cap or plug the open connections to reduce fuel loss and prevent entry of dirt.
19 For improved access, remove the battery, as described in Chapter 5A, Section 3.
20 Unclip the plastic cover, then unscrew the union nut and disconnect the high-pressure pipe from the fuel pump **(see illustration)**. Cap or plug the open connections to reduce fuel loss and prevent entry of dirt.
21 Disconnect the quick-release fuel supply and return hoses from the

9.14a Disconnect the wiring connectors …

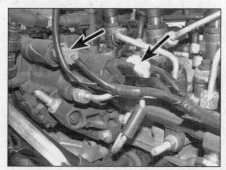

9.14b … from the fuel pump sensors

9.15a Remove the fuel pipe …

9.15b … and hoses from the pump

9.18 Disconnect the fuel pipe (arrowed) from the fuel rail

9.20 Remove the plastic cover (arrowed) from the fuel connection

9.21 Disconnect the fuel supply hose (arrowed)

9.22a Unscrew the mounting bolts …

9.22b …withdraw the pump from the cylinder head …

high-pressure pump and plug the openings **(see illustration)**.

22 Progressively unscrew the mounting bolts then withdraw the high-pressure pump from the cylinder head. Remove the O-ring seal from the groove, a new one will be required for refitting **(see illustrations)**.

23 If necessary, the pinion may be removed from the high-pressure pump drive shaft **(see illustration)**. To do this, first lock the pinion in a soft-jawed vice and unscrew the retaining nut. A puller will now be required to remove the pinion from the drive shaft.

Refitting

Note: *The manufacturers stipulate that the high-pressure pipe is renewed whenever it is removed.*

24 Refitting is a reversal of removal, but take care not to place the new high-pressure pipe under any stress. If fitting a new pump, it is highly recommended that the pump is primed with diesel on the bench before fitting.

25 On 2.0 litre engines, fit a new O-ring seal to the pump and new retaining bolts.

26 New high-pressure pipes are supplied with a lubricant for the threads on the pipe. If no lubricant is supplied the pipes are self-lubricating and lubricant should not be applied.

27 Tighten all nuts and bolts to the specified torque and angle as applicable.

28 Prime and bleed the fuel system as described in Section 5.

29 Before restarting the engine, it may be necessary to use a diagnostic tool to clear any faults that may be stored in the engine control module (ECM).

10 Fuel injectors – testing, removal and refitting

> **Warning: Exercise extreme caution when working on the high-pressure fuel system. Do not attempt to test the fuel injectors or disconnect the high-pressure lines with the engine running. Never expose the hands or any part of the body to injector spray, as the high working pressure can cause the fuel to penetrate the skin, with possibly fatal results. You are strongly advised to have any work that involves testing the injectors under pressure carried out by a dealer or fuel injection specialist. Refer to the precautions given in Section 1 of this Chapter before proceeding. After switching off the engine, allow the engine to cool for 5 to 10 minutes to allow the fuel pressure to drop before disconnecting any of the high-pressure fuel pipes.**

Note: *Each new injector is supplied with a unique code, which specifies its flow characteristics. This code must be programmed into the engine management ECM with a special diagnostic tool; therefore*

this work should be entrusted to a Nissan dealer or suitably equipped garage.

Testing

1 It is not possible to test the fuel injectors without specialist equipment, therefore, if they are thought to be faulty, consult a Nissan dealer or diesel specialist.

Removal

Note: *Take care not to allow dirt into the injectors or fuel pipes during this procedure; clean around the area before commencing work. Note that all high-pressure pipes removed must be renewed as a matter of course. The injector flame shield washers must also be renewed.*

2 Disconnect the battery negative lead (refer to *Disconnecting the battery* in the Reference Chapter).

1.5 litre engine

3 Remove the upper protective cover from the top of the cylinder head as described in Section 9, paragraphs 2 to 5.

4 Before removal thoroughly clean the area around the fuel injectors.

5 Disconnect the wiring connector from the top of the fuel injector **(see illustration)**.

6 While holding the injector central unions with one spanner, unscrew the high-pressure pipe union nuts with a further spanner. Use some cloth around the pipe unions to soak up the spilt fuel, and then loosen them. Similarly, unscrew the union nuts from the fuel rail, and

9.22c …and remove the O-ring seal

9.23 High-pressure pump pinion

10.5 Disconnect the injector wiring connectors

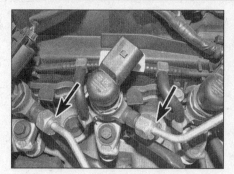

10.6a Unscrew the fuel injector pipe union nuts …

10.6b … and also at the fuel rail

10.7 Release the leak-off pipe retaining clips (arrowed)

then remove the pipes **(see illustrations)**. As a precaution against remaining pressure in the pipes, first wrap them loosely in cloth/rag. Discard the fuel pipe, as a new one will be required for refitting. Plug all fuel apertures to prevent entry of dust and dirt.

7 Using a thin screwdriver, release the securing clip and disconnect the fuel leak-off pipe from the side of the injector **(see illustration)**. Tape over or plug all fuel apertures to prevent entry of dust and dirt.

8 Unscrew the bolt securing each injector clamp plate to the cylinder head **(see illustration)**. Lift off the clamp plates and remove the injectors then recover the flame shield washers between the injectors and the cylinder head.

2.0 litre engines

9 Remove the cylinder head cover from the top of the engine with reference to Chapter 2D.

10 Undo the retaining bolts and remove the oil separator from the top of the cylinder head **(see illustration)**.

11 Carefully clean around the fuel injectors and injector pipe union nuts.

12 Disconnect the wiring connectors from the fuel injectors **(see illustration)**.

13 Note the fitted position of the leak-off pipes, and then disconnect them from the fuel injectors **(see illustration)**.

14 Unscrew the union nuts securing the injector pipes to the fuel rail whilst being prepared for some fuel spillage, then unscrew the union nuts and disconnect the pipes from the injectors. Where necessary, undo the pipe support clamp

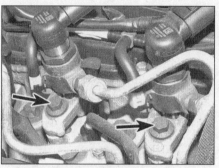

10.8 Injector plate retaining bolts (arrowed)

10.12 Disconnect the injector wiring connectors

bolts **(see illustrations)**. As a precaution against remaining pressure in the pipes, first wrap them loosely in cloth/rag. Plug all fuel apertures to prevent entry of dust and dirt.

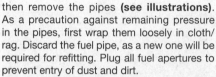

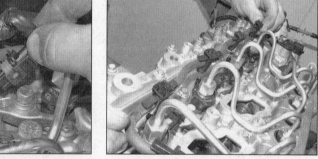

10.10 Remove the oil separator (arrowed)

10.13 Removing the leak-off pipes from the injectors

15 Using a felt-tipped pen, mark each injector for its position (No 1 cylinder at the timing chain end). This is important because the engine management ECM recognises

10.14a Unscrew the union nuts …

10.14b … where necessary undo the pipe support clamp bolts …

10.14c … and disconnect the pipes from the injectors and fuel rail

each injector by the cylinder it is located in. If new injectors are obtained, the code on each injector must be noted and programmed into the ECM.

16 Unscrew the bolt securing each injector clamp plate, lift off the clamp plates and withdraw the injectors. Recover the flame shield washer between the injectors and the cylinder head **(see illustrations)**.

Refitting

17 Take care not to drop the injectors or allow the needles at their tips to become damaged. The injectors are precision-made to fine limits and must not be handled roughly. In particular, do not mount them in a bench vice. It is recommended that the injectors are stored vertically at all times.

18 Clean the cylinder head, taking care to prevent foreign matter entering the fuel apertures. The injectors can be cleaned with a lint-free cloth soaked in brake cleaning fluid or fresh diesel. **Do not** clean them with a wire brush or emery cloth.

19 Obtain new injector sealing washers and new fuel pipes for refitting.

20 Fit new sealing shims between the injectors and the cylinder head. Insert the injectors then fit the clamp plates. Tighten the clamp plate bolts to the specified torque.

21 Fit new injector pipes, and tighten the union nuts on the injectors and the fuel rail by hand at first. Make sure the pipe clamps are in their previously noted positions. Bearing in mind the high vibration levels with a diesel engine, if the clamps are wrongly positioned or missing, problems may be experienced with pipes breaking or splitting. With all the pipes in place tighten them to the specified torque setting.

22 Renew the injector leak-off pipes, and refit in the position noted on removal.

23 Reconnect the fuel injector wiring.

24 Refit the engine cylinder cover with reference to Chapter 2C or 2D.

25 Reconnect the battery negative lead (refer to *Disconnecting the battery* in the Reference Chapter).

26 If new injectors have been fitted, have the code programmed into the engine management ECM by a Nissan dealer.

27 Start the engine. If difficulty is experienced, bleed the fuel system as described in Section 5.

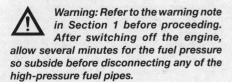

11 Injector rail (common rail) – removal and refitting

⚠ *Warning: Refer to the warning note in Section 1 before proceeding. After switching off the engine, allow several minutes for the fuel pressure to subside before disconnecting any of the high-pressure fuel pipes.*

10.16a Unscrew the retaining bolts ...

10.16b ... remove the clamp plates ...

10.16c ... then withdraw the injector ...

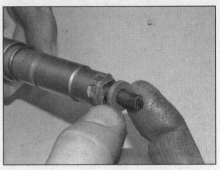

10.16d ... and recover the flame shield washer

Note: *Take care not to allow dirt into the fuel pipes during this procedure, clean around the area before commencing work. Note that all high-pressure pipes removed must be renewed as a matter of course.*

Removal

1 Disconnect the battery negative lead (refer to *Disconnecting the battery* in the Reference Chapter).

2 Remove the plastic engine cover (where fitted) from the top of the engine.

1.5 litre engine

3 Remove the upper and lower protective covers from around the fuel rail, as described in Section 9, paragraphs 2 to 10.

4 Disconnect the wiring connectors from the

heater (glow) plugs and move the wiring loom to one side **(see illustration)**.

5 Undo the union nuts and remove the high-pressure fuel pipe from the fuel pump to the fuel rail **(see illustration)**. As a precaution against remaining pressure in the pipes, first wrap them loosely in cloth/rag. Discard the fuel pipe, as a new one will be required for refitting. Plug all fuel apertures to prevent entry of dust and dirt.

6 While holding the injector central unions with one spanner, unscrew the high-pressure pipe union nuts with a further spanner. As a precaution against remaining pressure in the pipes, first wrap them loosely in cloth/rag. Similarly, unscrew the union nuts from the fuel rail, and then remove the pipes. Discard the fuel pipes, as new ones will be required for refitting. Plug all fuel apertures to prevent entry of dust and dirt.

11.4 Disconnect the heater plug wiring connector

11.5 Remove the high pressure fuel pipe (arrowed)

11.7 Undo the fuel rail mounting nuts (arrowed)

11.9a Disconnect the pressure sensor wiring connector (arrowed)

11.9b Disconnect the pressure control valve wiring connector (arrowed)

11.10 Disconnect the fuel return hose (arrowed)

11.12 Undo the fuel pipe union nut and release the pipe retaining clamp bolt (arrowed)

11.13 Remove the four injector-to-fuel rail pipes

7 Unbolt and remove the fuel rail from the front of the cylinder head (see illustration).

2.0 litre engine

8 The fuel rail is located on the side of the camshaft housing, with the injector and pump connections emerging from inside the housing upper cavity. First, remove the cylinder head cover and the oil separator from the top of the engine with reference to Chapter 2D.

9 Disconnect the wiring connectors from the fuel rail switches, at each end of the fuel rail (see illustrations). **Note:** *The one on the left-hand end of the rail is the fuel rail pressure sensor, and the one on the right-hand end of the fuel rail is the fuel rail pressure control valve (as viewed from the drivers seat).*

10 Disconnect the fuel return hose from the right-hand end of the fuel rail (see illustration).

11 Unclip the plastic cover, then unscrew the union nut and disconnect the high-pressure pipe from the fuel pump, see Section 9. As a precaution against remaining pressure in the pipes, first wrap them loosely in cloth/rag.

12 Unscrew the union nut and disconnect the high-pressure pipe from the fuel rail, undo the pipe securing clamp bolt and remove the pipe from the engine (see illustrations). Discard the fuel pipes, as new ones will be required for refitting.

13 With reference to Section 10, unscrew the union nuts and disconnect the fuel supply pipes from the injectors and fuel rail, new ones will be required for refitting (see illustration). Release the fuel pipes and unclip from any retaining clips, note their position for refitting. Discard the fuel pipes, as new ones will be required for refitting.

14 Cover or plug all fuel apertures to prevent entry of dust and dirt into the fuel system.

15 Unbolt and remove the fuel rail from the front of the cylinder head (see illustrations).

Refitting

16 Refitting is a reversal of removal, but take care not to place the new high-pressure pipe under any stress. Before fitting the new pipe, lubricate the threads of the union nuts with oil from the sachet provided, and finger-tighten the nuts before tightening them to the specified torque. When tightening the pipe union nuts onto the injectors, counter-hold the injectors with a further spanner.

17 On completion, prime and bleed the fuel system as described in Section 5. Run the engine, and check for fuel leaks.

12 Inlet manifold – removal and refitting

1.5 litre engines

1 The inlet manifold on 1.5 litre diesel engines is incorporated into the cylinder head and therefore cannot be removed separately.

2.0 litre engines

2 The inlet manifold is located on the front of the cylinder head. First, remove the engine top cover, then remove the battery and battery tray as described in Chapter 5A.

11.15a Undo the mounting bolts ...

11.15b ...and lower the fuel rail to withdraw

12.5a Remove the EGR cooler pipe …

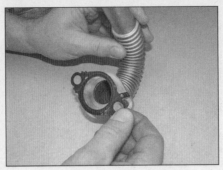

12.5b … and gaskets

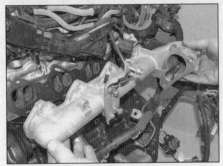

12.6a Remove the inlet manifold …

12.6b … and recover the gasket

13.7a Remove the exhaust manifold …

13.7b … and recover the gasket

13.10a Unbolt the EGR rigid pipe from the exhaust manifold …

13.10b … and recover the gasket

3 Remove the intake air ducting and intercooler inlet pipe from the front of the engine.

4 Remove the throttle valve housing, as described in Section 8.

5 Unbolt the EGR cooler pipe from the inlet manifold and cooler and recover the gaskets **(see illustrations)**.

6 Unscrew and remove the mounting bolts and withdraw the inlet manifold from the cylinder head. Recover the gasket and discard it as a new gasket must be used on refitting **(see illustrations)**. Also obtain new gaskets for the EGR cooler pipe.

7 Refitting is the reverse of removal using new gaskets, and tightening the manifold retaining bolts to the specified torque.

13 Exhaust manifold – removal and refitting

Removal

1 The exhaust manifold is located on the rear of the cylinder head. Remove the engine top cover, and then disconnect the battery negative terminal.

2 Apply the handbrake, and then jack up the front of the vehicle and support it on axle stands (*see Jacking and vehicle support*).

3 Disconnect the exhaust front pipe/ particle filter (where fitted), with reference to Section 17.

4 Remove the turbocharger as described in Section 15. If the reason for removing the manifold is simply to renew the gasket, the turbocharger can remain attached to the manifold.

1.5 litre engines

5 Loosen the two clamps, then remove the EGR metal tube between the inlet and exhaust manifolds. The manufacturers recommend that the metal tube and clamps are renewed as a matter of course.

6 Unscrew the mounting bolts and remove the EGR unit from the inlet manifold.

7 Progressively unscrew the mounting nuts and remove the exhaust manifold from the studs on the cylinder head. Recover the metal gasket **(see illustrations)**.

8 Clean the surfaces of the cylinder head and exhaust manifold, then locate a new gasket on the cylinder head studs.

2.0 litre engines

9 Unscrew the bolts securing the EGR rigid pipe to the exhaust manifold and cylinder head, then unbolt and remove the heat shield from the rigid pipe.

10 Unbolt the EGR rigid pipe from the EGR cooler and exhaust manifold, and recover the gaskets **(see illustrations)**.

11 Unscrew and remove the nuts and spacers and withdraw the exhaust manifold from the cylinder head. Recover the manifold gasket and discard it as a new gasket must

13.11a Unscrew the nuts and remove the spacers ...

13.11b ... remove the exhaust manifold ...

13.11c ... and recover the gasket

be used on refitting **(see illustrations)**. Also obtain new EGR rigid pipe seals. Nissan state that the manifold nuts must also be renewed.
12 Check the condition of the exhaust manifold studs and renew them if necessary. Tighten into the cylinder head to the specified torque.

Refitting

13 Refitting is the reverse of removal using a new gasket and seals, and tightening the manifold retaining nuts to the specified torque. When positioning the gasket on the studs, the gasket end tab must be towards the flywheel end of the engine.

14 Turbocharger – description and precautions

1 A turbocharger increases engine efficiency by raising the pressure in the inlet manifold above atmospheric pressure. Instead of the air simply being sucked into the cylinders, it is forced in. Additional fuel is supplied in proportion to the increased air intake.
2 Energy for the operation of the turbocharger comes from the exhaust gas. The gas flows through a specially shaped housing (the turbine housing) and in so doing, spins the turbine wheel. The turbine wheel is attached to a shaft, at the end of which is another vaned wheel known as the compressor wheel. The compressor wheel spins in its own housing and compresses the inducted air on the way to the inlet manifold.
3 Between the turbocharger and the inlet manifold, the compressed air passes through an intercooler. This is an air-to-air heat exchanger, mounted behind the front bumper, in front of the air conditioning condenser and the coolant radiator. The purpose of the intercooler is to remove some of the heat gained in being compressed from the inducted air. Because cooler air is denser, removal of this heat further increases engine efficiency.
4 Boost pressure (the pressure in the inlet manifold) is limited by a wastegate, which diverts the exhaust gas away from the turbine wheel in response to a pressure-sensitive

actuator. Turbocharging pressure is controlled by a pressure sensor located on the air intake **(see illustrations)**.
5 The boost control solenoid valve is located at the left-hand rear of the engine compartment by the air cleaner housing **(see illustrations 2.4a and 2.4b)**.
6 The turbo shaft is pressure-lubricated by an oil feed pipe from the main oil gallery. The shaft 'floats' on a cushion of oil. A drain pipe returns the oil to the sump.
7 On some models, there is an electric coolant pump located on the rear of the subframe, below the transmission, to help cool the turbocharger. There is a relay in the engine compartment fusebox to operate this electric coolant pump **(see illustrations)**.

Precautions

• The turbocharger operates at extremely

high speeds and temperatures. Certain precautions must be observed to avoid premature failure of the turbo or injury to the operator.
• Do not race the engine immediately after start-up, especially if it is cold. Give the oil a few seconds to circulate.
• Always allow the engine to return to idle speed before switching it off – do not blip the throttle and switch off, as this will leave the turbo spinning without lubrication.
• Allow the engine to idle for several minutes before switching off after a high speed run.
• Observe the recommended intervals for oil and filter changing, and use a reputable oil of the specified quality. Neglect of oil changing, or use of inferior oil, can cause carbon formation on the turbo shaft and subsequent failure.

14.4a Turbo pressure sensor location (arrowed) – 1.5 litre engine

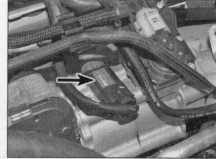

14.4b Turbo pressure sensor location (arrowed) – 2.0 litre engine

14.7a Electric coolant pump for turbocharger on subframe

14.7b Relay for electric coolant pump (arrowed)

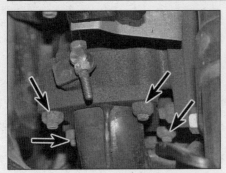

15.9 Nuts securing the catalytic converter to the turbocharger

15.10 Unbolt the strut from the side of the catalytic converter

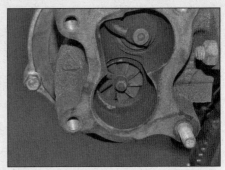

15.11 View of the turbocharger wastegate (upper) and vanes (lower) with the catalytic converter removed

 Warning: Do not operate the turbo with any parts exposed. Foreign objects falling onto the rotating vanes could cause damage and (if ejected) personal injury.

15 Turbocharger – removal and refitting

Note: *New turbocharger-to-exhaust manifold nuts must be used on refitting.*

Note: *New oil supply pipe O-rings and copper washers must be used on refitting.*

1 Apply the handbrake, then jack up the front of the vehicle, and support securely on axle stands (see *Jacking and vehicle support*). Remove the right-hand front roadwheel.

2 Disconnect the battery negative lead (refer to *Disconnecting the battery* in the Reference Chapter).

3 Remove the engine top cover, and then remove the air cleaner unit as described in Section 2.

Removal

1.5 litre engines

4 At the rear of the engine, disconnect the wiring from the downstream air temperature sensor and EGR solenoid valve.

15.13a Removing the oil supply pipe and copper sealing rings from the turbocharger

15.13b Removing the oil supply pipe from the cylinder head

5 Disconnect the tube from the turbocharger pressure adjustment valve on the air duct.

6 Loosen the clips and disconnect the air ducts from between the EGR unit and turbocharger.

7 Unbolt and remove the engine lifting eye from the right-hand rear of the cylinder head.

8 Unscrew the bolt and remove the air inlet metal tube.

9 Unscrew the four nuts securing the catalytic converter to the turbocharger **(see illustration)**.

10 Working under the front of the car, unscrew the nuts and disconnect the intermediate pipe flexible flange from the catalytic converter. Also, unbolt the strut from

the side of the catalytic converter and block **(see illustration)**.

11 Unbolt the catalytic converter and lower it as far as possible **(see illustration)** or remove it completely.

12 In the engine compartment, unbolt the heat shield from the EGR solenoid valve.

13 Unscrew the union and disconnect the oil supply pipe from the turbocharger, collect the copper sealing rings, then unscrew the union nut and disconnect the pipe from the cylinder head **(see illustrations)**.

14 Unscrew the bolts and detach the oil return pipe from the bottom of the turbocharger – if necessary, remove the pipe from the cylinder block **(see illustrations)**.

15.14a Oil return pipe flange bolts on the bottom of the turbocharger

15.14b Removing the oil return pipe

15.15a Turbocharger upper mounting nuts . . .

15.15b . . . and lower mounting nut

15 Unscrew the turbocharger upper and lower mounting nuts **(see illustrations)**, then remove the turbocharger together with the oil return pipe from the exhaust manifold. With the assembly on the bench, remove the oil return pipe. Do not attempt to separate the inlet and exhaust sections of the turbocharger.

2.0 litre engines

16 Where fitted, remove the exhaust particle filter (refer to Section 17).
17 Remove the catalytic converter as described in Section 17.
18 Loosen the clips and remove the air duct from the air mass meter and turbocharger.
19 Disconnect the wiring and vacuum pipe **(see illustration)**.
20 Unscrew the union bolt and flange nuts and disconnect the oil supply and return pipes from the turbocharger. Unscrew the support bolt and remove the pipes from the cylinder block **(see illustration)**.
21 Unscrew the nuts/bolts and remove the turbocharger and mounting bracket from the exhaust manifold.
22 Remove the gasket noting that its end tab is facing the flywheel end of the engine.
23 Unbolt and remove the mounting bracket.

Refitting

24 Refitting is a reversal of removal, but renew any damaged hose clamps, and use new turbocharger-to-exhaust manifold nuts which should be tightened to the specified torque. Fit new oil supply pipe O-rings and copper seals, then apply Loctite Frenetanch (or similar sealant) to the union threads before refitting the pipe and tightening the union nuts to the specified torque. Fit a new gasket to the top of the oil return pipe, and new O-ring seals to the grooves in the bottom of the pipe **(see illustrations)**. On completion, the following procedure must be observed before starting the engine in order to establish initial oil pressure in the turbocharger.

a) Disconnect the wiring from the fuel injectors.
b) Crank the engine on the starter motor until the instrument panel oil pressure warning light goes out (this may take several seconds).
c) Reconnect the wiring to the injectors, then start the engine using the normal procedure.
d) Run the engine at idle speed, and check the turbocharger oil unions for leakage.
e) After the engine has been run, check the engine oil level, and top–up if necessary.

15.19 Disconnecting the vacuum pipe

15.20 Removing the turbocharger oil supply and return pipes

15.24a Applying sealant to the threads of the oil supply pipe union

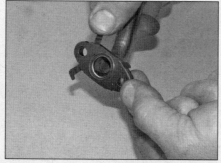

15.24b Fit a new gasket to the top of the oil return pipe . . .

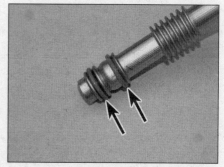

15.24c . . . and fit new O-ring seals to the grooves in the bottom of the pipe

16.3a Release the retaining clips ...

16.3b ... then remove the lower ...

16.3c ... and upper trim panels

16.4a Disconnect the hoses (arrowed) ...

16.4b ... at each end of the intercooler

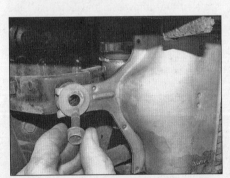

16.5a Undo the intercooler mounting bolts ...

16.5b ... and lift it out from its rubber mountings

17.2a Front exhaust joint – 1.5 litre engine

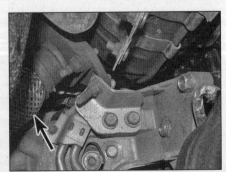

17.2b Front flexible exhaust pipe – 2.0 litre engine

16 Intercooler – removal and refitting

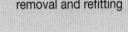

Removal

1 The intercooler is located behind the front bumper, in front of the air conditioning condenser.

2 Remove the front bumper as described in Chapter 11, Section 6.

3 Release the retaining clips and remove the plastic covers from each end of the condenser and intercooler (see illustrations).

4 Slacken the retaining clips and disconnect the air inlet and outlet hoses from each end of the intercooler (see illustrations).

5 Undo the intercooler mounting bolts (one at each end of the intercooler), then pull the intercooler upwards to release it from the lower rubber mountings, and remove it from the front of the vehicle (see illustrations).

Refitting

6 Refitting is a reversal of removal, making sure all the connections are securely fitted.

17 Exhaust system – general information and component renewal

General information

1 The exhaust system consists of the exhaust manifold (see Section 13), the turbocharger (see section 14), the catalytic converter, the front pipe/particle filter (depending on model) and the remaining exhaust section consisting of the intermediate pipe/tailpipe and silencer.

2 The front pipe is connected by a flexible flange joint on 1.5 litre engines, and a flexible length of pipe on 2.0 litre engines (see illustrations).

3 The system is suspended throughout its entire length by rubber mountings (see

17.3a Exhaust rubber mounting ...

17.3b ... some models have a mounting block on the front subframe

17.5 Undo the front pipe-to-catalytic converter bolts/nuts

illustrations), and all exhaust sections are joined by flanged joints, which are then secured together by nuts and/or bolts.

4 To remove the system or part of the system, firmly apply the handbrake, and then jack up the vehicle and support it securely on axle stands (see *Jacking and vehicle support*). Alternatively, position the car over an inspection pit, or on car ramps. Where fitted, remove the engine compartment undertray.

Front pipe (models without DPF)

5 Undo the nuts securing the front pipe to the catalytic converter (see illustration). With the nuts removed retrieve the washers and springs, and then separate the front pipe from the catalytic converter/manifold.

6 Slacken and remove the two bolts securing the front pipe/silencer flange joint to the intermediate pipe. Withdraw the front pipe from underneath the vehicle, and recover the gasket from the joint (see illustration).

Front pipe/particle filter (models with DPF)

7 Unscrew the pressure take-off unions from the side and base of the assembly (see illustrations). Undo the retaining nuts and disconnect any securing clamps from the pipes.

8 Disconnect the sensor wiring plug on the side of the exhaust system (see illustration).

9 Slacken the retaining nuts securing the front pipe/particle filter to the catalytic converter (see illustration 17.2b). Take care not to damage the flexible section of the front exhaust pipe.

10 Slacken and remove the two bolts securing the front pipe/particle filter flange joint to the intermediate pipe. Withdraw the front pipe/particle filter from underneath the vehicle, and recover the gasket from the joint (see illustration).

Intermediate pipe/silencer/tailpipe

11 Slacken and remove the two bolts securing the front pipe flange joint to the intermediate pipe and seperate. Support the disconnected front pipe so as not to place undue strain on the front part of the exhaust system.

12 With the aid of an assistant, working along the underside of the vehicle, unhook the intermediate pipe/silencer/tailpipe from its mounting rubbers, and then manoeuvre the pipe out from underneath the vehicle.

Catalytic converter

13 Remove the exhaust front pipe as described previously in this Chapter.

14 On 2.0 litre models, undo the retaining bolts and remove the heat shield from around the catalytic converter.

15 Undo the retaining bolts and remove the support bracket from the bottom of the catalytic converter.

16 Slacken the retaining nuts securing the catalytic converter to the turbocharger, and lower the catalytic converter from under the vehicle.

Heat shield(s)

17 The heat shields are secured in position by a mixture of fasteners. Some heatshields are fitted to the underside of the vehicle. And

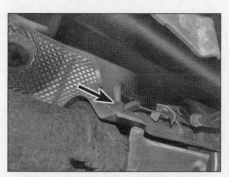

17.6 Undo the front pipe to intermediate pipe bolts

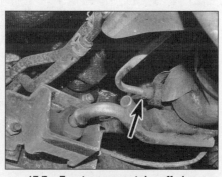

17.7a Front pressure take off pipe connection (arrowed) ...

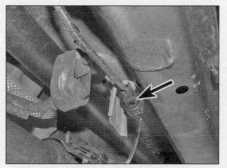

17.7b ... and rear pressure take-off pipe connection (arrowed)

17.8 Disconnect the sensor wiring connector (arrowed)

17.10 Undo the front pipe/particle filter to intermediate pipe bolts/nuts

17.17a Undo the retaining clips …

17.17b … and remove the heat shield

also some are fitted to parts of the exhaust system. When an exhaust section is renewed, transfer any relevant heat shields from the original over to the new section before installing the exhaust section on the vehicle **(see illustrations)**.

Refitting

18 Each section is refitted by a reverse of the removal sequence, noting the following points:

a) *Ensure that all traces of corrosion have been removed from the flanges, and renew all necessary gaskets* **(see illustrations)**.

b) *Inspect the rubber mountings for signs of damage or deterioration, and renew as necessary.*

c) *Prior to tightening the exhaust system fasteners, ensure that all rubber mountings are correctly located, and that*

there is adequate clearance between the exhaust system and vehicle underbody/suspension components, etc.

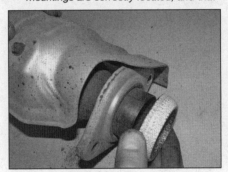

17.18a Fit new sealing rings to the silencer …

17.18b … and the exhaust front pipe

Chapter 4 Part C:
Emission control systems

Contents

Degrees of difficulty

Easy, suitable for novice with little experience	**Fairly easy,** suitable for beginner with some experience	**Fairly difficult,** suitable for competent DIY mechanic	**Difficult,** suitable for experienced DIY mechanic	**Very difficult,** suitable for expert DIY or professional

Specifications

Torque wrench settings	Nm	lbf ft
EGR cooler	16	12
EGR solenoid valve mounting bolts	8	6
Oxygen (lambda) sensor	45	33

1 General information

All petrol engine models have the ability to use unleaded petrol and also have various other features built into the fuel system to help minimise harmful emissions. On top of this, all models are equipped with the crankcase emission control system described below. All models are also equipped with a catalytic converter and an evaporative emission control system.

All diesel engine models are also designed to meet the strict emission requirements and are equipped with a crankcase emission control system. In addition to this certain models may also be fitted with a catalytic converter to reduce exhaust emissions. To further reduce emissions, they are also equipped with an exhaust gas recirculation (EGR) system.

The emission control systems function as follows.

Petrol models

Crankcase emission control

To reduce the emission of unburned hydrocarbons from the crankcase into the atmosphere, the engine is sealed and the blow-by gases and oil vapour are drawn from inside the crankcase, through a wire mesh oil separator, into the inlet tract to be burned by the engine during normal combustion.

Under conditions of high manifold depression (idling, deceleration) the gases will be sucked positively out of the crankcase. Under conditions of low manifold depression (acceleration, full-throttle running) the gases are forced out of the crankcase by the (relatively) higher crankcase pressure; if the engine is worn, the raised crankcase pressure (due to increased blow-by) will cause some of the flow to return under all manifold conditions.

Exhaust emission control

To minimise the amount of pollutants that escape into the atmosphere, all models are fitted with a catalytic converter in the exhaust system. The system is of the closed-loop type, in which one or two oxygen sensors in the exhaust system provides the fuel injection/ignition system ECM with constant feedback, enabling the ECM to adjust the mixture to provide the best possible conditions for the converter to operate.

The oxygen (lambda) sensors have a heating element built-in that is controlled by the ECM through the oxygen sensor relay to quickly bring the sensor's tip to an efficient operating temperature. The sensor's tip is sensitive to oxygen and sends the ECM a varying voltage depending on the amount of oxygen in the exhaust gases; if the inlet air/fuel mixture is too rich, the exhaust gases are low in oxygen so the sensors sends a low-voltage signal, the voltage rising as the mixture weakens and the amount of oxygen rises in the exhaust gases. Peak conversion efficiency of all major pollutants occurs if the inlet air/fuel mixture is maintained at the chemically correct ratio for the complete combustion of petrol of

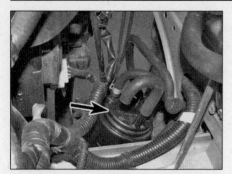

1.8 Location of charcoal canister

14.7 parts (by weight) of air to 1 part of fuel (the 'stoichiometric' ratio). The sensor output voltage alters in a large step at this point, the ECM using the signal change as a reference point and correcting the inlet air/fuel mixture accordingly by altering the fuel injector pulse width.

Evaporative emission control

To minimise the escape into the atmosphere of unburned hydrocarbons, an evaporative emissions control system is also fitted to all models. The fuel tank filler cap is sealed and a charcoal canister is mounted inside the engine compartment, behind the right-hand headlamp **(see illustration)**. The canister collects the petrol vapours generated in the tank when the car is parked and stores them until they can be cleared from the canister (under the control of the fuel injection/ignition system ECM) via the purge valve into the inlet tract to be burned by the engine during normal combustion.

To ensure the engine runs correctly when it is cold and/or idling and to protect the catalytic converter from the effects of an over-rich mixture, the purge control valve is not opened by the ECM until the engine has warmed-up, and the engine is under load; the valve solenoid is then modulated on and off to allow the stored vapour to pass into the inlet tract.

Diesel models

Crankcase emission control

Refer to petrol models.

Exhaust emission control

To minimise the level of exhaust pollutants released into the atmosphere, a catalytic converter is fitted in the exhaust system. The catalytic converter consists of a canister containing a fine mesh impregnated with a catalyst material, over which the hot exhaust gases pass. The catalyst speeds up the oxidation of harmful carbon monoxide, unburnt hydrocarbons and soot, effectively reducing the quantity of harmful products released into the atmosphere via the exhaust gases.

Exhaust gas recirculation system

This system is designed to recirculate small quantities of exhaust gas into the inlet tract, and therefore into the combustion process. This process reduces the level of oxides of nitrogen present in the final exhaust gas that is released into the atmosphere.

The volume of exhaust gas recirculated is controlled by signals supplied to the engine control module (ECM). An electrically operated EGR solenoid valve is fitted to the inlet manifold/throttle body housing to regulate the quantity of exhaust gas recirculated.

The Engine Control Module (ECM) receives information from the following components:
a) *Coolant temperature sensor.*
b) *Air temperature sensor.*
c) *Atmospheric pressure sensor.*
d) *Accelerator pedal position potentiometer.*
e) *Engine speed sensor.*
f) *Airflow meter.*
g) *Injection flow rate.*
h) *Turbocharging pressure sensor or solenoid valve.*

Particulate filter system

The particulate filter is combined with the exhaust front pipe in the exhaust system, and its purpose is to trap particles of carbon (soot) as the exhaust gases pass through, in order to comply with latest emission regulations.

The filter can be automatically regenerated (cleaned) by the system's ECM. The ECM automatically performs regeneration when the amount of particulate matter in the diesel particulate filter reaches the specified level. When performing regeneration, the ECM raises the exhaust gas temperature to activate

oxidation. The ECM performs the following functions to raise the temperature:
a) *Closes throttle valve to reduce the volume of air intake.*
b) *Retards the fuel injection timing.*
c) *Injects additional fuel into the cylinder during the exhaust stroke.*
d) *Performs EGR, exhaust fuel injector and thermoplunger control.*

When the exhaust gas temperature reaches the specified value, oxidation is activated. The trapped particulate matter is burned through the catalytic reaction, using exhaust gas heat of approx. 650°C.

2 Petrol engine emission control systems – testing and component renewal

Crankcase emission control

1 The components of this system require no attention other than to check that the hose(s) are clear and undamaged at regular intervals.
Note: *When removing hoses to check for condition or blockage, make sure their fitted positions are noted for reassembly.*

Evaporative emission control

Testing

2 If the system is thought to be faulty, disconnect the hoses from the charcoal canister and purge control valve and check that they are clear by blowing through them. If the purge control valve(s) or charcoal canister is thought to be faulty, they must be renewed.

Charcoal (fuel vapour) canister renewal

3 The charcoal canister is located inside the engine compartment behind the right-hand headlamp unit.
4 Using a thin screwdriver release the retaining clip and slide the canister upwards to remove it from the chassis leg **(see illustrations)**.
5 Note the fitted position and disconnect the hoses from the top of the canister **(see illustration)**.
6 Refitting is a reverse of the removal procedure, ensuring that the hoses are correctly reconnected.

2.4a Release the retaining clip ...

2.4b ... and slide the canister from the securing clip

2.5 Note the markings on the side of the canister

2.7 Location of the purge valve (arrowed)

2.9 Disconnect the hose and undo the two retaining screws (arrowed)

Purge control solenoid valve renewal

7 The purge valve is mounted onto the intake manifold, next to the throttle housing **(see illustration)**.

8 To renew the purge valve, disconnect the battery negative terminal then depress the retaining clip and disconnect the wiring connector from the valve.

9 Disconnect the hose from the valve, then undo the two retaining screws and remove it from the intake manifold **(see illustration)**.

10 Refitting is a reversal of the removal procedure, ensuring that a new o-ring seal

is fitted to the valve, before refitting to the manifold.

Exhaust emission control

Testing

11 The performance of the catalytic converter can be checked by measuring the exhaust gases using an exhaust gas analyser.

12 If the CO level at the tailpipe is too high, the vehicle should be taken to a Nissan dealer so that the complete fuel injection and ignition systems, including the oxygen sensor, can be thoroughly checked using the special

diagnostic equipment. Once these have been checked and are known to be free from faults, the fault must be in the catalytic converter, which must be renewed.

Catalytic converter renewal

13 Refer to Chapter 4A, Section 13.

Oxygen (lambda) sensor renewal

Note 1: *The oxygen sensor is delicate and will not work if it is dropped or knocked, if its power supply is disrupted, or if any cleaning materials are used on it.*

Note 2: *There are two oxygen sensors – one each side of the catalytic converter. The 'upstream' sensor may be in the exhaust manifold or in the downpipe. The 'downstream' sensor is in the exhaust pipe behind the catalytic converter.*

14 Firmly apply the handbrake then jack up the front of the vehicle and support it on axle stands (see *Jacking and vehicle support*). Remove the engine undershield.

15 Trace the wiring back from the oxygen sensor and disconnect its wiring connector, freeing the wiring from any relevant retaining clips or ties **(see illustrations)**.

16 Unscrew the sensor and remove it from the exhaust pipe or manifold **(see illustrations)**.

17 Refitting is a reverse of the removal procedure. Prior to installing the sensor apply a smear of high-temperature grease to the sensor threads. Tighten the sensor to the specified torque and ensure that the wiring is correctly routed and in no danger of contacting either the exhaust system or engine.

2.15a Upper oxygen sensor wiring connector (arrowed)

2.15b Lower oxygen sensor wiring connector (arrowed)

2.16a Upper oxygen sensor

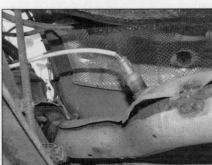

2.16b Lower oxygen sensor

3 Diesel engine emission control systems – testing and component renewal

Crankcase emission control

1 The components of this system require no attention other than to check that the hose(s) are clear and undamaged at regular intervals.

2 If the system is thought to be faulty, first

3.8 Location of the EGR valve (arrowed)

3.10 Disconnect the EGR valve wiring connector

check that the hoses are unobstructed and not damaged.

3 On high-mileage cars, particularly when regularly used for short journeys, a sludge-like deposit may be evident inside the system hoses and oil separators. If excessive deposits are present, the relevant component(s) should be removed and cleaned.

4 Periodically inspect the system components for security and damage, and renew them as necessary.

Exhaust emission control

Testing

5 The performance of the catalytic converter can be checked by measuring the exhaust gases using an exhaust gas analyser, which is suitable for diesel engines.

Catalytic converter renewal

6 Refer to Chapter 4B, Section 17.

Exhaust gas recirculation system

Testing

7 Testing of the system should be entrusted to a Nissan dealer, who will have the specialist diagnostic equipment to carry out any tests.

EGR valve renewal – 1.5 litre engine

8 The EGR valve is mounted on the inlet manifold at the rear of the cylinder head **(see illustration)**.

9 Disconnect the battery negative lead (refer to *Disconnecting the battery* in the Reference Chapter).

10 Remove the plastic engine cover and disconnect the wiring from the EGR solenoid valve **(see illustration)**.

11 Unbolt and remove the EGR valve **(see illustrations)**. Recover the gasket.

12 Thoroughly clean and inspect the EGR valve. Ensure the valve seats correctly **(see illustration)**.

13 Refitting is a reversal of removal, but a new gasket should be fitted.

EGR valve renewal – 2.0 litre engines

14 The EGR solenoid valve is located on the front of the intake manifold on the front of the engine. First disconnect the wiring from the unit.

15 Remove the plastic engine cover and disconnect the wiring from the EGR solenoid valve **(see illustration)**.

16 Undo the screws and lift the solenoid valve from the throttle valve housing **(see illustration)**. Recover the gasket.

17 Refitting is a reversal of removal, using a new gasket and ensuring that the valve and housing surfaces are clean and the bolts are securely tightened.

EGR pipework – 1.5 litre engine

18 If required, the pipework between the valve housing and exhaust manifold can be removed for cleaning and inspection.

19 Disconnect the hose from the turbocharger pressure adjustment valve on the air duct **(see illustration)**.

20 Loosen the clips and remove the air duct

3.11a Undo the mounting bolts …

3.11b … and remove the EGR valve

3.12 Clean and inspect the valve seat (arrowed)

3.15 Disconnect the EGR valve wiring connector

3.16 Undo the six EGR mounting screws

3.19 Disconnect the wastegate valve hose

3.20 Remove the air duct between the EGR valve and the turbo

3.22 Remove the inlet pipe

3.24a Release the clamps ...

from between the EGR unit and turbocharger **(see illustration)**.

21 Unbolt and remove the right-hand rear engine lifting eye.

22 Unscrew the bolt and remove the air inlet metallic tube **(see illustration)**.

23 Where fitted, remove the heat shield from over the EGR solenoid valve.

24 Loosen both clamps and remove the EGR convoluted metal tube from the EGR valve and exhaust manifold **(see illustrations)**.

25 Unscrew the mounting bolts and remove the EGR valve unit from its location on the inlet manifold. Note that the solenoid valve is not available separately.

26 Refitting is a reversal of removal, but renew the air inlet duct O-rings. Check the condition of the convoluted metal tube retaining clamps and if necessary, renew them – if the special tool is not available, use a pair of pincers to tighten the clamps until the clip is engaged **(see illustration)**.

EGR cooler renewal – 2.0 litre engine

27 The EGR cooler is located on the front of the engine, below the inlet manifold and throttle valve (damper) housing. First drain the cooling system as described in Chapter 1B, Section 29.

28 Remove the engine top cover, then remove the battery and battery tray as described in Chapter 5A, Section 3.

29 Remove the intake air ducting and inter-cooler inlet pipe from the front of the engine.

30 Remove the throttle valve housing (damper unit) as described in Chapter 4B.

31 Unbolt the EGR cooler pipe from the inlet manifold and cooler and recover the gaskets **(see illustrations)**.

32 Unscrew the bolts and disconnect the EGR transfer pipe from the cooler.

33 Loosen the clips and disconnect the coolant hoses from the cooler **(see illustrations)**.

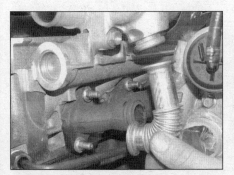

3.24b ... and remove the EGR convoluted metal tube

3.26 Use pincer type pliers to tighten the clamp

3.31a Unbolt and remove the EGR cooler pipe ...

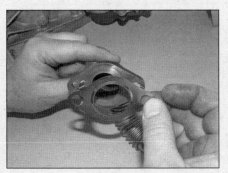

3.31b ... and recover the gasket

3.33a Disconnecting the inlet coolant hose (arrowed) ...

3.33b ...and outlet coolant hose from the cooler

3.34 EGR cooler mounting bolts (arrowed)

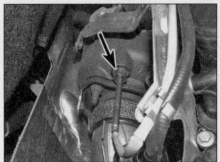

3.37a Particulate filter upper temperature sensor …

3.37b … and lower temperature sensor

34 Unbolt the EGR cooler from the front of the cylinder block **(see illustration)**.
35 Refitting is a reversal of removal, but tighten the bolts to the specified torque.

Particulate filter system

Particulate filter renewal

36 The particle filter is part of the exhaust front section. Remove the front pipe/particle filter, as described in Chapter 4B, Section 17.

Temperature sensors renewal

37 The temperature sensors monitor the exhaust gas temperature both upstream and downstream of the particulate filter during regeneration **(see illustrations)**. To remove the sensors, disconnect the wiring at the connector, unbolt the wiring support and unscrew the sensor from the exhaust.

4 Catalytic converter – general information and precautions

General information

The catalytic converter reduces harmful exhaust emissions by chemically converting the more poisonous gases to ones that (in theory at least) are less harmful. The chemical reaction is known as an 'oxidising' reaction, or one where oxygen is 'added'.

Inside the converter is a honeycomb structure, made of ceramic material and coated with the precious metals palladium, platinum and rhodium (the 'catalyst' which promotes the chemical reaction). The chemical reaction generates heat, which itself promotes the reaction – therefore, once the car has been driven several miles, the body of the converter will be very hot.

The ceramic structure contained within the converter is understandably fragile, and will not withstand rough treatment. Since the converter runs at a high temperature, driving through deep standing water (in flood conditions, for example) is to be avoided, since the thermal stresses imposed when plunging the hot converter into cold water may well cause the ceramic internals to fracture, resulting in a 'blocked' converter – a common cause of failure. A catalytic converter that has been damaged in this way can be checked by

shaking it, do not strike it – if a rattling noise is heard, this indicates probable failure.

Precautions

The catalytic converter is a reliable and simple device which needs no maintenance in itself, but there are some facts of which an owner should be aware if the converter is to function properly for its full service life.

Petrol models

a) DO NOT use leaded petrol (or lead-replacement petrol, LRP) in a car equipped with a catalytic converter – the lead (or other additives) will coat the precious metals, reducing their converting efficiency and will eventually destroy the converter.

b) Always keep the ignition and fuel systems well maintained in accordance with the manufacturer's schedule.

c) If the engine develops a misfire, do not drive the car at all (or at least as little as possible) until the fault is cured.

d) DO NOT push- or tow-start the car – this will soak the catalytic converter in unburned fuel, causing it to overheat when the engine does start.

e) DO NOT switch off the ignition at high engine speeds.

f) DO NOT use fuel or engine oil additives – these may contain substances harmful to the catalytic converter.

g) DO NOT continue to use the car if the engine burns oil to the extent of leaving a visible trail of blue smoke.

h) Remember that the catalytic converter operates at very high temperatures. DO NOT, therefore, park the car in dry undergrowth, over long grass or piles of dead leaves after a long run.

i) Remember that the catalytic converter is FRAGILE – do not strike it with tools during servicing work.

j) In some cases a sulphurous smell (like that of rotten eggs) may be noticed from the exhaust. This is common to many catalytic converter-equipped cars and once the car has covered a few thousand miles the problem should disappear.

k) The catalytic converter, used on a well-maintained and well-driven car, should last at least 100 000 miles – if the converter is no longer effective it must be renewed.

l) If a substantial loss of power is experienced, remember that this could be due to the converter being blocked. This can occur simply as a result of high mileage, but may be due to the ceramic element having fractured and collapsed internally (see paragraph 3). A new converter is the only cure in this instance.

m) As mentioned above, driving through deep water should be avoided if possible. The sudden cooling effect may fracture the ceramic honeycomb, damaging it beyond repair.

Diesel models

The catalytic converter fitted to diesel models is simpler than that fitted to petrol models, but it still needs to be treated with respect to avoid problems:

a) DO NOT use fuel or engine oil additives – these may contain substances harmful to the catalytic converter.

b) DO NOT continue to use the car if the engine burns (engine) oil to the extent of leaving a visible trail of blue smoke.

c) Remember that the catalytic converter operates at very high temperatures. DO NOT, therefore, park the car in dry undergrowth, over long grass or piles of dead leaves after a long run.

d) As mentioned above, driving through deep water should be avoided if possible. The sudden cooling effect will fracture the ceramic honeycomb, damaging it beyond repair.

e) Remember that the catalytic converter is FRAGILE – do not strike it with tools during servicing work, and take care handling it when removing it from the car for any reason.

f) If a substantial loss of power is experienced, remember that this could be due to the converter being blocked. This can occur simply as a result of high mileage, but may be due to the ceramic element having fractured and collapsed internally (see paragraph 3). A new converter is the only cure in this instance.

g) The catalytic converter, used on a well-maintained and well-driven car, should last at least 100 000 miles – if the converter is no longer effective, it must be renewed.

Chapter 5 Part A:
Starting and charging systems

Contents

Degrees of difficulty

Easy, suitable for novice with little experience	Fairly easy, suitable for beginner with some experience	Fairly difficult, suitable for competent DIY mechanic	Difficult, suitable for experienced DIY mechanic	Very difficult, suitable for expert DIY or professional

Specifications

System type . . . . 12 volt, negative earth

Battery
Type . . . . Low-maintenance or maintenance-free, depending on model
Charge condition:
  Poor . . . . 12.5 volts
  Normal . . . . 12.6 volts
  Good . . . . 12.7 volts

Alternator
Make . . . . Bosch or Mitsubishi
Type:
  HR16DE . . . . Mitsubishi A2TJ0291ZE
  MR20DE . . . . Mitsubishi A2TJ0281ZE
  K9K . . . . Bosch 0 124 525 082
  M9R . . . . Mitsubishi A3TJ2481ZE
Specifications for Mitsubishi alternators:
  Output rating:
    HR16DE and MR20DE . . . . 120 amp
    M9R . . . . 150 amp
  Regulated output voltage . . . . 14.1 to 14.7 Volts
  Minimum brush length . . . . 5.0 mm
  Slip ring minimum outer diameter . . . . 22.1 mm
  Rotor (field coil) resistance:
    HR16DE and MR20DE . . . . 1.7 to 2.2 ohms
    M9R . . . . 1.7 to 2.0 ohms

Starter motor
Make . . . . Mitsubishi, Hitachi or Valeo
Type:
  HR16DE . . . . Mitsubishi M000T32171
  MR20DE . . . . Hitachi S114-902A
  K9K . . . . Mitsubishi M000T87881
  M9R . . . . Valeo 194262

Torque wrench settings

	Nm	lbf ft
Alternator mounting bolts:		
HR16DE	21	15
MR20DE	25	18
K9K	21	15
M9R	25	18
Oil pressure switch:		
HR16DE	20	14
MR20DE	15	11
K9K	25	18
M9R	35	26
Oil level sensor:		
HR16DE	8	7
MR20DE, K9K and M9R	25	18
Starter motor mounting bolts:		
HR16DE	34	25
MR20DE	62	46
K9K	44	32
M9R	48	35

1 General information and precautions

General information

The engine electrical system consists mainly of the charging and starting systems. Because of their engine-related functions, these components are covered separately from the body electrical devices such as the lights, instruments, etc (which are covered in Chapter 12). Information on the ignition system is covered in Part B of this Chapter.

The electrical system is of the 12-volt negative earth type.

The battery is of the low-maintenance or 'maintenance-free' (sealed for life) type, and is charged by the alternator, which is belt-driven from the crankshaft pulley.

The starter motor is of the pre-engaged type, incorporating an integral solenoid. On starting, the solenoid moves the drive pinion into engagement with the flywheel ring gear before the starter motor is energised. Once the engine has started, a one-way clutch prevents the motor armature being driven by the engine until the pinion disengages from the flywheel.

Precautions

Further details of the various systems are given in the relevant Sections of this Chapter. While some repair procedures are given, the usual course of action is to renew the component concerned. The owner whose interest extends beyond mere component renewal should obtain a copy of *The Haynes Car Electrical Systems Manual*, available from the publishers of this manual.

It is necessary to take extra care when working on the electrical system, to avoid damage to semi-conductor devices (diodes and transistors), and to avoid the risk of personal injury. In addition to the precautions given in *Safety first!* at the beginning of this manual, observe the following when working on the system:

Always remove rings, watches, etc, before working on the electrical system. Even with the battery disconnected, capacitive discharge could occur if a component's live terminal is earthed through a metal object. This could cause a shock or nasty burn.

Do not reverse the battery connections. Components such as the alternator, ECCS control unit, or any other components having semi-conductor circuitry could be irreparably damaged.

If the engine is being started using jump leads and a slave battery, connect the batteries *positive-to-positive* and *negative-to-negative* (see *Jump starting*). This also applies when connecting a battery charger.

Never disconnect the battery terminals, the alternator, any electrical wiring, or any test instruments, when the engine is running.

Do not allow the engine to turn the alternator when the alternator is not connected.

Never 'test' for alternator output by 'flashing' the output lead to earth.

Never use an ohmmeter of the type incorporating a hand-cranked generator for circuit or continuity testing.

Always ensure that the battery negative terminal is disconnected when working on the electrical system.

Before using electric-arc welding equipment on the car, disconnect the battery, alternator and components such as electronic control units, to protect them from the risk of damage.

Several systems fitted to the vehicle require battery power to be available at all times, either to ensure their continued operation (such as the clock) or to maintain security codes which would be wiped if the battery were to be disconnected. To ensure that there are no unforeseen consequences of this action, refer to *Disconnecting the battery* in the Reference Chapter of this manual for further information.

2 Battery – checking, testing and charging

Checking

Standard and low-maintenance battery

1 In addition to the checks described in *Weekly checks* at the start of this manual, the battery electrolyte level should also be periodically checked as follows.

Batteries with a translucent casing

2 On this type of battery, the electrolyte level is visible through the casing. Make sure that the level in each cell is between the UPPER and LOWER level marks on the side of the battery casing.

3 If topping-up is necessary, remove the cell cap(s) and top-up the relevant cell to the UPPER level marking using only distilled water. **Note:** *Do not use ordinary tap water, as this will damage the battery.* Refit the cell cap(s), ensuring each one is securely fitted, and mop-up any spilt water.

Batteries with a solid (non-translucent) casing

4 On batteries where it is not possible to see the electrolyte level through the casing, the level is checked via the cell filler cap apertures. Remove the cap from each battery cell and, looking down through cap apertures, check that the electrolyte level is up to the base of the aperture neck.

5 If topping-up is necessary, top-up the relevant cell to the base of the neck using only distilled water. **Note:** *Do not use ordinary tap water, as this will damage the battery.* Refit the cell cap(s), ensuring each one is securely fitted, and mop-up any spilt water.

Testing

Standard and low-maintenance battery

6 If the vehicle covers a small annual mileage, it is worthwhile checking the specific gravity of the electrolyte every three months, to determine the state of charge of the battery. Use a hydrometer to make the check, and compare the results with the following table. Note that the specific gravity readings assume an electrolyte temperature of 15°C; for every 10°C below 15°C, subtract 0.007. For every 10°C above 15°C, add 0.007. However, for convenience, the temperatures quoted in the following table are **ambient** (outdoor air) temperatures, above or below 25°C:

	Above 25°C	Below 25°C
Fully-charged	1.210 to 1.230	1.270 to 1.290
70% charged	1.170 to 1.190	1.230 to 1.250
Discharged	1.050 to 1.070	1.110 to 1.130

7 If the battery condition is suspect, first check the specific gravity of electrolyte in each cell. A variation of 0.040 or more between any cells indicates loss of electrolyte, or deterioration of the internal plates.

8 If the specific gravity variation is 0.040 or more, a new battery should be fitted. If the cell variation is satisfactory but the battery is discharged, it should be charged as described later in this Section.

Maintenance-free battery

9 In cases where a 'sealed for life' maintenance-free battery is fitted, topping-up and testing of the electrolyte in each cell is not possible. The condition of the battery can therefore only be tested using a battery condition indicator or a voltmeter.

10 One type of maintenance-free battery, which may be fitted, is the 'Delco' type maintenance-free battery, with a built-in charge condition indicator **(see illustration)**. The indicator is located in the top of the battery casing, and indicates the condition of the battery from its colour. If the indicator shows green, then the battery is in a good state of charge. If the indicator turns darker, eventually to black, then the battery requires charging, as described later in this Section. If the indicator shows clear/yellow, then the electrolyte level in the battery is too low to allow further use, and the battery should be renewed. **Do not** attempt to charge, load or jump-start a battery when the indicator shows clear/yellow.

11 If testing the battery using a voltmeter, connect the voltmeter across the battery, and compare the result with those given in the Specifications under 'charge condition'. The test is only accurate if the battery has not been subjected to any kind of charge for the previous six hours. If this is not the case, switch on the headlights for 30 seconds, and then wait four to five minutes before testing the battery after switching off the headlights. All other electrical circuits must be switched off, so check that the doors and tailgate are fully shut when making the test.

12 If the voltage reading is less than 12.2 volts, then the battery is discharged, whilst a reading of 12.2 to 12.4 volts indicates a partially discharged condition.

13 If the battery is to be charged, remove it from the vehicle (Section 3) and charge it as described later in this Section.

Charging

Note: *The following is intended as a guide only. Always refer to the manufacturer's recommendations (often printed on a label attached to the battery) before charging a battery.*

Standard and low-maintenance battery

14 Charge the battery at a rate of 3.5 to 4 amps, and continue to charge the battery at this rate until no further rise in specific gravity is noted over a four-hour period.

15 Alternatively, a trickle charger charging at the rate of 1.5 amps can safely be used overnight.

16 Specially rapid 'boost' charges, which are claimed to restore the power of the battery in 1 to 2 hours, are not recommended, as they can cause serious damage to the battery plates through overheating.

17 While charging the battery, note that the temperature of the electrolyte should never exceed 38°C.

Maintenance-free battery

18 This battery type takes considerably longer to fully recharge than the standard type, the time taken being dependent on the extent of discharge, but it can take anything up to three days.

19 A constant-voltage type charger is required, to be set, when connected, to 13.9 to 14.9 volts, with a charger current below 25 amps. Using this method, the battery should be usable within three hours, giving a voltage reading of 12.5 volts, but this is for a partially discharged battery and, as mentioned, full charging can take considerably longer.

20 If the battery is to be charged from a fully discharged state (condition reading less than 12.2 volts), have it recharged by your Nissan dealer or local automotive electrician, as the charge rate is higher, and constant supervision during charging is necessary.

3 Battery – removal and refitting

Note: *Refer to 'Disconnecting the battery' in the Reference Chapter before proceeding.*

Removal

1 The battery is located on the left-hand side of the engine compartment.

2 Slacken the clamp nut/bolt, and disconnect the clamp from the battery negative terminal **(see illustration)**.

3 Remove the insulation cover (where fitted)

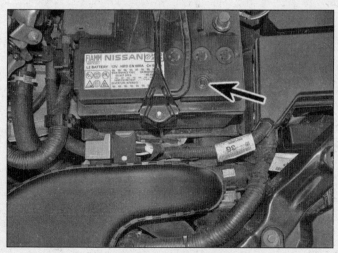

2.10 Battery charge condition indicator (arrowed)

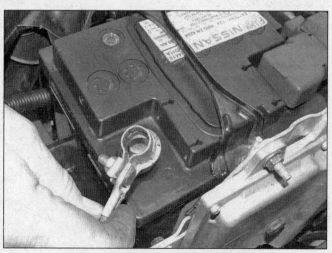

3.2 Disconnect the negative (earth) terminal

3.3 Slacken the bolt and disconnect the positive terminal

3.4a Slacken the two retaining nuts (arrowed) …

3.4b … unhook the threaded rods …

3.4c … and remove the battery securing bracket

3.5 Remove the plastic battery tray

and disconnect the positive clamp in the same way **(see illustration)**.

4 Slacken the two securing nuts, and remove the battery retaining clamp from over the top of the battery **(see illustrations)**.

5 Lift the battery out of the engine compartment, and then lift out the plastic battery tray **(see illustration)**.

6 If necessary, the battery mounting bracket can also be unbolted and removed from the engine compartment. First undo the retaining bolts and remove the engine management ECM from the rear of the battery mounting bracket as described in Chapter 4A, Section 10, or Chapter 4B, Section 8.

7 Depending on model, it will be necessary to disconnect wiring loom retaining clips and various brackets from the battery mounting bracket **(see illustrations)**.

8 Remove the air cleaner housing as described in Chapter 4A, Section 2, or Chapter 4B, Section 2.

9 The battery mounting bracket is part of the transmission mounting bracket, so the transmission will need to be supported by a trolley jack before the mounting bracket can be removed.

10 With the transmission supported, undo the retaining bolts and remove the mounting bracket from the chassis leg **(see illustration)**.

Refitting

11 Refitting is a reversal of removal, but smear petroleum jelly on the terminals after reconnecting the leads, and always reconnect the positive lead first, and the negative lead last.

4 Charging system – testing

Note: *Refer to the warnings given in 'Safety first!' and in Section 1 of this Chapter before starting work.*

1 If the ignition/no-charge warning light fails to come on when the ignition is switched on, first check the alternator wiring connections for security. If satisfactory, check that the warning light bulb has not blown, and that the bulbholder is secure in its location in the instrument panel. If the light still fails to come on, check the continuity of the warning light feed wire from the alternator to the bulbholder. If all is satisfactory, the alternator is at fault, and should be taken to an auto-electrician for testing and repair.

2 If the ignition warning light comes on when the engine is running, stop the engine as soon as possible. Check that the drivebelt is correctly tensioned (see Chapter 1A or 1B), that the drivebelt is not contaminated (with oil or water, for example), and that the alternator connections are secure. If all is so far satisfactory, the alternator should be renewed or taken to an auto-electrician for testing and repair.

3 If the alternator output is suspect, even though the warning light functions correctly, the regulated voltage may be checked as follows.

4 Connect a voltmeter across the battery terminals, and start the engine.

3.7a Unclip the wiring loom retaining clips …

3.7b … and remove the battery tray bracket

3.10 Support the transmission before removing the mounting bracket

5 Increase the engine speed until the voltmeter reading remains steady; the reading should be approximately 12 to 13 volts, and no more than 14 volts.

6 Switch on as many electrical accessories (e.g. the headlights, heated rear window and heater blower) as possible, and check that the alternator maintains the regulated voltage at around 13 to 14 volts.

7 If the regulated voltage is not as stated, the fault may be due to worn brushes, weak brush springs, a faulty voltage regulator, a faulty diode, a severed phase winding, or worn or damaged slip-rings. The alternator should be taken to an auto-electrician for testing and repair.

5.2 Remove the auxiliary belt from around the pulley

5.3 On turbo models, remove the intercooler hose

5 Alternator – removal and refitting

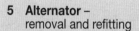

Removal

1 Disconnect the battery negative terminal (refer to *Disconnecting the battery* in the Reference Chapter).

2 Slacken the auxiliary drivebelt as described in Chapter 1A, Section 10 or Chapter 1B, Section 10, and then disengage it from the alternator pulley **(see illustration)**.

3 On turbo-diesel models, slacken the retaining clips and remove the intercooler air intake hose from above the alternator **(see illustration)**.

Caution: Cover the open ends of the

intercooler and hoses to prevent anything being dropped inside them.

4 Remove the rubber covers (where fitted) from the alternator terminals, then unscrew the retaining nut(s) and disconnect the wiring cable from the rear of the alternator **(see illustrations)**.

5 Release the locking clip and disconnect the wiring plug connector from the rear of the alternator **(see illustration)**.

6 Unscrew the alternator upper mounting bracket and lower mounting bolt and washers, and then manoeuvre the alternator away from its mounting brackets and out of position **(see illustrations)**.

7 On some models, the lower mounting bolt cannot be removed completely, as it contacts the body side member. On these models, the mounting bracket has a cut out to allow the alternator to be withdrawn with the bolt still in place **(see illustration)**.

Refitting

8 Refitting is a reversal of removal, tensioning the auxiliary drivebelt as described in Chapter 1A, Section 10 or Chapter 1B, Section 10, ensuring that the alternator mountings are tightened to the specified torque.

6 Alternator – testing and overhaul

If the alternator is thought to be suspect, it should be removed from the vehicle and taken to an auto-electrician for testing. Most auto-electricians will be able to supply fit new parts at reasonable cost. However, check on the cost of repairs before proceeding, as it may prove more economical to obtain a new or exchange alternator.

5.4a Undo the retaining nut …

5.4b … and disconnect the alternator wiring cable

5.5 Disconnect the wiring plug connector

5.6a Undo the two alternator mounting bolts (arrowed) …

5.6b … and withdraw the alternator

5.7 Recess in bracket to allow removal (arrowed) – 2.0 litre petrol shown

7 Starting system – testing

Note: *Refer to the precautions given in 'Safety first!' and in Section 1 of this Chapter before starting work.*

1 If the starter motor fails to operate when the ignition key is turned to the appropriate position, the following may be to blame:

  a) *The battery is faulty.*
  b) *The electrical connections between the switch, solenoid, battery and starter motor are somewhere failing to pass the necessary current from the battery through the starter to earth.*
  c) *The solenoid is faulty.*
  d) *The starter motor is mechanically or electrically defective.*

2 To check the battery, switch on the headlights. If they dim after a few seconds, this indicates that the battery is discharged – recharge (see Section 2) or renew the battery. If the headlights glow brightly, operate the ignition switch and observe the lights. If they dim, then this indicates that current is reaching the starter motor; therefore the fault must lie in the starter motor. If the lights continue to glow brightly (and no clicking sound can be heard from the starter motor solenoid),

this indicates that there is a fault in the circuit or solenoid – see following paragraphs. If the starter motor turns slowly when operated, but the battery is in good condition, then this indicates that either the starter motor is faulty, or there is considerable resistance somewhere in the circuit.

3 If a fault in the circuit is suspected, disconnect the battery leads (including the earth connection to the body), the starter/solenoid wiring and the engine/transmission earth strap (refer to Disconnecting the battery in the Reference Chapter of this manual). Thoroughly clean the connections, reconnect the leads and wiring, then use a voltmeter or test light to check that full battery voltage is available at the battery positive lead connection to the solenoid, and that the earth is sound. Smear petroleum jelly around the battery terminals to prevent corrosion – corroded connections are amongst the most frequent causes of electrical system faults.

4 If the battery and all connections are in good condition, check the circuit by disconnecting the wire from the solenoid blade terminal. Connect a voltmeter or test light between the wire end and a good earth (such as the battery negative terminal), and check that the wire is live when the ignition switch is turned to the 'start' position. If it is, then the circuit is sound

– if not, the circuit wiring can be checked as described in Chapter 12.

5 The solenoid contacts can be checked by connecting a voltmeter or test light between the battery positive feed connection on the starter side of the solenoid, and earth. When the ignition switch is turned to the 'start' position, there should be a reading or lighted bulb, as applicable. If there is no reading or lighted bulb, the solenoid is faulty and should be renewed.

6 If the circuit and solenoid are proved sound, the fault must lie in the starter motor. In this event, it may be possible to have the starter motor overhauled by a specialist, but check on the availability and cost of spares before proceeding, as it may prove more economical to obtain a new or exchange motor.

8 Starter motor – removal and refitting

Removal

1 Disconnect the battery negative terminal (refer to *Disconnecting the battery* in the Reference Chapter).

2 On turbo-diesel models, slacken the retaining clips and remove the intercooler air intake hose from above the starter motor **(see illustration)**.

Caution: Cover the open ends of the intercooler and hoses to prevent anything being dropped inside them.

3 Working down the front of the engine compartment, move the wiring loom and hoses to one side to access the starter motor **(see illustration)**, which is located at the front of the cylinder block, bolted to the transmission bell housing.

4 Pull back the rubber cover, and then slacken and remove the two retaining nuts. Disconnect the main battery cable, and the small solenoid wiring from the starter motor solenoid **(see illustrations)**.

8.2 On turbo models, remove the air intake hose

8.3 Unclip the wiring loom from the front of the transmission

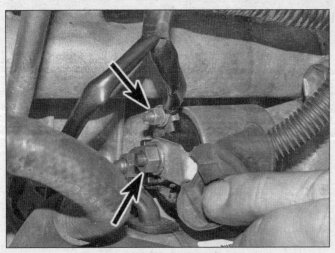

8.4a Undo the retaining nuts (arrowed) ...

8.4b ... and disconnect the starter wiring cables

8.5a Undo the starter motor mounting bolts (arrowed) – 2.0 litre petrol

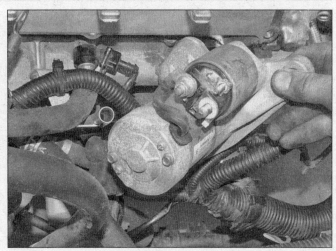

8.5b Remove the starter motor from the transmission housing

5 Unscrew the starter motor mounting bolts **(see illustrations)**, supporting the motor as the bolts are withdrawn, and manoeuvre the starter motor out from its location.

Refitting

6 Refitting is a reversal of removal.

9 Starter motor – testing and overhaul

If the starter motor is thought to be suspect, it should be removed from the vehicle and taken to an auto-electrician for testing. Most auto-electricians will be able to supply fit new parts at reasonable cost. However, check on the cost of repairs before proceeding, as it may prove more economical to obtain a new or exchange motor.

10 Ignition switch – removal and refitting

The ignition switch is integral with the steering column lock, and can be removed as described in Chapter 10, Section 13.

11 Oil pressure warning light switch – removal and refitting

Removal

1 On some models, access to the switch is improved if the vehicle is jacked up and supported on axle stands (see *Jacking and vehicle support*), so that the switch can be reached from underneath. Remove the engine undershield.

2 On petrol engines, the switch is located at the front of the cylinder block, above the oil filter **(see illustration)**. On diesel engines, the switch is located at the front of the cylinder block, screwed into the oil filter housing

3 Disconnect the battery negative terminal (refer to *Disconnecting the battery* in the Reference Chapter).

4 Disconnect the wiring connector from the oil pressure switch **(see illustration)**.

5 Unscrew the switch and recover the sealing washer (where fitted). Be prepared for oil spillage. If the switch is to be left removed from the engine for any length of time, plug the hole to prevent excessive oil loss.

Warning: Do not start the engine with the oil pressure switch removed.

Refitting

6 Where the switch was fitted with a sealing washer, examine the sealing washer for signs of damage or deterioration, and if necessary

11.2 Location of oil pressure switch (arrowed)

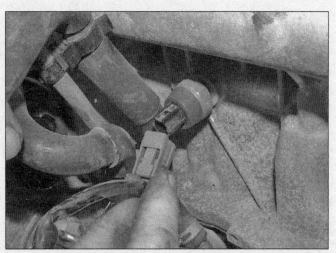

11.4 Disconnect the pressure switch wiring connector

12.2a Location of oil level sensor (arrowed) – 1.6 litre petrol

12.2b Location of oil level sensor (arrowed) – 2.0 litre petrol

12.4 Disconnect the level sensor wiring connector

renew it. Where no sealing washer was fitted, clean the switch and apply a smear of sealant to its threads.

7 Refit the switch, tightening it securely, and reconnect the wiring connector.

8 Where applicable refit the engine undershield and lower the vehicle to the ground.

9 Check and if necessary, top-up the engine oil as described in *Weekly checks*.

12 Oil level sensor – removal and refitting

Removal

1 Access to the switch is improved if the vehicle is jacked up and supported on axle stands (see *Jacking and vehicle support*). Remove the engine undershield, so that the switch can be reached from underneath.

2 The sensors are located as follows:
  a) HR16DE petrol engine – At the front of the engine **(see illustration)**, *in the upper*

alloy sump housing below the oil filter and held in place by a securing bolt.
b) MR20DE petrol engine – At the front of the engine and screwed into the upper alloy sump housing **(see illustration)**, *next to the oil filter.*
c) K9K diesel engine – At the front of the engine and screwed into the top of the alloy sump housing, at the transmission end.
d) M9R diesel engine – At the rear of the engine and screwed into the lower part of the cylinder block, at the centre.

3 Disconnect the battery negative terminal (refer to *Disconnecting the battery* in the Reference Chapter).

4 Disconnect the wiring from the oil level sensor **(see illustration)**.

5 On 1.6 litre (HR16DE) petrol engine, undo the retaining bolt and withdraw the oil level sensor from the engine. Be prepared for oil spillage. If the switch is to be left removed from the engine for any length of time, plug the hole to prevent excessive oil loss.

⚠ **Warning: Do not start the engine with the oil level sensor removed.**

6 On all other models, unscrew the switch and recover the sealing washer (where fitted). Be prepared for oil spillage. If the switch is to be left removed from the engine for any length of time, plug the hole to prevent excessive oil loss.

Refitting

7 Where the sensor was fitted with a sealing washer, examine the sealing washer for signs of damage or deterioration, and if necessary renew it. Where no sealing washer was fitted, clean the sensor and apply a smear of sealant to its threads.

8 Refit the sensor, tightening to the torque setting specified, and reconnect the wiring connector.

9 Lower the vehicle to the ground, then check and if necessary, top-up the engine oil as described in *Weekly checks*.

Chapter 5 Part B:
Ignition system – petrol engines

Contents

Degrees of difficulty

Easy, suitable for novice with little experience	**Fairly easy,** suitable for beginner with some experience	**Fairly difficult,** suitable for competent DIY mechanic	**Difficult,** suitable for experienced DIY mechanic	**Very difficult,** suitable for expert DIY or professional

Specifications

General

System type	Distributorless electronic ignition, controlled by ECCS control unit
Firing order	1-3-4-2 (No 1 cylinder at timing chain end)
Ignition timing	Not adjustable – controlled by ECM

Torque wrench setting

	Nm	lbf ft
Ignition coil mounting bolts	7	6
Spark plug	20	14

1 General information

The system is a self-contained engine management system, which controls both the fuel injection and ignition. This Chapter deals with the ignition system components only – refer to Chapter 4A for details of the fuel system components.

The ignition system fitted to all models is of the increasingly popular 'distributorless' (DIS – Distributorless Ignition System) or 'static' type (there are no moving parts). The ignition system fitted to the Nissan Qashqai has four separate coils, one fitted to each spark plug **(see illustration)**. Each spark plug has its own dedicated 'plug-top' HT coil that fits directly onto the spark plug (no HT leads are therefore

needed); on these models a spark is only generated at each plug once every engine cycle. Therefore, these systems have no distributor cap, rotor arm, or even HT leads, resulting in a simpler, more reliable system requiring even less maintenance.

Because there is no distributor to adjust, the ignition timing cannot be adjusted by conventional means, and the advance and retard functions are carried out by the Electronic Control Module (ECM).

The ignition system consists of the spark plugs, four separate coils, and the ECM together with its associated sensors and wiring.

The component layout varies from system to system, but the basic operation is the same for all models: the ECM supplies a voltage to the input stage of the ignition coil, which causes the primary windings in the coils to be energised. The supply voltage is

periodically interrupted by the ECM and this results in the collapse of primary magnetic field, which then induces a much larger voltage in the secondary coil, called the HT voltage. The spark plug electrodes form a gap small enough for the HT voltage to arc across, and the resulting spark ignites the fuel/air mixture in the cylinder. The timing of this sequence of events is critical, and is regulated solely by the ECM.

The ECM calculates and controls the ignition timing primarily according to engine speed, crankshaft position, camshaft position, and inlet airflow rate information, received from sensors mounted on and around the engine. Other parameters that affect ignition timing are throttle position and rate of opening, inlet air temperature and coolant temperature, monitored via sensors mounted on the engine. Note that most of these sensors have a dual role, in that the information they provide is

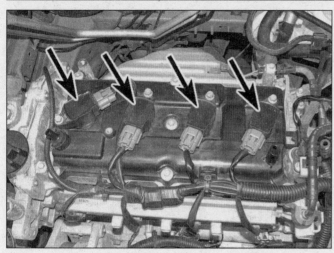

1.2 Individual ignition coils fitted (arrowed)

1.12 Vehicle diagnostic plug connector (arrowed)

equally useful in determining the fuelling requirements as in deciding the optimum ignition or firing point – therefore, removal of some of the sensors mentioned below is described in Chapter 4A.

The ECM computes engine speed and crankshaft position from toothed impulse rotor attached to the engine flywheel, with an engine speed sensor whose inductive head runs just above rotor. As the crankshaft (and flywheel) rotate, the rotor 'teeth' pass the engine speed sensor, which transmits a pulse to the ECM every time a tooth passes it. At the top dead centre (TDC) position, there is one missing tooth in the rotor periphery, which results in a longer pause between signals from the sensor. The ECM recognises the absence of a pulse from the engine speed sensor at this point, and uses it to establish the TDC position for No 1 piston. The time interval between pulses, and the location of the missing pulse, allow the ECM to accurately determine the position of the crankshaft and its speed. The camshaft position sensor enhances this information by detecting whether a particular piston is on an inlet or an exhaust cycle.

Information on engine load is supplied to the ECM via the air mass meter (or via the inlet manifold pressure sensor, as applicable), and from the throttle position sensor. The engine load is determined by computation based on the quantity of air being drawn into the engine.

Sensors monitoring coolant temperature, throttle position, roadspeed, and (where applicable) automatic transmission gear position and air conditioning system operation, provide additional input signals to the ECM on vehicle operating conditions. From all this constantly changing data, the ECM selects, and if necessary modifies, a particular ignition advance setting from a map of ignition characteristics stored in its memory.

The ECM also uses the ignition timing to

finely adjust the engine idle speed, in response to signals from the power steering switch or air conditioning switch (to prevent stalling), or if the alternator output voltage falls too low.

In the event of a fault in the system due to loss of a signal from one of the sensors, the ECM reverts to an emergency ('limp-home') program. This will allow the car to be driven, although engine operation and performance will be limited. A warning light on the instrument panel will illuminate if the fault is likely to cause an increase in harmful exhaust emissions.

It should be noted that comprehensive fault diagnosis of all the engine management systems described in this Chapter is only possible with dedicated electronic test equipment. In the event of a sensor failing or other fault occurring, a fault code will be stored in the ECM's fault log, which can only be extracted from the ECM using a dedicated fault code reader. The on-board diagnostic (OBD) plug is located below the fuses, in the passenger compartment fusebox, at the lower right-hand side of the facia panel (see illustration). A Nissan dealer or specialist will obviously have such a reader, but they are also available from other suppliers. It is unlikely to be cost-effective for the private owner to purchase a fault code reader, but a well-equipped local garage or auto-electrical specialist will have one. Once the fault has been identified, the removal/refitting sequences detailed in the following Sections will then allow the appropriate component(s) to be renewed as required.

2 Ignition system – testing

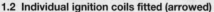

⚠️ **Warning: Due to the high voltages produced by the electronic ignition system, extreme care must be taken when working on**

the system with the ignition switched on. Persons with surgically implanted cardiac pacemaker devices should keep well clear of the ignition circuits, components and test equipment.

1 If a fault appears in the ignition system, first ensure that the fault is not due to a poor electrical connection or poor maintenance; i.e. check that the air cleaner filter element is clean, that the spark plugs are in good condition and correctly gapped, that the engine breather hoses are clear and undamaged, referring to Chapter 1A for further information. If the engine is running very roughly, check the compression pressures and the valve clearances are correct. Refer to Chapter 2A, Section 2, for 1.6 litre engines and Chapter 2B, Section 2, for 2.0 litre engines.

2 The only specific ignition system checks that can be carried out by the home mechanic are those described in Chapter 1A, Section 25, relating to the spark plugs. If necessary, the system wiring and wiring connectors can be checked as described in Chapter 12, ensuring that the control unit wiring connectors have first been disconnected.

3 If the above checks fail to reveal the cause of the problem, the vehicle should be taken to a suitably equipped Nissan dealer for testing.

3 HT coil(s) – removal and refitting

Removal

1 The ignition coil units are mounted on top of each spark plug.

2 Make sure the ignition is switched off (take out the key), and disconnect the battery negative terminal (refer to *Disconnecting the battery* in the Reference Chapter).

3 Remove the inlet manifold as described in Chapter 4A, Section 11.

3.4a Disconnect the coil wiring connector – 1.6 litre engine

3.4b Disconnect the coil wiring connector – 2.0 litre engine

3.5a Undo the retaining bolt ...

3.5b ... and withdraw the ignition coil

4 Unplug the wiring plug connector from the ignition coil (see illustrations).
5 Undo the retaining bolt and withdraw the ignition coil from the cylinder head (see illustrations).

Refitting

6 Refitting is a reversal of the removal procedure, noting the following points:
   a) Securely tighten the coil mounting bolts.

   b) Make sure the wiring connectors are fitted correctly.
   c) Refit the inlet manifold, refer to Chapter 4A, Section 11.

4 Ignition timing – checking and adjustment

The ignition timing is under the control of

the engine management system ECM and is not manually adjustable without access to dedicated electronic test equipment. A basic setting cannot be quoted because the ignition timing is constantly being altered to control engine (see Section 1 for details).

The vehicle must be taken to a Nissan dealer if the timing requires checking or adjustment.

Chapter 5 Part C:
Pre/post-heating system – diesel engines

Contents

Degrees of difficulty

Easy, suitable for novice with little experience	**Fairly easy,** suitable for beginner with some experience	**Fairly difficult,** suitable for competent DIY mechanic	**Difficult,** suitable for experienced DIY mechanic	**Very difficult,** suitable for expert DIY or professional

Specifications

Glow plugs
Resistance . . . . 0.6 ohms

Fuel temperature sensor
Resistance at 25°C . . . . 2.2 kohms

Torque wrench setting

	Nm	lbf ft
Glow plugs	15	11

---

1 General information

1 The preheating/post-heating system consists of glow plugs screwed into the combustion chambers, a control unit mounted next to the battery on the left-hand side of the engine compartment, and a coolant temperature sensor located on the thermostat housing. The control unit is itself activated by the engine management ECM.

2 The glow plugs are supplied with current from the control unit in several phases, namely variable preheating, fixed preheating, starting heating, and variable post-heating.

3 The variable preheating phase occurs when the ignition is switched on, and during this phase the preheating warning light is illuminated on the instrument panel. The period of preheating depends on the temperature of the coolant and battery voltage. The maximum

period of 15 seconds occurs if the coolant temperature is low and the battery voltage is less than 9.3 volts. The period varies from 15 seconds to zero seconds according to the temperature of the coolant, and when the temperature reaches 80°C, no preheating occurs. With normal battery voltage the maximum period is 10 seconds.

4 The fixed preheating phase occurs straight after the variable phase finishes, after the warning light has extinguished, and lasts for up to 5 seconds. Normally, the driver will start the engine at some point during this phase.

5 During the period when the starter motor is in operation, the glow plugs are continuously supplied with current.

6 The variable post-heating phase occurs immediately after the engine has been started, and the period of post-heating depends on the temperature of the coolant. The maximum period of variable post-heating is 60 seconds, at which point the system is switched off. Variable post-heating will cease if the coolant temperature exceeds 80°C.

2 Pre/post-heating system – testing

1 If the system malfunctions, testing is best carried out by a Nissan dealer or suitably equipped garage using dedicated test equipment, however, some preliminary checks may be made as follows.

2 Connect a voltmeter or 12 volt test lamp between the glow plug supply cable and earth (engine or vehicle metal). Make sure that the live connection is kept clear of the engine and bodywork.

3 Have an assistant switch on the ignition and check that voltage is applied to the glow plugs. Note the time for which the warning light is lit and the total time for which voltage is applied before the system cuts out Switch off the ignition and compare to the times given in the previous Section.

4 If there is no supply at all, the relay, control unit or associated wiring is at fault.

5 To locate a defective glow plug, disconnect the main supply cable and the interconnecting wire from the top of the glow plugs.

6 Use a continuity tester, or 12-volt test lamp connected to the battery positive terminal, to check for continuity between each glow plug terminal and earth. The resistance of a glow plug in good condition is very low (less than 1 ohm), so if the test lamp does not light or the continuity tester shows a high resistance, the glow plug is defective.

7 If an ammeter is available, the current draw of each glow plug can be checked. After an initial surge of around 15 to 20 amps, each plug should draw around 10 amps. Any plug that draws much more or less than 10 amps is probably defective.

8 As a final check, the glow plugs can be removed and inspected as described in Section 3.

9 If the pre/post-heating system is faulty, first check the wiring to each individual component. If this does not locate the fault, ideally each component should be substituted with known good units until the fault is located. If this is not possible, take the vehicle to a Nissan dealer or diesel specialist who will have the diagnostic equipment necessary to pin point the fault quickly.

3 Glow plugs – removal, inspection and refitting

Caution: If the preheating system has just been energised, or if the engine has been running, the glow plugs may be very hot.

Removal

1 Disconnect the battery negative (earth) lead and position it away from the terminal (refer to *Disconnecting the battery* in the Reference Section).

1.5 litre engine

2 Remove the plastic trim cover from the top of the engine **(see illustration)**.

3 Slacken the retaining clip and disconnect the intercooler pipe rubber hose **(see illustration)**.

4 Undo the retaining bolt, then release the securing clip at the turbo end of the pipe and pull the pipe upwards to remove it from across the top of the engine **(see illustrations)**.

5 Undo the upper bolt and retaining nut, release the two lower securing clips and remove the upper protective cover **(see illustrations)**.

6 Pull the plastic leg to disconnect the wiring plugs from the glow plugs **(see illustration)**.

7 Clean the surrounding area, then unscrew

3.2 Remove the engine upper trim cover

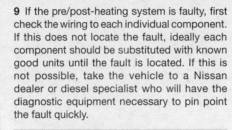

3.3 Disconnect the intercooler hose

3.4a Undo the retaining bolt (arrowed) ...

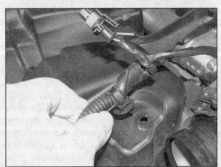

3.4b ... and release the securing clip (arrowed) to remove the pipe

3.5a Undo the nut and bolt (arrowed) ...

3.5b ...release the securing clips ...

3.5c ... unclip the wiring clip ...

3.5d ... and remove the upper plastic cover

3.6 Disconnect the wiring connector – 1.5 litre engine

3.7 Unscrew the glow plug (arrowed) from the cylinder head

3.10 Disconnect the wiring connector – 2.0 litre engine

3.11 Unscrew the glow plugs from the cylinder head

3.16 Tighten the glow plugs to the correct torque

and remove the glow plugs from the cylinder head **(see illustration)**.

2.0 litre engine

8 Remove the plastic trim cover from the top of the engine.

9 Slacken the retaining clips and disconnect the intercooler pipe rubber hoses from across the top of the engine.

10 Pull the plastic leg to disconnect the wiring plugs from the glow plugs **(see illustration)**.

11 Clean the surrounding area, then unscrew and remove the glow plugs from the cylinder head **(see illustration)**.

Inspection

12 Inspect the glow plugs for physical damage. Burnt or eroded glow plug tips can be caused by a bad injector spray pattern. Have the injectors checked if this sort of damage is found.

13 If the glow plugs are in good physical condition, check them electrically using a 12-volt test lamp or continuity tester with reference to the previous Section.

14 The glow plugs can be energised by applying 12-volts to them, this will verify that they heat up evenly and in the required time. Observe the following precautions:

a) *Support the glow plug by clamping it carefully in a vice or self-locking pliers. Remember it will become red-hot.*

b) *Make sure that the power supply or test lead incorporates a fuse or overload trip to protect against damage from a short-circuit.*

c) *After testing, allow the glow plug to cool for several minutes before attempting to handle it.*

15 A glow plug in good condition will start to glow red at the tip after drawing current for 5 seconds or so. Any plug that takes much longer to start glowing, or which starts glowing in the middle instead of at the tip, is defective.

Refitting

16 Refit by reversing the removal operations. Apply a smear of copper based anti-seize compound to the plug threads and tighten the glow plugs to the specified torque **(see illustration)**. Do not overtighten, as this can damage the glow plug element.

4 Pre/post-heating system control unit – removal and refitting

Removal

1 The pre/post-heating control unit is located on a bracket in front of the battery, on the left-hand side of the engine compartment

4.1a Location of the pre/post heating control unit (arrowed) – 1.5 litre engine

4.1b Location of the pre/post heating control unit (arrowed) – 2.0 litre with automatic transmission

4.2 Remove the air intake ducting – 2.0 litre engine

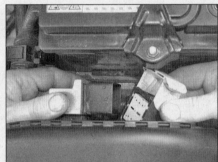

4.3a Release the wiring connector – 1.5 litre engine

(see illustrations). Before proceeding, make sure that the ignition is switched off.

2 On 2.0 litre engine models, to gain better access release the retaining clips, and then remove the air intake ducting from the front left-hand side of the engine compartment (see illustration).

3 Disconnect the wiring from the control unit (see illustrations).

4 Unscrew the mounting nuts/bolts and remove the control unit from the mounting bracket (see illustrations).

Refitting

5 Refitting is a reversal of removal.

4.3b Release the wiring connector – 2.0 litre with automatic transmission

4.4a Undo the mounting bolt – manual transmission models

4.4b Undo the mounting bolt – automatic transmission models

Chapter 6
Clutch

Contents

Degrees of difficulty

Easy, suitable for novice with little experience	Fairly easy, suitable for beginner with some experience	Fairly difficult, suitable for competent DIY mechanic	Difficult, suitable for experienced DIY mechanic	Very difficult, suitable for expert DIY or professional

Specifications

Type	Single dry plate with diaphragm spring. Hydraulic with master cylinder and operating (slave) cylinder

Friction disc

Outer diameter:
HR16DE	200 mm
MR20DE	225 mm
K9K	225 mm
M9R	250 mm

Inner diameter (of friction materiel):
HR16DE	140 mm
MR20DE	160 mm
K9K	150 mm
M9R	165 mm

Friction material thickness (new):
HR16DE	3.5 mm
MR20DE	3.2 mm
K9K	3.1 mm
M9R	3.75 mm

Minimum friction material-to-rivet head depth:
HR16DE, MR20DE and M9R	0.3 mm
K9K	1.0 mm
Maximum friction disc run-out	1.0 mm

Torque wrench settings

	Nm	lbf ft
Clutch pedal bracket nuts	14	10
Concentric slave cylinder (CSC) retaining bolts	21	15
Pressure plate (clutch cover) retaining bolts:		
HR16DE:		
Stage 1	20	14
Stage 2	25	19
MR20DE:		
Stage 1	15	11
Stage 2	25	19
K9K	12	9
M9R	25	18

1 General information

The clutch consists of a friction disc, a pressure plate assembly, a release bearing and the release mechanism. All of these components are contained in the large cast-aluminium alloy bellhousing, and sandwiched between the engine and the transmission. The release mechanism is hydraulic, operated by a master cylinder and a slave cylinder, which is part of the release bearing. The hydraulic master cylinder is located in the pedal bracket on the bulkhead, and the clutch fluid reservoir is shared with the brake fluid reservoir on the top of the brake master cylinder. Inside the reservoir each circuit has its own compartment, so that in the event of fluid loss in the clutch circuit, the brake circuit remains fully operational.

The friction disc/plate is fitted between the engine flywheel and the clutch pressure plate, and is allowed to slide on the transmission input shaft splines. It consists of two circular facings of friction material to provide the clutch bearing surface, and a spring-cushioned hub to damp out transmission shocks.

The pressure plate assembly is bolted to the engine flywheel, and is located by dowel pins. When the engine is running, drive is transmitted from the crankshaft via the flywheel to the friction disc (these components being clamped securely together by the pressure plate assembly), and from the friction disc to the transmission input shaft.

To interrupt the drive, the spring pressure must be relaxed. This is achieved by a sealed release bearing fitted concentrically around the transmission input shaft; when the driver depresses the clutch pedal, the release bearing is pressed against the fingers at the centre of the diaphragm spring. The pressure at its centre causes the springs to deform, so that it flattens and thus releases the clamping force it exerts at its periphery on the pressure plate.

When the pedal is released, the diaphragm spring forces the pressure plate into contact with the friction linings on the friction

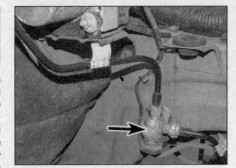

1.6 Pulsation damper location (arrowed)

plate. The disc is now firmly sandwiched between the pressure plate and the flywheel, thus transmitting engine power to the transmission.

Wear of the friction material on the friction plate is automatically compensated for by the operation of the hydraulic system. As the friction material on the friction plate wears, the pressure plate moves towards the flywheel causing the clutch diaphragm spring inner fingers to move outwards. When the clutch pedal is released, excess fluid is expelled through the master cylinder into the fluid reservoir. There is a pulsation damper fitted in the hydraulic hose from the master cylinder to the (concentric) slave cylinder. It is located in the left-hand rear corner of the engine compartment below the air cleaner assembly (see illustration).

 Warning: Hydraulic fluid is poisonous, thoroughly wash off spills from bare skin without delay. Seek immediate medical advice if any fluid is swallowed or gets into the eyes. Certain types of hydraulic fluid are inflammable and may ignite when brought into contact with hot components. Hydraulic fluid is also an effective paint stripper. If spillage occurs onto painted bodywork or fittings, it should be washed off immediately, using copious quantities of cold water. It is also hygroscopic (i.e. it can absorb moisture from the air) which then renders it useless. Old fluid may have suffered contamination, and should never be re-used.

2 Hydraulic system – bleeding

Note: *Refer to the warning at the beginning of Section 1, regarding the hazards of working with hydraulic fluid.*

1 If any part of the hydraulic system is dismantled, or if air has accidentally entered the system, the system will need to be bled. The presence of air is characterised by the pedal having a spongy feel and it results in difficulty in changing gear.

2 Obtain a clean container, a suitable length of rubber or clear plastic tubing that is a tight fit over the bleed screw on the clutch slave cylinder, and a container of the specified hydraulic fluid. The help of an assistant will also be required. (If a one-man do-it-yourself bleeding kit for bleeding the brake hydraulic system is available, this can be used quite satisfactorily for the clutch also. Full information on the use of these kits may be found in Chapter 9, Section 2.)

3 Remove the air cleaner inlet ducting from the front left-hand side of the engine compartment (see Chapter 4A, Section 2 or Chapter 4B, Section 2), to access the clutch bleed screw.

4 Remove the filler cap from the brake master cylinder reservoir, and if necessary top-up the fluid. Keep the reservoir topped-up during subsequent operations.

5 Remove the dust cap from the bleed screw at the hydraulic connection, located on the lower front facing side of the transmission **(see illustration)**.

6 Connect one end of the bleed tube to the bleed screw, and insert the other end of the tube in the container with sufficient clean hydraulic fluid to keep the end of the tube submerged **(see illustration)**.

7 With the tube on the bleed screw, press down on the hose retaining clip **(see illustration)**, and then carefully pull the clutch fluid hose outwards from the bell housing, by 5mm on 5-speed transmissions, and 10mm on 6-speed transmissions. Be careful not to pull the clutch fluid hose completely out from the connection.

2.5 Remove the dust cap from the bleed screw

2.6 Air bleed bottle connected to bleed screw

2.7 Release the retaining clip (arrowed)

3.2 Unclip the trim panel from under the facia

3.3a Unclip the kick panel ...

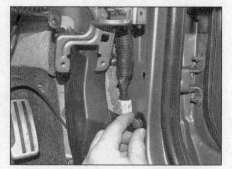

3.3b ... release the retaining clip ...

3.3c ... and withdraw the heater ducting

3.4a Disconnect the switch wiring connector ...

3.4b ... and unclip the wiring loom retaining clip (arrowed)

8 Have your assistant depress the clutch pedal and then slowly release it. Continue this procedure until clean hydraulic fluid, free from air bubbles, emerges from the tube. At the end of a downstroke, push the clutch fluid hose back into position, making sure the retaining clip secures the hose in place.

9 Make sure that the brake master cylinder reservoir is checked frequently to ensure that the level does not drop too far, allowing air into the system.

10 Check the operation of the clutch pedal. After a few strokes it should feel normal. Any sponginess would indicate air still present in the system, if so; carry out the procedure once again.

11 On completion remove the bleed tube and refit the dust cover. Top-up the master cylinder reservoir if necessary and refit the cap. Fluid expelled from the hydraulic system should now be discarded, as it will be contaminated

with moisture, air and dirt, making it unsuitable for further use.

3 Clutch pedal – removal and refitting

Removal

1 Disconnect the battery negative (earth) lead and position it away from the terminal (refer to *Disconnecting the battery* in the Reference Section).

2 Working inside the vehicle in the driver's side footwell, unclip the facia lower trim panel **(see illustration)**.

3 Undo the plastic retaining nut and then unclip the kick panel from the driver's side front footwell. Release the retaining clip and remove the heater ducting from across

the top of the drivers pedal assembly **(see illustrations)**.

4 Disconnect the wiring connector from the clutch pedal switch, and unclip the wiring loom securing clips from the pedal mounting bracket **(see illustrations)**.

5 Release the securing clips, and then using a flat bladed screwdriver, prise the master cylinder pushrod end from the pedal pin **(see illustration)**.

6 Hold the clutch pedal down and remove the return spring from the locating pegs on the mounting bracket and pedal **(see illustration)**.

7 Slacken and remove the clutch pedal mounting bracket retaining nuts, then withdraw the pedal and mounting bracket out from under the facia **(see illustration)**.

8 Check the condition of the pedal, pivot bush and return spring assembly and renew any components as necessary.

3.5 Release the end of the pushrod from the pedal

3.6 Unclip the return spring from the pedal and mounting bracket

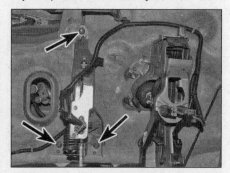

3.7 Clutch pedal mounting bracket nuts (arrowed)

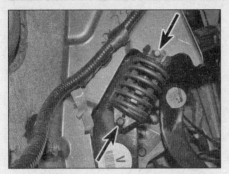

3.10 Make sure the return spring is located on the pegs correctly

4.3 Remove the bulkhead soundproofing

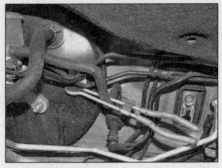

4.5 Clamp the fluid pipe from the reservoir

Refitting

9 Lubricate the pedal pivot bolt with multipurpose grease, then manoeuvre and locate the pedal and mounting bracket on the bulkhead. Refit the retaining nuts and tighten securely.

10 Reconnect the return spring to the pedal and pedal bracket; making sure it locates correctly **(see illustration)**.

11 Reconnect the clutch master cylinder pushrod to the clutch pedal.

12 Depress the pedal two or three times and check the operation of the clutch release mechanism.

13 Reconnect the wiring connector to the clutch switch, and then secure the wiring loom back into position with the retaining clips on the pedal mounting bracket.

14 Refit the heater ducting back across the top of the pedal assembly and then refit the facia lower trim panels.

15 Reconnect the battery negative (earth) lead (refer to *Disconnecting the battery* in the Reference Section).

4 Master cylinder – removal and refitting

Note: *Refer to the warning at the beginning of Section 1 regarding the hazards of working with hydraulic fluid.*

Removal

1 Working inside the driver's footwell, release the securing clips, and then prise the master

cylinder pushrod end from the pedal pin **(see illustration 3.5)**. Press on the securing clips to free the pushrod from the pedal.

2 To minimise hydraulic fluid loss, remove the brake master cylinder reservoir filler cap then tighten it down onto a piece of polythene to obtain an airtight seal.

3 Working inside the engine compartment, undo the fasteners and remove the sound proofing protector from down the back of the engine compartment **(see illustration)**.

4 Place absorbent rags under the clutch master cylinder pipe connections in the engine compartment and be prepared for some hydraulic fluid loss.

5 Clamp the upper hydraulic fluid supply hose leading from the brake fluid reservoir to the clutch master cylinder using a brake hose clamp **(see illustration)**.

6 Release the master cylinder hydraulic pressure pipe from the retaining clip on the engine compartment bulkhead. Be prepared for some hydraulic fluid loss, then prise out the retaining wire clip and disconnect the pipe from the master cylinder **(see illustration)**. Suitably plug or cap the pipe end to prevent further fluid loss and dirt entry.

7 Be prepared for some hydraulic fluid loss and disconnect the fluid supply hose from the top of the master cylinder. Suitably plug or cap the pipe end to prevent further fluid loss and dirt entry.

8 Rotate the master cylinder 45 degrees clockwise, and remove it from the bulkhead.

Refitting

9 Refitting the master cylinder is the reverse

sequence to removal, bearing in mind the following points.
a) Ensure that the pedal-to-master cylinder pushrod is correctly fitted.
b) Ensure all retaining clips are correctly refitted.
c) Remove the piece of polythene from the top of the reservoir.
d) On completion, bleed the clutch hydraulic system as described in Section 2.

5 Concentric slave cylinder (CSC) – removal and refitting

The clutch slave cylinder (Concentric Slave Cylinder) is part of the release bearing assembly; refer to Section 7, for the removal and refitting procedure.

6 Clutch assembly – removal, inspection and refitting

⚠️ *Warning: Dust created by clutch wear and deposited on the clutch components may contain asbestos, which is a health hazard. DO NOT blow it out with compressed air, or inhale any of it. DO NOT use petrol or petroleum-based solvents to clean off the dust. Brake system cleaner or methylated spirit should be used to flush the dust into a suitable receptacle. After the clutch components are wiped clean with rags, dispose of the contaminated rags and cleaner in a sealed, marked container.*
Note: *Although some friction materials may no longer contain asbestos, it is safest to assume that they DO, and to take precautions accordingly*

Removal

1 Unless the complete engine/transmission is to be removed from the car, and separated for major overhaul (see Chapter 2E), the clutch can be reached by removing the transmission as described in Chapter 7A, Section 6.

2 Before disturbing the clutch, use a dab of quick-drying paint or a marker pen to mark the relationship of the pressure plate assembly to the flywheel **(see illustration)**.

4.6 Disconnect the fluid pipes from the master cylinder

6.2 Mark the position of the pressure plate on the flywheel

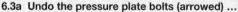

6.3a Undo the pressure plate bolts (arrowed) ...

6.3b ... using a homemade tool to prevent the flywheel from turning

3 Working in a diagonal sequence, slacken the pressure plate bolts by half a turn at a time, until the spring pressure is released and the bolts can be unscrewed by hand **(see illustrations)**. If required lock the flywheel to prevent it from turning, by locking the ring gear teeth.

4 Prise the pressure plate assembly off its locating dowels, and collect the friction disc, noting which way round the friction disc is fitted **(see illustration)**.

Inspection

Note: *Due to the amount of work necessary to remove and refit clutch components, it is usually considered good practice to renew the clutch friction disc, pressure plate assembly and release bearing as a matched set, even if only one of these is actually worn enough to require renewal. It is worth considering the renewal of the clutch components on a preventative basis if the engine and/or transmission have been removed for some other reason.*

5 When cleaning clutch components, first read the warning at the beginning of this Section. Remove the dust only as described – working with dampened cloths will help to keep dust levels to a minimum. Wherever possible, work in a well-ventilated atmosphere.

6 Check the friction disc facings for signs of wear, damage or oil contamination. If the friction material is cracked, burnt, scored or damaged, or if it is contaminated with oil or grease (shown by shiny black patches), the friction disc must be renewed.

7 If the friction material is still serviceable, check that the centre boss splines are unworn, that the torsion springs are in good condition and securely fastened, and that all the rivets are tightly fastened. If excessive wear or damage is found, the friction disc must be renewed.

8 If the friction material is fouled with oil, this must be due to an oil leak from the crankshaft left-hand oil seal, from the sump-to-cylinder block joint, or from the transmission input shaft. Renew the seal or repair the joint, as appropriate, as described in Chapter 2A, 2B, 2C or 2D or Chapter 7A, before installing the new friction disc, or the new disc will quickly go the same way.

9 Check the pressure plate assembly for obvious signs of wear or damage; shake it to check for loose rivets, or worn or damaged fulcrum rings. Check that the drive straps securing the pressure plate to the cover do not show signs (such as a deep yellow or blue discoloration) of overheating. If the diaphragm spring is worn or damaged, or if its pressure

is in any way suspect, the pressure plate assembly should be renewed.

10 Examine the machined bearing surfaces of the pressure plate and of the flywheel; they should be clean, completely flat, and free from scratches or scoring. If either is discoloured from excessive heat, or shows signs of cracks, it should be renewed; however, minor damage of this nature can sometimes be polished away using emery paper.

11 Check that the release bearing contact surface rotates smoothly and easily, with no sign of noise or roughness, and that the surface itself is smooth and unworn, with no signs of cracks, pitting or scoring. If there is any doubt about its condition, the bearing must be renewed

Refitting

12 On reassembly, ensure that the bearing surfaces of the flywheel and pressure plate are completely clean, smooth, and free from oil or grease. Use solvent to remove any protective grease from new components.

13 Fit the friction disc/plate so that its spring hub assembly faces away from the flywheel; there may also be a marking showing which way round the plate is to be refitted **(see illustration)**.

14 Refit the pressure plate assembly, aligning the marks made on dismantling (if the original pressure plate is re-used), and locating the pressure plate on its locating dowels. Fit the pressure plate bolts, but tighten them only finger-tight so that the friction disc can still be moved.

15 The friction disc must now be centralised, so that when the transmission is refitted, its input shaft will pass through the splines at the centre of the friction disc.

16 Centralisation can be achieved by passing a screwdriver or other long bar through the friction disc, and into the hole in the crankshaft. The friction disc can then be moved around until it is centred on the crankshaft hole. Alternatively, a clutch-aligning tool can be

6.4 Remove the pressure plate complete with friction disc

6.13 Markings on friction disc – P.P.SIDE (pressure plate side)

6.16a Using a special tool to centralise the friction disc ...

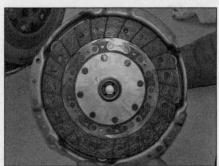

6.16b ... on the pressure plate

6.17a Align the pressure plate on the dowels on the flywheel

6.17b Tighten the bolts to the correct torque setting

used to eliminate the guesswork; these can be obtained from most accessory shops **(see illustrations)**.

17 When the friction disc is centralised, tighten the pressure plate bolts evenly and in a diagonal sequence to the specified torque setting **(see illustrations)**. Lock the ring gear to prevent the flywheel from turning, using the method employed when dismantling.

18 Apply a thin smear of high melting-point grease to the splines of the friction disc and the transmission input shaft.

19 Refit the transmission as described in Chapter 7A, Section 6.

---

7   Clutch release mechanism
– removal, inspection and refitting

Note: *Refer to the warning concerning the dangers of asbestos dust at the beginning of Section 6.*

Removal

1 Unless the complete engine/transmission is to be removed from the car, and separated for major overhaul (see Chapter 2E), the clutch release mechanism can be reached by removing the transmission as described in Chapter 7A, Section 6.

2 With the transmission removed, undo the two mounting bolts from inside the bellhousing **(see illustration)**.

3 Withdraw the concentric slave cylinder/ release bearing by sliding it over the transmission input shaft. Withdraw it complete with plastic fluid pipe out from the bellhousing.

4 If required, withdraw the securing clip from the plastic fluid pipe **(see illustration)**, to disconnect it from the clutch slave cylinder/ release bearing.

Inspection

5 Check the release mechanism, renewing any component, which is worn or damaged. Carefully check all bearing surfaces and points of contact.

6 When checking the release bearing itself, note that it is often considered worthwhile to renew it as a matter of course, given that a significant amount of work is required to gain access to it. Check that the contact surface rotates smoothly and easily, with no sign of noise or roughness. Also check that the surface itself is smooth and unworn, with no signs of cracks, pitting or scoring. If there is any doubt about its condition, the bearing must be renewed.

Refitting

7 Slide the concentric slave cylinder/release bearing over the transmission input shaft and tighten the retaining bolts to the specified torque setting.

8 Refit the transmission as described in Chapter 7A, Section 6.

7.2 Undo the concentric slave cylinder (CSC) mounting bolts

7.4 Retaining clip (arrowed) securing plastic pipe to the slave cylinder

Chapter 7 Part A:
Manual transmission

Contents

Degrees of difficulty

Easy, suitable for novice with little experience	Fairly easy, suitable for beginner with some experience	Fairly difficult, suitable for competent DIY mechanic	Difficult, suitable for experienced DIY mechanic	Very difficult, suitable for expert DIY or professional

Specifications

General

Type .... Manual, five or six forward speeds and reverse. Synchromesh on all forward speeds

Designation:
  Petrol engines:
    1.6 litre (HR16DE) engine .... RS5F92R – (5 speed)
    2.0 litre (MR20DE) engine:
      2WD (two wheel drive) .... RS6F94R – (6 speed)
      4WD (four wheel drive) .... RS6F52A – (6 speed)
  Diesel engines:
    1.5 litre (K9K) engine .... RS6F94R – (6 speed)
    2.0 litre (M9R) engine (2WD and 4WD) .... RS6F52A – (6 speed)
Models code:
  Petrol engines:
    HR16DE – RS5F92R JD00A
    MR20DE – RS6F94R (2WD) JD200
    MR20DE – RS6F52A (4WD) JG20C
  Diesel engines:
    K9K – RS6F94R JD500
    M9R – RS6F52A – (2WD) JG70E
    M9R – RS6F52A – (4WD) JG75E

Lubrication

Oil capacities:
  5-speed transmissions .... 2.3 litres
  6-speed transmissions .... 2.0 litres

Torque wrench settings

	Nm	lbf ft
Engine-to-transmission fixing bolts:		
HR16DE	48	35
MR20DE	62	46
K9K	48	35
M9R	48	35
Oil drain plug	25	18
Oil filler/level plug (plastic plug)	3	2
Reversing light switch	23	17

1 General information

The transmission is contained in a cast-aluminium alloy casing bolted to the left-hand end of the engine, and consists of the gearbox and final drive differential, often called a transaxle.

Drive is transmitted from the crankshaft via the clutch to the input shaft, which has a splined extension to accept the clutch friction disc, and rotates in sealed ball-bearings. From the input shaft, drive is transmitted to the output shaft, which rotates in a roller bearing at its right-hand end, and a sealed ball-bearing at its left-hand end. From the output shaft, the drive is transmitted to the differential crownwheel, which rotates with the differential case and planetary gears, thus driving the sun gears and driveshafts. The rotation of the planetary gears on their shaft allows the inner roadwheel to rotate at a slower speed than the outer roadwheel when the car is cornering.

The input and output shafts are arranged side-by-side, parallel to the crankshaft and driveshafts, so that their gear pinion teeth are in constant mesh. In the neutral position, the output shaft gear pinions rotate freely, so that drive cannot be transmitted to the crownwheel.

Gear selection is via a floor-mounted lever and dual cable arrangement. The selector cables cause the appropriate selector fork to move its respective synchro-sleeve along the shaft, to lock the gear pinion to the synchro-hub. Since the synchro-hubs are splined to the output shaft, this locks the pinion to the shaft so that drive can be transmitted. To ensure that gearchanging can be made quickly and quietly, a synchromesh system is fitted to all forward gears, consisting of baulk rings and spring-loaded fingers, as well as the gear pinions and synchro-hubs; the synchromesh cones are formed on the mating faces of the baulk rings and gear pinions.

2 Transmission – draining and refilling

1 This operation is much quicker and more efficient if the car is first taken on a journey of sufficient length to warm the engine/transmission up to normal operating temperature.

2 Park the car on level ground, switch off the ignition and apply the handbrake firmly. For improved access, jack up the front of the car and support it securely on axle stands (see *Jacking and vehicle support*). Note that the car must be lowered to the ground and be level to ensure accuracy when refilling and checking the oil level.

3 Undo the retaining bolts and remove the plastic undershield from below the engine/transmission.

4 Wipe clean the area around the filler/level plug, which is:

a) Screwed into the front of the transmission housing on 5-speed transmissions (**see illustration**).
b) Screwed into the left-hand side of the transmission, to the rear of the driveshaft, on 6-speed transmissions (**see illustration**).

5 Remove the oil filler/level plug, be prepared for some oil spillage as the plug is removed.

6 Position a suitable container under the drain plug, which is situated at the lower rear of the transmission differential housing (**see illustrations**).

7 Remove the drain plug and allow the oil to drain completely into the container (**see illustration**). If the oil is hot, take precautions against scalding. Clean both the filler/level and the drain plug, discard the sealing washers, as new ones will be required on refitting.

8 When the oil has finished draining, clean the drain plug threads and those of the transmission casing, then fit the new sealing washer and refit the drain plug (**see illustration**), tightening it to the specified torque wrench setting. If the car was raised for the draining operation, lower it to the ground, to make sure it is level.

9 Refilling the transmission is an awkward operation. Above all, allow plenty of time for the oil level to settle properly before checking it. Note that the car must be parked on flat level ground when checking the oil level.

10 Refill the transmission with the exact amount of the specified type of oil, then check the oil level as described in Chapter 1A,

2.4a Oil filler/level plug (arrowed) – 5-speed transmission

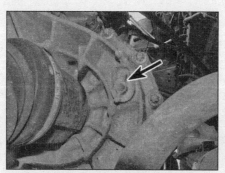

2.4b Oil filler/level plug (arrowed) – 6-speed transmission

2.6a Oil drain plug (arrowed) – 5-speed transmission

2.6b Oil drain plug (arrowed) – 6-speed transmission

2.7 Drain the transmission oil

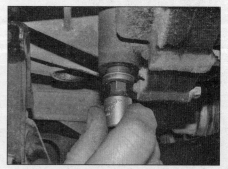

2.8 Use a new sealing washer when refitting the drain plug

Section 21 or Chapter 1B, Section 23; if the correct amount was poured into the transmission, and a large amount flows out on checking the level, refit the filler/level plug and take the car on a short journey so that the new oil is distributed fully around the transmission components, then check the level again on your return.

11 When the level is correct, refit the filler/level plug **(see illustration)**, tightening it to the specified torque wrench setting. Wash off any spilt oil.

3 Gearchange linkage – removal and refitting

Removal

Gear lever assembly

1 Remove the centre console as described in Chapter 11, Section 25.

2 Release the white securing clips and disconnect the two cables from the ball joints on the gear change selector levers **(see illustrations)**.

3 Pull out the locating pin and withdraw the two outer cables from the gear change housing **(see illustrations)**.

4 With the cables disconnected, undo the four mounting bolts from the bottom of the gear change housing **(see illustration)**, and manoeuvre the gear lever assembly out of position.

Gear change cables

5 Release the cables from the gear lever assembly, as described in paragraphs 1 to 3.

6 Remove the battery as described in Chapter 5A, Section 3.

7 Also to make access to the cables on top of the transmission housing easier, remove the air cleaner housing, as described in Chapter 4A, Section 2 or Chapter 4B, Section 2.

8 Release the white securing clips and disconnect the two cables from the ball joints on the gear change selector levers **(see illustrations)**.

2.11 Refit the filler/level plug when fluid is correct

3.2a Release the locking clips ...

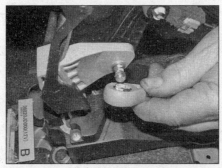

3.2b ... and disconnect the cables from the ball joint

3.3a Pull out the locating pins ...

3.3b ... and unclip the outer cables ...

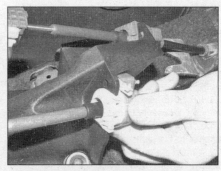

3.3c ... from the gear lever bracket

3.4 Undo the gear change mounting bracket bolts (arrowed)

3.8a Release the locking clips (arrowed) ...

3.8b ... and disconnect the cables from the ball joint

3.9a Pull out the locating pins ...

3.9b ... and unclip the outer cables from the transmission bracket

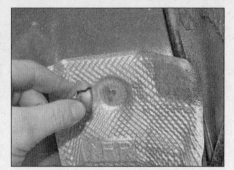

3.11a Undo the retaining clips ...

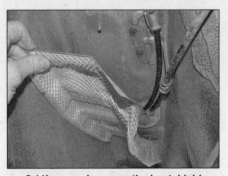

3.11b ... and remove the heatshield

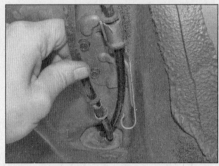

3.12a Release the cables from the retaining bracket ...

3.12b ... and remove the rubber grommet from the floor panel

9 Pull out the locating pin and withdraw the two outer cables from the transmission mounting bracket **(see illustrations)**.

10 Firmly apply the handbrake, and then jack up the front of the vehicle and support it securely on axle stands (see *Jacking and vehicle support*).

11 From underneath the vehicle, release the fasteners and remove the heat shield from under the centre tunnel of the vehicle **(see illustrations)**. Note depending on model, it may be necessary to remove the exhaust front pipe or prop shaft (4WD models) to give better access to the heat shield.

12 Unclip the outer cables from the mounting bracket on the underside of the vehicle, and then release the rubber grommet from the floor panel and withdraw the cables from under the vehicle **(see illustrations)**.

13 Inspect all the gear linkage components

for signs of wear or damage, paying particular attention to the cables, renew worn components as necessary.

Refitting

14 Refitting is a reversal of the removal procedure, applying a smear of multipurpose grease to the gear lever pivot ball and bushes.

Adjustment

15 Adjustment is made from inside the vehicle, on the gear lever end of the left-hand selector cable **(see illustration)**.

16 Remove the centre console as described in Chapter 11, Section 25.

17 Slide the centre clip and withdraw the locking clip from the end of the gear change cable; this will disengage the inner cable.

18 Position the gear lever so that the slot in

the lever aligns with the hole in the gear lever housing **(see illustration)**, and then insert a 3mm locating pin (drill bit) to lock the gear lever in position.

19 With the gear lever in position, slide the centre locking clip back into position, securing the cable in position.

20 When completed remove the 3mm locating pin and move the gear lever through all gears to check smooth operation.

21 Refitting is a reversal of the removal procedure.

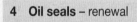

4 Oil seals – renewal

Driveshaft oil seal

1 Firmly apply the handbrake, and then jack up the front of the vehicle and support it securely on axle stands (see *Jacking and vehicle support*). Remove the appropriate front roadwheel.

2 Drain the transmission oil as described in Section 2.

3 Working as described in Chapter 8, Section 2, free the inner end of the driveshaft from the transmission, and place it clear of the seal, noting that there is no need to completely remove the driveshaft; the driveshaft can be left secured to the hub. Support the driveshaft, to avoid placing any strain on the driveshaft joints or gaiters.

3.15 Release the locking clip (arrowed) to adjust the cable

3.18 Insert pin through slot in the gear lever (arrowed)

4 Before removing the seal, use a vernier gauge to check the seal depth in the transmission casing (see illustration). This will give you the position of the seal in the transmission casing for refitting, see following measurements:

On 5-speed (RS5F92R) transmissions:
Left-hand side seal should be 5.7 to 6.3 mm
Right-hand side seal should be 2.4 to 3.0 mm
On 6-speed (RS6F94R) transmissions:
Left-hand side seal should be 1.2 to 1.8 mm
Right-hand side seal should be 2.7 to 3.3 mm
On 6-speed (RS6F52A) transmissions the left and right-hand side seals should be flush with casing
On Automatic (RE6F01A) transmissions:
Left-hand side seal should be 5.7 to 6.2 mm
Right-hand side seal should be 22.7 to 23.5 mm
On 4WD transmissions, the transfer box side seal should be set at 7.5 to 8.0 mm depth

5 Carefully prise the oil seal out of the transmission using a large flat-bladed screwdriver (see illustration). Take care not to damage the transmission casing as the seal is removed.
6 Remove all traces of dirt from the area around the oil seal aperture, then apply a smear of oil to the lip of the new oil seal, and locate it in its aperture (see illustration).
7 Drive the seal squarely into position, using a suitable tubular drift (such as a socket), which bears only on the hard outer edge of the seal (see illustration). Drive the seal into position until it is at the depth noted on removal.
8 On 4WD models, see Chapter 7C, Section 4, for transfer gearbox seals.
9 Refit the driveshaft as described in Chapter 8, Section 2.
10 Refill the transmission with the specified quantity of oil, as described in Section 2. Refer to end of *Weekly Checks* for the specified type of oil used.

Input shaft oil seal

11 To renew the input shaft seal, the transmission must be dismantled. This task should therefore be entrusted to a Nissan dealer.

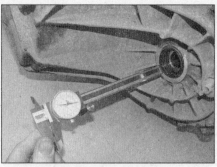

4.4 Using a vernier gauge to measure the seal depth

4.6 Fit the new seal squarely to the transmission …

5 Reversing light switch – testing, removal and refitting

Testing

1 The reversing light circuit is controlled by a plunger-type switch that is:
a) Screwed into the base of the transmission housing on its left-hand side on 5-speed transmissions (see illustration).
b) Screwed into the front of the transmission housing on 6-speed transmissions (see illustration).
2 If a fault develops in the circuit, first ensure that the circuit fuse has not blown (see Chapter 12).
3 To test the switch, disconnect the wiring

4.5 Use a large flat-bladed screwdriver to prise out the driveshaft oil seals

4.7 … and tap it into position using a tubular drift/socket

connector, and use a multi-meter (set to the resistance function) or a battery-and-bulb test circuit to check that there is continuity between the switch terminals only when reverse gear is selected. If this is not the case, and there are no obvious breaks or other damage to the wires, the switch is faulty and must be renewed.

Removal

4 Firmly apply the handbrake, and then jack up the front of the vehicle and support it securely on axle stands (see *Jacking and vehicle support*).
5 On models with 5-speed transmission, drain the oil as described in Section 2, or be prepared for some oil loss as the switch is removed.
6 Disconnect the wiring connector from the reversing light switch (see illustration).

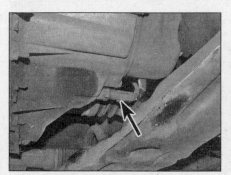

5.1a Location of reversing light switch – 5-speed transmission

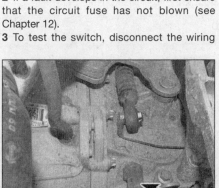

5.1b Location of reversing light switch – 6-speed transmission

5.6 Disconnect the switch wiring connector

7 Unscrew the switch from the transmission, and remove it. On 5-speed transmissions, plug the housing aperture, to minimise oil loss (if the transmission has not been drained), and to prevent dirt entry.

Refitting

8 Fit a new sealing washer to the switch, and then screw it back into the transmission housing.

9 Tighten the switch to the specified torque, then reconnect the wiring connector and check the operation of the circuit.

10 Lower the vehicle to the ground, and top-up/refill the transmission oil (as applicable) as described in Section 2.

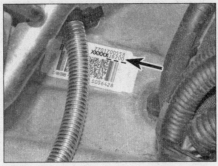

6.0 Label with transmission model code

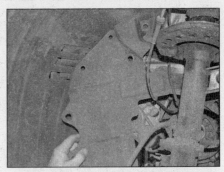

6.1 Remove the inner wing panel

---

6 Manual transmission – removal and refitting

Note: *This Section describes the removal of the transmission leaving the engine in position in the car. Alternatively the engine and transmission can be removed together, as described in Chapter 2E, and then separated on the bench.*

Note: *Transmission model code number is on a label on the top of the transmission housing* **(see illustration)***; see specifications at the beginning of this Chapter.*

Removal

1 Firmly apply the handbrake, and then jack up the front of the vehicle and support it securely on axle stands (see *Jacking and vehicle support*). Remove both front roadwheels. Undo the retaining screws, and remove the plastic undershields from beneath the engine/transmission, and the covers from underneath both wheel arches **(see illustration)**.

2 Drain the transmission oil as described in Section 2, then refit the drain and filler/level plugs and tighten them to their specified torque settings.

3 Remove the battery as described in Chapter 5A, Section 3.

6.10 Using a dummy shaft in the differential

4 Remove the front subframe as described in Chapter 10, Section 12.

5 Remove the starter motor as described in Chapter 5A, Section 8.

6 Remove the air cleaner assembly as described in Chapter 4A, Section 2 or Chapter 4B, Section 2.

7 Remove the exhaust system front pipe as described in Chapter 4A, Section 13 or Chapter 4B, Section 17.

8 On 4WD models, remove the transfer gearbox as described in Chapter 7C, Section 3.

9 Release the gearchange cables from the transmission as described in Section 3.

10 Working as described in Chapter 8, Section 2, remove the two front driveshafts from the transmission. Note that there is no

6.11 Undo the earth cable retaining bolt (arrowed)

need to unscrew the driveshaft retaining nuts – each driveshaft can be left secured to the hub. But take care and support the driveshafts, to avoid placing any strain on the driveshaft joints or gaiters. With the driveshafts out of the transmission, insert a dummy shaft into differential recess **(see illustration)**.

11 Undo the retaining bolt and disconnect the earth cable from the left-hand end of the transmission **(see illustration)**.

12 Disconnect the wiring connector from the reversing light switch, see Section 5 for reversing light switch location.

13 Be prepared for some fluid loss as the pipe is disconnected, place some cloth around the fitting. Release the retaining spring clip and disconnect the clutch fluid hose from the slave cylinder connector pipe **(see illustrations)**.

6.13a Release the locking clip (arrowed) ...

6.13b ... and disconnect the clutch fluid hose

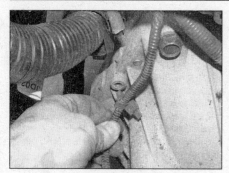

6.14a Release the wiring loom ...

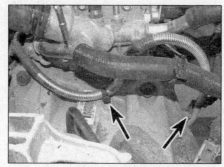

6.14b ... retaining clips (arrowed) from the transmission

6.16 Support the transmission with a trolley jack

Plug the ends of the slave cylinder pipe and clutch fluid hose to prevent fluid leakage and dirt ingress.

14 Work around the transmission and free the wiring loom from any relevant retaining clips **(see illustrations)**, and position the wiring clear of the transmission.

15 Make sure the breather pipe on top of the transmission housing is not secured to any other components. This does not have to be completely removed and left across the top of the transmission.

16 Place a jack with interposed block of wood beneath the engine, to take the weight of the engine **(see illustration)**. Alternatively, attach a hoist or support bar to the engine and take the weight of the engine.

17 Also place a jack and block of wood beneath the transmission, and raise the jack to take the weight of the transmission.

18 Slacken and remove the nut from the centre stud on the left-hand engine/ transmission mounting. Undo the two bolts securing the mounting to the bracket, and remove the rubber mounting **(see illustration)**. For further information on engine/transmission mounting removal, see the relevant part of Chapter 2A, B, C or D.

19 Unclip the clutch fluid pipe from the clip on the mounting bracket, and then undo the three bolts and remove the mounting from the top of the transmission **(see illustration)**.

20 With the jack positioned beneath the transmission taking the weight, slacken

and remove the remaining bolts securing the transmission housing to the engine **(see illustrations)**. Note the correct fitted positions of each bolt (and the relevant brackets) as they are removed, to use as a reference on refitting – the bolts are of different lengths. Note that it may be necessary to raise the transmission slightly to gain access to the lower bolts.

21 Make a final check that all necessary components have been disconnected, and are positioned clear of the transmission so that they will not hinder the removal procedure.

22 Move the trolley jack and transmission to the left to free it from its locating dowels. Keep the transmission fully supported until the input shaft is free of the engine.

23 Once the transmission is free, lower the

6.18 Remove the transmission mounting

6.19 Undo the mounting bracket retaining bolts

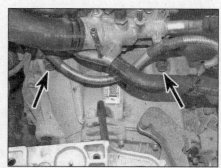

6.20a Remove the upper mounting bolts ...

6.20b ... rear mounting bolts ...

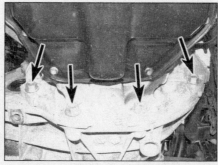

6.20c ... lower mounting bolts ...

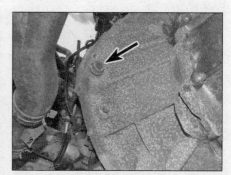

6.20d ... and front mounting bolt – 6-speed transmission shown

6.23 Lower the transmission from under the vehicle

jack and manoeuvre the unit out from under the car **(see illustration)**. If they are loose, remove the locating dowels from the transmission or engine, and keep them in a safe place.

Refitting

24 The transmission is refitted by a reversal of the removal procedure, bearing in mind the following points:

a) *Apply a little high melting-point grease to the splines of the transmission input shaft. Do not apply too much; otherwise there is a possibility of the grease contaminating the clutch friction disc.*

b) *Ensure that the locating dowels are correctly positioned prior to installation.*

c) *Insert the transmission-to-engine bolts into their original locations, as noted on removal. Tighten all nuts and bolts to the specified torque (where given).*

d) *Refit the driveshafts as described in Chapter 8, Section 2. If required renew the driveshaft oil seals using the information given in Section 4.*

e) *Bleed the clutch system as described in Chapter 6, Section 2.*

f) *Refit the gearchange cables as described in Section 3, and check operation.*

g) *On completion, refill the transmission with the specified type and quantity of lubricant as described in Section 2.*

7 Manual transmission overhaul – general information

Overhauling a manual transmission is a difficult and involved job for the DIY home mechanic. In addition to dismantling and reassembling many small parts, clearances must be precisely measured and, if necessary, changed by selecting shims and spacers.

Internal transmission components are also often difficult to obtain, and in many instances, extremely expensive. Because of this, if the transmission develops a fault or becomes noisy, the best course of action is to have the unit overhauled by a specialist repairer, or to obtain an exchange reconditioned unit.

Nevertheless, it is not impossible for the more experienced mechanic to overhaul the transmission, if the special tools are available, and the job is done in a deliberate step-by-step manner so that nothing is overlooked.

The tools necessary for an overhaul include internal and external circlip pliers, bearing pullers, a slide hammer, a set of pin punches, a dial test indicator, and possibly a hydraulic press. In addition, a large, sturdy workbench and a vice will be required.

During dismantling of the transmission, make careful notes of how each component is fitted, to make reassembly easier and accurate.

Before dismantling the transmission, it will help if you have some idea which area is malfunctioning. Certain problems can be closely related to specific areas in the transmission, which can make component examination and renewal easier. Refer to the *Fault finding* Section in the Reference Chapter for more information.

Chapter 7 Part B:
Automatic transmission

Contents

Degrees of difficulty

Easy, suitable for novice with little experience	Fairly easy, suitable for beginner with some experience	Fairly difficult, suitable for competent DIY mechanic	Difficult, suitable for experienced DIY mechanic	Very difficult, suitable for expert DIY or professional

Specifications

General

Type	Automatic, six forward speeds and reverse
Designation:	
2.0 litre (M9R) diesel engine	RE6F01A
Model Code	1XN0A or 1XN1A
Fluid Capacity	7.5 litres
Gear Ratio:	
1st	4.199
2nd	2.405
3rd	1.583
4th	1.161
5th	0.855
6th	0.685
Reverse	3.457
Final Drive	4.072

Torque wrench settings

	Nm	lbf ft
Drain plug (hexagon outer plug)	8	7
Fluid level tube (inner plug/tube)	8	7
Turbine revolution sensor	6	5
Turbine revolution sensor	6	5
Park/Neutral Position (PNP) switch:		
Mounting bolts	6	5
Lever retaining nut	17	13
Selector cable-to-transmission lever nut	14	10
Engine-to-transmission fixing bolts:		
Bolts length 55mm long	48	35
Bolts length 70mm long	20	15
Torque converter-to-driveplate bolts	50	38

1 General information

A six-speed fully-automatic transmission is available as an option on 2.0 litre diesel models. The transmission consists of a torque converter, an epicyclic geartrain, and hydraulically operated clutches and brakes.

The torque converter provides a fluid coupling between engine and transmission, which acts as an automatic clutch, and also provides a degree of torque multiplication when accelerating.

The epicyclic gear train provides either of the six forward or one reverse gear ratios, according to which of its component parts are held stationary, or are allowed to turn. The components of the geartrain are held or released by brakes and clutches, which are activated by a hydraulic control unit. A fluid pump within the transmission provides the necessary hydraulic pressure to operate the brakes and clutches.

Due to the complexity of the automatic transmission, some repair or overhaul work must be left to a Nissan dealer with the necessary special equipment for fault diagnosis and repair. The contents of the following Sections are therefore mainly confined to supplying general information, and any service information and instructions that can be used by the owner.

2 Automatic transmission – fluid renewal

Note: *The fluid temperature must be at 40°C, before the following procedure can be carried out. Nissan have special equipment for this procedure, so if in any doubt contact your local dealer.*

Note: *Some transmissions do not have a fluid drain/level check plug; on these transmissions it will be necessary to have the fluid level check carried out by a Nissan dealer or transmission specialist.*

Draining

1 This operation is much quicker and more efficient if the car is first taken on a journey of sufficient length to warm the engine/transmission up to temperature (40°C). **Note:** *The fluid in the transmission will reach approximately 40°C, after ten minutes of the engine idling.*

2 Park the car on level ground, switch off the ignition and apply the handbrake firmly. For improved access, jack up the front of the car and support it securely on axle stands (see *Jacking and vehicle support*). Undo the fasteners and remove the engine/transmission undershield (where fitted).

3 Position a suitable container under the drain plug, situated on the base of the transmission. Unscrew the hexagon outer plug and recover the sealing washer, then inside the housing is the second part of the plug, which is the level tube, this needs to be removed to drain the transmission. Allow the fluid to drain completely into the container.

 Warning: If the fluid is hot, take precautions against scalding.

4 Clean the drain plug, being especially careful to wipe off any metallic particles. Discard the sealing washer; it should be renewed whenever it is disturbed.

5 When the fluid has finished draining, clean both parts of the drain plug, also clean the threads and those of the transmission casing. Fit new sealing washers (where applicable) and refit the inner level tube first and then the hexagon outer plug, tightening it to the specified torque wrench setting. If the car was raised for the draining operation, now lower it to the ground.

Refilling

6 There is no filler plug on this transmission, so the sensor in the top of the transmission housing has to be removed and the fluid is poured in through the sensor mounting hole. To improve access to the sensor, remove the battery as described in Chapter 5A, Section 3.

7 Locate the turbine revolution sensor on top of the transmission and wipe clean the area around the sensor **(see illustration)**.

Disconnect the wiring connector, and then undo the retaining bolt and remove the sensor from the top of the transmission housing. Nissan recommend that the O-ring and retaining bolt be renewed when refitting.

8 Carefully refill the transmission with the correct amount of oil as specified at the beginning of this Chapter. Refer to end of *Weekly Checks* for the specified type of oil used

9 Fit the new O-ring seal to the sensor, and then refit the sensor to the top of the transmission housing, tightening the new bolt to the specified torque.

10 Refit the battery as described in Chapter 5A, Section 3.

11 Take the vehicle on a short journey to warm the transmission up to normal operating temperature.

12 On your return, check the transmission fluid level as described in Chapter 1A, Section 20.

3 Selector cable – adjustment

1 Position the gear selector lever inside the vehicle in the Park (P) position.

2 Remove the battery as described in Chapter 5A, Section 3.

3 Using a screwdriver to support the lever on top of the Park/Neutral Position (PNP) switch, undo the retaining nut and disconnect the selector cable from the lever **(see illustrations)**. The lever has an elongated hole to allow for adjustment of the cable.

Caution: Support the lever when turning the selector cable retaining nut, do not apply any force to the switch as this will cause damage.

4 Make sure the lever on the PNP switch is in the Park (P) position, and then refit the selector cable and tighten the nut to the specified torque setting. Make sure the lever is supported when tightening the nut, as damage to the switch may occur.

5 Refit the battery as described in Chapter 5A, Section 3.

6 Check the operation of the selector lever,

2.7 Turbine revolution sensor location (arrowed)

3.3a Support the lever with a screwdriver …

3.3b … and disconnect the selector cable

ensuring that it moves smoothly and easily, without any sign of the cable binding.

7 Also make the following checks:

a) *Make sure the gear selector can be moved out of Park, when the brake pedal is depressed.*

b) *Check that the gear selector lever cannot be moved out of Park, when the brake pedal is not applied.*

c) *Check the engine only starts in Park and Neutral positions.*

d) *Check that the position of the gear selector lever, matches the position shown by the indicator on the trim panel.*

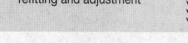

4 Shift lock system – removal, refitting and adjustment

Key interlock cable

1 Move the selector lever to Park (P) position.

2 Disconnect the battery negative terminal (refer to *Disconnecting the battery* in the Reference Chapter).

3 Remove the centre console as described in Chapter 11, Section 25.

4 Release the locking clip on the key interlock cable, then release the outer cable from the front of the gear lever mounting bracket, and withdraw the cable to one side **(see illustrations)**.

5 Undo the retaining screws and remove the steering column shrouds, as described in Chapter 11, Section 26.

6 The other end of the key interlock cable is fitted to the rear of the ignition switch **(see illustration)**.

7 Withdraw the securing clip by sliding it downwards, and then withdraw the cable from the rear of the ignition switch **(see illustrations)**.

8 Working along the cable, release it from any securing clips and withdraw it from behind the facia, taking care not to bend or twist the cable **(see illustration)**.

9 Refitting is a reversal of the removal procedure.

Cable adjustment

10 Move the selector lever to Park (P) position.

4.4a Release the locking clip (arrowed) ...

4.4b ... and unclip the outer cable

4.6 Interlock cable is fitted to the rear of the ignition barrel

4.7a Withdraw the locking clip ...

4.7b ... and disengage the cable

4.8 Unclip the cable from the bracket on the facia (arrowed)

11 Remove the centre console as described in Chapter 11, Section 25.

12 Unclip the plastic cup from the bottom of the gear knob and remove the retaining clip, then withdraw the gear knob and plastic cup from the top of the gear lever **(see illustrations)**.

13 Slide the white plastic collar forwards to

4.12a Unclip the plastic cup ...

4.12b ... remove the securing clip ...

4.12c ... and then withdraw the gear knob

4.13 Slide the locking collar forwards in the direction of the arrow

4.14a Press down on the gear lever detent rod (arrowed) …

4.14b … and then slide the locking collar in the direction of the arrow…

4.14c … until the collar locks into place

4.17a Location of the shift lock solenoid (arrowed)

4.17b Disconnect the wiring connector (arrowed)

allow the interlock rod and interlock cable to move independently of each other **(see illustration)**.

14 Press down on the detent rod in the top of the gear selector lever, whilst holding the detent rod fully down, slide the white plastic locking collar back into place to secure the interlock rod and interlock cable together **(see illustrations)**.

15 Refitting is a reversal of the removal procedure.

Shift lock solenoid

16 Remove the centre console as described in Chapter 11, Section 25.

17 The shift lock solenoid is located in the right-hand side of the selector housing disconnect the wiring connector and unclip the

solenoid from the housing **(see illustrations)**.

18 If the gear selector lever cannot be moved out of Park (P), a thin screwdriver can be inserted into the top of the selector panel to press down on the lock release button **(see illustration)**.

19 Refitting is a reversal of the removal procedure.

5   Selector cable – removal and refitting

Removal

1 Firmly apply the handbrake, and then jack up the front of the vehicle and support it securely on axle stands (see *Jacking and*

vehicle support). Position the selector lever in the P position.

2 Remove the battery as described in Chapter 5A, Section 3.

3 Remove the centre console as described in Chapter 11, Section 25.

4 Unclip the selector cable ball joint from the lower part of the gear lever (noting its fitted position), then release the outer cable from the front of the gear lever mounting bracket, and withdraw the cable from the gear selector assembly **(see illustrations)**.

5 To make access to the selector cable on top of the transmission housing easier, remove the air cleaner housing, as described in Chapter 4A, Section 2 or Chapter 4B, Section 2.

6 Undo the retaining bolt and move the coolant pipe bracket to one side **(see illustration)**. If

4.18 Using a thin screwdriver to release the selector lever

5.4a Unclip the selector cable ball joint …

5.4b … and then release the outer cable

5.6 Undo the coolant pipe bracket securing bolt (arrowed)

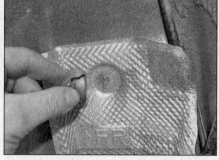

5.10 Remove the heat shield retaining clips ...

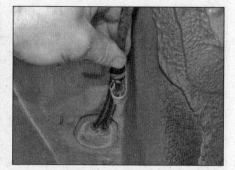

5.11 ... and release the gear selector cable from the bracket

required, to make access to the selector cable easier, drain the cooling system and remove the coolant hoses from the metal coolant pipe bracket.

7 Using a screwdriver to support the lever on top of the Park/Neutral Position (PNP) switch, undo the retaining nut and disconnect the selector cable from the lever **(see illustrations 3.3a and 3.3b)**. The lever has an elongated hole to allow for adjustment of the cable, note its fitted position for refitting.

Caution: Support the lever when turning the selector cable retaining nut, do not apply any force to the switch as this will cause damage.

8 Pull out the locking plate from the outer cable and withdraw the outer cables from the transmission mounting bracket.

9 Firmly apply the handbrake, and then

jack up the front of the vehicle and support it securely on axle stands (see *Jacking and vehicle support*).

10 From underneath the vehicle, release the fasteners and remove the heat shield from under the centre tunnel of the vehicle **(see illustration)**. Note depending on model, it may be necessary to remove the exhaust front pipe or prop shaft (4WD models) to give better access to the heat shield.

11 Unclip the outer cable from the mounting bracket on the underside of the vehicle, and then release the rubber grommet from the floor panel and withdraw the cable from under the vehicle **(see illustration)**.

12 Inspect all the gear linkage components for signs of wear or damage, paying particular attention to the cables, renew worn components as necessary.

Refitting

13 Refitting is a reversal of the removal procedure, applying a smear of multipurpose grease to the gear lever pivot ball and bushes. Tighten all the linkage nuts and bolts to their specified torque settings (where given) and adjust the selector cable, as described in Section 3.

6 Selector lever assembly – removal and refitting

Removal

1 Firmly apply the handbrake, and then jack up the front of the vehicle and support it securely on axle stands (see *Jacking and vehicle support*). Position the selector lever in the P position.

2 Disconnect the battery negative terminal (refer to *Disconnecting the battery* in the Reference Chapter).

3 Remove the centre console as described in Chapter 11, Section 25.

4 Move the selector lever to Neutral (N) position.

5 If the gear knob needs to be removed, unclip the plastic cup from the bottom of the gear knob and remove the retaining clip **(see illustrations 4.12a, 4.12b and 4.12c)**.

6 Unclip the wiring and remove the gear selector illumination light bulb from the right-hand side of the gear selector assembly **(see illustrations)**.

7 Release the retaining clips at each side of the housing and remove the selector trim panel from the top of the gear lever assembly **(see illustrations)**.

8 Unclip the selector cable ball joint from the lower part of the gear lever (noting its fitted position), then release the outer cable from the front of the gear lever mounting bracket, and then move the cable to one side **(see illustrations 5.4a and 5.4b)**.

9 Release the locking clip on the key interlock cable, then release the outer cable from the front of the gear lever mounting bracket,

6.6a Unclip the wiring from the gear lever housing ...

6.6b ... and remove the gear selector bulb holder

6.7a Release the retaining clips (arrowed) ...

6.7b ... and remove the selector trim panel

6.10 Disconnect the wiring connector (arrowed)

6.11 Gear lever assembly mounting bolts – one side shown

and withdraw the cable to one side **(see illustrations 4.4a and 4.4b)**.

10 Disconnect the wiring loom connector at the rear of the gear lever mounting bracket **(see illustration)**.

11 With the cables and wiring disconnected, undo the four mounting bolts from the bottom of the gear selector housing, and manoeuvre the gear lever assembly out of position **(see illustration)**.

12 If required the shift lock solenoid can be removed from the right-hand side of the selector housing, disconnect the wiring connector and unclip the solenoid from the housing, see Section 4.

Refitting

13 The selector lever assembly is refitted by a reversal of the removal procedure, bearing in mind the following points:

a) Make sure the selector lever assembly is tightened down securely.

b) Adjust the key interlock cable as described in Section 4.

c) Refit the selector cable as described in Section 5.

d) Check the operation of the selector lever.

e) Refit the centre console as described in Chapter 11, Section 25.

f) On completion, road test the vehicle to check gear selection is correct.

7 Oil seals – renewal

Driveshaft seals

1 Refer to the information given in Chapter 7A, Section 4, noting that the seals must be correctly positioned.

Selector shaft seal

2 Renewal of the selector shaft seal is complex task, requiring much dismantling of the transmission, and should therefore be entrusted to a Nissan dealer.

Torque converter seal

3 Remove the transmission unit as described in Section 11.

4 Carefully slide the torque converter off the transmission shaft whilst being prepared for fluid spillage.

5 Note the correct fitted position of the O-ring seal on the transmission side of the torque converter and then remove, taking care not to mark the housing.

6 Remove all traces of dirt from the area around the oil seal aperture. Lubricate the seal with some clean transmission fluid, and then fit the new O-ring seal.

7 Engage the two slots on the rear of the

torque converter with the transmission dog gears and slide it into position, taking care not to damage the oil seal.

8 Refit the transmission unit as described in Section 11.

8 Electronic control unit (ECU) and sensors

Electronic Control Unit (ECU)

Note: *The automatic transmission ECU is electronically coded for the vehicle to which it is fitted; therefore new units are supplied without a code. If the ECU is being removed to enable a new unit to be fitted, a Nissan dealer must program the new unit with the information from the old ECU.*

1 The ECU is located in the left-hand side of the engine compartment, in front of the battery **(see illustration)**.

2 First disconnect the battery negative lead (refer to *Disconnecting the battery* in the Reference Section).

3 To gain better access release the retaining clips, and then remove the air intake ducting from the front left-hand side of the engine compartment **(see illustration)**.

4 Disconnect the wiring from the control unit **(see illustration)**.

8.1 Location of the transmission ECU

8.3 Remove the air intake ducting

8.4 Disconnect the ECU wiring connector

8.5 ECU is secured to mounting bracket by three nuts

8.7 Location of the vehicle speed sensor (arrowed)

8.11 Disconnect the sensor wiring connector

5 Unscrew the mounting nuts/bolts and remove the control unit from the mounting bracket **(see illustration)**.

6 Refitting is a reversal of removal.

Vehicle speed sensor

Note: *The sensor, O-ring seal and retaining bolt must not be re-used. If the sensor is removed from the transmission housing, then a new sensor, O-ring seal and retaining bolt must be purchased.*

7 The vehicle speed sensor is located in the top of the transmission casing **(see illustration)**.

8 Remove the battery as described in Chapter 5A, Section 3.

9 To make access easier, undo the retaining bolts and remove the engine management ECU and mounting bracket from the rear of the battery tray as described in Chapter 4A, Section 10 or Chapter 4B, Section 8.

10 Remove all traces of dirt from around the sensor before proceeding.

11 Disconnect the wiring connector from the sensor, undo the retaining bolt and remove the sensor **(see illustration)**.

12 Refitting is a reversal of removal, using a new sensor, O-ring and retaining bolt.

Turbine revolution sensor

Note: *The sensor, O-ring seal and retaining bolt must not be re-used. If the sensor is removed from the transmission housing, then a new sensor, O-ring seal and retaining bolt must be purchased.*

13 The turbine revolution sensor is located

in the top of the transmission casing **(see illustration 7.7)**.

14 Remove the battery as described in Chapter 5A, Section 3.

15 Remove all traces of dirt from around the sensor before proceeding.

16 Disconnect the wiring connector from the sensor, undo the retaining bolt and remove the sensor **(see illustration)**.

17 Refitting is a reversal of removal, using a new sensor, O-ring and retaining bolt.

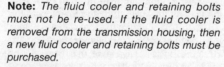

9 Fluid cooler – removal and refitting

Note: *The fluid cooler and retaining bolts must not be re-used. If the fluid cooler is removed from the transmission housing, then a new fluid cooler and retaining bolts must be purchased.*

Removal

1 The fluid cooler is located on the rear left-hand side of the transmission, above the driveshaft **(see illustration)**.

2 To gain access to the fluid cooler, chock the rear wheels jack up the front of the vehicle and support it on axle stands (see *Jacking and vehicle support*). Remove the left-hand front road wheel and inner wheel arch liner.

3 Remove all traces of dirt from around the fluid cooler before proceeding.

4 Using a hose clamp or similar, clamp both

the fluid cooler coolant hoses to minimise coolant loss during subsequent operations.

5 Release the retaining clips, and disconnect both coolant hoses from the fluid cooler – be prepared for some coolant spillage **(see illustration)**. Wash off any spilt coolant immediately with cold water, and dry the surrounding area before proceeding further.

6 Slacken and remove the fluid cooler retaining bolts, and remove the cooler from the transmission.

Caution: Be careful not to allow dirt into the transmission unit during this procedure.

Refitting

7 Locate the new fluid cooler on the transmission housing, ensure the cooler is correctly positioned, and then tighten the new retaining bolts.

8 Reconnect the coolant hoses to the fluid cooler, and secure them in position with their retaining clips. Remove the hose clamps.

9 Refit the wheel arch liner and roadwheel as applicable.

10 Top-up the cooling system as described in *Weekly checks* and check the transmission unit fluid level as described in Chapter 1A, Section 20.

10 Park/Neutral (PNP) switch – removal and refitting

Note: *The PNP switch, lever, washer, nut and retaining bolts must not be re-used. If the*

8.16 Disconnect the revolution sensor wiring connector

9.1 Location of the transmission fluid cooler (arrowed)

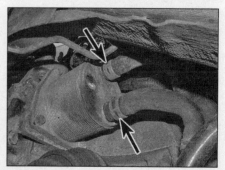

9.5 Disconnect the hoses (arrowed) from the cooler

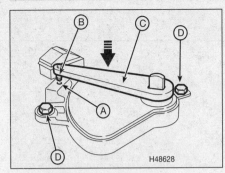

10.0 Switch resetting special tool

A) Adjustment setting hole
B) Locking pin on end of tool
C) Special tool
D) Switch securing bolts

PNP switch is removed from the transmission housing, then a switch, lever, washer, nut and retaining bolts must be purchased.
Note: *When refitting the PNP switch, Nissan use a special tool to reset the switch and lever in the correct position. Once the lever has been removed the special tool fits over the flats on the lever stud, and then the other end has a locating pin that aligns with the hole in the switch assembly* (see illustration).

Removal

1 Position the gear selector lever inside the vehicle in the Neutral (N) position.
2 Remove the battery as described in Chapter 5A, Section 3.
3 Using a screwdriver to support the lever on top of the Park/Neutral Position (PNP) switch, undo the retaining nut and disconnect the selector cable from the lever (see illustrations 3.3a and 3.3b). Note its fitted position for refitting.
Caution: Support the lever when turning the selector cable retaining nut, do not apply any force to the switch as this will cause damage.
4 Release the locking clip and disconnect the wiring connector from the switch (see illustration).
5 Make alignment marks on the transmission and switch to aid refitting, then undo the retaining nut and remove the lever from the stud through the switch (see illustration).

10.9 Hole for resetting the switch (arrowed), when using special tool

Make sure the lever is supported when removing the nut, as damage to the switch may occur.
6 Make alignment marks on the transmission and switch to aid refitting, then undo the two retaining bolts and remove Park/ Neutral Position switch from the top of the transmission housing.

Refitting

7 Make sure the gear selector lever inside the vehicle is still in the Neutral (N) position.
8 Refit the new Park/Neutral Position switch to the top of the transmission housing, fit the new retaining bolts, but do not fully tighten at this point.
9 If the Nissan special tool (SST: KV31300QAD) is available (see illustration 10.0), fit it over the flats on the lever stud, and then locate the pin on the other end of the tool with the hole in the switch assembly (see illustration).
10 If the tool is not available, use the markings made on removal to align the new switch and lever.
11 Refit the new lever to the PNP switch, fit the new washer and then tighten the new nut to the specified torque setting. Make sure the lever is supported when tightening the nut, as damage to the switch may occur.
12 With the switch correctly positioned, tighten the mounting bolts to their specified torque setting.
13 Reconnect the wiring connector to the Switch.
14 Refit the selector cable to the switch lever and adjust as described in Section 3.

11.1 Remove the inner wing panel

10.4 Disconnect the switch wiring connector

10.5 Undo the lever retaining nut (arrowed)

15 If required, have your local Nissan dealer do the final adjustments on the switch, using their special tools.

11 Automatic transmission – removal and refitting

Note: *This Section describes the removal of the transmission leaving the engine in position in the car. Alternatively the engine and transmission can be removed together, as described in Chapter 2E, and then separated on the bench.*

Removal

1 Firmly apply the handbrake, and then jack up the front of the vehicle and support it securely on axle stands (see *Jacking and vehicle support*). Remove both front roadwheels. Undo the retaining screws, and remove the plastic undershields from beneath the engine/ transmission, and the covers from underneath both wheel arches (see illustration).
2 Drain the transmission oil as described in Section 2, then refit the drain and filler/level plugs and tighten them to their specified torque settings.
3 Drain the cooling system as described in Chapter 1A, Section 27 or Chapter 1B, Section 29.
4 Remove the battery as described in Chapter 5A, Section 3.
5 Remove the front subframe as described in Chapter 10, Section 12.
6 Remove the starter motor as described in Chapter 5A, Section 8.
7 Remove the air cleaner assembly as described in Chapter 4A, Section 2 or Chapter 4B, Section 2.
8 Remove the exhaust system front pipe as described in Chapter 4A, Section 13 or Chapter 4B, Section 17.
9 On 4WD models, remove the transfer gearbox as described in Chapter 7C, Section 3.
10 Release the gear selector cable from the transmission as described in Section 3.
11 Disconnect the wiring connector from the Park/Neutral Position switch on top of the transmission (see illustration 10.4).
12 Unscrew the main electrical bayonet

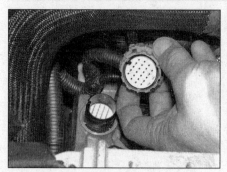

11.12 Unscrew the main wiring loom connector

11.13 Disconnect the wiring connectors from sensors (arrowed)

11.14 Using a dummy shaft in the differential

connector from the top of the transmission, at the front edge **(see illustration)**.

13 Disconnect the wiring connectors from the vehicle speed and turbine revolution sensors on top of the transmission **(see illustration)**.

14 Working as described in Chapter 8, Section 2, remove the two front driveshafts from the transmission. Note that there is no need to unscrew the driveshaft retaining nuts – each driveshaft can be left secured to the hub. But take care and support the driveshafts, to avoid placing any strain on the driveshaft joints or gaiters. With the driveshafts out of the transmission, insert a dummy shaft into differential recess **(see illustration)**.

15 Undo the retaining bolt and disconnect the earth cable from the left-hand end of the transmission **(see illustration)**.

16 Disconnect the coolant hoses from the fluid cooler on the rear of the transmission. Undo the retaining bolt and disconnect the coolant hose bracket from the rear of the transmssion **(see illustrations)**.

17 Work around the transmission and free the wiring loom from any relevant retaining clips, and position the wiring clear of the transmission.

18 Make sure the breather pipe on top of the transmission housing is not secured to any other components. This does not have to be completely removed and left across the top of the transmission.

19 Place a jack with interposed block of wood beneath the engine, to take the weight of the engine **(see illustration)**. Alternatively, attach a hoist or support bar to the engine and take the weight of the engine.

20 Also place a jack and block of wood beneath the transmission, and raise the jack to take the weight of the transmission.

21 Access to the torque converter retaining bolts is gained through the starter motor aperture at the rear of the cylinder block. Use a socket and extension bar to rotate the crankshaft pulley to align the first bolt with the aperture. Unscrew the nut then rotate the crankshaft 90º. Remove the second nut/bolt then rotate the crankshaft another 90º and unscrew the third bolt and then finally another 90º to remove the final bolt and discard all four bolts; new ones must be used on refitting.

22 Slacken and remove the mounting bolts, then remove the transmission mounting **(see illustration)**. Refer to the relevant part of Chapter 2A, B, C or D for further information on engine/transmission mounting removal.

23 Undo the three bolts and remove the mounting bracket from the top of the

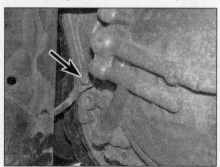

11.15 Undo the earth cable retaining bolt (arrowed)

transmission.

24 With the jack positioned beneath the transmission taking the weight, slacken and remove the remaining bolts securing the transmission housing to the engine. Note the correct fitted positions of each bolt (and the relevant brackets) as they are removed, to use as a reference on refitting – the bolts are of different lengths. Note that it may be necessary to raise the transmission slightly to gain access to the lower bolts.

25 Make a final check that all necessary components have been disconnected, and are positioned clear of the transmission so that they will not hinder the removal procedure.

26 Move the trolley jack and transmission to the left to free it from its locating dowels. Keep the transmission fully supported until the input shaft is free of the engine.

27 Once the transmission is free, lower the jack and manoeuvre the unit out from under the car. If

11.16a Disconnect the coolant hoses ...

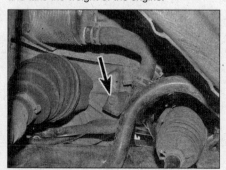

11.16b ... and undo the hose bracket securing bolt (arrowed)

11.19 Support the transmission with a trolley jack

11.22 Remove the transmission mounting

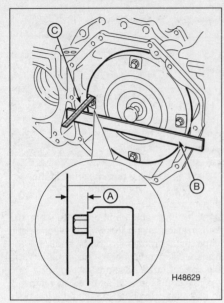

11.28a Measurement from torque converter to transmission surface

A = at least 20.4mm

they are loose, remove the locating dowels from the transmission or engine, and keep them in a safe place. Make sure the torque converter stays in place in the bell housing as the transmission is removed.

Refitting

28 The transmission is refitted by a reversal

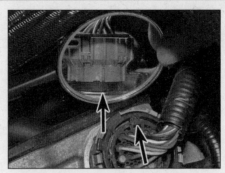

11.28b Make sure the markings on the connector align (viewed in mirror)

of the removal procedure, bearing in mind the following points:

a) *Prior to installing the transmission, ensure that the torque converter is correctly engaged with the transmission. This can be checked by measuring the distance from the torque converter to the transmission mating surface; if the converter is correctly seated, this distance will be at least 20.4 mm* **(see illustration).**

b) *When refitting the main wiring loom bayonet connector, turn the locking ring until the arrow head markings on the connector align with each other* **(see illustration).**

c) *Ensure that the locating dowels are correctly positioned prior to installation.*

d) *Align the torque converter studs with*

the driveplate holes then engage the transmission unit with the engine.

e) *Insert the transmission-to-engine bolts into their original locations, as noted on removal. Tighten all nuts and bolts to the specified torque (where given).*

f) *Refit the driveshafts as described in Chapter 8, Section 2. If required renew the driveshaft oil seals using the information given in Chapter 7A, Section 4.*

g) *Adjust the selector cable as described in Sections 3 of this Chapter.*

h) *Refit the gearchange cables as described in Section 5, and check operation.*

i) *On completion, refill the transmission with the specified type and quantity of lubricant as described in Section 2.*

12 Automatic transmission overhaul – general information

In the event of a fault occurring on the transmission, it is first necessary to determine whether it is of an electrical, mechanical or hydraulic nature, and to do this, special test equipment is required. It is therefore essential to have the work carried out by a Nissan dealer if a transmission fault is suspected.

Do not remove the transmission from the car for possible repair before professional fault diagnosis has been carried out, since most tests require the transmission to be in the vehicle.

Chapter 7 Part C:
Transfer gearbox and final drive – 4WD models

Contents

Degrees of difficulty

| **Easy,** suitable for novice with little experience | 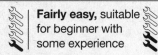 | **Fairly easy,** suitable for beginner with some experience | | **Fairly difficult,** suitable for competent DIY mechanic | | **Difficult,** suitable for experienced DIY mechanic | | **Very difficult,** suitable for expert DIY or professional | |

Specifications

Transfer gearbox

Model	TY30A
Gear ratio	0.656
Drive pinion (number of teeth)	32
Drive gear (number of teeth)	21
Flange runout limit	0.1 mm
Backlash (ring gear to drive gear)	0.13 to 0.19 mm
Drive pinion bearing pre-load	0.52 to 1.01 Nm
Total pre-load:	
With all oil seals fitted	0.76 to 0.96 Nm
Without adaptor case oil seal fitted	0.55 to 0.75 Nm

Final drive

Model	R145
Gear ratio	2.466
Drive pinion (number of teeth)	15
Drive gear (number of teeth)	37
Flange runout limit	0.13 mm
Drive gear (back face runout)	0.05 mm
Backlash (drive gear to drive pinion gear)	0.10 to 0.15 mm
Pre-load:	
Pinion bearing	0.69 to 1.18 Nm
Side bearing	0.64 to 0.98 Nm
Side bearing to pinion bearing (total pre-load)	1.33 to 2.16 Nm
Drive pinion adjustment spacer type	Collapsible

Lubrication

Capacity:	
Transfer gearbox	0.36 litre
Final drive	0.55 litre
Recommended oil type	See *Lubricants and fluids*

Torque wrench settings

	Nm	lbf ft
Electric controlled coupling mounting bolts.....................	16	12
Final drive:		
Filler/level plug..	35	26
Drain plug..	35	26
Transfer box:		
Filler/level plug..	35	26
Drain plug..	35	26
Transfer box-to-transmission mounting bolts	44	32
Transfer box mounting bracket bolts:		
Bracket-to-transfer gearbox..............................	48	35
Bracket-to-cylinder block................................	50	37
Transfer gearbox pinion retaining nut * (collapsible washer)	127 to 294	94 to 216
Final drive mounting bolts:		
Front bolts...	63	46
Rear nut..	78	58
Final drive front flange locknut: *		
2.0 litre (MR20DE) petrol	111	82
2.0 litre (MR20DE) petrol (+2)...........................	140	103
2.0 litre (M9R) diesel....................................	140	103
Propeller shaft bolts *....................................	49	36

* Note: *Use new bolts/nuts.*

1 General information

The four-wheel drive (4WD) system controls the distribution of drive between the front and rear wheels, according to signals from various sensors. The 4WD control unit, which is located behind the glovebox, transmits and receives signals from the ABS, Engine Control Module and Steering angle sensors.

AUTO Mode

The electronic control module allows optimal distribution of torque to the front and rear wheels to match the road conditions. Four-wheel drive mode makes stable driving, with no wheel spin on slippery surfaces. On road surfaces that do not require 4WD, AUTO mode contributes to improve fuel economy by putting more drive power to the front wheels. The sensors detect tight cornering or heavy braking; this then puts more torque to the rear wheels.

LOCK Mode

In this mode the front and rear wheels are fixed, ensuring stable driving when climbing slopes. It will switch to AUTO mode if the vehicle speed increases. If the vehicle speed then decreases, the vehicle automatically returns to direct four-wheel drive. If there is a significant difference in tyre pressures, full vehicle speed will not be available. LOCK mode may also be prohibited, or speeds at which LOCK mode is enabled may be restricted.

2 Transfer gearbox – draining and refilling

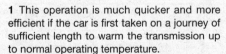

1 This operation is much quicker and more efficient if the car is first taken on a journey of sufficient length to warm the transmission up to normal operating temperature.

2 Park the car on level ground, switch off the ignition and apply the handbrake firmly. For improved access, jack up the front of the car and support it securely on axle stands (see *Jacking and vehicle support*). Note that the car must be lowered to the ground and be level to ensure accuracy when refilling and checking the oil level.

3 Undo the retaining bolts and remove the plastic undershield from below the engine/transmission.

4 Wipe clean the area around the filler/level plug, which is screwed into the right-hand side of the transfer gearbox casing, above the driveshaft **(see illustration)**.

5 Remove the oil filler/level plug, be prepared for some oil spillage as the plug is removed.

6 Position a suitable container under the drain plug, which is situated at the lower rear of the transmission differential housing **(see illustration)**. Make sure the correct plug is removed from the lower part of the casing, as there are two plugs fitted. The plug nearest the right-hand side of the casing is the drain plug; this also has a sealing washer that will need to be renewed if the plug is removed

7 Remove the drain plug and allow the oil to drain completely into the container. If the oil is hot, take precautions against scalding. Clean both the filler/level and the drain plug, discard the sealing washer, as a new one will be required on refitting.

8 When the oil has finished draining, clean the drain plug threads and those of the transfer gearbox casing, then fit the new sealing washer and refit the drain plug, tightening it to the specified torque wrench setting. If the car was raised for the draining operation, lower it to the ground, to make sure it is level.

9 Refilling the transfer gearbox is an awkward operation. Above all, allow plenty of time for the oil level to settle properly before checking it. Note that the car must be parked on flat level ground when checking the oil level.

10 Refill the transfer gearbox with the exact amount of the specified type of oil, then check the oil level as described in Chapter 1A, Section 23 or Chapter 1B, Section 25; if the correct amount was poured into the transfer gearbox, and a large amount flows out on checking the level, refit the filler/level plug and take the car on a short journey so that the new oil is distributed fully around the transfer

2.4 Filler/level plug location (arrowed)

2.6 Drain plug location (arrowed)

3.4 Undo the propeller shaft front flange bolts

3.5 Driveshaft support mounting bracket

3.6 Undo the retaining bolts (arrowed)

gearbox components, then check the level again on your return.

11 When the level is correct, fit a new sealing washer and refit the filler/level plug, tightening it to the specified torque wrench setting. Wash off any spilt oil.

3 Transfer gearbox –
removal and refitting

Removal

1 Firmly apply the handbrake, and then jack up the front of the vehicle and support it securely on axle stands (see *Jacking and vehicle support*).

2 Drain the transfer gearbox oil, as described in Section 2.

3 Remove the exhaust front pipe and exhaust manifold.

4 Make alignment marks on the propeller shaft and the flange, to make sure that it is fitted in the same position on refitting. Undo the four retaining bolts and disconnect the front of the propeller shaft from the flange on the rear of the transfer gearbox **(see illustration)**. Discard the retaining bolts, as new ones will be required for refitting.

5 Remove the right-hand side driveshaft, as described in Chapter 8, Section 2. Then undo the retaining bolts and remove the driveshaft support mounting bracket form the rear of the cylinder block **(see illustration)**.

6 On automatic transmission models, undo the retaining bolt and disconnect the hose mounting bracket from the transfer gearbox mounting bracket **(see illustration)**.

7 On 2.0 litre diesel engines, undo the retaining bolts and remove the mounting bracket from the right-hand side of the transfer gearbox **(see illustration)**.

8 To make access to the transfer gearbox easier, undo the retaining bolts and remove the lower rear torque arm (mounting link arm), from the subframe **(see illustration)**. Insert a block of wood between the engine and the subframe, to make more room for removal of the transfer gearbox. Take care not to put any stress on any other components when doing this.

9 Undo the transfer gearbox securing bolts and withdraw it from the right-hand side of the transmission. Note, there are five bolts securing the transfer gearbox to the transmission; four are bolted from the transfer gearbox side into the transmission casing and one is bolted from the transmission side into the transfer gearbox.

10 Remove the O-ring seal from between the transfer gearbox and the transmission and discard it, as a new one will be required for refitting.

Refitting

11 Refitting is a reversal of the removal procedure, noting the following points.

a) *Make sure a new outer O-ring seal is fitted to the transfer gearbox before refitting.*

b) *Apply a small amount of multi-purpose grease, evenly to the seal before refitting to the transfer gearbox.*

c) *Fit new retaining bolts to the propeller shaft and tighten to the specified torque setting.*

d) *Align the marks made on removal, when refitting the propeller shaft.*

e) *When completed, refill the transfer gearbox oil, as described in Section 2.*

4 Transfer gearbox oil seals –
renewal

Note: *Although the seals in the adapter plate can be removed and refitted as described in this Section, Nissan recommend that the backlash, tooth contact, pre-load and flange*

3.7 Undo the mounting bracket retaining bolts (arrowed)

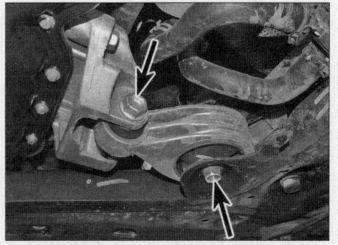

3.8 Remove the engine lower torque arm

runout should be checked if dismantled. Take the transfer gearbox to your local Nissan dealer or specialist to have this checked before refitting.

Note: *The only seal that can be renewed without any dismantling is the outer O-ring seal.*

1 Remove the transfer gearbox, as described in Section 3.

Adapter case O-ring seals

2 Remove the outer O-ring seal from the transfer gearbox and discard it, as a new one will be required for refitting.

3 Undo the five adapter plate securing bolts and withdraw it from the transfer gearbox. This may be a tight fit on the dowels, lightly tap the adapter plate with a plastic hammer to remove.

4 With the adapter plate removed, remove the inner O-ring seal from the inside the transfer gearbox and discard it, as a new one will be required for refitting.

5 Refitting is a reversal of the removal procedure, noting the following points. Make sure a new O-ring seals are fitted correctly to the transfer gearbox. Apply a small amount of multi-purpose grease, evenly to the seals before refitting to the transfer gearbox. When completed, refit the transfer gearbox, as described in Section 3.

Adapter case oil seals

6 There are also, inner and outer seals fitted to the centre of the adapter plate.

7 If not already done undo the five retaining bolts and remove the adapter plate from the transfer gearbox.

8 Note the fitted position of the seals, and then carefully lever them out from their position in the adapter plate. Use a large flat-bladed screwdriver, taking care not to damage the adapter plate.

9 Clean the seal housing in the adapter plate, and polish off any burrs or raised edges, which may have caused the seals to fail in the first place.

10 Apply a small amount of multi-purpose grease, evenly to the lips of the seals, and gear oil onto the outer circumference, before fitting them back to the adapter plate. Carefully ease the seals into position, taking care not to damage its sealing lip. Using a drift drive the seals into the adapter plate, in the position noted on removal. Take care not to damage the seal lips during fitting.

11 Refit the adapter plate and new O-ring seals, as described in paragraphs 2 to 5.

12 Refit the transfer gearbox, as described in Section 3.

5 Transfer gearbox – overhaul

Overhauling a transfer gearbox is a difficult and involved job for the DIY home mechanic. In addition to dismantling and

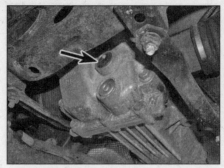

6.4 Filler/level plug location (arrowed)

reassembling many small parts, clearances must be precisely measured and, if necessary, changed by selecting shims and spacers. Internal components are also often difficult to obtain, and in many instances, extremely expensive. Because of this, if the transfer gearbox develops a fault or becomes noisy, the best course of action is to have the unit overhauled by a specialist repairer, or to obtain an exchange reconditioned unit.

Nevertheless, it is not impossible for the more experienced mechanic to overhaul the transfer gearbox, if the special tools are available, and the job is done in a deliberate step-by-step manner so that nothing is overlooked.

The tools necessary for an overhaul include internal and external circlip pliers, bearing pullers, a slide hammer, a set of pin punches, a dial test indicator, and possibly a hydraulic press. In addition, a large, sturdy workbench and a vice will be required.

During dismantling of the transfer gearbox, make careful notes of how each component is fitted, to make reassembly easier and accurate.

Before dismantling the transfer gearbox, it will help if you have some idea which area is malfunctioning. Certain problems can be closely related to specific areas in the transmission, which can make component examination and renewal easier.

6 Final drive – draining and refilling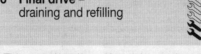

1 This operation is much quicker and more efficient if the car is first taken on a journey of sufficient length to warm the transmission up to normal operating temperature.

2 Park the car on level ground, switch off the ignition and apply the handbrake firmly. For improved access, jack up the rear of the car and support it securely on axle stands (see *Jacking and vehicle support*).

3 Note that the car must be lowered to the ground and be level to ensure accuracy when refilling and checking the oil level.

4 Wipe clean the area around the filler/level plug, which is screwed into the rear of the final drive casing **(see illustration)**.

6.6 Drain plug location (arrowed)

5 Remove the oil filler/level plug, be prepared for some oil spillage as the plug is removed.

6 Position a suitable container under the drain plug, which is situated at the lower rear of the final drive unit **(see illustration)**.

7 Remove the drain plug and allow the oil to drain completely into the container. If the oil is hot, take precautions against scalding. Clean both the filler/level and the drain plug, discard the sealing washer, as a new one will be required on refitting.

8 When the oil has finished draining, clean the drain plug threads and those of the final drive casing, then fit the new sealing washer and refit the drain plug, tightening it to the specified torque wrench setting. If the car was raised for the draining operation, lower it to the ground, to make sure it is level.

9 Refilling the final drive is an awkward operation. Above all, allow plenty of time for the oil level to settle properly before checking it. Note that the car must be parked on flat level ground when checking the oil level.

10 Refill the final drive with the exact amount of the specified type of oil, then check the oil level as described in Chapter 1A, Section 22 or Chapter 1B, Section 24; if the correct amount was poured into the final drive, and a large amount flows out on checking the level, refit the filler/level plug and take the car on a short journey so that the new oil is distributed fully around the final drive components, then check the level again on your return.

11 When the level is correct, fit a new sealing washer and refit the filler/level plug, tightening it to the specified torque wrench setting. Wash off any spilt oil.

7 Final drive – removal and refitting

Removal

1 Firmly apply the handbrake, and then jack up the rear of the vehicle and support it securely on axle stands (see *Jacking and vehicle support*).

2 Drain the final drive unit, as described in Section 6.

3 Undo the four retaining bolts and disconnect the rear of the propeller shaft from the flange

7.3 Undo the propeller shaft rear flange bolts

7.5 Disconnect the wiring connector (arrowed)

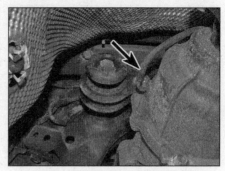

7.6 Disconnect the breather pipe (arrowed)

on the final drive flange **(see illustration)**. Make alignment marks on the propeller shaft and the flange to make sure that it is fitted in the same position on refitting. Discard the retaining bolts, as new ones will be required for refitting.

4 Working as described in Chapter 8, Section 2, remove both rear driveshafts from the final drive unit.

5 Disconnect the wiring connector to the coupling, then undo the retaining bolt and move the wiring loom bracket to one side **(see illustration)**.

6 Disconnect the breather pipe from the right-hand side of the coupling and move it to one side **(see illustration)**.

7 Place a jack with interposed block of wood beneath the final drive unit, to take the weight.

8 Slacken and remove the two front upper mounting bolts, and then undo the rear mounting nut **(see illustrations)**.

9 Support the final drive unit on the trolley jack, and then lower it down and out from under the vehicle. As the final drive is lowered, disconnect the breather hose from the top of the unit at the rear; note its fitted position for refitting.

Refitting

10 Refitting is a reversal of the removal procedure, noting the following points.
a) Make sure the electric coupling wiring connector is secure.
b) Make sure breather pipes are fitted correctly and not trapped.

7.8a Undo the front mounting bolts (arrowed) ...

c) Fit new retaining bolts to the propeller shaft.
d) Tighten bolts to the specified torque setting, where given.
e) Align the marks made on removal, when refitting the propeller shaft.
f) When completed, refill the final drive unit, as described in Section 6.

8 Final drive oil seals – renewal

Front (electric coupling) oil seal

1 Firmly apply the handbrake, and then jack up the rear of the vehicle and support it securely on axle stands (see *Jacking and vehicle support*).

2 Undo the four retaining bolts and disconnect the rear of the propeller shaft from the flange on the final drive flange **(see illustration 7.3)**. Make alignment marks on the propeller shaft and the flange to make sure that it is fitted in the same position on refitting.

3 Use a length of bar, bolted to two of the holes in the flange, hold the flange on the front of the final drive unit in place, and then undo the flange lock nut. Make alignment marks on the flange and the shaft to make sure that it is fitted in the same position on refitting. Discard the locknut, as a new one will be required on refitting.

4 With the flange removed, note the fitted position of the seal, and then carefully lever it out from the front of the housing. Use a large

7.8b ... and the rear mounting nut (arrowed)

flat-bladed screwdriver, taking care not to damage the casing.

5 Clean the seal housing in the front of the final drive unit, and polish off any burrs or raised edges, which may have caused the seal to fail in the first place.

6 Apply a small amount of multi-purpose grease; evenly to the lips of the seal, and gear oil onto the outer circumference, before fitting the seal back to the housing. Making sure the seal is sitting square in the housing, carefully ease it into position, taking care not to damage its sealing lip. Using a drift drive the seal into the adapter plate, in the position noted on removal. Take care not to damage the seal lips during fitting.

7 Refitting is a reversal of the removal procedure, noting the following points.
a) Align the marks made on removal, when refitting the flange to the shaft.
b) Fit a new locknut to the flange and tighten to the specified torque setting.
c) Align the marks made on removal, when refitting the propeller shaft.
d) When completed, if required, refill the final drive unit, as described in Section 6.

Side (driveshaft) oil seals

8 Firmly apply the handbrake, and then jack up the rear of the vehicle and support it securely on axle stands (see *Jacking and vehicle support*).

9 Drain the final drive unit oil as described in Section 6.

10 Working as described in Chapter 8, Section 2, free the inner end of the driveshaft from the final drive unit, and place it clear of the seal, noting that there is no need to completely remove the driveshaft; the driveshaft can be left secured to the outer hub. Support the driveshaft, to avoid placing any strain on the driveshaft joints or gaiters.

11 Before removing the seal, use a vernier gauge to check the seal depth in the transmission casing. This will give you the position of the seal for refitting.

12 Carefully prise the oil seal out of the final drive casing using a large flat-bladed screwdriver. Take care not to damage the casing as the seal is removed.

13 Remove all traces of dirt from the area around the oil seal aperture, then apply a

10.2 Four-wheel drive ECU location (arrowed)

10.3 Disconnect the wiring connector and undo the two retaining screws

11.6 Undo the six bolts from around the coupling housing

small amount of multi-purpose grease; evenly to the lips of the new seal, and gear oil onto the outer circumference, and locate it in its aperture.

14 Drive the seal squarely into position, using a suitable tubular drift (such as a socket), which bears only on the hard outer edge of the seal. Drive the seal into position until it is at the depth noted on removal.

15 Refit the driveshaft as described in Chapter 8, Section 2.

16 Refill the final drive with the specified quantity of oil, as described in Section 6. Refer to end of *Weekly Checks* for the specified type of oil used

9 Final drive – overhaul

Overhauling a final drive is a difficult and involved job for the DIY home mechanic. In addition to dismantling and reassembling many small parts, clearances must be precisely measured and, if necessary, changed by selecting shims and spacers. Internal components are also often difficult to obtain, and in many instances, extremely expensive. Because of this, if the final drive unit develops a fault or becomes noisy, the best course of action is to have the unit overhauled by a specialist repairer, or to obtain an exchange reconditioned unit.

Nevertheless, it is not impossible for the more experienced mechanic to overhaul the final drive unit, if the special tools are available, and the job is done in a deliberate step-by-step manner so that nothing is overlooked.

The tools necessary for an overhaul include internal and external circlip pliers, bearing pullers, a slide hammer, a set of pin punches, a dial test indicator, and possibly a hydraulic press. In addition, a large, sturdy workbench and a vice will be required.

During dismantling of the final drive unit, make careful notes of how each component is fitted, to make reassembly easier and accurate.

Before dismantling the final drive, it will help if you have some idea which area

is malfunctioning. Certain problems can be closely related to specific areas in the final drive, which can make component examination and renewal easier.

10 Four wheel drive (4WD) control unit – removal and refitting

Removal

1 Remove the glovebox, as described in Chapter 11, Section 26.

2 The control unit is located on a bracket, screwed to the facia rear crossmember **(see illustration)**.

3 Disconnect the wiring connector from the control unit, undo the two retaining screws, and then remove the control unit from the mounting bracket **(see illustration)**.

Refitting

4 Refitting is a reversal of the removal procedure, making sure the wiring connector is secure, and then refit the glovebox back into the facia panel.

11 Final drive electric controlled coupling – removal and refitting

Removal

1 Firmly apply the handbrake, and then jack up the rear of the vehicle and support it securely on axle stands (see *Jacking and vehicle support*).

2 Undo the four retaining bolts and disconnect the rear of the propeller shaft from the flange on the final drive flange **(see illustration 7.3)**. Make alignment marks on the propeller shaft and the flange to make sure that it is fitted in the same position on refitting.

3 Use a length of bar, bolted to two of the holes in the flange, hold the flange on the front of the final drive unit in place, and then undo the flange lock nut. Make alignment marks on the flange and the shaft to make sure that it is fitted in the same position on refitting. Discard the locknut, as a new one will be required on refitting.

4 Disconnect the wiring connector to the coupling, then undo the retaining bolt and move the wiring loom bracket to one side **(see illustration 7.5)**.

5 Disconnect the breather pipe from the right-hand side of the coupling and move it to one side **(see illustration 7.6)**.

6 Undo the six bolts from around the electric controlled coupling housing, then withdraw the housing, complete with electric coupling from the front of the final drive unit **(see illustration)**.

Refitting

7 Renew the oil seal in the front of the electric controlled coupling housing, as described in Section 8.

8 On refitting, fit the electric controlled coupling to the front of the final drive casing. Align the locating pin on the right-hand side of the coupling with the slot in the final drive casing. Also align the splines on the rear of the coupling with the final drive shaft, taking care not to damage the seal on the inside of the final drive unit.

9 Clean the contact face of the final drive casing and the coupling housing, then apply a bead of sealant around the coupling housing mating surface approx. 3mm diameter

10 Fit the coupling housing, making sure it is the correct way up (arrow facing up, at the bottom right-hand corner). As the housing is fitted over the electric coupling, make sure the wiring loom is located correctly in the housing to prevent it getting trapped.

11 Fit the housing bolts, starting with the ones at each side of the housing and carefully pull the housing into position over the electric controlled coupling. Tighten all the bolts evenly to their specified torque setting.

12 The remainder of the refitting procedure is the reversal of the removal procedure, noting the following points.

a) *Align the marks made on removal, when refitting the flange to the shaft.*

b) *Fit a new locknut to the flange and tighten to the specified torque setting.*

c) *Align the marks made on removal, when refitting the propeller shaft.*

d) *When completed, refill the final drive unit, as described in Section 6.*

Chapter 8
Driveshafts and propeller shafts

Contents

Degrees of difficulty

| **Easy,** suitable for novice with little experience | | **Fairly easy,** suitable for beginner with some experience | | **Fairly difficult,** suitable for competent DIY mechanic | | **Difficult,** suitable for experienced DIY mechanic | | **Very difficult,** suitable for expert DIY or professional | |

Specifications

General

Driveshaft type:

Front	Unequal length, solid steel shafts, splined to inner and outer constant velocity joints
Rear	Equal length, solid steel shafts, splined to inner and outer constant velocity joints
Propeller shaft type	Two piece variable length steel tube with centre joint

Overhaul

Lubricant type	Nissan grease supplied with gaiter repair kit

Front driveshafts

Lubricant quantity:

HR16DE:

Wheel end	100 to 120g
Transmission end	155 to 175g

MR20DE:

Wheel end	115 to 135g
Transmission end	200 to 220g

K9K:

Wheel end	115 to 135g
Transmission end	215 to 235g

M9R:

Wheel end	175 to 205g
Transmission end	165 to 175g

Front driveshafts (continued)

Driveshaft boot installed length:
  HR16DE:
    Wheel end .... 131.0 mm
    Transmission end:
      Left driveshaft .... 180.4 mm
      Right driveshaft .... 172.4 mm
  MR20DE:
    Wheel end .... 133.5 mm
    Transmission end:
      Left driveshaft (2WD manual transmission) .... 190.8 mm
      Left driveshaft (automatic transmission)................. 185.6 mm
      Left driveshaft (4WD manual transmission) .... 189.6 mm
      Right driveshaft .... 177.6 mm
  K9K:
    Wheel end .... 133.5 mm
    Transmission end:
      Left driveshaft .... 186.3 mm
      Right driveshaft .... 173.1 mm
  M9R:
    Wheel end .... 163.4 mm
    Transmission end:
      Left driveshaft .... 173.1 mm
      Right driveshaft .... 181.1 mm
Dynamic damper fitted position from wheel end bearing face:
  HR16DE .... 287 to 291 mm
  MR20DE:
    2WD – manual transmission.......................... 269 to 273 mm
    2WD – automatic transmission......................... 282 to 286 mm
    4WD – manual transmission.......................... 219 to 223 mm
    4WD – automatic transmission......................... 238 to 242 mm
  K9K .... 281 to 285 mm
  M9R:
    2WD – all models .... 229.5 to 235.5 mm
    4WD – manual transmission .... 194 to 200 mm
    4WD – automatic transmission .... 236.8 to 242.8 mm

Rear driveshafts (4WD models)

Lubricant quantity (all models):
  Wheel end .... 75 to 85g
  Final drive end .... 85 to 95g
Driveshaft boot installed length:
  Wheel end .... 90.2 to 92.2 mm
  Final drive end .... 125.8 to 127.8 mm

Propeller shaft (4WD models)

Model 3F SPL18-DOJ75
Joints:
  Front .... Universal joint (Cardan type)
  Centre .... Constant velocity joint (CVJ)
  Rear .... Universal joint (Cardan type)
Coupling method to:
  Transfer gearbox .... Flange type (4 x bolts)
  Final drive .... Flange type (4 x bolts)
Shaft length:
  2.0 litre (MR20DE) petrol engine:
    Front part of propeller shaft .... 1091 mm
    Rear part of propeller shaft (2 rows of seats).............. 831 mm
    Rear part of propeller shaft (3 rows of seats) .... 962 mm
  2.0 litre (M9R) diesel engine:
    Front part of propeller shaft .... 1106 mm
    Rear part of propeller shaft (2 rows of seats).............. 827 mm
    Rear part of propeller shaft (3 rows of seats) .... 962 mm
Shaft outer diameter:
  Front part of propeller shaft .... 57 mm
  Rear part of propeller shaft .... 70 mm
Propeller shaft runout.................................... 0.6 mm

Torque wrench settings

	Nm	lbf ft
Driveshaft front hub nut	125	92
Driveshaft rear hub nut	125	92
Right-hand front driveshaft retaining plate bolts	25	18
Right-hand front driveshaft centre bearing housing bolts:		
MR20DE	48	35
M9R	44	32
Propeller shaft front and rear flange bolts*	49	36
Propeller shaft centre bearing nuts*	45	33
Roadwheel nuts	113	83

New nut(s) must be used.

1 General information

2WD models

Drive is transmitted from the differential to the front wheels by means of two solid steel driveshafts of unequal length.

Both driveshafts are splined at their outer ends, to accept the wheel hubs, and are threaded so that each hub can be fastened to the driveshaft by a large nut and locked in position with a split pin. The inner end of each driveshaft is splined, to accept the differential sun gear.

Constant velocity (CV) joints are fitted to each end of the driveshafts, to ensure the smooth and efficient transmission of power at all suspension and steering angles. The outer constant velocity joints are of the ball-and-cage type, and the inner joints are of the tripod type.

4WD models

The front wheels are driven the same as it is on 2-wheel drive models by means of two solid steel driveshafts of unequal length.

Drive is transmitted from the transfer gearbox to the rear final drive unit through a two-piece propeller shaft with three joints. The joints on each end are a flange type connecting to the transfer gearbox and final drive unit, and there is a CV joint at the centre.

The rear final drive unit then transmits the drive through two solid steel driveshafts of equal length to the both rear wheels. Both driveshafts are splined at their outer ends, to accept the wheel hubs, and are threaded so that each hub can be fastened to the driveshaft by a large nut and locked in position with a split pin. The inner end of each driveshaft is splined, to accept the gears in the final drive unit.

Constant velocity (CV) joints are fitted to each end of the driveshafts, to ensure the smooth and efficient transmission of power at all suspension and steering angles. The outer constant velocity joints are of the ball-and-cage type, and the inner joints are of the tripod type.

2 Driveshafts – removal and refitting

Note: *A new split-pin and driveshaft inner joint circlip must be used on refitting.*

Front driveshaft

Removal

1 Firmly apply the handbrake, and then jack up the front of the vehicle and support it securely on axle stands (see *Jacking and vehicle support*). Remove the appropriate roadwheel(s).

2 To reduce spillage when the inner end of the driveshaft is withdrawn from the transmission, drain the transmission oil/fluid as described in Chapter 7A, Section 2 or Chapter 7B, Section 2.

2.3 Remove the split pin

2.6 Disconnect the track rod end

3 Remove the split-pin from the outer end of the driveshaft, discard the split-pin - a new one must be used on refitting **(see illustration)**.

4 The front hub must now be held stationary in order to loosen the driveshaft nut. Ideally, the hub should be held by a suitable tool bolted into place using two of the roadwheel nuts **(see illustration 2.41)**. Alternatively, have an assistant firmly apply the brake pedal to prevent the hub from rotating.

5 Using a socket and extension bar, slacken and remove the driveshaft retaining nut **(see illustration)**.

6 Undo the retaining nut and disconnect the track rod end from the hub carrier **(see illustration)**. Refer to Chapter 10, Section 17, for further information.

7 Undo the retaining nut and disconnect the lower drop link ball joint from the anti-roll bar **(see illustration)**. Refer to Chapter 10, Section 6, for further information.

2.5 Undo the driveshaft nut

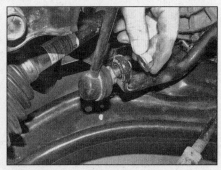
2.7 Disconnect the drop link lower ball joint

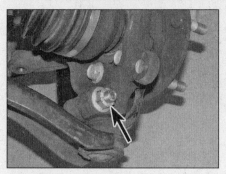

2.8a Remove the lower ball joint retaining bolt ...

2.8b ... and lever the lower arm away from the hub

2.10 Withdraw the driveshaft from the hub

8 Undo the retaining nut and withdraw the bolt from the lower ball joint. Use a length of bar, chain and a block of wood to lever the lower arm downwards and disconnect the lower ball joint from the hub carrier **(see illustrations)**.

9 If the shaft is a tight fit in the splines in the hub, temporarily refit the driveshaft nut to the end of the driveshaft, to prevent damage to the driveshaft threads. Using a soft-faced mallet, carefully tap the driveshaft to free it from the hub carrier. If required, a suitable puller can be used to force the end of the shaft from the hub.

10 Once the driveshaft is free, remove the driveshaft nut, tip the hub carrier outwards, and fully withdraw the outer end of the driveshaft from the hub **(see illustration)**. On models with ABS, take care not to strain the ABS wheel sensor wiring during this operation – if necessary, unscrew the bolt securing the

sensor to the hub carrier, withdraw the sensor and position it clear of the work area.

11 Proceed as follows, according to transmission type.

Left-hand driveshaft

12 If the transmission oil has not been drained (see paragraph 2), have a clean container ready to catch the transmission oil/fluid as the driveshaft is withdrawn.

13 The driveshaft is held into the transmission by a spring circlip, which can take some effort to release. Using a suitable lever, on the shoulder of the driveshaft inner joint, prise it out from the transmission, and then remove the driveshaft **(see illustrations)**.

14 When the shaft is removed, insert a dummy shaft into the transmission **(see illustration)**.

Right-hand driveshaft

15 If the transmission oil has not been drained (see paragraph 2), have a clean container ready to catch the transmission oil/fluid as the driveshaft is withdrawn.

16 There is a support bearing, which is bolted to the rear of the cylinder block. Undo the two bolts and remove the retaining plate from the bearing housing **(see illustrations)**. Note its fitted position for refitting, as there is a cut away in the retaining plate. **Note:** *Nissan recommends that this retaining plate be renewed each time it is removed.*

17 Using a suitable drift, on the shoulder of the driveshaft inner joint, carefully tap it out from the transmission, and then remove the driveshaft **(see illustration)**.

18 If the bearing is a tight fit in the housing,

2.13a Lever the driveshaft to release the spring clip ...

2.13b ... and remove the driveshaft from the transmission

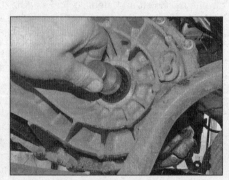

2.14 Using a dummy shaft inside the differential

2.16a Undo the two retaining bolts ...

2.16b ... and remove the retaining plate

2.17 Withdraw the right-hand driveshaft from the vehicle

2.18a Undo the bearing housing (arrowed) mounting bolts …

2.18b … and remove it with the driveshaft

2.24 Apply a small amount of oil to the end of the driveshaft

undo the retaining bolts and remove the bearing housing from the rear of the cylinder block, and remove the driveshaft complete with bearing housing from under the vehicle (see illustrations).

19 When the shaft is removed, insert a dummy shaft into the transmission (see illustration 2.14).

Refitting

20 Where fitted, remove the dummy shaft from the transmission.

21 Before installing a driveshaft, examine the driveshaft oil seal in the transmission for signs of damage or deterioration and, if necessary, renew it, referring to Chapter 7A, Section 4 or Chapter 7B, Section 7 for further information (it is advisable to renew the seal as a matter of course).

22 Thoroughly clean the driveshaft splines, and the apertures in the transmission and hub assembly. Apply a thin film of grease to the oil seal lips, and to the driveshaft splines and shoulders. Check that all driveshaft gaiter clips are securely fastened.

23 Note that the circlip at the inner end of the driveshaft **must** be renewed on refitting.

24 When refitting a driveshaft, great care must be taken to prevent damage to the driveshaft oil seals. Nissan specify the use of special tools, which guide the shafts through the seal lips on refitting. Provided that the seal lips and the shaft ends are lightly greased/oiled (see illustration), and that care is taken on refitting, these tools should not be necessary.

25 Insert the inner end of the driveshaft into the transmission, taking care not to damage the oil seal.

26 Grasp the inner joint body firmly, and check that the circlip is correctly engaged by attempting to pull the driveshaft from the transmission.

27 Apply a thin film of grease to the outer driveshaft joint splines, then engage the outer end of the driveshaft with the hub, ensuring that the splines engage correctly.

28 Refit the new driveshaft nut, but do not tighten the nut fully at this stage.

29 Reconnect the lower ball joint to the bottom of the hub carrier (see illustration). If required, use a length of bar, chain and a block of wood to lever the lower arm downwards, as described on removal. Fit new bolt and nut to the lower ball joint and tighten to the specified torque setting.

30 On right-hand driveshafts secure the support bearing back into position, on the rear of the cylinder block and tighten the bolts to the specified torque setting, where given. Make sure the retaining plate is positioned back into place on the housing, as noted on removal.

31 Reconnect the lower drop link ball joint to the anti-roll bar and tighten the retaining nut. Refer to Chapter 10, Section 6, for further information.

32 Reconnect the track rod end to the hub carrier and tighten the retaining nut.

Refer to Chapter 10, Section 17, for further information.

33 If removed, refit the ABS wheel sensor and tighten its retaining bolt securely.

34 Hold the front hub stationary as during removal, then tighten the new driveshaft nut to the specified torque.

35 Fit a new split-pin and bend over the split-pin legs (see illustration).

36 Refit the roadwheel(s), and lower the vehicle to the ground.

37 Refill the transmission with oil/fluid as described in Chapter 7A, Section 2 or Chapter 7B, Section 2.

Rear driveshaft

Removal

38 Firmly apply the handbrake, chock the front wheels and then jack up the rear of the vehicle and support it securely on axle stands (see Jacking and vehicle support). Remove the appropriate roadwheel(s).

39 To reduce spillage when the inner end of the driveshaft is withdrawn from the final drive unit, drain the final drive oil, as described in Chapter 7C, Section 6.

40 Remove the split-pin from the outer end of the driveshaft, discard the split-pin – a new one must be used on refitting (see illustration).

41 The rear hub must now be held stationary in order to slacken the driveshaft retaining nut. Ideally, the hub should be held by a suitable tool bolted into place using two of the

2.29 Reconnect the lower arm ball joint to the hub

2.35 Fit a new split pin to the end of the driveshaft

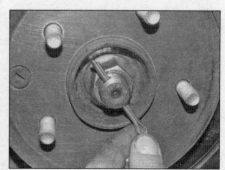

2.40 Remove the split pin

2.41 Using a fabricated tool to hold the hub stationary whilst the driveshaft nut is slackened

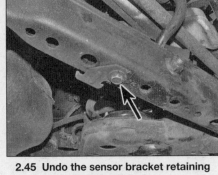

2.45 Undo the sensor bracket retaining bolt (arrowed)

2.46 Support the rear trailing arm with a trolley jack

roadwheel nuts **(see illustration)**. Alternatively, have an assistant firmly apply the brake pedal to prevent the hub from rotating.

42 Using a socket and extension bar, completely remove the driveshaft retaining nut.

43 Remove the rear brake caliper as described in Chapter 9, Section 10.

44 Remove the rear ABS sensor as described in Chapter 9, Section 20.

45 On models with headlight leveling sensor, undo the retaining bolt and disconnect the sensor bracket from the lower arm **(see illustration)**.

46 Support the rear trailing arm with a trolley jack **(see illustration)**.

47 Undo the retaining nut and disconnect the anti-roll bar drop link lower balljoint from the lower suspension arm **(see illustration)**.

48 Undo the retaining nut and bolt, and then disconnect the damper lower mounting from the lower suspension arm **(see illustration)**.

49 Undo the retaining nut and bolt, and then disconnect the lower suspension arm from the hub assembly **(see illustration)**.

50 Undo the retaining nut and bolt, and then disconnect the upper suspension arm from the hub assembly **(see illustration)**.

51 Lower the trolley jack and carefully pull the hub assembly outwards to allow for the driveshaft outer joint to be withdrawn from the splines in the hub **(see illustration)**. Take care that the coil spring does not become unseated from the trailing arm, as it is lowered.

52 If the final drive oil has not been drained (see paragraph 39), have a clean container ready to catch the final drive oil/fluid as the driveshaft is withdrawn.

53 The driveshaft is held into the final drive by a spring circlip, which can take some effort to release. Using a suitable lever, on the shoulder of the driveshaft inner joint, prise it out from the final drive, and then remove the driveshaft from under the vehicle **(see illustration)**.

Refitting

54 Before installing a driveshaft, examine the driveshaft oil seal in the final drive for signs of damage or deterioration and, if necessary, renew it, referring to Chapter 7C, Section 8, for further information (it is advisable to renew the seal as a matter of course).

55 Thoroughly clean the driveshaft splines, and the apertures in the final drive and hub assembly. Apply a thin film of grease to the oil seal lips, and to the driveshaft splines and shoulders. Check that all driveshaft gaiter clips are securely fastened.

56 Note that the circlip at the inner end of the driveshaft **must** be renewed on refitting.

2.47 Disconnect the anti-roll bar drop link lower balljoint

2.48 Disconnect the damper lower mounting

2.49 Undo the lower suspension arm nut and bolt (arrowed)

2.50 Undo the upper suspension arm nut and bolt

2.51 Withdraw the driveshaft from the rear hub

2.53 Lever the driveshaft from the final drive

2.60 Refit the outer end of the driveshaft to the rear hub

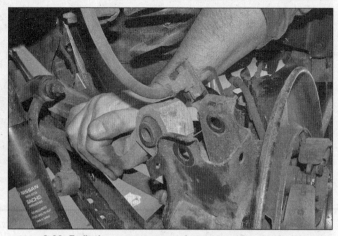

2.63 Refit the upper suspension arm to the rear hub

57 When refitting a driveshaft, great care must be taken to prevent damage to the driveshaft oil seals. Nissan specify the use of special tools, which guide the shafts through the seal lips on refitting. Provided that the seal lips and the shaft ends are lightly greased, and that care is taken on refitting, these tools should not be necessary.

58 Insert the inner end of the driveshaft into the final drive, taking care not to damage the oil seal.

59 Grasp the inner joint body firmly, and check that the circlip is correctly engaged by attempting to pull the driveshaft from the final drive.

60 Apply a thin film of grease to the outer driveshaft joint splines, then engage the outer end of the driveshaft with the hub **(see illustration)**, ensuring that the splines engage correctly.

61 Raise the trolley jack and carefully put the hub assembly back into position to allow the driveshaft outer joint to slide back into the splines in the hub. Make sure the coil spring is seated in the correct position on the trailing arm, as it is raised.

62 Refit the new driveshaft nut, but do not tighten the nut fully at this stage.

63 Reconnect the upper suspension arm to the hub assembly **(see illustration)**, do not tighten the nut fully at this stage.

64 Reconnect the lower suspension arm to

the hub assembly and fit the nut and bolt, do not tighten the nut fully at this stage.

65 Reconnect the damper lower mounting to the lower suspension arm and fit the nut and bolt, do not tighten the nut fully at this stage.

66 Reconnect the anti-roll bar drop link lower balljoint to the lower suspension arm. Fit the nut, do not tighten the nut fully at this stage.

67 With all suspension bolts back in position, lower and remove the trolley jack from under the training arm.

68 On models with headlight leveling sensor, reconnect the sensor bracket to the lower arm and tighten the retaining bolt.

69 Refit the rear ABS sensor, as described in Chapter 9, Section 20.

70 Refit the rear brake caliper, as described in Chapter 9, Section 10.

71 Hold the rear hub stationary as during removal, then tighten the new driveshaft nut to the specified torque.

72 Fit a new split-pin and bend over the split-pin legs **(see illustration)**.

73 Refit the roadwheel(s), lower the vehicle to the ground and tighten to the specified torque setting.

74 Refill the final drive unit with oil/fluid as described in Chapter 7C, Section 6.

75 With the vehicle on its wheels, and at normal ride height position, tighten all the rear suspension bolts to their specified torque setting.

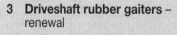

2.72 Fit a new split pin to the end of the driveshaft

3 Driveshaft rubber gaiters – renewal

Outer joint

1 Remove the driveshaft as described in Section 2.

2 Release the rubber gaiter retaining clips **(see illustrations)**. If required, cut through them using a junior hacksaw. Spread the clips and remove them from the gaiter.

3 Pull the gaiter back to expose the outer constant velocity joint then scoop out the excess grease **(see illustration)**.

3.2a Remove the outer …

3.2b … and inner retaining clips

3.3 Pull back the gaiter and clean out the old grease

3.5a Using a soft metal drift …

3.5b … to release the outer joint

3.6a Remove the old spring clip …

4 If the original joint is to be re-used, make alignment marks between the joint and the driveshaft, so that it is refitted in the same position.

5 Using a brass drift and hammer, sharply strike the centre part of the outer joint to drive it off the end of the shaft **(see illustrations)**. The joint is retained on the driveshaft by a circlip, and striking the joint in this manner forces the circlip into its groove, so allowing the joint to slide off.

6 Remove the circlip from the groove in the driveshaft splines, and discard it, then slide the old gaiter from the end of the shaft **(see illustrations)**. A new circlip must be fitted on reassembly.

7 With the constant velocity joint removed from the driveshaft, thoroughly clean the joint using paraffin, or a suitable solvent, and dry it thoroughly. Carry out a visual inspection of the joint.

8 Move the inner splined driving member from side-to-side, to expose each ball in turn at the top of its track. Examine the balls for cracks, flat spots, or signs of surface pitting.

9 Inspect the ball tracks on the inner and outer members. If the tracks have widened, the balls will no longer be a tight fit. At the same time, check the ball cage windows for wear or cracking between the windows.

10 If any of the constant velocity joint components are found to be worn or

damaged, it will be necessary to renew the complete joint assembly, as the internal parts are not available separately. If the joint is in satisfactory condition, obtain a repair kit consisting of a new gaiter, circlips, retaining clips **(see illustration)**, and use the correct type of grease.

11 Commence reassembly by sliding the smaller gaiter securing clip onto the driveshaft, followed by the gaiter **(see illustrations)**.

12 Fit a new joint retaining circlip to the groove in the end of the shaft **(see illustration)**.

13 Before fitting the outer joint, squeeze half of the grease supplied with the kit into the outer joint **(see illustration)**.

14 Fit the outer joint to the shaft, and engage

3.6b … and slide the old gaiter off the shaft

3.10 Driveshaft joint and gaiter kit

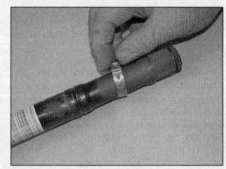

3.11a Fit the new inner retaining clip on the shaft …

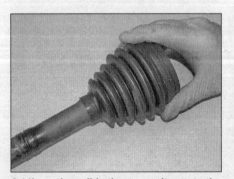

3.11b … then slide the new gaiter onto the shaft

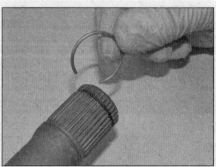

3.12 Fit the new spring clip to its groove in the driveshaft splines

3.13 Squeeze some of the grease inside the joint

3.14a Locate the outer joint on the splines, and slide it into position …

3.14b … making sure the spring clip is located correctly

3.15 Tap the joint into place, check that the joint is secured by the spring clip

it with the shaft splines **(see illustrations)**. If the original joint is re-used, align the previously made marks on the joint and the end of the driveshaft.

15 Take care not to damage the joint threaded end, and use a copper mallet to tap the joint onto the shaft until the circlip engages correctly behind the joint cage **(see illustration)**.

16 Use the remainder of the grease to pack the joint with the correct amount of the specified grease (supplied with the gaiter kit), then twist the joint to ensure that all the recesses are filled **(see illustration)**.

17 Check that the smaller end of the gaiter is located in the driveshaft groove, and then slide the gaiter onto the outer joint **(see illustration)**.

18 Check that the gaiter does not swell or deform when fitted. Use a screwdriver to get rid of the air inside the gaiter, and then position the gaiter at the setting dimension given in the specifications **(see illustrations)**.

19 Slide the smaller securing clip over the gaiter, and secure it in place **(see illustrations)**.

20 Fit the new outer gaiter large securing clip, and secure it in place **(see illustration)**.

21 Refit the driveshaft as described in Section 2.

Inner joint

22 Remove the driveshaft as described in Section 2.

3.16 Pack the joint with grease, working it into the ball tracks while twisting the joint

3.17 Slide the gaiter into position over the outer joint

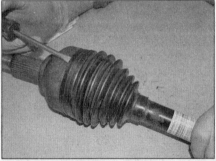

3.18a Using a screwdriver to displace the air inside the gaiter …

3.18b … measure the fitted position of the gaiter – see specifications

3.19a Slide the inner retaining clip into position …

3.19b …and secure the retaining clip with crimping pliers

3.20 Secure the outer retaining clip with crimping pliers

3.23a Release the retaining clips from the gaiter ...

3.23b ... using a screwdriver to prise up the ends

23 Release the rubber gaiter retaining clips **(see illustrations)**. If required, cut through them using a junior hacksaw. Slide the gaiter off the joint towards the middle of the driveshaft.

24 If the original joint is to be re-used, make alignment marks between the joint body and the driveshaft **(see illustrations)**.

25 Withdraw the gaiter from the joint outer body and release the retaining clip from inside the tripod joint. Wipe off the excess grease

from the joint and slide the tripod joint out from the outer body **(see illustrations)**.

26 If the original tripod joint is to be re-used, mark the relationship of the tripod joint and the driveshaft, then using circlip pliers, remove the circlip securing the tripod joint to the end of the shaft **(see illustrations)**. Discard the circlip – a new one should be used on refitting.

27 Withdraw the tripod joint and the gaiter from the end of the shaft **(see illustrations)**.

28 Thoroughly clean the constant velocity joint components and the end of the driveshaft using paraffin, or a suitable solvent, and dry thoroughly. Carry out a visual inspection of the joint. If any of the joint components are worn, the tripod joint assembly or the joint body can be renewed separately as complete units, but no other spare parts are available. If the joint is in satisfactory condition, obtain a repair kit consisting of a new gaiter, circlips, retaining

3.24a Mark the position of the inner joint ...

3.24b ... on the driveshaft

3.25a Pull back the gaiter and use a thin screwdriver ...

3.25b ... to remove the joint retaining clip

3.26a Make alignment marks on the tripod for refitting ...

3.26b ... then remove the circlip from the end of the shaft

3.27a Using a punch to ...

3.27b ... remove the tripod from the shaft ...

3.27c ... then withdraw the old gaiter from the shaft

clips **(see illustration)**, and use the correct type of grease.

29 Commence reassembly by sliding the smaller gaiter securing clip onto the driveshaft, followed by the gaiter **(see illustrations)**.

30 Refit the tripod joint, aligning the marks made previously if the original one is being used **(see illustration)**.

31 Fit a new circlip to secure the tripod joint to the driveshaft **(see illustration)**.

32 Peel back the rubber gaiter and fit the new tripod joint retaining clip around the shaft **(see illustration)**.

33 Before fitting the tripod joint into the outer body, squeeze half of the grease supplied with the kit into the outer body.

34 Fit the joint body over the tripod joint. If the original body is being refitted, align the marks made between the body and the driveshaft before removal **(see illustration)**.

35 Slide the tripod joint into the outer body and

3.28 Driveshaft joint and gaiter kit

3.29a Fit the new inner retaining clip on the shaft …

fit the new securing clip into the grooves on the inner side of the outer body **(see illustrations)**.

36 Use the remainder of the grease to pack the joint with the correct amount of the specified grease (supplied with the gaiter kit),

and then twist the joint to ensure that all the recesses are filled **(see illustration)**.

37 Check that the smaller end of the gaiter is located in the driveshaft groove, and then slide the gaiter onto the outer body **(see illustration)**.

3.29b … then slide the new gaiter onto the shaft

3.30 Using a soft metal drift to refit the tripod joint, noting the alignment marks

3.31 Fit the new circlip to the groove in the end of the shaft

3.32 Fit the new retaining clip around the shaft

3.34 Slide the joint back into position, noting the alignment marks

3.35a Fit the retaining clip back into the body …

3.35b … making sure it locates securely in the groove

3.36 Pack the joint with grease, working it into the joint while twisting the shaft

3.37 Peel the gaiter back into position over the outer body

3.38a Using a screwdriver to displace the air inside the gaiter ...

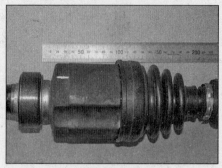

3.38b ... measure the fitted position of the gaiter – see specifications

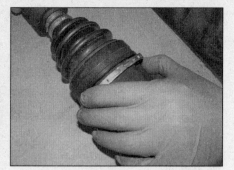

3.39a Slide the retaining clips into position ...

3.39b ...and secure them into position

3.40 Make sure the gaiter clips are secure

38 Check that the gaiter does not swell or deform when fitted. Use a screwdriver to get rid of the air inside the gaiter, and then position the joint at the setting dimension

given in the specifications **(see illustrations)**.
39 Fit the new gaiter large securing clip, and tighten it in place **(see illustrations)**.

40 Locate the smaller gaiter securing clip on the end of the gaiter, and secure it as described previously **(see illustration)**.
41 Refit the driveshaft as described in Section 2.

---

4 Driveshaft – inspection and overhaul

1 If any of the checks described in Chapter 1A, Section 12 or Chapter 1B, Section 13, reveal wear in any driveshaft joint, first remove the roadwheel trim or centre cap (as appropriate).
2 Check that the driveshaft nut is correctly tightened; if in doubt, remove the split-pin. Check that the nut is tightened to the specified torque, and then refit a new split-pin. Refit the roadwheel trim or centre cap (as applicable), and repeat the check on the remaining driveshaft nut.
3 Road test the vehicle, and listen for a metallic clicking from the front as the vehicle is driven slowly in a circle on full-lock. If a clicking noise is heard, this indicates wear in the outer constant velocity joint.
4 If vibration, consistent with roadspeed, is felt through the car when accelerating, there is a possibility of wear in the inner constant velocity joints.
5 To check the joints for wear, remove the driveshafts, then dismantle them as described in Section 3. If any wear or free play is found, the relevant joint, or joint components must be renewed.

Right-hand front driveshaft bearing

6 Remove the right-hand front driveshaft as described in Section 2.
7 If the bearing housing was removed with the driveshaft, the shaft will need to be carefully pressed from the housing **(see illustration)**.
8 Note the fitted position of the metal dust cap, and then remove it from the inner end of the driveshaft **(see illustration)**.
9 Remove the metal shield from the bearing, and then using circlip pliers, remove the circlip from the driveshaft **(see illustrations)**.

4.7 Using a press to remove the bearing housing

4.8 Remove the dust cap, noting its fitted position

4.9a Remove the metal shield ...

4.9b ... then remove the circlip

4.10 Using a long puller to remove the bearing from the shaft

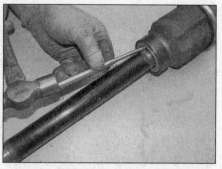

4.11 Carefully tap the new bearing back on the shaft

4.12 Fit a new circlip to secure the bearing

10 Using a long puller withdraw the bearing from the driveshaft **(see illustration)**.

11 Fit the new bearing onto the driveshaft and carefully tap it into position on the shaft **(see illustration)**.

12 Fit the new circlip making sure it is located in the groove in the shaft **(see illustration)**.

13 Fit the new metal shield onto the driveshaft and carefully tap it into position on the shaft **(see illustration)**.

14 Fit the new metal dust cap onto the driveshaft and carefully tap it into the position noted on removal **(see illustration)**.

15 Where applicable bolt the bearing housing to the rear of the cylinder block, then refit the driveshaft as described in Section 2.

4.13 Refit the bearing shield

4.14 Refit the dust cap to the position noted on removal

5 Propeller shaft – removal and refitting

Removal

1 Make sure the vehicle transmission is in the neutral position, and the handbrake released.

2 Jack up the front and rear of the vehicle and support it securely on axle stands (see *Jacking and vehicle support*).

3 Remove the exhaust front pipe as described in Chapter 4A, Section 13 or Chapter 4B, Section 17.

4 Make alignment marks on the propeller shaft and front and rear universal joint flanges,

to make sure that it is fitted in the same position on refitting.

5 Release the retaining clips and remove the heat shield from the propeller shaft centre mounting **(see illustrations)**.

6 Note the fitted position of the upper and lower bracket, and then remove the two plastic locating clips, one each side of the mounting bracket.

7 Slacken the two retaining nuts from the centre bearing bracket, do not remove completely at this stage **(see illustration)**. **Note**: *The upper mounting bracket has an arrow stamped on it, this should point to the front of the vehicle, when fitted.*

Caution: Do not allow the propeller shaft to hang unsupported, as damage may occur to the universal joints.

5.5a Undo the fasteners …

8 Support the propeller shaft, and then undo four retaining bolts and disconnect the front of the propeller shaft from the flange

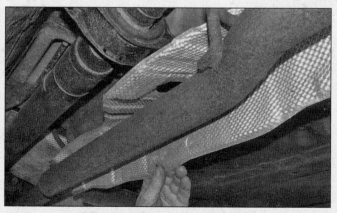

5.5b … and remove the heat shield

5.7 Centre bearing mounting bracket securing nuts

5.8 Front flange retaining bolts

5.10 Rear flange retaining bolts

on the rear of the transfer gearbox **(see illustration)**. Discard the retaining bolts, as new ones will be required for refitting.

9 Now fully remove the centre bearing retaining nuts, and remove the lower bracket. As the propeller shaft is lowered, withdraw the upper bracket, noting its fitted position. Discard the nuts, as new ones will be required for refitting.

10 Undo the four retaining bolts and disconnect the rear of the propeller shaft from the flange on the final drive flange **(see illustration)**. Withdraw the propeller shaft from under the vehicle. Discard the retaining bolts, as new ones will be required for refitting.

Refitting

11 Refitting is a reversal of the removal procedure, noting the following points.
   a) *Align the marks made on the flanges on removal.*
   b) *Fit the centre bearing upper and lower brackets in the position noted on removal. The upper bracket has an arrow facing forwards on it.*
   c) *Fit new retaining bolts and nuts to the propeller shaft joints.*
   d) *Tighten bolts to the specified torque setting, where given.*
   e) *Make sure the heads of the propeller shaft*

bolts are sitting in their recesses in the flange when tightened.
   f) *Refit the exhaust front pipe as described in Chapter 4A, Section 13 or Chapter 4B, Section 17.*

6 Propeller shaft –
inspection and overhaul

Inspection

1 Wear in the universal/constant velocity joints is characterized by vibration in the transmission, clonks on taking up the drive, and in extreme cases (lack of lubrication), unpleasant metallic noises as the bearings/surfaces break up.

2 To test the universal joints (Cardan type) for wear with the propeller shaft in place apply the handbrake and chock the wheels.

3 Working under the vehicle, apply leverage between the yokes using a large screwdriver or flat metal bar. Wear is indicated by movement between the shaft yoke and the coupling flange yoke.

4 Check for play between the constant velocity joint housing and the shaft tubes. Any play or stiffness/roughness indicates the joint is defective; therefore the complete propeller shaft will need to be renewed.

5 If there is any bend, dents, cracks or damage to the propeller shaft, the complete shaft will need to be replaced.

Overhaul

6 If any of the joints are defective, the complete propeller shaft must be renewed, it would appear that no new components are available. Check with a Nissan dealer or parts specialist.

7 If vibration occurs, disconnect the propeller shaft from the final drive flange and turn it 90°, reconnect it and then carry out a roadtest. If there is vibration the propeller shaft can be turned a further 90° and then road tested again. If there is still vibration the propeller shaft can be turned a further 90° and then road tested again. At this point if there is still vibration then the propeller shaft will need to be renewed, as a further 90° will bring it back to where it started.

8 To check the runout of the propeller shaft, use a dial test indicator (DTI), and turn the propeller shaft by hand. See the following illustration for checking points on the propeller shaft **(see illustrations)**

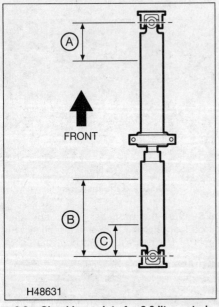

6.8a Checking points for 2.0 litre petrol models

Dimension A = 200mm   Dimension B = 639mm
Dimension C = 159mm

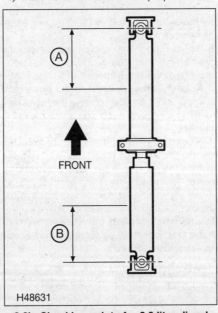

6.8b Checking points for 2.0 litre diesel models

Dimension A = 495mm
Dimension B = 416mm

Chapter 9
Braking system

Contents

Degrees of difficulty

| Easy, suitable for novice with little experience | | Fairly easy, suitable for beginner with some experience | | Fairly difficult, suitable for competent DIY mechanic | | Difficult, suitable for experienced DIY mechanic | | Very difficult, suitable for expert DIY or professional | |

Specifications

General

System type . . . . Dual hydraulic circuit with Anti-lock braking system (ABS) fitted. Front ventilated disc brakes on all models. Solid rear disc brakes, with handbrake shoes in the centre of the disc/drum. Vacuum servo-assistance on all models. Cable-operated handbrake acting on rear wheels

Front brakes

Type	Ventilated disc, with single-piston sliding caliper
Disc diameter	296 mm
Front brake disc:	
Vehicles with – 2 seat rows:	
Standard thickness of brake disc	26.00 mm
Wear limit thickness of brake disc	24.00 mm
Vehicles with – 3 seat rows:	
Standard thickness of brake disc	28.00 mm
Wear limit thickness of brake disc	26.00 mm
Maximum disc run-out	0.035 mm
Minimum pad friction material thickness	2.0 mm

Rear disc brakes

Type	Solid disc with single-piston sliding caliper
Disc diameter	292 mm
Rear brake disc:	
Vehicles with – 2 seat rows:	
Standard thickness of brake disc	9.00 mm
Wear limit thickness of brake disc	8.00 mm
Vehicles with – 3 seat rows:	
Standard thickness of brake disc	16.00 mm
Wear limit thickness of brake disc	14.00 mm
Maximum disc run-out	0.035 mm
Minimum pad friction material thickness	1.5 mm

Handbrake

Type	Drum (inside centre of disc), with leading and trailing shoes operated by cables

Drum/disc inner diameter:

New	172 mm
Maximum inner diameter	173 mm
Maximum out-of-round	0.02 mm
Minimum shoe lining thickness	1.5 mm
Number of notches (when handbrake fully applied)	7 to 8 notches
Number of notches (for warning light to be ON)	1 notch

Brake pedal

Free height	130.2 to 140.2 mm

Pedal switch

Clearance (between pedal bracket and threads of switch)	0.74 to 1.96 mm

Brake master cylinder

Cylinder bore diameter	23.8 mm

Vacuum servo

Servo diameter	250 mm
Output rod length....................................	30.5 mm
Input rod length	124.5 to 125.5 mm

Torque wrench settings

	Nm	lbf ft
ABS wheel sensor securing bolts............................	10	7
Brake bleed screw	8	6
Brake fluid hose union banjo bolts...........................	18	13
Brake servo/pedal bracket securing nuts	15	11
Front brake caliper guide pin bolts...........................	34	25
Front brake caliper mounting bracket bolts.....................	150	112
Handbrake lever mounting bolts	14	10
Master cylinder securing nuts	15	11
Rear brake caliper guide pin bolts...........................	43	32
Rear brake caliper mounting bracket bolts	84	62

1 General information

The braking system is of the servo-assisted, dual-circuit hydraulic type. The arrangement of the hydraulic system is such that each circuit operates one front and one rear brake from a tandem master cylinder. Under normal circumstances, both circuits operate in unison. However, in the event of hydraulic failure in one circuit, full braking force will still be available at two diagonally opposite wheels.

All models are fitted with front and rear disc brakes. The front disc brakes are actuated by single-piston sliding type calipers, which ensure that equal pressure is applied to each disc pad. The rear disc brakes are also actuated by single-piston sliding type caliper, but have a separate drum brake arrangement in the centre of the brake disc to provide a separate means of handbrake application.

To prevent the possibility of the rear wheels locking before the front wheels under heavy braking, pressure-regulating valves are incorporated in the hydraulic circuit to the rear brakes. All models have ABS fitted, there are valves located in a separate unit mounted in the left-hand rear corner of the engine compartment behind the air cleaner housing.

Note: *When servicing any part of the system, work carefully and methodically; also observe scrupulous cleanliness when overhauling any part of the hydraulic system. Always renew components (in axle sets, where applicable) if in doubt about their condition, and use only genuine Nissan parts, or at least those of known good quality. Note the warnings given in 'Safety first!' and at relevant points in this Chapter concerning the dangers of asbestos dust and hydraulic fluid.*

2 Hydraulic system – bleeding

⚠ *Warning: Brake hydraulic fluid is poisonous; wash off immediately and thoroughly in the case of skin contact, and seek immediate medical advice if any fluid is swallowed, or gets into the eyes. Certain types of hydraulic fluid are inflammable, and may ignite when allowed into contact with hot components. When servicing any hydraulic system, it is safest to assume that the fluid IS inflammable, and to take precautions against the risk of fire as though it is petrol that is being handled. Hydraulic fluid is also an effective paint stripper, and will attack plastics; if any is spilt, it should be washed off immediately, using copious quantities of fresh water. Finally, it is hygroscopic (it absorbs moisture from the air) – old fluid may be contaminated and unfit for further use. When topping-up or renewing the fluid, always use the recommended type, and ensure that it comes from a freshly opened sealed container.*

General

1 The correct operation of any hydraulic system is only possible after removing all air from the components and circuit; and this is achieved by bleeding the system.

2 During the bleeding procedure, add only clean, unused brake hydraulic fluid of the recommended type; never re-use fluid that has already been bled from the system.

Ensure that sufficient fluid is available before starting work.

3 If there is any possibility of incorrect fluid being already in the system, the brake components and circuit must be flushed completely with uncontaminated, correct fluid, and new seals should be fitted throughout the system.

4 If hydraulic fluid has been lost from the system, or air has entered because of a leak, ensure that the fault is cured before proceeding further.

5 Park the vehicle on level ground, switch off the engine and select first or reverse gear (or P), then chock the wheels and release the handbrake.

6 Check that all pipes and hoses are secure, unions tight and bleed screws closed. Remove the dust caps (where applicable), and clean any dirt from around the bleed screws.

7 Unscrew the master cylinder reservoir cap, and top the master cylinder reservoir up to the MAX level line; refit the cap loosely. Remember to maintain the fluid level at least above the MIN level line throughout the procedure; otherwise there is a risk of further air entering the system.

8 There is a number of one-man, do-it-yourself brake bleeding kits currently available from motor accessory shops. It is recommended that one of these kits is used whenever possible, as they greatly simplify the bleeding operation, and also reduce the risk of expelled air and fluid being drawn back into the system. If such a kit is not available, the basic (two-man) method must be used, which is described in detail below.

9 If a kit is to be used, prepare the vehicle as described previously, and follow the kit manufacturer's instructions, as the procedure may vary slightly according to the type being used; generally, they are as outlined below in the relevant sub-section.

10 Whichever method is used, the same sequence must be followed (paragraphs 11 and 12) to ensure that the removal of all air from the system.

Bleeding sequence

11 If the system has been only partially disconnected, and suitable precautions were taken to minimise fluid loss, it should be necessary to bleed only that part of the system (i.e. the primary or secondary circuit).

12 If the complete system is to be bled, then it should be done working in the following sequence:

a) Left-hand rear wheel.
b) Right-hand rear wheel.
c) Left-hand front wheel.
d) Right-hand front wheel.

Bleeding

Caution: On models equipped with ABS, switch off the ignition and disconnect the battery negative terminal (refer to 'Disconnecting the battery' in the Reference Chapter), before carrying out the bleeding procedure.

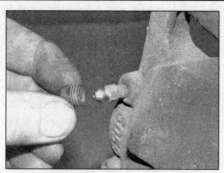

2.14a Remove the dust cap

2.14b Connect the bleed kit to the bleed screw

Basic (two-man) method

13 Collect a clean glass jar, a suitable length of plastic or rubber tubing which is a tight fit over the bleed screw, and a ring spanner to fit the screw. The help of an assistant will also be required.

14 Remove the dust cap from the first screw in the sequence. Fit a suitable spanner and tube to the screw, place the other end of the tube in the jar, and pour in sufficient fluid to cover the end of the tube **(see illustrations)**.

15 Ensure that the master cylinder reservoir fluid level is maintained at least above the MIN level line throughout the procedure.

16 Have the assistant fully depress the brake pedal several times to build-up pressure, and then maintain it on the final down stroke.

17 While pedal pressure is maintained, unscrew the bleed screw (approximately one turn) and allow the compressed fluid and air to flow into the jar. The assistant should maintain pedal pressure, following the pedal down to the floor if necessary, and should not release the pedal until instructed to do so. When the flow stops, tighten the bleed screw again, have the assistant release the pedal slowly, and recheck the reservoir fluid level.

18 Repeat the steps given in paragraphs 16 and 17 until the fluid emerging from the bleed screw is free from air bubbles. If the master cylinder has been drained and refilled, and air is being bled from the first screw in the sequence, allow approximately five seconds between cycles for the master cylinder passages to refill.

19 When no more air bubbles appear, tighten the bleed screw securely, remove the tube and spanner, and refit the dust cap. Do not over tighten the bleed screw.

20 Repeat the procedure on the remaining screws in the sequence, until all air is removed from the system, and the brake pedal feels firm again.

Using a one-way valve kit

21 As their name implies, these kits consist of a length of tubing with a one-way valve fitted, to prevent expelled air and fluid being drawn back into the system; some kits include a translucent container, which can be positioned so that the air bubbles can be more easily seen flowing from the end of the tube.

22 The kit is connected to the bleed screw, which is then opened. The user returns to the driver's seat, depresses the brake pedal with a smooth, steady stroke, and slowly releases it; this is repeated until the expelled fluid is clear of air bubbles.

23 Note that these kits simplify work so much that it is easy to forget the master cylinder reservoir fluid level; ensure that this is maintained at least above the MIN level line at all times.

Using a pressure-bleeding kit

24 These kits are usually operated by the reservoir of pressurised air contained in the spare tyre. However, note that it will probably be necessary to reduce the pressure to a lower level than normal; refer to the instructions supplied with the kit.

25 By connecting a pressurised, fluid-filled container to the master cylinder reservoir, bleeding can be carried out simply by opening each screw in turn (in the specified sequence), and allowing the fluid to flow out until no more air bubbles can be seen in the expelled fluid.

26 This method has the advantage that the large reservoir of fluid provides an additional safeguard against air being drawn into the system during bleeding.

27 Pressure-bleeding is particularly effective when bleeding 'difficult' systems, or when bleeding the complete system at the time of routine fluid renewal.

All methods

28 When bleeding is complete, and firm pedal feel is restored, wash off any spilt fluid, tighten the bleed screws securely, and refit their dust caps.

29 Check the hydraulic fluid level in the master cylinder reservoir, and top up if necessary.

30 Discard any hydraulic fluid that has been bled from the system; it will not be fit for re-use.

31 Check the feel of the brake pedal. If it feels at all spongy, air must still be present in the system, and further bleeding is required. Failure to bleed satisfactorily after a reasonable repetition of the bleeding procedure may be due to worn master cylinder seals.

3.1 Using a brake hose clamp

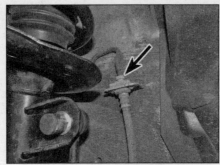

3.2 Slacken the union nut (arrowed) and then remove the spring clip

3.6 Make sure the spring clips (arrowed) are secure

3 Hydraulic pipes and hoses – renewal

Note: *Before starting work, refer to the note at the beginning of Section 2 concerning the dangers of hydraulic fluid.*

1 If any pipe or hose is to be renewed, minimise fluid loss by first removing the master cylinder reservoir cap, then tighten the cap down onto a piece of polythene to obtain an airtight seal. Alternatively, flexible hoses can be sealed, if required, using a proprietary brake hose clamp **(see illustration)**; metal brake pipe unions can be plugged (if care is taken not to allow dirt into the system) or capped immediately they are disconnected. Place a wad of rag under any union that is to be disconnected, to catch any spilt fluid.

2 If a flexible hose is to be disconnected, unscrew the brake pipe union nut before removing the spring clip, which secures the hose to its mounting bracket **(see illustration)**.

3 To unscrew the union nuts, it is preferable to obtain a brake pipe spanner of the correct size; these are available from most large motor accessory shops. Failing this, a close-fitting open-ended spanner will be required, though if the nuts are tight or corroded their flats may be rounded-off if the spanner slips. In

such a case, a self-locking wrench is often the only way to unscrew a stubborn union, but it follows that the pipe and the damaged nuts must be renewed on reassembly. Always clean a union and surrounding area before disconnecting it. If disconnecting a component with more than one union, make a careful note of the connections before disturbing any of them.

4 If a brake pipe is to be renewed, it can be obtained, cut to length and with the union nuts and end flares in place, from Nissan dealers. All that is then necessary is to bend it to shape, following the line of the original, before fitting it to the vehicle. Alternatively, most motor accessory shops can make up brake pipes from kits, but this requires very careful measurement of the original, to ensure that the new one is of the correct length. The safest answer is usually to take the original to the shop as a pattern.

5 On refitting, do not over tighten the union nuts. It is not necessary to exercise brute force to obtain a sound joint.

6 Ensure that the pipes and hoses are correctly routed, with no kinks, and that they are secured in the clips or brackets provided **(see illustration)**. After fitting, remove the polythene from the reservoir, and bleed the hydraulic system as described in Section 2. When completed, wash off any spilt fluid, and then check carefully for any fluid leaks.

4 Front brake pads – renewal

 Warning: Renew BOTH sets of front brake pads at the same time – NEVER renew the pads on only one wheel, as uneven braking may result.

Warning: Note that the dust created by wear of the pads may contain asbestos, which is a health hazard. Never blow it out with compressed air, and don't inhale any of it. An approved filtering mask should be worn when working on the brakes. DO NOT use petrol or petroleum-based solvents to clean brake parts; use brake cleaner or methylated spirit only.

1 Firmly apply the handbrake, and then jack up the front of the vehicle and support it securely on axle stands (see *Jacking and vehicle support*). Remove the front roadwheels.

2 Working on one side of the vehicle, push the caliper piston into its bore by pulling the caliper outwards.

3 Unscrew the caliper lower guide pin bolt (if necessary, use a slim open-ended spanner to counterhold the head of the guide pin), then remove the bolt **(see illustration)**.

4 Pivot the caliper body upwards to expose the brake pads and secure the caliper in place **(see illustrations)**. **Do not** depress the brake

4.3 Remove the caliper lower guide pin bolt ...

4.4a ... then pivot the caliper upwards and away from the brake pads ...

4.4b ... and tie it to the suspension strut

4.6a Withdraw the inner ...

4.6b ... and outer brake pad from the caliper mounting bracket

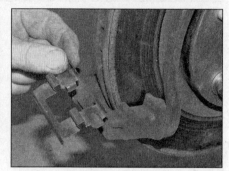

4.6c Remove the lower ...

4.6d ... and upper anti-rattle shims, if required

4.7 Remove the shim (where fitted) from the brake pad

4.8 Measure the thickness of the pads friction material

pedal until the caliper is refitted. Take care not to strain the brake fluid hose.

5 Note the locations and orientation of the shims fitted to the rear of each pad, and the anti-rattle clips fitted to the top and bottom of the pads.

6 Lift out the brake pads and shims, followed by the anti-rattle clips **(see illustrations)**.

7 Separate the shims from the brake pads, noting that there are two shims fitted to the inboard pad **(see illustration)**.

8 First measure the thickness of each brake pad's friction material **(see illustration)**. If either pad is worn at any point to the specified minimum thickness or less, all four pads must be renewed. Also, the pads should be renewed if any are fouled with oil or grease; there is no satisfactory way of degreasing

friction material, once contaminated. If any of the brake pads are worn unevenly, or are fouled with oil or grease, trace and rectify the cause before reassembly. New brake pads and shim/clip kits are available from Nissan dealers. Do not be tempted to swap brake pads over to compensate for uneven wear.

9 If the brake pads are still serviceable, carefully clean them using a clean, fine wire brush or similar, paying particular attention to the sides and back of the metal backing. Where applicable, clean out the grooves in the friction material, and pick out any large embedded particles of dirt or debris.

10 Clean the anti-rattle clips, shims, and the brake pad locations in the caliper body/ mounting bracket.

11 Prior to fitting the pads, check that the

guide pins are free to slide easily in the caliper body/mounting bracket, and check that the rubber guide pin gaiters are undamaged **(see illustrations)**.

12 Brush the dust and dirt from the caliper and piston, but *do not* inhale it, as it is a health hazard. Inspect the dust seal around the piston for damage, and the piston for evidence of fluid leaks, corrosion or damage. If attention to any of these components is necessary, refer to Section 9.

13 If new brake pads are to be fitted, the caliper piston must be pushed back into the cylinder, to make room for them. Either use a G-clamp or similar tool **(see illustration)**, or use suitable pieces of wood as levers. Provided that the master cylinder reservoir has not been overfilled with hydraulic fluid,

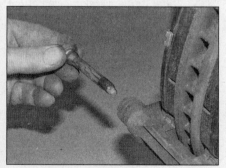

4.11a Check the condition of the guide pins ...

4.11b ... and the guide pin gaiters

4.13 Open the bleed screw and push the piston back (piston retraction tool shown)

4.14a Use the special grease to lubricate the rear of the brake pads ...

4.14b ... and the ends that slide in the caliper

4.15a Ensure the shims at the top and bottom of the caliper mounting bracket are correctly fitted

4.15b Refit the inner ...

4.15c ... and outer brake pads

4.16 Pivot the caliper down and over the pads

there should be no spillage, but keep a careful watch on the fluid level while retracting the piston. If the fluid level rises above the MAX level line at any time, the surplus should be syphoned off or ejected via a plastic tube connected to the bleed screw (see Section 2).

 Warning: Do not syphon the fluid by mouth, as it is poisonous; use a syringe or an old antifreeze tester.

14 Apply a little anti-squeal brake grease to the contact surfaces of the pad backing plates and the shims, but take great care not to allow any grease onto the pad friction linings **(see illustrations)**. Similarly, apply brake grease to the contact surfaces of the anti-rattle clips – again take care not to apply excess grease, which may contaminate the pads.

15 Refit the anti-rattle clips to the caliper

mounting bracket, and then refit the pads and shims in the positions noted before removal, ensuring that the pad friction material is against the disc **(see illustrations)**.

16 Pivot the caliper back into position, over the pads and mounting bracket **(see illustration)**.

17 Refit the caliper lower guide pin bolt, and then tighten it to the specified torque.

18 Check that the caliper body slides smoothly on the guide pins.

19 Repeat the procedure on the remaining front caliper.

20 With both sets of front brake pads refitted, depress the brake pedal repeatedly until the pads are pressed into firm contact with the brake disc, and normal pedal pressure is restored.

21 Refit the roadwheels, and lower the vehicle to the ground.

22 Finally, check the brake hydraulic fluid level as described in *Weekly checks*.

23 Note that new pads will not give full braking efficiency until they have bedded-in. Be prepared for this, and avoid hard braking as far as possible for the first hundred miles or so after pad renewal.

5 Rear brake pads – renewal

 Warning: Renew BOTH sets of rear brake pads at the same time – NEVER renew the pads on only one wheel, as uneven braking may result.

 Warning: Before starting work, refer to the warning given at the beginning of Section 4, concerning the dangers of asbestos dust.

1 Chock the front wheels, then jack up the rear of the car and support it on axle stands (see *Jacking and vehicle support*). Remove the rear roadwheels, and release the handbrake fully.

2 Working on one side of the vehicle, push the caliper piston into its bore by pulling the caliper outwards.

3 Unscrew the caliper lower guide pin bolt (noting that it is also the guide pin), and then remove from the caliper **(see illustrations)**.

4 Pivot the caliper body upwards to expose the brake pads and secure the caliper in place

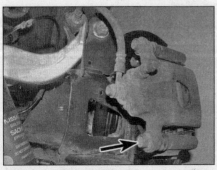

5.3a Remove the caliper lower guide pin bolt (arrowed) ...

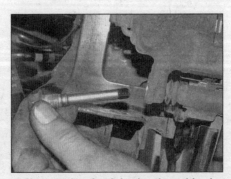

5.3b ... noting that it is also the guide pin

5.4 Pivot the caliper upwards and tie it to the suspension

5.6a Withdraw the outer …

5.6b … and inner brake pad from the caliper mounting bracket

5.6c Remove the lower …

5.6d … and upper anti-rattle shims, if required

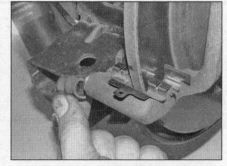

5.11 Check the condition of the guide pin gaiters

(see illustration). **Do not** depress the brake pedal until the caliper is refitted. Take care not to strain the brake fluid hose.

5 Note the locations and orientation of the shims fitted to the rear of each pad, and the anti-rattle clips fitted to the top and bottom of the pads.

6 Lift out the brake pads and shims, followed by the anti-rattle clips (see illustrations).

7 Separate the shims from the brake pads, noting there fitted position.

8 First measure the thickness of each brake pad's friction material (see illustration 4.8). If either pad is worn at any point to the specified minimum thickness or less, all four pads must be renewed. Also, the pads should be renewed if any are fouled with oil or grease; there is no satisfactory way of degreasing friction material, once contaminated. If any of the brake pads are worn unevenly, or are fouled with oil or grease, trace and rectify the cause before reassembly. New brake pads and shim/clip kits are available from Nissan dealers. Do not be tempted to swap brake pads over to compensate for uneven wear.

9 If the brake pads are still serviceable, carefully clean them using a clean, fine wire brush or similar, paying particular attention to the sides and back of the metal backing. Where applicable, clean out the grooves in the friction material, and pick out any large embedded particles of dirt or debris.

10 Clean the anti-rattle clips, shims, and the brake pad locations in the caliper body/ mounting bracket.

11 Prior to fitting the pads, check that the rubber guide pin gaiters are undamaged (see illustration).

12 Brush the dust and dirt from the caliper and piston, but *do not* inhale it, as it is a health hazard. Inspect the dust seal around the piston for damage, and the piston for evidence of fluid leaks, corrosion or damage. If attention to any of these components is necessary, refer to Section 9.

13 If new brake pads are to be fitted, the caliper piston must be pushed back into the cylinder, to make room for them. Either use a G-clamp or similar tool (see illustration), or use suitable pieces of wood as levers. Provided that the master cylinder reservoir has not been overfilled with hydraulic fluid, there should be no spillage, but keep a careful watch on the fluid level while retracting the piston. If the fluid level rises above the MAX level line at any time, the surplus should be syphoned off or ejected via a plastic tube connected to the bleed screw (see Section 2).

 Warning: Do not syphon the fluid by mouth, as it is poisonous; use a syringe or an old antifreeze tester.

14 Apply a little anti-squeal brake grease to the contact surfaces of the pad backing plates and the shims, but take great care not to allow any grease onto the pad friction linings (see illustrations 4.14a and 4.14b). Similarly, apply brake grease to the contact surfaces of the anti-rattle clips – again take care not to apply excess grease, which may contaminate the pads.

15 Refit the anti-rattle clips to the caliper mounting bracket, and then refit the pads and shims in the positions noted before removal, ensuring that the pad friction material is against the disc (see illustration).

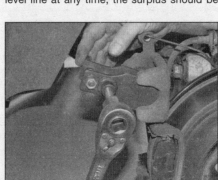

5.13 Open the bleed screw and push the piston back (piston retraction tool shown)

5.15 Refit the anti-rattle shims and the brake pads

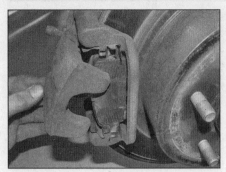

5.16 Pivot the caliper down and over the pads

16 Pivot the caliper back into position, over the pads and mounting bracket **(see illustration)**.

17 Refit the caliper lower guide pin bolt, and then tighten it to the specified torque.

18 Check that the caliper body slides smoothly on the guide pins.

19 Repeat the procedure on the remaining front caliper.

20 With both sets of front brake pads refitted, depress the brake pedal repeatedly until the pads are pressed into firm contact with the brake disc, and normal pedal pressure is restored.

21 Refit the roadwheels, and lower the vehicle to the ground.

22 Finally, check the brake hydraulic fluid level as described in *Weekly checks*.

23 Note that new pads will not give full braking efficiency until they have bedded-in. Be prepared for this, and avoid hard braking as far as possible for the first hundred miles or so after pad renewal.

6 Handbrake shoes – renewal

⚠️ *Warning: Renew BOTH sets of handbrake shoes at the same time – NEVER renew the shoes on only one wheel, as uneven braking may result.*

⚠️ *Warning: Before starting work, refer to the warning given at the beginning of Section 4, concerning the dangers of asbestos dust.*

1 Chock the front wheels, then jack up the rear of the car and support it on axle stands (see *Jacking and vehicle support*). Remove the rear roadwheels, and release the handbrake fully.

2 Working inside the vehicle, unclip the plastic trim/cup holder from the top of the centre console **(see illustration)**.

3 The handbrake cable adjustment nut can be accessed through the top of the centre console. Measure the length of thread, protruding through the nut, as a guide for refitting **(see illustration)**.

4 Slacken the handbrake cable adjusting nut, until it gets to the end of the thread. Note the nut does not have to be completely removed.

5 Remove the rear brake disc, as described in Section 8.

6 Working carefully, and taking the necessary precautions, remove all traces of brake dust from the brake drum, backplate and shoes.

7 Measure the thickness of the friction material of each brake shoe at several points; if either shoe is worn at any point to the specified minimum thickness or less, all four shoes must be renewed as a set. The shoes should also be renewed if any are fouled with oil or grease; there is no satisfactory way of degreasing friction material, once contaminated.

8 If any of the brake shoes are worn unevenly, or fouled with oil or grease, trace and rectify the cause before reassembly.

9 Before removing the brake shoes, note the position of each shoe, and the location of the return and adjuster springs. Also make a note of the adjuster component locations, to aid refitting later **(see illustrations)**.

10 Using pliers, depress the shoe hold-down spring and turn the retaining pin through 90º, then lift off the shoe hold down spring **(see illustrations)**. Carry out the same procedure on the remaining brake shoe.

11 Using a pair of long nose pliers, open up the lower ends of the brake shoes and remove

6.2 Unclip the cup holder trim from the centre console

6.3 Measure the amount of thread on the handbrake adjuster

6.9a Make a note of the brake shoes, springs ...

6.9b ... and adjusters fitted position

6.10a Turn the retaining pin ...

6.10b ... and remove the spring clip

6.11 Open up the brake shoes and remove the adjuster

6.12a Release the upper spring …

6.12b … and remove the front brake shoe

6.13a Release the upper spring …

6.13b … and remove the strut plate

6.14 Release the handbrake lever from the rear brake shoe

the adjuster strut, noting its fitted position **(see illustration)**.

12 Release the upper return spring, then withdraw the front brake shoe from the back plate and unhook the lower adjuster spring **(see illustrations)**. The one end of the return springs can be left fitted to the brake shoe, to aid refitting.

13 Release the upper return spring, and then withdraw the strut plate from the rear brake shoe and handbrake lever **(see illustrations)**.

14 When the rear shoe is withdrawn from the back plate, release the handbrake lever from the brake shoe **(see illustration)**.

15 If required, the other end of the handbrake lever can be released from the cable by pulling back the return spring **(see illustration)**.

16 Check the condition of the forked end from the adjuster strut, and carefully examine the assembly for signs of wear or damage. Pay particular attention to the threads and the toothed adjuster wheel, and renew if necessary.

17 Check the condition of all return springs and renew any that show signs of distortion or other damage.

18 Prior to installation, clean the backplate, and apply a thin smear of high-temperature brake grease or anti-seize compound to all those surfaces of the backplate which bear on the shoes **(see illustration)**. Do not allow the lubricant to foul the friction material.

19 If removed, refit the end of the handbrake

lever to the cable by pulling back the return spring.

20 Refit the handbrake lever back to the rear

6.15 Release the handbrake cable from the lever, if required

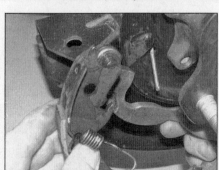

6.20a Refit the handbrake lever to the rear brake shoe …

brake shoe, and then refit the upper return spring **(see illustrations)**.

21 Slide the strut plate back into position, in

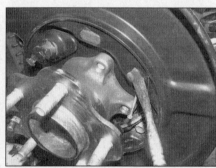

6.18 Use the special grease to lubricate the back plate

6.20b … and hook the spring over the upper bracket

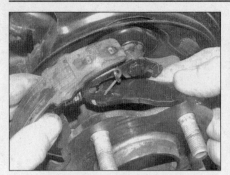

6.21a Insert the strut plate …

6.21b … making sure the end of the spring locates in the hole (arrowed)

the slot in the rear brake shoe and handbrake lever, locating the end of the spring in the hole in the strut plate **(see illustrations)**.

22 Refit the upper return spring to the front brake shoe, and then reconnect it to the upper mounting bracket **(see illustrations)**.

23 Make sure the upper strut plate is fitted into the slot in the front brake shoe **(see illustration)**.

24 Refit the lower return spring to the lower part of the brake shoes **(see illustration)**.

25 Shorten the adjuster strut to its minimum length by turning the toothed wheel, and apply a smear of brake grease to the contact faces at each end of the adjuster strut.

26 With the spring in place, use a pair of long nose pliers to open up the lower part of the brake shoes, and then slide the adjuster strut back into position **(see illustrations)**. Make sure the adjuster strut is fitted the correct way around (as noted on removal), and that the ends are fitted to the slots in the brake shoes.

27 Use a flat bladed screwdriver to hold the retaining pins in position, and then fit the two hold-down springs to both of the brake shoes, turning the retaining pins through 90° to secure the hold-down springs in position **(see illustrations)**.

6.22a Insert the upper spring in the brake shoe …

6.22b … and hook the other end of the spring over the upper bracket

6.23 Make sure the springs and strut plate are fitted correctly

6.24 Fit the lower spring to the brake shoes

6.26a Open up the brake shoes and fit the adjuster …

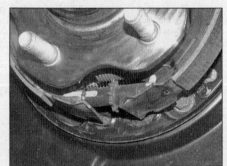

6.26b … making sure it is fitted the correct way around

6.27a Hold the retaining pin in place and fit the spring clip

6.27b Turn the retaining pin …

6.27c … and lock the spring clip in place

28 Check that all components have been correctly refitted, and check that the adjuster mechanism operates correctly.

29 Using a screwdriver, turn the adjuster strut toothed wheel to expand the shoes until the brake disc/drum just slides over the shoes.

30 Refit the rear brake disc, as described in Section 8.

31 Repeat the above procedure on the remaining rear brake.

32 Check and adjust the handbrake cable as described in Chapter 1A, Section 6 or Chapter 1B, Section 7.

33 Refit the plastic trim/cup holder to the top of the centre console.

34 Refit the roadwheels, and then lower the vehicle to the ground.

---

7 Front brake disc – inspection, removal and refitting

Warning: Before starting work, refer to the warning at the beginning of Section 4 concerning the dangers of asbestos dust.

Note: *If either disc requires renewal, BOTH should be renewed at the same time, to ensure even and consistent braking. New brake pads should also be fitted.*

Inspection

1 Firmly apply the handbrake, and then jack up the front of the vehicle and support it securely on axle stands (see *Jacking and vehicle support*). Remove the appropriate front roadwheel.

2 Slowly rotate the brake disc so that the full area of both sides can be checked; remove the brake pads (see Section 4) if better access is required to the inboard surface. Light scoring is normal in the area swept by the brake pads, but if heavy scoring or cracks are found, the disc must be renewed.

3 It is normal to find a lip of rust and brake dust around the disc's perimeter; this can be scraped off if required. If, however, a lip has formed due to excessive wear of the brake pad swept area, then the disc's thickness must be measured using a micrometer **(see illustration)**. Take measurements at several places around the disc, at the inside and outside of the pad swept area; if the disc has worn at any point to the specified minimum thickness or less, the disc must be renewed.

4 If the disc is thought to be warped, it can be checked for run-out. Either use a dial gauge mounted on any convenient fixed point, while the disc is slowly rotated **(see illustrations)**, or use feeler blades to measure (at several points all around the disc) the clearance between the disc and a fixed point, such as the caliper mounting bracket. If the measurements obtained are at the specified maximum or beyond, the disc is excessively warped, and must be renewed; however, it is worth checking first that the hub bearing is in good condition (Chapters 1 and/or 10). Also try the effect of removing the disc and turning it through 180°, to reposition it on the hub; if the run-out is still excessive, the disc must be renewed.

5 Check the disc for cracks, especially around the wheel stud holes, and any other wear or damage, and renew if necessary.

Removal

6 If not already done, firmly apply the handbrake, and then jack up the front of the vehicle and support it securely on axle stands (see *Jacking and vehicle support*). Remove the appropriate front roadwheel.

7 Unscrew the two bolts securing the caliper mounting bracket to the hub carrier **(see illustrations)**. Withdraw the caliper assembly, and suspend it using wire or string. Take care not to strain the brake fluid hose – if necessary release the hose from the securing clip(s).

8 If the original disc is to be refitted, mark the relationship between the disc and the hub, then pull the disc from the roadwheel studs **(see illustration)**.

Refitting

9 Ensure that the mating faces of the disc and the hub are clean and flat. If necessary, wipe the mating surfaces clean.

10 If the original disc is being refitted, align the marks made on the disc and hub before removal, then refit the disc.

11 If a new disc has been fitted, use a suitable solvent to wipe any preservative coating from the disc.

12 Refit the caliper, ensuring that the pads locate correctly over the disc. Then tighten the caliper mounting bracket securing bolts to the specified torque. Where applicable, refit the brake fluid hose to the clip(s).

13 Depress the brake pedal repeatedly until the

7.3 Checking the thickness of the brake disc with a micrometer

7.4a Secure the disc with washer and wheel nuts …

7.4b … then check the run out of the disc with a DTI gauge

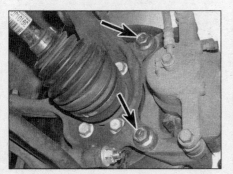

7.7a Slacken the two caliper mounting bracket bolts (arrowed) …

7.7b … and withdraw the assembly from over the brake disc

7.8 Remove the brake disc from the hub

8.5a Slacken the two caliper mounting bracket bolts (arrowed) ...

8.5b ... and support the caliper, so as not to strain the brake hose

8.6 Remove the brake disc from the hub

pads are pressed into firm contact with the brake disc, and normal pedal pressure is restored.

14 Repeat the above procedure on the remaining brake, if a new disc was fitted.

15 Refit the roadwheel, and lower the vehicle to the ground.

8 Rear brake disc – inspection, removal and refitting

> ⚠ *Warning: Before starting work, refer to the warning at the beginning of Section 4 concerning the dangers of asbestos dust.*

Note: *If either disc requires renewal, BOTH should be renewed at the same time, to ensure even and consistent braking. New brake pads should also be fitted.*

Inspection

1 Chock the front wheels then jack up the rear of the vehicle and support it securely on axle stands (see *Jacking and vehicle support*). Remove the appropriate rear roadwheel.

2 Fully release the handbrake.

3 Proceed as described for the front disc in Section 7, but refer to Section 5 if the brake pads are to be removed.

Removal

4 If not already done, chock the front wheels then jack up the rear of the vehicle and support it securely on axle stands (see *Jacking and vehicle support*). Remove the appropriate rear roadwheel and release the handbrake.

5 Unscrew the two bolts securing the caliper mounting bracket to the hub carrier **(see illustrations)**. Withdraw the caliper assembly, and suspend it using wire or string. Take care not to strain the brake fluid hose – if necessary release the hose from the securing clip(s).

6 If the original disc is to be refitted, mark the relationship between the disc and the hub, then pull the disc from the roadwheel studs **(see illustration)**.

7 If the disc cannot be withdrawn easily, it may be necessary to slacken the adjuster on the handbrake shoes inside the centre of the brake disc. Remove the grommet in the centre of the brake disc, and then slacken the handbrake shoe adjuster **(see illustrations)**. Remove brake disc from over the handbrake shoes.

Refitting

8 Ensure that the mating faces of the disc and the hub are clean and flat. If necessary, wipe the mating surfaces clean.

9 If the original disc is being refitted, align the marks made on the disc and hub before removal, then refit the disc.

10 If a new disc has been fitted, use a suitable solvent to wipe any preservative coating from the disc.

11 Refit the caliper, ensuring that the pads locate correctly over the disc. Then tighten the caliper mounting bracket securing bolts to the specified torque. Where applicable, refit the brake fluid hose to the clip(s).

12 Depress the brake pedal repeatedly until the pads are pressed into firm contact with the brake disc, and normal pedal pressure is restored.

13 Repeat the above procedure on the remaining brake, if a new disc was fitted.

14 Check and adjust the handbrake cable as described in Chapter 1A, Section 6 or Chapter 1B, Section 7.

15 Refit the roadwheel, and lower the vehicle to the ground.

9 Front brake caliper – removal, overhaul and refitting

> ⚠ *Warning: Before starting work, refer to the note at the beginning of Section 2 concerning the dangers of hydraulic fluid, and to the warning at the beginning of Section 4 concerning the dangers of asbestos dust.*

Removal

1 Firmly apply the handbrake, and then jack up the front of the vehicle and support it securely on axle stands (see *Jacking and vehicle support*). Remove the appropriate front roadwheel.

2 To minimise fluid loss during the following operations, remove the master cylinder reservoir cap, then tighten it down onto a piece of polythene to obtain an airtight seal. Alternatively, use a brake hose clamp, a G-clamp or a similar tool to clamp the flexible hose running to the caliper **(see illustration 3.1)**.

3 Clean the area around the fluid hose union on the caliper, and then unscrew the hose union banjo bolt **(see illustration)**. Recover the two sealing washers noting that new

8.7a Remove the rubber grommet ...

8.7b ... and slacken the adjuster wheel (arrowed)

9.3 Unscrew the brake hose union bolt (arrowed)

9.6 Undo the upper bolt and withdraw the brake caliper

9.7 Caliper mounting bracket bolts (arrowed)

washers will be required for refitting. Cover the open ends of the banjo and the caliper, to prevent dirt ingress.

4 Remove the brake pads as described in Section 4.

5 Unscrew the caliper upper guide pin bolt. If necessary, use a slim open-ended spanner to counterhold the head of the guide pin.

6 Withdraw the caliper from the mounting bracket **(see illustration)**.

7 If desired, the caliper mounting bracket can be unbolted from the hub carrier **(see illustration)**.

Overhaul

Note: Before commencing work, check with your local dealer for the availability of parts, and ensure that the appropriate caliper overhaul kit is obtained.

8 With the caliper on the bench, wipe away all traces of dust and dirt, but *avoid inhaling the dust, as it is a health hazard.*

9 Extract the caliper guide pins, if necessary by screwing the bolts into the pins, and pulling on the bolts to withdraw the pins. Peel off the rubber dust cover from each guide pin.

10 Place a small block of wood between the caliper body and the piston. Remove the piston, including the dust seal, by applying a jet of low-pressure compressed air, such as that from a tyre pump, to the fluid inlet port. *Caution: The piston may be ejected with some force. Only low pressure should be required, such as is generated by a foot pump.*

11 Peel the dust seal off the piston, and use a blunt instrument, such as a knitting needle, to extract the piston seal from the caliper cylinder bore.

12 Thoroughly clean all components, using only methylated spirit or clean hydraulic fluid. Never use mineral-based solvents such as petrol or paraffin, which will attack the hydraulic system rubber components.

13 The caliper piston seal and the dust seal, the guide pin dust covers, and the bleed nipple dust cap, are only available as part of a seal kit. Since the manufacturers recommend that the piston seal and dust seal are renewed whenever they are disturbed, all of these components should be discarded, and new

ones fitted on reassembly as a matter of course.

14 Carefully examine all parts of the caliper assembly, looking for signs of wear or damage. In particular, the cylinder bore and piston must be free from any signs of scratches, corrosion or wear. If there is any doubt about the condition of any part of the caliper, the relevant part should be renewed; note that if the caliper body or the mounting bracket are to be renewed, they are available only as part of the complete assembly.

15 The manufacturers recommend that minor scratches, rust, etc, may be polished away from the cylinder bore using fine emery paper, but the piston must be renewed to cure such defects. The piston surface is plated, and **must not** be polished with emery or similar abrasives.

16 Check that the threads in the caliper body and the mounting bracket are in good condition. Check that both guide pins are undamaged, and (when cleaned) a reasonably tight sliding fit in the mounting bracket bores.

17 Use compressed air to blow clear the fluid passages.

> ⚠ *Warning: Wear eye protection when using compressed air.*

18 Before commencing reassembly, ensure that all components are spotlessly clean and dry.

19 Soak the new piston seal in clean hydraulic fluid, and fit it to the groove in the cylinder bore, using your fingers only (no tools) to manipulate it into place.

20 Fit the new dust seal inner lip to the cylinder groove, smear clean hydraulic fluid over the piston and caliper cylinder bore, and twist the piston into the dust seal. Press the piston squarely into the cylinder, then slide the dust seal outer lip into the groove in the piston.

21 Fit a new rubber dust cover to each guide pin, and apply a smear of brake grease to the guide pins before refitting them to their bores **(see illustration 4.11a and 4.11b)**.

Refitting

22 Where applicable, refit the caliper mounting bracket to the hub carrier, and tighten the mounting bolts to the specified torque.

23 Place the caliper in position, refit the upper

guide pin bolt, and tighten it to the specified torque.

24 Refit the brake pads as described in Section 4.

25 Check that the caliper slides smoothly on the mounting bracket.

26 Check that the hydraulic fluid hose is correctly routed, without being twisted, and then reconnect the union to the caliper, using two new sealing washers. Refit the union banjo bolt, and tighten to the specified torque.

27 Remove the polythene from the master cylinder reservoir cap, or remove the clamp from the fluid hose, as applicable.

28 Bleed the hydraulic fluid circuit as described in Section 2. Note that if no other part of the system has been disturbed, it should only be necessary to bleed the relevant front circuit.

29 Depress the brake pedal repeatedly to bring the pads into contact with the brake disc, and ensure that normal pedal pressure is restored.

30 Refit the roadwheel, and lower the vehicle to the ground.

10 Rear brake caliper – removal and refitting

> ⚠ *Warning: Before starting work, refer to the note at the beginning of Section 2 concerning the dangers of hydraulic fluid, and to the warning at the beginning of Section 4 concerning the dangers of asbestos dust.*

Removal

1 Chock the front wheels then jack up the rear of the vehicle and support it securely on axle stands (see *Jacking and vehicle support*). Remove the appropriate rear roadwheel.

2 To minimise fluid loss during the following operations, remove the master cylinder reservoir cap, then tighten it down onto a piece of polythene to obtain an airtight seal. Alternatively, use a brake hose clamp, a G-clamp or a similar tool to clamp the flexible hose running to the caliper **(see illustration)**.

3 Clean the area around the fluid hose union on the caliper, and then unscrew the hose

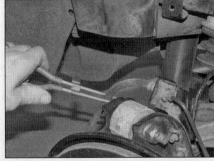

10.2 To minimise fluid loss, fit a brake hose clamp to the flexible hose

10.3 Unscrew the brake hose union bolt (arrowed)

10.5 Lift up the caliper and withdraw the upper guide bolt from the mounting bracket

10.7a Undo the caliper mounting bracket bolts (arrowed) ...

union banjo bolt **(see illustration)**. Recover the two sealing washers noting that new washers will be required for refitting. Cover the open ends of the banjo and the caliper, to prevent dirt ingress.

4 Remove the brake pads as described in Section 5.

5 Lift the caliper and then slide the upper guide pin bolt from the mounting bracket. If necessary unscrew the upper guide pin bolt from the caliper **(see illustration)**.

6 Withdraw the caliper from the mounting bracket.

7 If desired, the caliper mounting bracket can be unbolted from the hub carrier **(see illustrations)**.

Refitting

8 Where applicable, refit the caliper mounting bracket to the hub carrier, and tighten the mounting bolts to the specified torque.

9 Place the caliper in position, refit the caliper upper guide pin bolt and tighten it to the specified torque.

10 Refit the brake pads as described in Section 5.

11 Check that the caliper slides smoothly on the mounting bracket.

12 Check that the brake fluid hose is correctly routed, without being twisted, and then reconnect the union to the caliper **(see illustration)**. Refit the union banjo bolt, using two new sealing washers, and then tighten to the specified torque.

13 Remove the polythene from the master cylinder reservoir cap, or remove the clamp from the fluid hose, as applicable.

14 Bleed the hydraulic fluid circuit as described in Section 2. Note that if no other part of the system has been disturbed, it should only be necessary to bleed the relevant rear circuit.

15 Depress the brake pedal repeatedly to bring the pads into contact with the brake disc, and ensure that normal pedal pressure is restored.

16 Refit the roadwheel, and lower the vehicle to the ground.

11 Master cylinder – removal and refitting

Caution: Make sure the ignition switch is in the OFF position before disconnecting any braking system hydraulic union and do not switch it on until after the hydraulic system has been bled. Failure to do this could lead to air entering the ABS modulator unit. If air enters the modulator pump, it will prove very difficult to bleed the unit.

Note: *Before starting work, refer to the warning*

at the beginning of Section 2 concerning the dangers of hydraulic fluid.

Removal

1 Disconnect the battery negative terminal (refer to *Disconnecting the battery* in the Reference Section).

2 Remove the master cylinder fluid reservoir cap, and syphon the hydraulic fluid from the reservoir. Alternatively, open two bleed screws in the system (one in each of the dual circuit), and gently pump the brake pedal to expel the fluid through a tube connected to the bleed screws (see Section 2).

⚠ *Warning: Do not syphon the fluid by mouth, as it is poisonous; use a syringe or an old antifreeze tester.*

3 Disconnect the wiring connector from the brake fluid level sender unit on the side of the reservoir **(see illustration)**. Unclip the wiring loom retaining clip from the lower front part of the reservoir.

4 On models with manual transmission, use a brake hose clamp, a G-clamp or a similar tool, to clamp the supply hose to the clutch master cylinder, and then disconnect the hose from the reservoir **(see illustrations)**.

5 Wipe clean the area around the brake pipe unions on the side of the master cylinder, and place absorbent rags beneath the pipe unions to catch any surplus fluid. Make a note of the correct fitted positions of the unions, then

10.7b ... and withdraw it from the brake disc

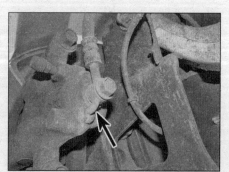

10.12 Make sure the brake hose is located correctly on the caliper

11.3 Disconnect the level sensor wiring plug

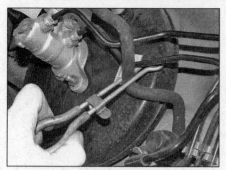

11.4a Fit a brake hose clamp to the clutch supply hose ...

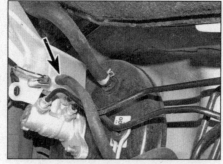

11.4b ... and then disconnect the hose from the reservoir (arrowed)

11.5 Slacken the brake fluid pipes (arrowed)

unscrew the union nuts and carefully withdraw the pipes (see illustration). Plug or tape over the pipe ends and master cylinder orifices, to minimise the loss of brake fluid, and to prevent the entry of dirt into the system. Wash off any spilt fluid immediately with cold water.

6 Slacken and remove the two nuts securing the master cylinder to the vacuum servo unit (see illustration), and then withdraw the master cylinder complete with reservoir from the engine compartment.

7 If required, undo the retaining screw at the lower part of the reservoir (see illustration), and then pull the reservoir upwards to release it from the master cylinder.

11.6 Master cylinder securing nuts (arrowed)

11.7 Reservoir securing screw (arrowed)

Refitting

8 Remove all traces of dirt from the master cylinder and servo unit mating surfaces.

9 If removed, refit the reservoir to the top of the master cylinder making sure the rubber seals are fitted correctly, and tighten the reservoir retaining screw.

10 Fit the master cylinder to the servo unit, ensuring that the servo unit pushrod enters the master cylinder bore centrally. Refit the master cylinder mounting nuts, and tighten them to the specified torque.

11 Place absorbent rags around and beneath the master cylinder, and then fill the reservoir with fresh hydraulic fluid.

12 Have an assistant slowly depress the brake pedal fully, and then hold it in the fully depressed position. Cover the outlet ports on the master cylinder body with your fingers

then have the assistant slowly release the brake pedal. Continue this procedure until the fluid emerging from the master cylinder is free from air bubbles. Take care to collect the expelled fluid in the rags and wash off any spilt fluid immediately with cold water.

13 When all air has been bled from the master cylinder, wipe clean the brake pipe unions, then refit them to the correct master cylinder ports, as noted before removal, and tighten the union nuts securely.

14 On manual transmission models, refit the clutch supply hose to the reservoir and remove the hose clamp. There should be no need to bleed the clutch system, but if required the clutch can be bled, as described in Chapter 6, Section 2.

15 Reconnect the wiring connector to the brake fluid level sender unit on the side of the

reservoir, clip the wiring loom retaining clip back into position.

16 On completion, bleed the complete hydraulic system as described in Section 2.

12 Brake pedal – removal, refitting and adjustment

Removal

1 To improve access, if not already done, remove the driver's side lower facia panel as described in Chapter 11, Section 26.

2 Working in the driver's foot well, remove the R clip from the end of the servo pushrod clevis pin, and then withdraw the clevis pin (see illustrations).

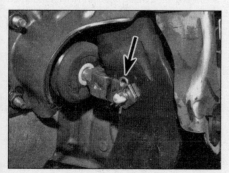

12.2a Remove the R-clip ...

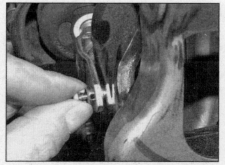

12.2b ... squeeze the clips together ...

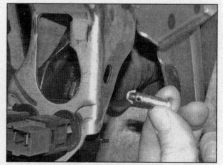

12.2c ... and remove the clevis pin

12.3 Disconnect the switch wiring connector(s)

12.4 Disconnect the accelerator pedal wiring connector

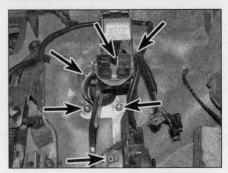

12.5 Undo the brake pedal assembly mounting bolts (arrowed)

3 Disconnect the wiring plug(s) from the stop-light switch(es) **(see illustration)**.
4 Disconnect the wiring plug from the accelerator pedal unit **(see illustration)**.
5 Unscrew the nuts securing the pedal bracket to the bulkhead (note that these nuts also secure the vacuum servo) **(see illustration)**.
6 Withdraw the pedal/bracket assembly from the bulkhead and out through the footwell.
7 The brake pedal is integral with the bracket assembly, and cannot be renewed individually.

Refitting

8 Refitting is a reversal of removal (on completion, check the pedal height as described later in this Section).

Adjustment

9 The pedal free height should be measured from the top face of the pedal to the floor reinforcement panel.
10 If desired, to improve access, remove the driver's side lower facia panel, as described in Chapter 11, Section 26. Lift the carpet to give the correct measurement.
11 Measure the pedal free height **(see illustration)**. Check the measured height against the value given in the Specifications.
12 If the height of the pedal requires adjustment, proceed as follows.
13 Loosen the locknut on the servo pushrod, and turn the pushrod as required

until the specified height is achieved **(see illustration 14.8)**. Retighten the locknut on completion.
14 Check that the stop-lights go out when the pedal is released. If not, adjust the switch as described in Section 18.
15 On completion, refit the trim panel.

13 Vacuum pump (diesel engines) – removal, refitting and testing

Note: *The vacuum pump is bolted to the transmission end of the cylinder head; a new gasket will be required before refitting.*

Removal

1 Where applicable, remove the plastic trim cover from the top of the engine **(see illustration)**.
2 If required to give better access to the vacuum pump, remove the air intake hose and brackets.
3 Release the retaining clip and disconnect the vacuum hoses from the pump **(see illustration)**.
4 Slacken and remove the mounting bolts securing the pump to the end of the cylinder head, then remove the pump **(see illustrations)**. Recover the gasket and discard, as a new one will be required for refitting.

Refitting

5 Ensure that the pump and cylinder head

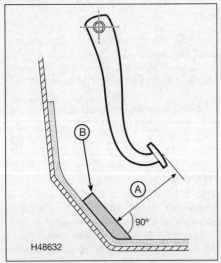

12.11 Check the height of the brake pedal (A) from the accelerator stopper plate (B)

13.1 Remove the engine upper trim cover (where fitted)

13.3 Disconnect the vacuum hose (arrowed)

13.4a Undo the two retaining bolts (arrowed) – one out of view

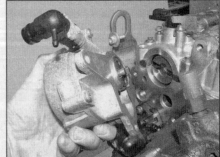

13.4b Removing the vacuum pump – 2.0 litre engine

13.5 Fit a new gasket to the vacuum pump

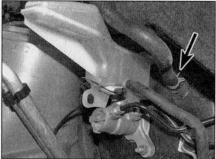

14.3 Disconnect the vacuum hose (arrowed) from the servo

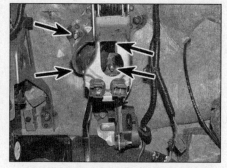

14.6 Undo the four servo mounting nuts (arrowed)

mating surfaces are clean and dry, and then fit the new gasket **(see illustration)**.

6 Manoeuvre the pump into position, aligning the drive gear with the slot in the end of the camshaft. Refit the pump mounting bolts and tighten securely.

7 Reconnect the vacuum hoses to the pump, making sure that the hoses are clipped into their relevant retaining clips.

8 If removed refit the air intake hoses and brackets, as described in Chapter 4B, then refit the engine trim cover.

9 On completion, test the operation of the brakes as follows.

Testing

10 The operation of the braking system can be checked using a vacuum gauge.

11 Disconnect the vacuum hoes from the pump and connect the gauge to the pump using a length of hose.

12 Start the engine and allow it to idle, and then measure the vacuum created by the pump. As a guide after one minute, a minimum of approx. 500 mm Hg should be recorded.

13 If the vacuum registered is significantly less than this, it is likely that the pump is faulty. However seek the advice of a specialist, before condemning the pump.

14 Overhaul of the vacuum pump may not be possible; check the availability of spares.

14 Vacuum servo unit – removal and refitting

Removal

1 Disconnect the battery negative terminal (refer to *Disconnecting the battery* in the Reference Chapter).

2 Remove the brake master cylinder, with reference to Section 11.

3 Disconnect the vacuum hose from the servo **(see illustration)**.

4 Remove the driver's side lower facia panel, as described in Chapter 11, Section 26.

5 Working in the driver's footwell, remove the spring clip from the end of the servo pushrod clevis pin, and then withdraw the clevis pin **(see illustrations 12.2a, 12.2b and 12.2c)**. If desired,

6 Again working in the driver's footwell, unscrew

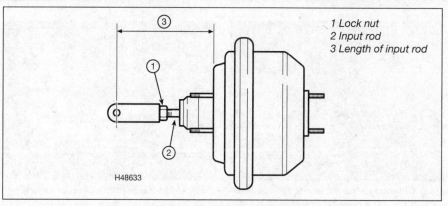

14.8 Servo input rod adjustment

1 Lock nut
2 Input rod
3 Length of input rod

the four nuts securing the brake pedal mounting bracket to the servo studs **(see illustration)**.

7 Working in the engine compartment, withdraw the servo.

Refitting

8 Refitting is a reversal of removal, bearing in mind the following points:

a) Before refitting the servo, check that the length of the pushrod is as specified (see Specifications), and adjust if necessary by loosening the locknut and turning the pushrod **(see illustration)**.

b) Where applicable, tighten all fixings to the specified torque.

c) Refit the master cylinder as described in Section 11.

d) On completion, check the brake pedal height as described in Section 12.

15 Vacuum servo unit check valve – removal, testing and refitting

Removal

1 The valve is located in the vacuum hose leading to the servo, and is secured to the body panel by a clip.

2 Release the valve from the securing clip. Take note of the direction of the arrow on the valve body, which should point in the direction of the hose connected to the engine.

3 Release the retaining clips (where fitted), and disconnect the vacuum hoses from the valve, then withdraw the valve.

Testing

4 Examine the check valve for signs of damage, and renew if necessary. The valve may be tested by blowing through it in both directions. Air should flow through the valve in one direction only – when blown through from the servo unit end of the valve. Renew the valve if this is not the case.

Refitting

5 Refitting is a reversal of removal, ensuring that the arrow on the valve body and hoses, points towards the engine.

6 On completion, start the engine and check the hose connections to the valve for air leaks.

16 Handbrake lever – removal and refitting

Removal

1 Disconnect the battery negative terminal (refer to *Disconnecting the battery* in the Reference Chapter).

2 Remove the centre console as described in Chapter 11, Section 25.

3 Chock the wheels, and fully release the handbrake.

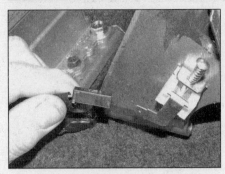

16.4 Disconnect the switch wiring connector

16.5a Measure the amount of threads …

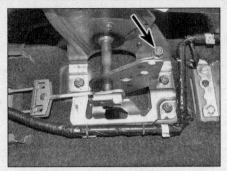

16.5b … then slacken the adjuster nut to the end of the threads

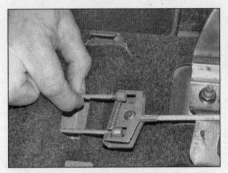

16.6 Disengage the cable end fittings from the equaliser plate

16.7 Undo the handbrake lever mounting nuts

4 Disconnect the wiring plug from the handbrake 'on' warning light switch **(see illustration)**.

5 Measure the number of exposed threads on the front cable adjuster (for reference when refitting), then unscrew the adjuster nut to the end of the threads **(see illustrations)**.

6 Disconnect the two rear handbrake cables from the equalizer bracket at the rear of the handbrake lever **(see illustration)**.

7 Remove the three securing nuts, and withdraw the handbrake lever assembly from the floor panel **(see illustration)**.

Refitting

8 Refitting is a reversal of removal, bearing in mind the following point:
a) *Screw the adjuster nut onto the front cable to give the measurement noted before removal, then check the handbrake operation, and adjust if necessary, as described in Chapter 1A, Section 6 or Chapter 1B, Section 7.*
b) *Before refitting the centre console, check the operation of the handbrake 'on' warning light.*

---

17 Handbrake cables – removal and refitting

17.4a Undo the handbrake cable securing nut …

17.4b … and withdraw the cable from the back plate

Rear cables

Removal

1 There are two rear handbrake cables, one on each side of the vehicle. To renew either rear cable, proceed as follows.

2 Chock the front wheels then jack up the rear of the vehicle and support it securely on axle stands (see *Jacking and vehicle support*). Release the handbrake fully.

3 Remove the handbrake shoes, as described in Section 6.

4 Unclip the handbrake cable spring, undo the retaining bolt and withdraw the handbrake cable from the brake back plate **(see illustrations)**.

5 Undo the retaining bolts and disconnect the handbrake cable securing clips from the top of the rear trailing arms and underbody of the vehicle **(see illustrations)**.

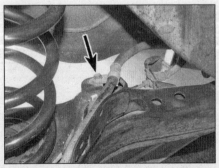

17.5a Undo the handbrake cable retaining clips (arrowed) …

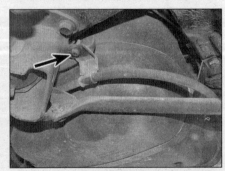

17.5b … bolted to the underside of the vehicle

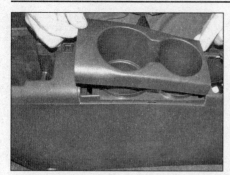

17.6 Unclip the cup holder from the centre console

17.7 Disconnect the cables from the equalizer plate (arrowed)

17.8 Withdraw the cables through the floor panel

6 Working inside the vehicle, remove the cup holder/trim from the top of the centre console **(see illustration)**.

7 Reaching inside the centre console, disconnect the two rear handbrake cables from the equalizer plate at the rear of the handbrake lever **(see illustration)**.

8 With the cables disconnected from the equalizer, from under the vehicle withdraw the cables from the floor panel **(see illustration)**. Note that on certain models it will be necessary to remove the exhaust heat shield for access to where the handbrake cables go through the floor panel.

Refitting

9 Refitting is a reversal of removal, bearing in mind the following points:
 a) Refit the handbrake shoes, as described in Section 6.
 b) On completion, check the handbrake adjustment, as described in Chapter 1A, Section 6 or Chapter 1B, Section 7.

Front cable

Removal

10 Working inside the vehicle, remove the cup holder/trim from the top of the centre console **(see illustration 17.6)**.

11 Measure the number of exposed threads on the front cable adjuster (for reference when refitting), then unscrew the adjuster nut from the end of the threads **(see illustration 16.5a)**.

12 Reaching inside the centre console, disconnect the two rear handbrake cables from the equalizer bracket at the rear of the handbrake lever **(see illustration 17.7)**.

13 Withdraw the front cable complete with equalizer plate out from inside the centre console.

Refitting

14 Refitting is a reversal of removal, bearing in mind the following points:
 a) Screw the adjuster nut onto the front cable to give the measurement noted before removal.
 b) Check the handbrake operation, and adjust if necessary, as described in Chapter 1A, Section 6 or Chapter 1B, Section 7.

18 Stop-light switch – removal, adjustment and refitting

Removal

1 Remove the driver's side lower facia panel, as described in Chapter 11, Section 26.

2 Disconnect the switch wiring connector from the switch **(see illustration 12.3)**. Note on some models, there are two switches fitted to the brake pedal mounting bracket. One of the switches is to give information to the ECM for the cruise control.

3 Twist the switch body and withdraw it from the pedal bracket **(see illustration)**.

4 When refitting the switch, hold the pedal upwards, and then push the switch back into the mounting bracket until the plunger on the end of the switch is fully pressed back into the switch **(see illustration)**. Once in place, turn the switch clockwise to lock it back in position in the mounting bracket.

5 Measure the pedal to switch clearance **(see illustration)**. Check the measurement against the value given in the Specifications.

6 Re-connect the wiring connector(s), and then check that the stop-lights are extinguished when the brake pedal is released, and illuminated within the first few millimeters of brake pedal travel.

7 If adjustment is required, remove the switch as described previously, and then when refitting the switch, fit it further inwards or outwards on the mounting bracket, until the pedal to switch clearance is correct and the lights operate correctly.

8 When completed, refit the driver's side lower facia panel, as described in Chapter 11, Section 26.

19 Handbrake 'on' warning light switch – removal and refitting

Removal

1 Working inside the vehicle, remove the cup holder/trim from the top of the centre console **(see illustration 17.6)**.

18.3 Rotate the switch and remove it from the mounting bracket

18.4 Press the pedal down and fit the switch

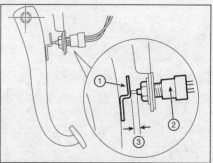

18.5 Check the pedal to switch clearance

1 Pedal bracket   2 Switch   3 Clearance

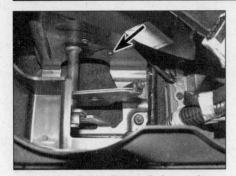

19.2 Handbrake light switch securing screw (arrowed)

2 Reaching inside the centre console, undo the securing screw, securing the switch to the handbrake lever mounting bracket **(see illustration)**.

3 As the switch is withdrawn, disconnect the wiring connector.

Refitting

4 Refitting is a reversal of removal, check that the warning light comes on after the specified number of handbrake clicks (see Specifications).

20 Anti-lock braking system (ABS) – general information and component renewal

General information

Anti-lock braking is available as standard equipment on the models covered by this manual. The system is fail-safe, and is fitted in addition to the conventional braking system, meaning that the vehicle retains conventional braking in the event of an ABS failure.

To prevent wheel locking, the system provides a means of modulating (varying) the hydraulic pressure in the braking circuits, to control the amount of braking effort at each wheel. To achieve this, sensors mounted at all four wheels monitor the rotational speeds of the wheels, and are thus able to detect when there is a risk of wheel locking (low rotational speed, relative to vehicle speed). Solenoid valves are positioned in the brake circuits to each wheel, and the solenoid valves are incorporated in a modulator assembly, which is controlled by an electronic control unit. The electronic control unit controls the braking effort applied to each wheel, according to the information supplied by the wheel sensors.

Should an ABS fault develop, the system can only be satisfactorily tested using specialist diagnostic equipment available to a Nissan dealer. For safety reasons, owners are strongly advised against attempting to diagnose complex problems with the ABS using standard workshop equipment.

Component renewal

Wheel speed sensors

1 Jack up the front or rear of the vehicle (as applicable), and support it securely using axle stands (see *Jacking and vehicle support*). Remove the relevant roadwheel.

2 The front speed sensors are located on the rear side of each wheel hub carrier, whilst the rear sensors are located on the inner face of the stub axle assembly on 2WD models and on the rear of the wheel hub carrier on 4WD models **(see illustrations)**.

20.2a Location of front wheel speed sensor

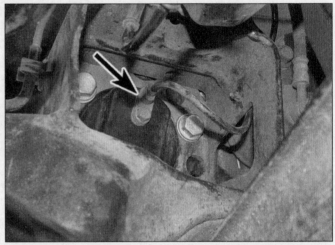

20.2b Location of rear wheel speed sensor (arrowed) - 2WD models

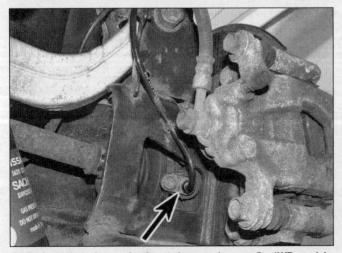

20.2c Location of rear wheel speed sensor (arrowed) – 4WD models

20.3 Remove the inner wing trim panel

20.4a Disconnect the front sensor wiring connector (arrowed) …

20.4b … and release the wiring from the support bracket

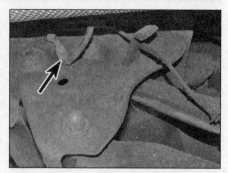

20.4c Disconnect the rear sensor wiring connector (arrowed) …

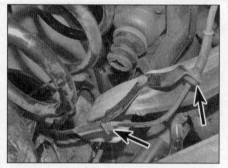

20.4d … and release the wiring from the support bracket

20.5a Remove the front wheel sensor

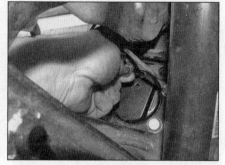

20.5b Remove the rear wheel sensor-2WD models

3 For access to the front wheel sensor connector, release the retaining clips and remove the plastic inner trim from inside the wheel arch **(see illustration)**.

4 Trace the sensor wiring back to the connector, and separate the two halves of the wiring plug. Release the wiring from any retaining brackets/clips **(see illustrations)**.

5 Undo the retaining bolt and pull the sensor from the hub carrier/stub axle assembly **(see illustrations)**. If the sensor is reluctant to move, apply releasing/penetrating fluid to the assembly, and leave it to soak for a few minutes before trying again. If the sensor still will not move, the hub carrier or rear brake disc must be removed, and the sensor driven from place.

6 Refitting is the reversal of removal, noting the following points:

a) *Ensure the mating faces of the hub carrier/stub axle assembly and sensor are clean and free from corrosion.*

b) *Apply a thin smear of anti-seize compound to mounting surfaces of the sensor and hub carrier/stub axle assembly.*

c) *Tighten the sensor retaining bolt to the specified torque.*

Actuator (Modulator)

7 The actuator is located in the left-hand rear corner of the engine compartment **(see illustration)**. Disconnect the battery negative lead (refer to *Disconnecting the battery* in the Reference Chapter).

8 Open two bleed screws in the system (one in each of the dual circuit), and gently pump the brake pedal to expel the fluid through a tube connected to the bleed screws (see Section 2). Alternatively, have some caps handy to plug the open ends of the brake pipes once they are disconnected from the actuator.

9 Remove the air cleaner assembly as described in Chapter 4A, Section 2 or Chapter 4B, Section 2.

10 Release the locking clip, and then disconnect the wiring plug from the side of the actuator **(see illustration)**.

11 Note their fitted locations, then undo the union nuts and disconnect the brake pipes

20.5c Remove the rear wheel sensor-4WD models

20.7 Location of ABS actuator

20.10 Release the wiring plug locking lever (arrowed)

20.11 Mark the location of the various brake pipes before disconnecting them from the actuator

20.12 Undo the actuator mounting nuts

from the ABS actuator **(see illustration)**. If the system has not been drained, be prepared for fluid spillage. Plug the end of the pipes to prevent dirt ingress.

12 Undo the actuator mounting nuts **(see illustration)**, and manoeuvre the actuator from the mounting bracket.

13 To refit the actuator, align the locating lug at the bottom of the unit with the corresponding hole in the mounting bracket, and then tighten the mounting nuts securely.

14 The remainder of refitting is a reversal of removal, bleeding the brake system as described in Section 2.

Chapter 10
Suspension and steering

Contents

Degrees of difficulty

| Easy, suitable for novice with little experience | 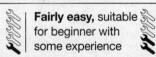 | Fairly easy, suitable for beginner with some experience | | Fairly difficult, suitable for competent DIY mechanic | | Difficult, suitable for experienced DIY mechanic | | Very difficult, suitable for expert DIY or professional | |

Specifications

Front suspension
Type . . . .   Independent by MacPherson struts, with coil springs and integral shock absorbers, and lower arms. Anti-roll bar fitted to all models

Rear suspension
Type . . . .   Independent multi-link with coil springs and shock absorbers

Steering
Type . . . .   Rack-and-pinion, electrically power-assisted.

Wheel bearings
Maximum endfloat at hub (front and rear) . . . .   0.05 mm

Roadwheels and tyres
See *Weekly checks* and Chapter 1A or Chapter 1B

Front wheel alignment
Front wheel toe setting. . . . .   2.0 mm ± 2.0 mm toe-in

Torque wrench settings

	Nm	lbf ft
Front suspension		
Anti-roll bar drop link-to-anti-roll bar nuts	75	55
Anti-roll bar drop link-to-strut nuts.	75	55
Anti-roll bar mounting bracket bolts.	29	21
Subframe mounting bolts.	87	65
Hub carrier-to-suspension strut retaining bolt nuts*	168	124
Lower arm balljoint-to-hub carrier bolt/nut*	87	65
Front hub nut (renew split pin)	125	92
Front wheel bearing hub assembly bolts:		
2WD models.	62	46
4WD models.	88	65
Lower arm front mounting-to-subframe bolts	171	126
Lower arm rear mounting-to-subframe bolt/nut*	97	72
Subframe tie bar-to-body bolts	87	65
Suspension strut damper rod top nut*	62	46
Suspension strut upper mounting bolts.	15	11
Rear suspension		
Anti-roll bar drop link-to-anti-roll bar nuts*	85	62
Anti-roll bar drop link-to-lower arm nuts*	110	81
Anti-roll bar mounting bracket nuts	36	27
Lower suspension arm inner mounting bolt/nut*	117	86
Lower suspension arm outer mounting bolt/nut*	150	111
Upper suspension arm inner mounting bolt/nut*	150	111
Upper suspension arm outer mounting bolt/nut*	150	111
Rear hub nut (renew split pin).	125	92
Rear centre subframe mounting bolts	115	85
Rear wheel bearing hub assembly bolts	93	69
Suspension damper upper mounting bolt/nut*	117	86
Suspension damper lower mounting bolt/nut*	117	86
Trailing arm-to-front mounting bracket bolt/nut*	117	86
Trailing arm front mounting bracket-to-body bolts	130	95
Steering		
Steering column securing nuts.	17	13
Steering column upper universal joint clamp bolt	31	23
Steering column lower universal joint clamp bolt:		
Black bolt with silver cam nut	32	24
Silver bolt with silver cam nut.	40	30
Steering gear mounting bracket bolts/nuts	145	107
Steering wheel securing nut.	35	26
Track rod end locknut.	88	65
Track rod end-to-steering arm/hub carrier nut.	34	25
Roadwheels		
Roadwheel nuts	113	83

* Use new nut(s)

1 General information

Front suspension

The independent front suspension is of the MacPherson strut type, incorporating coil springs and integral telescopic shock absorbers. The upper ends of the MacPherson struts are connected to the bodyshell front suspension turrets; the lower ends are bolted to the hub carriers, which carry the wheel bearings, brake calipers and hub/disc assemblies. The hub carriers are located at their lower ends by transverse lower arms. A front anti-roll bar is fitted to all models.

Rear suspension

The rear suspension is of the independent multi-link type, with two trailing arms. The rear coil springs sit on top of the rear trailing arms and the telescopic dampers (shock absorbers) are connected to the rear of the trailing arms. The same rear suspension arms and subframe are fitted to both two-wheel and four-wheel drive models.

Steering

The steering column has a universal joint fitted at its lower end, which is clamped to both the steering column shaft and the steering gear pinion by means of clamp bolts.

The steering gear is mounted on the rear of the engine/transmission subframe, and is connected to the steering arms projecting rearwards from the hub carriers. The track rods are fitted with balljoints at their inner and outer ends, to allow for suspension movement, and are threaded to facilitate adjustment.

Electric power steering is fitted as standard on all models. The electric motor is part of the steering column assembly inside the passenger compartment.

2 Front hub bearings – renewal

Note: *The bearing is part of the centre hub assembly and can only be replaced as a complete assembly.*

Removal

1 Firmly apply the handbrake, and then jack up the front of the vehicle and support it securely on axle stands (see *Jacking and vehicle support*). Remove the appropriate roadwheel.

2.4 Disconnect the driveshaft from the hub

2.5 Remove the two strut-to-hub retaining bolts

2.6 Hub/bearing assembly mounting bolts

2 Remove the brake disc, as described in Chapter 9, Section 7.

3 On models with ABS, if not already done, unbolt the ABS wheel sensor, as described in Chapter 9, Section 20. Suspend the sensor away from the working area, to avoid the possibility of damage.

4 Disconnect the outboard end of the driveshaft from the hub carrier **(see illustration)**, as described in Chapter 8, Section 2. Note that there is no need to drain the transmission oil/fluid, or disconnect the inboard end of the driveshaft from the transmission. **Do not** allow the end of the driveshaft to hang down under its own weight – support the end of the driveshaft using wire or string.

5 Undo the two upper hub carrier-to-strut retaining bolt/nuts, and then remove the hub carrier from the strut **(see illustration)**. Note the fitted position of the retaining bolts for refitting; discard the nuts, as new ones will be required for refitting.

6 Slacken the four hub/bearing retaining bolts **(see illustration)**. Remove two of the bolts completely, and then leave the other two bolts screwed most of the way into the rear of the hub/bearing.

7 Using a copper hammer, hit the heads of the two bolts that remain in the rear of the hub/bearing, whilst holding the assembly on the bench **(see illustrations)**. If the hub/bearing is reluctant to move, apply releasing/penetrating fluid to the assembly, and leave it to soak for a few minutes before trying again.

8 With the hub/bearing removed from the

carrier, remove the brake disc back plate, noting its fitted position **(see illustration)**.

9 Using a press (or similar), press the centre wheel flange part of the hub out from the bearing **(see illustration)**.

10 Note that one half of the bearing inner race may remain on the centre wheel flange. If so, support the wheel hub in a vice then draw off the bearing inner race, using a suitable puller.

Refitting

11 Before installing the new bearing, thoroughly clean the wheel flange, hub and the bearing location in the hub carrier.

12 Press the new bearing onto the centre wheel flange until it contacts the shoulder on the flange. This can be achieved using metal tubing, or large sockets of suitable diameter, together with threaded bar, spacers and nuts to pull the components together.

2.7a Using a copper hammer to free the bearing assembly …

2.7b … then withdraw it from the hub/steering knuckle

13 With the bearing fully home, fit the brake disc back plate into position (as noted on removal), and then fit the hub/bearing unit to the carrier and tighten the retaining bolts.

14 Refit the hub/bearing carrier back to the lower part of the strut and fit the retaining bolts and new nuts, in the position noted on removal **(see illustration)**. Tighten the retaining bolts to the specified torque setting.

15 Refit the outer end of the driveshaft back into the hub, as described in Chapter 8, Section 2.

16 Refit the wheel speed sensor back into the rear of the hub carrier, as described in Chapter 9, Section 20.

17 Refit the front brake disc, as described in Chapter 9, Section 7.

18 On completion, refit the roadwheel and lower the vehicle to the ground.

2.8 Remove the brake disc back plate

2.9 The centre hub will need to be pressed out of the bearing

2.14 Fit new nuts to the lower strut bolts

3.2 Release the brake pipe securing clip

3.3 Unclip the wheel sensor wiring from the support bracket

3.4 Undo the drop link upper retaining nut

3 Front suspension strut – removal, overhaul and refitting

Note: *New hub carrier-to-suspension strut retaining nuts must be used on refitting.*

Removal

1 Firmly apply the handbrake, and then jack up the front of the vehicle and support it securely on axle stands (see *Jacking and vehicle support*). Remove the appropriate roadwheel.

2 Extract the retaining clip and release the brake hydraulic hose from the support bracket on the suspension strut **(see illustration)**.

3 Unclip the ABS wiring loom from the support bracket on the lower part of the suspension strut **(see illustration)**.

4 Undo the retaining nut and disconnect the drop link upper ball joint retaining nut from the suspension strut **(see illustration)**.

5 Undo the two nuts and withdraw the bolts securing the suspension strut to the hub carrier **(see illustration)**. Discard the nuts, as new ones must be used on refitting.

6 Open the bonnet, release the securing clips and remove the scuttle panel from the rear of the engine compartment **(see illustration)**. See Chapter 11, Section 21 for further information on the removal of the scuttle panel.

7 Have an assistant support the strut from underneath the wheel arch then, working in the engine compartment, unscrew the three bolts securing the top of the strut to the suspension turret **(see illustration)**.

8 Release the lower end of the strut from the hub carrier, and then withdraw the assembly

from under the wheel arch. Note the fitted position of the top mounting to the inner wing panel for refitting **(see illustrations)**.

⚠️ **Warning: Do not unscrew the centre damper rod nut at this stage.**

Overhaul

Note: *Coil spring compressor tools will be required for this operation, and a new damper rod top nut must be used on reassembly.*

9 Using an Allen key to hold the damper centre rod, slacken the strut upper mounting nut. **Do not** remove the nut; only slacken to the top of the threads, so the nut is still fully on the threads.

10 Fit spring compressors to the spring, and compress the spring sufficiently to enable the upper spring seat to be turned by hand **(see illustration)**.

3.5 Remove the two strut-to-hub retaining bolts

3.6 Remove the scuttle grill panel

3.7 Undo the three strut upper mounting bolts

3.8a Remove the strut assembly ...

3.8b ... noting the position of the upper mounting

3.10 Fit the coil compressors to the springs

3.11 The damper rod nut can now be completely removed

3.12 Remove the upper mounting complete with gaiter

3.13a Carefully withdraw the spring and compressors ...

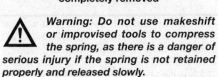

Warning: Do not use makeshift or improvised tools to compress the spring, as there is a danger of serious injury if the spring is not retained properly and released slowly.

11 Fully unscrew and remove the damper rod top nut. Note that it may be necessary to counterhold the damper rod, using an Allen key, as the nut is unscrewed **(see illustration)**. Discard the nut – a new one must be used on reassembly.

12 Withdraw the upper mounting plate, upper mounting insulator, bearing, upper spring seat, and the dust cover and bump rubber from the damper **(see illustration)**.

13 Withdraw the spring, complete with the compressors, and then withdraw the lower spring seat rubber, noting its fitted position **(see illustrations)**.

14 With the strut assembly now dismantled, examine all the components for wear, damage or deformation. Check the rubber components for deterioration **(see illustration)**. Renew any of the components as necessary.

15 Remove the upper bearing from the strut top mounting assembly. Release the retaining clips and split the lower part of the cover from the bearing upper cover. Remove the bearing race, then clean out the bearings and re-grease with new grease **(see illustrations)**.

16 Examine the damper for signs of fluid leakage. Check the damper rod for signs of pitting along its entire length, and check the strut body for signs of damage. While holding it in an upright position, test the operation of

3.13b ... and then remove the lower rubber spring seat

the strut by moving the damper rod through a full stroke, and then through short strokes of 50 to 100 mm. In both cases, the resistance felt should be smooth and continuous. If the resistance is jerky, or uneven, or if there is any visible sign of wear or damage to the strut, renewal is necessary. Note that the damper cannot be renewed independently, and if leakage or damage is evident, the complete strut/damper assembly must be renewed (in which case, the spring, upper mounting components, bushes, and associated components can be transferred to the new strut).

17 If any doubt exists about the condition of the coil spring, carefully remove the spring compressors, and check the spring for distortion and signs of cracking. Renew the spring if it is damaged or distorted, or if there is any doubt as to its condition.

3.14 Unclip the gaiter from the upper mounting

18 Commence reassembly by refitting the lower spring seat rubber, ensuring that it is correctly located in the recess in the lower spring seat, as noted on removal.

19 Ensure that the coil spring is compressed sufficiently to enable the upper mounting components to be fitted, and then locate the spring on the strut, ensuring that the lower end of the spring is correctly located on the lower spring seat rubber.

20 If previously separated, refit the dust cover and bump rubber to the upper spring seat, ensuring that the dust cover is fully engaged in the upper spring seat.

21 Refit the upper mounting plate, upper mounting insulator, bearing, upper spring seat, and the dust cover and bump rubber to the damper.

22 Fit a new damper rod top nut, and then tighten the top nut to the specified torque,

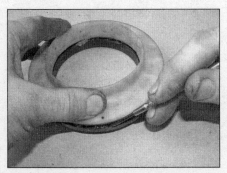

3.15a Release the retaining clips ...

3.15b ... and split the upper bearing covers ...

3.15c ... remove the bearing disc and grease the bearings

3.25 Fit new nuts to the lower strut bolts

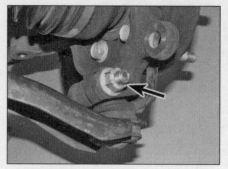

4.2a Remove the ball joint retaining nut and bolt …

4.2b … then lever the lower arm down to release the ball joint

counterholding the damper rod as during dismantling.

23 Check that the spring ends are correctly located in the upper and lower spring seats, and then remove the spring compressors.

Refitting

24 Manoeuvre the strut assembly into position under the wheel arch and up into the suspension turret. Make sure the upper mounting is in the correct position, as it is fitted inside the inner wheel arch, as noted on removal. Fit the upper mounting bolts, and tighten them to the specified torque.

25 Engage the lower end of the strut with the hub carrier and refit the securing bolts with the bolt heads toward the rear of the vehicle (see illustration). Fit the new nuts to the bolts, and tighten to the specified torque.

26 Refit the drop link upper ball joint to

the suspension strut, and then tighten the retaining nut to the specified torque.

27 Locate the brake hydraulic hose and ABS wiring loom back in the support bracket on the suspension strut. Securing the brake hose with the retaining clip.

28 Refit the scuttle panel with reference to Chapter 11, Section 21.

29 On completion, refit the roadwheel and lower the vehicle to the ground.

4 Front suspension lower arm – removal, inspection and refitting

Note: The lower arm balljoint retaining nut must be renewed on refitting.

Removal

1 Firmly apply the handbrake, and then

jack up the front of the vehicle and support it securely on axle stands (see Jacking and vehicle support). Remove the appropriate roadwheel.

2 Undo the retaining nut and withdraw the bolt from the lower ball joint. Use a length of bar, chain and a block of wood to lever the lower arm downwards and disconnect the lower ball joint from the hub carrier (see illustrations). Discard the nut – a new one must be used on refitting.

3 Undo the bolt and nut securing the lower arm rear mounting to the subframe (see illustration). Discard the nut – a new one must be used on refitting.

4 Unscrew the lower arm front mounting bolts, and then withdraw the lower arm from the subframe (see illustrations).

Inspection

5 With the lower arm removed; examine the lower arm itself, and the mounting bushes for wear, cracks or damage.

6 Check the balljoint for wear, excessive play, or stiffness (see illustration). Also check the balljoint dust boot for cracks or damage.

Rear bush renewal

7 Depending how tight the rear bush is in the lower arm, it may be possible, to remove and refit it using an assortment of spacers and a threaded bar.

8 Measure the fitted depth of the bush in the lower arm, and also mark it for orientation in the arm (see illustrations).

9 Using a length of threaded bar and different

4.3 Remove the lower arm rear mounting bolt and nut

4.4a Remove the lower arm front mounting bolts …

4.4b … and remove the lower arm from the vehicle

4.6 Checking the ball joint and gaiter

4.8a Checking the fitted position of the bush using a vernier gauge …

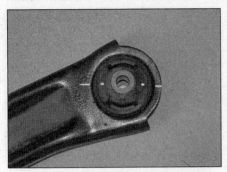

4.8b ... and marking the position of the bush in relation with the lower arm

4.9a Using different size spacers and a threaded bar ...

4.9b ... tighten the nuts each side ...

size spacers, press the bush out from the lower arm **(see illustrations)**. The larger spacer sitting against the lower arm and the smaller spacer pressing on the outer sleeve of the bush.

10 Clean the lower arm, making sure there are no burrs around the edge of the recess for the bush.

11 Fit the new bush in the position noted on removal, and then press the bush into the lower arm, using the same arrangement as removal. Make sure the bush is only pressed the same distance into the arm as noted before removal **(see illustrations)**.

12 If the bush is a tight fit, then a hydraulic press may be needed, this should therefore be entrusted to a Nissan dealer or specialist with access to the necessary equipment.

13 The front mounting bush and balljoint assembly are integral with the lower arm, and cannot be renewed independently. If either the bush or the balljoint is worn or damaged, the complete lower arm assembly must be renewed.

Refitting

14 Slide the rear of the lower arm into position in the subframe, and then refit the bolts to the front mounting on the lower arm **(see illustration)**. Tighten the bolts to the specified torque.

15 Refit the bolt and new nut to the rear lower arm mounting bush **(see illustration)**, and then tighten to the specified torque.

16 Reconnect the lower ball joint to the bottom of the hub carrier **(see illustration)**. If

4.9c ... to press out the mounting bush

4.11b ... and press the new bush into the arm ...

4.11a Align the marks made on removal ...

4.11c ... to the depth noted on removal

required, use a length of bar, chain and a block of wood to lever the lower arm downwards, as described on removal. Fit the retaining bolt and new nut to the lower ball joint, and then tighten to the specified torque setting.

17 Refit the roadwheel and lower the vehicle to the ground.

18 On completion the front wheel alignment should be checked, with reference to Chapter 1A, Section 13 or Chapter 1B, Section 14.

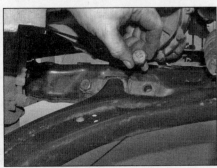

4.14 Refit the lower arm front mounting bolts

4.15 Fit a new nut to the rear mounting bolt

4.16 Refit the ball joint to the front hub assembly

6.2a Use a spanner to counterhold the ball joint ...

6.2b ... and disconnect the drop link from the anti-roll bar

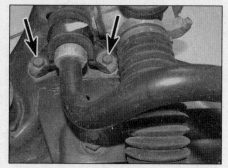

6.4 Undo the anti-roll bar clamp bolts (one side shown)

6.9 Where fitted, remove the plastic cap from the securing nut

6.11a Use a spanner to counterhold the ball joint ...

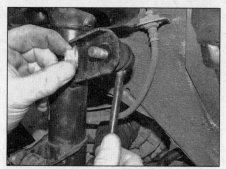

6.11b ... and disconnect the drop link from the strut

5 Front suspension lower arm balljoint – renewal

At the time of writing the lower arm balljoint was not available separately and is integral with the suspension lower arm. If the balljoint is worn or damaged, the complete lower arm must be renewed as described in Section 4.

6 Front suspension anti-roll bar – removal and refitting

Anti-roll bar

Removal

1 Firmly apply the handbrake, and then jack up the front of the vehicle and support it securely on axle stands (see *Jacking and vehicle support*). Remove the front roadwheels.
2 Working at one side of the anti-roll bar, use an open ended spanner to counterhold the drop link ball joint, then unscrew the nut securing the end of the anti-roll bar to the drop link **(see illustrations)**.
3 Repeat the operation on the other side of the anti-roll bar.
4 Unscrew the bolts, and withdraw the clamps securing the anti-roll bar to the top of the front subframe **(see illustration)**.
5 Manipulate the anti-roll bar out from under the vehicle.

Refitting

6 Inspect the mounting clamp rubbers for cracks or deterioration. If renewal is necessary, slide the old rubbers from the bar, and fit the new rubbers. Note that the rubbers should be positioned with the paint marks on the bar against their inner edges.
7 Refitting is a reversal of removal.

Drop link

Removal

8 To improve access, firmly apply the handbrake, and then jack up the front of the vehicle and support it securely on axle stands (see *Jacking and vehicle support*). Remove the relevant front roadwheel.
9 Where fitted, unclip the plastic cover from the drop link securing nuts **(see illustration)**.
10 Counterhold the drop link lower ball joint, and then unscrew the nut securing the end of the anti-roll bar to the drop link **(see illustrations 6.2a and 6.2b)**.
11 Again, counterhold the drop link ball joint, and then unscrew the nut securing the drop link upper ball joint to the suspension strut **(see illustrations)**.
12 With both upper and lower ball joints disconnected, withdraw the drop link from under the wheel arch.

Refitting

13 Check the condition of the drop link bushes, and renew if necessary.
14 Refitting is a reversal of removal, making sure that drop link securing nuts are tightened to the specified torque.

7 Rear hub bearings – renewal

1 The rear hub bearings are integral with the rear hubs, and cannot be renewed independently. If the bearings require renewal, the complete hub assembly must be renewed as follows.
2 Chock the front wheels then jack up the rear of the vehicle and support it securely on axle stands (see *Jacking and vehicle support*). Remove the appropriate rear roadwheel and release the handbrake fully.

4WD models

3 Remove the split-pin from the outer end of the driveshaft, discard the split-pin – a new one must be used on refitting **(see illustration)**.

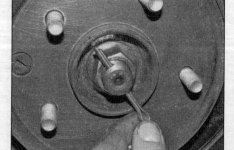

7.3 Remove the split pin

7.4 Using a homemade tool to hold the hub stationary

7.7a Undo the handbrake cable securing bolt (arrowed) …

7.7b … and withdraw the cable from the backplate

7.9a Undo the four mounting bolts …

7.9b … and remove the hub/bearing assembly

7.11 Make sure the handbrake shoe retaining pins are in place before refitting

4 The rear hub must now be held stationary in order to slacken the driveshaft retaining nut. Ideally, the hub should be held by a suitable tool bolted into place using two of the roadwheel nuts **(see illustration)**. Alternatively, have an assistant firmly apply the brake pedal to prevent the hub from rotating.

5 Using a socket and extension bar, completely remove the driveshaft retaining nut.

All models

6 Remove the handbrake shoes from inside the rear brake disc, as described in Chapter 9, Section 6.

7 Unbolt the handbrake cable and withdraw it from the lower part of the brake back plate **(see illustrations)**.

8 Remove the wheel speed sensor from the

rear of the hub, as described in Chapter 9, Section 20.

9 Working at the rear of the hub assembly undo the four mounting bolts, and then withdraw the hub complete with back plate from the trailing arm **(see illustrations)**.

10 Remove the back plate from the rear of the old hub/bearing and fit to the new one.

11 Thoroughly clean the back plate and trailing arm, and then slide the new hub assembly and back plate into position. Make sure the two handbrake shoe retaining pins are in place in the back plate before refitting **(see illustration)**.

12 Fit the hub assembly to the trailing arm and then tighten the four retaining bolts to the specified torque. Note on 4WD models, it will be necessary to slide the hub onto the driveshaft splines as it is fitted.

13 Check that the hub spins freely, and then

refit the handbrake shoes and brake disc, as described in Chapter 9, Section 6.

14 Refit the ABS wheel speed sensor and tighten its retaining bolt to the specified torque (see Chapter 9, Section 20).

15 On 4WD models, hold the rear hub stationary as during removal, then tighten the new driveshaft nut to the specified torque. Fit a new split-pin and bend over the split-pin legs **(see illustration)**.

16 Refit the roadwheel(s), lower the vehicle to the ground and tighten to the specified torque setting.

8 Rear shock absorber (damper) – removal, testing and refitting

Note: *New damper upper and lower securing nuts must be used on refitting. Also it is advisable to always renew dampers in pairs on the same axle.*

Removal

1 Chock the front wheels then jack up the rear of the vehicle and support it securely on axle stands (see *Jacking and vehicle support*). For better access remove the appropriate rear roadwheel.

2 Using a trolley jack, raise the rear trailing arm, until the damper is slightly compressed **(see illustration)**.

3 Slacken the damper lower mounting bolt retaining nut, and then withdraw the bolt,

7.15 Fit new split pin to the driveshaft threads

8.2 Use a trolley jack to support the trailing arm

8.3a Undo the retaining nut ...

8.3b ... and disconnect the lower part of the damper

8.4 Damper upper securing bolt (arrowed)

disengaging the lower part of the damper from the trailing arm (see illustrations).

4 Slacken the damper upper mounting bolt, and then withdraw the bolt and disengage the top of the damper from the upper mounting bracket (see illustration).

5 Withdraw the damper from under the rear of the vehicle.

Testing

6 Examine the damper for signs of fluid leakage. Check the damper rod for signs of pitting along its entire length, and check the body for signs of damage. While holding it in an upright position, test the operation by moving the damper rod through a full stroke, and then through short strokes of 50 to 100 mm. In both cases, the resistance felt should be smooth and continuous. If the resistance is jerky, or uneven, or if there is any visible sign of wear or damage to the damper, renewal is necessary. Also check the rubber mounting bushes for damage or deterioration, and inspect the mounting bolts for signs of wear or damage; renew if necessary.

Refitting

7 Offer up the top of the damper into its mounting bracket, then refit it's mounting bolt, fit the new retaining nut and tighten by hand at this stage.

8 Align the damper lower mounting with the trailing arm and refit the lower mounting bolt. Fit the new nut, also tightening it by hand at this stage.

9 Refit the rear roadwheel then lower the vehicle to the ground and tighten the wheel bolts to the specified torque.

10 With the vehicle down on its wheels, in the normal ride height position; tighten the upper and lower damper mounting bolts/nuts to the specified torque.

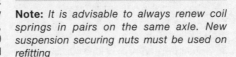

9 Rear coil spring – removal and refitting

Note: *It is advisable to always renew coil springs in pairs on the same axle. New suspension securing nuts must be used on refitting*

Removal

1 Chock the front wheels then jack up the rear of the vehicle and support it securely on axle stands (see *Jacking and vehicle support*). Remove the appropriate rear roadwheel.

4WD models

2 Remove the split-pin from the outer end of the driveshaft, discard the split-pin – a new one must be used on refitting (see illustration 7.3).

3 The rear hub must now be held stationary in order to slacken the driveshaft retaining nut. Ideally, the hub should be held by a suitable tool bolted into place using two of

the roadwheel nuts (see illustration 7.4). Alternatively, have an assistant firmly apply the brake pedal to prevent the hub from rotating.

4 Using a socket and extension bar, completely remove the driveshaft retaining nut. This will allow the outer joint of the shaft to slide from the hub as the suspension is lowered.

All models

5 Using a trolley jack, raise the rear trailing arm, until the damper is slightly compressed (see illustration 8.2).

6 Slacken the damper lower mounting bolt retaining nut, and then withdraw the bolt, disengaging the lower part of the damper from the trailing arm (see illustration 8.3a and 8.3b).

7 On models with Xenon headlights, undo the retaining bolt and disconnect the level sensor linkage bracket from the lower suspension arm (see illustration).

8 Undo the retaining nut and disconnect the anti-roll bar drop link lower ball joint from the lower suspension arm (see illustration).

9 Undo the retaining nut and bolt, and then disconnect the outer part of the upper suspension arm from the trailing arm (see illustration).

10 Carefully lower the trailing arm on the trolley jack, taking care not to put any strain on the brake hose or wheel speed sensor wiring.

11 Withdraw the coil spring complete with

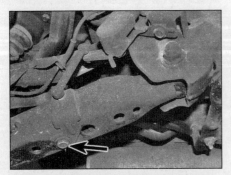

9.7 Undo the level sensor bracket retaining bolt (arrowed)

9.8 Disconnect the drop link from the lower arm

9.9 Remove the upper arm retaining bolt

9.11 Withdraw the coil spring from under the vehicle

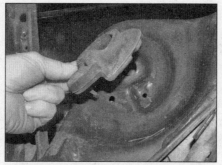

9.12 Check the coil spring lower rubber seat

9.13 Make sure the upper and lower rubber seats are in place

upper rubber mounting from under the rear of the vehicle **(see illustration)**.

12 If required, unclip the spring lower rubber mounting from the trailing arm **(see illustration)**.

Refitting

13 Refit the coil spring back into position between the underbody and the trailing arm, making sure the upper and lower rubber mountings **(see illustration)**.

14 Carefully raise the trolley jack; making sure trailing arm aligns with the upper arm. On 4WD models, make sure the splines on the outer end of the driveshaft, slide back into the hub assembly, without damaging the driveshaft.

15 Reconnect the upper suspension arm to the trailing arm, then fit the mounting bolt and tighten it by hand at this stage.

16 Reconnect the anti-roll bar drop link ball joint to the lower suspension arm, then fit the retaining nut and tighten it by hand at this stage.

17 On models with Xenon headlights, reconnect the level sensor linkage bracket to the lower suspension arm and tighten the retaining bolt.

18 Align the damper lower mounting with the trailing arm and refit the lower mounting bolt. Fit the new nut, also tightening it by hand at this stage.

19 On 4WD models, hold the rear hub stationary as during removal, then tighten the new driveshaft nut to the specified torque. Fit

a new split-pin and bend over the split-pin legs **(see illustration 7.15)**.

20 Refit the rear roadwheel then lower the vehicle to the ground and tighten the wheel bolts to the specified torque.

21 With the vehicle down on its wheels, in the normal ride height position; tighten the upper suspension arm bolt, lower damper mounting bolt and the anti-roll bar drop link securing nut to the specified torque.

---

10 Rear suspension arms –
removal, overhaul and refitting

Note: *New suspension securing nuts must be used on refitting.*

Upper suspension arm

Removal

1 Chock the front wheels then jack up the rear of the vehicle and support it securely on axle stands (see *Jacking and vehicle support*). Remove the appropriate rear roadwheel.

2 Undo the retaining bolt and disconnect the ABS wheel speed sensor wiring bracket from the front of the upper suspension arm **(see illustration)**.

3 Using a trolley jack, raise the rear trailing arm, until the damper is slightly compressed **(see illustration 8.2)**.

4 Slacken the damper lower mounting bolt retaining nut, and then withdraw the bolt, disengaging the lower part of the damper

from the trailing arm **(see illustration 8.3a and 8.3b)**. This will allow movement up and down to allow for room to withdraw the upper suspension arm, when it is disconnected.

5 Slacken and remove the upper arm-to-trailing arm mounting bolt; discard the nut, as a new one will be required for refitting **(see illustration)**.

6 Slacken and remove the upper arm-to-rear axle subframe mounting bolt; discard the nut, as a new one will be required for refitting **(see illustration)**.

7 If required, to give further movement of the rear suspension on the trolley jack, undo the retaining nut and disconnect the anti-roll bar drop link lower ball joint from the lower suspension arm **(see illustration 9.8)**.

8 Withdraw the upper suspension arm from under the rear of the vehicle **(see illustration)**.

10.2 Undo the wheel sensor wiring bracket bolt (arrowed)

10.5 Remove the upper arm outer retaining nut and bolt

10.6 Remove the upper arm inner retaining nut and bolt (arrowed)

10.8 Withdraw the upper arm from under the vehicle

10.14 Disconnect the drop link to lower arm retaining nut (arrowed)

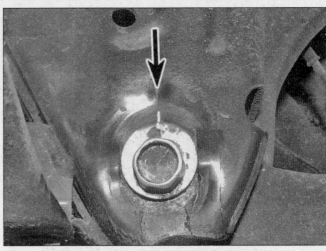

10.15a Make alignment marks on the subframe ...

Refitting

9 Refitting is the reverse of removal, noting the following points:
a) *Refit the rear roadwheel and tighten to the specified torque.*
b) *Before fully tightening the suspension nuts/bolts, lower the vehicle to the ground, to its normal ride height position, and then tighten to the specified torque.*
c) *Use new suspension arm retaining nuts on refitting.*

Lower suspension arm

Note: *The inner mounting bolt, securing the lower arm to the rear axle subframe is adjustable.*

Removal

10 Chock the front wheels then jack up the rear of the vehicle and support it securely on axle stands (see *Jacking and vehicle support*). Remove the appropriate rear roadwheel.

11 On models with Xenon headlights, undo the retaining bolt and disconnect the level sensor linkage bracket from the lower suspension arm **(see illustration 9.7)**.

12 Using a trolley jack, raise the rear trailing arm, until the damper is slightly compressed **(see illustration 8.2)**.

13 Slacken the damper lower mounting bolt retaining nut, and then withdraw the bolt, disengaging the lower part of the damper from the trailing arm **(see illustration 8.3a and 8.3b)**.

14 Undo the retaining nut and disconnect the anti-roll bar drop link lower ball joint from the lower suspension arm **(see illustration)**.

15 Before removing the lower arm inner mounting bolt, make alignment marks on the subframe and adjustable eccentric washers, as this adjusts the rear suspension **(see illustrations)**.

16 Slacken and remove the lower arm-to-rear axle subframe mounting bolt; remove the nut and washer noting the alignment marks **(see illustrations)**. Discard the nut, as a new one will be required for refitting.

17 Slacken and remove the lower arm-to-

trailing arm mounting bolt; discard the nut, as a new one will be required for refitting **(see illustration)**.

18 Withdraw the lower suspension arm from under the rear of the vehicle.

Refitting

19 Refitting is the reverse of removal, noting the following points:
a) *Refit the rear roadwheel and tighten to the specified torque.*
b) *Before fully tightening the suspension nuts/bolts, lower the vehicle to the ground, to its normal ride height position, and then tighten to the specified torque.*

10.15b ... and on the adjustable eccentric washers

10.16b ... and eccentric washer

c) *Use new suspension arm retaining nuts on refitting.*
d) *On completion, have the rear suspension alignment checked at your local specialist.*

Trailing arm

Note: *New shock absorber lower mounting nut and suspension arm retaining nuts must be used on refitting.*

Removal

20 Chock the front wheels then jack up the rear of the vehicle and support it securely on axle stands (see *Jacking and vehicle support*). Remove the rear roadwheels.

10.16a Remove the retaining nut ...

10.17 Remove the lower arm outer retaining nut and bolt

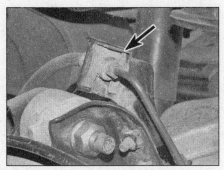

10.23a Release the brake pipe retaining clip (arrowed) ...

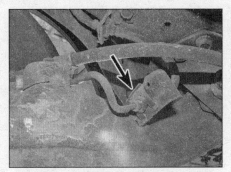

10.23b ... and the pipe retaining clip (arrowed) under the trailing arm

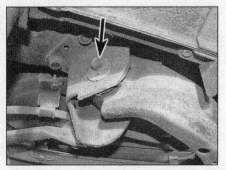

10.29 Remove the trailing arm retaining nut and bolt

21 Remove the rear hub/bearing assembly, as described in Section 7.

22 Slacken the damper lower mounting bolt retaining nut, and then withdraw the bolt, disengaging the lower part of the damper from the trailing arm **(see illustration 8.3a and 8.3b).**

23 With reference to Chapter 9, Section 3, slacken the brake hose connections and release the retaining clips securing the brake pipe along the top of the trailing arm **(see illustrations). Note:** *Be prepared for brake fluid spillage. Before starting work, refer to the note at the beginning of Chapter 9, Section 2 concerning the dangers of hydraulic fluid.*

24 Slacken and remove the upper arm-to-trailing arm mounting bolt; discard the nut, as a new one will be required for refitting **(see illustration 10.5).**

25 Slacken and remove the lower arm-to-trailing arm mounting bolt; discard the nut,

as a new one will be required for refitting **(see illustration 10.17).**

26 Check along the length of the trailing arm, making sure there is nothing else still connected to it.

27 On 4WD models, support the outer end of the driveshaft to prevent it from getting damaged when the trailing arm is removed. If required, remove the rear driveshaft completely, as described in Chapter 8, Section 2.

28 Before removing the trailing arm front mounting bolt, make alignment marks on the mounting bracket and adjustable eccentric washers **(see illustration 10.15a),** as this adjusts the rear suspension.

29 Carefully lower the rear end of the trailing arm slightly, using the trolley jack, and then undo the retaining nut and bolt at the front of the trailing arm **(see illustration).** Remove the bolt and withdraw the trailing arm from under the rear of the vehicle.

Refitting

30 Refitting is the reverse of removal, noting the following points:

a) *Refit the rear roadwheel and tighten to the specified torque.*

b) *Before fully tightening the suspension nuts/bolts, lower the vehicle to the ground, to its normal ride height position, and then tighten to the specified torque.*

c) *Use new suspension retaining nuts on refitting.*

d) *On completion, have the rear suspension alignment checked at your local specialist.*

11 Steering wheel – removal and refitting

⚠️ *Warning: The airbag is mounted in the steering wheel centre pad. Make sure that the safety recommendations given in Chapter 12, Section 20, are followed to prevent personal injury.*

Removal

1 Ensure that the ignition is switched off, and then disconnect the battery negative terminal (refer to *Disconnecting the battery* in the Reference Chapter). *Wait for at least ten minutes before carrying out any further work.*

2 Remove the airbag unit from the centre of the steering wheel, as described in Chapter 12, Section 21.

3 Release the steering lock by inserting the ignition key and set the front wheels in the straight-ahead position.

4 Undo and remove the steering wheel retaining nut **(see illustration).**

5 Check for alignment marks between the steering wheel and the end of the steering column shaft for refitting **(see illustration).** Make your own alignment marks, if required.

6 Withdraw the wheel from the column shaft and feed the wiring connectors through the steering wheel as the wheel is withdrawn **(see illustration).**

7 With the steering wheel removed, check the position of the rotary/spiral switch, tape in position to prevent it from moving, if required **(see illustration).**

11.4 Undo the steering wheel retaining nut

11.5 Note the alignment marks for refitting

11.6 Remove the steering wheel from the column

11.7 Make sure the rotary switch is not turned while wheel is removed

12.2a Remove the plastic cover to access the lower steering column joint ...

12.2b ... note the position and undo the retaining bolt ...

12.2c ... disconnect the joint from the pinion shaft

Refitting

8 Refitting is a reversal of removal, bearing in mind the following points:

  a) *Ensure that the front wheels are in the straight-ahead position.*

  b) *Remove the tape (where fitted) from the rotary/spiral unit, making sure it is in the correct position.*

  c) *Ensure that the direction indicator switch is in the central (cancelled/off) position, otherwise the switch may be damaged as the wheel is refitted.*

  d) *Make sure all the wiring connectors are secure and clipped into position.*

  e) *Align the marks on the wheel and the steering column shaft before removal, and align the steering wheel with the rotary switch.*

  f) *Tighten the steering wheel securing nut to the specified torque.*

  g) *Refit the airbag unit to the steering wheel as described in Chapter 12, Section 21.*

12 Front suspension subframe – removal and refitting

Note: *The steering rack, anti-roll bar and lower suspension arms will be still bolted to the subframe, as it is removed. Always renew any self-locking nuts when working on the suspension/steering components.*

Removal

1 Chock the rear wheels, firmly apply the handbrake, slacken the front roadwheel bolts,

and then jack up the front of the vehicle and support it on axle stands (see *Jacking and vehicle support*). Remove both front roadwheels.

2 Working inside the drivers footwell, remove the plastic cover, then note the position of the steering column lower joint on the steering rack pinion shaft. Undo the retaining bolt and disconnect the steering column joint from the steering rack pinion shaft **(see illustrations)**.

3 Working under the vehicle, slacken and remove the engine/transmission rear lower mounting bolt and nut, then undo the nut and bolt securing the link rod to the subframe and remove the link **(see illustration)**.

4 Slacken and remove both front lower ball joint retaining nut and bolts and free the ball joint shank from the front hub carriers **(see illustrations 4.2a and 4.2b)**. Discard the nuts, as new ones will be required for refitting.

5 Counterhold the drop link lower ball joint, and then unscrew the nut securing the

end of the anti-roll bar to the drop link **(see illustrations 6.2a and 6.2b)**.

6 Undo the retaining nut and disconnect the track rod end from the hub carrier **(see illustration)**. Refer to Section 17, for further information.

7 On some turbo models, undo the retaining bolt and remove the electric coolant pump and bracket from the rear of the subframe **(see illustration)**.

8 Make a final check that all cables/hoses that are attached to the subframe have been released and positioned clear so that they will not hinder the removal procedure.

9 Place a jack and a suitable block of wood under the subframe to support the subframe as it is lowered.

10 Slacken and remove the subframe rear mounting bolts and remove the support bracket from the rear of the subframe **(see illustrations)**.

12.3 Remove the rear lower mounting from the subframe

12.6 Disconnect the track rod ends

12.7 Electric coolant pump –where fitted

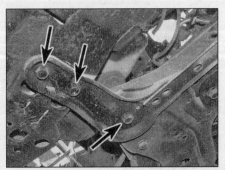

12.10a Undo the subframe rear mounting bolts ...

12.10b ... and remove the rear support brace

12.11a Undo the subframe front mounting bolts ...

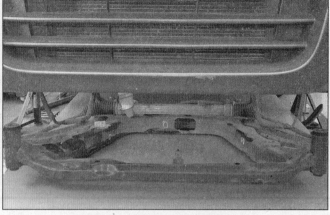

12.11b ... and lower the subframe

11 Slacken and remove the subframe front mounting bolts then carefully lower the subframe assembly out of position and remove it from underneath the vehicle, taking great care to ensure that the subframe assembly does not catch anything as it is lowered out of position **(see illustrations)**.

Refitting

12 Refitting is a reversal of the removal procedure, noting the following points:

a) Use new lower ball joint, and steering track rod end nuts.

b) Use a new bolt for the steering column lower joint, making sure the captivated nut is fitted correctly.

c) Tighten all nuts and bolts to the specified torque settings (where given).

d) On completion check and, if necessary, adjust the front wheel alignment as described in Chapter 1A, Section 13 or Chapter 1B, Section 14.

13 Ignition switch/steering column lock – removal and refitting

Note: New shear-bolts must be used when refitting the lock assembly.

Removal

1 Disconnect the battery negative terminal (refer to Disconnecting the battery in the Reference Chapter).

2 Lower the steering column to its lowest point, and then remove the steering column shrouds as described in Chapter 11, Section 26.

3 Disconnect the two wiring connectors from the left-hand side of the steering column **(see illustrations)**.

4 On models with intelligent key system, disconnect the wiring connector from the top of the ignition switch **(see illustration)**.

5 Disconnect the wiring connector to the transponder ring around the ignition switch, undo the retaining screw and then withdraw the transponder ring from around the switch **(see illustrations)**.

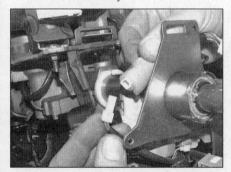

13.3a Disconnect the wiring connectors ...

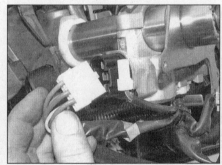

13.3b ... from the left-hand side of the column

13.4 Disconnect the wiring connector (arrowed)

13.5a Disconnect the wiring connector (arrowed) ...

13.5b ... undo the retaining screw ...

13.5c ... and withdraw the transponder ring

13.6a Slide out the retaining clip …

13.6b … and withdraw the selector locking cable

13.7 Drill out the lock assembly shear bolts (arrowed)

6 On automatic transmission models, release the retaining clip and withdraw the selector locking cable from the front of the ignition switch barrel **(see illustrations)**.

7 To remove the lock assembly, drill out and remove the two shear-bolts from the top of the steering column **(see illustration)**, then withdraw the two sections of the lock casting from the steering column. Note that the lock assembly cannot be removed from the casting.

Refitting

8 Refitting is a reversal of removal, but when refitting the lock assembly, use two new shear-bolts, and tighten the bolts until the heads break off.

14 Steering column/motor –
removal and refitting

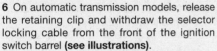

⚠ **Warning: All models are equipped with an airbag system. Ensure that the safety recommendations given in Chapter 12, Section 20, are followed to prevent personal injury.**
Note: *The steering column comprises the electric power steering (EPS) motor, the electronic control unit and the steering column itself. All these components form one assembly and cannot be individually separated or dismantled.*

Removal

1 Disconnect the battery negative terminal (refer to *Disconnecting the battery* in the Reference Chapter).
2 Remove the steering wheel as described in Section 11.
3 Remove the steering column stalk switches with reference to Chapter 12, Section 4.
4 Disconnect the wiring connectors from the ignition switch, refer to Section 13.
5 To improve access remove the driver's side lower facia panel as described in Chapter 11, Section 26.
6 Temporarily refit the steering wheel, and turn the steering column shaft as necessary for access to the universal joint clamp bolt.
7 Remove the plastic cover, then note the position of the steering column lower joint on the steering rack pinion shaft. Undo the retaining bolt and disconnect the steering

column joint from the pinion shaft **(see illustrations 12.2a, 12.2b and 12.2c)**.
8 Fasten a cable tie around the lower end of the steering column, to prevent it from extending as the steering column is removed **(see illustration)**.
9 Check along the steering column and, free the wiring loom from the retaining clips along the column **(see illustrations)**. Note its fitted position, and position it clear so that it does not hinder column removal.
10 The steering column/motor assembly is very heavy, it will be necessary to have the aid of an assistant or have something inside the footwell of the vehicle, to support the steering column/motor as it is removed.
11 Slacken and remove the four mounting nuts from the top of the column **(see illustrations)**. Slide the column assembly upwards, and free the upper locating plate from the metal crossbeam.

14.8 Secure the lower part of the steering column with cable ties (arrowed)

14.9a Unclip the wiring loom retaining clips …

14.9b … from steering column brackets

14.11a Undo the column mounting nuts (arrowed) …

14.11b … and release the upper part of the column from the locating bracket (arrowed)

14.12a Lowering the steering column
assembly onto an axle stand …

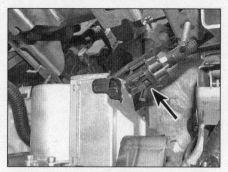

14.12b … then disconnect the wiring
connectors …

14.12c … from the top of the electric
power steering motor/control unit

12 Carefully lower the steering column and support it while disconnecting the wiring connectors from the top of the steering column motor **(see illustrations)**.

13 When the steering column/motor is free from any wiring, withdraw it from inside the vehicle **(see illustration)**.

Refitting

14 Refitting is a reversal of removal, bearing in mind the following points:

a) *Use new steering column bolts/nuts.*

b) *Tighten all bolts to their specified torque setting, where given.*

c) *Refit the steering column switches, as described in Chapter 12, Section 4.*

d) *Refit the steering wheel, as described in Section 11.*

e) *Refit the steering column shrouds, as described in Chapter 11, Section 26.*

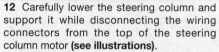

15 Steering gear assembly
– removal, inspection and refitting

⚠️ *Warning: All models are equipped with an airbag system. Ensure that the safety recommendations given in Chapter 12, Section 20, are followed to prevent personal injury.*

Note: *A balljoint separator tool may be required for this operation. New track rod end retaining nuts must be used on refitting.*

Removal

1 Firmly apply the handbrake, and then jack up

14.13 Lift the steering column assembly
from the vehicle

the front of the vehicle and support it securely on axle stands (see *Jacking and vehicle support*). Remove the front roadwheels.

2 Remove the front subframe as described in Section 12. It may be possible to lower the subframe and not completely remove it, to allow for enough room for the steering gear assembly to be withdrawn from between the underbody and the subframe.

3 Unscrew the bolts securing the steering gear to the top of the subframe and then withdraw the steering gear out through the side of the vehicle **(see illustration)**.

Inspection

4 Examine the assembly for obvious signs of wear or damage.

5 Check the rack for smooth operation through its full stroke of movement, and check that there is no binding or free play.

6 Check the track rods for deformation and cracks.

7 Check the condition of the steering gear rubber gaiters, and renew if necessary with reference to Section 16.

8 Examine the track rod ends for wear or damage, and renew if necessary with reference to Section 17.

9 Apart from renewal of the track rod ends and steering gear rubber gaiters, any further overhaul necessary should be entrusted to a Nissan dealer or specialist.

Refitting

10 Refitting is a reversal of removal, bearing in mind the following points:

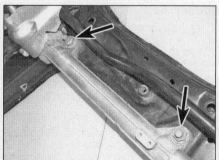

15.3 Steering rack assembly mounting
bolts

a) *Use new lower balljoint and steering track rod end nuts.*

b) *Use a new bolt for the steering column lower joint, making sure the captivated nut is fitted correctly.*

c) *Tighten all nuts and bolts to the specified torque settings (where given).*

16 Steering gear rubber gaiters
– renewal

Note: *New gaiter retaining clips should be used on refitting.*

1 Remove the relevant track rod end as described in Section 17.

2 If not already done, unscrew the track rod end locknut from the end of the track rod.

3 Mark the correct fitted position of the gaiter on the track rod, then release the gaiter securing clips **(see illustration)**. Slide the gaiter from the steering gear, and off the end of the track rod.

4 Thoroughly clean the track rod and the steering gear housing, using fine abrasive paper to polish off any corrosion, burrs or sharp edges that might damage the new gaiter sealing lips on installation. Scrape off all the grease from the old gaiter, and apply it to the track rod inner balljoint. (This assumes that grease has not been lost or contaminated as a result of damage to the old gaiter. Use fresh grease if in doubt.)

5 Carefully slide the new gaiter onto the track rod, and locate it on the steering gear housing.

16.3 Steering rack gaiter securing clips
(arrowed)

Align the outer edge of the gaiter with the mark made on the track rod prior to removal, and then secure it in position with new retaining clips.

6 Screw the track rod end locknut onto the end of the track rod.

7 Refit the track rod end as described in Section 17.

17 Track rod end – removal and refitting

Note: *A balljoint separator tool will be required for this operation. A new track rod end retaining nut must be used on refitting.*

Removal

1 Firmly apply the handbrake, and then jack up the front of the vehicle and support it securely on axle stands (see *Jacking and vehicle support*). Remove the relevant front roadwheel.

2 Using a Torx key to prevent the ball joint from turning, slacken the nut securing the track rod end to the steering arm **(see illustration)**.

3 Using a balljoint separator tool, separate the track rod end from the steering arm **(see illustrations)**. Remove the nut and discard, as a new one must be used on refitting.

4 Clean the threads on the track rod arm with a wire brush and lubricate. Counterhold the track rod arm using the flats provided, and then slacken the track rod end **(see illustration)**.

5 Counting the exact number of turns required to remove the track rod end, unscrew it from the track rod arm.

Refitting

6 Carefully clean the track rod end and the track rod threads.

17.2 Using a Torx socket to prevent the ball joint from turning

17.3b ... to release the tapered shank

17.3a Use a balljoint separator ...

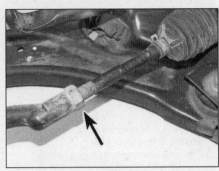

17.4 Slacken the track rod end locknut (arrowed)

7 Renew the track rod end if the rubber dust cover is cracked, split or perished, or if the movement of the balljoint is either sloppy or too stiff. Also check for other signs of damage such as worn threads.

8 Screw the track rod end onto the track rod by the number of turns noted before removal.

9 Counterhold the track rod arm using the flats provided, and then securely tighten the track rod lock nut.

10 Ensure that the balljoint taper is clean, and then engage the taper with the steering arm on the hub carrier.

11 Refit a new nut to the track rod end, and tighten to the specified torque.

12 Refit the roadwheel, and lower the vehicle to the ground.

13 Check the front wheel alignment with reference to Chapter 1A, Section 13 or Chapter 1B, Section 14.

Chapter 11
Bodywork and fittings

Contents

Degrees of difficulty

Easy, suitable for novice with little experience	**Fairly easy,** suitable for beginner with some experience	**Fairly difficult,** suitable for competent DIY mechanic	**Difficult,** suitable for experienced DIY mechanic	**Very difficult,** suitable for expert DIY or professional

Specifications

Torque wrench settings	Nm	lbf ft
Door hinge nuts	23	17
Door lock striker bolts	15	11
Front seat securing bolts	40	30
Rear seat securing bolts:		
2 seat row models	25	18
3 seat row models	65	48
Rear +2 seat securing bolts:		
Front anchorage bolts	25	18
Rear anchorage bolts	65	48
Front seat belt mounting bolts:		
Upper pillar anchorage	25	18
Lower sill anchorage	49	36
Seat belt inertia reel bolt	40	30
Pre-tensioner-to-sill bolt	50	37
Rear seat belt mounting bolts (all bolts)	49	36

1 General information

The bodyshell is made of pressed-steel sections, and is available in 5-seater (Qashqai) or 7-seater (Qashqai +2) versions. Most components are welded together, but some use is made of structural adhesives and some body components are bolted on.

Nissan vehicles have been designed with a rigid passenger safety compartment with reinforced pillars and sills, including safety 'waist' beams inside the doors. The use of high-strength steel in structural areas of the body enhances the rigidity of the structure.

Extensive use is made of plastic materials, mainly in the interior, but also in exterior components. The outer sections of the front and rear bumpers are injection-moulded from a synthetic material, which is very strong, and yet light. Plastic components such as wheel arch liners are fitted to the underside of the vehicle, to improve the body's resistance to corrosion.

2 Maintenance – bodywork and underframe

The general condition of a vehicle's bodywork is the one thing that significantly affects its value. Maintenance is easy, but needs to be regular. Neglect, particularly after minor damage, can lead quickly to further deterioration and costly repair bills. It is important also to keep watch on those parts of the vehicle not immediately visible, for instance the underside, inside all the wheel arches, and the lower part of the engine compartment.

The basic maintenance routine for the bodywork is washing – preferably with a lot of water, from a hose. This will remove all the loose solids, which may have stuck to the vehicle. It is important to flush these off in such a way as to prevent grit from scratching the finish. The wheel arches and underframe need washing in the same way, to remove any accumulated mud, which will retain moisture and tend to encourage rust. Paradoxically enough, the best time to clean the underframe and wheel arches is in wet weather, when the mud is thoroughly wet and soft. In very wet weather, the underframe is usually cleaned of large accumulations automatically, and this is a good time for inspection.

Periodically, except on vehicles with a wax-based underbody protective coating, it is a good idea to have the whole of the underframe of the vehicle steam-cleaned, engine compartment included, so that a thorough inspection can be carried out to see what minor repairs and renovations are necessary. Steam cleaning is available at many garages, and is necessary for the removal of the accumulation of oily grime, which sometimes is allowed to become thick in certain areas. If steam-cleaning facilities are not available, there are some excellent grease solvents available which can be brush-applied; the dirt can then be simply hosed off. Note that these methods should not be used on vehicles with wax-based underbody protective coating, or the coating will be removed. Such vehicles should be inspected annually, preferably just prior to winter, when the underbody should be washed down, and any damage to the wax coating repaired. Ideally, a completely fresh coat should be applied. It would also be worth considering the use of such wax-based protection for injection into door panels, sills, box sections, etc, as an additional safeguard against rust damage, where such protection is not provided by the vehicle manufacturer.

After washing paintwork, wipe off with a chamois leather to give an unspotted clear finish. A coat of clear protective wax polish will give added protection against chemical pollutants in the air. If the paintwork sheen has dulled or oxidised, use a cleaner/polisher combination to restore the brilliance of the shine. This requires a little effort, but such dulling is usually caused because regular washing has been neglected. Care needs to be taken with metallic paintwork, as special non-abrasive cleaner/polisher is required to avoid damage to the finish. Always check that the door and ventilator opening drain holes and pipes are completely clear, so that water can be drained out. Brightwork should be treated in the same way as paintwork. Windscreens and windows can be kept clear of the smeary film, which often appears, by the use of proprietary glass cleaner. Never use any form of wax or other body or chromium polish on glass.

3 Maintenance – upholstery and carpets

Mats and carpets should be brushed or vacuum-cleaned regularly, to keep them free of grit. If they are badly stained, remove them from the vehicle for scrubbing or sponging, and make quite sure they are dry before refitting. Seats and interior trim panels can be kept clean by wiping with a damp cloth. If they do become stained (which can be more apparent on light-coloured upholstery), use a little liquid detergent and a soft nail brush to scour the grime out of the grain of the material. Do not forget to keep the headlining clean in the same way as the upholstery. When using liquid cleaners inside the vehicle, do not over-wet the surfaces being cleaned. Excessive damp could get into the seams and padded interior, causing stains, offensive odours or even rot.

4 Minor body damage – repair

Minor scratches in bodywork

If the scratch is very superficial, and does not penetrate to the metal of the bodywork, repair is very simple. Lightly rub the area of the scratch with a paintwork renovator, or a very fine cutting paste, to remove loose paint from the scratch, and to clear the surrounding bodywork of wax polish. Rinse the area with clean water.

Apply touch-up paint to the scratch using a fine paintbrush; continue to apply fine layers of paint until the surface of the paint in the scratch is level with the surrounding paintwork. Allow the new paint at least two weeks to harden, and then blend it into the surrounding paintwork by rubbing the scratch area with a paintwork renovator or a very fine cutting paste. Finally, apply wax polish.

Where the scratch has penetrated right through to the metal of the bodywork, causing the metal to rust, a different repair technique is required. Remove any loose rust from the bottom of the scratch with a penknife, and then apply rust-inhibiting paint to prevent the formation of rust in the future. Using a rubber or nylon applicator, fill the scratch with body stopper paste. If required, this paste can be mixed with cellulose thinners to provide a very thin paste, which is ideal for filling narrow scratches. Before the stopper-paste in the scratch hardens, wrap a piece of smooth cotton rag around the top of a finger. Dip the finger in cellulose thinners, and quickly sweep it across the surface of the stopper-paste in the scratch; this will ensure that the surface of the stopper-paste is slightly hollowed. The scratch can now be painted over as described earlier in this Section.

Dents in bodywork

When deep denting of the vehicle's bodywork has taken place, the first task is to pull the dent out, until the affected bodywork almost attains its original shape. There is little point in trying to restore the original shape completely, as the metal in the damaged area will have stretched on impact, and cannot be reshaped fully to its original contour. It is better to bring the level of the dent up to a point, which is about 3 mm below the level of the surrounding bodywork. In cases where the dent is very shallow anyway, it is not worth trying to pull it out at all. If the underside of the dent is accessible, it can be hammered out gently from behind, using a mallet with a wooden or plastic head. Whilst doing this, hold a suitable block of wood firmly against the outside of the panel, to absorb the impact from the hammer blows and thus prevent a large area of the bodywork from being 'belled-out'.

Should the dent be in a section of the bodywork, which has a double skin, or some other factor making it inaccessible from behind, a different technique is called for. Drill several small holes through the metal inside the area - particularly in the deeper section. Then screw long self-tapping screws into the holes, just sufficiently for them to gain a good purchase in the metal. Now the dent can be pulled out by pulling on the protruding heads of the screws with a pair of pliers.

The next stage of the repair is the removal of the paint from the damaged area, and from an inch or so of the surrounding 'sound' bodywork. This is accomplished most easily by using a wire brush or abrasive pad on a power drill, although it can be done just as effectively by hand, using sheets of abrasive paper. To complete the preparation for filling, score the surface of the bare metal with a screwdriver or the tang of a file, or alternatively, drill small holes in the affected area. This will provide a really good 'key' for the filler paste.

To complete the repair, see the Section on filling and re-spraying.

Rust holes/gashes in bodywork

Remove all paint from the affected area, and from an inch or so of the surrounding 'sound' bodywork, using an abrasive pad or a wire brush on a power drill. If these are not available, a few sheets of abrasive paper will do the job most effectively. With the paint removed, you will be able to judge the severity of the corrosion, and therefore decide whether to renew the whole panel (if this is possible) or to repair the affected area. New body panels are not as expensive as most people think, and it is often quicker and more satisfactory to fit a new panel than to attempt to repair large areas of corrosion.

Remove all fittings from the affected area, except those, which will act as a guide to the original shape of the damaged bodywork (e.g. headlight shells etc). Then, using tin snips or a hacksaw blade, remove all loose metal and any other metal badly affected by corrosion. Hammer the edges of the hole inwards, in order to create a slight depression for the filler paste.

Wire-brush the affected area to remove the powdery rust from the surface of the remaining metal. Paint the affected area with rust-inhibiting paint, if the back of the rusted area is accessible, treat this also.

Before filling can take place, it will be necessary to block the hole in some way. This can be achieved by the use of aluminium or plastic mesh, or aluminium tape.

Aluminium or plastic mesh, or glass-fibre matting, is probably the best material to use for a large hole. Cut a piece to the approximate size and shape of the hole to be filled, then position it in the hole so that its edges are below the level of the surrounding body-work. It can be retained in position by several blobs of filler paste around its periphery.

Aluminium tape should be used for small or very narrow holes. Pull a piece off the roll, trim it to the approximate size and shape required, then pull off the backing paper (if used) and stick the tape over the hole; it can be overlapped if the thickness of one piece is insufficient. Burnish down the edges of the tape with the handle of a screwdriver or similar, to ensure that the tape is securely attached to the metal underneath.

Filling and respraying

Before using this Section, see the Sections on dent, deep scratch, rust holes and gash repairs.

Many types of bodyfiller are available, but generally speaking, those proprietary kits, which contain a tin of filler paste and a tube of resin hardener, are best for this type of repair. A wide, flexible plastic or nylon applicator will be found invaluable for imparting a smooth and well-contoured finish to the surface of the filler.

Mix up a little filler on a clean piece of card or board – measure the hardener carefully (follow the maker's instructions on the pack), otherwise the filler will set too rapidly or too slowly. Using the applicator, apply the filler paste to the prepared area; draw the applicator across the surface of the filler to achieve the correct contour and to level the surface. As soon as a contour that approximates to the correct one is achieved, stop working the paste – if you carry on too long, the paste will become sticky and begin to 'pick-up' on the applicator. Continue to add thin layers of filler paste at 20-minute intervals, until the level of the filler is just proud of the surrounding bodywork.

Once the filler has hardened, the excess can be removed using a metal plane or file. From then on, progressively finer grades of abrasive paper should be used, starting with a 40-grade production paper, and finishing with a 400-grade wet-and-dry paper. Always wrap the abrasive paper around a flat rubber, cork, or wooden block – otherwise the surface of the filler will not be completely flat. During the smoothing of the filler surface, the wet-and-dry paper should be periodically rinsed in water. This will ensure that a very smooth finish is imparted to the filler at the final stage.

At this stage, the 'dent' should be surrounded by a ring of bare metal, which in turn should be encircled by the finely 'feathered' edge of the good paintwork. Rinse the repair area with clean water, until all of the dust produced by the rubbing-down operation has gone.

Spray the whole area with a light coat of primer – this will show up any imperfections in the surface of the filler. Repair these imperfections with fresh filler paste or bodystopper, and once more smooth the surface with abrasive paper. Repeat this spray-and-repair procedure until you are satisfied that the surface of the filler, and the feathered edge of the paintwork, are perfect. Clean the repair area with clean water, and allow to dry fully.

The repair area is now ready for final spraying. Paint spraying must be carried out in a warm, dry, windless and dust-free atmosphere. This condition can be created artificially if you have access to a large indoor working area, but if you are forced to work in the open, you will have to pick your day very carefully. If you are working indoors, dousing the floor in the work area with water will help to settle the dust, which would otherwise be in the atmosphere. If the repair area is confined to one body panel, mask off the surrounding panels; this will help to minimise the effects of a slight mis-match in paint colours. Bodywork fittings (e.g. chrome strips, door handles etc) will also need to be masked off. Use genuine masking tape, and several thicknesses of newspaper, for the masking operations.

Before commencing to spray, agitate the aerosol can thoroughly, and then spray a test area (an old tin, or similar) until the technique is mastered. Cover the repair area with a thick coat of primer; the thickness should be built up using several thin layers of paint, rather than one thick one. Using 400-grade wet-and-dry paper, rub down the surface of the primer until it is really smooth. While doing this, the work area should be thoroughly doused with water, and the wet-and-dry paper periodically rinsed in water. Allow to dry before spraying on more paint.

Spray on the top coat, again building up the thickness by using several thin layers of paint. Start spraying at one edge of the repair area, and then, using a side-to-side motion, work until the whole repair area and about 2 inches of the surrounding original paintwork is covered. Remove all masking material 10 to 15 minutes after spraying on the final coat of paint.

Allow the new paint at least two weeks to harden, then, using a paintwork renovator, or a very fine cutting paste, blend the edges of the paint into the existing paintwork. Finally, apply wax polish.

Plastic components

With the use of more and more plastic body components by the vehicle manufacturers (e.g. bumpers. spoilers, and in some cases major body panels), rectification of more serious damage to such items has become a matter of either entrusting repair work to a specialist in this field, or renewing complete components. Repair of such damage by the DIY owner is not really feasible, owing to the cost of the equipment and materials required for effecting such repairs. The basic technique involves making a groove along the line of the crack in the plastic, using a rotary burr in a power drill. The damaged part is then welded back together, using a hot-air gun to heat up and fuse a plastic filler rod into the groove. Any excess plastic is then removed, and the area rubbed down to a smooth finish. It is important that a filler rod of the correct plastic is used, as body components can be made of a variety of different types (e.g. polycarbonate, ABS, polypropylene).

Damage of a less serious nature (abrasions, minor cracks etc) can be repaired by the DIY owner using a two-part epoxy filler repair material. Once mixed in equal proportions, this is used in similar fashion to the bodywork filler used on metal panels. The filler is usually cured in twenty to thirty minutes, ready for sanding and painting.

If the owner is renewing a complete component himself, or if he has repaired it with epoxy filler, he will be left with the problem of finding a suitable paint for finishing which is compatible with the type of plastic used. At one time, the use of a universal paint was not possible, owing to the complex range of plastics encountered in body component applications. Standard paints, generally speaking, will not bond to plastic or rubber satisfactorily. However, it is now possible to obtain a plastic body parts finishing kit, which

consists of a pre-primer treatment, a primer and coloured top coat. Full instructions are normally supplied with a kit, but basically, the method of use is to first apply the pre-primer to the component concerned, and allow it to dry for up to 30 minutes. Then the primer is applied, and left to dry for about an hour before finally applying the special-coloured top coat. The result is a correctly coloured component, where the paint will flex with the plastic or rubber, a property that standard paint does not normally possess.

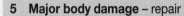

5 Major body damage – repair

Where serious damage has occurred, or large areas need renewal due to neglect,

it means that complete new panels will need welding-in, and this is best left to professionals. If the damage is due to impact, it will also be necessary to check completely the alignment of the bodyshell, and this can only be carried out accurately by a Nissan dealer or specialist, using special jigs. If the body is left misaligned, it is primarily dangerous, as the car will not handle properly, and secondly, uneven stresses will be imposed on the steering, suspension and possibly transmission, causing abnormal wear, or complete failure, particularly to such items as the tyres.

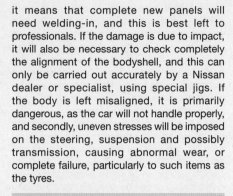

6 Front bumper – removal and refitting

Removal

1 Firmly apply the handbrake, and then jack up the front of the vehicle and support it securely on axle stands (see *Jacking and vehicle support*). To make access inside the wheel arch easier, remove the front roadwheels.

2 Working under the front of the vehicle, undo the retaining screws securing the engine undershield to the lower edge of the bumper.

3 Still working under the front of the vehicle, unscrew the lower securing screws at each end of the bumper **(see illustration)**.

4 Carefully lever the wheel arch trim to release the retaining clips from the ends of the bumper **(see illustrations)**. **Note:** *The wheel arch trims do not have to be completely removed from the front wing panels, they just need to be released from the ends of the bumper. Take care not to damage them as the bumper is removed.*

5 Remove the securing clips from inside the wheel arch liner, then ease the liner away and undo the bolt securing the upper corner of the bumper to the front wing **(see illustrations)**. Repeat the procedure on the other side of the vehicle.

6 Release the upper retaining clips from the top of the bumper and grille panel **(see illustrations)**.

6.3 **Undo the lower securing screws**

6.4a **Unclip the wheel arch trim ...**

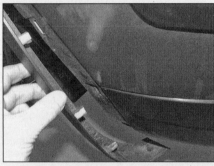

6.4b **... away from the front bumper**

6.5a **Pull back the wheel arch liner ...**

6.5b **... and undo the bolt securing the upper part of the bumper**

6.6a **Release the retaining clips ...**

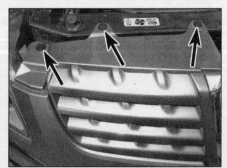

6.6b **... along the top of the bumper trim (one side shown)**

7 Reaching up behind the bumper, disconnect the foglight wiring connectors **(see illustration)**.

8 Where fitted, disconnect the parking sensor wiring connector and headlight washer pipes.

9 Have an assistant support one end of the bumper, and then unclip the outer ends of the bumper from the front wing panels **(see illustration)**. If not completely removed, take care not to damage the wheel arch trims, as the bumper is removed.

10 Check that there is nothing still connected to the bumper, and then with the aid of an assistant, draw the bumper forwards and remove it from the vehicle.

Refitting

11 Refitting is a reversal of removal.

6.7 Disconnect the foglight wiring connector

6.9 Release the bumper at each side, noting the locating slots

<table>
<tr><td>

7   **Rear bumper –**
    removal and refitting

</td><td></td></tr>
</table>

Removal

1 Firmly apply the handbrake, and then jack up the rear of the vehicle and support it securely on axle stands (see *Jacking and vehicle support*). To make access inside the wheel arch easier, remove the rear roadwheels.

2 Working under the rear of the vehicle, release the retaining clips securing the lower edge of the bumper **(see illustrations)**.

3 Working at the rear of the wheel arches, undo the two retaining screws, release the retaining clip and remove the lower plastic trim **(see illustrations)**.

4 Still working under the rear of the vehicle, undo the lower securing screw and carefully lever the wheel arch trim to release the retaining clips from the ends of the bumper **(see illustrations)**. **Note:** *The wheel arch trims do not have to be completely removed from the rear wing panels, they just need to be released to access the ends of the bumper. Take care not to damage them as the bumper is removed.*

5 Release the six retaining clips (three clips

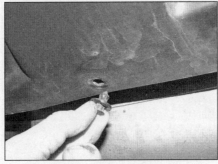
7.2a Release the retaining clips ...

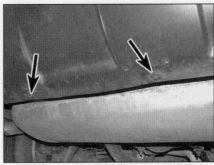
7.2b ... along the lower edge of the bumper (arrowed)

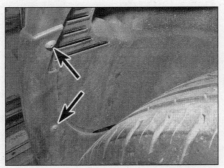
7.3a Undo the two retaining screws (arrowed) ...

7.3b ... release the retaining clip ...

7.3c ... and remove the lower plastic trim

7.4a Undo the retaining bolt (arrowed) ...

7.4b ... and unclip the wheel arch trim

7.5a Release the retaining clips ...

7.5b ... from the inner wheel arch liner

7.6 Undo the bolt securing the upper part of the bumper

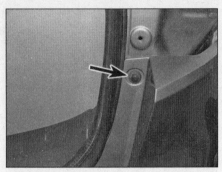

7.8 Undo the bumper upper securing bolt

7.9 Peel back the tailgate aperture seal

each side), from the inner wheel arch liner to the ends of the bumper (see illustrations).

6 Unscrew the two bolts (one each side) securing the upper corners of the bumper to the rear wing and body brackets (see illustration).

7 Open the rear tailgate and remove the rear light units, as described in Chapter 12, Section 7.

8 Undo the upper bumper securing bolts (one each side) inside the tailgate aperture (see illustration).

9 Peel back the rubber seal from the lower edge of the tailgate aperture (see illustration).

10 Have an assistant support one end of the bumper, and then unclip the outer ends of the bumper from the rear wing panels (see illustrations).

11 Working down between the bumper and the rear body panel, lift the retaining clips to release the three bumper securing clips, and then withdraw the bumper from the rear of the vehicle (see illustrations). If not completely removed, take care not to damage the wheel arch trims, as the bumper is removed.

12 On models with rear parking sensors, disconnect the wiring connectors as the bumper is removed.

Refitting

13 Refitting is a reversal of removal.

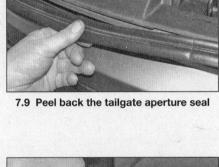

7.10a Release the bumper at each side of the wing panel ...

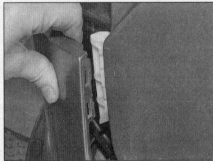

7.10b ... noting the locating slots

7.11a Lift up the centre clips ...

7.11b ... along the rear of the bumper ...

7.11c ... to release the retaining clips

8.2 Bonnet hinge retaining nuts

9.3a The bonnet release cable (arrowed) ...

9.3b ... to the right and under the headlight unit

8 Bonnet – removal, refitting and adjustment

Removal

1 Open the bonnet and have an assistant support it. Using a pencil or felt tip pen, mark the outline of each bonnet hinge relative to the bonnet, to use as a guide on refitting.
2 With the help of an assistant to support one side of the bonnet, unscrew the nuts securing the hinges to the bonnet (see illustration). Carefully lift the bonnet clear of the vehicle and store it out of the way in a safe place.
3 Inspect the bonnet hinges for signs of wear and free play at the pivots, and if necessary renew. Each hinge is secured to the body by bolts.

Refitting

4 With the aid of an assistant, offer up the bonnet, and loosely fit the retaining nuts. Align the hinges with the marks made on removal, and then tighten the retaining nuts securely.
5 Adjust the alignment of the bonnet as follows.

Adjustment

6 Close the bonnet, and check for alignment with the adjacent panels. If necessary, slacken the hinge nuts/bolts and re-align the bonnet to suit. Once the bonnet is correctly aligned, tighten the relevant hinge bolts securely.
7 Once the bonnet is correctly aligned, check that the bonnet fastens and releases in a satisfactory manner. If adjustment is necessary, slacken the bonnet lock retaining bolts (see illustration 10.2), and adjust the position of the lock to suit. Once the lock is operating correctly, securely tighten its retaining bolts.
8 If necessary, align the front edge of the bonnet with the wing panels by turning the rubbers screwed into the body front panel, to raise or lower the front edge as required.

9 Bonnet release cable – removal and refitting

Removal

1 Open and support the bonnet.
2 Remove the bonnet lock from the front panel, as described in Section 10.
3 The bonnet release cable travels from the bonnet lock, along the front panel, and then under the right-hand headlight unit (see illustrations).

4 To make access easier, remove the front bumper as described in Section 6.
5 Working along the length of the cable, release it from any securing clips to the vehicle body.
6 Working in the driver's footwell, undo the two retaining bolts and unclip the bonnet release lever mounting bracket from the facia (see illustrations).
7 Unclip the outer cable from the bracket, and then unhook the end of the bonnet release cable from the bonnet release lever (see illustration).
8 Note the routing of the cable, and release it from any clips in the engine compartment, then feed the cable through the bulkhead grommet into the passenger compartment. It is advisable to tie a length of string to the end of the cable before removal, to aid refitting. Pull the cable through into the passenger compartment, then untie the string and leave it place until the new cable is to be refitted.

Refitting

9 Refitting is a reversal of removal, but use the string to pull the cable into position, and ensure that the bulkhead grommet is securely located. Make sure that the cable is routed as noted before removal, and reposition the cable in its securing clips in the engine compartment. Check the bonnet release mechanism for correct operation on completion.

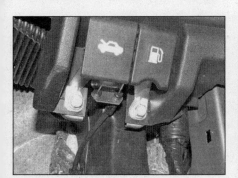

9.6a Undo the two retaining bolts ...

9.6b ... and unclip the release levers from the facia

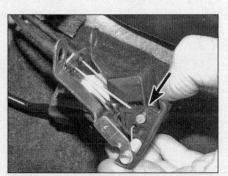

9.7 Unhook the cable from the release lever

10.2 Undo the three retaining bolts ...

10.3 ... and unhook the cable from the bonnet catch

10 Bonnet lock – removal and refitting

Removal

1 Open and support the bonnet.
2 Undo the three securing bolts, and withdraw the lock assembly from the body panel (see illustration).
3 Unclip the outer cable from the bracket, and then unhook the end of the bonnet release cable from the lock lever (see illustration).
4 The bonnet lock assembly can then be removed from the vehicle.

Refitting

5 Refitting is a reversal of removal. If necessary see adjustment, as described in Section 8.

11 Door – removal, refitting and adjustment

Removal

1 Disconnect the battery negative terminal (refer to *Disconnecting the battery* in Reference).
2 On rear doors, open the door and unclip the rubber gaiter from the door pillar, withdraw the wiring block connector from within the door pillar and disconnect (see illustrations).
3 On front doors, open the door and unclip the sill trim panel, then undo the retaining nut and remove the kick panel from inside the front door pillar. Disconnect the wiring connector and withdraw it through the door pillar (see illustrations).
4 Undo the bolt securing the door check strap to the body panel (see illustration).
5 Mark the positions of the hinges on the door, to aid alignment of the door on refitting.
6 Have an assistant support the door, then unscrew the nuts securing the door hinges

11.2a Unclip the gaiter from the door pillar ...

11.2b ... and disconnect the wiring block connector

11.3a Unclip the sill trim panel ...

11.3b ... and the front kick trim panel

11.3c Disconnect the wiring block connector ...

11.3d ... and pull the door wiring out from the front pillar

11.4 Undo the door check strap bolt

to the door, and lift the door from the vehicle **(see illustrations)**.

7 Examine the hinges for wear and damage. If necessary, the hinges can be unbolted from the body and renewed.

Refitting

8 Refitting is a reversal of removal, but align the hinges with the marks made on the body before removal, and before finally tightening the hinge securing bolts, check the door adjustment as described in the following paragraphs.

Adjustment

9 Close the door (**carefully**, in case the alignment is incorrect, which may cause scratching on the door or the body as the door is closed), and check the fit of the door with the surrounding panels.

10 If adjustment is required, loosen the hinge securing bolts (the hinge-to-door and the hinge-to-body bolt holes are elongated), and move the hinges as required to achieve satisfactory alignment. Tighten the securing bolts to the specified torque when the alignment is satisfactory.

11 Check the operation of the door lock. If necessary, slacken the securing bolts, and adjust the position of the lock striker on the body pillar to achieve satisfactory alignment **(see illustration)**.

12 Door inner trim panel – removal and refitting

Front door trim panel

1 Disconnect the battery negative terminal (refer to *Disconnecting the battery* in Reference).

2 Carefully unclip the switch panel from the top of the armrest and disconnect the wiring connectors **(see illustrations)**.

3 Unclip the trim finisher and remove it from the grab handle **(see illustrations)**.

4 Undo the two retaining screws and remove the grab handle and surround from the door trim panel **(see illustrations)**. Pull the door release lever outwards, as the trim is removed.

11.6a Undo the upper hinge retaining nuts …

11.6b … and lower hinge retaining nuts

11.11 Door lock striker plate (arrowed)

12.2a Unclip the switch panel …

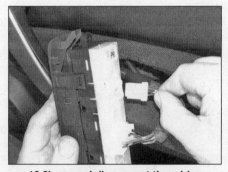
12.2b … and disconnect the wiring connectors

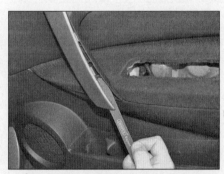
12.3a Carefully lever the trim panel …

12.3b … to release the securing clips

12.4a Undo the two retaining screws …

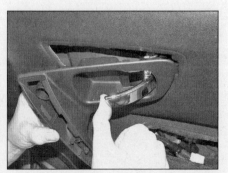
12.4b … and remove the door handle trim

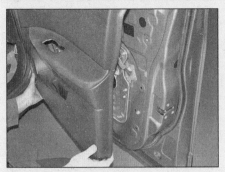

12.5 Lift and remove the trim panel from the door

12.8a Carefully lever the handle trim panel ...

12.8b ... to release the securing clips

5 Working your way around the edge of the panel, release the retaining clips securing the trim panel to the door. Using a suitable forked tool, release the internal securing clips around the edge of the trim panel, then lift the panel upwards to release it from the door frame **(see illustration)**.

6 Refitting is a reversal of removal, bearing in mind the following points:
a) *Make sure that the trim panel securing clips engage correctly with the door panel. Renew any broken clips.*
b) *Check the upper weatherstrip engages correctly with the door trim panel as the panel is refitted.*

Rear door trim panel (early models)

7 Disconnect the battery negative terminal (refer to *Disconnecting the battery* in the Reference Chapter).

8 Carefully prise the trim from around the door inner release lever **(see illustrations)**.
9 Carefully unclip the switch panel from the top of the armrest and disconnect the wiring connector **(see illustrations)**.
10 Working your way around the edge of the panel, release the retaining clips securing the trim panel to the door. Using a suitable forked tool, release the internal securing clips around the edge of the trim panel, then lift the panel upwards to release it from the door frame **(see illustration)**.
11 If work is to be carried out on the door internal components, it will be necessary to remove the plastic sealing sheet. Undo the retaining bolts and remove the strengthener plate from the door panel. Then using a sharp knife, carefully release the sealant bead and pull the plastic sealing sheet from the door **(see illustrations)**. Try to keep the sealant intact as far as possible, to ease refitting.

12 Refitting is a reversal of removal, bearing in mind the following points:
a) *Ensure that the sealing sheet is correctly refitted, and sealed around its edge. It should be possible to use the original mastic sealant, but if necessary, new sealant can be obtained from a Nissan dealer.*
b) *Make sure that the trim panel securing clips engage correctly with the door panel. Renew any broken clips.*
c) *Check the upper weatherstrip engages correctly with the door trim panel as the panel is refitted.*

Rear door trim panel (later models)

13 Disconnect the battery negative terminal (refer to *Disconnecting the battery* in the Reference Chapter).
14 Carefully prise the trim from around the door inner release lever **(see illustration)**.

12.9a Unclip the switch panel ...

12.9b ... from the door trim panel

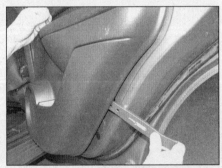

12.10 Using a forked tool, release the retaining clips around the door trim

12.11a Undo the strengthener plate retaining bolts ...

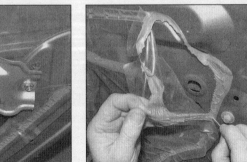

12.11b ... and use a knife to remove the sealing sheet

12.14 Carefully unclip the release lever trim panel

12.15a Unclip the switch panel ...

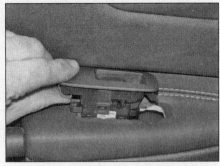

12.15b ... from the door trim panel

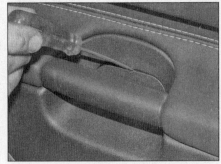

12.16a Unclip the plastic trim cover ...

15 Carefully unclip the switch panel from the top of the armrest and disconnect the wiring connector **(see illustrations)**.

16 Unclip the trim finisher and undo the two retaining bolts for the grab handle **(see illustrations)**.

17 Working your way around the edge of the panel, release the retaining clips securing the trim panel to the door. Using a suitable forked tool, release the internal securing clips around the edge of the trim panel, then lift the panel upwards to release it from the door frame **(see illustration)**.

18 If work is to be carried out on the door internal components, it will be necessary to remove the plastic sealing sheet (where fitted). Using a sharp knife, carefully release the sealant bead and pull the plastic sealing sheet from the door **(see illustration 12.11a and 12.11b)**. Try to keep the sealant intact as far as possible, to ease refitting.

19 Refitting is a reversal of removal, bearing in mind the following points:

a) *Ensure that the sealing sheet is correctly refitted, and sealed around its edge. It should be possible to use the original mastic sealant, but if necessary, new sealant can be obtained from a Nissan dealer.*

b) *Make sure that the trim panel securing clips engage correctly with the door panel. Renew any broken clips.*

c) *Check the upper weatherstrip engages correctly with the door trim panel as the panel is refitted.*

12.16b ... and undo the two retaining bolts

12.17 Using a forked tool, release the retaining clips around the door trim

13.2a Undo the retaining bolt ...

13.2b ... then slide the release lever bracket from the door

13 Door handles and lock components – removal and refitting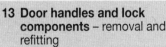

Interior door release handle/lever

1 Remove the door inner trim panel and plastic sealing sheet (where fitted), as described in Section 12.

2 Undo the securing bolt and slide the release lever to the rear of the door to withdraw it from the door panel **(see illustrations)**.

3 Unclip the operating cable outer sleeve from the release lever bracket, and then unclip the inner part of the operating cable from the lever **(see illustrations)**.

13.3a Release the outer cable ...

13.3b ... and disconnect the inner operating cable

13.5 Remove the piece of tape covering the access hole

13.6a Slacken the retaining screw ...

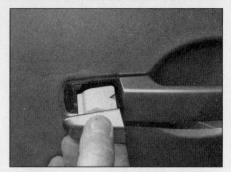

13.6b ... and withdraw the door push button

13.7 Slide the handle to the rear and pull it out to disengage it from the door

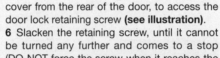

13.8 Remove the seals from the door handle recess

8 If required unclip the rubber seals from around the handle recess in the door panel **(see illustration)**.

9 Refitting is a reversal of removal, but ensure that the handle locates securely inside the door lock housing. When fitting the rear of the door handle, make sure the leg on the rear of the handle is positioned behind the lever on the support bracket inside the door panel, before refitting the push button **(see illustration)**.

Exterior door handle (front doors)

Note: *When removing the door lock cylinder the plastic lever on the rear of the lock will get damaged, a new one will be required on refitting.*

10 Open the door, undo the retaining screw and remove the plastic plug from the rear of the door, to access the door lock retaining screw **(see illustration)**.

11 Remove the door inner trim panel and plastic sealing sheet (where fitted), as described in Section 12.

12 Remove the window regulator, as described in Section 14. On models with intelligent key system, disconnect the wiring connectors inside the door panel, to the

4 Refitting is a reversal of removal, bearing in mind the following points:

  a) *Ensure that the lock operating cables are routed as noted before removal.*

  b) *Check the operation of the release lever/ lock mechanism before refitting the door inner trim panel.*

  c) *Refit the door inner trim panel with reference to Section 12.*

Exterior door handle (rear doors)

5 Open the door and peel back the plastic

cover from the rear of the door, to access the door lock retaining screw **(see illustration)**.

6 Slacken the retaining screw, until it cannot be turned any further and comes to a stop (DO NOT force the screw when it reaches the stop). The screw does not come completely out from the door panel. Carefully withdraw the push button out from the door handle assembly **(see illustrations)**. Take care not to damage the paintwork as it is removed.

7 Detach the handle by sliding it to the rear of the door, and then pulling it out from the handle recess **(see illustration)**.

13.9 Make sure the handle hooks around the door lock lever (arrowed)

13.10 Undo the screw and remove the plastic plug

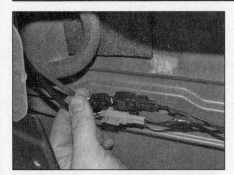

13.12 On models with intelligent key system, disconnect the wiring connectors

13.13a Unclip the plastic lever (arrowed) …

13.13b … from the rear of the door lock button

door handle antenna and door switch **(see illustration)**.

13 Reaching inside the door panel to the rear of the door lock button, use a thin screwdriver to unclip the plastic lever from the rear of the door lock button **(see illustrations)**.

14 Slacken the retaining screw, until it cannot be turned any further and comes to a stop (DO NOT force the screw when it reaches the stop). The screw does not come completely out from the door panel. Carefully withdraw the push button/lock cylinder out from the door handle assembly **(see illustrations)**. Take care not to damage the paintwork as it is removed.

15 Detach the handle by sliding it to the rear

of the door, and then pulling it out from the handle recess. On models with intelligent key system, withdraw the wiring cables out through the handle recess **(see illustrations)**.

16 If required unclip the rubber seals from around the handle recess in the door panel **(see illustrations)**.

17 Refitting is a reversal of removal, bearing in mind the following points:

a) *Fit a new plastic lever to the rear of the door lock button* **(see illustration)**.

b) *Make sure the leg on the rear of the handle is positioned behind the lever on the support bracket inside the door panel* **(see illustration 13.9)**.

c) *Ensure that the lock operating cable/rods are routed as noted before removal.*

d) *Check the operation of the release lever/ lock mechanism before refitting the door inner trim panel.*

e) *Refit the window regulator assembly with reference to Section 14.*

f) *Refit the door inner trim panel with reference to Section 12.*

Front door lock

18 Remove the door inner trim panel and plastic sealing sheet (where fitted), as described in Section 12.

19 Remove the window regulator, as described in Section 14.

20 Remove the interior door release lever, as described in paragraphs 1 to 4.

13.14a Slacken the retaining screw …

13.14b … and withdraw the door lock cylinder/push button

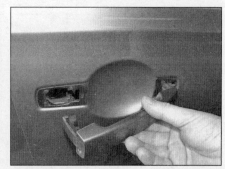

13.15a Slide the handle to the rear and pull it out to disengage it from the door

13.15b On models with intelligent key system, withdraw the wiring out from the door panel

13.16 Remove the seals from the door handle recess

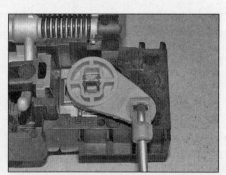

13.17 Fit new lever to the rear of the door lock

13.22a Undo the retaining bolt (arrowed) …

13.22b … and also second retaining bolt (arrowed) …

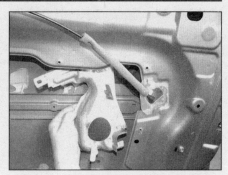

13.23 … then remove the lock protection shield

13.24 Undo the retaining bolt and remove the wiring retaining plate

13.25 Disconnect the wiring connector

21 Remove the exterior door handle, as described in paragraphs 10 to 17.

22 Peel back the plastic covers from the door panel, to access the door lock protection shield retaining bolts **(see illustrations)**.

23 Undo the retaining bolts and remove the door lock protection shield from inside the door panel **(see illustration)**.

24 Undo the retaining bolt and remove the wiring connector retaining plate, from inside the door panel **(see illustration)**.

25 Disconnect the wiring connector from the door lock assembly **(see illustration)**.

26 Unclip the operating cable plastic shield from the door panel **(see illustration)**.

27 Working at the rear edge of the door, unscrew the three lock securing screws, release the handle support bracket from the inside of the door panel, and then withdraw the lock assembly through the door aperture **(see illustrations)**.

28 Refitting is a reversal of removal, bearing in mind the following points:

a) Before refitting the door lock assembly, make sure the lock button retaining bracket is fitted correctly in the handle support bracket **(see illustration)**.

b) Fit a new plastic lever to the rear of the door lock button **(see illustration 13.17)**.

c) Make sure the leg on the rear of the handle is positioned behind the lever on the support bracket inside the door panel **(see illustration 13.9)**.

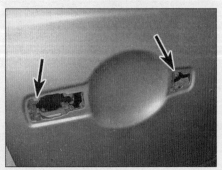

13.26 Unclip the operating cable plastic shield

13.27a Undo the three screws securing the lock …

13.27b … release the handle support from the handle recess …

13.27c … then withdraw the assembly from inside the door

13.28 Make sure the lock/button retaining bracket is fitted

13.32a Undo the three screws securing the lock …

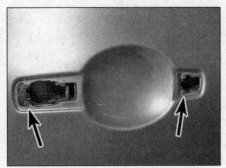

13.32b … release the handle support from the handle recess …

13.32c … then withdraw the assembly from inside the door

d) *Ensure that the lock operating cable/rods are routed as noted before removal.*

e) *Check the operation of the release lever/ lock mechanism before refitting the door inner trim panel.*

f) *Refit the window regulator assembly with reference to Section 14.*

g) *Refit the door inner trim panel with reference to Section 12.*

Rear door lock

29 With the window fully raised, remove door inner trim panel, plastic sealing sheet and strengthener panel, as described in Section 12.

30 Remove the interior door release lever, as described in paragraphs 1 to 4.

31 Remove the exterior door handle, as described in paragraphs 10 to 17.

32 Working at the rear edge of the door, unscrew the three lock securing screws, release the handle support bracket from the inside of the door panel, and then withdraw the lock assembly through the door aperture **(see illustrations)**.

33 Disconnect the wiring connector from the door lock assembly as it is removed **(see illustration)**.

34 Refitting is a reversal of removal, bearing in mind the following points:

a) *Before refitting the door lock assembly, make sure the push button retaining bracket is fitted correctly in the handle support bracket (see illustration 13.28).*

13.33 Disconnect the wiring connector as it is removed

b) *Ensure that the lock operating cables are correctly reconnected and routed, as noted before removal.*

c) *Check the operation of the handle/lock mechanism before refitting the door inner trim panel.*

d) *Refit the door inner trim panel as described in Section 12.*

14 Door window glass and regulator – removal and refitting

Front window glass

1 Remove the door inner trim panel, as described in Section 12.

14.2 Remove the sealing covers

2 Peel back and remove the round sealing covers from the window regulator assembly **(see illustration)**.

3 Temporarily reconnect the electric window switch (and the battery negative terminal, if removed), and lower or raise the window until the two bolts securing the lower edge of the window glass to the regulator mechanism are accessible through the holes in the window regulator assembly. Support the glass, and then undo the two bolts **(see illustration)**.

4 Ease the inner sealing weather strip from the top of the door frame **(see illustration)**.

5 Disengage the window glass from the regulator, raise the glass at the rear, and then withdraw it from the outside of the door frame **(see illustration)**.

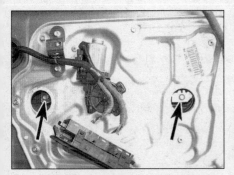

14.3 Undo the two window glass securing bolts (arrowed)

14.4 Carefully prise up the inner door seal

14.5 Withdraw the window glass from the door

14.8a Unclip the wiring loom retaining clip …

14.8b … and disconnect the motor wiring connector

14.9 Remove the window motor/regulator assembly from the door

6 Refitting is a reversal of removal, bearing in mind the following points:

a) *Take care not to dislodge the weather strips when fitting the glass.*

b) *Check the operation of the window mechanism before refitting the door inner trim panel.*

c) *Refit the door inner trim panel with reference to Section 12.*

Front window regulator

7 Remove the front window glass as described in paragraphs 1 to 5 in this Section.

8 Unclip the wiring loom from the mounting bracket, and then disconnect the wiring connector from the window regulator motor **(see illustrations)**.

9 Undo the window regulator assembly securing bolts, then manipulate the complete motor/regulator assembly out through the aperture in the door **(see illustration)**.

10 The window regulator/motor assembly comes as a complete unit **(see illustration)**, Check with your Nissan dealer for the availability of parts.

11 Refitting is a reversal of removal, bearing in mind the following points:

a) *Refit the front window glass with reference to paragraph 6.*

b) *Check the operation of the window mechanism before refitting the door inner trim panel.*

Rear window glass

12 Remove the door inner trim panel and plastic sealing sheet, as described in Section 12.

13 If not already done, temporarily reconnect the electric window switch (and the battery negative terminal, if removed), and raise the window glass to the top of the doorframe.

14 Undo the retaining bolt and remove the rear window guide from inside the door panel **(see illustration)**.

15 Unclip the plastic trim from the rear of the window frame **(see illustration)**.

16 Lower the window glass, and then ease the inner sealing weather strip from the top of the door frame **(see illustration)**.

17 Working your way around the upper door frame, carefully remove the inner window channel/seal **(see illustration)**. Note this is one piece that is inserted all around the upper window frame; take care not to damage it, as it is removed.

18 Raise the window until the two bolts securing the lower edge of the window glass to the regulator mechanism are accessible through the holes in the doorframe. Support the glass, and then undo the two bolts **(see illustration)**.

19 Disengage the window glass from the

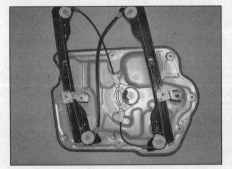

14.10 The window motor/regulator is a complete assembly

14.14 Remove the window guide

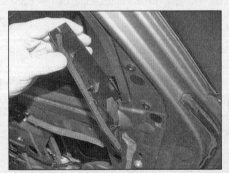

14.15 Unclip the plastic trim panel

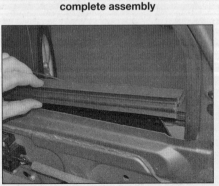

14.16 Carefully prise up the inner door seal

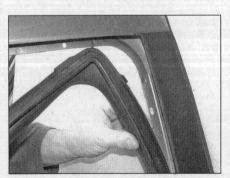

14.17 Carefully prise out the seal

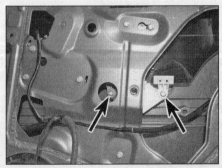

14.18 Undo the two window glass securing bolts

14.19 Withdraw the window glass out from the door

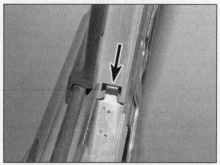

14.20 Make sure the locating peg (arrowed) is located correctly in the door frame

14.23 Tape the window to the top of the frame

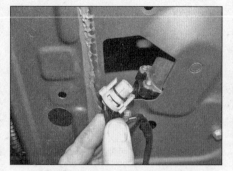

14.24 Disconnect the motor wiring connector

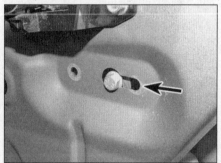

14.25a This bolt does not have to be completely removed

14.25b There are two hooks (arrowed) to support the motor

regulator, raise the glass at the rear, and then withdraw it from the outside of the door frame **(see illustration)**.

20 Refitting is a reversal of removal, bearing in mind the following points:

a) *When fitting the rear window guide, make sure the upper part is located correctly in the door frame* **(see illustration)**.

b) *Take care not to dislodge the weather strips when fitting the glass.*

c) *Check the operation of the window mechanism before refitting the door inner trim panel.*

d) *Refit the door inner trim panel with reference to Section 12.*

Rear window regulator

21 Remove the door inner trim panel and plastic sealing sheet, as described in Section 12.

22 Temporarily reconnect the electric window switch (and the battery negative terminal, if removed), and lower or raise the window until the two bolts securing the lower edge of the window glass to the regulator mechanism are accessible through the holes in the window regulator assembly. Support the glass, and then undo the two bolts.

23 Disengage the window glass from the regulator and slide it to the top of the

window frame and tape it in position **(see illustration)**.

24 Disconnect the wiring connector from the window regulator motor **(see illustration)**.

25 Note the upper right-hand regulator bolt does not have to be removed completely, as the mounting hole is elongated. Also the window motor has two locating pegs that hook onto the door frame, to prevent it falling down inside the door panel, when the bolts are removed **(see illustrations)**.

26 Undo the window regulator and motor securing bolts, and then manipulate the complete motor/regulator assembly out through the aperture in the door **(see illustrations)**.

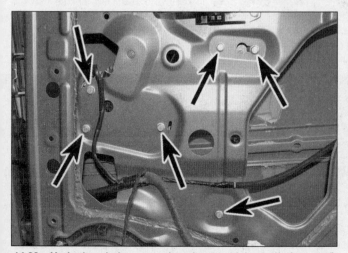

14.26a Undo the window motor/regulator retaining bolts (arrowed)

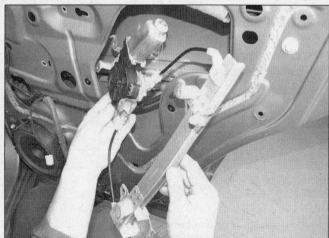

14.26b Remove the window motor/regulator from the door

27 Refitting is a reversal of removal, bearing in mind the following points:
a) *Refit the window glass and tighten the retaining bolts.*
b) *Check the operation of the window mechanism before refitting the door inner trim panel.*
c) *Refit the door inner trim panel with reference to Section 12.*

15 Tailgate and support struts – removal, refitting and adjustment

Tailgate
Removal

1 Disconnect the battery negative terminal (refer to *Disconnecting the battery* in Reference).

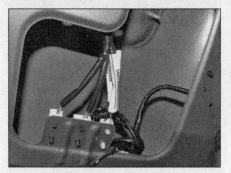
15.3 Disconnect the wiring block connectors inside the tailgate

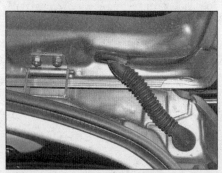
15.5b ... from both sides of the vehicle

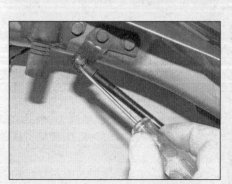
15.16a Prise out the securing clip ...

2 Remove the tailgate interior trim panels as described in Section 24.
3 Working inside the tailgate, disconnect the wiring plugs to the wiper motor, the heated rear window element, the rear number plate lights, the rear light clusters, and the high-level stop-light. Also unbolt any earth lead(s). Check for any other wiring connectors, which must be disconnected to facilitate tailgate removal, and then release the harness securing cable ties **(see illustration)**.
4 Remove the tailgate high level brake light, as described in Chapter 12, Section 5, and disconnect the washer fluid hose.
5 Tie a length of string to the wiring harness and washer hose, then prise the wiring harness grommets from the both corners of the tailgate **(see illustrations)**. Feed the wiring harness through the aperture in the tailgate on the left-hand side and the washer fluid hose

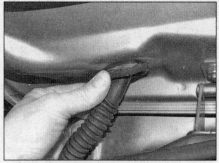
15.5a Unclip the wiring gaiters ...

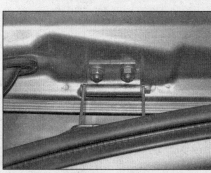
15.8 Undo the hinge retaining nuts

15.16b ... and pull the strut from the upper balljoint

on the right-hand side. Untie the string from the wiring harness, and leave the string in place in the tailgate, to aid refitting.
6 Have an assistant support the tailgate in the open position.
7 Remove the securing clips and release both support struts from their upper mounting point on the tailgate **(see illustrations 15.16a and 15.16b)**.
8 Using a pencil or felt tip pen, mark the outline of each hinge relative to the tailgate, to use as a guide on refitting. Unscrew the nuts securing the hinges to the tailgate **(see illustration)**, and then lift the tailgate from the vehicle.

Refitting

9 Refitting is a reversal of removal, bearing in mind the following points.
10 Tie the string to the wiring harness and washer fluid hose, and use the string to pull them back through the aperture and into the tailgate.
11 Do not fully tighten the hinge securing nuts until the tailgate adjustment has been checked, as described in the following paragraphs.

Adjustment

12 Close the tailgate (**carefully**, in case the alignment is incorrect, which may cause scratching on the tailgate or the body as the tailgate is closed), and check for alignment with the adjacent panels.
13 If adjustment is required, it will be necessary to slacken the hinge retaining nuts and re-align the tailgate to suit. Once the tailgate is correctly aligned, tighten the hinge retaining nuts fully.
14 Once the tailgate is correctly aligned, check that the tailgate fastens and releases in a satisfactory manner. If adjustment is necessary, slacken the tailgate lock striker retaining screws, and adjust the position of the catch, as described in Section 16. Once the tailgate lock is operating correctly, securely tighten the retaining screws.

Support struts

15 To remove a strut, first ensure that the tailgate is adequately supported.
16 Remove the securing clips and release both support struts from their upper and lower mounting points **(see illustrations)**.

15.16c Prise out the clip and pull the strut from the lower balljoint

15.17a Upper strut bracket retaining bolts

15.17b Lower strut bracket retaining bolts

17 If required, unscrew the two bolts securing the support strut upper and lower mounting plates to the body **(see illustrations)**. Lift away the support strut.

18 Refitting is a reversal of removal.

16 Tailgate lock components – removal and refitting

Tailgate lock

1 Disconnect the battery negative terminal (refer to *Disconnecting the battery* in Reference).

2 Remove the tailgate inner trim panel as described in Section 24.

3 Unscrew the two lock securing bolts and manipulate the lock out through the aperture in the tailgate **(see illustrations)**.

4 Disconnect the wiring connector as the lock is removed **(see illustration)**

5 Refitting is a reversal of removal, but before refitting the trim panel, check that the tailgate fastens and releases in a satisfactory manner. If adjustment is necessary, slacken the tailgate lock retaining bolts, and adjust the position of the lock to suit. Once the lock is operating correctly, securely tighten its retaining bolts.

Tailgate lock striker

6 Unclip the small trim panel from the rear of the luggage compartment panel **(see illustration)**.

7 Note the position of the striker plate,

then unscrew the two securing screws, and withdraw the lock striker from the rear panel **(see illustration)**.

8 Refitting is a reversal of removal, but check the operation of the tailgate release mechanism.

9 Check that the tailgate fastens and releases in a satisfactory manner. If adjustment is necessary, slacken the striker retaining screws, and adjust the position of the striker to suit. Once the lock is operating correctly, securely tighten the striker retaining screws.

Tailgate exterior switch

10 Remove the tailgate inner trim panel as described in Section 24.

11 Reach inside the tailgate and disconnect the wiring connector(s) for the tailgate switch and number plate lights **(see illustration)**.

16.3a Undo the two bolts …

16.3b … and withdraw the lock from the tailgate

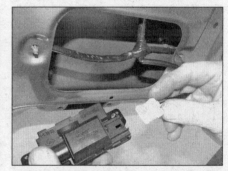

16.4 Disconnect the lock wiring plug connector

16.6 Unclip the plastic trim …

16.7 … and undo the two screws to remove the lock striker

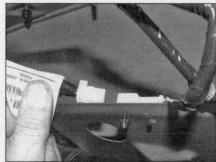

16.11 Disconnect the wiring plug connector …

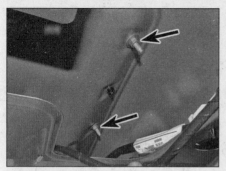

16.12a Undo the retaining nuts (two shown) …

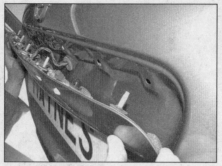

16.12b … and remove the tailgate trim panel

6.13 Release the wiring rubber grommet from the tailgate

12 Undo the five nuts, securing the switch trim panel to the tailgate, working inside the tailgate undo the nuts and withdraw the trim panel from the tailgate **(see illustrations)**.

13 As the trim panel is withdrawn, release the wiring loom rubber grommet from the tailgate **(see illustration)**.
14 To remove the switch, disconnect the

wiring connector, release the securing clips and withdraw the switch from the trim panel **(see illustrations)**.
15 Refitting is a reversal of removal.

---

17 Central locking system components – removal and refitting

Body Control Module (BCM)

Removal

1 The electronic body control unit is located above the glovebox, on the left-hand side of the facia **(see illustration)**.
2 Disconnect the battery negative terminal (refer to *Disconnecting the battery* in Reference).
3 Remove the glovebox as described in Section 26.
4 Remove the four securing bolts **(see illustration)**, and then withdraw the unit, complete with the mounting bracket, and then disconnect the wiring plugs.

Refitting

5 Refitting is a reversal of removal.

Door lock motor

6 The motor is integral with the door lock assembly. Removal and refitting of the lock assembly is described in Section 13.

Tailgate lock motor

7 Removal of the tailgate lock motor is described as part of the tailgate lock removal and refitting procedure described in Section 16.

Door switches

8 Disconnect the battery negative terminal (refer to *Disconnecting the battery* in Reference).
9 Undo the retaining screw and withdraw the relevant switch from the door pillar **(see illustration)**.
10 Disconnect the wiring connector and remove the switch.
11 Refitting is a reversal of removal.

Remote control battery renewal

12 Unclip the cover from the end of the remote control **(see illustration)**.

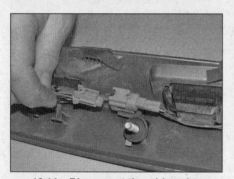

16.14a Disconnect the wiring plug connector …

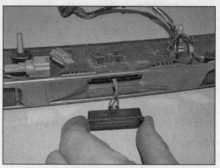

16.14b … and release the switch from the trim panel

17.1 Body Control Module (BCM) location

17.4 Undo the bracket retaining screws (arrowed)

17.9 Remove the door switch from the pillar

17.12 Unclip the cover from the key remote

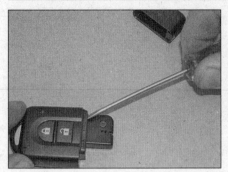

17.13a Twist a small screwdriver in the slot ...

17.13b ... and unclip one side of the transmitter

17.14 Lift the battery from its location in the remote

13 Using a small screwdriver, carefully prise the two halves of the transmitter apart **(see illustrations)**.

14 Carefully unclip the battery from its position in the transmitter housing, noting its fitted position **(see illustration)**.

15 Fit the new battery, observing the correct polarity, and clip the transmitter housing back together.

18 Mirrors and associated components – removal and refitting

Exterior mirror assembly

1 If working on an electric mirror, disconnect the battery negative terminal (refer to *Disconnecting the battery* in Reference).

2 Remove the door inner trim panel, as described in Section 12.

3 Carefully prise off the mirror interior trim panel **(see illustration)**.

4 Disconnect the mirror wiring connector and, where applicable, unclip the wiring from the door, noting its routing **(see illustration)**.

5 Remove the three securing bolts, and withdraw the mirror from the outside of the door **(see illustrations)**.

6 Refitting is a reversal of removal, ensuring that the mirror wiring is routed as noted before removal.

Exterior mirror glass

7 Carefully press the mirror glass in at the top, and then working through the gap at the bottom edge of the mirror glass, use a lever to release the clips that secure the mirror glass to the mirror body **(see illustration)**.

8 Withdraw the glass, and (where applicable) disconnect the heating element wiring connectors **(see illustrations)**.

9 To refit, carefully push the mirror glass

18.3 Unclip the plastic trim cover

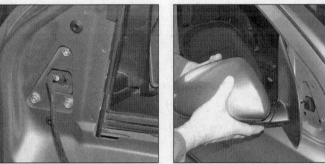

18.4 Disconnect the wiring connector

18.5a Undo the three securing bolts ...

18.5b ... and remove the mirror assembly

18.7 Carefully lever the lower edge of the mirror glass

18.8a Unclip the mirror from the mirror base ...

18.8b ... and disconnect the wiring connectors

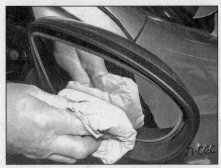

18.9 Carefully push the mirror glass back into position

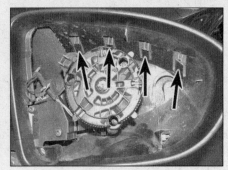

18.11a Release the retaining clips (arrowed) …

18.11b … and remove the mirror outer shell

evenly until the securing clips lock into position on the mirror adjuster base **(see illustration)**.

 Warning: It is advisable to wear gloves to protect your hands, even if the glass is not broken, due to the risk of glass breakage.

Exterior mirror outer shell

10 Remove the mirror glass as described previously in this Section.
11 Working from inside the mirror housing, release the retaining clips, and then carefully remove the mirror shell from the mirror body **(see illustrations)**.
12 To refit, carefully push the mirror shell onto the mirror body until the securing clips lock into position.
13 Refit the mirror glass as described previously in this Section.

Exterior mirror electric motor

14 Remove the mirror glass as described previously in this Section.
15 Working from inside the mirror housing, undo the three retaining screws and withdraw the motor from the mirror body **(see illustration)**.
16 Disconnect the wiring connector as it is removed **(see illustration)**.
17 Refitting is a reversal of removal, ensuring that the mirror glass is fitted securely as described previously in this Section.

Interior mirror

18 Using a small flat-bladed screwdriver carefully prise apart the two plastic covers, from around the mirror base **(see illustrations)**.

19 Disconnect the wiring plug connector at the rear of the mirror base **(see illustration)**.
20 The mirror can now be pushed upwards, to release it from the mounting base on the windscreen. Note the mirror can be a tight fit on the base, take care not to damage the windscreen as this is removed.
21 To refit the interior mirror to the base, offer it up and slide it downwards back into place. Reconnect the wiring connector and refit the plastic trim covers.

19 Windscreen, tailgate glass and fixed windows – general information

These areas of glass are secured by the tight fit of the weatherstrip in the body aperture, and are bonded in position with a special adhesive. Renewal of such fixed glass is a difficult, messy and time-consuming task, which is considered beyond the scope of the home mechanic. It is difficult, unless one has plenty of practice, to obtain a secure, waterproof fit. Furthermore, the task carries a high risk of breakage; this applies especially to the laminated glass windscreen. In view of this, owners are strongly advised to have this sort of work carried out by one of the many specialist windscreen fitters.

For those possessing the necessary skills and equipment to carry out this task, some preliminary removal of the vehicle interior trim and associated components is necessary, as follows, referring to the procedures contained in the Sections and Chapters indicated.

18.15 Undo the three motor retaining screws (arrowed) …

18.16 … and disconnect the wiring connector

18.18a Unclip the upper trim …

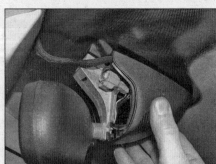

18.18b … the lower trim …

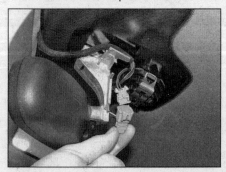

18.19 … and then disconnect the wiring connector

Windscreen

1 Remove both wiper arms (Chapter 12, Section 11).
2 Remove the windscreen scuttle grille panel (Section 21 of this Chapter).
3 Remove the front pillar trim on both sides (Section 24 of this Chapter).
4 Remove the sunvisors (Section 24 of this Chapter).

Rear fixed side window glass

5 Remove the relevant luggage compartment trim panels (Section 24 of this Chapter).

Tailgate window glass

6 Remove the tailgate trim panels (Section 24 of this Chapter).

20 Sunroof – general information

Due to the complexity of the sunroof mechanism, considerable expertise is required to repair, renew or adjust the sunroof components successfully. Removal of the roof first requires the headlining to be removed, which is a tedious operation, and not a task to be undertaken lightly. Any problems with the sunroof should be referred to a Nissan dealer.

21 Body exterior fittings – removal and refitting

Windscreen scuttle grille panel

1 Open and support the bonnet.
2 Remove the windscreen wiper arms as described in Chapter 12, Section 11.
3 Disconnect the washer fluid hose from the right-hand side of the scuttle panel (**see illustration**).
4 Working along the front edge of the scuttle panel, pull out the centre pin and release the scuttle panel retaining clips (**see illustration**).
5 Lift the scuttle grille panel away from the wiper spindles, unclipping it from around the bonnet hinges (**see illustrations**).
6 Refitting is a reversal of removal.

21.3 Disconnect the washer fluid hose

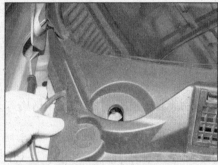

21.5a Unclip the outer edges …

Wheel arch liners/shields

7 The wheel arch liners are secured by expanding plastic rivets, screws, nuts or bolts.
8 Firmly apply the handbrake, and then jack up the vehicle and support it securely on axle stands (see *Jacking and vehicle support*). To improve access to the fasteners, remove roadwheel(s).
9 To remove the liners, release the centre pins, and then prise the complete plastic rivet from place. Undo the retaining screws from under the lower edges of the liner. On the front, if the engine undershield is fitted undo the retaining bolts. With all the fasteners removed, manoeuvre the liner from the wheel arch (**see illustrations**).

Body trim strips and badges

10 The various body trim strips and badges are held in position with a special adhesive

21.4 Release the retaining clips

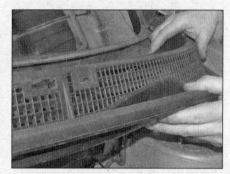

21.5b … then remove the scuttle panel

tape. Removal requires the trim/badge to be heated, to soften the adhesive, and then cut away from the surface. Due to the high risk of damage to the vehicle paintwork during this operation, it is recommended that this task should be entrusted to a Nissan dealer.

22 Seats – removal and refitting

Front seat

⚠️ *Warning: Certain later models are equipped with side airbags built into the outer sides of the front seats. Refer to Chapter 12, Section 20, for the precautions, which should be observed when dealing with an airbag system. Do not tamper with the airbag unit in any way, and do not attempt to test any airbag*

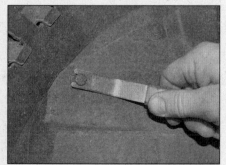

21.9a Release the plastic securing clips …

21.9b … and remove the inner wheel arch panel …

21.9c … then remove the inner wheel arch liner

22.3 Undo the two bolts (arrowed) at the rear of the seat rails

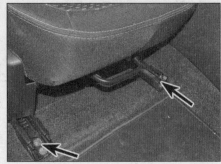

22.4 Undo the two bolts at the front of the seal rails (arrowed)

22.5 Disconnect the seat wiring plug connectors

system components. Note that the airbag is triggered if the mechanism is supplied with an electrical current (including via an ohmmeter), or if the assembly is subjected to a temperature of greater than 100°C.

1 On models with side airbags in the front seats, de-activate the airbag system as described in Chapter 12, Section 20, before attempting to remove the seat.

2 Release the retaining clips and withdraw the headrest out from the top of the seat backrest. This will give more room, when removing the seat out through the door aperture.

3 Move the seat fully forwards and undo the two retaining bolts from the rear of the seat rails **(see illustration)**.

4 Slide the seat fully rearwards, and then unscrew the seat rail front securing bolts **(see illustration)**.

5 Tilt the seat backwards and disconnect the wiring connectors, then release the wiring

loom from any retaining clips under the seat base **(see illustration)**. Lift the seat, complete with the rails out from the vehicle, taking care that the seat rails do not catch on the vehicle paintwork as it is being removed.

6 Refitting is a reversal of removal, but tighten the securing bolts to the specified torque.

Rear seat cushion (2 row model)

7 Lift the seat cushion at the front, and then give a sharp pull upwards, to release the securing clip from the vehicle floor panel **(see illustration)**.

8 Slide the seat cushion forward, releasing the rear locating clips **(see illustration)**.

9 Then lift the seat cushion upwards and withdraw the seat belt buckles from the seat cushion **(see illustration)**.

10 Refitting is a reversal of removal.

Rear seat backs (2 row model)

11 Remove the rear seat cushions as

described in paragraphs 7 to 9, previously in this Section.

12 Release the catches on the rear seat backs and fold them forward

13 Unclip the plastic inner wheel arch trim from each side of the vehicle, as described in Section 24, paragraph 20.

14 With both seat backs forward, undo the two nuts securing the outer part of the hinge bracket to the vehicle inner wing panel **(see illustration)**.

15 Lift the right-hand seat back upwards, and then pull it away from the left-hand seat back to disengage the inner hinge peg **(see illustration)**. Remove the right-hand seat back from the vehicle.

16 The left-hand seat back can now be removed, undo the two nuts securing the outer part of the hinge bracket to the vehicle inner wing panel **(see illustration)**.

17 Undo the centre hinge bracket bolt/nut

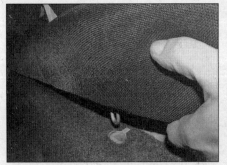

22.7 Release the front securing clip

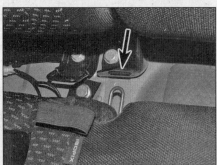

22.8 Slide the seat forwards from the locating bracket (arrowed)

22.9 Release the seat belt buckles from the seat

22.14 Undo the two retaining nuts …

22.15 … and remove the right-hand seat back

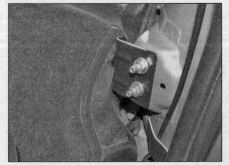

22.16 Undo the outer two retaining nuts …

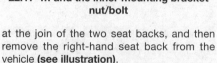

22.17 ... and the inner mounting bracket nut/bolt

22.19 Unclip the rear sill trim panel

22.20 Unclip the plastic covers from the seat rail ...

at the join of the two seat backs, and then remove the right-hand seat back from the vehicle **(see illustration)**.
18 Refitting is a reversal of removal, tightening the hinge bolt/nut securely.

Rear sliding seats (3 row model)

19 Unclip the plastic inner sill trim from each side of the vehicle **(see illustration)**.
20 Unclip the plastic trim panels from front of each seat rail **(see illustration)**.
21 Slide the seat fully rearwards, and then unscrew the seat rail front securing bolts **(see illustration)**.
22 Move the seat fully forwards and undo the two retaining bolts from the rear of the seat rails **(see illustration)**.
23 Tilt the seat backwards and release the wiring loom from any retaining clips under the seat base, then disconnect the wiring connectors **(see illustration)**. Lift the seat,

complete with the rails out from the vehicle, taking care that the seat rails do not catch on the vehicle paintwork as it is being removed.
24 The rear seat on the other side of the vehicle can be removed using the same method.
25 Refitting is a reversal of removal.

Rear +2 seats (3 row model)

26 Open the tailgate, release the rear seat locking catches and tilt the seat forwards.
27 Remove the securing clips and release both support struts from each side of the rear seat **(see illustration)**. With the struts removed lower the seat back down, but do not clip the seat back into the rear seat catches.
28 Working at the front of the seat, unclip the plastic trim from the two front seat hinges **(see illustration)**.
29 Undo the mounting bolts from the two front seat hinges, and withdraw the complete

rear seat out through the back of the tailgate aperture **(see illustration)**.
30 Refitting is a reversal of removal.

23 Seat belt components – removal and refitting

Note: *Record the positions of the washers and spacers on the seat belt anchors, and ensure they are refitted in their original positions.*

Front seat belt

⚠️ *Warning: On certain models, the front seat belt inertia reels are equipped with a mechanical or pyrotechnic pretensioner mechanism. Refer to the airbag system precautions contained in Chapter 12, Section 20, which apply equally to the seat belt pretensioners.*

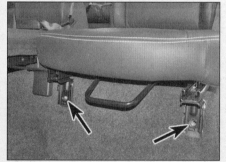

22.21 ... and undo the seat front mounting bolts

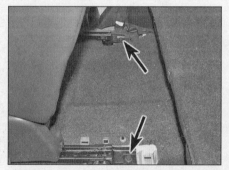

22.22 Undo the two bolts (arrowed) at the rear of the seat rails

22.23 Disconnect the seat wiring plug connectors

22.27 Prise out the securing clip and pull the strut from the balljoint

22.28 Unclip the plastic covers from the seat mounting bracket ...

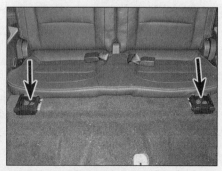

22.29 ... and undo the seat front mounting bolts

23.4a Insert a thin screwdriver …

23.4b … to release the seat belt from the pretensioner

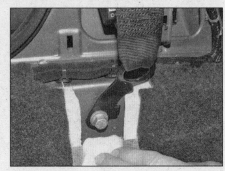

23.5 Undo the seat belt lower anchor bolt

23.6 Disconnect the wiring connector (arrowed) from the inertia reel

23.7 Undo the seat belt reel mounting bolt

23.8 Undo the seat belt upper anchor bolt

Do not tamper with the inertia reel pretensioner unit in any way, and do not attempt to test the unit.

1 De-activate the airbag system (which will also de-activate the pyrotechnic pretensioner mechanism, where fitted) as described in Chapter 12, Section 20, before attempting to remove the seatbelt.

2 To make access easier, remove the relevant front seat as described in Section 22.

3 Remove the centre pillar trim panels as described in Section 24.

4 On models with seat belt pre-tensioners fitted, use a small screwdriver to disconnect the lower end of the seat belt from the seat belt pre-tensioner **(see illustrations)**.

5 On models without seat belt pre-tensioners fitted, undo the seat belt lower anchorage bolt **(see illustration)**. Note the locating

peg fitted to the slot in the sill panel for refitting.

6 Release the locking clip and disconnect the wiring connector from the inertia reel **(see illustration)**.

7 Unscrew the seat belt inertia reel mounting bolt **(see illustration)**, noting the fitted position of the inertial reel in the mounting bracket.

8 Undo the seat belt upper anchorage bolt, then remove the seat belt assembly from the vehicle **(see illustration)**.

9 Refitting is a reversal of removal, ensuring that all mounting bolts are tightened to the specified torque.

Front seat belt stalk

10 Remove the relevant front seat as described in Section 22.

11 Trace the wiring back from the seat

belt stalk and under the seat cushion, then unclip it from the wiring securing clips **(see illustration)**.

12 Unscrew the bolt and withdraw the stalk assembly from the side of the front seat **(see illustration)**.

13 Refitting is a reversal of removal, but tighten the stalk anchor bolt to the specified torque.

Rear side seat belt (2 row model)

14 Remove the relevant rear seat as described in Section 22.

15 Working as described in Section 24, remove the relevant rear pillar trim panels for access to the inertia reel.

16 Unscrew the lower anchor bolts, from the rear floor panel **(see illustration)**.

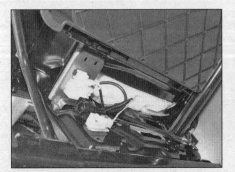

23.11 Unclip the wiring loom from the seat frame

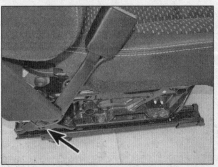

23.12 Undo the seat belt stalk anchor bolt (arrowed)

23.16 Undo the seat belt lower anchor bolt

23.17 Undo the seat belt reel mounting bolt

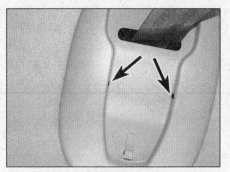

23.19a Using a thin screwdriver through the two holes (arrowed) …

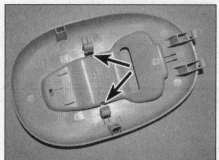

23.19b … release the two retaining clips (arrowed) …

17 Unscrew the seat belt inertia reel mounting bolt, then remove the seat belt assembly from the vehicle **(see illustration)**. Note the fitted position of the inertial reel on the mounting bracket before removal.

18 Refitting is a reversal of removal, ensuring that all mounting bolts are tightened to the specified torque.

Rear centre seat belt (2 row model)

19 Using a thin screwdriver, release the retaining clips and remove the plastic trim cover from the headlining **(see illustrations)**. Slide the seat belt through the plastic trim panel and remove.

20 Unscrew the inertia reel securing bolts/nut, and carefully withdraw the seat belt assembly from the roof panel **(see illustration)**. Take care not to damage the headlining as the seat belt assembly is removed.

21 Refitting is a reversal of removal, ensuring that all mounting bolts/nut are tightened to the specified torque.

Rear seat belt stalk (2 row model)

22 Remove the rear seat cushion, as described in Section 22.

23 Trace the wiring back from the seat belt stalk and disconnect the wiring connector.

24 Unscrew the bolt and withdraw the stalk assembly from the floor panel **(see illustration)**.

25 Refitting is a reversal of removal, but tighten the stalk anchor bolt to the specified torque.

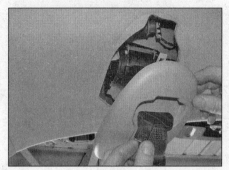

23.19c … and withdraw the trim from the seat belt

Rear side seat belt (3 row model)

26 Remove the relevant rear seat as described in Section 22.

27 Working as described in Section 24, remove the relevant parcel shelf support panel and rear pillar trim panels for access to the inertia reel.

28 Unscrew the lower anchor bolts, from the rear floor panel.

29 Unscrew the seat belt inertia reel mounting bolt, then remove the seat belt assembly from the vehicle **(see illustration)**. Note the fitted position of the inertial reel on the mounting bracket before removal.

30 Refitting is a reversal of removal, ensuring that all mounting bolts are tightened to the specified torque. After the trim panels have been refitted as described in Section 24, tighten the upper seat belt anchorage bolts

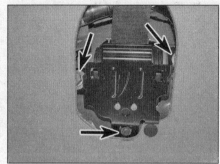

23.20 Undo the seat belt reel mounting bolts/nut

to the specified torque setting, then fit the plastic covers to the mounting bolts **(see illustration)**.

24 Interior trim panels – removal and refitting

General

1 The interior trim panels are secured by a combination of metal and plastic clips and screws. When releasing certain types of securing clips, a suitable forked tool will prove invaluable to avoid damage to the panel and clips. A degree of force will be necessary to pull some of the panels from their locations, especially where numerous internal retaining clips are used. Be prepared for some of the

23.24 Undo the seat belt stalk retaining bolt (arrowed)

23.29 Undo the seat belt reel mounting bolt/nut (arrowed)

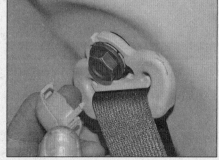

23.30 Fit the plastic covers to the seat belt upper anchor bolts

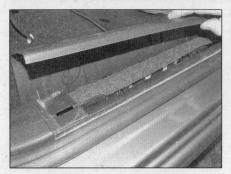

24.3a Unclip the front sill trim ...

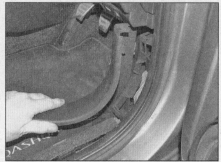

24.3b ... releasing it from the front kick panel trim

24.4a Undo the plastic retaining nut ...

24.4b ... and unclip the kick panel trim

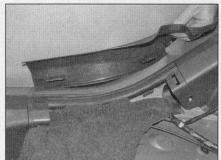

24.5 Unclip the rear sill trim panel

24.7 Peel back the door weather seal

plastic clips to break when their relevant panel is being removed.

Door inner trim

2 Refer to Section 12.

Footwell sill trim panels

3 Unclip the front sill trim panel from the bottom of the B-pillar trim, and then from the front footwell side/kick trim panel **(see illustrations)**.
4 Undo the plastic securing nut, and then unclip the footwell side/kick trim panel from the bottom of the A-pillar **(see illustrations)**.
5 Unclip the rear sill trim panel from the bottom of the B-pillar trim, and the rear inner wheel arch trim panel **(see illustration)**.
6 Refitting is a reversal of removal.

Front A-pillar trim panels

7 Carefully prise the front door weatherstrip from along the edge of the panel **(see illustration)**.
8 Pull the upper part of the panel from the pillar, then lift the panel up to disengage the lower lugs from the facia and remove the trim panel **(see illustration)**.
9 Refitting is a reversal of removal, ensuring the weatherstrip is correctly seated.

Centre B-pillar trim panels

10 To make access easier, slide the front seat as far forward as possible.
11 On models with seat belt pre-tensioners fitted, use a small screwdriver to disconnect the lower end of the seat belt from the seat belt pre-tensioner **(see illustrations 23.4a and 23.4b)**.
12 On models without seat belt pre-tensioners fitted, unclip the small plastic trim from around the seat belt **(see illustration)**.
13 Remove the sill trim panels from the front and rear door apertures, as described in paragraphs 3 to 5 in this Section.

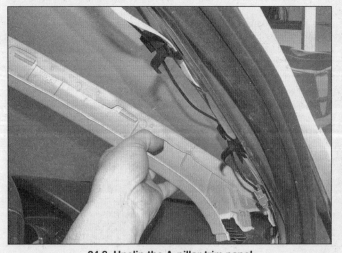

24.8 Unclip the A-pillar trim panel

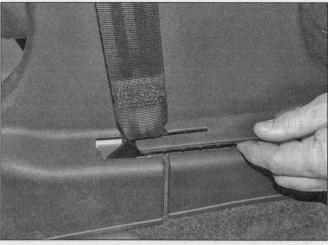

24.12 Unclip the small plastic trim panel

24.15a Unclip the B-pillar lower trim panel ...

24.15b ... pass the seat belt through the slot ...

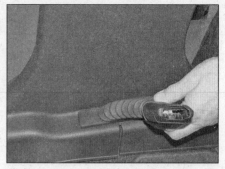

24.15c ... or unclip the gaiter from the trim panel

14 Carefully prise the front and rear door weatherstrip from the edges of the centre B-pillar trim panels.

15 Unclip the lower trim panel from the B-pillar, and then disengage the seat belt/ rubber gaiter through the slot in the trim panel (see illustrations). The lower trim panel can then be unclipped from the B-pillar.

16 Unclip the upper trim panel from the B-pillar, and then pull it downwards to disengage the upper part from behind the headlining (see illustrations).

17 The upper trim panel can then be completely removed, by sliding the seat belt out through the slot in the panel (see illustration). On models without seat belt pre-tensioners fitted, undo the seat belt lower anchorage bolt (with reference to Section 23, paragraph 5), to remove the seat belt from the upper trim panel.

18 Refitting is a reversal of removal, ensuring that all retaining clips are fully engaged. If removed, refit the seat belt anchor bolt in the position noted during removal, then tighten to the specified torque.

Rear pillar trim panels (2 row seat model)

19 If the trim panel is to be completely removed it may be easier to remove the rear seats as described in Section 22. If required, remove the rear luggage compartment trim panel as described later in this Section.

20 Unclip the plastic inner wheel arch trim from each side of the vehicle (see illustration).

21 Unscrew the lower anchor bolts, from the rear floor panel (see illustration 23.16).

22 Unclip the small plastic trim from around the seat belt (see illustration).

24.16a Unclip the lower part of the trim ...

24.17 Withdraw the seat belt out through the panel

23 Carefully prise the upper trim panel to release the securing clips, and then disengage it from the rear pillar (see illustrations).

24 The upper trim panel can then be

24.16b ... then pull downwards to release it from the roof panel

24.20 Unclip the rear wheel arch trim panel

24.22 Unclip the small plastic trim from around the seat belt

24.23a Using a lever, carefully release the retaining clips ...

24.23b ... and unclip the upper trim panel

24.24 Withdraw the seat belt out through the panel

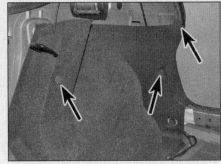

24.25a Release the retaining clips …

24.25b … and remove the lower side carpet

completely removed, by sliding the seat belt out through the slot in the panel **(see illustration)**.

25 To remove the lower carpet trim panel,

release the retaining clips and withdraw the carpet trim from the inner rear wheel arch **(see illustrations)**.

26 Refitting is a reversal of removal, ensuring

that all retaining clips are fully engaged. If removed, refit the seat belt anchor bolt in the position noted during removal, then tighten to the specified torque.

Rear pillar trim panels (3 row seat model)

27 Remove the rear seats as described in Section 22. Remove the rear luggage compartment trim panel as described later in this Section.

28 Unclip the plastic cover and remove the retaining bolt from the grab handle at the front of the lower panel **(see illustration)**.

29 Unclip the plastic cover and remove the retaining bolt from the tie-down anchor at the rear of the lower panel **(see illustration)**.

30 Carefully prise the lower trim panel to release the securing clips, and then disengage it from the rear inner wheel arch **(see illustrations)**.

31 Remove the plastic covers from the upper seat belt anchorage bolts, and undo the anchorage bolts from the rear pillars **(see illustration)**.

32 Undo the retaining screw from the rear parcel shelf support panel **(see illustration)**.

33 Unscrew the seat belt lower anchor bolts, from the rear floor panel.

34 Carefully prise the upper trim panel to release the securing clips, and then disengage it from the rear pillars **(see illustrations)**. Note there are five upper metal clips along the top edge, and then seven lower plastic clips.

35 As the upper trim panel is being removed,

24.28 Unclip the cover and undo the retaining bolt

24.29 Undo the retaining bolt and remove the anchor point

24.30a Using a lever, carefully release the retaining clips …

24.30b … and unclip the lower trim panel

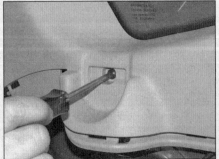

24.31 Unclip the cover and undo the upper anchorage bolt

24.32 Undo the side trim retaining screw

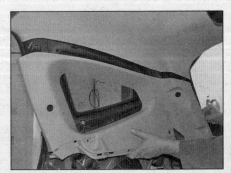

24.34a Remove the upper trim panel …

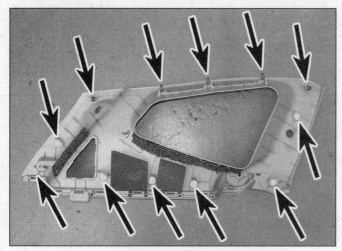

24.34b ... releasing it from its retaining clips

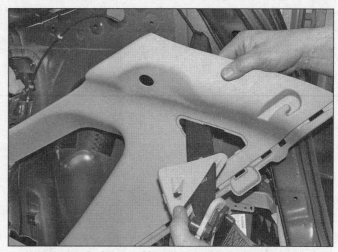

24.35 Pass the seat belt through the trim on removal

unclip the small plastic cover to allow for the rear seat belt to pass through the trim panel (see illustration).

36 Refitting is a reversal of removal, ensuring that all retaining clips are fully engaged. Refit the seat belt anchor bolts in the position noted during removal, then tighten to the specified torque.

Tailgate inner trim (early models)

37 Remove the securing screw from the grab handle on the inner edge of the tailgate (see illustration).

38 Carefully working your way around the outer edge of the trim panel, release the retaining clips and remove the panel from the tailgate (see illustration).

39 Unclip the trim panels from each side of the rear screen (see illustration).

40 Unclip the trim panel from the top inner edge of the rear screen (see illustration).

41 Refitting is a reversal of removal,

but ensure that all clips are securely engaged.

Tailgate inner trim (later models)

42 Remove the securing bolt and remove the grab handle from the lower edge of the tailgate trim (see illustration).

43 Pull out the centre pins, and then release the two securing clips, from the lower edge of the tailgate trim (see illustration).

44 Carefully working your way around the trim

24.37 Undo the retaining screw

24.38 Unclip and remove the tailgate trim panel

24.39 Unclip the tailgate side trim panels

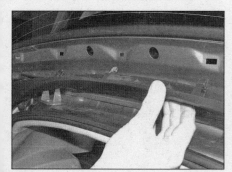

24.40 Unclip the tailgate upper trim panel

24.42 Undo the retaining bolt and remove the grab handle trim

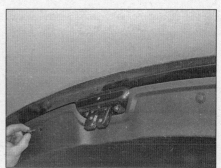

24.43 Release the two retaining clips from the lower edge

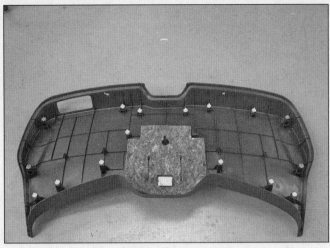

24.44 Tailgate trim retaining clips

24.49 Unclip the trim from the lock striker

panel, release the retaining clips and remove the panel from the tailgate **(see illustration)**.

45 Unclip the trim panels from each side of the rear screen.

46 Unclip the trim panel from the top inner edge of the rear screen.

47 Refitting is a reversal of removal, but ensure that all clips are securely engaged.

Rear luggage compartment trim panel (early models)

48 Open the tailgate and remove the luggage compartment floor panel.

49 Unclip the small plastic trim panel from the lock catch **(see illustration)**.

50 Pull out the centre pins, and then release the two securing clips (one at each end), from the inner edge of the luggage compartment rear trim **(see illustration)**.

51 Unclip the trim panel from the rear of the luggage compartment, releasing it at the centre from the locating peg **(see illustrations)**.

52 Refitting is a reversal of removal, but ensure that all clips are securely engaged.

Rear luggage compartment trim panel (later models)

53 Open the tailgate and remove the luggage compartment floor panel.

54 Pull out the centre pins, and then release the four securing clips from the inner edge of the luggage compartment rear trim **(see illustrations)**.

55 Unclip the trim panel from the rear of the luggage compartment, releasing it at the centre from the locating peg **(see illustrations)**.

24.50 Release the retaining clips inside the rear trim panel

24.51a Remove the luggage compartment rear trim panel …

24.51b … releasing it at the centre from the body panel

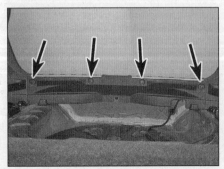

24.54 Release the four retaining clips inside the rear trim panel

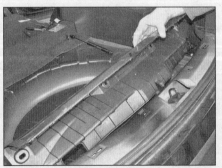

24.55a Remove the luggage compartment rear trim panel …

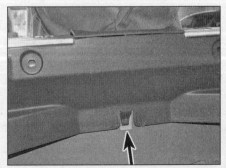

24.55b … releasing it at the centre from the body panel

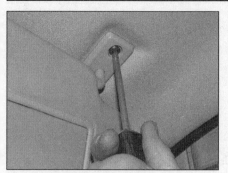

24.57 Undo the retaining screw

24.58 Disconnect the wiring connector as the sunvisor is withdrawn

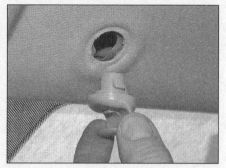

24.59 Twist the sunvisor retaining clip to remove

56 Refitting is a reversal of removal, but ensure that all clips are securely engaged.

Sunvisor

57 Remove the securing screw and remove the sunvisor from the roof panel **(see illustration)**.
58 As the sunvisor is removed, disconnect the wiring connector for the vanity mirror lighting **(see illustration)**.
59 To remove the sunvisor retaining clip, turn it through 90°, and pull it out from the roof panel **(see illustration)**.
60 Refitting is a reversal of removal.

Grab handles

61 Using a thin screwdriver release the two plastic retaining pegs from the grab handle mounting bracket **(see illustration)**.
62 With both retaining pegs released, pull the grab handle to remove it from the roof panel **(see illustration)**.
63 Refitting is a reversal of removal, but ensure that all retaining pegs are securely engaged.

---

25 Centre console – removal and refitting

Removal

1 Disconnect the battery negative terminal (refer to *Disconnecting the battery* in Reference).

2 Working at the front of the centre console, unclip the two front trim panels, from inside the front footwells **(see illustrations)**.
3 Release the lower securing clips and upper

retaining screws, from the front end of the centre console **(see illustrations)**.
4 Unclip the cup holder trim panel from the top of the centre console **(see illustration)**.

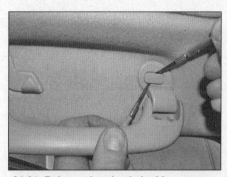

24.61 Release the plastic locking pegs ...

24.62 ... and remove the grab handle from the roof panel

25.2a Unclip the trim covers ...

25.2b ... from each side of the centre console

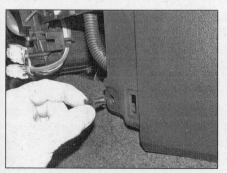

25.3a Release the retaining clips ...

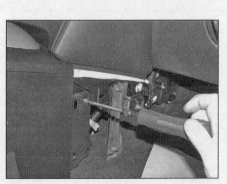

25.3b ... and screws from the front of the console

25.4 Unclip the cup holder from the console

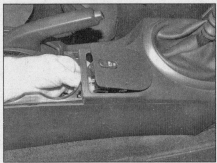

25.5 Unclip the switch panel

25.6a Unclip the gear lever gaiter trim …

25.6b … or selector trim panel on automatic models

5 Unclip the switch panel from the top of the centre console, and disconnect the wiring connectors as it is removed **(see illustration)**.
6 Unclip the gear lever gaiter and trim panel from the front of the centre console **(see illustrations)**.

7 Carefully unclip the heater control trim panel from the centre of the facia panel, and then disconnect the wiring connectors as it is removed **(see illustration)**.
8 Undo the two retaining screws from the front of the centre console **(see illustration)**.
9 Working at the rear of the centre console, unclip the rear trim panel **(see illustration)**.
10 Disconnect the wiring connector and release the wiring loom from the securing clip at the rear of the centre console **(see illustrations)**.
11 Slide the front seats forward, and then undo the mounting screws, from the rear of the centre console **(see illustration)**.
12 Measure the length of thread on the handbrake adjustment rod **(see illustration)**, and then slacken the adjustment nut until it reaches the end of the thread. This will allow for the handbrake lever to be pulled up further to allow for easier removal of the centre console.
13 Lift the console up at the rear, manipulate it over the handbrake and gear lever, and then remove the console from the vehicle **(see illustration)**.

25.7 Unclip the trim panel from around the heater controls

25.8 Undo the two retaining screws from the front of the console

25.9 Unclip the trim panel from the rear of the console

25.10a Release the wiring loom …

25.10b … and disconnect the wiring connectors

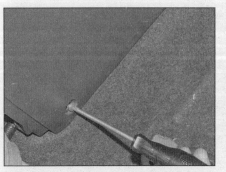

25.11 Undo the two screws at the rear of the console

25.12 Measure the amount of threads on the handbrake adjuster

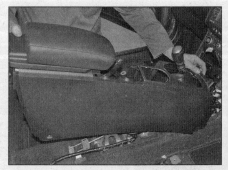

25.13 Remove the centre console from the vehicle

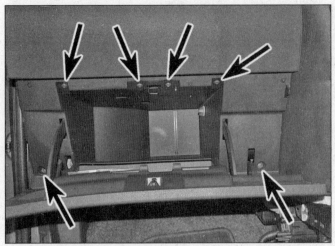

26.1 Undo the glovebox retaining screws

26.2 Unclip the facia end cover

Refitting

14 Refitting is a reversal of removal. Making sure that the handbrake adjustment nut is screwed back down the threads to the measurement noted before removal.

26 Facia panels – removal and refitting

> ⚠ **Warning: Certain models are equipped with an airbag system. The driver's airbag is mounted in the steering wheel centre pad and, where fitted, the passenger's airbag is mounted in the passenger's side of the facia. Make sure that the safety recommendations given in Chapter 12 are followed, to prevent personal injury.**

Glovebox

1 Open the glovebox, and undo the retaining screws from the upper and lower edge of the assembly **(see illustration)**.
2 Unclip the left-hand trim panel from the end of the facia **(see illustration)**.

3 Reach inside the end of the facia panel and unclip the glovebox illumination light bulb holder from the top of the glovebox **(see illustration)**.
4 Withdraw the glovebox from the facia **(see illustration)**. Check for any wiring connectors still connected, as the glovebox is withdrawn.
5 Refitting is a reversal of removal.

Driver's side lower panel

6 Undo the two retaining bolts and unclip the bonnet and fuel flap release levers, from the lower edge of the trim panel **(see illustrations)**.
7 Open the small flap that covers the fusebox, and release the diagnostic plug from the bottom trim panel **(see illustration)**.
8 Carefully pull the trim panel from the facia to release the retaining clips, and then as the panel is withdrawn, disconnect the wiring connector and air tubing from the

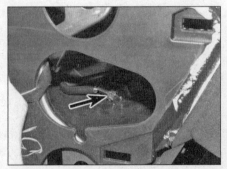

26.3 Release the glovebox light from the top of the glovebox

26.4 Withdraw the glovebox from the facia

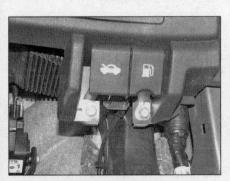

26.6a Undo the two retaining bolts ...

26.6b ... and unclip the release levers from the facia

26.7 Release the diagnostic plug from the facia

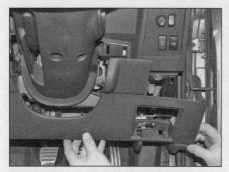

26.8a Unclip the trim panel ...

26.8b ... and disconnect the air vent pipe and wiring connector

26.10 Unclip the trim panel from around the heater controls

26.11a Release the retaining clips ...

26.11b ... and unclip the upper trim panel from the facia

26.12 Disconnect the wiring connectors

left-hand side of the trim panel **(see illustrations)**.

9 Refitting is a reversal of removal.

Centre ventilation trim panel

10 Carefully unclip the heater control trim panel from the centre of the facia panel, and then disconnect the wiring connectors as it is removed **(see illustration)**.

11 Unclip the upper vent trim panel from the centre of the facia. Release the trim panel by carefully levering at each side of the trim, to release the securing clips **(see illustrations)**.

12 As the trim panel is withdrawn disconnect the wiring connectors from the rear of the panel **(see illustration)**.

13 Refitting is a reversal of removal.

Steering column shrouds

14 Unclip the plastic trim from around the ignition switch **(see illustration)**.

15 Release the height adjustment lever and move the steering column downwards to its fully lowered position.

16 Working under the steering column lower shroud, undo the shroud securing screws.

26.14 Unclip the trim from around the switch

Release the clips securing the lower shroud to the upper shroud and then withdraw it from under the steering column **(see illustrations)**.

17 Release the two retaining clips securing the upper part of the shroud to the lower part

26.16a Undo the retaining screws (arrows)...

26.16b ... release the clips at the front ...

26.16c ... and sides ...

26.16d ... then remove the lower trim panel

26.17a Unclip the upper trim panel ...

26.17b ... from the top of the steering column

26.19 Using a lever to prise up the shroud ...

of the instrument panel, and then withdraw it from the top of the steering column **(see illustrations)**.

18 Refitting is a reversal of removal, but ensure that the shroud halves engage correctly with each other.

Instrument panel upper shroud

19 Using a lever, carefully prise the instrument panel upper shroud, to release the retaining clips **(see illustration)**.

20 Ease the upper shroud away from the facia, disengaging the retaining clips and then remove it from the vehicle **(see illustration)**.

21 Refitting is a reversal of removal.

Facia end trim panels

22 Using a lever, carefully prise the trim panel from the end of the facia **(see illustrations)**.

23 On the left-hand (passenger) side, disconnect the wiring connector from the airbag switch as it is removed **(see illustration)**.

24 Refitting is a reversal of removal.

Complete assembly

Note: *This is an involved procedure, and it is suggested that this complete Section is read through thoroughly before beginning the operation. It is advisable to make careful note of all wiring connections, and the routing of all wiring, to aid refitting.*

Removal

25 Disconnect the battery negative terminal

26.20 ... then release it from the facia

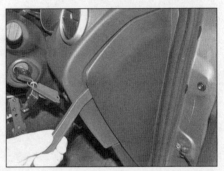

26.22 Using a lever to remove the facia side trim

(refer to *Disconnecting the battery* in the Reference Chapter).

26 Remove the front footwell trim panels as described in Section 24.

27 Remove the front A-pillar trim panels as described in Section 24.

28 Remove the centre console as described in Section 25.

29 Remove the following facia panels, as described previously in this Section. Note the routing of all wiring, and keep all securing screws and fixings with the relevant panels to avoid confusion on refitting.

a) Glovebox.
b) Driver's side lower facia panel.
c) Centre ventilation nozzle trim panel.
d) Steering column shrouds.
e) Instrument panel upper shroud.
f) Facia end trim panels

30 Remove the heater/ventilation control unit, as described in Chapter 3, Section 9.

31 Remove the radio/CD player, as described in Chapter 12. Section 15.

32 Remove the instrument panel, as described in Chapter 12, Section 9.

33 Remove the passenger's airbag as described in Chapter 12, Section 21.

34 Remove the upper facia speakers as described in Chapter 12, Section 16.

35 Carefully prise out the switch panel on the driver's side **(see illustration)**, disconnect the switch wiring connectors and remove the panel.

36 Undo the facia mounting nuts/bolts/screws from the following locations:

a) *Two screws securing the centre of the facia to the metal crossmember* **(see illustration)**.
b) *One screw inside the instrument panel*

26.23 Disconnect the switch as the panel is removed

26.35 Unclip the switch panel from the facia

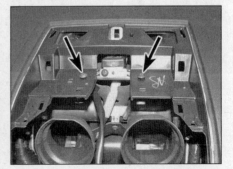

26.36a Undo the two screws (arrowed) ...

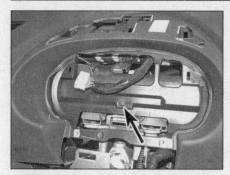

26.36b ... one screw in the instrument aperture ...

26.36c ... one screw at each end ...

26.36d ... one bolt at each end of the upper facia ...

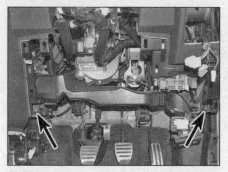

26.36e ... two screws on the lower edge ...

26.36f ... one screw in the glovebox aperture

aperture, securing the facia to the metal crossmember **(see illustration)**.

c) Two screws (one each side) securing the ends of the facia to the metal crossmember **(see illustration)**.

d) One bolt each side **(see illustration)**, securing the top edge of the facia to the body (behind the previously removed speaker grilles).

e) Two screws securing the lower part of the facia, at the driver's side of the vehicle **(see illustration)**.

f) One screw inside the glovebox aperture, securing the facia to the metal crossmember **(see illustration)**.

37 Make a final check to ensure that all relevant wiring has been disconnected, and any wiring loom retaining clips disconnected **(see illustrations)**.

38 With the aid of an assistant, pull the upper part of the facia panel towards the rear of the car to disengage it from the scuttle – some manipulation may be required. Once the facia panel has been released, withdraw it through the door aperture **(see illustration)**.

39 If required, the metal crossmember can be removed from across the front of the vehicle **(see illustration)**. This will need to be removed to access the heating/ventilation housing.

40 Referring to Chapter 10, Section 14,

26.37a Disconnect the wiring connector

26.37b Release the wiring loom retaining clips

26.38 Carefully lift the facia panel out from the vehicle

26.39 Vehicle front safety crossmember

26.41 Remove the support bracket

26.42 Undo the bolt above the steering column

26.43a Disconnect the wiring connectors ...

26.43b ... from the front door pillars

26.44a Remove the plastic caps ...

remove the steering column/motor assembly from the metal crossmember.

41 Undo the retaining bolts and remove the metal bracket from the right-hand side of the heater housing **(see illustration)**.

42 Undo the retaining bolt at the top of the bulkhead, above the steering column mounting bracket **(see illustration)**.

43 Working along the length of the metal crossmember, trace the wiring loom and disconnect the wiring plugs from any components or wiring plug connectors **(see illustrations)**. Make a note, or take pictures of the connections to refer to on refitting. Wiring connectors will need to be disconnected from the following locations:

a) Along the centre console area, to the airbag ECU, handbrake warning light, console switches etc....

b) Around the heating ventilation housing to the air flap control modules and sensors.

b) At the upper and lower sides of the A-pillar on both sides of the vehicle.

44 Working at the left-hand side of the vehicle, remove the plastic covers and slacken the crossmember securing bolts **(see illustrations)**. An open-ended spanner will be required to counter hold the crossmember adjustment nut.

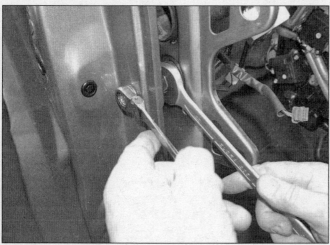

26.44b ... and slacken the bolts ...

26.44c ... leaving the adjuster nut in the left-hand side of the crossmember

45 Working at the right-hand side of the vehicle, remove the plastic covers and slacken the crossmember securing bolts **(see illustrations)**. Note the bolt furthest away cannot be completely removed, as it comes up against the door. **DO NOT** try and close the door while this bolt is unscrewed.

46 Make a final check along the length of the metal crossmember, to check that there is nothing still connected and lift the crossmember complete with wirng loom, out through the door aperture **(see illustration)**.

Refitting

47 Refitting is essentially a reversal of the removal procedure, bearing in mind the following points:

a) Tighten the right-hand crossmember bolts first, and then tighten the left-hand side crossmember bolts, using an open-ended spanner to counter hold the adjustment nuts.

b) Ensure that all wiring is correctly reconnected, and routed.

c) Refit all surrounding facia panels with reference to the relevant paragraphs of this Section.

26.45a Undo the crossmember mounting bolts …

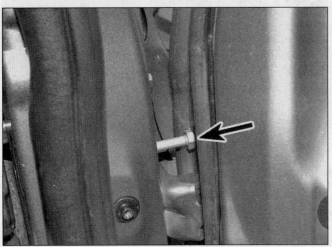

26.45b … noting the inner one cannot be completely removed (Do Not Close Door)

26.46 Carefully lift the crossmember complete with wiring loom out from the vehicle

Chapter 12
Body electrical systems

Contents

Degrees of difficulty

Easy, suitable for novice with little experience	**Fairly easy,** suitable for beginner with some experience	**Fairly difficult,** suitable for competent DIY mechanic
Difficult, suitable for experienced DIY mechanic	**Very difficult,** suitable for expert DIY or professional	

Specifications

Bulb ratings

	Watts
Front direction indicator light	21
Front direction indicator repeater light	5
Front foglight (H11)	55
Front sidelight	5
Headlights:	
Main beam (H7)	55
Dipped beam – Halogen (H7)	55
Dipped beam – Xenon (D1S)	35
High-level stop-light	LED
Luggage compartment light	5
Map reading lights	5
Interior reading lights	5
Rear direction indicator light	21
Rear foglight	21
Rear number plate light	5
Reversing light	21
Stop/tail light	21/5

Torque wrench setting

	Nm	lbf ft
Airbag unit retaining bolts	20	15

1 General information and precautions

General information

The electrical system is of 12-volt negative earth type. Power for the lights and all electrical accessories is supplied by a lead-acid type battery, which is charged by the alternator.

This Chapter covers repair and service procedures for the various electrical components not associated with the engine. Information on the battery, alternator and starter motor can be found in Chapter 5A.

It should be noted that, prior to working on any component in the electrical system, the battery negative terminal should first be disconnected, to prevent the possibility of electrical short-circuits and/or fires (refer to *Disconnecting the battery* in the Reference Chapter).

Precautions

⚠ **Warning: Before carrying out any work on the electrical system, read through the precautions given in 'Safety first!' at the beginning of this manual, and in Chapter 5A.**

⚠ **Warning: All models are equipped with an airbag system and pyrotechnic seat belt pretensioners. When working on the electrical system, refer to the precautions given in Section 20 to avoid the possibility of personal injury.**

2 Electrical fault finding – general information

Note: *Refer to the precautions given in 'Safety first!' and in Section 1 of this Chapter before starting work. The following tests relate to testing of the main electrical circuits, and should not be used to test delicate electronic circuits (such as engine management systems or anti-lock braking systems), particularly where an electronic control unit is used.*

General

1 A typical electrical circuit consists of an electrical component; any switches, relays, motors, fuses, fusible links or circuit breakers related to that component, and the wiring and connectors which link the component to both the battery and the chassis. To help to pinpoint a problem in an electrical circuit, wiring diagrams are included at the end of this chapter.

2 Before attempting to diagnose an electrical fault, first study the appropriate wiring diagram, to obtain a more complete understanding of the components included in the particular circuit concerned. The possible sources of a fault can be narrowed down by noting whether other components related to the circuit are operating properly. If several components or circuits fail at one time, the problem is likely to be related to a shared fuse or earth connection.

3 Electrical problems usually stem from simple causes, such as loose or corroded connections, a faulty earth connection, a blown fuse, a melted fusible link, or a faulty relay (refer to Section 3 for details of testing relays). Visually inspect the condition of all fuses, wires and connections in a problem circuit before testing the components. Use the wiring diagrams to determine which terminal connections will need to be checked, in order to pinpoint the trouble spot.

4 The basic tools required for electrical fault finding include a circuit tester or voltmeter (a 12 volt bulb with a set of test leads can also be used for certain tests); a self-powered test light (sometimes known as a continuity tester); an ohmmeter (to measure resistance); a battery and set of test leads; and a jumper wire, preferably with a circuit breaker or fuse incorporated, which can be used to bypass suspect wires or electrical components. Before attempting to locate a problem with test instruments, use the wiring diagram to determine where to make the connections.

5 To find the source of an intermittent wiring fault (usually due to a poor or dirty connection, or damaged wiring insulation), a 'wiggle' test can be performed on the wiring. This involves wiggling the wiring by hand, to see if the fault occurs as the wiring is moved. It should be possible to narrow down the source of the fault to a particular section of wiring. This method of testing can be used in conjunction with any of the tests described in the following sub-Sections.

6 Apart from problems due to poor connections, two basic types of fault can occur in an electrical circuit – open-circuit, or short-circuit.

7 Open-circuit faults are caused by a break somewhere in the circuit, which prevents current from flowing. An open-circuit fault will prevent a component from working, but will not cause the relevant circuit fuse to blow.

8 Short-circuit faults are normally caused by a breakdown in wiring insulation, which allows a feed wire to touch either another wire, or an earthed component such as the bodyshell. This allows the current flowing in the circuit to 'escape' along an alternative route, usually to earth. As the circuit does not now follow its original complete path, it is known as a 'short' circuit. A short-circuit fault will normally cause the relevant circuit fuse to blow.

Finding an open-circuit

9 To check for an open-circuit, connect one lead of a circuit tester or voltmeter to either the negative battery terminal or a known good earth.

10 Connect the other lead to a connector in the circuit being tested, preferably nearest to the battery or fuse.

11 Switch on the circuit, bearing in mind that some circuits are live only when the ignition switch is moved to a particular position.

12 If voltage is present (indicated either by the tester bulb lighting or a voltmeter reading, as applicable), this means that the section of the circuit between the relevant connector and the battery is problem-free.

13 Continue to check the remainder of the circuit in the same fashion.

14 When a point is reached at which no voltage is present, the problem must lie between that point and the previous test point with voltage. Most problems can be traced to a broken, corroded or loose connection.

Finding a short-circuit

15 To check for a short circuit; first disconnect the load(s) from the circuit (loads are the components which draw current from a circuit, such as bulbs, motors, heating elements, etc).

16 Remove the relevant fuse from the circuit, and connect a circuit tester or voltmeter to the fuse connections.

17 Switch on the circuit, bearing in mind that some circuits are live only when the ignition switch is moved to a particular position.

18 If voltage is present (indicated either by the tester bulb lighting or a voltmeter reading, as applicable), this means that there is a short circuit.

19 If no voltage is present, but the fuse still blows with the load(s) connected, this indicates an internal fault in the load(s).

Finding an earth fault

20 The battery negative terminal is connected to 'earth' – the metal of the engine/transmission and the car body – and most systems are wired so that they only receive a positive feed, the current returning via the metal of the car body. This means that the component mounting and the body form part of that circuit. Loose or corroded mountings can therefore cause a range of electrical faults, ranging from total failure of a circuit, to a puzzling partial fault. In particular, lights may shine dimly (especially when another circuit sharing the same earth point is in operation), motors (e.g. wiper motors or the radiator cooling fan motor) may run slowly, and the operation of one circuit may have an apparently unrelated effect on another. Note that on many vehicles, earth straps are used between certain components, such as the engine/transmission and the body, usually where there is no metal-to-metal contact between components, due to flexible rubber mountings, etc.

21 To check whether a component is properly earthed, disconnect the battery, and connect one lead of an ohmmeter to a known good earth point. Connect the other lead to the wire or earth connection being tested. The resistance reading should be zero; if not, check the connection as follows.

22 If an earth connection is thought to be faulty, dismantle the connection, and clean back to bare metal both the bodyshell and

the wire terminal or the component earth connection mating surface. Be careful to remove all traces of dirt and corrosion, and then use a knife to trim away any paint, so that a clean metal-to-metal joint is made. On reassembly, tighten the joint fasteners securely; if a wire terminal is being refitted, use serrated washers between the terminal and the bodyshell, to ensure a clean and secure connection. When the connection is remade, prevent the onset of corrosion in the future by applying a coat of petroleum jelly or silicone-based grease, or by spraying on (at regular intervals) a proprietary ignition sealer.

3 Fuses and relays –
general information

Fuses

1 Fuses are designed to break a circuit when a predetermined current is reached, in order to protect the components and wiring, which could be damaged by excessive current flow. Any excessive current flow will be due to a fault in the circuit, usually a short-circuit (see Section 2).
2 The main fuses are located in the fusebox on the driver's side of the facia.
3 For access to the fuses, pull open the cover flap **(see illustration)**.
4 Additional fuses and circuit-breakers are located in an auxiliary fusebox in the engine compartment, next to the battery **(see illustration)**.
5 The Intelligent Power Distribution Module (IPDM) is also located in the engine compartment, next to the fusebox **(see illustrations)**.
6 Depending on model. It may be necessary to remove the air intake ducting, to access the engine compartment fuseboxes **(see illustrations)**.
7 A blown fuse can be recognised from its melted or broken wire. Before removing a fuse, first ensure that the relevant circuit is switched off.
8 Using the plastic tool clipped inside the main fusebox, pull the fuse from its location **(see illustration)**.

3.3 Vehicle passenger compartment fusebox

9 Spare fuses are usually provided in the main fusebox.
10 Before renewing a blown fuse, trace and rectify the cause, and always use a fuse of the correct rating (fuse ratings are usually specified on the inside of the fusebox cover flap). Never substitute a fuse of a higher rating, or make temporary repairs using wire or metal foil; more serious damage, or even fire, could result.
11 Note that the fuses are colour-coded as follows.

Colour	Rating
Orange	5A
Red	10A
Blue	15A
Yellow	20A
Clear or White	25A
Green	30A

3.5a Vehicle IPDM also has fuses ...

3.4 Vehicle engine compartment fusebox

Relays

12 A relay is an electrically operated switch, which is used for the following reasons:
a) *A relay can switch a heavy current remotely from the circuit in which the current is flowing, therefore allowing the use of lighter-gauge wiring and switch contacts.*
b) *A relay can receive more than one control input, unlike a mechanical switch.*
c) *A relay can have a timer function – for example, the intermittent wiper relay.*
13 Various relays are located behind the facia, next to the fusebox, and in the relay box on the right-hand side of the engine compartment **(see illustration 3.4)**.
14 If a circuit or system controlled by a relay develops a fault, and the relay is suspect, operate the system. If the relay is functioning,

3.5b ... with fuse ratings and location on the side

3.6a Release the retaining clips ...

3.6b ... and remove the air intake ducting

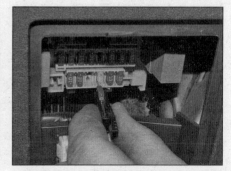

3.8 Pull the fuse from its position in the fusebox

it should be possible to hear it 'click' as it is energised, If this is the case, the fault lies with the components or wiring of the system. If the relay is not being energised, then either the relay is not receiving a main supply or a switching voltage, or the relay itself is faulty. Testing is by the substitution of a known good unit, but be careful – while some relays are identical in appearance and in operation, others look similar but perform different functions.

15 To remove a relay, first ensure that the relevant circuit is switched off. The relay can then simply be pulled out from the socket, and pushed back into position.

4 Switches – removal and refitting

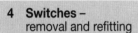
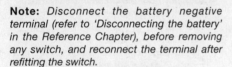

Note: *Disconnect the battery negative terminal (refer to 'Disconnecting the battery' in the Reference Chapter), before removing any switch, and reconnect the terminal after refitting the switch.*

Ignition switch/steering lock

1 Remove the ignition switch/steering lock, as described in Chapter 10, Section 13.

Steering column switches

2 Remove the steering column shrouds, as described in Chapter 11, Section 26.
3 Release the retaining clips and slide the

4.3a Release the clips and withdraw the switch …

4.3b … then disconnect the wiring connector

wiper stalk/switch out from the right-hand side of the combination switch housing, then disconnect the wiring connector as it is being withdrawn **(see illustrations)**.
4 Release the retaining clips and slide the lighting stalk/switch out from the left-hand side of the combination switch housing **(see illustrations)**.
5 Refitting is a reversal of removal.

Heater/ventilation switches

6 The heater/ventilation switches are integral with the heater control panel, remove the heater control panel, as described in Chapter 3, Section 9.

Heated front and rear windscreen switches

7 The heated windscreen switches are

integral with the heater control panel, remove the heater control panel, as described in Chapter 3, Section 9.

Driver's side panel switches

8 These switches include the electric door mirror switch, the electronic stability programme (ESP) switch, cruise control on/off switch and the headlight beam adjustment switch, according to model.
9 Carefully unclip the switch panel from the facia, and then disconnect the wiring connectors on removal **(see illustrations)**.
10 To remove the relevant switch, turn the trim panel over, release the retaining clips and withdraw the switch from the trim panel **(see illustrations)**.
11 Refit the relevant switch and trim panel, using a reversal of the removal procedure.

4.4a Release the securing clips …

4.4b … and withdraw the switch

4.9a Unclip the switch panel from the facia …

4.9b … and disconnect the switch wiring connectors

4.10a Release the securing clips …

4.10b … and release the switch from the trim panel

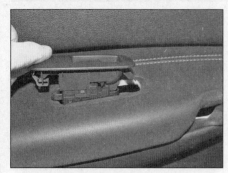

4.12 Unclip the trim panel from the door panel ...

4.13 ... and disconnect the wiring connector

4.14a Release the securing clips and remove the switch

4.14b On the driver's door the switches are a complete assembly

4.17a Release the securing clips ...

4.17b ... and release the switch from the front of the trim panel

Electric window switches

Front door switch

12 Unclip the door switch trim panel from the top of the armrest in the door trim panel (see illustration).
13 Disconnect the wiring connector from the switch panel as it is removed (see illustration).
14 To remove the relevant switch, release the retaining clips and withdraw the switch from the rear of the trim panel (see illustrations).

15 Refit the relevant switch and trim panel, using a reversal of the removal procedure.

Hazard warning light switch

16 The hazard warning switch is fitted to the centre ventilation trim panel, remove the ventilation trim panel, as described in Chapter 11, Section 26.
17 To remove the switch, release the retaining clips and withdraw the switch through the front of the trim panel (see illustrations).

18 Refit the switch and trim panel, using a reversal of the removal procedure.

Centre console switches

19 These switches include the heated seat switches, central door-locking switch and 4WD/2WD/Automatic-setting switch, according to model.
20 Carefully unclip the switch panel from the top of the centre console, and then disconnect the wiring connectors on removal (see illustrations).

4.20a Unclip the switch panel from the centre console ...

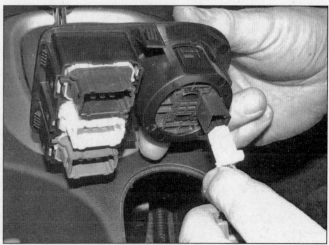

4.20b ... and disconnect the switch wiring connectors

4.21a Release the securing clips ...

4.21b ... and remove the switches from the rear of the trim panel

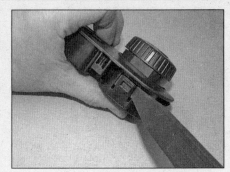

4.21c Release the securing clips ...

4.21d ... and remove the 4WD switch from the front of the trim panel

4.28 Disconnect the earth wire

21 To remove the relevant switch, turn the trim panel over, release the retaining clips and withdraw the switch from the trim panel **(see illustrations)**.

22 Refit the relevant switch and trim panel, using a reversal of the removal procedure.

Courtesy light/door warning switches

23 The door warning switches are part of the central locking system components, remove the switches as described in Chapter 11, Section 17.

Luggage area light switch

24 The switch is integral with the boot lid/tailgate lock. Removal and refitting details for the boot lid/tailgate lock are provided in Chapter 11, Section 16.

Map reading/courtesy light switches

25 The switches are integral with the interior light assembly and cannot be renewed independently. See Section 6 for interior light bulb renewal.

Steering wheel switches

26 These switches include the audio control switches to the left-hand side of the steering wheel, and cruise control system operation to the right-hand side of the steering wheel, according to model.

⚠ **Warning: When working on the airbag system, refer to the precautions given in Section 20 to avoid the possibility of personal injury.**

27 Remove the airbag from the centre of the steering wheel, as described in Section 21.

28 Disconnect the earth wire connection from the rear of the airbag unit **(see illustration)**.

29 Undo the retaining screws, and disconnect the switch panel from the side of the airbag **(see illustrations)**.

30 Refit the switch and trim panel, using a reversal of the removal procedure. Refer to Section 21, when refitting the airbag.

Passenger airbag switch

31 Carefully prise the trim panel from the left-hand end of the facia **(see illustration)**.

32 Disconnect the wiring connector from

4.29a Undo the switch retaining screws (arrowed) ...

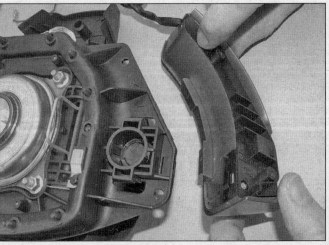

4.29b ... and remove the switch from the airbag

4.31 Unclip the trim from the end of the facia panel

4.32 Disconnect the wiring connector from the switch

4.33 Release the securing clips and remove the airbag switch

the switch as the trim is removed **(see illustration)**.

33 Release the retaining clips and withdraw the switch from the end trim panel **(see illustration)**.

34 Refit the switch and trim panel, using a reversal of the removal procedure.

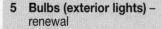

5 Bulbs (exterior lights) – renewal

General

1 Whenever a bulb is renewed, note the following points:

a) *Disconnect the battery negative terminal (refer to 'Disconnecting the battery' in the Reference Chapter).*

b) *Remember that, if the light has just been in use, the bulb may be extremely hot.*

c) *Always check the bulb contacts and holder, ensuring that there is clean metal-to-metal contact between the bulb and its live contact(s) and earth. Clean off any corrosion or dirt before fitting a new bulb.*

d) *Wherever bayonet-type bulbs are fitted, ensure that the live contact(s) bear firmly against the bulb contact.*

e) *Always ensure that the new bulb is of the correct rating (see Specifications), and that it is completely clean before fitting it; this applies particularly to headlight/foglight bulbs (see following paragraphs).*

Headlights

2 Open the bonnet and depending on model, to improve access to the left-hand headlight, remove the air inlet ducting **(see illustrations 3.6a & 3.6b)**.

3 When handling the new bulb, use a tissue or clean cloth to avoid touching the glass with the fingers; moisture and grease from the skin can cause blackening and rapid failure of this type of bulb. If the glass is accidentally touched, wipe it clean using methylated spirit.

Halogen headlight

Dipped beam

4 Reach behind the headlamp, and unclip the dipped beam's protective cover and remove it **(see illustration)**.

5 Twist the bulb holder anti-clockwise and release it from the retaining clip in the headlight **(see illustration)**.

6 Pull the bulb to release it from the bulb holder **(see illustration)**.

7 Install the new bulb, ensuring that the bulb holder is located correctly in the headlight unit **(see illustration)**. When handling a new bulb, use a tissue or clean cloth to avoid touching the glass with the fingers; moisture and grease from the skin can cause blackening and rapid failure of this type of bulb. If the glass is accidentally touched, wipe it clean using methylated spirit.

8 Refit the protective cover.

5.4 Unclip the headlight bulb protective cover

5.6 Remove the bulb from its holder

Main beam

Note: *The procedure is as described for the Xenon main beam described in paragraphs 15 to 19.*

Xenon headlight

Dipped beam

⚠ *Warning: Before carrying out any operations on xenon headlight units, it is recommended that protective gloves and safety glasses be worn. It is essential that the wiring connectors are disconnected from the rear of the headlight unit, and then wait until the module and bulbs have cooled down before removal. DO NOT switch the headlights on with the bulb removed, as it is harmful to the eyes.*

9 Make sure the battery negative terminal

5.5 Twist the bulb holder to release it

5.7 Make sure the holder is located correctly in the headlight unit

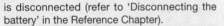

5.10 High voltage warnings on the rear of the bulb holder

5.11 Disconnect the wiring connector from the high voltage pack

5.12 Twist the high voltage unit to release it from the headlight

is disconnected (refer to 'Disconnecting the battery' in the Reference Chapter).

10 Reach behind the headlamp, and twist the plastic protective cover to remove it from the rear of the headlight. Take notice of the warnings on the high voltage unit on the rear of the headlight bulb **(see illustration)**. If in any doubt, go to your local Nissan dealer to have the bulb replaced.

11 Disconnect the wiring connector from the high voltage unit on the rear of the headlight bulb **(see illustration)**.

12 Twist the high voltage unit and bulb holder anti-clockwise and release it from the retaining clip in the headlight **(see illustration)**.

13 Install the new bulb, ensuring that the bulb holder/high voltage unit is located correctly in the headlight unit. When handling the new bulb, use a tissue or clean cloth to avoid touching the glass with the fingers;

moisture and grease from the skin can cause blackening and rapid failure of this type of bulb. If the glass is accidentally touched, wipe it clean using methylated spirit.

14 Refit the protective cover.

Main beam

15 Reach behind the headlamp, and unclip the main beam's protective cover and remove it **(see illustration)**.

16 Twist the bulb holder anti-clockwise and release it from the retaining clip in the headlight **(see illustration)**.

17 Pull the bulb to release it from the bulb holder **(see illustration)**.

18 Install the new bulb, ensuring that the bulb holder is located correctly in the headlight unit **(see illustration)**. When handling the new bulb, use a tissue or clean cloth to avoid touching the glass with the fingers;

moisture and grease from the skin can cause blackening and rapid failure of this type of bulb. If the glass is accidentally touched, wipe it clean using methylated spirit.

19 Refit the protective cover.

Sidelight

20 Open the bonnet and depending on model, to improve access to the left-hand headlight, remove the air inlet ducting **(see illustrations 3.6a & 3.6b)**.

21 Disconnect the wiring connector from the side light bulb holder at the top of the headlight unit.

22 Twist the bulb holder and withdraw the sidelight bulb and holder from the rear of the headlight unit **(see illustration)**.

23 The bulb is a push-fit in the bulbholder, pull the sidelight bulb to remove it from the bulb holder **(see illustration)**.

5.15 Unclip the headlight bulb protective cover

5.16 Twist the bulb holder to release it

5.17 Remove the bulb from its holder

5.18 Make sure the holder is located correctly in the headlight unit

5.22 Rotate the bulbholder to remove ...

5.23 ... then pull the bulb from its holder

5.26a Rotate the bulbholder anti-clockwise ...

5.26b ... and remove it from the headlight unit

5.27 Press in the bulb and rotate it anti-clockwise to remove it

5.29 Carefully unclip the light unit

5.30 Remove the bulb holder ...

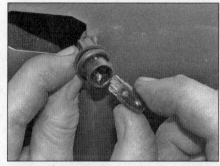

5.31 ... then pull the bulb from its holder

24 Fit the new bulb using a reversal of the removal procedure.

Front indicator

25 Open and support the bonnet.
26 Twist the bulbholder anti-clockwise and withdraw it from the headlight light unit **(see illustrations)**.
27 The bulb is a bayonet fit in the bulbholder, push lightly and turn anti-clockwise to remove the bulb **(see illustration)**.
28 Fit the new bulb using a reversal of the removal procedure.

Front indicator side repeater

29 Carefully unclip one end of the light unit and release it from the wing panel **(see illustration)**.

30 Withdraw the light unit, and then twist the bulbholder anti-clockwise to release it from the light unit **(see illustration)**.
31 The bulb is a push-fit in the bulbholder **(see illustration)**.
32 Fit the new bulb using a reversal of the removal procedure.

Front foglight

33 Remove the inner wheel arch liner as described in Chapter 11, Section 21 **(see illustration)**.
34 Reach behind the bumper and disconnect the wiring connector from the bulbholder **(see illustration)**.
35 Turn the bulbholder anti-clockwise and withdraw it from the rear of the foglight **(see illustration)**.

36 The bulb can then be removed from the bulbholder, check new bulb before removing the bulb from its holder, as some new bulbs come with the bulb holder as part of the bulb. When handling the new bulb, use a tissue or clean cloth to avoid touching the glass with the fingers; moisture and grease from the skin can cause blackening and rapid failure of this type of bulb. If the glass is accidentally touched, wipe it clean using methylated spirit.
37 Fit the new bulb using a reversal of the removal procedure.

Rear lights (indicator/stop/tail lights)

38 Open the tailgate and remove the rear light unit as described in Section 7.
39 Release the retaining clips and withdraw

5.33 Pull back the inner wheel arch liner

5.34 Disconnect the foglight wiring plug

5.35 Rotate the bulbholder anti-clockwise to remove

5.39 Unclip the bulb holder from the light unit

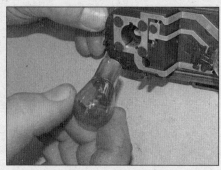

5.40 Press in the bulb and rotate it anti-clockwise to remove it

5.42a Carefully unclip the light unit ...

5.42b ... releasing the retaining clips

5.43 Rotate the bulbholder anti-clockwise to remove

the bulbholder from the rear of the light unit **(see illustration)**.

40 The bulbs are a bayonet fit in the bulbholder, push lightly and turn anti-clockwise to remove the relevant bulb **(see illustration)**.

41 Fit the new bulb using a reversal of the

removal procedure. Note that the stop/tail light bulb has offset pins, on the side of the end cap, to ensure correct installation.

Rear fog light

42 Carefully prise the rear fog light from the rear bumper **(see illustrations)**.

43 Turn the bulbholder anti-clockwise and withdraw it from the rear of the foglight **(see illustration)**.

44 The bulb is a bayonet fit in the bulbholder, push lightly and turn anti-clockwise to remove the bulb **(see illustration)**.

45 Fit the new bulb using a reversal of the removal procedure.

Reversing light

46 Open the tailgate and remove the inner tailgate trim, as described in Chapter 11, Section 24.

47 Turn the bulbholder anti-clockwise and withdraw it from the rear of the reversing light **(see illustration)**.

48 The bulb is a bayonet fit in the bulbholder, push lightly and turn anti-clockwise to remove the bulb **(see illustration)**.

49 Fit the new bulb using a reversal of the removal procedure.

Number plate light

50 Unclip the light unit from the tailgate trim **(see illustrations)**.

51 Turn the bulbholder anti-clockwise and

5.44 Press in the bulb and rotate it anti-clockwise to remove it

5.47 Rotate the bulbholder anti-clockwise to remove

5.48 Press in the bulb and rotate it anti-clockwise to remove it

5.50a Carefully unclip the light unit ...

5.50b ... and release it from the rear trim panel

5.51 Twist the bulb holder to remove ...

5.52 ... then pull the bulb from its holder

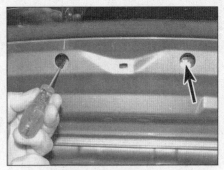

5.55a Release the two retaining clips (arrowed) ...

5.55b ... and remove the light unit from the tailgate

5.56a Disconnect the wiring connector ...

5.56b ... and washer fluid hose

withdraw it from the number plate light **(see illustration)**.
52 The bulb is a push-fit in the bulbholder, pull the sidelight bulb to remove it from the bulb holder **(see illustration)**.
53 Fit the new bulb using a reversal of the removal procedure.

High-level stop-light

54 Open the tailgate and remove the upper tailgate trim panel, as described in Chapter 11, Section 24.
55 Working on the inside of the tailgate, release the two retaining clips and withdraw the high-level brake light from the top of the tailgate **(see illustrations)**.
56 Disconnect the wiring connector and washer fluid hose, as it is removed **(see illustrations)**.
57 The light unit has LED's (Light Emitting Diodes), and can only be renewed as a complete unit. Fit the new light unit using a reversal of the removal procedure.

6 Bulbs (interior lights) – renewal

General

1 Refer to Section 5, paragraph 1.

Map reading/courtesy light (front)

2 Carefully prise the lens from the light unit

(if necessary, carefully use a flat-bladed screwdriver) **(see illustration)**.
3 Pull the bulb from the light unit; note that the bulb is a capless type **(see illustration)**.

4 If required, release the securing clips to release the light unit from the headlining **(see illustrations)**.
5 Fit the new bulb using a reversal of the removal procedure.

6.2 Carefully prise the light lens from place ...

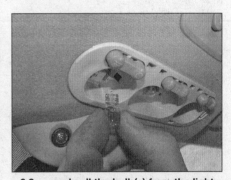

6.3 ... and pull the bulb(s) from the light unit

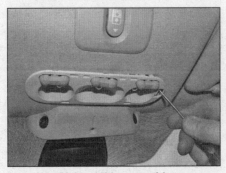

6.4a Using a thin screwdriver ...

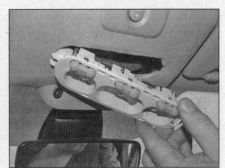

6.4b ... to release the light unit from the roof panel

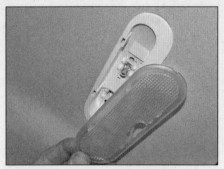

6.6 Carefully prise the light lens from the light unit

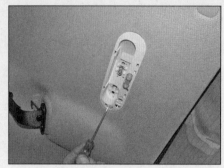

6.8 Release the light unit from the roof panel

6.10 Carefully prise the light unit from the roof panel ...

6.11 ... and disconnect the wiring connector

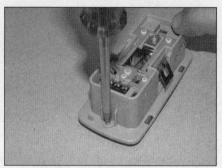

6.12a Undo the retaining screw ...

6.12b ... unclip the light lens ...

Courtesy light (rear)

6 Carefully prise the lens from the light unit (if necessary, carefully use a flat-bladed screwdriver) **(see illustration)**.

7 Pull the bulb from the light unit; note that the bulb is a capless type **(see illustration 6.3)**.

8 If required, release the securing clips to release the light unit from the headlining **(see illustration)**.

9 Fit the new bulb using a reversal of the removal procedure.

Courtesy light (side)

10 Carefully prise the light unit from the side of the roof panel **(see illustration)**.

11 Disconnect the wiring connector and remove the light unit **(see illustration)**.

12 Undo the retaining screw and remove

the lens from the front of the light unit **(see illustrations)**.

13 Pull the bulb from the light unit; note that the bulb is a festoon type **(see illustration)**.

14 Fit the new bulb using a reversal of the removal procedure.

Vanity mirror light

15 Carefully prise the lens from the light unit (if necessary, carefully use a small thin screwdriver) **(see illustration)**.

16 Pull the bulb from the light unit; note that the bulb is a capless type **(see illustration)**.

17 Fit the new bulb using a reversal of the removal procedure.

Luggage area light

18 Open the tailgate.

19 Unclip the light unit from the trim panel.

20 Disconnect the wiring connector and remove the light unit, the bulb is a push-fit in the light assembly.

21 Fit the new bulb using a reversal of the removal procedure.

Instrument panel lights

22 The instrument panel is a complete unit and is lit by LEDs. If there is a fault on the illumination of the panel the complete unit will need to be renewed, as described in Section 9.

Heater control illumination

23 The heater control panel is a complete unit and is lit by LEDs. If there is a fault on the illumination of the panel the complete unit will need to be renewed.

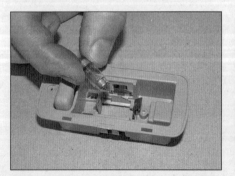

6.13 ... and remove the bulb from the light unit

6.15 Carefully prise the light lens from place ...

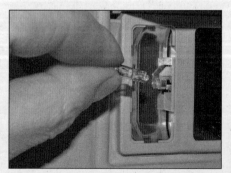

6.16 ... and pull the bulb from the light unit

Seat belt warning light illumination

24 The warning light panel is fitted to the lower edge of the centre ventilation trim panel, remove the ventilation trim panel, as described in Chapter 11, Section 26.

25 To remove the warning light panel, undo the two retaining screws, and withdraw the warning lights from the trim panel **(see illustrations)**.

26 The warning light unit has LED's (Light Emitting Diodes), and can only be renewed as a complete unit.

27 Refit the warning light and trim panel, using a reversal of the removal procedure.

Switch illumination bulbs

28 All of the switches are fitted with illuminating bulbs, and some are also fitted with a bulb to show when the circuit concerned is operating.

29 In most cases, if a bulb blows, the complete switch must be renewed, but on certain models, some of the switch bulbs can be renewed. Check with a Nissan dealer for information on the availability of spare bulbs.

30 The electric mirror switch has a bulb fitted to the side of the switch. Remove the relevant switch as described in Section 4, then using a small screwdriver, turn the bulbholder and remove the bulb and holder from the switch **(see illustrations)**. The bulbs are integral with the bulbholders.

31 Fit the new bulb using a reversal of the removal procedure.

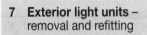

| 7 | Exterior light units – removal and refitting |

Note: *Disconnect the battery negative terminal (refer to 'Disconnecting the battery' in the Reference Chapter), before removing any light unit, and reconnect the terminal after refitting the light.*

Headlight

1 Remove the front bumper, as described in Chapter 11, Section 6.

6.25a Undo the two retaining screws ...

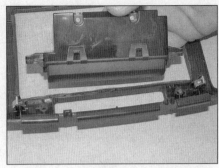

6.25b ... and remove the warning light assembly

6.30a Turn the bulb holder ...

6.30b ... and remove it from the switch

2 Unscrew the two headlight lower securing bolts **(see illustration)**.

3 Unscrew the two headlight upper securing bolts **(see illustration)**.

4 Remove the headlight unit, and disconnect the wiring connectors as the headlamp is withdrawn from the vehicle **(see illustration)**.

5 Refitting is a reversal of removal. On completion, it is wise to have the headlight beam alignment checked (see Section 8).

Front sidelight

6 The front sidelight unit is part of the headlamp unit and cannot be renewed separately.

Front indicator

7 The indicator unit is part of the headlamp unit and cannot be renewed separately.

Front indicator side repeater

8 The procedure is described as part of the bulb renewal procedure in Section 5.

Front foglight

9 Remove the inner wheel arch liner as described in Chapter 11, section 21 **(see illustration 5.33)**.

10 Disconnect the wiring connector from the bulbholder **(see illustration 5.34)**.

7.2 Headlight lower mounting bolts (arrowed)

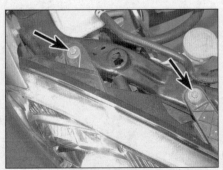

7.3 Headlight upper mounting bolts (arrowed)

7.4 Disconnect the wiring connectors

7.11a Undo the fog light retaining bolts ...

7.11b ...and remove the light unit

11 Undo the two securing bolts and remove the light unit from the rear of the bumper (see illustrations).
12 Refitting is a reversal of removal.

Rear light

13 Open the tailgate and working at the side of the luggage compartment aperture, undo the two rear light unit mounting bolts (see illustration).
14 Withdraw the light unit from the rear of the vehicle, disengaging the two locating pegs from the rear wing panel (see illustration).
15 Disconnect the wiring connector at the rear of the light unit as it is removed (see illustration).
16 Refit the light unit using a reversal of the removal procedure.

Rear fog light

17 The procedure is described as part of the bulb renewal procedure in Section 5.

Reversing light

18 Open the tailgate and remove the inner tailgate trim, as described in Chapter 11, Section 24.
19 Disconnect the wiring connector at the rear of the light unit as it is removed (see illustration).
20 Undo the three light unit securing nuts, and then remove the light unit from the tailgate (see illustrations).
21 Refit the light unit using a reversal of the removal procedure.

Number plate light

22 The procedure is described as part of the bulb renewal procedure in Section 5.

High-level stop-light

23 The procedure is described as part of the bulb renewal procedure in Section 5.

> **8 Headlight beam adjustment components** – general information, removal and refitting

General information

1 Models with Halogen headlights are equipped with a headlight beam adjustment system, controlled by a switch located on the facia, which allows the aim of the headlights to be adjusted to compensate for the varying loads carried in the vehicle. The switch should be positioned according to the load being carried in the vehicle – e.g. position 0 for driver with no passengers or luggage, then increase the position to 1, 2, or 3 as the load is increased, or when towing.
2 Models with Xenon headlights are equipped with an automatic levelling system, which is controlled from a level sensor fitted to the rear suspension. If a fault occurs in the system, a warning light will show up on the instrument panel, and the headlights will be angled down to avoid dazzling on coming traffic. If happens, the driving speed must be adjusted accordingly to allow for decreased visibility.

⚠ *Warning: Before carrying out any operations on xenon headlight units, it is recommended that protective gloves and safety glasses be worn. It is essential that the wiring connectors are*

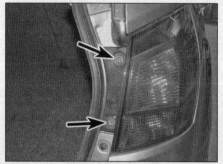

7.13 Undo the rear light retaining bolts

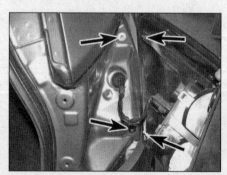

7.14 Pull the light unit to disengage the two locating pegs (arrowed)

7.15 Disconnect the rear light wiring connector

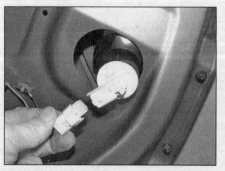

7.19 Disconnect the reversing light wiring connector

7.20a Undo the retaining nuts (arrowed) ...

7.20b ... and remove the reversing light unit

8.5 Disconnect the headlight adjuster wiring connector (arrowed)

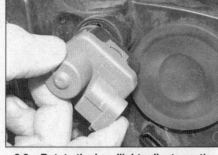

8.6a Rotate the headlight adjuster anti-clockwise …

8.6b … and remove it from the headlight unit

disconnected from the rear of the headlight unit, and then wait until the module and bulbs have cooled down before removal. DO NOT switch the headlights on with the bulb removed, as it is harmful to the eyes.

3 Accurate adjustment of the headlight beam is only possible using optical beam-setting equipment, and this work should therefore be carried out by a Nissan dealer or suitably-equipped workshop. To make temporary adjustment of the headlights, position the vehicle on a level surface, 10 metres from a wall. The tyres must be all at the correct pressures, the fuel tank half full, and a person be sitting in the drivers seat. Turn on the ignition, and check that, where fitted, the manual adjustment inside the vehicle is set at 0. Measure the distance from the ground to the centre of the headlight, and then deduct 5.0cm for models with halogen headlights, and 7.5cm for models with xenon headlights. Draw a mark on the wall at this height, and then adjust the headlight beam centre point onto this mark by turning the adjustment screws on the rear of the headlight unit.

Headlight adjuster

4 Open the bonnet and depending on model, to improve access to the left-hand headlight, remove the air inlet ducting (see illustrations 3.6a & 3.6b).
5 Disconnect the wiring connector from the headlight adjuster unit on the rear of the headlight (see illustration).
6 Twist the adjuster anti-clockwise, to disengage the adjuster from the headlight housing (see illustrations).
7 Remove the headlight bulb rear protective

8.7 Hold the light unit reflector back to release the ball joint

cover and pull the headlight bulbholder back, to aid removing and refitting the ball joint to the reflector (see illustration). Withdraw the adjuster, and then unclip the ball joint from the slot in the retaining clip on the inner reflector.
8 Refit the adjuster to the rear of the headlight unit using a reversal of the removal procedure.

Headlight adjuster switch

9 The procedure for removing the switch is described in Section 4.

Xenon high voltage unit

Note: *Take note of the warnings at the beginning of this Section, when working on headlight units with Xenon bulbs.*
10 Remove the headlight unit, as described in Section 7.
11 Undo the two retaining screws and then withdraw the unit from the bottom of the headlight unit (see illustration). Disconnect the wiring connector as it is removed.

8.11 High voltage unit retaining screws (arrowed)

12 Refit the high voltage unit using a reversal of the removal procedure.

Xenon headlight level sensor

13 A level sensor is fitted to the rear suspension. This forms an integral part of the headlight adjustment system for the Xenon headlights.
14 To remove sensor jack up the rear of the vehicle and support it on axle stands (see *Jacking and vehicle support*).
15 Disconnect the wiring connector from the sensor, and then undo the two retaining bolts and remove it from the rear suspension (see illustrations).

Manual adjustment

16 For reference, the outer adjusting screw (nearest the vehicle wing) is used to adjust the vertical alignment, and the inner screw (located nearest to the radiator) is used to adjust the horizontal alignment (see illustration). Note that on models with

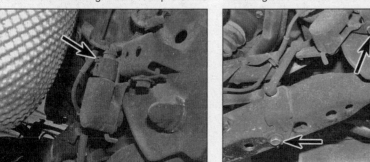

8.15a Disconnect the wiring connector (arrowed) …

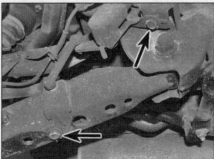

8.15b … and undo the two retaining bolts (arrowed)

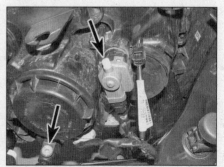

8.16 Headlight alignment manual adjustment screws (arrowed)

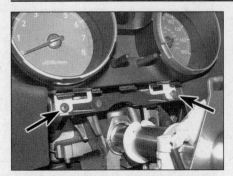

9.3 Undo the two instrument panel retaining screws (arrowed)

9.4a Withdraw the instrument panel ...

9.4b ... and disconnect the wiring connector

10.3 Disconnect the wiring connector

10.4 Undo the horn mounting bracket retaining bolt

2 Remove the front bumper, as described in Chapter 11, Section 6.

3 Disconnect the wiring connector from the horn **(see illustration)**.

4 Unscrew the securing bolt, and withdraw the horn complete with its mounting bracket **(see illustration)**

Refitting

5 Refitting is a reversal of removal.

11 Wiper arm – removal and refitting

electric headlight beam adjustment, the adjustment switch must be set to position 0 when carrying out beam alignment.

9 Instrument panel – removal and refitting

Instrument panel

Removal

1 Disconnect the battery negative terminal (refer to *Disconnecting the battery* in the Reference Chapter).

2 Remove the steering column upper and lower shrouds, as described in Chapter 11, Section 26.

3 Remove the instrument panel two lower securing screws **(see illustration)**.

4 Pull the instrument panel forwards, and disconnect the wiring connectors from the rear of the panel **(see illustrations)**. Withdraw the instrument panel from the facia.

Refitting

5 Refitting is a reversal of removal.

10 Horn – removal and refitting

Removal

1 Disconnect the battery negative terminal (refer to *Disconnecting the battery* in the Reference Chapter).

Removal

1 Operate the wiper motor, and then switch it off so that the wiper arm returns to the at-rest/parked position.

2 If a windscreen or tailgate wiper is being removed, stick a piece of tape alongside the edge of the wiper blade, to use as an alignment aid on refitting. On some models there are marks on the screen to aid refitting.

3 Unclip the plastic cover from the wiper arm spindle nut, then slacken and remove the nut **(see illustrations)**.

4 Lift the blade off the glass, and pull the wiper arm off its spindle **(see illustration)**.

5 If necessary, the arm can be removed from the spindle, by using a suitable puller **(see illustration)**. If both windscreen wiper arms are removed, note their locations, as different

11.3a Unclip the plastic cap ...

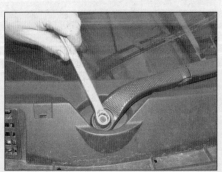

11.3b ... and undo the retaining nut

11.3c Rear wiper arm retaining nut

11.4 Remove the wiper arm ...

11.5 ... if it is tight on the spindle, use a puller

12.3 Disconnect the wiper motor wiring plug

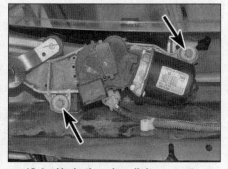

12.4a Undo the wiper linkage centre retaining bolts ...

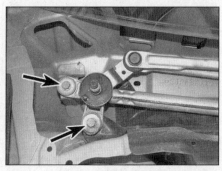

12.4b ... and right-hand retaining bolts ...

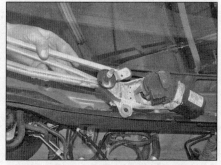

12.4c ... then remove the wiper motor assembly

arms are fitted to the driver and passenger's sides.

Refitting

6 Ensure that the wiper arm and spindle splines are clean and dry.

7 When refitting a windscreen or tailgate wiper arm, refit the arm to the spindle, aligning the wiper blade with the mark on the screen or tape fitted before removal.

8 If both front windscreen wiper arms have been removed, ensure that the arms are refitted to their correct positions as noted before removal.

9 Refit the spindle nut, tighten it securely and, clip the plastic nut cover back into position.

12 Windscreen wiper motor and linkage – removal and refitting

Removal

1 Disconnect the battery negative terminal (refer to *Disconnecting the battery* in the Reference Chapter).

2 Remove the windscreen scuttle grille panels as described in Chapter 11, Section 21.

3 Disconnect the wiring connector from the wiper motor **(see illustration)**.

4 Unscrew the motor and linkage securing bolts, and withdraw it from the scuttle panel **(see illustrations)**.

Refitting

5 Refitting is a reversal of removal.

13 Tailgate wiper motor – removal and refitting

Removal

1 Disconnect the battery negative terminal (refer to *Disconnecting the battery* in the Reference Chapter).

2 Open the tailgate and remove the inner tailgate trim, as described in Chapter 11, Section 24.

3 Remove the rear wiper arm with reference to Section 11.

4 Disconnect the tailgate wiper motor wiring connector **(see illustration)**.

13.4 Disconnect the wiper motor wiring plug

5 Unscrew the three bolts securing the wiper motor assembly to the tailgate and withdraw it from the tailgate **(see illustration)**.

Refitting

6 Refitting is a reversal of removal.

14 Windscreen/tailgate washer system components – removal and refitting

Washer fluid reservoir

Removal

1 Working in the engine compartment, release the retaining clip and then pull the filler neck upwards to remove it from the top

13.5 Undo the rear wiper motor mounting bolts

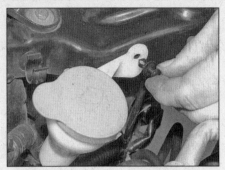

14.1a Release the securing clip ...

14.1b ... and withdraw the filler neck

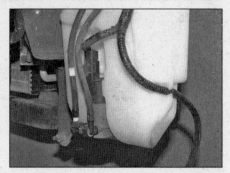

14.4 Unclip the wiring and the hoses from the reservoir

of the reservoir **(see illustrations)**. Make sure the washer fluid level is low before removing the reservoir; be prepared for some spillage.

2 Disconnect the battery negative terminal (refer to *Disconnecting the battery* in the Reference Chapter).

3 Remove the front bumper, as described in Chapter 11, Section 6.

4 Release the wiring harness and fluid hoses

from the retaining clips in the reservoir **(see illustration)**, and move the harness and hoses to one side to allow sufficient clearance to remove the reservoir.

5 Disconnect the fluid hose(s) from the washer pump **(see illustration)** – if the reservoir still contains fluid, be prepared for fluid spillage.

6 Disconnect the wiring connector(s) from the washer pump(s), and from the fluid level sensor, where applicable **(see illustration)**.

7 Remove the reservoir securing bolts, and then lower the reservoir from under the wheel arch **(see illustrations)**.

Refitting

8 Refitting is a reversal of removal.

Washer pump

Removal

9 Proceed as described in paragraphs 2 to 6.

10 Pull the washer pump from the reservoir and recover the grommet **(see illustration)**. If the reservoir still contains fluid, be prepared for fluid spillage.

Refitting

11 Refitting is a reversal of removal, making sure the grommet is fitted correctly in the reservoir before refitting the washer pump.

Windscreen washer nozzle

Removal

12 Open and support the bonnet, then unclip the small grille panel from the scuttle panel **(see illustration)**.

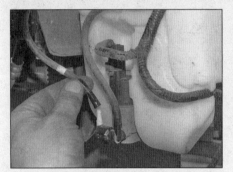

14.5 Disconnect the hoses from the washer pump

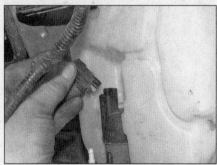

14.6 Disconnect the washer pump wiring plug connector

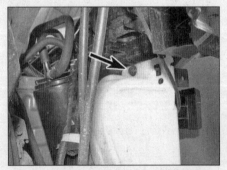

14.7a Undo the upper mounting bolt (arrowed) ...

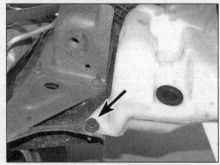

14.7b ... lower mounting bolt ...

14.7c ... then remove the reservoir

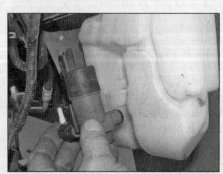

14.10 Ease the washer pump from the reservoir

14.12 Unclip the grille panel

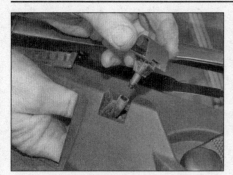

14.13 Unclip the washer nozzle from the scuttle panel

14.14 Turn the washer jet for adjustment position onto the windscreen

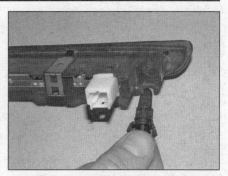

14.17 Unclip the rear washer jet from the light unit

13 Reach inside the scuttle panel, and then release the windscreen washer nozzle from the scuttle panel. Disconnect the washer fluid hose and remove washer nozzle **(see illustration)**.

14 To adjust the position of the washer nozzle, unclip it from the scuttle panel. Then using a small screwdriver adjust the position of the washer nozzle **(see illustration)**.

Refitting

15 Refitting is a reversal of removal.

Tailgate washer nozzle

Removal

16 Remove the high-level brake light unit, as described in Section 5. The tailgate washer nozzle is located in the right-hand end of the high-level brake light unit.

17 Carefully unclip the washer nozzle from the end of the high-level brake light unit **(see illustration)**.

Refitting

18 Refitting is a reversal of removal.

Headlight washer nozzle

Removal

19 Remove the front bumper, as described in Chapter 11, Section 6.

20 If not already done, disconnect the washer fluid hose from the headlight washer nozzle **(see illustration)**.

21 Working on the outside of the bumper, pull the washer nozzle cover out, and then carefully unclip the cover from the end of the washer nozzle **(see illustration)**.

22 Working on the inside of the bumper, release the retaining clips, and then withdraw the washer nozzle assembly from the inside of the bumper **(see illustration)**.

Refitting

23 Refitting is a reversal of removal.

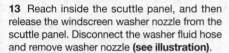

15 Radio/CD player –
removal and refitting

Removal

1 Disconnect the battery negative terminal (refer to *Disconnecting the battery* in the Reference Chapter).

2 Remove the facia centre ventilation trim panel, as described in Chapter 11, Section 26.

14.21 Unclip the washer jet cover

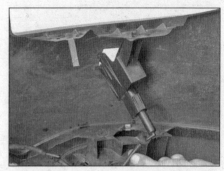

14.20 Disconnect the washer fluid hose

3 Remove the four now-exposed securing screws **(see illustration)**.

4 Pull the unit forwards from the facia, and then disconnect the wiring connectors and the aerial lead from the rear of the unit **(see illustrations)**.

14.22 Unclip the assembly from the inside of the bumper

15.3 Undo the four retaining screws (arrowed)

15.4a Withdraw audio unit from the facia ...

15.4b ... and disconnect the wiring plug connectors

16.3 Disconnect the speaker wiring connector

16.4 Undo the screws and remove the speaker

16.6 Unclip the grille panel ...

16.7 ... and remove the speaker

Refitting

5 Refitting is a reversal of removal, ensuring that the wiring is freely routed behind the unit.

16 Loudspeakers – removal and refitting

1 Disconnect the battery negative terminal (refer to *Disconnecting the battery* in the Reference Chapter).

Door-mounted loudspeakers

2 Remove the door inner trim panel as described in Chapter 11, Section 12.
3 Disconnect the wiring connector from the door speaker (see illustration).
4 Undo the three securing screws, and then withdraw the loudspeaker from the door panel (see illustration).

5 Refitting is a reversal of removal, but refit the inner door trim panel with reference to Chapter 11, Section 12.

Facia-mounted loudspeakers

6 Working in the top corner of the facia panel, carefully unclip the speaker grille (see illustration).
7 Release the loudspeaker from the top of the facia and disconnect the wiring connector (see illustration).
8 Refitting is a reversal of removal.

17 Radio aerial – removal and refitting

Removal

1 Working inside the vehicle unclip the rear courtesy light from the rear of the headlining, as described in section 6
2 Undo the retaining nut and disconnect the aerial lead, remove the aerial from the roof (see illustration).

Refitting

3 Refitting is a reversal of removal, but ensure that the aerial lead is securely connected.

18 Anti-theft system and engine immobiliser – general information

All models in the range are equipped as standard with a central locking system incorporating an electronic engine immobiliser function.

The electronic engine immobiliser is operated by a transponder fitted to the ignition key, in conjunction with an analogue module fitted around the ignition switch.

When the ignition key is inserted in the switch and turned to the ignition 'on' position, the control module sends a preprogrammed recognition code signal to the analogue module on the ignition switch. If the recognition code signal matches that of the transponder on the ignition key, an unlocking request signal is sent to the engine management ECU allowing the engine to be started. If the ignition key signal is not recognised, the engine management system remains immobilised.

When the ignition is switched off, a locking signal is sent to the ECU and the engine is immobilised until the unlocking request signal is again received.

19 Intelligent key system components – general information

1 The intelligent key system is a keyless entry system, which allows you to operate your vehicle without using an actual key. This can only be used when the Intelligent Key remote is within a specified operating distance (80cm with new battery) from the antennas or ignition switch. The antennas are located in the following positions around the vehicle:
a) Rear of the centre console (see illustration).

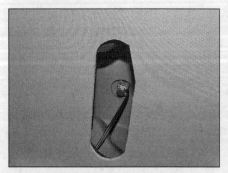

17.2 Roof aerial mounting nut

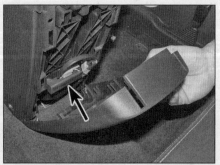

19.1a Antenna at rear of centre console

19.1b Antenna in luggage compartment

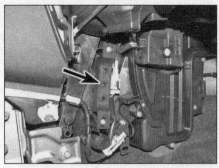

19.1c Antenna right-hand side of heater unit

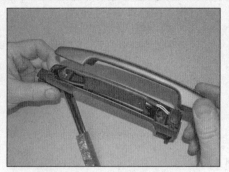

19.1d Antenna inside door handle

19.2 Warning buzzer behind front bumper

b) *In luggage compartment* **(see illustration).**
c) *Right-hand side of heater housing* **(see illustration).**
d) *Left-hand front door handle* **(see illustration).**
e) *Right-hand front door handle*
f) *Behind rear bumper*

2 As the battery discharges over time, the operating distance becomes less, so a new battery will be required. Do not hold the Intelligent Key remote too close to the door, as this may also cause it to not function correctly. If a door is not closed securely, this will cause the Intelligent Key not to function properly. There is also a warning buzzer, which is positioned behind the front bumper **(see illustration).**

20 Airbag system – general information, precautions and system de-activation

General information

A driver's and passenger's airbag are fitted as standard on all models. The driver's airbag is located in the steering wheel centre pad and the passenger's airbag is located above the glovebox in the facia. Side airbags are also available on certain models and are located in the front seats. Curtain airbags are also fitted to some models and are located behind the headlining around the outer edge.

The system is armed only when the ignition is switched on; however, a reserve power source maintains a power supply to the system in the event of a break in the main electrical supply. The steering wheel and facia airbags are activated by a sensor (deceleration sensor), and controlled by an electronic control unit located under the centre console. The side and curtain airbags are activated by severe side impact and operate in conjunction with the main system.

The airbags are inflated by a gas generator, which forces the bag out from its location in the steering wheel, facia or seat back frame.

Precautions

⚠️ **Warning: The following precautions must be observed when working on vehicles equipped with an airbag system, to prevent the possibility of personal injury.**

General precautions

a) *Do not disconnect the battery with the engine running.*
b) *Before carrying out any work in the vicinity of the airbag, removal of any of the airbag components, or any welding work on the vehicle, de-activate the system as described in the following sub-Section.*
c) *Do not attempt to test any of the airbag system circuits using test meters or any other test equipment.*
d) *If the airbag warning light comes on, or any fault in the system is suspected, consult a Nissan dealer without delay.* **Do not** *attempt to carry out fault diagnosis, or any dismantling of the components.*

Precautions when handling an airbag

a) *Transport the airbag by itself, bag upward.*
b) *Do not put your arms around the airbag.*
c) *Carry the airbag close to the body, bag outward.*
d) *Do not drop the airbag or expose it to impacts.*
e) *Do not attempt to dismantle the airbag unit.*
f) *Do not connect any form of electrical equipment to any part of the airbag circuit.*

Precautions when storing an airbag

a) *Store the unit in a cupboard with the airbag upward.*
b) *Do not expose the airbag to temperatures above 80°C.*
c) *Do not expose the airbag to flames.*
d) *Do not attempt to dispose of the airbag – consult a Nissan dealer.*
e) *Never refit an airbag that is known to be faulty or damaged.*

De-activation of airbag system

The system must be de-activated before carrying out any work on the airbag components or surrounding area:
a) *Switch on the ignition and check the operation of the airbag warning light on the instrument panel. The light should illuminate when the ignition is switched on, then extinguish.*
b) *Switch off the ignition.*
c) *Remove the ignition key.*
d) *Switch off all electrical equipment.*

e) *Disconnect the battery negative terminal (refer to 'Disconnecting the battery' in the Reference Chapter).*
f) *Insulate the battery negative terminal and the end of the battery negative lead to prevent any possibility of contact.*
g) *Wait for at least ten minutes before carrying out any further work.*

Activation of airbag system

To activate the system on completion of any work, proceed as follows:
a) *Ensure that there are no occupants in the vehicle, and that there are no loose objects around the vicinity of the steering wheel. Close the vehicle doors and windows.*
b) *Ensure that the ignition is switched off then reconnect the battery negative terminal.*
c) *Open the driver's door and switch on the ignition, without reaching in front of the steering wheel. Check that the airbag warning light illuminates briefly then extinguishes.*
d) *Switch off the ignition.*
e) *If the airbag warning light does not operate as described in paragraph c), consult a Nissan dealer before driving the vehicle.*

21 Airbag system components – removal and refitting

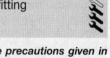

Warning: Refer to the precautions given in Section 20 before attempting to carry out work on any of the airbag components. Any suspected faults with the airbag system should be referred to a Nissan dealer – under no circumstances attempt to carry out any work other than removal and refitting of the front airbag unit(s) and/or the rotary connector, as described in the following paragraphs.
Note: *Disconnect the battery negative terminal (refer to Disconnecting the battery in the Reference Chapter), before the removal and refitting of components in the airbag system.*

Airbag electronic control units

1 The ECU is located under the centre

21.2 Disconnect the wiring connectors

21.3 Note the arrow must face forward when fitted

21.5 Insert a screwdriver through the sides of the steering wheel

21.6 ... to release the airbag securing clips (arrowed)

21.7a Lift up the locking clips ...

21.7b ... and disconnect the wiring connectors from the airbag

console in front of the handbrake, and is accessible after removal of the centre console as described in Chapter 11, Section 25.

2 Disconnect the wiring connectors from the control unit, then undo the retaining bolts and remove the control unit from the floor panel **(see illustration)**.

3 The arrow on the top of the unit must face forward when refitted **(see illustration)**.

Driver's airbag unit

Removal

4 De-activate the airbag system as described in Section 20.

5 Working at each side of the steering wheel, insert a screwdriver (or similar) through the holes in the rear of the steering wheel, to release the securing clips on the rear of the airbag unit **(see illustration)**.

6 Carefully lever the airbag, and release it from the steering wheel **(see illustration)**.

7 Using a thin screwdriver, release the centre retaining clips and disconnect the airbag wiring connectors from the rear of the airbag unit **(see illustrations)**.

8 Disconnect the wiring connector for the steering wheel switches **(see illustration)**.

9 Disconnect the earth wire connector **(see illustration)**, and then carefully remove the airbag from the steering wheel.

10 If the airbag unit is to be stored for any length of time, refer to the storage precautions given in Section 20.

Refitting

11 Refitting is a reversal of removal, bearing in mind the following points:

a) *Do not strike the airbag unit, or expose it to impacts during refitting.*

b) *On completion of refitting, activate the airbag system as described in Section 20.*

Airbag rotary switch assembly

Removal

12 Remove the driver's airbag unit, as described previously in this Section.

13 With the steering in the straight–ahead position, remove the steering wheel as described in Chapter 10, Section 11.

14 Remove the steering column upper and lower shrouds, as described in Chapter 11, Section 26.

15 Remove the steering column switches (if required), as described in Section 4.

16 Disconnect the wiring connectors, below the steering column from the rear of the rotary switch assembly **(see illustration)**.

21.8 Disconnect the switch wiring connector

21.9 Disconnect the earth wiring connector

21.16 Disconnect the switch wiring connectors

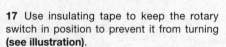

21.17 Secure the rotary switch in place using duct tape

21.18a Release the retaining clips …

21.18b … and withdraw the rotary switch assembly

17 Use insulating tape to keep the rotary switch in position to prevent it from turning (**see illustration**).

18 Release the retaining clips and withdraw the rotary switch assembly from the steering column (**see illustrations**).

Refitting

19 Refitting is a reversal of removal, bearing in mind the following points:

a) *Make sure the rotary switch has not been turned and the insulating tape is still in position.*

b) *Ensure that the roadwheels are in the straight–ahead position before refitting the rotary connector and steering wheel.*

c) *Before refitting the steering column shrouds, ensure that the rotary connector wiring harness is correctly routed as noted before removal.*

d) *Refit the steering wheel as described in Chapter 10, Section 11, and refit the airbag unit as described previously in this Section.*

Passenger's airbag unit

Removal

20 The passenger's airbag is fitted to the upper part of the facia, above the glovebox.

21 De–activate the airbag system as described in Section 20.

22 Remove the glovebox as described in Chapter 11, Section 26.

23 Disconnect the airbag wiring connectors (**see illustration**).

24 Undo the bolts securing the airbag assembly to the facia support rail, and then carefully withdraw the airbag from the facia (**see illustrations**).

25 If the airbag unit is to be stored for any length of time, refer to the storage precautions given in Section 20.

Refitting

26 Refitting is a reversal of removal, bearing in mind the following points:

a) *Use new bolts to secure the airbag unit*

and tighten the bolts to the specified torque.

b) *Do not strike the airbag unit, or expose it to impacts during refitting.*

c) *On completion of refitting, activate the airbag system as described in Section 20.*

Side airbag units

27 The side airbags are located internally within the front seat back and no attempt should be made to remove them. Any suspected problems with the side airbag system should be referred to a Nissan dealer.

Curtain airbag units

28 The curtain airbags are located internally behind the headlining and no attempt should be made to remove them. Any suspected problems with the curtain airbag system should be referred to a Nissan dealer.

21.23 Disconnect the airbag wiring connectors

21.24a Undo the airbag mounting bolts …

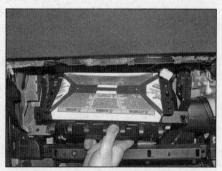

21.24b … and remove it from under the facia

Nissan Qashqai wiring diagrams

Diagram 1

WARNING: This vehicle is fitted with a supplemental restraint system (SRS) consisting of a combination of driver (and passenger) airbag(s), side impact protection airbags and seatbelt pre-tensioners. The use of electrical test equipment on any SRS wiring systems may cause the seatbelt pre-tensioners to abruptly retract and airbags to explosively deploy, resulting in potentially severe personal injury. Extreme care should be taken to correctly identify any circuits to be tested to avoid choosing any of the SRS wiring in error.

For further information see airbag system precautions in body electrical systems chapter.

Note: The SRS wiring harness can normally be identified by yellow and/or orange harness or harness connectors.

Key to symbols

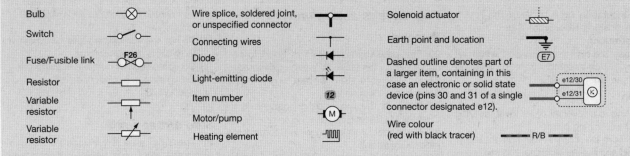

Engine fusebox 6

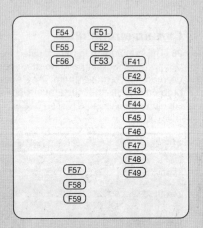

Passenger fusebox 7

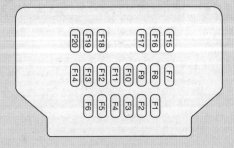

For fuse ratings consult fusebox lid

Fusible link box 4

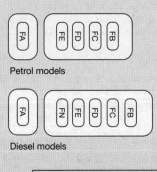

Petrol models

Diesel models

Fuse & fusible link box 5

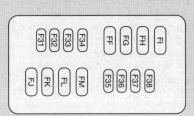

Earth locations

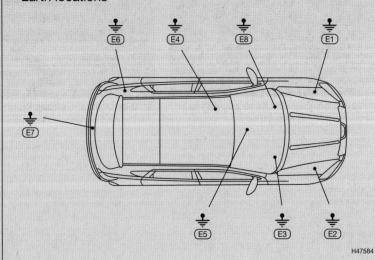

H47584

Wire colours

B	Black	O	Orange
Y	Yellow	L	Blue
BR	Brown	W	White
GR	Grey	LG	Light Green
V	Purple	SB	Light Blue
R	Red	DG	Dark Green
P	Pink	CH	Dark Brown
G	Green		

*Diesel models

Key to items

1 Battery
2 Alternator
3 Starter motor
4 Fusible link box
5 Fuse & fusible link box
6 Engine fusebox
  a = starter relay
  b = ignition relay
  c = control unit
  d = cooling fan relay 1
  e = cooling fan relay 2

7 Passenger fusebox
  a = accessory relay
8 Ignition switch
9 Horn
10 Steering wheel clock springs
11 Horn switch
12 Horn relay
13 Front accessory socket/cigar lighter
14 Rear accessory socket
15 Rear accessory socket relay
16 Engine cooling fan

17 Engine cooling fan resistor
18 Engine management control unit
19 Coolant temperature sensor

Diagram 2

H47585

Starting & charging

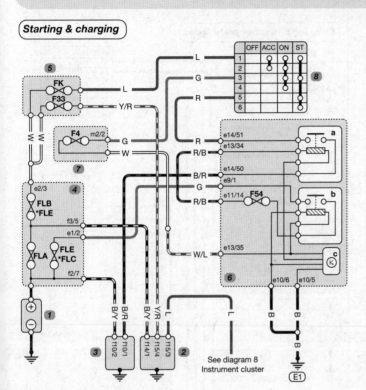

Horn

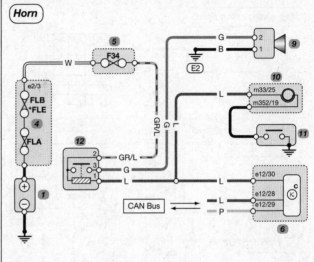

Engine cooling fan

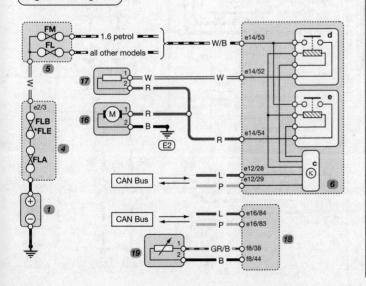

Cigar lighter & accessory socket

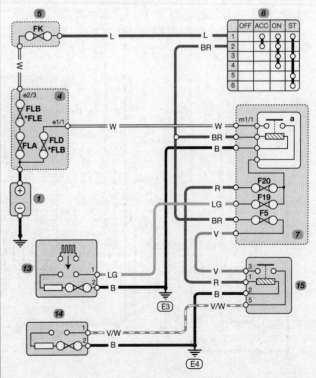

Wire colours

B	Black	O	Orange
Y	Yellow	L	Blue
BR	Brown	W	White
GR	Grey	LG	Light Green
V	Purple	SB	Light Blue
R	Red	DG	Dark Green
P	Pink	CH	Dark Brown
G	Green		

* Diesel models

Key to items

1 Battery
4 Fusible link box
5 Fuse & fusible link box
6 Engine fusebox
  b = ignition relay
  c = control unit
  f = tail light relay
7 Passenger fusebox
8 Ignition switch
20 Gear selector position switch
  (models with automatic transmission)
21 Gear selector position switch
  (models with CVT)
22 Gear selector position switch
  (models with manual transmission)
23 Stop light switch
24 Body control unit
25 LH rear light unit
  a = stop light
  b = tail light
26 RH rear light unit
  (a & b as above)

27 High level stop light
28 LH reversing light
29 RH reversing light
30 LH side light
31 RH side light
32 LH number plate light
33 RH number plate light
34 Combination switch
35 Driver's door switch

Diagram 3

H47586

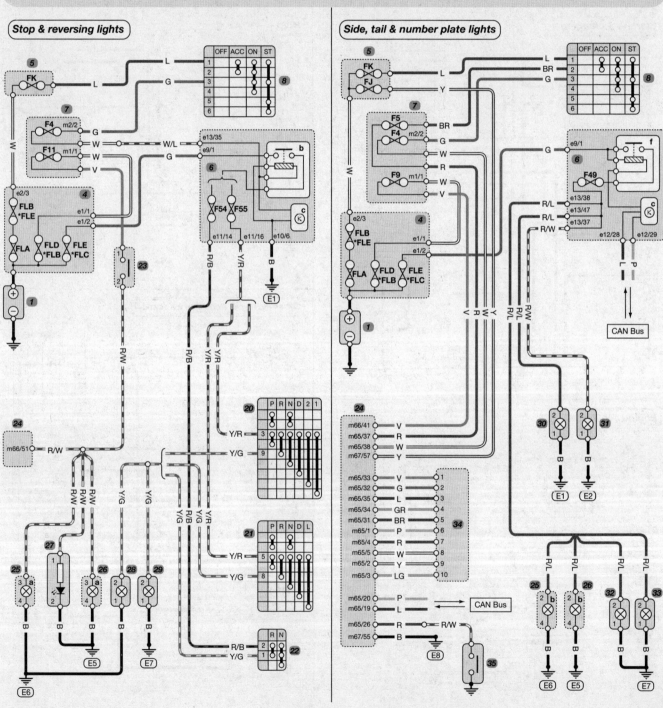

Stop & reversing lights

Side, tail & number plate lights

Wire colours

B	Black	O	Orange
Y	Yellow	L	Blue
BR	Brown	W	White
GR	Grey	LG	Light Green
V	Purple	SB	Light Blue
R	Red	DG	Dark Green
P	Pink	CH	Dark Brown
G	Green		

*Diesel models

Key to items

1 Battery
4 Fusible link box
5 Fuse & fusible link box
6 Engine fusebox
  c = control unit
  g = main beam relay
  h = dip beam relay
7 Passenger fusebox
8 Ignition switch
24 Body control unit
25 LH rear light unit
  c = direction indicator

26 RH rear light unit
  c = direction indicator
34 Combination switch
35 Driver's door switch
37 LH headlight
  a = main beam
  b = dip beam (HID)
38 RH headlight
  (a & b as above)
39 LH front direction indicator
40 LH indicator side repeater
41 RH front direction indicator

42 RH indicator side repeater
43 Hazard warning switch

Diagram 4

H47587

Headlights

Direction indicators & hazard warning lights

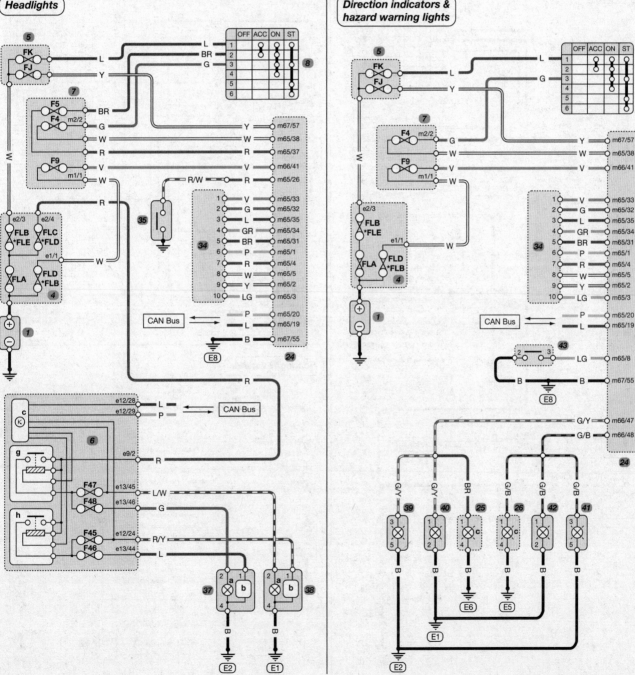

Wire colours

B	Black	O	Orange
Y	Yellow	L	Blue
BR	Brown	W	White
GR	Grey	LG	Light Green
V	Purple	SB	Light Blue
R	Red	DG	Dark Green
P	Pink	CH	Dark Brown
G	Green		

* Diesel models

Key to items

1 Battery
4 Fusible link box
5 Fuse & fusible link box
6 Engine fusebox
 c = control unit
 f = tail light relay
 h = dip beam relay
 i = front foglight relay
7 Passenger fusebox
8 Ignition switch
24 Body control unit
34 Combination switch
45 LH front foglight
46 RH front foglight
47 Rear foglight
48 LH headlight levelling adjuster
49 RH headlight levelling adjuster
50 Headlight levelling control unit
51 Diagnostic connector
52 Headlight washer relay
53 Headlight washer pump

Diagram 5

H47588

Front & rear foglight

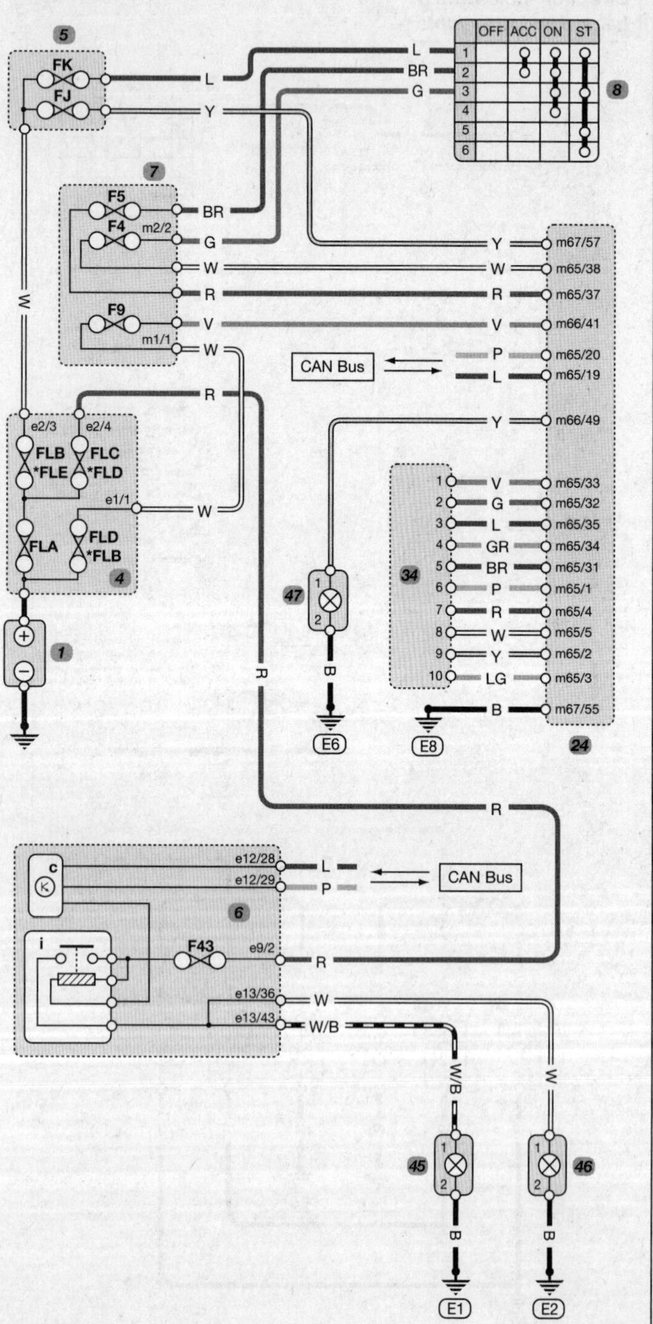

Headlight levelling

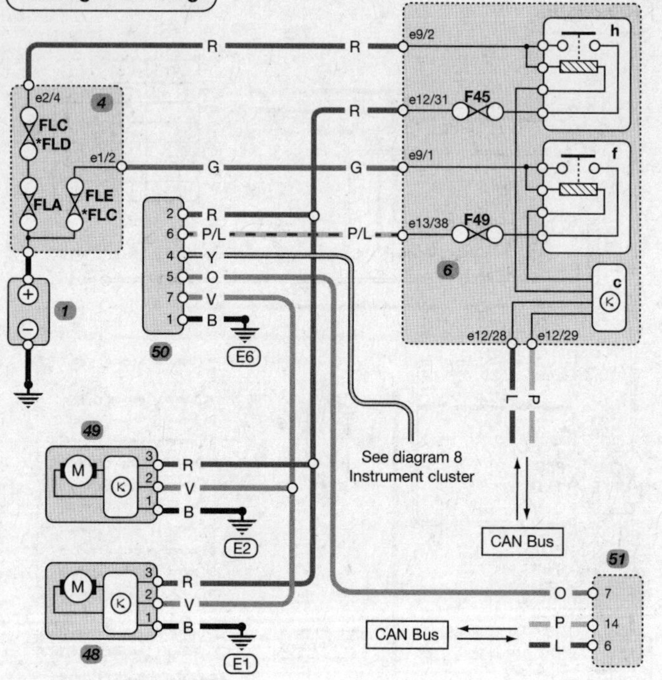

See diagram 8
Instrument cluster

Headlight washer

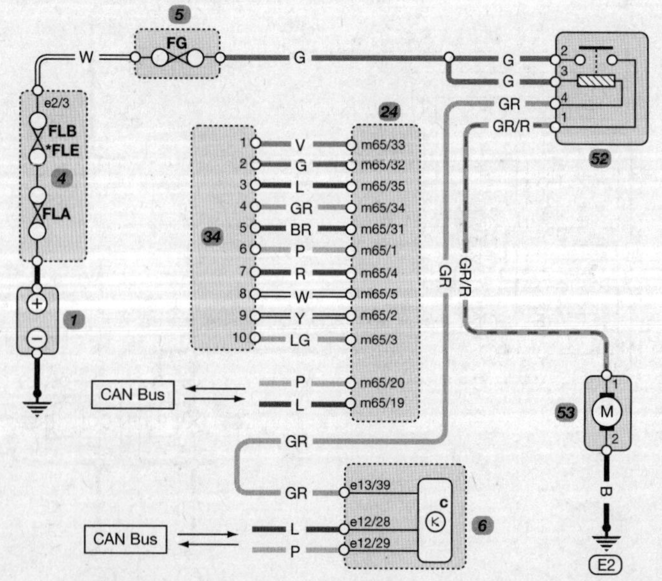

Wire colours

B	Black	**O**	Orange
Y	Yellow	**L**	Blue
BR	Brown	**W**	White
GR	Grey	**LG**	Light Green
V	Purple	**SB**	Light Blue
R	Red	**DG**	Dark Green
P	Pink	**CH**	Dark Brown
G	Green		

* Diesel models

Key to items

1 Battery
4 Fusible link box
5 Fuse & fusible link box
6 Engine fusebox
   c = control unit
   j = front wiper relay
   k = rear wiper relay
   l = heated rear window relay

7 Passenger fusebox
   a = accessory relay
8 Ignition switch
24 Body control unit
34 Combination switch
55 Rain/light sensor
56 Washer pump
57 Front wiper motor

58 Rear wiper motor
59 Heater control panel
   (heated mirror/window switch)
60 Heated rear window
61 Mirror control switch
62 Driver's mirror assembly
63 Passenger's mirror assembly

Diagram 6

H47589

Wash/wipe

Heated rear window

Electric mirrors

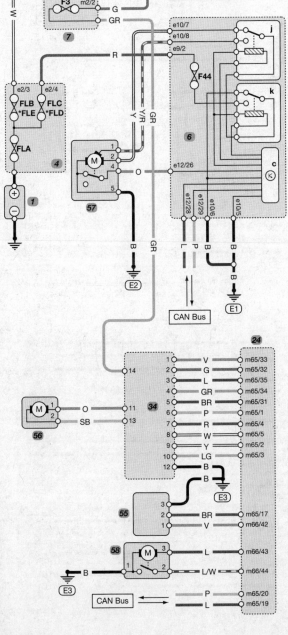

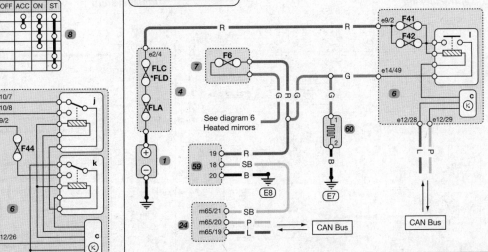

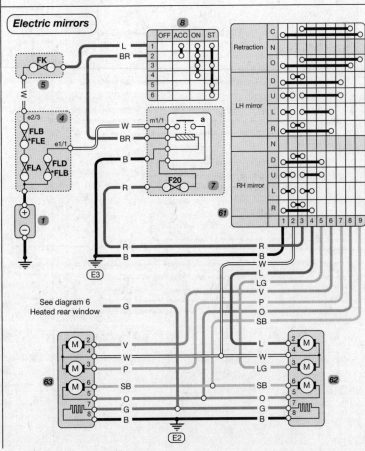

Wire colours

B	Black	**O**	Orange
Y	Yellow	**L**	Blue
BR	Brown	**W**	White
GR	Grey	**LG**	Light Green
V	Purple	**SB**	Light Blue
R	Red	**DG**	Dark Green
P	Pink	**CH**	Dark Brown
G	Green		

* Diesel models

Key to items

1	Battery
4	Fusible link box
5	Fuse & fusible link box
7	Passenger fusebox
8	Ignition switch
10	Steering wheel clock springs
24	Body control unit
35	Driver's door switch
65	Key switch
66	Door lock master switch
67	SRS control unit
68	Driver's door lock motor
69	Passenger's door lock motor
70	LH rear door lock motor
71	RH rear door lock motor
73	Passenger's door switch
74	LH rear door lock switch
75	RH rear door lock switch
76	Tailgate lock switch
77	Steering wheel remote controls
79	Microphone
80	LH front door speaker
81	LH tweeter
82	RH front door speaker
83	RH tweeter
84	LH rear speaker
85	RH rear speaker
86	Antenna
87	Audio unit

Diagram 7

H47590

Central locking

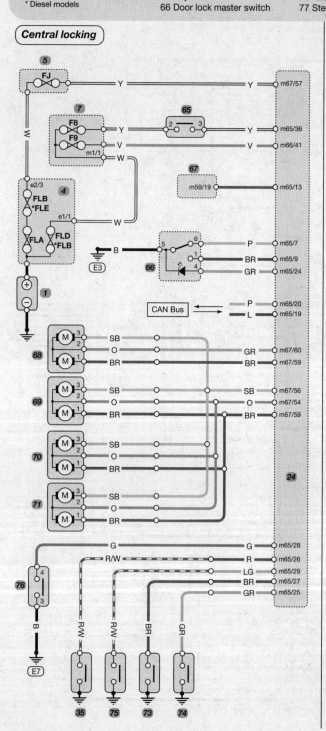

Audio system

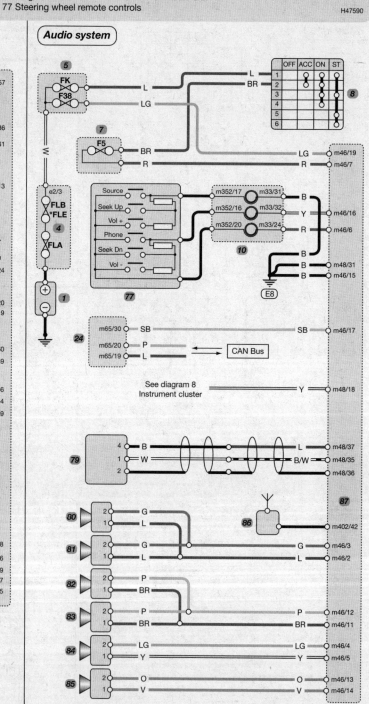

Wire colours

B	Black	O	Orange
Y	Yellow	L	Blue
BR	Brown	W	White
GR	Grey	LG	Light Green
V	Purple	SB	Light Blue
R	Red	DG	Dark Green
P	Pink	CH	Dark Brown
G	Green		

* Diesel models

Key to items

1 Battery
4 Fusible link box
5 Fuse & fusible link box
6 Engine fusebox
  b = ignition relay
  c = control unit
  m = a/c relay
7 Passenger fusebox
  b = heater blower relay
8 Ignition switch
10 Steering wheel clock springs
18 Engine management control unit

24 Body control unit
59 Heater control panel
  (air conditioning switch)
67 SRS control unit
78 Instrument cluster
90 Compressor clutch
91 Heater blower motor
92 Heater blower resistors
93 Heater blower switch
94 High level vent switch
95 High level vent door motor
96 Intake door motor

97 Refridgerant pressure sensor
98 Oil level sensor
99 Handbrake switch
100 Outside air temperature sensor
101 Fuel gauge sesnder unit
102 Brake fluid level switch
103 Driver's seatbelt switch
104 Passenger's seatbelt switch
105 Passenger's occupancy sensor
106 Automatic transmission control device
107 Trip computer switch

Diagram 8

H47591

Air conditioning

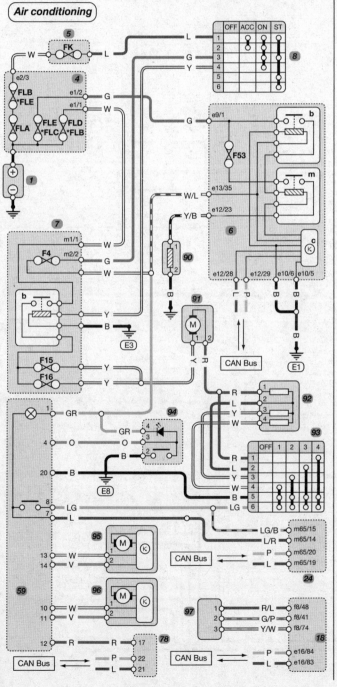

Instrument cluster

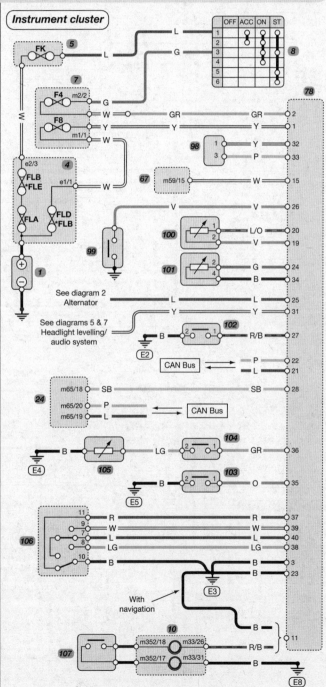

Wire colours

B	Black	O	Orange
Y	Yellow	L	Blue
BR	Brown	W	White
GR	Grey	LG	Light Green
V	Purple	SB	Light Blue
R	Red	DG	Dark Green
P	Pink	CH	Dark Brown
G	Green		

* Diesel models

Key to items

1 Battery
4 Fusible link box
5 Fuse & fusible link box
6 Engine fusebox
  c = control unit
  f = tail light relay
7 Passenger fusebox
8 Ignition switch
10 Steering wheel clock springs
24 Body control unit
34 Combination switch
35 Driver's door switch
43 Hazard warning switch
59 Heater control panel
61 Mirror control switch
65 Key switch
66 Door lock master switch
73 Passenger's door switch
74 LH rear door lock switch
75 RH rear door lock switch
76 Tailgate lock switch
78 Instrument cluster
87 Audio unit
94 High level vent switch
106 Automatic transmission control device
110 ESP switch
111 Glovebox light
112 Steering wheel illumination
113 Map reading light
114 Luggage compartment light
115 Interior light
116 Driver's vanity mirror illumination
117 Passenger's vanity mirror illumination

Diagram 9

H47592

Interior lighting & illumination

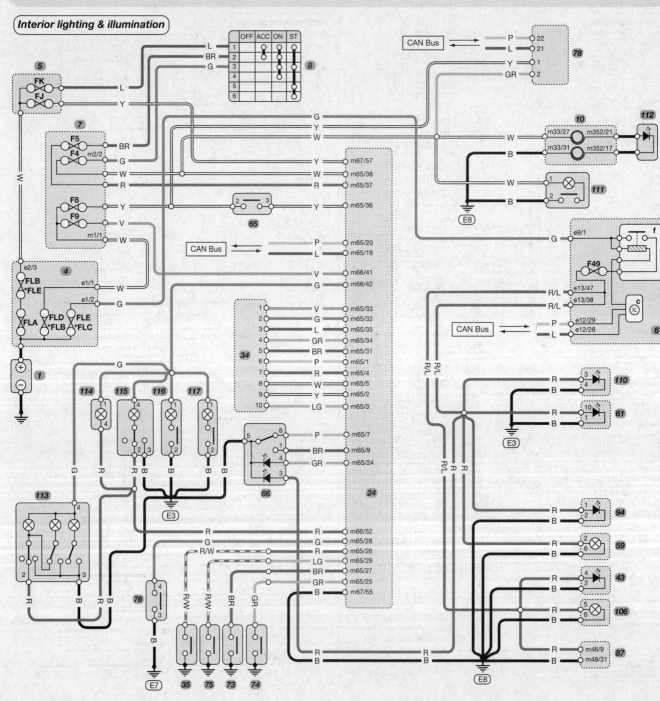

Dimensions and weights

Note: *All figures are approximate, and may vary according to model. Refer to manufacturer's data for exact figures.*

Dimensions

Overall length:
    5-seater models . . . . 4332 mm
    7-seater models . . . . 4542 mm
Overall width:
    5-seater models . . . . 1780 mm
    7-seater models . . . . 1780 mm
Overall height (unladen):
    5-seater models:
        Without roof rails . . . . 1605 mm
        With roof rails . . . . 1622 mm
    7-seater models . . . . 1645 mm
Wheelbase:
    5-seater models . . . . 2630 mm
    7-seater models . . . . 2765 mm
Front track:
    5-seater models . . . . 1540 mm
    7-seater models . . . . 1540 mm
Rear track:
    5-seater models . . . . 1545 mm
    7-seater models . . . . 1550 mm

Weights

Vehicle weights are listed on the VIN label on the driver's side door pillar **(see illustration)**.
    First (kg) figure is . . . . *Gross vehicle weight*
    Second (kg) figure is . . . . *Gross vehicle weight + Gross trailer weight*
    Third (kg) figure is . . . . *Gross axle weight (front)*
    Fourth (kg) figure is . . . . *Gross axle weight (rear)*

Conversion factors

Length (distance)

Inches (in)	x 25.4	= Millimetres (mm)	x 0.0394	= Inches (in)
Feet (ft)	x 0.305	= Metres (m)	x 3.281	= Feet (ft)
Miles	x 1.609	= Kilometres (km)	x 0.621	= Miles

Volume (capacity)

Cubic inches (cu in; in^3)	x 16.387	= Cubic centimetres (cc; cm^3)	x 0.061	= Cubic inches (cu in; in^3)
Imperial pints (Imp pt)	x 0.568	= Litres (l)	x 1.76	= Imperial pints (Imp pt)
Imperial quarts (Imp qt)	x 1.137	= Litres (l)	x 0.88	= Imperial quarts (Imp qt)
Imperial quarts (Imp qt)	x 1.201	= US quarts (US qt)	x 0.833	= Imperial quarts (Imp qt)
US quarts (US qt)	x 0.946	= Litres (l)	x 1.057	= US quarts (US qt)
Imperial gallons (Imp gal)	x 4.546	= Litres (l)	x 0.22	= Imperial gallons (Imp gal)
Imperial gallons (Imp gal)	x 1.201	= US gallons (US gal)	x 0.833	= Imperial gallons (Imp gal)
US gallons (US gal)	x 3.785	= Litres (l)	x 0.264	= US gallons (US gal)

Mass (weight)

Ounces (oz)	x 28.35	= Grams (g)	x 0.035	= Ounces (oz)
Pounds (lb)	x 0.454	= Kilograms (kg)	x 2.205	= Pounds (lb)

Force

Ounces-force (ozf; oz)	x 0.278	= Newtons (N)	x 3.6	= Ounces-force (ozf; oz)
Pounds-force (lbf; lb)	x 4.448	= Newtons (N)	x 0.225	= Pounds-force (lbf; lb)
Newtons (N)	x 0.1	= Kilograms-force (kgf; kg)	x 9.81	= Newtons (N)

Pressure

Pounds-force per square inch (psi; lbf/in^2; lb/in^2)	x 0.070	= Kilograms-force per square centimetre (kgf/cm^2; kg/cm^2)	x 14.223	= Pounds-force per square inch (psi; lbf/in^2; lb/in^2)
Pounds-force per square inch (psi; lbf/in^2; lb/in^2)	x 0.068	= Atmospheres (atm)	x 14.696	= Pounds-force per square inch (psi; lbf/in^2; lb/in^2)
Pounds-force per square inch (psi; lbf/in^2; lb/in^2)	x 0.069	= Bars	x 14.5	= Pounds-force per square inch (psi; lbf/in^2; lb/in^2)
Pounds-force per square inch (psi; lbf/in^2; lb/in^2)	x 6.895	= Kilopascals (kPa)	x 0.145	= Pounds-force per square inch (psi; lbf/in^2; lb/in^2)
Kilopascals (kPa)	x 0.01	= Kilograms-force per square centimetre (kgf/cm^2; kg/cm^2)	x 98.1	= Kilopascals (kPa)
Millibar (mbar)	x 100	= Pascals (Pa)	x 0.01	= Millibar (mbar)
Millibar (mbar)	x 0.0145	= Pounds-force per square inch (psi; lbf/in^2; lb/in^2)	x 68.947	= Millibar (mbar)
Millibar (mbar)	x 0.75	= Millimetres of mercury (mmHg)	x 1.333	= Millibar (mbar)
Millibar (mbar)	x 0.401	= Inches of water (inH$_2$O)	x 2.491	= Millibar (mbar)
Millimetres of mercury (mmHg)	x 0.535	= Inches of water (inH$_2$O)	x 1.868	= Millimetres of mercury (mmHg)
Inches of water (inH$_2$O)	x 0.036	= Pounds-force per square inch (psi; lbf/in^2; lb/in^2)	x 27.68	= Inches of water (inH$_2$O)

Torque (moment of force)

Pounds-force inches (lbf in; lb in)	x 1.152	= Kilograms-force centimetre (kgf cm; kg cm)	x 0.868	= Pounds-force inches (lbf in; lb in)
Pounds-force inches (lbf in; lb in)	x 0.113	= Newton metres (Nm)	x 8.85	= Pounds-force inches (lbf in; lb in)
Pounds-force inches (lbf in; lb in)	x 0.083	= Pounds-force feet (lbf ft; lb ft)	x 12	= Pounds-force inches (lbf in; lb in)
Pounds-force feet (lbf ft; lb ft)	x 0.138	= Kilograms-force metres (kgf m; kg m)	x 7.233	= Pounds-force feet (lbf ft; lb ft)
Pounds-force feet (lbf ft; lb ft)	x 1.356	= Newton metres (Nm)	x 0.738	= Pounds-force feet (lbf ft; lb ft)
Newton metres (Nm)	x 0.102	= Kilograms-force metres (kgf m; kg m)	x 9.804	= Newton metres (Nm)

Power

Horsepower (hp)	x 745.7	= Watts (W)	x 0.0013	= Horsepower (hp)

Velocity (speed)

Miles per hour (miles/hr; mph)	x 1.609	= Kilometres per hour (km/hr; kph)	x 0.621	= Miles per hour (miles/hr; mph)

Fuel consumption*

Miles per gallon, Imperial (mpg)	x 0.354	= Kilometres per litre (km/l)	x 2.825	= Miles per gallon, Imperial (mpg)
Miles per gallon, US (mpg)	x 0.425	= Kilometres per litre (km/l)	x 2.352	= Miles per gallon, US (mpg)

Temperature

Degrees Fahrenheit = (°C x 1.8) + 32   Degrees Celsius (Degrees Centigrade; °C) = (°F - 32) x 0.56

It is common practice to convert from miles per gallon (mpg) to litres/100 kilometres (l/100km), where mpg x l/100 km = 282

Spare parts are available from many sources, including maker's appointed garages, accessory shops, and motor factors. To be sure of obtaining the correct parts, it will sometimes be necessary to quote the vehicle identification number. If possible, it can also be useful to take the old parts along for positive identification. Items such as starter motors and alternators may be available under a service exchange scheme - any parts returned should be clean.

Our advice regarding spare parts is as follows.

Officially appointed garages

This is the best source of parts which are peculiar to your car, and which are not otherwise generally available (e.g. badges, interior trim, certain body panels, etc). It is also the only place at which you should buy parts if the vehicle is still under warranty.

Accessory shops

These are very good places to buy materials and components needed for the maintenance of your car (oil, air and fuel filters, light bulbs, drivebelts, greases, brake pads, touch-up paint, etc). Components of this nature sold by a reputable shop are usually of the same standard as those used by the car manufacturer.

Besides components, these shops also sell tools and general accessories, usually have convenient opening hours, charge lower prices, and can often be found close to home. Some accessory shops have parts counters where components needed for almost any repair job can be purchased or ordered.

Motor factors

Good factors will stock the more important components, which wear out comparatively quickly, and can sometimes supply individual components needed for the overhaul of a larger assembly (e.g. brake seals and hydraulic parts, bearing shells, pistons, valves). They may also handle work such as cylinder block reboring, crankshaft regrinding, etc.

Tyre and exhaust specialists

These outlets may be independent, or members of a local or national chain. They frequently offer competitive prices when compared with a main dealer or local garage, but it will pay to obtain several quotes before making a decision. When researching prices, also be sure to ask what "extras" may be added - for instance, fitting a new valve, balancing the wheel, and checking the tracking (front wheels) are all commonly charged on top of the price of a new tyre.

Other sources

Beware of parts or materials obtained from market stalls, car boot sales or similar outlets. Such items are not invariably sub-standard, but there is little chance of compensation if they do prove unsatisfactory. In the case of safety-critical components such as brake pads, there is the risk not only of financial loss, but also of an accident causing injury or death.

Second-hand components or assemblies obtained from a car breaker can be a good buy in some circumstances, but this sort of purchase is best made by the experienced DIY mechanic.

Disconnecting the battery

Several systems fitted to the vehicle require battery power to be available at all times, either to ensure their continued operation (such as the clock) or to maintain control unit memories which could be erased if the battery were to be disconnected. Whenever the battery is to be disconnected therefore, first note the following, to ensure that there are no unforeseen consequences of this action:

a) *On any vehicle with central locking, it is a wise precaution to remove the key from the ignition, and to keep it with you, so that it does not get locked in if the central locking should engage accidentally when the battery is reconnected.*

b) *If a security-coded audio unit is fitted, and the unit and/or the battery is disconnected, the unit will not function again on reconnection until the correct security code is entered. Details of this procedure, which varies according to the unit fitted and vehicle model, are given in the vehicle owner's handbook. Where necessary, ensure you have the correct code before you disconnect the battery. If*

you do not have the code or details of the correct procedure, but can supply proof of ownership and a legitimate reason for wanting this information, a Nissan dealer may be able to help.

c) *The engine management system electronic control unit is of the 'self-learning' type, meaning that as it operates, it also monitors and stores the settings which give optimum engine performance under all operating conditions. When the battery is disconnected, these settings are lost and the ECU reverts to the base settings programmed into its memory at the factory. On restarting, this may lead to the engine running/idling roughly for a short while, until the ECU has re-learned the optimum settings. This process is best accomplished by taking the vehicle on a road test (for approximately 15 minutes), covering all engine speeds and loads, concentrating mainly in the 2500 to 3500 rpm region.*

d) *When reconnecting the battery after*

disconnection, switch on the ignition and wait 10 seconds to allow the electronic vehicle systems to stabilise and re-initialise.

Devices known as 'memory-savers' (or 'code-savers') can be used to maintain an electrical supply to various circuits. Precise details vary according to the device used. Typically, it is plugged into the cigarette lighter, and is connected by its own wires to a spare battery; the vehicle's own battery is then disconnected from the electrical system, leaving the 'memory-saver' to pass sufficient current to maintain audio unit security codes and any other memory values, and also to run permanently-live circuits such as the clock.

⚠️ **Warning: Some of these devices allow a considerable amount of current to pass, which can mean that many of the vehicle's systems are still operational when the main battery is disconnected. If a 'memory- saver' is used, ensure that the circuit concerned is actually 'dead' before carrying out any work on it!**

Whenever servicing, repair or overhaul work is carried out on the car or its components, observe the following procedures and instructions. This will assist in carrying out the operation efficiently and to a professional standard of workmanship.

Joint mating faces and gaskets

When separating components at their mating faces, never insert screwdrivers or similar implements into the joint between the faces in order to prise them apart. This can cause severe damage which results in oil leaks, coolant leaks, etc upon reassembly. Separation is usually achieved by tapping along the joint with a soft-faced hammer in order to break the seal. However, note that this method may not be suitable where dowels are used for component location.

Where a gasket is used between the mating faces of two components, a new one must be fitted on reassembly; fit it dry unless otherwise stated in the repair procedure. Make sure that the mating faces are clean and dry, with all traces of old gasket removed. When cleaning a joint face, use a tool which is unlikely to score or damage the face, and remove any burrs or nicks with an oilstone or fine file.

Make sure that tapped holes are cleaned with a pipe cleaner, and keep them free of jointing compound, if this is being used, unless specifically instructed otherwise.

Ensure that all orifices, channels or pipes are clear, and blow through them, preferably using compressed air.

Oil seals

Oil seals can be removed by levering them out with a wide flat-bladed screwdriver or similar implement. Alternatively, a number of self-tapping screws may be screwed into the seal, and these used as a purchase for pliers or some similar device in order to pull the seal free.

Whenever an oil seal is removed from its working location, either individually or as part of an assembly, it should be renewed.

The very fine sealing lip of the seal is easily damaged, and will not seal if the surface it contacts is not completely clean and free from scratches, nicks or grooves. If the original sealing surface of the component cannot be restored, and the manufacturer has not made provision for slight relocation of the seal relative to the sealing surface, the component should be renewed.

Protect the lips of the seal from any surface which may damage them in the course of fitting. Use tape or a conical sleeve where possible. Where indicated, lubricate the seal lips with oil before fitting and, on dual-lipped seals, fill the space between the lips with grease.

Unless otherwise stated, oil seals must be fitted with their sealing lips toward the lubricant to be sealed.

Use a tubular drift or block of wood of the appropriate size to install the seal and, if the seal housing is shouldered, drive the seal down to the shoulder. If the seal housing is unshouldered, the seal should be fitted with its face flush with the housing top face (unless otherwise instructed).

Screw threads and fastenings

Seized nuts, bolts and screws are quite a common occurrence where corrosion has set in, and the use of penetrating oil or releasing fluid will often overcome this problem if the offending item is soaked for a while before attempting to release it. The use of an impact driver may also provide a means of releasing such stubborn fastening devices, when used in conjunction with the appropriate screwdriver bit or socket. If none of these methods works, it may be necessary to resort to the careful application of heat, or the use of a hacksaw or nut splitter device. Before resorting to extreme methods, check that you are not dealing with a left-hand thread!

Studs are usually removed by locking two nuts together on the threaded part, and then using a spanner on the lower nut to unscrew the stud. Studs or bolts which have broken off below the surface of the component in which they are mounted can sometimes be removed using a stud extractor.

Always ensure that a blind tapped hole is completely free from oil, grease, water or other fluid before installing the bolt or stud. Failure to do this could cause the housing to crack due to the hydraulic action of the bolt or stud as it is screwed in.

For some screw fastenings, notably cylinder head bolts or nuts, torque wrench settings are no longer specified for the latter stages of tightening, "angle-tightening" being called up instead. Typically, a fairly low torque wrench setting will be applied to the bolts/nuts in the correct sequence, followed by one or more stages of tightening through specified angles.

When checking or retightening a nut or bolt to a specified torque setting, slacken the nut or bolt by a quarter of a turn, and then retighten to the specified setting. However, this should not be attempted where angular tightening has been used.

Locknuts, locktabs and washers

Any fastening which will rotate against a component or housing during tightening should always have a washer between it and the relevant component or housing.

Spring or split washers should always be renewed when they are used to lock a critical component such as a big-end bearing retaining bolt or nut. Locktabs which are folded over to retain a nut or bolt should always be renewed.

Self-locking nuts can be re-used in non-critical areas, providing resistance can be felt when the locking portion passes over the bolt or stud thread. However, it should be noted that self-locking stiffnuts tend to lose their effectiveness after long periods of use, and should then be renewed as a matter of course.

Split pins must always be replaced with new ones of the correct size for the hole.

When thread-locking compound is found on the threads of a fastener which is to be re-used, it should be cleaned off with a wire brush and solvent, and fresh compound applied on reassembly.

Special tools

Some repair procedures in this manual entail the use of special tools such as a press, two or three-legged pullers, spring compressors, etc. Wherever possible, suitable readily-available alternatives to the manufacturer's special tools are described, and are shown in use. In some instances, where no alternative is possible, it has been necessary to resort to the use of a manufacturer's tool, and this has been done for reasons of safety as well as the efficient completion of the repair operation. Unless you are highly-skilled and have a thorough understanding of the procedures described, never attempt to bypass the use of any special tool when the procedure described specifies its use. Not only is there a very great risk of personal injury, but expensive damage could be caused to the components involved.

Environmental considerations

When disposing of used engine oil, brake fluid, antifreeze, etc, give due consideration to any detrimental environmental effects. Do not, for instance, pour any of the above liquids down drains into the general sewage system, or onto the ground to soak away. Many local council refuse tips provide a facility for waste oil disposal, as do some garages. You can find your nearest disposal point by calling the Environment Agency on 08708 506 506 or by visiting www.oilbankline.org.uk.

Note: It is illegal and anti-social to dump oil down the drain. To find the location of your local oil recycling bank, call 08708 506 506 or visit www.oilbankline.org.uk.

Modifications are a continuing and unpublicised process in vehicle manufacture, quite apart from major model changes. Spare parts manuals and lists are compiled upon a numerical basis, the individual vehicle identification numbers being essential to correct identification of the component concerned. When ordering spare parts, always give as much information as possible. Quote the car model; year of manufacture, body and engine numbers as appropriate.

The vehicle identification number is stamped into the bulkhead behind the plastic scuttle panel and there is an additional sticker on the driver's side door pillar (see illustrations). The VIN is also visible through the windscreen, at the lower left hand corner (see illustration).

The *engine number* is stamped on a machined surface on the front side of the cylinder block, at the flywheel end on petrol engines (see illustration). On diesel engines, the number is stamped on a plate on the front of the cylinder block. The first part of the engine number gives the engine code – e.g. MR20DE.

The *transmission number* is on a label on top of the transmission housing.

VIN plate location on driver's side B-pillar

Remove the grille panel ...

... to access Chassis number on rear bulkhead panel

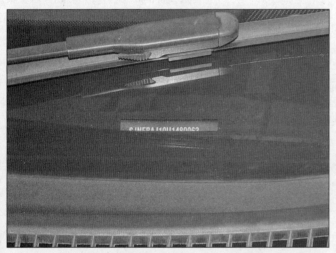

... and on a plate visible through the base of the windscreen

Engine number on front of cylinder block

Jacking and vehicle support

The jack supplied with the vehicle tool kit should only be used for changing the roadwheels in an emergency – see *Wheel changing* at the front of this manual. When carrying out any other kind of work, raise the vehicle using a hydraulic (or 'trolley') jack, and always supplement the jack with axle stands positioned under the vehicle jacking points.

When using a hydraulic jack or axle stands, always position the jack head or axle stand head under one of the relevant jacking points (see illustration) (note that the jacking points for use with the vehicle jack are different from those for a hydraulic trolley jack). Nissan recommend the use of adapters when supporting the vehicle with axle stands – the adapters should be grooved, and fit over the sill edge to prevent the vehicle weight damaging the sill. **Do not** jack the vehicle under the sump or any of the steering or suspension components other than those indicated.

 Warning: Never work under, around, or near a raised vehicle, unless it is adequately supported in at least two places.

The jacking point as indicated by two cut-outs on the lower edge of the sill

Introduction

A selection of good tools is a fundamental requirement for anyone contemplating the maintenance and repair of a motor vehicle. For the owner who does not possess any, their purchase will prove a considerable expense, offsetting some of the savings made by doing-it-yourself. However, provided that the tools purchased meet the relevant national safety standards and are of good quality, they will last for many years and prove an extremely worthwhile investment.

To help the average owner to decide which tools are needed to carry out the various tasks detailed in this manual, we have compiled three lists of tools under the following headings: *Maintenance and minor repair, Repair and overhaul*, and *Special*. Newcomers to practical mechanics should start off with the *Maintenance and minor repair* tool kit, and confine themselves to the simpler jobs around the vehicle. Then, as confidence and experience grow, more difficult tasks can be undertaken, with extra tools being purchased as, and when, they are needed. In this way, a *Maintenance and minor repair* tool kit can be built up into a *Repair and overhaul* tool kit over a considerable period of time, without any major cash outlays. The experienced do-it-yourselfer will have a tool kit good enough for most repair and overhaul procedures, and will add tools from the *Special* category when it is felt that the expense is justified by the amount of use to which these tools will be put.

Maintenance and minor repair tool kit

The tools given in this list should be considered as a minimum requirement if routine maintenance, servicing and minor repair operations are to be undertaken. We recommend the purchase of combination spanners (ring one end, open-ended the other); although more expensive than open-ended ones, they do give the advantages of both types of spanner.

- [ ] *Combination spanners:*
  Metric - 8 to 19 mm inclusive
- [ ] *Adjustable spanner - 35 mm jaw (approx.)*
- [ ] *Spark plug spanner (with rubber insert) - petrol models*
- [ ] *Spark plug gap adjustment tool - petrol models*
- [ ] *Set of feeler gauges*
- [ ] *Brake bleed nipple spanner*
- [ ] *Screwdrivers:*
  Flat blade - 100 mm long x 6 mm dia
  Cross blade - 100 mm long x 6 mm dia
  Torx - various sizes (not all vehicles)
- [ ] *Combination pliers*
- [ ] *Hacksaw (junior)*
- [ ] *Tyre pump*
- [ ] *Tyre pressure gauge*
- [ ] *Oil can*
- [ ] *Oil filter removal tool (if applicable)*
- [ ] *Fine emery cloth*
- [ ] *Wire brush (small)*
- [ ] *Funnel (medium size)*
- [ ] *Sump drain plug key (not all vehicles)*

Repair and overhaul tool kit

These tools are virtually essential for anyone undertaking any major repairs to a motor vehicle, and are additional to those given in the *Maintenance and minor repair* list. Included in this list is a comprehensive set of sockets. Although these are expensive, they will be found invaluable as they are so versatile - particularly if various drives are included in the set. We recommend the half-inch square-drive type, as this can be used with most proprietary torque wrenches.

The tools in this list will sometimes need to be supplemented by tools from the *Special* list:

- [ ] *Sockets to cover range in previous list (including Torx sockets)*
- [ ] *Reversible ratchet drive (for use with sockets)*
- [ ] *Extension piece, 250 mm (for use with sockets)*
- [ ] *Universal joint (for use with sockets)*
- [ ] *Flexible handle or sliding T "breaker bar" (for use with sockets)*
- [ ] *Torque wrench (for use with sockets)*
- [ ] *Self-locking grips*
- [ ] *Ball pein hammer*
- [ ] *Soft-faced mallet (plastic or rubber)*
- [ ] *Screwdrivers:*
  Flat blade - long & sturdy, short (chubby), and narrow (electrician's) types
  Cross blade – long & sturdy, and short (chubby) types
- [ ] *Pliers:*
  Long-nosed
  Side cutters (electrician's)
  Circlip (internal and external)
- [ ] *Cold chisel - 25 mm*
- [ ] *Scriber*
- [ ] *Scraper*
- [ ] *Centre-punch*
- [ ] *Pin punch*
- [ ] *Hacksaw*
- [ ] *Brake hose clamp*
- [ ] *Brake/clutch bleeding kit*
- [ ] *Selection of twist drills*
- [ ] *Steel rule/straight-edge*
- [ ] *Allen keys (inc. splined/Torx type)*
- [ ] *Selection of files*
- [ ] *Wire brush*
- [ ] *Axle stands*
- [ ] *Jack (strong trolley or hydraulic type)*
- [ ] *Light with extension lead*
- [ ] *Universal electrical multi-meter*

Sockets and reversible ratchet drive

Brake bleeding kit

Torx key, socket and bit

Hose clamp

Angular-tightening gauge

Special tools

The tools in this list are those which are not used regularly, are expensive to buy, or which need to be used in accordance with their manufacturers' instructions. Unless relatively difficult mechanical jobs are undertaken frequently, it will not be economic to buy many of these tools. Where this is the case, you could consider clubbing together with friends (or joining a motorists' club) to make a joint purchase, or borrowing the tools against a deposit from a local garage or tool hire specialist.

The following list contains only those tools and instruments freely available to the public, and not those special tools produced by the vehicle manufacturer specifically for its dealer network. You will find occasional references to these manufacturers' special tools in the text of this manual. Generally, an alternative method of doing the job without the vehicle manufacturers' special tool is given. However, sometimes there is no alternative to using them. Where this is the case and the relevant tool cannot be bought or borrowed, you will have to entrust the work to a dealer.

- [ ] *Angular-tightening gauge*
- [ ] *Valve spring compressor*
- [ ] *Valve grinding tool*
- [ ] *Piston ring compressor*
- [ ] *Piston ring removal/installation tool*
- [ ] *Cylinder bore hone*
- [ ] *Balljoint separator*
- [ ] *Coil spring compressors (where applicable)*
- [ ] *Two/three-legged hub and bearing puller*
- [ ] *Impact screwdriver*
- [ ] *Micrometer and/or vernier calipers*
- [ ] *Dial gauge*
- [ ] *Tachometer*
- [ ] *Fault code reader*
- [ ] *Cylinder compression gauge*
- [ ] *Hand-operated vacuum pump and gauge*
- [ ] *Clutch plate alignment set*
- [ ] *Brake shoe steady spring cup removal tool*
- [ ] *Bush and bearing removal/installation set*
- [ ] *Stud extractors*
- [ ] *Tap and die set*
- [ ] *Lifting tackle*

Buying tools

Reputable motor accessory shops and superstores often offer excellent quality tools at discount prices, so it pays to shop around.

Remember, you don't have to buy the most expensive items on the shelf, but it is always advisable to steer clear of the very cheap tools. Beware of 'bargains' offered on market stalls, on-line or at car boot sales. There are plenty of good tools around at reasonable prices, but always aim to purchase items which meet the relevant national safety standards. If in doubt, ask the proprietor or manager of the shop for advice before making a purchase.

Care and maintenance of tools

Having purchased a reasonable tool kit, it is necessary to keep the tools in a clean and serviceable condition. After use, always wipe off any dirt, grease and metal particles using a clean, dry cloth, before putting the tools away. Never leave them lying around after they have been used. A simple tool rack on the garage or workshop wall for items such as screwdrivers and pliers is a good idea. Store all normal spanners and sockets in a metal box. Any measuring instruments, gauges, meters, etc, must be carefully stored where they cannot be damaged or become rusty.

Take a little care when tools are used. Hammer heads inevitably become marked, and screwdrivers lose the keen edge on their blades from time to time. A little timely attention with emery cloth or a file will soon restore items like this to a good finish.

Working facilities

Not to be forgotten when discussing tools is the workshop itself. If anything more than routine maintenance is to be carried out, a suitable working area becomes essential.

It is appreciated that many an owner-mechanic is forced by circumstances to remove an engine or similar item without the benefit of a garage or workshop. Having done this, any repairs should always be done under the cover of a roof.

Wherever possible, any dismantling should be done on a clean, flat workbench or table at a suitable working height.

Any workbench needs a vice; one with a jaw opening of 100 mm is suitable for most jobs. As mentioned previously, some clean dry storage space is also required for tools, as well as for any lubricants, cleaning fluids, touch-up paints etc, which become necessary.

Another item which may be required, and which has a much more general usage, is an electric drill with a chuck capacity of at least 8 mm. This, together with a good range of twist drills, is virtually essential for fitting accessories.

Last, but not least, always keep a supply of old newspapers and clean, lint-free rags available, and try to keep any working area as clean as possible.

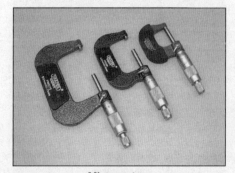

Micrometers

Dial test indicator ("dial gauge")

Oil filter removal tool (strap wrench type)

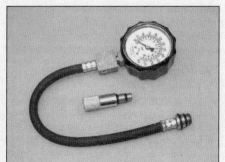

Compression tester

Bearing puller

This is a guide to getting your vehicle through the MOT test. Obviously it will not be possible to examine the vehicle to the same standard as the professional MOT tester. However, working through the following checks will enable you to identify any problem areas before submitting the vehicle for the test.

It has only been possible to summarise the test requirements here, based on the regulations in force at the time of printing. Test standards are becoming increasingly stringent, although there are some exemptions for older vehicles.

An assistant will be needed to help carry out some of these checks.

The checks have been sub-divided into four categories, as follows:

1 Checks carried out **FROM THE DRIVER'S SEAT**

2 Checks carried out **WITH THE VEHICLE ON THE GROUND**

3 Checks carried out **WITH THE VEHICLE RAISED AND THE WHEELS FREE TO TURN**

4 Checks carried out on **YOUR VEHICLE'S EXHAUST EMISSION SYSTEM**

---

1 Checks carried out **FROM THE DRIVER'S SEAT**

Handbrake (parking brake)

☐ Test the operation of the handbrake. Excessive travel (too many clicks) indicates incorrect brake or cable adjustment.
☐ Check that the handbrake cannot be released by tapping the lever sideways. Check the security of the lever mountings.

☐ If the parking brake is foot-operated, check that the pedal is secure and without excessive travel, and that the release mechanism operates correctly.
☐ Where applicable, test the operation of the electronic handbrake. The brake should engage and disengage without excessive delay. If the warning light does not extinguish when the brake is disengaged, this could indicate a fault which will need further investigation.

Footbrake

☐ Depress the brake pedal and check that it does not creep down to the floor, indicating a master cylinder fault. Release the pedal, wait a few seconds, then depress it again. If the pedal travels nearly to the floor before firm resistance is felt, brake adjustment or repair is necessary. If the pedal feels spongy, there is air in the hydraulic system which must be removed by bleeding.

☐ Check that the brake pedal is secure and in good condition. Check also for signs of fluid leaks on the pedal, floor or carpets, which would indicate failed seals in the brake master cylinder.
☐ Check the servo unit (when applicable) by operating the brake pedal several times, then keeping the pedal depressed and starting the engine. As the engine starts, the pedal will move down slightly. If not, the vacuum hose or the servo itself may be faulty.

Steering wheel and column

☐ Examine the steering wheel for fractures or looseness of the hub, spokes or rim.
☐ Move the steering wheel from side to side and then up and down. Check that the steering wheel is not loose on the column, indicating wear or a loose retaining nut. Continue moving the steering wheel as before, but also turn it slightly from left to right.

☐ Check that the steering wheel is not loose on the column, and that there is no abnormal movement of the steering wheel, indicating wear in the column support bearings or couplings.
☐ Check that the ignition lock (where fitted) engages and disengages correctly.
☐ Steering column adjustment mechanisms (where fitted) must be able to lock the column securely in place with no play evident.

Windscreen, mirrors and sunvisor

☐ The windscreen must be free of cracks or other significant damage within the driver's field of view. (Small stone chips are acceptable.) Rear view mirrors must be secure, intact, and capable of being adjusted.

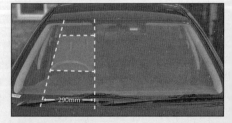

☐ The driver's sunvisor must be capable of being stored in the "up" position.

Seat belts and seats

Note: *The following checks are applicable to all seat belts, front and rear.*

☐ Examine the webbing of all the belts (including rear belts if fitted) for cuts, serious fraying or deterioration. Fasten and unfasten each belt to check the buckles. If applicable, check the retracting mechanism. Check the security of all seat belt mountings accessible from inside the vehicle, ensuring any height adjustable mountings lock securely in place.

☐ Seat belts with pre-tensioners, once activated, have a "flag" or similar showing on the seat belt stalk. This, in itself, is not a reason for test failure.

☐ The front seats themselves must be securely attached and the backrests must lock in the upright position.

Doors

☐ Both front doors must be able to be opened and closed from outside and inside, and must latch securely when closed.

Bonnet and boot/tailgate

☐ The bonnet and boot/tailgate must latch securely when closed.

2 Checks carried out WITH THE VEHICLE ON THE GROUND

Vehicle identification

☐ Number plates must be in good condition, secure and legible, with letters and numbers correctly spaced – spacing at (A) should be 33 mm and at (B) 11 mm. At the front, digits must be black on a white background and at the rear black on a yellow background. Other background designs (such as honeycomb) are not permitted.

☐ The VIN plate and/or homologation plate must be permanently displayed and legible.

Electrical equipment

☐ Switch on the ignition and check the operation of the horn.

☐ Check the windscreen washers and wipers, examining the wiper blades; renew damaged or perished blades. Also check the operation of the stop-lights.

☐ Check the operation of the sidelights and number plate lights. The lenses and reflectors must be secure, clean and undamaged.

☐ Check the operation and alignment of the headlights. The headlight reflectors must not be tarnished and the lenses must be undamaged.

☐ Switch on the ignition and check the operation of the direction indicators (including the instrument panel tell-tale) and the hazard warning lights. Operation of the sidelights and stop-lights must not affect the indicators - if it does, the cause is usually a bad earth at the rear light cluster. Indicators should flash at a rate of between 60 and 120 times per minute – faster or slower than this could indicate a fault with the flasher unit or a bad earth at one of the light units.

☐ Check the operation of the rear foglight(s), including the warning light on the instrument panel or in the switch.

☐ The warning lights must illuminate in accordance with the manufacturer's design. For most vehicles, the ABS and other warning lights should illuminate when the ignition is switched on, and (if the system is operating properly) extinguish after a few seconds. Refer to the owner's handbook.

Footbrake

☐ Examine the master cylinder, brake pipes and servo unit for leaks, loose mountings, corrosion or other damage. If ABS is fitted, this unit should also be examined for signs of leaks or corrosion.

☐ The fluid reservoir must be secure and the fluid level must be between the upper (**A**) and lower (**B**) markings.

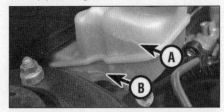

☐ Inspect both front brake flexible hoses for cracks or deterioration of the rubber. Turn the steering from lock to lock, and ensure that the hoses do not contact the wheel, tyre, or any part of the steering or suspension mechanism. With the brake pedal firmly depressed, check the hoses for bulges or leaks under pressure.

Steering and suspension

☐ Have your assistant turn the steering wheel from side to side slightly, up to the point where the steering gear just begins to transmit this movement to the roadwheels. Check for excessive free play between the steering wheel and the steering gear, indicating wear or insecurity of the steering column joints, the column-to-steering gear coupling, or the steering gear itself.

☐ Have your assistant turn the steering wheel more vigorously in each direction, so that the roadwheels just begin to turn. As this is done, examine all the steering joints, linkages, fittings and attachments. Renew any component that shows signs of wear or damage. On vehicles with power steering, check the security and condition of the steering pump, drivebelt and hoses.

☐ Check that the vehicle is standing level, and at approximately the correct ride height.

Shock absorbers

☐ Depress each corner of the vehicle in turn, then release it. The vehicle should rise and then settle in its normal position. If the vehicle continues to rise and fall, the shock absorber is defective. A shock absorber which has seized will also cause the vehicle to fail.

Exhaust system

☐ Start the engine. With your assistant holding a rag over the tailpipe, check the entire system for leaks. Repair or renew leaking sections.

3 Checks carried out
WITH THE VEHICLE RAISED AND THE WHEELS FREE TO TURN

Jack up the front and rear of the vehicle, and securely support it on axle stands. Position the stands clear of the suspension assemblies. Ensure that the wheels are clear of the ground and that the steering can be turned from lock to lock.

Steering mechanism

☐ Have your assistant turn the steering from lock to lock. Check that the steering turns smoothly, and that no part of the steering mechanism, including a wheel or tyre, fouls any brake hose or pipe or any part of the body structure.
☐ Examine the steering rack rubber gaiters for damage or insecurity of the retaining clips. If power steering is fitted, check for signs of damage or leakage of the fluid hoses, pipes or connections. Also check for excessive stiffness or binding of the steering, a missing split pin or locking device, or severe corrosion of the body structure within 30 cm of any steering component attachment point.

Front and rear suspension and wheel bearings

☐ Starting at the front right-hand side, grasp the roadwheel at the 3 o'clock and 9 o'clock positions and rock gently but firmly. Check for free play or insecurity at the wheel bearings, suspension balljoints, or suspension mount-ings, pivots and attachments.
☐ Now grasp the wheel at the 12 o'clock and 6 o'clock positions and repeat the previous inspection. Spin the wheel, and check for roughness or tightness of the front wheel bearing.

☐ If excess free play is suspected at a component pivot point, this can be confirmed by using a large screwdriver or similar tool and levering between the mounting and the component attachment. This will confirm whether the wear is in the pivot bush, its retaining bolt, or in the mounting itself (the bolt holes can often become elongated).

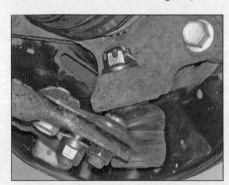

☐ Carry out all the above checks at the other front wheel, and then at both rear wheels.

Springs and shock absorbers

☐ Examine the suspension struts (when applicable) for serious fluid leakage, corrosion, or damage to the casing. Also check the security of the mounting points.
☐ If coil springs are fitted, check that the spring ends locate in their seats, and that the spring is not corroded, cracked or broken.
☐ If leaf springs are fitted, check that all leaves are intact, that the axle is securely attached to each spring, and that there is no deterioration of the spring eye mountings, bushes, and shackles.

☐ The same general checks apply to vehicles fitted with other suspension types, such as torsion bars, hydraulic displacer units, etc. Ensure that all mountings and attachments are secure, that there are no signs of excessive wear, corrosion or damage, and (on hydraulic types) that there are no fluid leaks or damaged pipes.
☐ Inspect the shock absorbers for signs of serious fluid leakage. Check for wear of the mounting bushes or attachments, or damage to the body of the unit.

Driveshafts (fwd vehicles only)

☐ Rotate each front wheel in turn and inspect the constant velocity joint gaiters for splits or damage. Also check that each driveshaft is straight and undamaged.

Braking system

☐ If possible without dismantling, check brake pad wear and disc condition. Ensure that the friction lining material has not worn excessively, (A) and that the discs are not fractured, pitted, scored or badly worn (B).

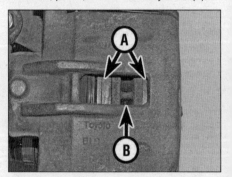

☐ Examine all the rigid brake pipes underneath the vehicle, and the flexible hose(s) at the rear. Look for corrosion, chafing or insecurity of the pipes, and for signs of bulging under pressure, chafing, splits or deterioration of the flexible hoses.
☐ Look for signs of fluid leaks at the brake calipers or on the brake backplates. Repair or renew leaking components.
☐ Slowly spin each wheel, while your assistant depresses and releases the footbrake. Ensure that each brake is operating and does not bind when the pedal is released.

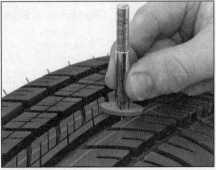

□ Examine the handbrake mechanism, checking for frayed or broken cables, excessive corrosion, or wear or insecurity of the linkage. Check that the mechanism works on each relevant wheel, and releases fully, without binding.

□ It is not possible to test brake efficiency without special equipment, but a road test can be carried out later to check that the vehicle pulls up in a straight line.

Fuel and exhaust systems

□ Inspect the fuel tank (including the filler cap), fuel pipes, hoses and unions. All components must be secure and free from leaks. Locking fuel caps must lock securely and the key must be provided for the MOT test.

□ Examine the exhaust system over its entire length, checking for any damaged, broken or missing mountings, security of the retaining clamps and rust or corrosion.

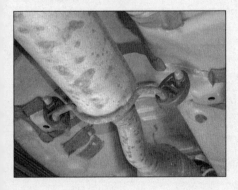

Wheels and tyres

□ Examine the sidewalls and tread area of each tyre in turn. Check for cuts, tears, lumps, bulges, separation of the tread, and exposure of the ply or cord due to wear or damage. Check that the tyre bead is correctly seated on the wheel rim, that the valve is sound and properly seated, and that the wheel is not distorted or damaged.

□ Check that the tyres are of the correct size for the vehicle, that they are of the same size and type on each axle, and that the pressures are correct.

□ Check the tyre tread depth. The legal minimum at the time of writing is 1.6 mm over the central three-quarters of the tread width. Abnormal tread wear may indicate incorrect front wheel alignment or wear in steering or suspension components.

□ If the spare wheel is fitted externally or in a separate carrier beneath the vehicle, check that mountings are secure and free of excessive corrosion.

Body corrosion

□ Check the condition of the entire vehicle structure for signs of corrosion in load-bearing areas. (These include chassis box sections, side sills, cross-members, pillars, and all suspension, steering, braking system and seat belt mountings and anchorages.) Any corrosion which has seriously reduced the thickness of a load-bearing area (or is within 30 cm of safety-related components such as steering or suspension) is likely to cause the vehicle to fail. In this case professional repairs are likely to be needed.

□ Damage or corrosion which causes sharp or otherwise dangerous edges to be exposed will also cause the vehicle to fail.

Towbars

□ Check the condition of mounting points (both beneath the vehicle and within boot/hatchback areas) for signs of corrosion, ensuring that all fixings are secure and not worn or damaged. There must be no excessive play in detachable tow ball arms or quick-release mechanisms.

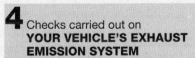

4 Checks carried out on **YOUR VEHICLE'S EXHAUST EMISSION SYSTEM**

Petrol models

□ The engine should be warmed up, and running well (ignition system in good order, air filter element clean, etc).

□ Before testing, run the engine at around 2500 rpm for 20 seconds. Let the engine drop to idle, and watch for smoke from the exhaust. If the idle speed is too high, or if dense blue or black smoke emerges for more than 5 seconds, the vehicle will fail. Typically, blue smoke signifies oil burning (engine wear); black smoke means unburnt fuel (dirty air cleaner element, or other fuel system fault).

□ An exhaust gas analyser for measuring carbon monoxide (CO) and hydrocarbons (HC) is now needed. If one cannot be hired or borrowed, have a local garage perform the check.

CO emissions (mixture)

□ The MOT tester has access to the CO limits for all vehicles. The CO level is measured at idle speed, and at 'fast idle' (2500 to 3000 rpm). The following limits are given as a general guide:

At idle speed – Less than 0.5% CO
At 'fast idle' – Less than 0.3% CO
Lambda reading – 0.97 to 1.03

□ If the CO level is too high, this may point to poor maintenance, a fuel injection system problem, faulty lambda (oxygen) sensor or catalytic converter. Try an injector cleaning treatment, and check the vehicle's ECU for fault codes.

HC emissions

□ The MOT tester has access to HC limits for all vehicles. The HC level is measured at 'fast idle' (2500 to 3000 rpm). The following limits are given as a general guide:

At 'fast idle' – Less then 200 ppm

□ Excessive HC emissions are typically caused by oil being burnt (worn engine), or by a blocked crankcase ventilation system ('breather'). If the engine oil is old and thin, an oil change may help. If the engine is running badly, check the vehicle's ECU for fault codes.

Diesel models

□ The only emission test for diesel engines is measuring exhaust smoke density, using a calibrated smoke meter. The test involves accelerating the engine at least 3 times to its maximum unloaded speed.

Note: *On engines with a timing belt, it is VITAL that the belt is in good condition before the test is carried out.*

□ With the engine warmed up, it is first purged by running at around 2500 rpm for 20 seconds. A governor check is then carried out, by slowly accelerating the engine to its maximum speed. After this, the smoke meter is connected, and the engine is accelerated quickly to maximum speed three times. If the smoke density is less than the limits given below, the vehicle will pass:

Non-turbo vehicles: 2.5m-1
Turbocharged vehicles: 3.0m-1

□ If excess smoke is produced, try fitting a new air cleaner element, or using an injector cleaning treatment. If the engine is running badly, where applicable, check the vehicle's ECU for fault codes. Also check the vehicle's EGR system, where applicable. At high mileages, the injectors may require professional attention.

Engine

- [ ] Engine fails to rotate when attempting to start
- [ ] Engine rotates, but will not start
- [ ] Engine difficult to start when cold
- [ ] Engine difficult to start when hot
- [ ] Starter motor noisy or excessively-rough in engagement
- [ ] Engine starts, but stops immediately
- [ ] Engine idles erratically
- [ ] Engine misfires at idle speed
- [ ] Engine misfires throughout the driving speed range
- [ ] Engine hesitates on acceleration
- [ ] Engine stalls
- [ ] Engine lacks power
- [ ] Engine backfires
- [ ] Oil pressure warning light illuminated with engine running
- [ ] Engine runs-on after switching off
- [ ] Engine noises

Cooling system

- [ ] Overheating
- [ ] Overcooling
- [ ] External coolant leakage
- [ ] Internal coolant leakage
- [ ] Corrosion

Fuel and exhaust systems

- [ ] Excessive fuel consumption
- [ ] Fuel leakage and/or fuel odour
- [ ] Excessive noise or fumes from exhaust system

Clutch

- [ ] Pedal travels to floor – no pressure or very little resistance
- [ ] Clutch fails to disengage (unable to select gears)
- [ ] Clutch slips (engine speed increases, with no increase in vehicle speed)
- [ ] Judder as clutch is engaged
- [ ] Noise when depressing or releasing clutch pedal

Manual transmission

- [ ] Noisy in neutral with engine running
- [ ] Noisy in one particular gear
- [ ] Difficulty engaging gears
- [ ] Jumps out of gear
- [ ] Vibration
- [ ] Lubricant leaks

Automatic transmission

- [ ] Fluid leakage
- [ ] Transmission fluid brown, or has burned smell
- [ ] General gear selection problems
- [ ] Transmission will not downshift (kickdown) with accelerator fully depressed
- [ ] Engine will not start in any gear, or starts in gears other than Park or Neutral
- [ ] Transmission slips, shifts roughly, is noisy, or has no drive in forward or reverse gears

Driveshafts

- [ ] Clicking or knocking noise on turns (at slow speed on full-lock)
- [ ] Vibration when accelerating or decelerating

Braking system

- [ ] Vehicle pulls to one side under braking
- [ ] Noise (grinding or high-pitched squeal) when brakes applied
- [ ] Excessive brake pedal travel
- [ ] Brake pedal feels spongy when depressed
- [ ] Excessive brake pedal effort required to stop vehicle
- [ ] Judder felt through brake pedal or steering wheel when braking
- [ ] Brakes binding
- [ ] Rear wheels locking under normal braking

Suspension and steering systems

- [ ] Vehicle pulls to one side
- [ ] Wheel wobble and vibration
- [ ] Excessive pitching and/or rolling around corners, or during braking
- [ ] Wandering or general instability
- [ ] Excessively-stiff steering
- [ ] Excessive play in steering
- [ ] Lack of power assistance
- [ ] Tyre wear excessive

Electrical system

- [ ] Battery will not hold a charge for more than a few days
- [ ] Ignition/no-charge warning light remains illuminated with engine running
- [ ] Ignition/no-charge warning light fails to come on
- [ ] Lights inoperative
- [ ] Instrument readings inaccurate or erratic
- [ ] Horn inoperative, or unsatisfactory in operation
- [ ] Windscreen/tailgate wipers inoperative, or unsatisfactory in operation
- [ ] Windscreen/tailgate washers inoperative, or unsatisfactory in operation
- [ ] Electric windows inoperative, or unsatisfactory in operation
- [ ] Central locking system inoperative, or unsatisfactory in operation

Introduction

The vehicle owner who does his or her own maintenance according to the recommended service schedules should not have to use this section of the manual very often. Modern component reliability is such that, provided those items subject to wear or deterioration are inspected or renewed at the specified intervals, sudden failure is comparatively rare. Faults do not usually just happen as a result of sudden failure, but develop over a period of time. Major mechanical failures in particular are usually preceded by characteristic symptoms over hundreds or even thousands of miles.

Those components, which do occasionally fail without warning, are often small and easily carried in the vehicle.

With any fault-finding, the first step is to decide where to begin investigations. Sometimes this is obvious, but on other occasions, a little detective work will be necessary. The owner who makes half a dozen haphazard adjustments or replacements may be successful in curing a fault (or its symptoms), but will be none the wiser if the fault recurs, and ultimately may have spent more time and money than was necessary. A calm and logical approach will be found to be more satisfactory in the long run. Always take into account any warning signs or abnormalities that may have been noticed in the period preceding the fault – power loss, high or low gauge readings, unusual smells, etc – and remember that failure of components such as fuses or spark plugs may only be pointers to some underlying fault.

The pages that follow provide an easy-reference guide to the more common problems, which may occur during the operation of the vehicle. These problems and their possible causes are grouped under headings denoting various components or systems, such as Engine, Cooling system, etc. The general Chapter that deals with the problem is also shown in brackets; refer to the relevant part of that Chapter for system-specific information. Whatever the fault, certain basic principles apply. These are as follows:

Verify the fault. This is simply a matter of being sure that you know what the symptoms are before starting work. This is particularly important if you are investigating a fault for someone else, who may not have described it very accurately.

Don't overlook the obvious. For example, if the vehicle won't start, is there petrol in the tank? (Don't take anyone else's word on this particular point, and don't trust the fuel gauge either!) If an electrical fault is indicated, look for loose or broken wires before digging out the test gear.

Cure the disease, not the symptom. Substituting a flat battery with a fully charged one will get you off the hard shoulder, but if the underlying cause is not attended to, the new battery will go the same way. Similarly, changing oil-fouled spark plugs for a new set

will get you moving again, but remember that the reason for the fouling (if it wasn't simply an incorrect grade of plug) will have to be established and corrected.

Don't take anything for granted. Particularly, don't forget that a 'new' component may itself be defective (especially if it's been rattling around in the boot for months), and don't leave components out of a fault diagnosis sequence just because they are new or recently fitted. When you do finally diagnose a difficult fault, you'll probably realise that all the evidence was there from the start.

Engine

Engine fails to rotate when attempting to start

- ☐ Battery terminal connections loose or corroded *(Weekly Checks)*.
- ☐ Battery discharged or faulty (Chapter 5A).
- ☐ Broken, loose or disconnected wiring in the starting circuit (Chapter 5A).
- ☐ Defective starter solenoid or switch (Chapter 5A).
- ☐ Defective starter motor (Chapter 5A).
- ☐ Starter pinion or flywheel ring gear teeth loose or broken (Chapter 2A).
- ☐ Engine earth strap broken or disconnected (Chapter 5A).
- ☐ Automatic transmission not in Park/Neutral position or starter inhibitor switch faulty (Chapter 7B).

Engine rotates, but will not start

- ☐ Fuel tank empty.
- ☐ Battery discharged (engine rotates slowly) (Chapter 5A).
- ☐ Battery terminal connections loose or corroded *(Weekly Checks)*.
- ☐ Ignition components damp or damaged (Chapters 1 and 5B).
- ☐ Broken, loose or disconnected wiring in the ignition circuit (Chapters 1 and 5B).
- ☐ Worn, faulty or incorrectly-gapped spark plugs (Chapter 1).
- ☐ Fuel injection/engine management system fault (Chapter 4A or 4B).
- ☐ Major mechanical failure (e.g. camshaft drive) (Chapter 2A or 2B).

Engine difficult to start when cold

- ☐ Battery discharged (Chapter 5A).
- ☐ Battery terminal connections loose or corroded *(Weekly Checks)*.
- ☐ Worn, faulty or incorrectly-gapped spark plugs (Chapter 1).
- ☐ Fuel injection/engine management system fault (Chapter 4A or 4B).
- ☐ Other ignition system fault (Chapters 1 and 5A).
- ☐ Low cylinder compressions (Chapter 2A).

Engine difficult to start when hot

- ☐ Air filter element dirty or clogged (Chapter 1).
- ☐ Fuel injection/engine management system fault (Chapter 4A or 4B).
- ☐ Other ignition system fault (Chapters 1 and 5A).
- ☐ Low cylinder compressions (Chapter 2A).

Starter motor noisy or excessively rough in engagement

- ☐ Starter pinion or flywheel ring gear teeth loose or broken (Chapters 2A and 5A).
- ☐ Starter motor mounting bolts loose or missing (Chapter 5A).
- ☐ Starter motor internal components worn or damaged (Chapter 5A).

Engine starts, but stops immediately

- ☐ Loose or faulty electrical connections in the ignition circuit (Chapters 1 and 5B).
- ☐ Vacuum leak at the throttle housing or inlet manifold (Chapter 4A or 4B).
- ☐ Fuel injection/engine management system fault (Chapter 4A or 4B).

Engine idles erratically

- ☐ Air filter element clogged (Chapter 1).
- ☐ Vacuum leak at the throttle housing, inlet manifold or associated hoses (Chapter 4A or 4B).
- ☐ Worn, faulty or incorrectly-gapped spark plugs (Chapter 1).
- ☐ Uneven or low cylinder compressions (Chapter 2A).
- ☐ Camshaft lobes worn (Chapter 2A).
- ☐ Timing chain(s) incorrectly fitted (Chapter 2A).
- ☐ Fuel injection/engine management system fault (Chapter 4A or 4B).

Engine misfires at idle speed

- ☐ Worn, faulty or incorrectly-gapped spark plugs (Chapter 1).
- ☐ Vacuum leak at the throttle housing, inlet manifold or associated hoses (Chapter 4A or 4B).
- ☐ Fuel injection/engine management system fault (Chapter 4A or 4B).
- ☐ Uneven or low cylinder compressions (Chapter 2A).
- ☐ Disconnected, leaking, or perished crankcase ventilation hoses (Chapter 4B).

Engine misfires throughout the driving speed range

- ☐ Fuel filter choked (Chapter 1).
- ☐ Fuel pump faulty, or delivery pressure low (Chapter 4A).
- ☐ Fuel tank vent blocked, or fuel pipes restricted (Chapter 4A).
- ☐ Vacuum leak at the throttle housing, inlet manifold or associated hoses (Chapter 4A or 4B).
- ☐ Worn, faulty or incorrectly-gapped spark plugs (Chapter 1).
- ☐ Faulty ignition coil (Chapter 5B).
- ☐ Uneven or low cylinder compressions (Chapter 2A).
- ☐ Fuel injection/engine management system fault (Chapter 4A or 4B).

Engine hesitates on acceleration

- ☐ Worn, faulty or incorrectly-gapped spark plugs (Chapter 1).
- ☐ Vacuum leak at the throttle housing, inlet manifold or associated hoses (Chapter 4A or 4B).
- ☐ Fuel injection/engine management system fault (Chapter 4A or 4B).

Engine stalls

- ☐ Vacuum leak at the throttle housing, inlet manifold or associated hoses (Chapter 4A or 4B).
- ☐ Fuel filter choked (Chapter 1).
- ☐ Fuel pump faulty, or delivery pressure low (Chapter 4A).
- ☐ Fuel tank vent blocked, or fuel pipes restricted (Chapter 4A).
- ☐ Fuel injection/engine management system fault (Chapter 4A or 4B).

Engine (continued)

Engine lacks power

- [ ] Timing chain(s) incorrectly fitted (Chapter 2A).
- [ ] Fuel filter choked (Chapter 1).
- [ ] Fuel pump faulty, or delivery pressure low (Chapter 4A).
- [ ] Uneven or low cylinder compressions (Chapter 2A).
- [ ] Worn, faulty or incorrectly-gapped spark plugs (Chapter 1).
- [ ] Vacuum leak at the throttle housing, inlet manifold or associated hoses (Chapter 4A or 4B).
- [ ] Fuel injection/engine management system fault (Chapter 4A or 4B).
- [ ] Brakes binding (Chapters 1 and 9).
- [ ] Clutch slipping – manual transmission models (Chapter 6).

Engine backfires

- [ ] Timing chain(s) incorrectly fitted (Chapter 2A).
- [ ] Vacuum leak at the throttle housing, inlet manifold or associated hoses (Chapter 4A or 4B).
- [ ] Fuel injection/engine management system fault (Chapter 4A or 4B).

Oil pressure warning light illuminated with engine running

- [ ] Low oil level, or incorrect oil grade (Weekly Checks).
- [ ] Faulty oil pressure warning light switch (Chapter 5A).
- [ ] Worn engine bearings and/or oil pump (Chapter 2A or 2B).
- [ ] High engine operating temperature (Chapter 3).
- [ ] Oil pressure relief valve defective (Chapter 2A).
- [ ] Oil pick-up strainer clogged (Chapter 2A).

Engine runs-on after switching off

- [ ] Excessive carbon build-up in engine (Chapter 2A).
- [ ] High engine operating temperature (Chapter 3).
- [ ] Fuel injection/engine management system fault (Chapter 4A or 4B).

Engine noises

Pre-ignition (pinking) or knocking during acceleration or under load

- [ ] Ignition timing incorrect/ignition system fault (Chapters 1 and 5B).
- [ ] Incorrect grade of spark plug (Chapter 1).
- [ ] Incorrect grade of fuel (Chapter 4A).
- [ ] Vacuum leak at the throttle housing, inlet manifold or associated hoses (Chapter 4A or 4B).
- [ ] Excessive carbon build-up in engine (Chapter 2A).
- [ ] Fuel injection/engine management system fault (Chapter 4A or 4B).

Whistling or wheezing noises

- [ ] Leaking inlet manifold or throttle housing gasket (Chapter 4A).
- [ ] Leaking exhaust manifold gasket or pipe-to-manifold joint (Chapter 4A).
- [ ] Leaking vacuum hose (Chapters 4A, 4B, 5B and 9).
- [ ] Blowing cylinder head gasket (Chapter 2A).

Tapping or rattling noises

- [ ] Worn valve gear or camshaft (Chapter 2A).
- [ ] Ancillary component fault (coolant pump, alternator, etc) (Chapters 3, 5A, etc).

Knocking or thumping noises

- [ ] Worn big-end bearings (regular heavy knocking, perhaps less under load) (Chapter 2B).
- [ ] Worn main bearings (rumbling and knocking, perhaps worsening under load) (Chapter 2B).
- [ ] Piston slap (most noticeable when cold) (Chapter 2B).
- [ ] Ancillary component fault (coolant pump, alternator, etc) (Chapters 3, 5A, etc).

Cooling system

Overheating

- [ ] Insufficient coolant in system (Weekly Checks).
- [ ] Thermostat faulty (Chapter 3).
- [ ] Radiator core blocked, or grille restricted (Chapter 3).
- [ ] Electric cooling fan faulty (Chapter 3).
- [ ] Pressure cap faulty (Chapter 3).
- [ ] Ignition timing incorrect/ignition system fault (Chapters 1 and 5B).
- [ ] Inaccurate temperature gauge sender unit (Chapter 3).
- [ ] Airlock in cooling system (Chapter 1).

Overcooling

- [ ] Thermostat faulty (Chapter 3).
- [ ] Inaccurate temperature gauge sender unit (Chapter 3).

External coolant leakage

- [ ] Deteriorated or damaged hoses or hose clips (Chapter 1).
- [ ] Radiator core or heater matrix leaking (Chapter 3).
- [ ] Pressure cap faulty (Chapter 3).
- [ ] Coolant pump seal leaking (Chapter 3).
- [ ] Boiling due to overheating (Chapter 3).
- [ ] Cylinder block core plug leaking (Chapter 2B).

Internal coolant leakage

- [ ] Leaking cylinder head gasket (Chapter 2A).
- [ ] Cracked cylinder head or cylinder bore (Chapter 2A or 2B).

Corrosion

- [ ] Infrequent draining and flushing (Chapter 1).
- [ ] Incorrect coolant mixture or inappropriate coolant type (Chapter 1).

Fuel and exhaust systems

Excessive fuel consumption

- [ ] Air filter element dirty or clogged (Chapter 1).
- [ ] Fuel injection/engine management system fault (Chapter 4A or 4B).
- [ ] Ignition timing incorrect/ignition system fault (Chapters 1 and 5B).
- [ ] Tyres under-inflated (Weekly Checks).

Fuel leakage and/or fuel odour

- [ ] Damaged or corroded fuel tank, pipes or connections (Chapter 4A or 4B).

Excessive noise or fumes from exhaust system

- [ ] Leaking exhaust system or manifold joints (Chapters 1 or 4B).
- [ ] Leaking, corroded or damaged silencers or pipe (Chapters 1 or 4B).
- [ ] Broken mountings causing body or suspension contact (Chapter 1).

Clutch

Pedal travels to floor – no pressure or very little resistance

- ☐ Leaking hydraulic fluid (Chapter 6).
- ☐ Faulty slave or master cylinder (Chapter 6).
- ☐ Broken clutch release bearing or fork (Chapter 6).
- ☐ Broken diaphragm spring in clutch pressure plate (Chapter 6).

Clutch fails to disengage (unable to select gears)

- ☐ Leaking hydraulic fluid (Chapter 6).
- ☐ Clutch friction plate sticking on gearbox input shaft splines (Chapter 6).
- ☐ Clutch friction plate sticking to flywheel or pressure plate (Chapter 6).
- ☐ Faulty pressure plate assembly (Chapter 6).
- ☐ Clutch release mechanism worn or incorrectly assembled (Chapter 6).

Clutch slips (engine speed increases, with no increase in vehicle speed)

- ☐ Leaking hydraulic fluid (Chapter 6).
- ☐ Clutch friction plate linings excessively worn (Chapter 6).
- ☐ Clutch friction plate linings contaminated with oil or grease (Chapter 6).
- ☐ Faulty pressure plate or weak diaphragm spring (Chapter 6).

Judder as clutch is engaged

- ☐ Clutch friction plate linings contaminated with oil or grease (Chapter 6).
- ☐ Clutch friction plate linings excessively worn (Chapter 6).
- ☐ Leaking hydraulic fluid (Chapter 6).
- ☐ Faulty or distorted pressure plate or diaphragm spring (Chapter 6).
- ☐ Worn or loose engine or gearbox mountings (Chapter 2A).
- ☐ Clutch friction plate hub or gearbox input shaft splines worn (Chapter 6).

Noise when depressing or releasing clutch pedal

- ☐ Worn clutch release bearing (Chapter 6).
- ☐ Worn or dry clutch pedal bushes (Chapter 6).
- ☐ Faulty pressure plate assembly (Chapter 6).
- ☐ Pressure plate diaphragm spring broken (Chapter 6).
- ☐ Broken clutch friction plate cushioning springs (Chapter 6).

Driveshafts

Clicking or knocking noise on turns (at slow speed on full-lock).

- ☐ Lack of constant velocity joint lubricant, possibly due to damaged gaiter (Chapter 8).
- ☐ Worn outer constant velocity joint (Chapter 8).

Vibration when accelerating or decelerating

- ☐ Worn inner constant velocity joint (Chapter 8).
- ☐ Bent or distorted driveshaft (Chapter 8).

Manual transmission

Noisy in neutral with engine running

- ☐ Input shaft bearings worn (noise apparent with clutch pedal released, but not when depressed) (Chapter 7A).*
- ☐ Clutch release bearing worn (noise apparent with clutch pedal depressed, possibly less when released) (Chapter 6).

Noisy in one particular gear

- ☐ Worn, damaged or chipped gear teeth (Chapter 7A).*

Difficulty engaging gears

- ☐ Clutch fault (Chapter 6).
- ☐ Oil level low (Chapter 1).
- ☐ Worn or damaged gearchange linkage (Chapter 7A).
- ☐ Worn synchroniser units (Chapter 7A).*

Jumps out of gear

- ☐ Worn or damaged gearchange linkage (Chapter 7A).

- ☐ Worn synchroniser units (Chapter 7A).*
- ☐ Worn selector forks (Chapter 7A).*

Vibration

- ☐ Lack of oil (Chapter 1).
- ☐ Worn bearings (Chapter 7A).*

Lubricant leaks

- ☐ Leaking driveshaft oil seal (Chapter 7A).
- ☐ Leaking housing joint (Chapter 7A).*
- ☐ Leaking input shaft oil seal (Chapter 7A).*
- ☐ Leaking selector shaft oil seal (Chapter 7A).

Although the corrective action necessary to remedy the symptoms described is beyond the scope of the home mechanic, the above information should be helpful in isolating the cause of the condition, so that the owner can communicate clearly with a professional mechanic.

Automatic transmission

Note: *Due to the complexity of the automatic transmission, it is difficult for the home mechanic to properly diagnose and service this unit. For problems other than the following, the vehicle should be taken to a dealer service department or automatic transmission specialist. Do not be too hasty in removing the transmission if a fault is suspected, as most of the testing is carried out with the unit still fitted.*

Fluid leakage

☐ Automatic transmission fluid is usually dark in colour. Fluid leaks should not be confused with engine oil, which can easily be blown onto the transmission by airflow.

☐ To determine the source of a leak, first remove all built-up dirt and grime from the transmission housing and surrounding areas using a degreasing agent, or by steam-cleaning. Drive the vehicle at low speed, so airflow will not blow the leak far from its source. Raise and support the vehicle, and determine where the leak is coming from. The following are common areas of leakage:

a) Oil pan (Chapter 1).
b) Dipstick tube (Chapter 1).
c) Transmission-to-fluid cooler pipes/unions (Chapter 7B).

Transmission fluid brown, or has burned smell

☐ Transmission fluid level low, or fluid in need of renewal (Chapter 1).

General gear selection problems

☐ Chapter 7B deals with checking and adjusting the selector cable on automatic transmissions. The following are common problems which may be caused by a poorly-adjusted cable:

a) Engine starting in gears other than Park or Neutral.
b) Indicator panel indicating a gear other than the one actually being used.
c) Vehicle moves when in Park or Neutral.
d) Poor gearshift quality or erratic gearchanges

☐ Refer to Chapter 7B for the selector cable adjustment procedure.

Transmission will not downshift (kickdown) with accelerator pedal fully depressed

☐ Low transmission fluid level (Chapter 1).
☐ Incorrect selector cable adjustment (Chapter 7B).
☐ Incorrect kickdown cable adjustment (Chapter 7B).

Engine will not start in any gear, or starts in gears other than Park or Neutral

☐ Incorrect selector cable adjustment (Chapter 7B).
☐ Incorrect starter inhibitor switch adjustment (Chapter 7B).

Transmission slips, is noisy, or has no drive in forward or reverse gears

☐ There are many probable causes for the above problems, but the home mechanic should be concerned with only one possibility – fluid level. Before taking the vehicle to a dealer or transmission specialist, check the fluid level and condition of the fluid as described in Chapter 1. Correct the fluid level as necessary, or change the fluid and filter if needed. If the problem persists, professional help will be necessary.

Braking system

Note: *Before assuming that a brake problem exists, make sure that the tyres are in good condition and correctly inflated, that the front wheel alignment is correct, and that the vehicle is not loaded with weight in an unequal manner. Apart from checking the condition of all pipe and hose connections, any faults occurring on the anti-lock braking system should be referred to a Nissan dealer for diagnosis.*

Vehicle pulls to one side under braking

☐ Worn, defective, damaged or contaminated brake pads/shoes on one side (Chapters 1 and 9).
☐ Seized or partially-seized front brake caliper or rear wheel cylinder/ caliper piston (Chapters 1 and 9).
☐ A mixture of brake pad/shoe lining materials fitted between sides (Chapters 1 and 9).
☐ Brake caliper or backplate mounting bolts loose (Chapter 9).
☐ Worn or damaged steering or suspension components (Chapters 1 and 10).

Noise (grinding or high-pitched squeal) when brakes applied

☐ Brake pad or shoe friction lining material worn down to metal backing (Chapters 1 and 9).
☐ Excessive corrosion of brake disc or drum. (May be apparent after the vehicle has been standing for some time (Chapters 1 and 9).
☐ Foreign object (stone chipping, etc) trapped between brake disc and shield (Chapters 1 and 9).

Excessive brake pedal travel

☐ Inoperative rear brake self-adjust mechanism – drum brake models (Chapters 1 and 9).
☐ Faulty master cylinder (Chapter 9).
☐ Air in hydraulic system (Chapter 9).
☐ Faulty vacuum servo unit (Chapters 1 and 9).

Brake pedal feels spongy when depressed

☐ Air in hydraulic system (Chapter 9).
☐ Deteriorated flexible rubber brake hoses (Chapters 1 and 9).
☐ Master cylinder mounting nuts loose (Chapter 9).
☐ Faulty master cylinder (Chapter 9).

Excessive brake pedal effort required to stop vehicle

☐ Faulty vacuum servo unit (Chapters 1 and 9).
☐ Disconnected, damaged or insecure brake servo vacuum hose (Chapter 9).
☐ Primary or secondary hydraulic circuit failure (Chapter 9).
☐ Seized brake caliper or wheel cylinder piston(s) (Chapter 9).
☐ Brake pads or brake shoes incorrectly fitted (Chapter 9).
☐ Incorrect grade of brake pads or brake shoes fitted (Chapter 9).
☐ Brake pads or brake shoe linings contaminated (Chapter 9).

Judder felt through brake pedal or steering wheel when braking

☐ Excessive run-out or distortion of discs/drums (Chapter 9).
☐ Brake pad or brake shoe linings worn (Chapters 1 and 9).
☐ Brake caliper or brake backplate mounting bolts loose (Chapter 9).
☐ Wear in suspension or steering components or mountings (Chapters 1 and 10).

Brakes binding

☐ Seized brake caliper or wheel cylinder piston(s) (Chapter 9).
☐ Incorrectly-adjusted handbrake mechanism (Chapter 1).
☐ Faulty master cylinder (Chapter 9).

Rear wheels locking under normal braking

☐ Rear brake pad/shoe linings contaminated (Chapters 1 and 9).
☐ Faulty brake pressure regulator (Chapter 9).

Suspension and steering

Note: *Before diagnosing suspension or steering faults, be sure that the trouble is not due to incorrect tyre pressures, mixtures of tyre types, or binding brakes.*

Vehicle pulls to one side

- [ ] Defective tyre *(Weekly Checks)*.
- [ ] Excessive wear in suspension or steering components (Chapters 1 and 10).
- [ ] Incorrect front wheel alignment (Chapter 1).
- [ ] Accident damage to steering or suspension components (Chapter 1).

Wheel wobble and vibration

- [ ] Front roadwheels out of balance (vibration felt mainly through the steering wheel) (Chapters 1 and 10).
- [ ] Rear roadwheels out of balance (vibration felt throughout the vehicle) (Chapters 1 and 10).
- [ ] Roadwheels damaged or distorted (Chapters 1 and 10).
- [ ] Faulty or damaged tyre *(Weekly Checks)*.
- [ ] Worn steering or suspension joints, bushes or components (Chapters 1 and 10).
- [ ] Wheel nuts loose (Chapters 1 and 10).

Excessive pitching and/or rolling around corners, or during braking

- [ ] Defective shock absorbers (Chapters 1 and 10).
- [ ] Broken or weak spring and/or suspension component (Chapters 1 and 10).
- [ ] Worn or damaged anti-roll bar or mountings (Chapter 10).

Wandering or general instability

- [ ] Incorrect front wheel alignment (Chapter 1).
- [ ] Worn steering or suspension joints, bushes or components (Chapters 1 and 10).
- [ ] Roadwheels out of balance (Chapters 1 and 10).
- [ ] Faulty or damaged tyre *(Weekly Checks)*.
- [ ] Wheel nuts loose (Chapters 1 and 10).
- [ ] Defective shock absorbers (Chapters 1 and 10).

Excessively-stiff steering

- [ ] Lack of steering gear lubricant (Chapter 10).

- [ ] Seized track rod end balljoint or suspension balljoint (Chapters 1 and 10).
- [ ] Broken or incorrectly-adjusted auxiliary drivebelt – power steering (Chapter 1).
- [ ] Incorrect front wheel alignment (Chapter 1).
- [ ] Steering rack or column bent or damaged (Chapter 10).

Excessive play in steering

- [ ] Worn steering track rod end balljoints (Chapters 1 and 10).
- [ ] Worn rack-and-pinion steering gear (Chapter 10).
- [ ] Worn steering or suspension joints, bushes or components (Chapters 1 and 10).

Lack of power assistance

- [ ] Broken or incorrectly-adjusted auxiliary drivebelt (Chapter 1).
- [ ] Incorrect power steering fluid level *(Weekly Checks)*.
- [ ] Restriction in power steering fluid hoses (Chapter 1).
- [ ] Faulty power steering pump (Chapter 10).
- [ ] Faulty rack-and-pinion steering gear (Chapter 10).

Tyre wear excessive

Tyres worn on inside or outside edges

- [ ] Tyres under-inflated (wear on both edges) *(Weekly Checks)*.
- [ ] Incorrect camber or castor angles (wear on one edge only) (Chapter 1).
- [ ] Worn steering or suspension joints, bushes or components (Chapters 1 and 10).
- [ ] Excessively-hard cornering.
- [ ] Accident damage.

Tyre treads exhibit feathered edges

- [ ] Incorrect toe setting (Chapter 1).

Tyres worn in centre of tread

- [ ] Tyres over-inflated *(Weekly Checks)*.

Tyres worn on inside and outside edges

- [ ] Tyres under-inflated *(Weekly Checks)*.

Tyres worn unevenly

- [ ] Tyres/wheels out of balance (Chapter 1).
- [ ] Excessive wheel or tyre run-out (Chapter 1).
- [ ] Worn shock absorbers (Chapters 1 and 10).
- [ ] Faulty tyre *(Weekly Checks)*.

Electrical system

Note: *For problems associated with the starting system, refer to the faults listed under 'Engine' earlier in this Section.*

Battery will not hold a charge for more than a few days

- [ ] Battery defective internally (Chapter 5A).
- [ ] Battery terminal connections loose or corroded *(Weekly Checks)*.
- [ ] Auxiliary drivebelt worn or incorrectly adjusted (Chapter 1).
- [ ] Alternator not charging at correct output (Chapter 5A).
- [ ] Alternator or voltage regulator faulty (Chapter 5A).
- [ ] Short-circuit causing continual battery drain (Chapters 5A and 12).

Ignition/no-charge warning light remains illuminated with engine running

- [ ] Auxiliary drivebelt broken, worn, or incorrectly adjusted (Chapter 1).
- [ ] Alternator brushes worn, sticking, or dirty (Chapter 5A).
- [ ] Alternator brush springs weak or broken (Chapter 5A).
- [ ] Internal fault in alternator or voltage regulator (Chapter 5A).
- [ ] Broken, disconnected, or loose wiring in charging circuit (Chapter 5A).

Electrical system (continued)

Ignition/no-charge warning light fails to come on

- [ ] Warning light bulb blown (Chapter 12).
- [ ] Broken, disconnected, or loose wiring in warning light circuit (Chapter 12).
- [ ] Alternator faulty (Chapter 5A).

Lights inoperative

- [ ] Bulb blown (Chapter 12).
- [ ] Corrosion of bulb or bulbholder contacts (Chapter 12).
- [ ] Blown fuse (Chapter 12).
- [ ] Faulty relay (Chapter 12).
- [ ] Broken, loose, or disconnected wiring (Chapter 12).
- [ ] Faulty switch (Chapter 12).

Instrument readings inaccurate or erratic

Fuel or temperature gauges give no reading

- [ ] Faulty gauge sender unit (Chapters 3 or 4A).
- [ ] Wiring open-circuit (Chapter 12).
- [ ] Faulty gauge (Chapter 12).

Fuel or temperature gauges give continuous maximum reading

- [ ] Faulty gauge sender unit (Chapters 3 or 4A).
- [ ] Wiring short-circuit (Chapter 12).
- [ ] Faulty gauge (Chapter 12).

Horn inoperative, or unsatisfactory in operation

Horn operates all the time

- [ ] Horn push either earthed or stuck down (Chapter 12).
- [ ] Horn cable-to-horn push earthed (Chapter 12).

Horn fails to operate

- [ ] Blown fuse (Chapter 12).
- [ ] Cable or cable connections loose, broken or disconnected (Chapter 12).
- [ ] Faulty horn (Chapter 12).

Horn emits intermittent or unsatisfactory sound

- [ ] Cable connections loose (Chapter 12).
- [ ] Horn mountings loose (Chapter 12).
- [ ] Faulty horn (Chapter 12).

Windscreen/tailgate wipers inoperative, or unsatisfactory in operation

Wipers fail to operate, or operate very slowly

- [ ] Wiper blades stuck to screen, or linkage seized or binding (Chapters 1 and 12).
- [ ] Blown fuse (Chapter 12).
- [ ] Cable or cable connections loose, broken or disconnected (Chapter 12).
- [ ] Faulty relay (Chapter 12).
- [ ] Faulty wiper motor (Chapter 12).

Wiper blades sweep over too large or too small an area of the glass

- [ ] Wiper arms incorrectly positioned on spindles (Chapter 1).
- [ ] Excessive wear of wiper linkage (Chapter 12).
- [ ] Wiper motor or linkage mountings loose or insecure (Chapter 12).

Wiper blades fail to clean the glass effectively

- [ ] Wiper blade rubbers worn or perished (Weekly Checks).
- [ ] Wiper arm tension springs broken, or arm pivots seized (Chapter 12).
- [ ] Insufficient windscreen washer additive to adequately remove road film (Weekly Checks).

Windscreen/tailgate washers inoperative, or unsatisfactory in operation

One or more washer jets inoperative

- [ ] Blocked washer jet (Chapter 1 or 12).
- [ ] Disconnected, kinked or restricted fluid hose (Chapter 12).
- [ ] Insufficient fluid in washer reservoir (Weekly Checks).

Washer pump fails to operate

- [ ] Broken or disconnected wiring or connections (Chapter 12).
- [ ] Blown fuse (Chapter 12).
- [ ] Faulty washer switch (Chapter 12).
- [ ] Faulty washer pump (Chapter 12).

Washer pump runs for some time before fluid is emitted from jets

- [ ] Faulty one-way valve in fluid supply hose (Chapter 12).

Electric windows inoperative, or unsatisfactory in operation

Window glass will only move in one direction

- [ ] Faulty switch (Chapter 12).

Window glass slow to move

- [ ] Incorrectly-adjusted door glass guide channels (Chapter 11).
- [ ] Regulator seized or damaged, or in need of lubrication (Chapter 11).
- [ ] Door internal components or trim fouling regulator (Chapter 11).
- [ ] Faulty motor (Chapter 11).

Window glass fails to move

- [ ] Incorrectly-adjusted door glass guide channels (Chapter 11).
- [ ] Blown fuse (Chapter 12).
- [ ] Faulty relay (Chapter 12).
- [ ] Broken or disconnected wiring or connections (Chapter 12).
- [ ] Faulty motor (Chapter 11).

Central locking system inoperative, or unsatisfactory in operation

Complete system failure

- [ ] Blown fuse (Chapter 12).
- [ ] Faulty relay (Chapter 12).
- [ ] Broken or disconnected wiring or connections (Chapter 12).
- [ ] Faulty control unit (Chapter 11).

Latch locks but will not unlock, or unlocks but will not lock

- [ ] Faulty master switch (Chapter 12).
- [ ] Broken or disconnected latch operating rods or levers (Chapter 11).
- [ ] Faulty relay (Chapter 12).
- [ ] Faulty control unit (Chapter 11).

One solenoid/motor fails to operate

- [ ] Broken or disconnected wiring or connections (Chapter 12).
- [ ] Faulty solenoid/motor (Chapter 11).
- [ ] Broken, binding or disconnected latch operating rods or levers (Chapter 11).
- [ ] Fault in door latch (Chapter 11).

Note: *References throughout this index are in the form "**Chapter number**" • "**Page number**". So, for example, 2C•15 refers to page 15 of Chapter 2C.*

Note: References throughout this index are in the form "Chapter number" • "Page number". So, for example, 2C•15 refers to page 15 of Chapter 2C.

Note: *References throughout this index are in the form "***Chapter number***" • "***Page number***". So, for example, 2C•15 refers to page 15 of Chapter 2C.*

Preserving Our Motoring Heritage

<
The Model J Duesenberg Derham Tourster. Only eight of these magnificent cars were ever built – this is the only example to be found outside the United States of America

Almost every car you've ever loved, loathed or desired is gathered under one roof at the Haynes Motor Museum. Over 300 immaculately presented cars and motorbikes represent every aspect of our motoring heritage, from elegant reminders of bygone days, such as the superb Model J Duesenberg to curiosities like the bug-eyed BMW Isetta. There are also many old friends and flames. Perhaps you remember the 1959 Ford Popular that you did your courting in? The magnificent 'Red Collection' is a spectacle of classic sports cars including AC, Alfa Romeo, Austin Healey, Ferrari, Lamborghini, Maserati, MG, Riley, Porsche and Triumph.

A Perfect Day Out

Each and every vehicle at the Haynes Motor Museum has played its part in the history and culture of Motoring. Today, they make a wonderful spectacle and a great day out for all the family. Bring the kids, bring Mum and Dad, but above all bring your camera to capture those golden memories for ever. You will also find an impressive array of motoring memorabilia, a comfortable 70 seat video cinema and one of the most extensive transport book shops in Britain. The Pit Stop Cafe serves everything from a cup of tea to wholesome, home-made meals or, if you prefer, you can enjoy the large picnic area nestled in the beautiful rural surroundings of Somerset.

>
John Haynes O.B.E., Founder and Chairman of the museum at the wheel of a Haynes Light 12.

<
Graham Hill's Lola Cosworth Formula 1 car next to a 1934 Riley Sports.

The Museum is situated on the A359 Yeovil to Frome road at Sparkford, just off the A303 in Somerset. It is about 40 miles south of Bristol, and 25 minutes drive from the M5 intersection at Taunton.
Open 9.30am - 5.30pm (10.00am - 4.00pm Winter) 7 days a week, *except Christmas Day, Boxing Day and New Years Day*
Special rates available for schools, coach parties and outings Charitable Trust No. 292048